# New in This Edition!!

If you have been using VFP 3.0, some
exciting new VFP 5.0 features include

D0851471

**Ch 1  Quick Review of Visual FoxPro's Interface**

- Edit using syntax coloring to quickly identify variables, commands, comments, and more.

**Ch 4  Advanced Database Management Concepts**

- Automatically include field captions, formats, input masks, and field comments when dragging fields to a form.

**Ch 8  Advanced Queries and Views**

- Master enhancements to SQL statements that make it easier to define left, right, and full outer joins.

**Ch 11  Building Applications with Simple Form Structures**

- Assign field mapping to use any VFP base classes or your own custom classes when dragging fields to a form.

**Ch 15  Organizing Components of an Application into a Project**

- Use Visual SourceSafe to control updates to code in a multi-developer environment.

**Ch 16  Error Detection and Removal**

- Debug your application with the new Debugger, which streamlines the process of finding and correcting bugs.

**Ch 19  Internet Support**

- Prepare your own VFP-powered Web site with the VFP WWW Search Page Wizard.

**BO 6  Sharing Data Through Automation and Using ActiveX™ Controls**

- Compile visual class libraries into ActiveX servers. These servers allow any application that can use Automation to use these libraries.

*Special Edition*

# USING
# VISUAL
# FOXPRO™ 5

**que**®

*Special Edition*

# USING
# VISUAL
# FOXPRO™ 5

*Written by Michael Antonovich with*

*Alice Atkins • Marl Atkins • Richard L. Curtis*
*Sandra Richardson-Lutzow • Jay van Santen*
*Richard Strahl • Arthur Young*

# Special Edition Using Visual FoxPro 5

Library of Congress Catalog No.: 96-70614

ISBN: 0-7897-0885-x

98 97 96    4 3 2 1

Interpretation of the printing code: the rightmost double-digit number is the year of the book's printing; the rightmost single-digit number, the number of the book's printing. For example, a printing code of 96-1 shows that the first printing of the book occurred in 1996.

Screen reproductions in this book were created using Collage Plus from Inner Media, Inc., Hollis, NH.

# Credits

**PRESIDENT**
Roland Elgey

**PUBLISHER**
Joseph B. Wikert

**EDITORIAL SERVICES DIRECTOR**
Elizabeth Keaffaber

**MANAGING EDITOR**
Sandy Doell

**PUBLISHING MANAGER**
Fred Slone

**SENIOR TITLE MANAGER**
Bryan Gambrel

**ACQUISITIONS EDITOR**
Tracy Dunkelberger

**ACQUISITIONS COORDINATOR**
Carmen Krikorian

**PRODUCTION EDITOR**
Juliet MacLean

**EDITOR**
Kathy Simpson

**DIRECTOR OF MARKETING MANAGER**
Lynn E. Zingraf

**STRATEGIC MARKETING MANAGER**
Barry Pruett

**PRODUCT MARKETING MANAGER**
Kim Margolius

**ASSISTANT PRODUCT MARKETING MANAGER**
Christy M. Miller

**TECHNICAL EDITOR**
Pablo Flores

**OPERATIONS COORDINATOR**
Patricia J. Brooks

**TECHNICAL SUPPORT SPECIALIST**
Nadeem Muhammed

**EDITORIAL ASSISTANTS**
Jennifer Condon
Andrea Duvall

**BOOK DESIGNER**
Ruth Harvey

**COVER DESIGNER**
Dan Armstrong

**PRODUCTION TEAM**
Stephen Adams
Debra Bolhuis
Marcia Brizendine
Kevin Cliburn
Melissa Coffey
Jason Hand
Daniel Harris
Bob LaRoche
Erich Richter
Laura Robbins
Marvin Van Tiem
Mary Beth Wakefield
Paul Wilson

**INDEXER**
Chris Wilcox

Composed in *Century Old Style* and *Franklin Gothic* by Que Corporation.

*This book is dedicated to my daughter Natasha.*

# About the Authors

**Michael P. Antonovich** is a consultant specializing in large database applications. His most recent systems have been for distributors and the retail industry, including advertisement tracking, trade promotion analysis, point-of-sale, and complete order tracking from entry through billing. He has also implemented applications for general business use and government agencies, including information systems, custom data collection and reporting systems, and loan tracking systems. He has extensive programming experience in several development systems, particularly, Visual Basic, Access, and dBASE. Mr. Antonovich has also taught programming and computer science classes for several colleges, including both regular and extension courses. He is the author of two prior FoxPro books. He received both his bachelor's degree in chemical engineering and his M.B.A. from Lehigh University.

**Marl** and **Alice Atkins** have collectively worked as technical writers/editors for well over ten years. Both have bachelor's degrees as well as collective writing experience in electronics, automation systems, laser systems, and many software programs. Now they work together in their own business, offering technical documentation, including on-line Help systems and graphic arts.

You can contact Alice and Marl Atkins via any of the following methods:

Phone: (407) 767-9016

FAX: (407) 767-5607

email: **amatkins@sundial.net**

**Richard L. Curtis** is vice president of development at Documation, Inc., Orlando, Florida, and a retired U.S. Naval Officer (submarine administration). With more than ten years experience in microcomputer database design and development, he is an accomplished programmer in MS Visual FoxPro, MS FoxPro, MS Access, and MS Visual Basic development languages. Mr. Curtis is a Certified Microsoft Product Specialist and Certified Microsoft Trainer. He received his bachelor's degree in business administration from Charleston Southern University. He can be reached at **rcurtis@ documationinc.com, rl_curtis@msn.com**, or **70571.1766@compuserve.com**.

**Sandra Richardson-Lutzow** specializes in database design and data normalization with additional talents in user interface design. She has played a major role in the development of custom applications for engineering and marketing institutions including calculation and scenario analyses, tracking systems, billing systems, and decision support systems. Sandra's experience with FoxPro has extended to over five years. She is currently a Microsoft Certified Professional and a member of the Information Technology group at a nationwide utilities engineering firm.

**Jay van Santen** was promised three careers by his high school guidance counselor, and currently is on his second. He came to FoxPro as many have—a friend needed a program. The capabilities of FoxPro promised a quality result to balance the time required to learn a new language. On many days, this was debatable. His background in Pascal provides a perspective on Fox as a computer language, rather than simply a database language. He hopes that his consulting work in analysis and programming is enhanced by earlier experience in ministry. Currently, he lives in downtown Indianapolis, in an Arts and Crafts vintage home.

**Rick Strahl** is an independent developer in Hood River, Oregon who specialized in FoxPro development on the Windows and DOS platforms. His consulting firm, West Wind Technologies, provides custom application development services in the Portland area. Rick has been involved in Xbase and FoxPro programming for over eight years. He is also the author of several popular FoxPro shareware applications, and a frequent contributor to *FoxPro Advisor* magazine.

**Arthur Young** is currently a programmer/analyst employed by LeConte Software in Orlando, Florida. He is involved in the conversion of a FoxPro 2.5 wholesale auto loan system, and a Clipper collateral management system to Visual FoxPro. He has been involved in software development since 1990, developing FoxPro applications since 1993 after three years of Clipper development. Arthur has worked with Visual FoxPro since mid-1995 as a beta tester while employed at the Harland Corporation. He has provided systems for both the resort and banking industries. He can be reached on CompuServe at **104567,50**.

## Authors from the Previous Edition

**Monte Mitzefelt** is currently employed by Candid Color Systems in Oklahoma City, Oklahoma. He functions primarily as a marketing database analyst and World Wide Web developer for Glamour Licensing, Inc., the franchisers of Glamour Shots®, Candid Color's sister Company. In recent memory, he has worked for Little Debbie® Snack Cakes near Chattanooga, Tennessee, as a FoxPro developer; the New Mexico Department of Taxation and Revenue developing systems to track law enforcement training and federal matching funds; and the New Mexico Department of Public Safety as an IS intern.

**Steven Miller** is a senior software engineer with microMANAGEMENT, Inc., a software development and computer consulting company in Troy, Michigan. He has contributed numerous articles to *FoxPro Advisor* and *FoxTalk*, and was on the beta team for Visual FoxPro 5.0 and 3.0. He is also founder and former vice president of the Detroit Area Fox Users Group.

**Rod Paddock** is president and founder of Dash Point Software, Inc. DPSI, based in Seattle, Washington, specializes in FoxPro, Visual Basic, and Microsoft Access database development. Rod's clients include SBT Accounting, Pinnacle Publishing, Intel, and Asalea Software. He is also an instructor for Application Developers Training Company. Rod writes for several database publications, including *Data Bases Advisor*, *Foxtalk*, and *dBASE Advisor*. He can be reached via Compuserve at address **76244,3116**.

# Acknowledgments

While writing this version of *Special Edition Using Visual FoxPro 5* was easier than the prior version for FoxPro 3.0, it still presented its own unique challenges and rewards. I decided early in the process to work with a group of local FoxPro developers whom I had gotten to know while working on a client project. Working with people who are your friends can be a two-edged sword. The biggest threat to that friendship is the stress of getting text written that everyone can agree on within a relatively limited amount of time. Editing is especially dangerous. But the benefit of working with people whose skills you are already familiar with and with whom you can be honest far outweighs the negatives. Therefore, I wish to publicly thank the people directly involved in the production of this book.

First, there are my primary coauthors: Richard, Sandi, and Arthur. I've known Richard Curtis for several years now. He is a meticulous programmer and believes in making his applications work perfectly. Thanks, Richard.

Sandi Lutzow has also developed into an excellent Visual FoxPro developer. Her dedication to getting a job done is unmatched. Although content to maintain a low profile, she has become one of the more knowledgeable FoxPro developers related to handling various database container issues and data dictionaries. (Sorry to have spilled the beans!) With the number of e-mail messages I received timestamped between 12:00 and 6 A.M., I have to wonder if she ever had time to sleep during this project. Thanks, Sandi.

Arthur Young, a BIG Dallas Cowbows fan, has considerable programming skills, too. He brings insights into multi-user issues and how to handle conflicts based on his own experience in developing multi-user applications as well as sharing some of his experience with basic Visual FoxPro features. Thanks, Arthur.

Several other people contributed to individual chapters.

Alice and Marl Atkins came into this project a little late specifically to handle the chapter on creating Windows-style help. She, along with her husband Marl, have their own documentation service business here in Orlando and have written several help systems for various projects. Thanks, Alice and Marl.

And a special thanks to Jay van Santen who did such a great job in writing the chapter "Creating a Design Plan" for the Visual FoxPro 3.0 book, that we kept it intact for this book. I guess proper design and planning are timeless. Thanks, Jay.

Finally, there is Rick Strahl. Rick was involved in the *Using Visual FoxPro 3.0* book and had subsequently become one of our industries leading experts on using the Internet with Visual FoxPro. Therefore, despite an extremely busy schedule, Rick took the time to share some of his knowledge on integrating Visual FoxPro and the Internet. He has even included his Web Connection utilities on the CD. Thanks, Rick.

Writing a book for a product months before it hits the book stores is a tremendous challenge. Not only do features of the product change on nearly a weekly basis, but even features that are there don't always work properly at the time we need to write about them. Attempting to discover what is "real" is almost magic. After all, many programmers still look at object programming as magic. It is, therefore, with immense gratitude that I thank:

Michael's family for their patience and support.

The developers of Visual FoxPro 5.0 at Microsoft for another job well done. May the tradition of FoxPro's cutting-edge features and superb performance continue.

All the dedicated people on the Beta Forum and Visual FoxPro Forum for their prompt responses to our questions.

The wide community of FoxPro beta testers and their suggestions, comments, and complaints as we all waded through the early beta days.

My coauthors without whose help (and sacrifice of golf, beach, or just plain goof-off time) it would have been impossible to write a book of this size with all the text and samples in time for the initial release of FoxPro 5.0.

The dozens of people at QUE responsible for editing and production.

# We'd Like to Hear from You!

As part of our continuing effort to produce books of the highest possible quality, Que would like to hear your comments. To stay competitive, we *really* want you, as a computer book reader and user, to let us know what you like or dislike most about this book or other Que products.

You can mail comments, ideas, or suggestions for improving future editions to the address below, or send us a fax at (317) 581-4663. For the online inclined, Macmillan Computer Publishing has a forum on CompuServe (type **GO QUEBOOKS** at any prompt) through which our staff and authors are available for questions and comments. The address of our Internet site is **http://www.mcp.com** (World Wide Web).

In addition to exploring our forum, please feel free to contact me personally to discuss your opinions of this book: I'm **104124,3145** on CompuServe, and **tdunkelberger@ que.mcp.com** on the Internet.

Thanks in advance—your comments will help us to continue publishing the best books available on computer topics in today's market.

*Tracy Dunkelberger*
Product Development Specialist
Que Corporation
201 W. 103rd Street
Indianapolis, Indiana 46290
USA

# Contents at a Glance

## Appendixes

## Bonus Chapters on the CD

# Table of Contents

## II  | Turning Data into Information

### 6   Selecting, Viewing, and Ordering Data   271

## IV | Techniques from the Pros

## Appendixes

# Introduction

*by Michael Antonovich*

Not since 1989, when FoxPro 1.0 succeeded FoxBase, did application developers in the FoxPro language have such a tremendous paradigm shift. I would argue that the current shift to objects in Visual FoxPro (VFP) represents an even greater shift than the 1989 shift to FoxPro 1.0.

It has now been more than a year since the original release of Visual FoxPro 3.0. The paradigm shift to object-oriented programming, however, has been so great for many developers that many have hesitated to jump in. If you have been waiting, there is no better time than now.

The FoxPro interface design style has always emphasized flexibility and user-friendly features. Yet power and raw speed have always set FoxPro apart from its competitors. Over the years, products from other database companies have created excellent user and programmer interfaces. Some have even moved into the object-oriented programming paradigm. But none has been able to challenge FoxPro's speed in performing database functions.

FoxPro's capability to quickly seek and extract records from databases with thousands, even millions, of records is unmatched. (True, Microsoft Access's performance has improved in many areas, but only by "borrowing" Rushmore features for its own Jet engine.)

This emphasis on power continues with VFP. At the same time, VFP now makes it easier to access other data files from ODBC-compliant databases. Open database connectivity (ODBC) is a standard protocol for database servers. As a result, you can access and use data from sources such as Access, Paradox, and dBASE files directly, without conversion.

The real revolution, however, is VFP's move into client/server features. It is now possible to easily store, retrieve, and manipulate company-critical information on a server platform. SQL Server may be the most popular platform, but ODBC also supports other servers, including Oracle.

Through third-party ODBC drivers, you can even connect to an IBM AS/400 using DB2 (an IBM database product included with the operating system on AS/400 systems). Then you can use VFP to create a user front end and Structured Query Language (SQL) calls to manipulate the data. You can even have the application work with the server and local fields simultaneously.

In the first release of VFP, the object-oriented features made many applications seem to run slower, primarily due to the overhead of those new features. In version 5.0, the development team at Microsoft searched for and found ways to improve the performance of most of these features. As a result, screens draw and refresh faster. Code based on objects runs faster. Overall, this release makes VFP an even more solid choice for developing database-intensive applications than ever before. ■

# The Visual FoxPro Programming Language

VFP is a full-featured programming language that supports an interactive environment and a compiled runtime environment. This means that although you need the full version of VFP to develop applications, you can create and distribute the necessary files to allow others to use them without having to own a copy of VFP.

Compiling VFP code is not quite the same as compiling Visual Basic or Visual C++. VFP does not compile FoxPro commands to machine code. Rather, it remains at an intermediate level called *tokenized code,* in which a command is represented by one or more bytes rather than a text string that calls appropriate functions from a Visual library.

Still, this does not slow VFP's performance, because these tokens reference blocks of true compiled code that actually perform the individual commands and functions. These commands and functions are part of VFP.EXE and related files; they also appear in the runtime files.

If you do not have the distribution kit, which is part of the Professional Edition, you can run VFP only interactively. It also means that you cannot distribute compiled applications to others who do not have VFP. But you certainly can give your application source files or compiled modules to another VFP user.

# What Is New in Visual FoxPro?

If you are still using FoxPro 2.x, much is new. Although VFP runs existing applications from previous Windows versions of FoxPro, to use its real power, you need to incorporate the new features, which include the following:

- The most obvious new feature in VFP is the use of object-oriented programming. VFP uses true classes with inheritance, encapsulation, and polymorphism. Each class has properties, events, and methods.

  Developers can take any of the base classes and develop new classes supplementing the built-in features or creating new classes. You can save these classes in class libraries and use them in your applications, reducing the need to redevelop and test the code.

- The redefined database introduces the concept of a data dictionary, which is new to many FoxPro developers. It provides a central storage "depot" of information about tables. This feature enables you to define long field and table names.

  More important, it allows developers to assign defaults, validations, and triggers for each table using stored procedures. Referential integrity can now be built directly into tables rather than programmed into applications.

- The collection of wizards has been expanded to handle more tasks, and builders have been added to help with additional tasks, such as defining properties for form objects.

- The Project Manager has been redesigned to combine the best features of the Catalog Manager (separation by application file type) and the capability to compile applications. It also allows you to compile and run individual modules.

- The VFP Distribution Kit handles the increasingly complex task of creating distribution disks for Windows applications. Windows applications need more support files, such as dynamic link libraries (DLLs)—utility routines that are separately compiled files and can be called into an application at runtime.

  The Setup Wizard makes including all the necessary files in a set of easy-to-use distribution disks much simpler.

If you have been using VFP 3.0, some of the most exciting new features include:

- A new debugger to replace the Trace and Debug windows. The new debugger adds to the functionality of these windows by making it easier to view memory-variable values, object properties, and the calling-stack sequence.

  But the two biggest additions to the debugger are the capability to track events to determine the order in which they fire and the capability to track coverage. Coverage tells you the number of times each of the lines in your application were executed.

- Enhancements to the SQL statement make it easier to define left, right, and full outer joins.

- VFP can compile visual class libraries into OLE servers. These servers allow any application that can use OLE automation to use these libraries.

- VFP's editor now uses syntax coloring, so that you can display commands, comments, variables, and other parts of your code in different colors. This feature allows you to quickly identify whether the variable that you entered is really a command or function name. It also makes different parts of your code, such as comments, stand out better.

- With field mapping, you no longer have to settle for using text boxes for all your fields when you drag them from a table into a form or use the Form Wizard. Now you can specify any of the VFP base classes for each field type. You can even develop your own classes and use them.

- Along with field mapping, VFP can automatically make use of other information from the database container in defining forms such as captions, formats, input masks, and field comments.

- Visual Source Safe is now integrated with VFP in the professional version. Source Safe is a version-control program that controls updates to code in a multi-developer environment. It also allows you to establish specific versions of each application, create branching applications, and merge branches back together.

- The VFP Internet Wizard allows you to create an interface between the Internet and your data so that visitors to your Web site can query your database. This feature can be useful for distributing data to other people in general or, more specifically, to your company's remote locations.

  The Internet provides a way to access computers across the country or around the world without the cost of dedicated or even public communication lines, because most calls can be local.

- More than 70 new properties, events, methods, commands, and system variables have been added to the language and object model.

# What Is a Relational Database?

Before beginning your study of the new VFP language, you must have a clear concept of what constitutes a relational database. In general terms, a *relational database* is a collection of data in separate files called *tables*. Each table is connected to at least one other table through a common field forming the relation.

Let's begin with the basic unit of a relational database: a field. *Fields* are individual pieces of information. Suppose that you want to track all the books you have read and their authors. You might start with a list like the one shown in Figure I.1.

**FIGURE I.1**

A simple list of books that you have read, organized in columns and rows, forms the basic visual representation of a table.

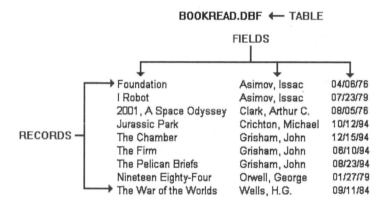

BOOKREAD.DBF ← TABLE

FIELDS

| | | |
|---|---|---|
| Foundation | Asimov, Issac | 04/06/76 |
| I Robot | Asimov, Issac | 07/23/79 |
| 2001, A Space Odyssey | Clark, Arthur C. | 08/05/76 |
| Jurassic Park | Crichton, Michael | 10/12/94 |
| The Chamber | Grisham, John | 12/15/94 |
| The Firm | Grisham, John | 06/10/94 |
| The Pelican Briefs | Grisham, John | 08/23/94 |
| Nineteen Eighty-Four | Orwell, George | 01/27/79 |
| The War of the Worlds | Wells, H.G. | 09/11/84 |

RECORDS —

Each column in this list defines a separate field or type of information. In each row, the information in the same column has the same meaning. For example, the book title is one field, the book author is another, and the date read is a third. If you want to store additional information, each piece of information constitutes another field.

For each book read, several fields further define that book. Taken together, these fields define a record. *Records* use one or more fields to collectively describe something. In this case, that something defines books that you have read. It is common to represent records as rows.

The records that define the books that you have read, when stored together, form a table. A table describes a higher-level grouping than a record; it defines what a group of records means.

Now suppose that you have a similar list that holds information about every book your favorite authors have written, whether you have read them or not. This list might include fields for the book name, author name, and maybe even a brief description of the book. Figure I.2 shows this table.

**FIGURE I.2**

A second table of all books by an author forms a list not unlike those used in library card catalogs.

AUTHORS.DBF ◄── [Second Table]

| | | |
|---|---|---|
| Congo | Crichton, Michael | An 8-person field expedition mysteriously dies brutally in a matter of minutes while Karen Ross watches a video transmission. Meanwhile in San |
| The Andromeda Strain | Crichton, Michael | Five biophysicists warn the U.S. gov't that returning space probes may be contaminated |
| Rising Sun | Crichton, Michael | Whilea grand opening celebration takes place on the 54-floor of a new Japanese conglomerate, a dead body of a beautiful woman is found on the |
| Jurassic Park | Crichton, Michael | An astronishing technique for recovering and cloning dinosaur DNA has been discovered and used to recreate a variety of species extinct for |
| Sphere | Crichton, Michael | A hugh vessel is discovered thousands of feet beneath the surface of the South Pacific ocean |
| The Terminal Man | Crichton, Michael | After being cured of violent seizures by a surgical procedure, Harry Benson has discovered how to |
| Eaters Of The Dead | Crichton, Michael | In A.D. 922 Ahmad Ibn Fadlan accompanies Vikings to the barbaric North where he combats a terror that slaughters the Vikings and devours their |

These two tables have a common element: author names. If you want to learn more about other books written by an author of the book you've read, you can use the second table to find this information. The author name forms a relation between the two tables, as shown in Figure I.3.

**FIGURE I.3**

A block diagram represents a simple database with two tables and their linking relationship.

RELATIONAL DATABASE

The combination of these two tables and the relationship between them forms a simple but complete relational database example. The rest of this book expands on relational tables to show how VFP helps you organize and manipulate data in meaningful and interesting ways.

# How to Use This Book

This book is divided into four sections and four appendixes. It assumes your basic familiarity with the FoxPro programming language and, concentrating on newer features, only briefly covers basic concepts in the appropriate sections.

## Part I: Introducing Visual FoxPro 5

This first part covers many basic concepts needed to understand features in later chapters. It begins with an overview of the VFP interface. It also introduces object-oriented terms and concepts, as well as basic database management.

Chapter 1, "Quick Review of Visual FoxPro's Interface," gets you started with VFP's interface, including the various menu options. It also covers configuration options that are available from within the program. Most of these options can also be set programmatically or in the VFP configuration file, CONFIG.FPW. The chapter concludes by showing how to use a developer's best friend: the online VFP help system.

Chapter 2, "Introducing Object-Oriented Programming," defines the language of object-oriented programming. Concepts such as inheritance, encapsulation, and polymorphism are new to VFP and to many FoxPro programmers. Yet these concepts make developing applications easier and less time-consuming. More important, they form the basis for understanding many of VFP's new features.

Chapter 3, "Defining Databases, Tables, and Indexes," explains how to create databases, tables, and indexes, using their new VFP definitions. For current FoxPro developers, the creation of tables and indexes should be familiar territory. The introduction of databases as containers for tables, however, adds a new dimension to data management. It is now possible to include relation and validation information directly in the database definition for each table. This chapter introduces the basic concepts of engine-based data management.

Chapter 4, "Advanced Database Management Concepts," expands on the concepts discussed in Chapter 3. It begins with a discussion of data normalization, a concept that often separates successful applications from failures. It then shows you how to use advanced database features, including record-level validation and triggers. Finally, the chapter explains how to use triggers to implement referential integrity.

Chapter 5, "Using Wizards for Rapid Application Development," shows how to use wizards to create "skeleton" applications in record time. These skeleton applications can be tested immediately to verify work flow, collect real data, and train users. From a developer's point of view, skeleton programs serve as prototypes for the final application modules, needing only the addition of customized code.

## Part II: Turning Data into Information

This section covers some of the tools that VFP provides to help convert data into information. Raw data is just a collection of character and numeric fields. The collection of data has no purpose if there is no way to perform calculations with it or to redisplay it in a more meaningful way.

Most businesses collect data documenting the number of hours that each employee spends on a project or in the creation of a product. They also collect data on the costs of buildings, equipment, supplies, utilities, and other things. But unless businesses can list and view the entered data and query it for specific results—such as billing rates, invoices, and profitability—the data has little value.

Chapter 6, "Selecting, Viewing, and Ordering Data," looks at basic ways to retrieve raw data from tables. It shows you how to retrieve records from single and multiple tables. It also looks at ways to retrieve selected records or selected ranges of records.

Chapter 7, "Creating Basic Queries," expands on the basic data-selection methods described in the preceding chapter. It introduces SQL, which, through the Query Designer, retrieves selected fields and records from one or more tables. The chapter also describes a variety of ways to output the resulting solution set.

Chapter 8, "Advanced Queries and Views," builds on the concepts in Chapter 7. It looks at multiple-query joins, inner joins, self joins, and outer joins. It also examines how Rushmore technology, introduced in FoxPro 2.0, optimizes a query's efficiency. Cross-tabs provide a method for looking at data differently from the way it is stored. Finally, updatable queries or views allow you to create special data sets that permit users to change individual field values.

Chapter 9, "Using BROWSE to View Data," examines the BROWSE command, one of the most powerful individual features of the FoxPro language. Not only does BROWSE display data in the traditional rows and columns of previous versions, but its related grid object for forms can hold additional objects, such as drop-down lists, buttons, and OLE links.

## Part III: Building Applications the Object Way

Although you can continue to build applications by using techniques you learned in FoxPro 2.x, they do not tap VFP's power unless they also include objects. Applications of any major size need up-front planning. This part examines the steps for designing a new application.

Part III reviews the available programming structures that VFP provides to implement a design. This part also explains how to use the major designers to create forms, menus, reports, and toolbars.

Chapter 10, "Programming Structures," returns to some basic but extremely important programming concepts for controlling the overall program flow. Although an overall program may seem to the user to be event-driven, individual procedures and functions are usually highly structured. This chapter describes how to best implement structured techniques with the new object-oriented paradigm.

Chapter 11, "Building Applications with Simple Form Structures," introduces the object paradigm as it applies to the creation of forms. *Forms* are containers for other objects, such as text boxes, check boxes, and labels. This chapter introduces forms and several basic controls that are common to most forms used for data entry and editing.

Chapter 12, "A Deeper Look at Object-Oriented Design," explores the creation and use of generalized custom objects in form design. In addition to showing you how to use the Class Browser, it shows how to create OLE Server objects. Any user action—such as a mouse click, mouse move, or key press—triggers a cascade of events. So this chapter also discusses how to determine the event sequence and how to select the appropriate event from which to execute methods.

Chapter 13, "Advanced Form Design Controls," looks at list boxes and combo boxes as two ways to give the user a series of choices. Page frames offer the flexibility of including more controls in a form than a traditional, single page form by layering pages. Grids provide a two-dimensional display object that holds not only field data, but also other controls. Finally, this chapter examines in more detail how to create and use custom control libraries.

Chapter 14, "Custom Report Generation," examines the use of VFP's powerful report generator. Through the use of multiple bands and custom expressions, the report generator can solve most report needs.

Chapter 15, "Organizing Components of an Application into a Project," shows how to organize your files into projects to avoid losing track of files. It also forms the basis for compiling programs into applications. This chapter also examines issues surrounding the distribution of applications to other users who may or may not have VFP on their systems.

## Part IV: Techniques from the Pros

This part explores in-depth issues ranging from error detection and debugging to enterprise data concerns. Various expert developers have contributed to this section to give you a broader perspective on development issues.

Chapter 16, "Error Detection and Removal," examines several errors that are common to many applications. It then looks at a few common practices that reduce errors in new code through the development of standards and reviews. Recognizing that some errors are inevitable, however, the chapter also examines the use of VFP's debugger. This enhanced tool expands on the capabilities of the Trace and Debug windows. The debugger also includes options that determine coverage during testing and event tracking to set the order in which events fire and coordinate with other objects.

Chapter 17, "Network Data Sharing," covers issues that affect applications running in a shared environment. The sharing of data involves the use of locks and data-integrity checks. VFP provides buffering and transaction processing as two new tools for handling multiuser situations, especially in client/server applications.

Chapter 18, "Data Dictionary Issues," first examines the features of the new database container to see how it can be used as the basis for a data dictionary in your application. It then expands on the basic features to increase functionality and shows you ways to recover damaged tables, indexes, and even database container files.

Chapter 19, "Internet Support," explains how to create a data interface for your Web page that connects to your corporate database through VFP. You can use such a connection to allow anyone to access data on your server. Alternatively, you can create a more secure system to give your employees around the country access to corporate data via the Internet (with far cheaper connection costs).

Chapter 20, "Creating On-Line Help," examines creating Windows-based help, using a word processor such as Microsoft Word to create RTF files. It reviews the features of several powerful utilities, including Doc-To-Help and RoboHelp, that take the pain out of creating Windows-based help.

## Appendixes

The appendixes provide additional information on special topics related to using VFP.

Appendix A, "Configuration Files," explains how to use the CONFIG.FPW file to define various configuration parameters. Although VFP stores default configuration parameters in the Registry, the settings in a configuration file override these defaults. It is possible to have different applications and even to have different users reference unique configuration files.

Appendix B, "The Resource File," examines the kinds of information that VFP stores in the resource file. You can also write your own code to store data in the resource file. The resource file is also one way to transfer information from one application to another. As with configuration files, you can have multiple resource files for different applications or users. To share a resource file across a network, however, you must mark the file read-only. Users and their applications cannot make changes in this read-only file.

Appendix C, "Optimizing Performance," documents some major settings that affect FoxPro's overall performance, including memory issues, Windows settings, and FoxPro configuration variables.

Appendix D, "Shortcut Keys, Function Keys, and Events," displays in table form the key-code values returned by INKEY() and READKEY(). It also shows the label equivalents of keys when you are using ON KEY LABEL versus ON KEY. Finally, it lists the default macros defined for function keys F2 through F9.

# Assumptions and Conventions

This book assumes that you have a basic familiarity with the FoxPro language. It also assumes that you have a basic familiarity with the Windows operating system. Chapter 1, "Quick Review of Visual FoxPro's Interface," does cover some basic Windows fundamentals, but it is not intended to be a tutorial on Windows itself.

The examples and screen shots use the fonts that come with Windows 95. If you use Windows NT or other fonts, sizes, or styles, your screens may differ slightly from those shown in this book.

## Selecting Options

An integral part of using any Windows-based product is using a mouse. Although some commands and actions include descriptions for both mouse and keyboard use, others mention only the mouse. Furthermore, for the sake of brevity in an already thick book, some terms (such as *click, drag,* and *select*) are used generically whether you use a mouse or the keyboard.

The term *click* is often used interchangeably with choosing an option. When VFP displays a menu or a list of options, you must choose the option that you want by doing one of the following things:

- Clicking the selection.
- Highlighting the option by pressing the arrow keys until the option that you want is displayed in a different color.
- Pressing one or more keys on the keyboard.

Clicking an option chooses and selects the option. Strictly speaking, choosing an option from the keyboard means highlighting it only. In a list, for example, the arrow keys usually move the highlight from one option to the next.

Moving the highlight to an option chooses it but does not select it. When the option is highlighted, double-clicking or pressing the Enter key selects and executes it.

You can access many commands by pressing one or more keys on the keyboard. If two keys are needed, one key typically is Alt or Ctrl. You should hold down the Alt or Ctrl key while pressing the other key.

To insert a blank record into a Browse window, for example, press Ctrl+Y, which means "Press and hold down the Ctrl key while pressing the Y key." Think of this technique like entering capital letters; you press and hold down the Shift key along with the letter that you want to capitalize.

## Type and Font Conventions

This book uses several type and font conventions to help make reading it easier.

Menu-bar selections have initial capital letters and are underlined (File, Edit, View, Database, Program, Window, and others). When these menu names have underlined letters, as shown here, the underlined letters also serve as *hot keys* that enable you to access the option quickly.

FoxPro commands and the names of disk files appear in text in uppercase (BROWSE, USE, and CUSTOMER.DBF).

Table alias names have their first letter capitalized (as in Customer, Payroll, and Orders), whereas table names themselves are in uppercase.

The naming convention used for table fields varies, because tables that are compatible with older versions of FoxPro limit field names to 10 characters. However, VFP allows longer field names. In these cases, field names follow, where possible, a naming convention that begins with a lowercase type identifier, followed by one or more words that identify the field.

Underscores are not recommended anywhere in a name, and spaces are not allowed. Still, some developers use underscores anyway, because VFP does not recognize case when it displays table fields. When shown in text, each "word" in a field name begins with a capital letter.

Although program listings can use mixed-case for field names, views of fields in tables can show field names in uppercase or lowercase. Some typical field names include cCustomerName, nRecordCnt, and dHireDate.

Memory variables follow a naming convention that begins with two lowercase characters that identify the variable's scope and type. These characters are followed by one or more words that identify the `variable`. Underscores should not appear anywhere in the name.

Some examples included with Microsoft, however, still use underscores. Each "word" in a `variable` name begins with a capital letter. Examples include gcCustomerName, lnRecordCnt, and pdHireDate.

*Italic* type is used to emphasize the author's points or to introduce new terms.

Screen messages, code listings, command samples, and code that the user may need to enter appear in a `monospace typeface`.

Placeholders are used to indicate places in commands where users should fill in their own information. To tell users to open a file, the text may say something like the following:

```
USE <filename>
```

In this example, <filename> means that users should supply the name of their own file and not literally type the characters *<filename>*.

## Command Sequences

Many actions need a command sequence, using several selections from the menu. To open a new form, for example, first open the File pull-down menu. Then select the New option, which opens a dialog box. Next, choose the file type by selecting Form.

Instead of going through this long descriptive instruction set every time, most instances shorten the command sequence to File, New, Form. Furthermore, if hot keys exist for a command, those keys are underlined.

In addition, Chapter 1, "Quick Review of Visual FoxPro's Interface," lists shortcut keys for many of the menu commands. The difference between a *hot key* and a *shortcut key* is that hot keys work only when the menu (or pull-down list) in which they appear is open, whereas shortcut keys work at any time.

# System Requirements

Microsoft recommends 10M of RAM for VFP 5.0—a small increase from VFP 3.0's requirement of 8M of RAM. Previous versions of FoxPro run on 4M of RAM, although slowly. The addition of at least 2M, for a total of 6M, makes a significant performance improvement.

For this reason, many developers have already upgraded to 8M. Although VFP 5.0 runs on systems with 8M, it runs even better with 32M. If you intend to use Automation, or if you typically run more than one application at a time, the additional memory improves performance substantially.

## Hardware Requirements

The following list shows the basic hardware needed to run VFP 5.0. As is true of all Windows applications, the more RAM, the better the performance. Furthermore, the number of applications running concurrently under Windows directly affects performance.

- An IBM-compatible computer with an 80486 50MHz processor or higher
- A mouse
- 10M RAM
- 15M of hard disk space for a minimum install (laptop), at least 100M for a typical install, and 240M to completely install all online documentation

- For network operation, a Windows-compatible network and a server with a hard disk
- A VGA monitor or better

Remember not to use all your hard disk space for programs. Windows uses hard disk space for temporary files and virtual memory.

**TIP** A useful rule of thumb is to leave empty at least the equivalent of twice your RAM, plus 10M. In other words, if you have 16M, reserve at least 42M of free space.

Another rule of thumb is to add memory until the hard disk light goes out when the programs are not actually accessing data.

## Software Requirements

In addition to the hardware needs, VFP has three software needs:

- Use Windows 95 or Windows NT 3.5 or later.
- For server applications, use Microsoft SQL Server '95 for Windows NT, MS SQL Server 4.x for Windows NT, MS SQL Server 4.x for OS/2, or Oracle Server 6.0 or later.
- Other networks that can link the server and client machine include Microsoft LAN Manager and any Windows-compatible network software, such as Novell NetWare.

# Using Visual FoxPro 5.0 Sample Files

On the CD

The CD-ROM that comes with this book contains many sample programs and data to illustrate commands and concepts. The program has a file called USINGFOX.BAT that creates the necessary directories and loads the files from the CD-ROM. Following is the structure that this program creates:

```
VFP5BOOK
        DATA
        PROGRAMS
                Chap01
                Chap02
                .
                .
                .
                Chapter 28
```

The program expects to find VFP in the \VFP\ directory on the same column or drive. It also expects to find the Tasmanian Trader example in \VFP\SAMPLES\TASTRADE\. If Microsoft changes these directories before the release of VFP, you may need to change some of the program examples to match the new directories before running them.

## Where Can You Go from Here?

VFP has developed into an incredibly rich programming environment. One book, regardless of the number of pages, cannot present all the possible ways of working with VFP for all levels of users. The first step on your journey, however, may be to learn and understand the techniques discussed here. ●

# Introducing Visual FoxPro 5

# Quick Review of Visual FoxPro's Interface

*by Michael Antonovich*

**O**ver the past several years, an increasing number of complex applications have been built with microcomputer database systems such as FoxPro. But even with the tools that these systems provide—such as screen and report generators, libraries, and project managers—the total time needed to complete many applications has increased. Furthermore, users want to access data stored in other formats, not only on their own machines, but also on central database servers.

Previous releases of FoxPro began to address these problems. Although progress occurred, something was still missing until the introduction of object programming. Many products have experimented with various degrees of object programming. Some products provide fixed definition objects, and the programmer has to use them as they are or not at all; they have no mechanism to start from a base object definition and build on it. Many people refer to this type of programming as *object-based*, not object-oriented. In fact, object-oriented developers look for features such as inheritance, polymorphism, subclassing, and event programming. Within the past couple of years, several

## Navigate the basic features of the Visual FoxPro Desktop

Visual FoxPro uses a variety of features in its interface. Learn how VFP uses menus, toolbars, and dialog boxes to make your tasks easier.

## Manipulate windows

Learn how to move between windows, resize them, minimize them, and maximize them as necessary.

## Use the Project Manager to store your files

The Project Manager should be your command center for starting all projects. Learn how to use the Project Manager to manage your files.

## Set basic configuration options

Visual FoxPro provides quite an array of options for customizing the working environment. Learn what options you can change to make Visual FoxPro work best for you.

## Get help from FoxPro's help system

Learn how to use Visual FoxPro's help system to learn syntax, as well as to get additional information about commands and functions.

products that have many of those features have been released. The authors feel, however, that Visual FoxPro presents the best implementation of an object-oriented, xBase-compatible database programming language to date.

This chapter introduces many basic concepts to ensure that all readers start from the same level. ■

# Getting FoxPro Up and Running

Assuming that you have Visual FoxPro 5.0 (VFP) installed on your machine, how do you start it? When VFP installs, it creates a new Windows group called Microsoft Visual FoxPro and/or installs Visual FoxPro in the Start menu. In Windows NT, this group appears in the Project Manager. Double-clicking the group icon opens the group window, revealing an icon named Microsoft Visual FoxPro 5.0. This icon represents the main program. In Windows 95, VFP installs a group (now called a folder) in the Programs menu of the Start button. By default, the program folder gets the name Microsoft Visual FoxPro. Clicking this option opens another menu level, showing the available programs installed with Visual FoxPro. These programs correspond to the programs shown in the Visual FoxPro group window of the Project Manager. Figure 1.1 shows the Windows 95 version of this screen. Click the menu item Microsoft Visual FoxPro 5.0 to start FoxPro. For details on installation, see Appendix A, "Configuration Files."

**FIGURE 1.1**

Open Visual FoxPro 5.0 by using the Microsoft Visual FoxPro menu in the Programs menu of the Start menu.

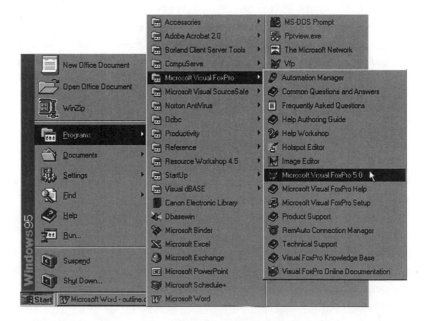

The Windows 95 Explorer provides another common way to start FoxPro. Use the Explorer to open the directory that contains Visual FoxPro, and select VFP.EXE from the file list, as shown in Figure 1.2.

**FIGURE 1.2**

Open Visual FoxPro 5.0 by selecting it from the file list in the Explorer.

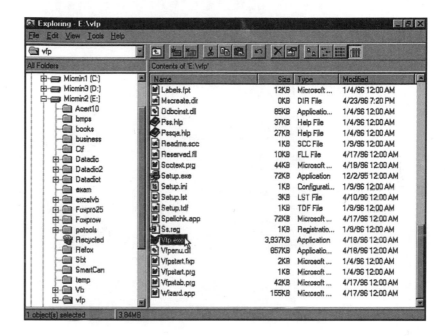

If you run Visual FoxPro frequently, as I do, you may want to create a shortcut for it on your desktop. To do so, open the Explorer as shown in Figure 1.2; but rather than double-click to start VFP, right-click and drag VFP.EXE from the Explorer onto the desktop. When you release the mouse button, a shortcut menu appears, with the following options:

Move Here

Copy Here

Create Shortcut(s) Here

Cancel

Choose Create Shortcut(s) Here. This option places an icon on your desktop that executes Visual FoxPro when it is clicked. Figure 1.3 shows the VFP shortcut in the process of being created.

Finally, you can run FoxPro from the Run option in the Start menu of Windows 95. Simply enter the program's fully qualified name, and select OK. (You also can use the Browse button to find the file, if you do not know its fully qualified name.) Figure 1.4 shows the Run dialog box.

**FIGURE 1.3**
Create a shortcut on your desktop for Visual FoxPro 5.0.

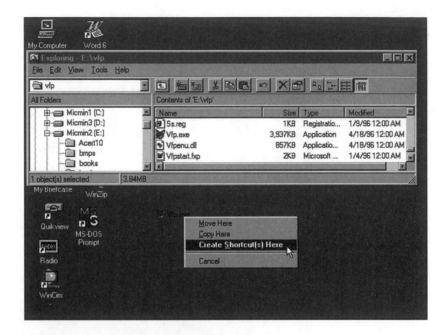

**FIGURE 1.4**
Start Visual FoxPro 5.0 by using the Run dialog box from the Start menu of Windows 95.

You can even start Visual FoxPro by double-clicking any program file (*PRG*) from within the Explorer, as long as you have associated the .PRG extension with the file VFP.EXE.

No matter how you start Visual FoxPro, it opens in its own main window, as shown in Figure 1.5; it also automatically opens the Command window inside the main window. (You may get an introductory splash screen. It includes options to create a new project; explore the sample applications; explore the online documentation; open an existing project; close the splash screen; and to never display the splash screen again. Because this feature adds just one more step before getting into VFP, most developers turn it off so you might not see it.) FoxPro refers to the main window as the *FoxPro desktop* or the *screen*. Later, as you write code that sends output to the screen (such as a report), FoxPro writes it in this window. FoxPro cannot write directly to the Windows desktop.

**FIGURE 1.5**
Visual FoxPro 5.0's
Desktop, or main
screen, opens with the
Command window
active.

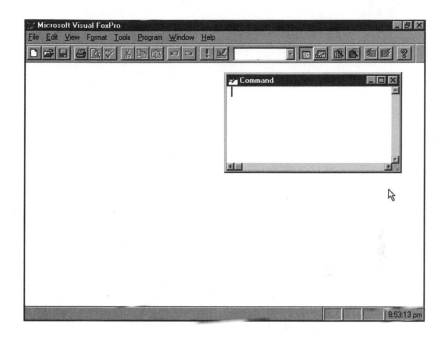

## The Title Bar

 Across the top of the main window or screen are five objects. The first object from the left is the application icon. When it is clicked (with either mouse button), the icon opens to display the Control menu. This menu has commands that move and resize the screen. You can even close FoxPro from this menu by double-clicking this icon.

Table 1.1 defines the options that are available from the Control menu.

| Table 1.1 | Control Menu Options |
| --- | --- |
| **Option** | **Definition** |
| Restore | Restores window to preceding size after minimization or maximization. |
| Move | Selects the main FoxPro window and allows you to move it by using the keyboard cursor controls. |
| Size | Selects the main FoxPro window and allows you to resize it by using the keyboard cursor controls. |
| Minimize | Reduces FoxPro to an icon. |
| Maximize | Maximizes the size of the main FoxPro window. When maximized, a window has no border. |
| Close | Closes FoxPro. |

The title Microsoft Visual FoxPro appears left-justified in Windows 95. You can easily personalize this title, however, just as you can any other property. You have three ways to change it. The old way is:

```
MODIFY WINDOW SCREEN TITLE 'Michael P. Antonovich'
```

And the new way is:

```
_SCREEN.caption = 'Michael P. Antonovich'
```

or

```
_VFP.caption = 'Michael Antonovich'
```

You'll probably want to put your own name in these commands.

The colored portion of the title bar also has a few other functions. First, you can click and drag it to move the window. Double-clicking it alternately maximizes and restores the window to its original size.

Finally, in case you are wondering, FoxPro gets the default color scheme for this title bar and all other window elements from the Windows Control Panel. Windows 95 stores color selections in the Registry.

 Several buttons appear at the right end of the title bar. In Windows 95, the first button shows a horizontal bar across the bottom of the image. This button represents minimizing the application, and it docks the application in the taskbar at the bottom of the screen. Visual FoxPro continues running while it is minimized. If you want to restore a minimized application, click its name in the taskbar. (Minimizing individual windows within Visual FoxPro docks the window title at the bottom of the Visual FoxPro desktop.)

 For the second button in this group, Windows 95 toggles between two buttons. The button used to maximize the Visual FoxPro desktop or the current window looks like a single window; the Restore button looks like two cascaded windows.

 Windows 95 also has a separate Close button on the right side of each window. Clicking this button, which contains an *X*, closes Visual FoxPro (or the current window when you are in application windows).

---

### Be Careful Which Button You Click

Many objects that open in their own windows display a similar Close button. Clicking this button closes the object. The potential danger is the fact that these controls often appear immediately below FoxPro's main Close button. Thus, you can easily click the wrong Close button. As a developer, you would find that restarting VFP after making this mistake several times during a session would be a major annoyance.

One solution stores the following program in FoxPro's main directory:

```
* This program intercepts a double-click on FoxPro's main
* screen and prompts the user to confirm that they want
* to leave FoxPro.
* Store this program as \VFP\REALQUIT.PRG

LOCAL lnMsgResult
lnMsgResult = MESSAGEBOX('Do you really want to quit FoxPro?', ;
    20, 'Exit FoxPro')
IF lnMsgResult = 6  && User selected YES button
  QUIT
ENDIF
```

Then, at the beginning of each session, type the following command to activate the accidental exit protection:

```
ON SHUTDOWN DO \VFP\REALQUIT
```

This routine runs not only when the user attempts to close Visual FoxPro directly, but also if the user attempts to close Windows without first closing FoxPro, or if the user includes the QUIT command in his or her program or types it in the Command window.

Rather than needing to remember to enter this command, consider adding it to the CONFIG.FPW file as a startup command, as follows:

```
COMMAND = ON SHUTDOWN DO \VFP\REALQUIT.PRG
```

## The Main Menu Bar

The main menu bar appears on the second screen line of FoxPro's desktop. In many ways, this menu bar is the equivalent of the tip of an iceberg. Each option in the menu, called a *menu pad*, displays a *menu popup* when you click it. A menu popup usually contains two or more *menu options*. Although a popup can have a single option, a better practice associates single actions with the menu pad directly.

You can select menu pads and their options in several ways. The most obvious method employs the mouse to click them. Pressing F10 activates the menu and highlights the first pad, File.

You may have noticed that each menu pad has one letter underlined. You can open that menu's popup directly by pressing the Alt key along with the underlined letter. To open the File menu, press Alt+F. With any menu popup open, use the left- or right-arrow key to move to other pads. The up- and down-arrow keys open the current pad's popup list and move through its options.

In any given popup, some menu options may appear dimmed. This formatting means that you cannot execute that option now. Usually, common sense tells you why the option is inappropriate. If you open the File popup before opening a table, database, program, or other file, for example, you cannot choose Save; you have nothing to save yet. Therefore, FoxPro automatically dims the Save option text.

While a popup is open, pressing the up- or down-arrow key moves the highlight from one option to the next. Pressing the left- or right-arrow key moves to the next menu pad and opens its menu popup—unless the highlighted option contains a right arrow along its right border, in which case pressing the right-arrow key opens a submenu that lists additional options. To choose a menu item, highlight it and press Enter. A mouse click works just as well. You can even press the underlined letter in the option, if it has one. Notice that in the popup menus, you do not press the Alt key with the underlined letter.

Some menu options have special key combinations, called *shortcut keys,* that allow you to jump to that option directly without going through the menu pads. FoxPro displays these shortcut keys along the right side of the popup menus. The shortcut key for File, New, for example, is Ctrl+N. This means that you can press Ctrl+N any time while you are in Visual FoxPro, with the System menu active, to open a new file. Table 1.2 summarizes the available shortcut keys.

**Table 1.2   Menu Option Shortcut Keys**

| Menu | Menu Option | Shortcut Key |
|------|-------------|--------------|
| File | New | Ctrl+N |
|      | Open | Ctrl+O |
|      | Save | Ctrl+S |
|      | Print | Ctrl+P |
| Edit | Undo | Ctrl+Z |
|      | Redo | Ctrl+R |
|      | Cut | Ctrl+X |
|      | Copy | Ctrl+C |
|      | Paste | Ctrl+V |
|      | Select All | Ctrl+A |
|      | Find | Ctrl+F |
|      | Find Again | Ctrl+G |
|      | Replace | Ctrl+L |
| Program | Do | Ctrl+D |
|         | Resume | Ctrl+M |
|         | Run current Program | Ctrl+E |
| Window | Cycle | Ctrl+F1 |
|        | Command Window | Ctrl+F2 |

### TROUBLESHOOTING

**I'm in the middle of a Visual FoxPro application and when I enter one of the hot keys, nothing happens.** Hot keys are defined through Visual FoxPro's system (or main) menu. You can override or even replace this menu with your own menu, however, when you create custom applications. If VFP's System menu or any individual menu pad is not active, these hot keys are not active, either.

A visual clue that has become a Windows-application standard is the use of an *ellipsis* (...) at the end of a menu option to indicate that selecting the option opens a dialog box with additional options. Choosing File, Open, for example, does not tell FoxPro what to open. Therefore, when you select this option, Visual FoxPro displays its standard Open dialog box. Menu options without ellipses (such as File, Close) execute immediately when they are selected.

A similar standard uses the right arrow to indicate that the option opens another menu level, as in Tools, Wizards.

**The File Menu Options**  The File menu popup list contains options related to accessing files (creating new files, opening existing ones, closing, saving, and printing). Table 1.3 describes these options.

**Table 1.3  File Menu Options**

| Menu Option | Description |
| --- | --- |
| New | Opens the New dialog box. The options in this dialog box enable you to create new projects, databases, tables, queries, connections, views, remote views, forms, reports, labels, programs, classes, text files, and menus. |
| Open | Opens the Open dialog box, which opens any file type listed under New. |
| Close | Closes the active window. If you press Shift and open the File menu, this option becomes Close All, which closes all open windows. |
| Save | Saves the file in the active window with its current name. For a new file that has no name, the option prompts the user for a file name. |
| Save As | Prompts the user for a new file name before saving the file. |
| Save As Class | Saves the current form or selected controls as a class definition (active only from within the Form Designer). |
| Revert | Cancels changes made in the current file during the current editing session. |
| Import | Imports a Visual FoxPro file or a file formatted by another application. You can also use this option to start the Import Wizard. |
| Export | Exports a Visual FoxPro file in another application's file format. |
| Page Setup | Changes the page layout and printer settings for reports. |

*continues*

**Table 1.3    Continued**

| Menu Option | Description |
| --- | --- |
| Page Preview | Displays pages in a window as they will appear when printed. |
| Print | Prints the contents of the current window, a file, or Visual FoxPro's Clipboard. |
| Send | Allows you to send e-mail. |
| <project files if any> | Provides quick access to reopen any of the last four opened projects. |
| Exit | Exits Visual FoxPro. Choosing this option is the same as typing **QUIT** in the Command window. |

**The Edit Menu Options**    The options in the Edit menu provide functions that are used for editing programs, forms, and reports. This menu also contains options that create *object linking and embedding (OLE)* objects. Table 1.4 lists the options that appear at various times in the Edit menu pad.

**Table 1.4    Edit Menu Options**

| Menu Option | Description |
| --- | --- |
| Undo | Reverses an unlimited number of changes made in the current edit session. Changes made before the last save, even if made during the same session, are not reversible. |
| Redo | Performs a reversed change again. |
| Cut | Removes selected text or object from current document, placing it on the Clipboard. |
| Copy | Makes a copy of the selected text or object on the Clipboard. |
| Paste | Copies the current contents of the Clipboard to the current insertion point. |
| Paste Special | Used to insert OLE objects from other applications into a general field. You can embed objects or merely link them. Visual FoxPro stores a copy of embedded objects in the current object. When merely an object is linked, FoxPro stores a path and name reference to the original object only. |
| Clear | Removes selected text without copying it to the Clipboard. |
| Select All | Selects all objects in the current window. This option is used often in form and report design to move or format all objects at the same time. |

| Menu Option | Description |
| --- | --- |
| Find | Displays the Find dialog box, which is used to locate text strings in files. Find options include the capability to ignore case, wrap around lines, match entire words, and search forward or backward. |
| Find Again | Repeats the last Find starting at the current insertion point position rather than the beginning of the document. |
| Replace | Displays the Replace dialog box, which is used to locate and replace text strings in files. |
| Go to Line | Used primarily during debugging to go to a specific line number in a program file. This option cannot be used with word wrap on. (Of course, you don't have word wrap on when you edit your FoxPro programs—*right?*) |
| Insert Object | Similar to Paste Special, except that it does not assume that the object already exists and is stored on the Clipboard. The option embeds objects in general type fields. When chosen, Insert Object opens the other application without exiting Visual FoxPro. After creating the object in the other application, Insert Object returns to Visual FoxPro and inserts the linked or embedded object. |
| Object | Provides options for editing a selected OLE object. |
| Links | Opens linked files (OLE) and allows you to edit the link. |
| Properties | Displays the Edit Properties dialog box, which allows you to affect the behavior, appearance, and save options of the edit windows. |

Several options from Table 1.4—Paste Special, Insert Object, Object, and Links—apply only to general fields and OLE. The rest of the options apply to editing programs and fields.

The Edit Properties dialog box, opened by the last option in the Edit menu, gives you control over the editor's many properties. The behavior properties, for example, turn on and off drag-and-drop editing, word wrap, and automatic indent. (Unless you are using Visual FoxPro editor as a word processor, I do not recommend using word wrap.)

You can also specify the following:

- Alignment of text (usually left for programs)
- Number of spaces in a tab
- Editor font
- Use of syntax coloring (a cool enhancement)
- Display of the column and row position of the insertion point

Finally, you can have VFP make a backup copy of the file when you edit it, compile the file when it is saved, save line feeds, and create an end-of-file marker. Figure 1.6 shows these features.

**FIGURE 1.6**
Use Edit Properties to customize the editor properties of Visual FoxPro 5.0.

**The View Menu Options**　This menu displays options that are appropriate for viewing the current table, if one is open. If you are not currently viewing a file, the menu displays a single option (Toolbar) that opens the Toolbar dialog box, which lists the available toolbars used by Visual FoxPro. On the other hand, if you already are browsing a table or editing a form, menu, or report, additional options appear, as described in Table 1.5.

**Table 1.5　View Menu Options**

| Menu Option | Description |
| --- | --- |
| Edit | Changes to an Edit layout style for viewing and changing records. The option displays fields vertically, and a horizontal line separates records (if grid lines are active). |
| Browse | Changes to a Browse layout style for viewing and changing records. The option displays fields horizontally; rows represent records, and columns represent fields. |
| Append Mode | Appends a blank record to the end of the table and moves the record pointer to the first field in it. |
| Design | Displays the Form, Label, or Report Designer. |
| Tab Order | Allows you to set the tab order in forms. |
| Preview | Shows a preview of labels or reports on-screen. |

| Menu Option | Description |
|---|---|
| Data Environment | Defines tables and relations used in a form, form set, or report. |
| Properties | Displays the Properties dialog box for forms and controls. |
| Code | Opens the code windows when you are editing object methods. |
| Form Controls Toolbar | Opens the Form Controls toolbar while you are in the Form Designer. |
| Report Controls Toolbar | Displays the Report Controls toolbar, which allows you to add controls to a report. |
| Layout Toolbar | Opens the Layout toolbar, which helps you align controls. |
| Color Palette Toolbar | Opens the Color Palette toolbar, which allows you to select foreground and background colors for a control. |
| Report Preview Toolbar | Provides buttons that move between pages of the preview, change the zoom factor, print the report, and exit preview mode. |
| Database Designer | Opens the Database Designer, which maintains tables, views, and relationships stored in a database. |
| Table Designer | Opens the Table Designer, which allows you to make structure modifications to associated and free tables and to their indexes. |
| Grid Lines | Toggles the display of grid lines on and off. |
| Show Position | Displays the position, height, and width of the selected object or form in the status bar. |
| General Options | Adds code in a menu when you are using the Menu Designer. |
| Menu Options | Adds code to specific menu options. |
| Toolbars | Displays a dialog box that lists every toolbar used by FoxPro, allowing you to customize the buttons in toolbars and to create your own. |

**The Format Menu Options**    The Format menu normally consists of options that control font characteristics, text indentation, and spacing. Additional options become available, however, when you are using the various Designers and are described in Table 1.6.

**Table 1.6    Format Menu Options**

| Menu Option | Description |
|---|---|
| Font | Selects a font and its characteristics. |
| Enlarge Font | Enlarges the font used in the current window. |
| Reduce Font | Reduces the font size used in the current window. |
| Single Space | Single-spaces the text in the current window. |
| 1 1/2 Space | Uses 1-1/2-line spacing for the text in the current window. |
| Double Space | Double-spaces the text in the current window. |
| Indent | Indents the current or selected lines in the current window. |
| Unindent | Removes the indent of the current or selected lines in the current window. |
| Comment | Comments out the selected lines. |
| Uncomment | Removes comments from the selected lines. |
| Align | Opens options that align selected objects. |
| Size | Opens options that size selected objects. |
| Horizontal Spacing | Provides options that adjust horizontal spacing between selected objects. |
| Vertical Spacing | Provides options that adjust vertical spacing between selected objects. |
| Bring to Front | Moves the selected object to the top of the objects in a form. |
| Send to Back | Moves the selected object to the back of the objects in a form. |
| Group | Associates a selection of objects in reports and allows you to work with them as a group. |
| Ungroup | Breaks a group definition into individual objects again. |
| Snap to Grid | When you are moving objects, repositions the top-left corner to the nearest grid intersection when the mouse button is released. |
| Set Grid Scale | Determines how far apart the vertical and horizontal grids are. |
| Text Alignment | Aligns text in the selected object. |
| Fill | Defines a fill pattern for shapes. |
| Pen | Defines a pen thickness and style for shapes. |
| Mode | Defines whether the background of an object is opaque or transparent. |

The Font option opens a dialog box that displays a list of available fonts, their styles, and sizes. The option also displays a small sample of the font in a preview window. The font list contains all fonts that are defined in Windows. Fonts that have *TT* before their names are *TrueType* fonts, which can print over a large range of font sizes and still look good. If you are editing a program file, fonts preceded by a blank are either screen or printer fonts. These fonts look good on-screen, but they have to be sent to the printer as bitmap images (which print slowly), or they use a "similar" font for printing. I recommend the use of TrueType fonts. You can also control some additional effects in reports, such as Strikeout, Underline, and Color.

**CAUTION**

If you develop applications for other people, be careful which fonts you use. Unless you have shareware fonts that permit distribution, keep in mind that many fonts cannot be distributed freely. If your application uses a font that other computers do not have, formatted screens and reports may not come out as planned. Common fonts that currently ship with Windows 95 include Arial, Courier New, Marlett, Symbol, Times New Roman, and Wingdings. Check your current Windows manual to verify this list.

**N O T E** When you use the Enlarge Font or Reduce Font option Visual FoxPro attempts to use font sizes stored in the font file, but it can calculate other font sizes based on multiples of existing font sizes or combinations of them. Visual FoxPro can create a 14-point font from information in the 6- and 8-point fonts, for example. ▪

Unlike the Single Space, 1 1/2 Space, and Double Space options, Indent modifies only the current or selected lines in the current window. The option indents the line by the equivalent of one tab position each time you choose it. You can set the number of characters represented by a tab position through the Properties dialog box (Edit menu).

The Unindent option removes the equivalent of one tab from the current or selected lines each time you choose it. The Comment option precedes the selected lines with the characters *!*. Only if the selected lines begin with these characters will Uncomment remove the comment characters.

**The Tools Menu Options**   This menu provides a variety of programmer tools, ranging from wizards to the debugger. Table 1.7 defines the options in the Tools menu.

**Table 1.7   Tools Menu Options**

| Menu Option | Description |
|---|---|
| Wizards | Lists and provides access to Visual FoxPro's wizards. (See Chapter 5, "Using Wizards for Rapid Application Development.") |
| Spelling | Primarily spell-checks text fields and memos. |
| Macros | Defines and maintains keyboard macros. |
| Class Browser | Examines the contents of any class to view its properties and methods or even the actual code used to create the object. |
| Beautify | Reformats program files to add indenting and capitalization. |
| Debugger | Opens the Debugger window. This improved replacement for the Debug and Trace window adds windows for watch variables, locals, call stack, and the capability to track events and analyze coverage during testing. |
| Options | Provides access to Visual FoxPro configuration options. |

FoxPro 2.6 introduced *wizards,* which are programs that guide the user through specific tasks, such as creating a table. A wizard uses a series of windows that ask questions about the object that is being created.

Visual FoxPro also includes a spelling checker, which you can use to check the spelling of any object's text, beginning at the current location of the insertion point. Although you can use this feature to spell check program listings, that is not the intent. Instead, use the spelling checker to spell check long text and memo fields.

▶ **See** "Keyboard Macros" in Bonus Chapter 03 located on the CD

The Macro dialog box enables you to create, edit, and view macro definitions. A *macro definition* consists of a series of Visual FoxPro commands that you can store and execute with a single keystroke. Previously FoxPro provided eight default macro definitions, which are assigned to function keys F2 through F9. Pressing F5, for example, executed the command DISPLAY STRUCTURE, which lists the structure of the current table. Table 1.8 shows the definitions of these default macros.

**Table 1.8   Default Macro Definitions for Function Keys**

| Key | Command | Description |
|---|---|---|
| F2 | SET | Opens the View window. |
| F3 | LIST | Lists records from the current table; opens the GETFILE window if no table is being used. |

| Key | Command | Description |
|-----|---------|-------------|
| F4 | DIR | Lists all tables in the current directory. |
| F5 | DISPLAY | Shows the field definitions of the current table; opens the STRUCTURE GETFILE window if no database is being used. |
| F6 | DISPLAY STATUS | Shows the table open in each area. If an index is also open, F6 displays its expression. The key also shows the settings of SET commands and other system information. |
| F7 | DISPLAY MEMORY | Displays the values stored in all memory variables, including system variables. F7 also shows the definitions of all menus, pads, popup lists, and windows. |
| F8 | DISPLAY | Displays the current record; opens the GETFILE window if no table is being used. |
| F9 | | Enters append mode for the current table. Opens the GETFILE window if no database is being used. |

Because these default macros are not currently provided with the beta version of VFP used to create this book, the file is \VFP5BOOK\CHAP01\DEFAULT.FKY. Simply install it in your VFP root directory and VFP will automatically find and use it.

In addition to these eight macros, you can define your own. In fact, because you can use a variety of key combinations to name macros, you can define more than 250 macros at one time.

▶ **See** "Using the Trace Window," **p. 652**

▶ **See** "Using the Watch Window," **p. 662**

The last option in the Tools menu is Options, which displays a multiple-page form that provides controls to customize the way that you work with Visual FoxPro. VFP divides these controls into 12 distinct groups: Controls, Data, Debug, Field Mapping, File Locations, Forms, General, Projects, Regional, Remote Data, Syntax Coloring, and View. These groups are covered in more detail in "Setting Configuration Options" later in this chapter.

**The Program Menu Options**    The Program menu consists of six options that are related to compiling and running a program. Table 1.9 defines the Program options.

**Table 1.9 Program Menu Options**

| Menu Option | Description |
| --- | --- |
| Do | Runs a program selected from a dialog box. |
| Cancel | Cancels the current program. |
| Resume | Resumes the current program from a suspended state. |
| Suspend | Stops the current program from executing but does not remove it from memory. |
| Compile | Translates a source file into object code. |
| Run | Runs the current program. (The option appears in the menu as Do, followed by the name of the PRG.) |

The Do command opens a dialog box that allows you to select the program that you want to run. (You can also execute a program from the Command window; enter **DO**, immediately followed by the name of the program that you want to run.) You do not have to compile a program before running it; you can run a PRG directly. VFP can compile the program automatically before running it.

**N O T E** You can have VFP compile a program each time you save it. You can use the Edit Properties dialog box to set this flag and save it for all PRG files. Subsequent new program files inherit this property, but it does not affect existing PRG files. To change those files to automatically compile on saving, you must set the property separately. ■

Choose Program, Do, and select the program from the Do dialog box which is similar to the Open dialog box. The Do option differs from the Run option (which appears in the menu as Do, followed by the name of the PRG), which executes the program in the current window.

VFP enables the Cancel option only when you are executing a program. To access this option, you must suspend the program or be stepping through it in the Trace window.

**N O T E** After suspending a program, you cannot edit the source code until you cancel the program. ■

Visual FoxPro enables Resume only while an executing program is suspended. The option resumes a suspended program to normal execution mode.

To suspend a program, you first need to interrupt it. You can do this while you are using the Trace window to step through the program. You also can interrupt a program by inserting breakpoints into the code, using the Trace window, or setting break conditions on variables or expressions.

The Compile option opens a window similar to the Open dialog box, allowing you to select a source file. The option takes the selected program source file (PRG) and compiles it. Click the More>> button to display several additional options related to encryption and debugging, as well as to create an error file (ERR), if desired.

▶ **See** "Understanding Methods for Tracking Down Errors," **p. 646**

▶ **See** "Building Visual FoxPro .APPs and .EXEs," **p. 593**

**The Window Menu Options**    The Window menu contains options that manage open windows on-screen. The menu provides options that allow you to Arrange All, Hide, Clear, and Cycle through windows. In addition, the menu allows you to bring to the front any window that is currently open. Table 1.10 lists the Window options.

**Table 1.10    Window Menu Options**

| Menu Option | Description |
| --- | --- |
| Arrange All | Arranges open windows as nonoverlapping tiles. |
| Hide | Hides the active window but does not remove it from memory. |
| Show All | Displays all defined windows. |
| Clear | Clears text from the application workspace or current output window. |
| Cycle | Moves from one open window to the next, making the next window the active one. |
| Command Window | Makes the Command window active and brings it to the top, opening it if necessary. |
| Data Session | Makes the Data Session window active and brings it to the top, opening it if necessary. This window serves as a valuable tool for monitoring which tables are open in each of the 32,767 work areas. |
| <Window List> | Displays the first nine defined windows. If more than nine windows have been defined, a final option—More Windows—appears. To change focus to any window, simply click its name. |

The Arrange All option resizes open windows to create nonoverlapping tiles. Arrange All will not resize a maximized window. With two open windows, it splits the screen in half vertically and puts the active window on the left side. With three open windows, it also splits the screen in half vertically, putting the active window on the left side. The option then splits the right half horizontally, however, to display the other two open windows. If you have four open windows, each window receives one-quarter of the screen; the active window is placed in the upper-left corner. For more windows, you'll have to experiment.

The Hide option removes the active window from the screen. You cannot redisplay a system window (such as an edit window for a program) without reissuing the command that created it. If you hide a user-defined window, however, that window remains in memory; you can redisplay it with the SHOW WINDOW command. If you hide the current output window, it continues to receive output even while it is hidden, which means that you cannot see it. Upon redisplaying the window, you again see anything that has been written to it.

**TIP**

Take advantage of the capability to write to a window while it is hidden to draw complex screens. Rather than amuse the user with a light show as your program paints a screen, hide the window, add the objects to it, and show the window fully developed.

Clear erases text from the current screen or active window. Notice that when you use the SHOW WINDOW command after hiding a window, that window does not automatically become the active window; its status depends on whether it was the active window when hidden and whether you activated another window in the meantime. (To ensure that a window is active, use the ACTIVATE WINDOW command.) Therefore, be careful about what you clear.

**CAUTION**

The CLEAR command and the Clear option in the Window menu are not the same as CLEAR WINDOW, which removes the window from both the screen and memory. The CLEAR command and the Clear option only remove the text from the window.

The Data Session option opens the Data Session dialog box, which displays a list of all tables that are open in the current session. The option also displays any relations defined among these tables, as shown in Figure 1.7.

In the middle of the Data Session dialog box is a set of six buttons. The Properties button opens a window that displays the current table properties, indicating the data-buffering options that are in effect and any data filter or index order. The window also allows you to determine whether to allow access to all fields in the work area or only to fields selected with a field filter. Figure 1.8 shows the Work Area Properties window.

▶ **See** "Modifying Table Structures," **p. 146**

**FIGURE 1.7**
The Data Session dialog box shows three work areas with defined tables and the relation set between two of them.

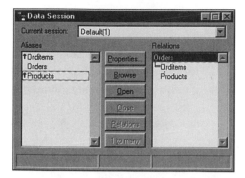

**FIGURE 1.8**
The Work Area Properties window is opened by choosing Properties in the Data Session window.

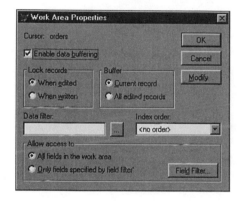

If you can open the table exclusively, you can change the structure by clicking the Modify button. This button opens the Table Designer, shown in Figure 1.9.

**FIGURE 1.9**
The Table Designer allows you to define not only the fields in a table, but also indexes, field properties, and table properties.

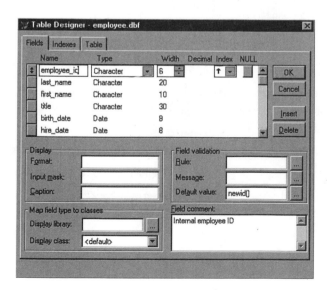

Part
I

Ch
1

This option allows you to change not only the fields for the selected table, but also the properties of those fields (captions, validations, defaults, and so on). You can also add, delete, or modify index expressions from the Indexes page of the Table Designer. The indexes defined here are part of the structural compound index for the current table. Finally, you can select the Table page to set record validations and triggers.

**N O T E** Visual FoxPro does not create indexes with .NDX extensions. The program can read .NDX indexes from earlier database systems, but it immediately converts them to its own internal index format, even though it may retain the .NDX extension. If you need to create a stand-alone index (.IDX) or a nonstructural compound index, you must do so from the Command window or from within a program, using the INDEX command. ■

To open a table in a new work area, click the Open button in the Data Session dialog box. The Open dialog box appears to help you select a table. With a table assigned to a work area, you can browse through its records by clicking the Browse button.

The Close button closes the table in the currently selected work area (the highlighted one).

The Relations button allows you to define relations between files. If you already defined persistent relations through the Database Designer, however (or if you plan to), do not repeat those relations here.

▶ **See** "Forming Persistent Relations," **p. 200**

**The Help Menu Options** Help is the final menu pad of the System menu. Table 1.11 lists the options available in this menu. The first two options present different ways to access the help file so as to get information on commands, functions, or features. The third option lists support options that are available from Microsoft. The last option opens the typical copyright screen for the product; it adds additional functionality by providing system information and allowing the user to run other applications from within FoxPro.

**Table 1.11  Format Menu Options**

| Menu Option | Description |
| --- | --- |
| Contents | Displays help information via an outline format. |
| Documentation | Opens the FoxPro online documentation. |
| Sample Applications | Describes the sample applications provided with Visual FoxPro. |
| Microsoft on the Web | Opens a second menu with options to use your Web browser to go to a variety of Visual FoxPro pages on the Web, the Microsoft Home Page, and several other locations. |

| Menu Option | Description |
|---|---|
| Technical Support | Provides a list of available resources from Microsoft that offer additional help. The list includes a section that answers common questions. |
| About Microsoft Visual FoxPro | Displays the copyright screen for the product, along with whom it is licensed to, version date, resource file name, default directory, and product ID. Additional features include the capability to list system information and to run other programs. |

The About Microsoft Visual FoxPro option displays an initial screen that contains the standard copyright and license information. The screen includes a special bonus: the System Info button. Click this button to display information about your system, as shown in Figure 1.10.

**FIGURE 1.10**

System Information is one of several categories of information for documenting your computer system that you can access from the About screen.

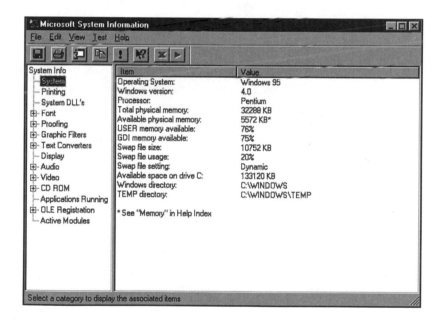

If you have problems with FoxPro and call Microsoft for assistance, print this screen first. In addition, you can display more than a dozen additional categories of available information by clicking the category name in the left window.

A bonus feature of the Microsoft System Info screen is the <u>R</u>un option in the <u>F</u>ile menu. Click this option to display a default list of applications that you can run. This list does not include every program on your system, but by clicking the <u>B</u>rowse button, you can open a window from which you can select any application that is available to your system. Your capability to run other programs, of course, may depend on the amount of available memory on your machine. Figure 1.11 shows the Run Application window.

**FIGURE 1.11**
The About screen has an option that permits you to run external programs from within Visual FoxPro.

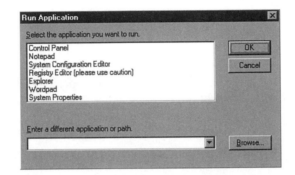

The Visual FoxPro System menu is dynamic; it changes as you perform different functions and use different VFP tools. Sometimes, the changes add or remove menu pads directly; at other times, the changes occur in the drop-down menus themselves.

▶ **See** "Creating a Menu" in Bonus Chapter 02 located on the CD

## The Toolbar

FoxPro has several toolbars, each of which is customized for the current task. This arrangement eliminates the confusion (and space problems) of having all buttons available at all times. This section briefly examines the main system toolbar, also called the Standard toolbar. Subsequent chapters examine the other toolbars as they are introduced.

The main system toolbar contains 20 buttons and one drop-down list. As you slowly pass your mouse over any button, a small box appears below it, displaying the button's name. This box is called a *ToolTip*. ToolTips remind you of what the pictures on the buttons represent, just in case you forget. Figure 1.12 shows the buttons in the Standard toolbar, along with their names.

Table 1.12 expands upon the button names, briefly describing the purpose of each button.

**FIGURE 1.12**
This figure shows the definitions of the buttons in the Standard toolbar.

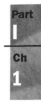

### Table 1.12   Buttons in the Standard Toolbar

| Button Name | Button | Description |
|---|---|---|
| New | | Opens the New File dialog box in preparation to create a new file. |
| Open | | Opens the Open File dialog box to open an existing file. |
| Save | | Saves changes made to the current file. By default, the button uses the file's original file name, except for a new file that has no name; then it prompts for a file name. |
| Print | | Prints the active file, Command window contents, or Clipboard contents. |
| Print Preview | | Uses a preview window to show what Print would output. |
| Spelling | | Activates the spell checker. |
| Cut | | Cuts the current selected text or object and places it on the Clipboard. |
| Copy | | Copies the current selected text or object and places it on the Clipboard. |

*continues*

**Table 1.12   Continued**

| Button Name | Button | Description |
| --- | --- | --- |
| Paste | | Copies the current contents of the Clipboard and pastes it at the current insertion-point location. |
| Undo | | Undoes the last action or command, with some limitations. The Undo button cannot undo a PACK command, for example. |
| Redo | | Repeats the last command or action. |
| Run | | Appears enabled if Visual FoxPro has an executable file open, such as a screen or program. |
| Modify Form | | Switches the currently executing form back into designer mode. |
| Database | | Lists the names of all open databases in a drop-down list. The current database appears in the text box. You can switch to a different database by selecting it from the list. |
| Command Window | | Opens or pops the Command window back into view and makes it the active window. |
| View Window | | Opens or pops the View window back into view and makes it the active window. |
| Form Wizard | | Launches the Form Wizard. |
| Report Wizard | | Launches the Report Wizard. |
| AutoForm Wizard | | Creates a form from the current table. |
| AutoReport Wizard | | Creates a report from the current table. |
| Help | | Displays Visual FoxPro's Help Contents screen. |

# The Status Bar

The status bar appears at the bottom of Visual FoxPro's main screen if SET STATUS is ON. The status bar itself has two main areas: the message area on the left and indicator boxes on the right.

The message area is blank when no table is open in the current work area. When a table is open, the message area displays the following:

- The table's name
- The table's database name (enclosed in parentheses, if appropriate)
- The current record number
- The total number of records in the table

The Designers use this area to display the position and size of objects.

Finally, the message area displays the current sharable status of the file or current record, using one of the following designations:

- Exclusive
- Record Unlocked
- Record Locked
- File Locked

Visual FoxPro also uses this portion of the status bar to display system messages that concern issues such as its progress during reindexing. Forms also use this area to display text messages associated with fields and controls, as well as position and size information, while you are in the Designers.

The right end of the status bar contains either three or four indicator boxes. The first box on the left indicates the status of the Insert key. This box is blank when VFP's editor is in insert mode; otherwise, the letters OVR appear, indicating overwrite mode. The next box displays NUM when the Num Lock key is on. The third box indicates the status of the Caps Lock key, displaying CAPS when the key is on. Finally, a fourth box may appear, displaying the current time.

**N O T E** The View page of the Options dialog box (choose Tools, Options to display this dialog box) controls whether to display time in the status bar. Alternatively, you can enter **SET CLOCK STATUS** to turn on the clock in the status bar. ■

# Controlling Windows

All windows, whether they are system windows or user-defined ones, have common features, although for any single window, one or more of the features may not be active. The following sections examine the Command window to help you become familiar with these features.

## Zooming Windows

   As mentioned earlier in this chapter, the title bar of a window has several buttons on the right side. The button with the lower horizontal line minimizes the window, representing it with an icon or docking it in the taskbar. (For windows within FoxPro, however, this button docks the icon on FoxPro's main screen, not the Windows desktop). The other button, with the single window image, maximizes the window. For a maximized window, the Restore button replaces the Maximize button; it has the image of two cascaded windows.

If you do not have a mouse, or if you just prefer not to take your hands off of the keyboard long enough to pick up the mouse, you can zoom the window by using shortcut keys. You can open the Windows 95 Window menu by pressing Alt+ –. This shortcut key displays the options, along with their shortcut keys. Table 1.13 lists the shortcut keys, which work consistently across all Windows applications.

| Table 1.13 | Commands in the Window Menu with Their Shortcut Keys | |
|---|---|---|
| **Command** | **Shortcut Key** | **Description** |
| Restore | Ctrl+F5 | Returns the window to its original size |
| Move | Ctrl+F7 | Allows you to move the window with the arrow keys |
| Size | Ctrl+F8 | Allows you to size the window with the arrow keys |
| Minimize | Ctrl+F9 | Minimizes the window and displays it as an icon |
| Maximize | Ctrl+F10 | Maximizes the window |
| Close | Ctrl+F4 | Closes the window |
| Next Window | Ctrl+F6 | Activates the next window |

**N O T E** The Next Window command in the Control menu duplicates the functionality of the Cycle option in the Window menu. Thus, you can use either Ctrl+F6 or Ctrl+F1 to cycle through open windows. ▪

## Resizing Windows

Maximizing or minimizing a window are not your only resizing choices; you can also "grab" any portion of the border to stretch the window. In fact, as you move the cursor around the border, you can see that Visual FoxPro divides the border into eight segments, one for each side and corner. Placing the mouse on any edge changes the cursor to show the direction in which the border stretches. Side segments stretch the window horizontally or vertically. Corners stretch the window in two directions at the same time.

If you don't have a mouse (but you really should get one before going much further with any Windows product; mice are relatively cheap and don't cat much), you can follow these steps to resize a window:

1. Press Ctrl+F1 to cycle through the open windows and activate the window that you want to resize.
2. Open the close box by pressing Alt+– (Alt plus the hyphen/minus-sign key).
3. Choose Size by pressing **S** or by selecting the option and then pressing Enter.
4. Now use the arrow keys to stretch the window. Notice that as you press the first arrow key, the cursor moves to the border in that same direction. If you continue to press the same arrow key, or the one for the opposite direction, the window expands or shrinks, respectively. If you press either of the two other arrow keys, the cursor moves to the corresponding corner first. Now you can use any arrow key to stretch or shrink the window from the current corner while the opposite corner remains fixed.
5. When you have the window sized the way that you want it, press Enter.

Later, when you create your own windows, you learn how to control which, if any, of these features remain active. Indeed, for some applications, you do not want the user to change the window's size.

## Moving Windows

The easiest way to move a window is with the mouse. Simply click the title bar and drag the entire window anywhere on the screen. If you try to drag the window off the screen, VFP stops the movement when the mouse reaches a screen edge. Therefore, you cannot drag the window completely off the screen by using the mouse.

You also can move the window by using the keyboard. Follow these steps:

1. Press Ctrl+F1 to cycle through the open windows and activate the window that you want to move.

2. Open the close box by pressing Alt+ – (Alt plus the hyphen/minus sign).

3. Choose <u>M</u>ove by pressing **M** or by selecting the option and then pressing Enter.

4. Now use the arrow keys to move the window.

5. When you have the window where you want it, press Enter.

## Understanding Common Window Objects

Many common components appear in Visual FoxPro's dialog boxes, as well as in custom-designed forms. Figure 1.13 shows the most common components used in the Visual FoxPro interface.

**FIGURE 1.13**

This image shows examples of common screen elements used in Visual FoxPro.

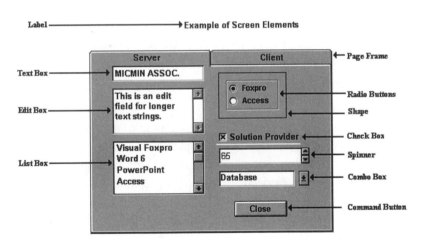

**Labels**   A *label* is a fixed text string displayed in a form. VFP uses labels for titles and to identify other objects in forms.

**Text Boxes**   *Text boxes* contain character variables. These boxes can obtain their values from tables, or they can represent memory variables. In either case, when text boxes appear in a form, you can edit them by selecting the text and making any changes.

Although a text box has a physical length on-screen, this physical length does not limit the length of the data that it contains. You control data length by using PICTURE clauses or by automatically truncating data to the length of table fields. You can also set the maximum length property of the text-box control. For longer values, text boxes can be more than one line high.

**Edit Boxes**    *Edit boxes* also allow you to edit character strings. The main advantage of an edit box is the scroll bar, which allows you to edit long strings and even memos.

**List Boxes**    The purpose of a *list box* is to display a series of options. Table 1.14 displays possible list sources.

**Table 1.14    List-Source Values for List Boxes**

| Source ID | Source |
| --- | --- |
| 0 | None |
| 1 | Value |
| 2 | Alias |
| 3 | SQL statement |
| 4 | Query (.QPR) |
| 5 | Array |
| 6 | Fields |
| 7 | Files |
| 8 | Structure |
| 9 | Popup |

**Option Groups**    *Option groups* (previously called *radio buttons*) limit the user to selecting one option from the group. Within a group of option buttons, you can select only one button at a time. In fact, the order of the option buttons in the group defines the value of a single variable. Should you click a second button, the preceding selection is released. The setup is just like the preset-station buttons on a car radio.

Remember that a variable can have only one value.

A selected button displays a black dot inside the circle. A deselected button is just an empty circle.

A box automatically surrounds the option group upon creation. This box is especially important if you have more than one option group in a form, because each group can have one—and only one—selected button.

**Check Boxes**    Visual FoxPro uses check boxes to represent binary states. Binary states are either on or off like a switch, thus the name: binary switch. Because many configuration options used by VFP are either on or off, forms that display them usually use check boxes. A selected check box, which represents the true state, contains a bold checkmark. Otherwise, the box is blank. Although a form can have more than one check box, each one represents a unique variable or field. Therefore, you can select as many check boxes as you want.

Check boxes now support a third value: null, which means neither true nor false; its value is unknown. To use this capability, you must represent the check-box value as a number ranging from 0 to 2. In this case, 0 represents false, 1 represents true, and 2 represents unknown. When a check box is set to null, its background is dimmed.

**Spinners**    *Spinners* provide an interesting way to select integer values. These elements use a text area to display the current value. To the right of this text area are two buttons, one on top of the other. The top button has an up arrow; the bottom one has a down arrow. Clicking the top button increments the spinner value; clicking the bottom button decrements the value. You also can change the value directly by selecting in the text area and entering a new value.

In most cases, spinners have minimum and maximum values. A good use for a spinner is to obtain the number of copies when you route a report to a printer. In this case, a minimum value might be 0 (no report) to 10 (10 copies).

Spinners can directly use only numeric variables, but you might reference the variable in this control to display and control other data types, such as dates or strings.

**Combo Boxes**    A *combo box* combines the best features of a text box with those of a list. Visual FoxPro uses two variations on combo boxes. The one shown in Figure 1.13 is a drop-down combo box, which allows the user to enter a new item in the box next to the button. The user can also click the arrow to the right of the box to display a list of predefined choices. The second type of combo box is called a drop-down list. The primary visual difference is that the arrow is connected to the text area in a drop-down list. Functionally, however, drop-down lists allow you only to select values that are in the list.

**Command Buttons**    *Command buttons* (or *push buttons*) appear as three-dimensional shaded rectangles. A command button usually displays a text caption or bitmap image that identifies its purpose. To execute the action associated with a button, simply click it.

Most Visual FoxPro dialog boxes have one command button that has a slightly darker border than the other buttons. This button executes as the default if you press Enter.

Some command buttons have ellipses (...) after their captions to indicate that they open another dialog box. Another common button convention uses the label MORE>>. When you click such a button, the current window expands to reveal additional options.

**Page Frames**    Finally, all of these controls (except for the initial label field) appear in a *page frame.* Each page in the page frame has a tab along the top. Sometimes, multiple rows of tabs are necessary. Clicking a tab displays a new page of options within the same window.

Effectively, page frames provide a mechanism to display more controls in a single window by dividing them into multiple pages. Another way to think of page frames is to think of them as layers.

Visual FoxPro supports other elements for creating forms. In addition, a large number of OCX controls are provided with Visual FoxPro. Also, many of the OCX controls provided by third-party tool suppliers work with Visual FoxPro, as well as with Access and Visual Basic. The controls described in this chapter are the basic controls included with Visual FoxPro; they provide the basis for interacting with VFP dialog boxes, builders, and designers.

# Introducing the Project Manager

The Project Manager has two primary purposes:

- First, it helps organize files for a project based on file type.
- Second, it provides a container for gathering components of an application in preparation for compiling them to an application (.APP) or executable (.EXE) file.

Consider the fully developed project file that comes with FoxPro: the Tastrade project. To open a project, enter the following command in the Command window:

```
MODIFY PROJECT \VFP\SAMPLES\TASTRADE\TASTRADE.PJX
```

(Alternatively, you can choose File, Open.)

In the dialog box that appears, change the contents of List Files of Type to Project, if necessary. Next, use the Drives and Directories options to switch to the drive and directory in which the Tastrade example is stored. You should see the project name TASTRADE.PJX in the selection box; to select it, simply double-click.

> **N O T E** You can also enter the full path name of the project file in the box immediately below the label File Name. ■

The Visual FoxPro Project Manager should open, as shown in Figure 1.14.

You should be aware of several features of the Project Manager. First, if you previously used FoxPro 2.x, the Project Manager no longer lists all files of all types in a single list; rather, it divides the files by type. Page tabs that identify the first group level appear across the top of the window. Each page further divides each major file group into specific file types. Using an outline structure, the following list shows the organization of files in a project:

Data
Databases
Free Tables
Queries
Documents
Forms
Reports
Labels
Class Libraries
Code
Programs
API Libraries
Applications
Other
Menus
Text Files
Other Files

**FIGURE 1.14**
Project Manager
initially displays all file
types for Tastrade.

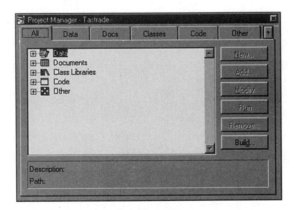

**N O T E**    Actually, you can get a single list by choosing Project, Project Info and then selecting
the Files page of the resulting dialog box to see an alphabetical list of all files in the
project. The list indicates the last-modified date and code page for each file, as well as whether it
is included in the project. ■

In fact, you can see each of these groups by clicking each of the tabs successively. In Visual FoxPro, this form structure is called a *page frame*. By using tabs across the top of the page frame, you can select different groups of data. This structure makes more information fit on a single screen by creating page overlays; it also helps users organize information. In this case, you can more easily find the names of programs when they are grouped by type than you can when all types appear in a single mixed-type list, as in earlier versions of FoxPro.

If you click the Data page (and if no one else has been working with the project), you should see three subgroup titles below Data: Databases, Free Tables, and Queries. Notice the plus sign before Databases. In this outline-like structure, a plus sign indicates that additional details are hidden in this item. To view these details, click the plus sign (an action that is also called *drilling down*).

In this case, only one item drops out of Databases: Tastrade. This fact means that the project has only a single database, named Tastrade.

Tastrade has a plus sign before it. Clicking the plus sign displays another set of categories:

> Tables
> Local Views
> Remote Views
> Connections
> Stored Procedures

Later chapters define tables, queries, views, and remote data access, and further explain what these groups mean. For now, concentrate on the Tables line, which is preceded by a plus sign. Click this plus sign to list the tables stored in database Tastrade.

At this point, I should clarify the terms *database* and *table*. In the past, FoxPro developers used these terms interchangeably, but the terms were never meant to be interchangeable. The misuse of the term *database* started in the early days of Ashton-Tate's dominance in the database market. Because of the company's dominance for many years, the term *database*, as used to refer to a single table, persisted.

In 1995, Visual FoxPro corrected the misuse of these terms by creating a separate object called a *database container*, which holds and/or organizes one or more tables. Most FoxPro programmers can associate a table with a single file that has a .DBF extension and that contains records and rows of data. The introduction of the database container, however, goes beyond the mere collection of tables. The database container also provides a platform to expand the traditional definition of a table by providing the following:

- Support for long tables and field names
- Record-validation clauses
- Field-validation clauses
- Default values
- Stored captions

■ Triggers for inserting, deleting, and updating records

■ Persistent relations among tables in the database

■ Referential integrity

▶ **See** "Creating a Database," **p. 162**

Finally, the project displays another level beyond the list that contains the table's fields. Figure 1.15 shows the first portion of a fully opened outline for Databases.

**FIGURE 1.15**
You can open
successive levels
of details about
databases until you
reach the list of table
fields and indexes.

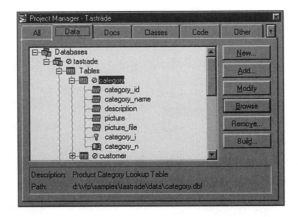

You may want to take a few moments to explore the contents of various levels of the Project Manager. Not every group contains the files in this example, but you get the idea of the way that the Project Manager organizes files.

## Adding and Removing Files

Adding a file is a simple process. First, select the group to which you want to add a file, and click either New or Add. Project Manager knows what type of file you want to add by the group that you selected. If you choose New, VFP first prompts you for a file name; it then opens an appropriate builder or designer to create that file. If you selected the Tables group in the Data category, for example, the Project Manager first prompts you to determine whether you want to use a wizard or a designer. If you choose the designer, you must assign a name to the created table. Then the Project Manager opens the Table Designer or wizard so that you can define the table's structure.

If the file already exists, click the Add button. Project Manager responds by prompting for the file name, using the Open dialog box, and then adding the file to the appropriate project group.

To remove a file, such as a table, highlight it and then click the Remove button. If the file is a database table, VFP displays a window, asking, `Do you want to remove the table from the database or delete it from the disk?` For other files, VFP asks a similar question: `Do you want to remove the file from the project or delete it from the disk?` In either case, deleting a file from the disk also removes it from the project.

 You can also see these options, like Remove, by right-clicking on the desired object.

## Viewing Files

When you are viewing a file, the Project Manager treats tables differently from most other file types. To view a table, highlight it and then click Browse. This action opens the table in a Browse window, where you can view the table's records (represented as rows) and fields (represented as columns). Think of this action as "running" the table. Clicking the Modify button opens the Table Designer.

If, instead, you want to view a program's code, highlight it and then click Modify. This action opens an edit window that lists the program code.

Similarly, click Modify to open and view a form, report, or label design. Each time you click Modify for one of these file types, VFP opens the appropriate designer tool.

You have just learned an important concept of object-oriented programming, called *polymorphism*. In each case in which you used Modify, the Project Manager opened the file with a different tool. Project Manager knew which tool to use because of the selected file type.

> **CAUTION**
>
> Using Modify to view a file can be dangerous, because you can save inadvertent changes to the file. If you know that you did not make any changes, but if VFP asks you to save your changes when you exit a file, just click No.

## Modifying Files

To return to tables for just a moment, you may ask why you would click Modify in the Project Manager. Actually, the preceding section stretched the terms a little by using Modify to view program code, forms, reports, or labels. The Modify button actually told Project Manager to modify those items, even though you only intended to view them. Therefore, as you may guess, the Modify button for tables takes you to the Table Designer, which allows you to modify the table's fields and indexes, not just view them.

Think of the Browse button as being the action button for a table. You cannot run a table, but you can look at it. On the other hand, you certainly can run a program, screen, report, or label. In this case, Run is the action button. Therefore, Project Manager renames the Run button Browse for tables.

Does this fact mean that you can store your PRG files in the Code-Programs group and then click the Run button to test them? *Absolutely!* It does not matter whether you intend to build an application from all the files in the project or whether you merely want to run individual programs, reports, or labels—use the Project Manager as your standard tool for file organization and testing. Also consider keeping a separate VFP project for each physical project that you work on. You can include the same file—whether it is a table, program, form, or whatever—in more than one project file.

Furthermore, you do not have to save all individual files in a project in the same directory. Therefore, you may want to organize your files by type. Consider storing order-entry files in one directory, inventory files in another, invoices in a third, and so on.

Remember that any one application may call on tables or other files from several areas. Merely add the file to each project that requires it.

Some additional project features related to compiling files into an application are covered in a later chapter of this book. You probably have been wondering, however, about another symbol in the group listings. This symbol—a circle with a slash through it—tells the compiler not to include this file in the compiled application or executable file.

Similarly, you may have noticed that one of the programs in the Code-Programs group is displayed in bold text. This formatting identifies the main program of an application to the compiler.

▶ **See** "Including and Excluding Files from Your .APPs and .EXEs," **p. 596**

▶ **See** "Setting a Main File," **p. 595**

# Setting Configuration Options

As mentioned earlier, Visual FoxPro allows the user to set a large number of parameters that determine how it works. In fact, VFP has so many options that they would never fit on a single screen page. But with a page-frame-style form, FoxPro can overlay several pages of options in a single window.

That is exactly what the Tools, Options command does. The resulting dialog box includes 12 tabs that divide the set options into the following logical sets:

- Controls
- Data
- Debug
- Field Mapping
- File Locations
- Forms
- General
- Projects
- Regional
- Remote Data
- Syntax Coloring
- View

## Controls Options

The Controls page allows you to select class libraries and OLE controls. A *class library* contains one or more custom visual classes that you define from FoxPro's base classes. An *OLE control* is a link to other OLE-supporting applications (insertable objects) and ActiveX controls. Class libraries and OLE controls selected in this page appear in the Form Controls Toolbar of the Form Designer when you click the View Classes button. Figure 1.16 shows the options in this page frame.

▶ **See** "Creating a Class Library," **p. 119**

**FIGURE 1.16**
The Controls page of the Options dialog box defines connections to visual class libraries and OLE (ActiveX) controls when you are creating forms.

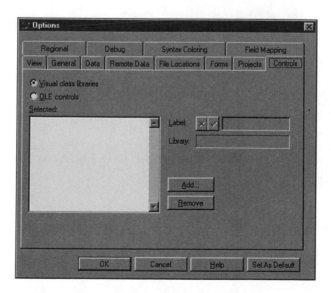

# Data Options

The Data page includes options related to the following:

- Accessing data (including sorting-sequence methods)
- Search-string comparison
- Locking and buffering parameters for shared access
- Memo-block size
- Refresh rates

Figure 1.17 shows these settings.

**FIGURE 1.17**

The Data page of the Options dialog box defines features related to data access, retrieval, and display.

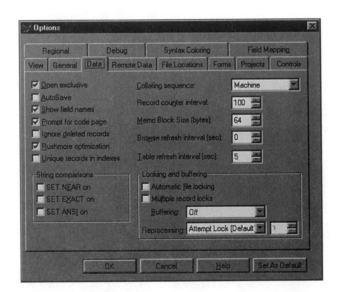

The Open Exclusive option determines how VFP opens a table in a shared environment. When this option is selected, VFP attempts to open the table exclusively, which means that no one else can have the table open. If you or someone else has the table open in another session or machine, VFP will not open it again; after VFP opens the table, no one else can open it.

Some commands require exclusive access to tables. These commands include:

- INDEX
- INSERT [BLANK]
- MODIFY STRUCTURE
- PACK

- REINDEX
- ZAP

 **TIP** If you work in a stand-alone environment, use SET EXCLUSIVE ON. Performance improves, because VFP does not have to check or maintain record lock tables (internal information that identifies which records or files are locked by a user editing them).

Autosave corresponds to the SET AUTOSAVE command. When this option is set, Visual FoxPro flushes file buffers back to disk when you exit a READ command or return to the Command window.

Show Field Names corresponds to SET HEADINGS and determines whether field names appear above columns during commands such as AVERAGE, DISPLAY, LIST, and SUM.

The Prompt for Code Page option determines whether to prompt users for a code page. *Code pages* perform character translations for international users when they are turned on; VFP displays the Code Page dialog box when you open a table exclusively and the table does not already have an associated code page. (See SET CPDIALOG in the VFP Online Help.)

Ignore Deleted Records determines how Visual FoxPro processes records that are marked for deletion when it performs a record-level function. First, you must understand that when you mark a record for deletion with the DELETE command, VFP does not physically delete the record; it merely marks the record in the table. Only the PACK command can physically delete marked records. Therefore, you need to decide whether you want to see or process records that are marked for deletion. In most cases, you probably don't want to process deleted records (unless you have a program option to recall deleted records). Therefore, you would check this option. When Ignore Deleted Records is not checked, VFP processes a record marked for deletion just as it does any other record in the table. This option corresponds to the SET DELETED command.

Since version 2.0, FoxPro has included a search-optimization technique called *Rushmore*, which uses existing indexes to perform data searches more rapidly. Under most conditions, you want to take advantage of Rushmore. At times, however, Rushmore may actually impede performance. You can globally control Rushmore with the Rushmore Optimization option. Most commands that use Rushmore also contain a clause that turns it off. Thus, you should turn on Rushmore in this page and turn it off only as needed in individual commands. (See SET OPTIMIZE in the VFP Online Help.)

The Unique Records in Indexes option controls the default that FoxPro uses in creating indexes. If this option is not selected, indexes can contain duplicate key values. In other words, if you index on last name, the index file can contain pointers to two or more

Smiths, for example. When the option is selected, indexes maintain pointers only to unique key values, even if multiple records with the same key value exist. In the case of the multiple Smiths, the index maintains a pointer to only the first one. If you do not select Unique Records in Indexes, you can selectively create unique indexes by using the UNIQUE clause of the INDEX command. While this option is set, you cannot create nonunique indexes programmatically. Unique Records in Indexes corresponds to SET UNIQUE.

▶ **See** "Basic Rules for Using Rushmore," **p. 361**

▶ **See** "Defining Normal and Unique Indexes," **p. 151**

Collating Sequence allows changes to the collating sequence during sorts to accommodate different character sets for users in other countries. The default, machine sequence, uses the ASCII equivalents of each character. This option corresponds to the SET COLLATE command. If you SET COLLATE to GENERAL, the indexes that you create will be case-insensitive.

Record-Counter Interval determines how frequently VFP reports its progress during commands such as REINDEX and PACK. This value can range from 1 to 32,787 records processed. Increasing the frequency can affect performance, however, because of the need for more frequent screen updates. (See SET ODOMETER in the VFP Online Help.)

Memo Block Size defines the number of bytes that VFP assigns to a memo at a time, from 33 bytes on up. Values of 1 to 32 allocate blocks of 512 bytes (1 = 512, 2 = 1,024, and so on). The smaller the number of allocated bytes, the less space you waste in the memo file. New to VFP is the capability to set the block size to 0, which actually allocates space in single bytes, resulting in no wasted space. You pay a performance penalty, however, if you make the block size too small. When VFP creates a memo file, the block size for it remains fixed. (See SET BLOCKSIZE in the VFP Online Help.)

The Browse-Refresh Interval option determines how frequently VFP resynchronizes data displayed in a Browse screen with the actual table source. Numbers between 1 and 3,600 refer to the number of seconds between each refresh. A value of 0 causes a refresh as soon as another user updates the table with a new value and unlocks the record. This option also corresponds to SET REFRESH.

Table-Refresh Interval determines how frequently VFP resynchronizes data displayed from a table with the actual table source. Numbers between 1 and 3,600 refer to the number of seconds between each refresh. A value of 0 does not cause a refresh when another user updates the table. (See SET REFRESH in the VFP Online Help.)

The next three options control how string comparisons are made.

SET NEAR controls what FoxPro does when a search fails. If this option is not selected, FoxPro leaves the record pointer at the end of the file. When this option is set, FoxPro leaves the record pointer at the next record alphabetically from the position where it expected to find the search value. This option corresponds to the SET NEAR command.

The SET EXACT option also controls how FoxPro performs a search. When this option is set, the search field must match the search criteria exactly, character for character and in total length. When this option is not set, the search must match character for character, up to the length of the value on the right side of the search expression. This option corresponds to the SET EXACT command.

SET ANSI controls how SQL performs string comparisons. When this option is selected, Visual FoxPro pads the shorter of the two strings with blanks to make both strings equal in length. Then VFP compares each string, character for character, to see whether the strings match. When this option is not set, it compares the strings character for character, up to the length of the shorter string (on either side of the expression). This option corresponds to SET ANSI.

The last set of options affects how Visual FoxPro handles file and record locks in a multi-user environment.

FoxPro automatically sets and releases file and record locks for file-related commands when it shares tables. Normally, you want to have the Automatic File Locking option turned on unless you intend to handle all locks manually through your code. This option corresponds to SET LOCK.

Normally, FoxPro releases the current record lock if you set a lock on a new record. You may want to lock several records at the same time, however, to update them simultaneously. In these cases, you want to select the Multiple Record Locks option. You can also set this option programmatically with the SET MULTILOCKS command. Only by setting multiple record locks can you activate buffering.

Buffering determines how to maintain data in a multi-user environment. Visual FoxPro has five buffering methods. For more information on buffering, see CURSORSETPROP( ) in the VFP help system.

▶ **See** "Buffering Edits," **p. 690**

The Reprocessing options determine how frequently or how long Visual FoxPro attempts to establish a lock when the lock fails. When you are working in a shared environment, you typically want FoxPro to retry setting locks if the first attempt fails. This option controls the number of retries, up to 32,000. In addition, values of –2, –1, and 0 have special meanings. For details on these options, see the command SET REPROCESS in the VFP Online Help.

▶ **See** "What to Do When the Record You Need Is Locked," **p. 688**

## Debug Options

The Debug options customize the way that the Debugger works. Figure 1.18 shows the options in the Debug page.

**FIGURE 1.18**
The Debug page of the Options dialog box controls FoxPro's default Debugger features.

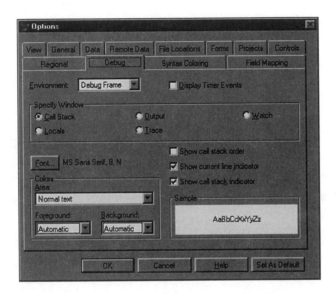

The first option allows you to select the environment for the Debugger. The environment option allows you to select either the Debug frame or the FoxPro frame. The Debug frame keeps all the debugger windows in one large frame called the Visual FoxPro Debugger. The FoxPro frame allows individual debugger windows to appear in the VFP main window. You can also display timer events during debugging. Be aware, however, that this option may result in a substantial increase in the debugger output.

Next, you can specify which window in the debugger you want to define properties for. Properties that you can set include the font and colors.

## Field Mapping Options

This feature, new to VFP 5.0, is one of the most useful for customizing the way that the form builders work. Previously, the type of object associated with each field type was fixed, and in most cases, that object was a text box. When you add a numeric field, you may not want to use a text box; you may want a spinner instead. Similarly, you probably want to use a check box as the default control for a logical field and an edit box as the default for a memo field. With the Field Mapping page, you can now set the default control associated with each field type, as shown in Figure 1.19.

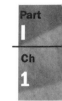

**FIGURE 1.19**
The Field Mapping page of the Options dialog box controls which base-class object is associated with each field type when you are using the Form Designer.

You can even associate a field type with a custom class in a class library. You could associate a logical or integer field with a group of option buttons, for example, as shown in Figure 1.20.

**FIGURE 1.20**
The Field Mapping page of the Options dialog box controls which base-class or custom object is associated with each field type by selecting Modify to display the Modify Field Mapping dialog box.

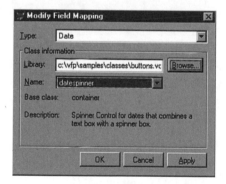

This page also allows you to determine whether to implement drag-and-drop field captions. When checked, this option gets the field caption from the table-structure property, Caption and includes it on the form when adding a field. Similarly, you can copy the field comments, input masks, and formats from comparable table-structure properties. These database options use the power of the data dictionary and help provide consistency across applications.

# File Locations Options

FoxPro uses many files, and it should not come as a surprise that those files do not all reside in the same directory. VFP uses the File Locations page to define the locations for 10 classes of files. Figure 1.21 shows this page, and the following paragraphs describe some of the auxiliary files and tools that require their file locations to be specified.

**FIGURE 1.21**

The File Locations page of the Options dialog box defines the paths of various auxiliary files and tools used by Visual FoxPro.

FoxPro first attempts to locate tables and program files in the default directory if you do not supply a full path name at the Default Directory prompt. The current directory can be any directory, not just the Visual FoxPro root directory. In fact, you can change the directory programmatically at any time with the SET DEFAULT TO command.

Use Search Path to tell VFP where to search for files that are not in the default directory. You can include multiple directories if you separate them with commas or semicolons. This option corresponds to the SET PATH command.

Although VFP attempts to keep as much data in memory as possible to improve performance, sometimes, it must create temporary files in response to commands. Visual FoxPro writes these files to a common directory specified in the Temporary Files text area. In a networked environment, keep temporary files on a local drive to improve performance.

Help File identifies the name and location of the help file. Usually, this is the FoxPro help file. If you create a custom help file for your users, however, you can identify it here. You can change the current file at any time, of course, by using the SET HELP TO command.

The resource file—which stores information about the way you work, edit preferences, window size and position values, color schemes, printer information, and much more—is designated in the Resource File text area and check box. Usually, VFP stores the resource file as FOXUSER.DBF in the VFP root directory. In a networked environment, however, you can either have individual resource files or a shared resource file. To be shared, a resource file must be read-only, which defeats some of its purpose. But would you want someone to change your color scheme to something like Hot Dog Stand in the middle of running a series of applications? In shared environments, you may need to write programs that work with two resource files: one private with read-write rights and one shared.

The converter application, in the Converter text area, takes objects such as screens and reports written for earlier versions of FoxPro, and converts them to Visual FoxPro 5.0. This conversion consists primarily of a file restructuring. If you begin with a DOS version of a screen, the converter creates a Windows screen, but it cannot add features that are unique to VFP; you must, alas, do that yourself.

Most larger applications use a main menu to tie together various parts of the system. Rather than write menu code manually, you can save time by using the menu builder. The Menu Builder locates this tool, using both the path and name.

To use the spell checker, you must identify its directory and name in the Spell Checker box, if it is not in the FoxPro root directory.

FoxPro includes builders for several objects, such as ComboBox and ListBox. *Builders* are tabbed dialog boxes used to create and modify the objects. Builders help set the properties for these objects.

Visual FoxPro comes with wizards that help develop various features of your application. All wizards must reside in the same directory and application file. The Wizards option identifies that directory.

## Forms Options

Almost every application requires at least one form. Using the Form Designer requires a few special options, including grids, screen resolution, tab order, and template classes. Figure 1.22 shows the Form options.

**FIGURE 1.22**

The Forms page of the Options dialog box controls features used in the Form Designer.

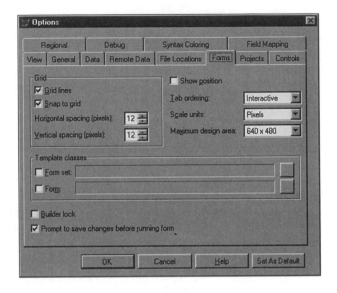

With Grid lines, you can elect to show a grid. Dotted horizontal and vertical lines appear on-screen, based on the spacing parameters defined later in the form page. You don't need to display the grid to use it; you can position objects in the grid's spaces by setting Snap to grid, regardless of whether the grid is actually displayed.

When turned on, Snap to grid automatically moves objects to the nearest grid intersection when you change their position or add new objects. The option does not affect the positions of objects that you placed previously unless you try to move them.

The Horizontal spacing option defines the number of pixels between horizontal grid lines.

The Vertical spacing option defines the number of pixels between vertical grid lines.

When selected, Show position displays the position of the upper-left corner and the size of the current object in the status bar.

Tab ordering determines how to sequence fields that receive focus as you press the Tab key when running the program. Tab ordering has two options: Interactive and by List. When Interactive is set, the user must press Shift while clicking the mouse to select the object order. At the same time, each object displays a small box with a number showing its current tab-sequence number. Alternatively, the tab order can be displayed as a list. You can reposition fields in the list by dragging them to a different position, thus changing the tab order.

In Windows, positioning of objects cannot be based on characters and rows; characters may vary in width and height from object to object. Instead, you position all objects based on pixels or foxels, which you can choose with the Scale units option. *Pixels* are individual dots of color on-screen. Most VGA monitors use a standard 640-by-480 pixel display. Visual FoxPro, however, defines a *foxel* as being equivalent to the average height and width of a character in the current window font.

 **TIP** Use foxels rather than pixels when you are transporting a screen from a character-based platform, such as DOS, to a graphical-based platform.

Use the Maximum design area option to match the resolution of the user's monitor and monitor driver. You can still develop using a higher resolution supported by your own display. The Maximum design area then limits the size of forms you can create so that they fit on the user's reduced-resolution screen.

> **CAUTION**
>
> If you develop applications for other people, beware of developing screens with a resolution larger than those people use—doing so will cause display problems when you attempt to install the application. Always use the lowest screen resolution of all your expected users.

You can define two template classes, which identify default templates for forms and form sets.

The button to the right of the Form set text box opens the Registered Library drop-down list of available class libraries selected in the Controls page. Simply select the form-set class that you want to use as a default in designing your application.

The button to the right of this text box opens the Registered Library drop-down list of available class libraries selected in the Controls page. Simply select the form class that you want to use as a default in designing your application.

Choose the Builder lock option to automatically display the builders when you add controls to a form.

▶ **See** "Using the Builder to Add Controls," **p. 448**

Finally, you can ask VFP to prompt you to save changes after you edit a form before running the form. If you don't do this, VFP automatically saves the changes before running the form.

## General Options

The next page defines general options, including those that deal with compatibility, color, confirmation, and sound issues. The page also includes options that affect programming and data entry. Figure 1.23 shows this page.

**FIGURE 1.23**

The General page of the Options dialog box sets miscellaneous options that do not fit in any of the other tabs.

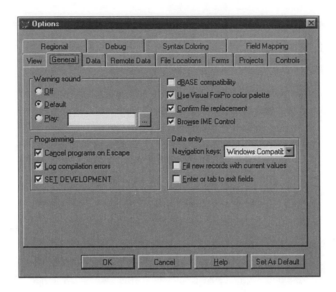

The Off option in the Warning Sound group determines whether to sound the bell when the user reaches the end of a field or enters invalid data. The corresponding command is SET BELL.

The Default option sets the bell frequency and duration to their default values. SET BELL TO [nFrequency, nDuration] supports frequencies from 19 through 10,000 Hz, with a default of 512. Duration ranges from 1 to 19 seconds, with a default of 2 seconds.

With Play, you also can choose a .WAV file to use instead of the impersonal beep. Click the button that has the ellipsis to display a dialog box from which you can pick a .WAV file.

**N O T E**  If VFP cannot locate the specified waveform, it uses a default defined in the Registry. If VFP finds no waveform there, it plays no sound. For you real techheads, the location of the default sound in the Registry is:

        HKEY_USERS/.DEFAULT/APP EVENTS/SCHEMES/APPS/.DEFAULT/.DEFAULT/.CURRENT

and

        HKEY_USERS/.DEFAULT/APP EVENTS/SCHEMES/APPS/.DEFAULT/.DEFAULT/.DEFAULT

I do not recommend, however, that you make changes in the Registry without first making a backup of the Registry. ■

The dBASE compatibility option controls the compatibility of Visual FoxPro with other xBase languages. By default, this option is not selected, thereby allowing Visual FoxPro to run programs written in earlier versions of FoxPro and FoxBase. When the option is selected, Visual FoxPro interprets the commands shown in Table 1.15 differently.

**Table 1.15   Commands Affected by the Set Compatible Command**

| Command | Compatible On | Compatible Off |
|---|---|---|
| @...GET...RANGE | Always checks range | Checks range only if data changes |
| @...SAY | Output to the FoxPro desktop scrolls as necessary | Output to the FoxPro desktop truncates after reaching the lower-right corner |
| @...SAY | Rounds the right-most digit in thePICTURE clause | Truncates the right-most digit in the PICTURE clause |
| ACTIVATE SCREEN | When activating the screen or a window, the cursor position is 0,0 | When activating the screen or a window, the cursor position is unchanged |
| APPEND MEMO | The default extension is TXT | No default extension |
| GO/GOTO (with SET TALK ON) | Outputs a message with the current work area and record number | No message |
| INKEY( ) | Home and Shift+Home returns 26; Ctrl+ Left returns 1 | Home and Shift+Home returns 1; Ctrl+L returns 26 |
| LIKE( ) | Trailing blanks in both expressions are trimmed before comparison | Trailing blanks are retained and are significant |
| MENU and POPUP | Popup lists are placed in the active output window with the cursor positioned on an option | Popup lists are placed in their own window while the cursor remains in the active window |
| Nested Reads | Performs an implicit CLEAR GETS when returning to a higher level | Pending GETS remain when returning to a higher level |
| Passed Parameters | Parameters passed by reference remain available in the called procedure | Parameters passed by reference are hidden in the called procedure |
| PLAY MACRO | Adds an implicit Alt+F10 before macros that begin with A–Z; adds an implicit Alt before macros F1–F9 | No implicit keystrokes are added |
| READ | Performs the VALID clause when you press Esc | Does not perform the VALID clause when you press Esc |

*continues*

**Table 1.15  Continued**

| Command | Compatible On | Compatible Off |
|---|---|---|
| RUN | Cursor moves to the first column in row 24 before beginning output; when done, scrolls output up three lines | Output begins at the cursor's current position; when done, scrolls output up two lines |
| SELECT( ) | Returns number of highest unused work area | Returns number of currently selected work area |
| SET MESSAGE | Displays the character expression in the last line of the screen | Displays the character expression only if SET STATUS is ON |
| SET PRINT TO | Output file has a default extension of .PRT | No default extension for output file |
| STORE | Cannot initialize all elements of an array | Can initialize all elements of an array |
| SUM | Uses the number of decimal places specified by SET DECIMALS | Uses the number of decimal places specified by the field being summed |
| SYS(2001,'COLOR') COLOR USE | Returns value of current SET COLOR. If a VFP path is set and USE includes a drive, VFP searches only that drive | Returns value of SET TO Color color pair. If a VFP path is set and USE includes a drive, VFP searches that drive first; then it searches the path |

When selected, the Use Visual FoxPro color palette option tells Visual FoxPro to use its own default color palette when displaying .BMP (bitmap) images. Otherwise, VFP uses the color palette used to create the .BMP. This option corresponds to the SET PALETTE command.

The Confirm File Replacement option determines whether VFP shows a warning message before overwriting an existing file. This option corresponds to the SET SAFETY command.

The Browse IME Control is only enabled when using a double-byte character system. It displays an Input Method Editor when you navigate to a text box in the Browse window. It corresponds to the IMESTATUS function

The General page includes three programming options, which primarily affect developers.

Selecting cancel program on escape allows the user to press the Esc key to terminate a program's execution. Although this capability is essential during development, you may not want to allow users to press Esc while they are running a production version of the application. The program code provides a better, more secure place to control this option by means of the SET ESCAPE command.

Log compilation errors, when you compile a PRG file to create an FXP, APP, or EXE, VFP displays errors to the screen. You may prefer to log compilation errors to an error file rather than interrupt the compilation for each one. Then you can go back to the log file and deal with each error individually. The error file has the same root name as the PRG (when you are compiling stand-alone PRGs) or the project file (when you are compiling projects), but it uses the extension .ERR.

If you select the SET DEVELOPMENT option, VFP checks to see whether any changes have been made in the source file before running a compiled FXP. Similarly, if you work with projects that contain groups of files, the option checks the source of each component with the last compile date of the APP or application file. If any of the source files have more recent time and date stamps, the option recompiles the project.

Finally, this page contains three data-entry options, which affect the way that users interact with the applications.

The Navigation keys option has two navigation options: Windows-Compatible and DOS-Compatible. This command corresponds to SET KEYCOMP. Some examples of differences between Windows and DOS navigation appear in Table 1.16.

**Table 1.16   Differences Between DOS and Windows Compatible Modes**

| Windows | DOS | Function/Action |
|---------|-----|-----------------|
| Enter | Ctrl+Enter | Selects the default button in a dialog box |
| Alt+letter | Single letter | Accesses keys for controls |
| Space bar, Alt+Up Arrow, Alt+Down Arrow | Enter or space bar | Opens a combo box that has focus |
| Up, Down Arrow | Tab | Moves between a group of option buttons |
| Selected | Not Selected | Status of browse field upon entry into cell |

The Fill new records with current values option tells Visual FoxPro to carry forward all fields from the current record to a new record. This feature has value if only a few fields change from one record to the next. This option corresponds to the SET CARRY command.

**TIP** SET CARRY includes a TO option that specifies which field values to carry forward. Often, this option is a better choice than carrying forward all fields.

When the user enters data in a field, Visual FoxPro automatically moves to the next field when it reaches the maximum number of characters for the current field. If SET BELL is ON, VFP beeps as it moves to the next field. If SET BELL is OFF, users have no warning that they are now in another field unless they are very observant. If you choose Enter or tab to exit fields, you have the option to force users to press the Enter or Tab key to move from one field to the next (SET CONFIRM). Although this option slows some data-entry people, it prevents them from accidentally writing data in the next field.

## Projects Options

The Projects options pertain to features associated with using the Project Manager to maintain and compile applications. The page also includes options that affect the user of Visual Source Safe with VFP. The only two project-specific options are Project double-click action and Prompt for Wizards. Figure 1.24 displays this page of options.

**FIGURE 1.24**
The Projects page of the Options dialog box defines both Project Manager and Visual SourceSafe options.

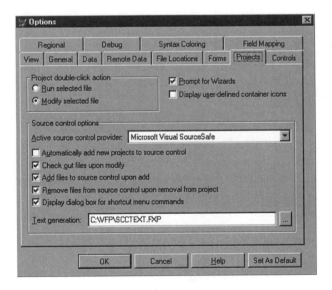

The first option determines the effect of double-clicking a file name in the Project Manager. Choose the Run selected file option if you want to run a file when you double-click it in the Project Manager. Choose the Modify selected file option to merely select the file for editing.

When checked, the second option—Prompt for Wizards—automatically asks whether you want to use a wizard when you are starting a new file from the Program Manager.

Display user-defined container icons tells VFP to display the icons of user-defined containers in the Project Manager.

This page also contains the source-control options. If you have Microsoft Visual SourceSafe (VSS) installed, it appears in the combo box next to the Active source control provider text. Otherwise, <None> appears, and all source-control options are inactive.

Visual Source Safe provides the following advantages:

- Keeps developer teams in sync and tracks changes
- Prevents developers from overwriting one another's work
- Allows older versions of code to be reviewed and restored
- Maintains multiple branching versions of an application

Next are five check boxes that control a few of the features of Visual Source Safe. The first check box, Automatically add new projects to source control, does exactly that. Usually, you want to make a conscious decision about when to add a project to VSS. (Simply open the project and choose Add Project to Source Control from the Project drop-down menu.)

The second option, Check out files upon modification automatically calls up VSS when you click the Modify button in the Project Manager. Yes, Source Safe still prompts you to check out the file, but the menu comes up automatically, and you need only click OK. Otherwise, you must manually check out the file before you attempt to open it; if you don't, the file will be opened as read-only. In either case, you will have to manually check the file back in after editing it.

The third option, Add files to source control upon add, automatically puts new project files into VSS. Similarly, the fourth option, Remove files from source control upon removal from project, removes references to the file in VSS when you remove the file from the project. Notice that removing a file from a project does not delete it from disk; neither does it remove all references to the file from the VSS database.

The fifth check box, Display dialog box for shortcut menu commands allows you to perform a VSS command from the project shortcut menu on multiple files.

The last option, Text generation, identifies a file that stores integration information between VFP and VSS. Specifically, the file creates text representations of screen, menu, report, and label files. Currently, you may not have any other alternatives for this utility. Because the source code is provided, however, you can make modifications to the version supplied with VFP. In this case, you probably want to save your revision with a different name and, therefore, need to change the reference here.

## Regional Options

Regional options customize your applications for local date, time, currency, and number conventions for international applications. If you click the first check box, Use System Settings, you cannot make any changes to the settings. Even if you need to make only one change, you must first deselect this box. Figure 1.25 shows the options available for Regional customization.

**FIGURE 1.25**

The Regional page of the Options dialog box defines formatting for dates and numbers.

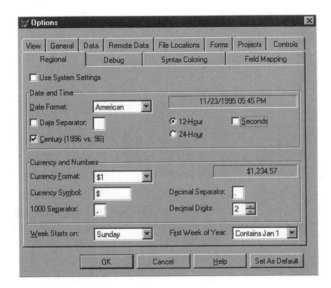

The first customization option, Date Format, controls the format that VFP uses to display the date and time. The default is American, but options exist for many other nations. There is even a difference between American and USA! (Hint: Watch the character between the month, day, and year.) You can even create and save your own custom format by following these steps:

1. Select the closest Date Format from the drop-down list.

2. To change the Date Separator, click the check box and enter a new character.

3. To turn the display of the century on or off, click the Century check box appropriately. This being only a few short years from the turn of the century, however, you may want to begin writing applications with Century turned on.

4. To select either a 12-Hour or 24-Hour clock, click the appropriate button. Remember that the suffix AM or PM appears only when you are using the 12-hour clock.

5. To display seconds, make sure to check the Seconds check box.

For each of these changes, you should see the corresponding result on a sample date and time string in the upper-right corner of this area.

The Currency Format option places the currency symbol either before or after the number. You can set this option programmatically with SET CURRENCY LEFT|RIGHT.

The Currency Symbol field defines the currency Symbol. You can use any valid symbol in the current character set, including combinations of up to nine characters. You can set this option with SET CURRENCY TO.

The 1000 Separator symbol appears at every third digit on the left side of the decimal separator when this option is selected. The command SET SEPARATOR performs the same function in programs.

The Decimal Separator symbol separates the whole portion from the fractional portion of a number.

The Decimal Digits value defines the minimum number of decimal places used to show expression results. This value can range from 0 to 18. This option's function is equivalent to SET DECIMALS TO.

Additional options related to date determine the default week start day and the definition of what constitutes the first week of the year.

You can select any day of the week for the Week Starts On option.

The First Week of Year feature has three possible values:

- Contains Jan 1
- First 4-Day Week
- First Full Week

This information determines the value returned by WEEK(). WEEK() can override these default values.

## Remote Data Options

The Remote Data options determine how Visual FoxPro establishes connections to remote data and works with remote data views. Figure 1.26 shows the available options.

**FIGURE 1.26**

The Remote Data page of the Options dialog box defines how Visual FoxPro establishes connections to remote data.

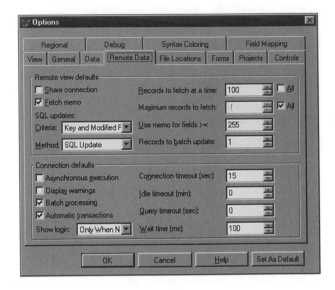

The first group of options establishes remote view defaults. A *remote view* is any data file that is not a Visual FoxPro table or database.

In many cases, a single remote ODBC connection allows you to open only a single view. By selecting Share connection, however, you can open additional views.

Fetching memos across a remote connection can greatly increase network traffic. Therefore, VFP recommends selecting the option Fetch memo, which retrieves the memo data only if the user activates the field.

Visual FoxPro provides several options for SQL updates. First are four Criteria options that determine whether VFP can update records in the source:

- Key Fields Only
- Key and Updatable Fields
- Key and Modified Fields
- Key and TimeStamp

These options determine conditions that allow SQL to succeed. This first one, for example, determines whether any of the key fields have changed in the source table since the data was retrieved. If so, the update fails.

The second SQL update option defines how to update the remote data. Visual FoxPro can perform an SQL Update on the selected records, or it can delete the old records and insert the modified ones by using the Method option.

The Records to fetch at a time option also limits traffic across a remote connection; it determines how many records to return from a query at one time. As you move through the records, the connection returns additional blocks of records until all records have been returned or you leave the view.

The Maximum records to fetch option places an upper limit on the total number of records returned by a query. You may want to consider using this option during testing, just in case your query incorrectly creates a Cartesian product view.

Some remote tables may support long character fields. The Use memo for fields >= option allows VFP to convert these long fields to memos automatically. Remember that a VFP character field supports a maximum 254 characters; therefore, 255 is a good default value for this option.

The Records to batch update option defines the number of records sent to the server in a single update statement. You can optimize network traffic if you batch multiple records in each update statement.

The Connection defaults define how your application communicates with the remote data.

The Asynchronous execution option determines whether control returns to your application immediately after it sends a SQL pass-through statement. In synchronous operation, control does not return until the entire result set is returned. In asynchronous execution, your application can do other things while it waits for the SQL to complete.

The Display warnings option determines whether to display error messages during the processing of a remote SQL pass-through.

Batch processing determines how to retrieve multiple result sets.

The Automatic transactions option determines whether SQL transactions are handled automatically by Visual FoxPro or whether the application must include its own SQLCOMMIT() and SQLROLLBACK() functions.

Some servers require that the user log in before accessing the data. The Show login option allows you to determine whether to show the login dialog box: always, never, or only when needed.

Connection timeout specifies the number of seconds to wait for a connection to be recognized by the server.

Idle timeout specifies the number of minutes that Visual FoxPro maintains the connection without activity. The default value, 0, requires that the application break the connection.

Part

I

Ch

1

Query timeout specifies how long (in seconds) Visual FoxPro waits for a result set to complete from a query before generating an error.

The <u>W</u>ait time option specifies the number of milliseconds before Visual FoxPro checks to see whether the SQL statement has completed.

▶ **See** "Using Views and Updatable Queries," **p. 368**

▶ **See** "Accessing Client-Server Data from Visual FoxPro" in Bonus Chapter 08 located on the CD

## Syntax Coloring Options

The Syntax Coloring options allow you to change the colors used to display different types of text while you are working in the Visual FoxPro editor. The use of color makes your programs easier to read. You may want to emphasize keywords, variables, or even comments in a different color to help them stand out. Figure 1.27 shows the options for syntax coloring.

**FIGURE 1.27**
Make your programs easier to read with syntax coloring.

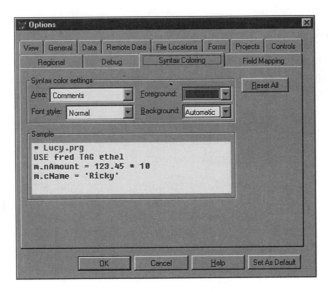

The types of text or <u>A</u>rea that you can color include:

- Comments
- Keywords
- Literals
- Normal
- Operators

- Strings
- Variables

For each type of text, you can select a Font styles from the following:

- Automatic
- Normal
- Bold
- Italic
- Bold Italic

Finally, you can change the Foreground and Background colors of each text type. The drop-down list displays 16 possible colors, along with Automatic. To make your comments really stand out, for example, make them bold white text on a black or dark-blue background.

## View Options

The View options determine how Visual FoxPro uses the status bar, if at all. These options also determine whether to display the recently used file list and whether VFP opens the last project automatically upon startup. Figure 1.28 shows these options.

**FIGURE 1.28**
The View page of the Options dialog box defines several features of the status bar, as well as whether to track project use.

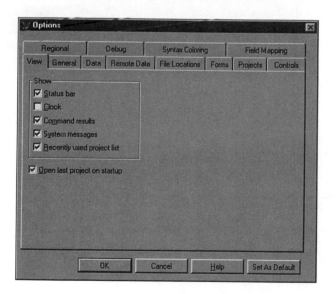

The Status bar option controls whether to display the status bar, which appears at the bottom of the screen. When the status bar is not shown, FoxPro displays messages in Wait windows in the upper-right corner of the screen.

To continuously display a clock in the status bar, select the Clock option, which places the current system time in a fourth box at the right end of the status bar.

To display command results in the status bar, click the Command results option. To see an example of a command result, open and pack a table. The messages in the status bar tell you how many records it has processed and the total number of records are command results. Indexing and reindexing also display messages as part of command results.

The System messages option enables or disables the display of selected system messages. One example of a system message is `Expression is Valid` displayed by the Expression Builder when you validate an expression. Another example is the `Attempting to lock...` message that appears when VFP attempts to obtain a record or file lock in a shared environment. These messages appear in the status bar (when it is present) or in a Wait window. This command corresponds to the SET NOTIFY command.

The Recently used project list option determines whether to display up to four recently used projects in the File menu.

The last option in this page—Open last project on startup—tells Visual FoxPro to automatically open the last project used before exiting Visual FoxPro on startup the next time.

 If you exit Options by clicking OK, the changes that you made affect only the current session. To make changes permanent, click the Set As Default option before you click OK.

 If you hold down the Shift key while clicking OK, VFP writes the equivalent SET commands to the Command window. Copy the commands from this window and place them in your code to customize a program's properties.

# Getting Help from Visual FoxPro

The last menu pad in the main menu is Help. You can active Help in four primary ways, two of which use this menu directly.

`Microsoft Visual FoxPro Help Topics`, which appears first in the Help menu, opens the main Help window. VFP uses a pageframe type format to display three ways to select help topics. The first tab, Contents, provides an outline-like approach to navigating help by successively drilling down through more detailed levels.

**N O T E**  Any time you press F1 with no text highlighted, VFP takes you to the Help Topics window. ■

The second page of the Help Topics page frame is labelled Index. This option requires a word or phrase that might appear in a help topic title. VFP uses this text string to search the available help topic titles, looking for a match. If VFP finds a match, it displays those topics.

The Find page of the Help Topics page frame lets you search by any keyword or phrase that might appear in the text of the help topics itself. This search requires more time, but allows you to locate all topics that might use a specific word.

Direct commands provide another way to access help. If you need help on a specific command or function, enter the keyword **HELP** in the Command window, followed by the command or function, as in this example:

```
HELP AINSTANCE()
```

Finally, you can highlight a word in any text-edit window and press F1. VFP copies the word to the Search dialog box. If it matches a topic exactly, VFP immediately displays the topic. Otherwise, VFP pastes the word in the Search dialog-box string area and allows you to select an appropriate topic manually.

The following sections take a closer look at each of the methods.

## Searching Help Via Contents

If you choose the Contents page from the Help Topics window, Visual FoxPro displays the top level of Visual FoxPro Help Contents. Figure 1.29 shows the initial screen.

This screen divides help into four topics:

- Glossary
- Language Reference
- Technical Reference
- Interface Reference

To open one of these topics, click the icon before the category name. Each topic may include additional topic levels. You can continue to drill down through the topics to find more specific information. Figure 1.30 shows the next help level that appears after you click the Language Reference icon.

**FIGURE 1.29**

The initial screen of the Visual FoxPro Help Contents shows five help categories.

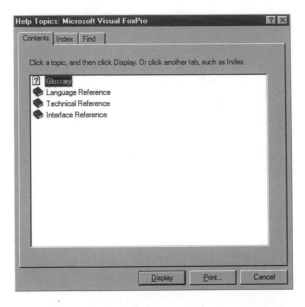

**FIGURE 1.30**

This figure shows the Language Reference topic open along with the Language Content topic showing the Language Reference A-Z topic.

Language Reference consists of four subcategories, beginning with an introduction. Each subcategory is preceded by the icon of a closed book. To open the topic, double-click the book. There can be "books" within "books." When you reach the level of a document, the icon displays a page with a question mark on it. Double-clicking a page icon opens that specific help topic in a separate window.

Figure 1.31 shows that the Language Reference A-Z option displays a scrollable list of all commands, events, functions, and properties in Visual FoxPro. You can scroll through the list to find the command or function you want.

**FIGURE 1.31**

The Language Reference A-Z topic combines a scrolling list with command buttons to help you find a help topic.

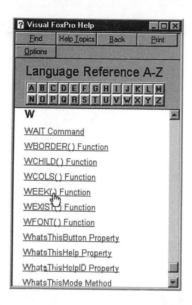

Notice the letter buttons at the top of the dialog box. Click one of these buttons to quickly move to the first command or function that begins with that letter. Suppose that you want to get more information on the command WEEK(). First, click the letter *W* to skip directly to commands and functions that begin with *W*. Next, scroll to WEEK(), and click the function to display its help text. Figure 1.32 shows the help text for WEEK().

In any help dialog box, when you click green text with a solid underline, you jump to that topic immediately. Therefore, this type of text is called a *jump*. Green text with a dotted underline displays a popup window that defines the underlined term. A popup window may itself have green text with either solid or dotted underlines. To close a popup window, click anywhere outside it or press Esc.

Many help topics contain an option called See Also, which appears directly below the topic title. Click this option to display cross-referenced topics. Sometimes, you may not be sure exactly what command you need to look for. But by starting at a command or function that is closely related to the one that you want, you may find it by surfing through these cross-references.

**FIGURE 1.32**

Help topics contain a brief description, syntax, return types, arguments, and remarks such as those shown for function WEEK().

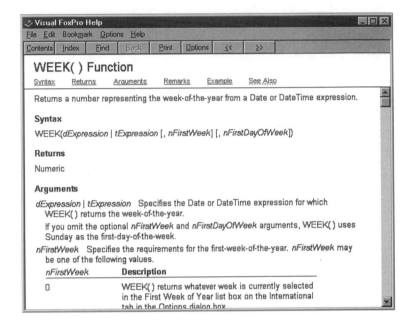

Another common feature of most topics in the Language Reference is examples. If the current help topic contains examples, the word *Example* also appears in green immediately below the topic title. Click the green *Example* text string to see sample command lines or even a small program segment that illustrates the command's use. Figure 1.33 shows the examples provided for WEEK().

**FIGURE 1.33**

Most commands and functions include examples, like this one for function WEEK().

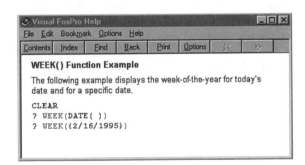

Notice that this window has both a menu with five options and a button bar with eight buttons. You can reach all the functions listed in the menu by using the buttons. Therefore, the following text reviews only the button options.

The button bar begins with the Contents button, which returns you to the Contents page of the Help Topics window. Similarly, the Index button corresponds to the second page of the pageframe, and returns you to the alphabetical listing of all help topics allowing you to jump to another topic easily. The Find button, corresponding to the third page of the pageframe, allows you to refine your help search by entering one or more words related to the help topic that you want to find.

The Back option takes you back to help topics that you looked at previously; it does not make side trips to the Contents, Index, or Find page. To return to these pages, click their buttons directly. The Print option sends the text of the current help topic to your default printer. The << and >> buttons move you backward and forward alphabetically through the help topics.

The Options button opens another menu that contains a series of options. These options include one that enables you to Annotate the current help topic, which means that you can add your own notes to this help topic. Your annotations become associated with the topic, and any user who accesses this help file sees them as well. You can use this feature to further clarify the help text, provide your own examples, or even add references to your favorite FoxPro book.

The Copy option places a complete copy of the current help-topic text in the Clipboard; from there, you can paste it into another document. The Print Topic option provides another way to print the current topic text. Font allows you to change the font. If the current help font is too small to read, you can enlarge it. You can even make the font smaller if you want to see more of the text at one time and don't mind squinting.

**NOTE** If you open an Example window, you must use the Options button in the button bar and choose Copy to place the example code into the Clipboard. From there, you can paste the code into a program file and test it. ■

The Keep Help on Top option is useful if you want to keep an example (or perhaps the syntax) of a command on the screen while you return to the program and make your changes. Finally, you can set the colors to the help system or revert to the system colors with the Use System Colors option.

## Searching for Help Via the Index

If you choose the Index from the Help Topics pageframe, VFP displays a dialog that lets you enter the first few letters of the term for which you want to search. You can also use the list to select topics directly. Suppose that you want help on Create Classlib. Just enter **create classlib** in the first text box. (The search string is not case-sensitive.) As you enter each letter, the list below the text box incrementally searches the help topics. The first letter, *c*, moves down the list to C. The second letter, *r*, moves further to *CREATE*. For the balance of the letters in the word *create*, the list does not change. But when you enter the *c* in *classlib*, the list moves again, this time to the topic *CREATE CLASS*. Only after you type the second *L* will the highlight move to the desired topic. For any search, you have to enter only enough characters to uniquely identify the topic; you do not have to complete the rest of the search string. You can also use the arrow keys or mouse to highlight the desired topic directly. Finally, click Display to show help on the highlighted topic. Figure 1.34 shows the screen just before it displays the topic.

**FIGURE 1.34**

Obtain help by performing a keyword search with Help's Index page, shown here finding the topic CREATE CLASSLIB.

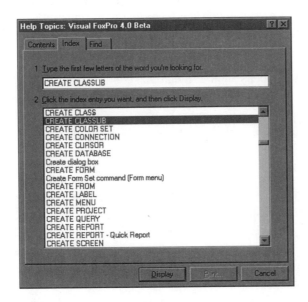

The Index option only searches the help topics. Sometimes, you may need to search for help, but you don't know the topic name. In such a case, you want to search based on the help contents rather than the topic name. To do so, choose the Find page of the Help Topics window. Figure 1.35 shows how to search for help based on words contained in the help text rather than in the topic.

In this dialog box, you can enter a series of words in the first text box (numbered 1) to search for (*trigger*, in this example), or you can select words from a scrollable list (numbered 2). Notice that after you enter one or more words in the first text box, the second text box shows selected related words to narrow your search. The next list (numbered 3), at the bottom of the dialog box, shows the topics that contain the selected word or words. You can select these topics for display or fine-tune your search with additional words. A text field near the bottom of the dialog box shows the number of topics that currently match the search criteria.

The Options button in this dialog box displays options that allow you to define how to conduct the search. Figure 1.36 shows these options.

**FIGURE 1.35**
Conduct a context
search of help by
using the Find options
to locate all topics
that contain selected
words.

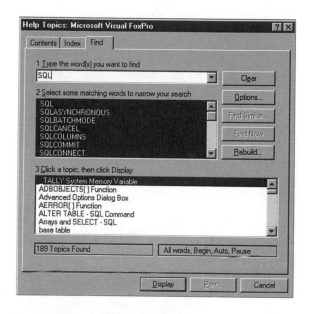

**FIGURE 1.36**
Customize your
context search by
telling Help how to
use the words and
characters that you
enter.

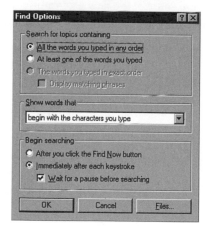

You can search for the following:

- Topics containing All the words you typed in any order
- Topics containing At least one of the words you typed
- Topics containing The words you typed in exact order

You also can search for topics that:

- Begin with the characters you type
- Contain the characters you type

- End with the characters you type
- Match the characters you type

Finally, you can have the search begin <u>I</u>mmediately after each keystroke (incremental search) or After you click the Find <u>N</u>ow button.

That is all you need to know to use Help effectively. After a little practice, you may find that you can get information from VFP's Help faster than you can from the manuals.

# From Here...

This chapter introduced many concepts that you must understand to use Visual FoxPro. In fact, almost every concept discussed in this chapter is important enough to be revisited in later chapters.

You can go from here in many directions, depending on your experience with FoxPro or other object-oriented languages. Most important, you must understand object-oriented concepts before you can understand some of the new programming capabilities of Visual FoxPro. Therefore, to learn more about object-oriented programming, refer to the following chapter:

- Chapter 2, "Introducing Object-Oriented Programming," explains the new concepts that you need to get started with this new programming paradigm.

If you already have a strong object-oriented background, jump straight to the following chapter:

- Chapter 3, "Defining Databases, Tables, and Indexes," shows you how to get started defining the basic objects needed to store data.

# Introducing Object-Oriented Programming

*by Michael Antonovich*

**M**any people in the industry believe that the current way of developing procedural code is failing. Some of their reasons include:

- Increasingly complex application requirements

  Today the emphasis is on letting the user control the application flow, rather than letting the application flow control the user. The user also expects many more different ways of interacting with the application.

- The need to reduce the time from conception to delivery

  The introduction of new tools, such as wizards and designers, and new programming paradigms like objects lets developers create applications in a fraction of the time typically required.

- The need for a more graphical approach to communicating with users

  Users expect different controls for different data entry types such as check boxes for logical fields, list and combo boxes to choose from arrays of possible values, spinners to change numeric fields, and option buttons to select one of several options.

**Define objects by using Visual FoxPro's base classes**

Base classes are the objects provided by Visual FoxPro to build your interface. They include everything from the form itself to labels, text boxes, check boxes, list boxes, command buttons, grids, and more.

**Add and modify properties and methods in those objects**

Each object has a series of properties that defines how it looks. Objects also have methods or things that they can do either as a result of a program event or the user's action.

**Recognize events and use them to trigger custom code**

The most widely recognized event is the click of the mouse. However, other events such as key presses, mouse movements, and so forth, can cause custom code to execute.

**Create custom nonvisual classes**

Not all objects are visual. In fact, any collection of information that has properties and methods can be put into an object.

**Create and use class libraries**

Just as you created program libraries in earlier versions of FoxPro to reuse procedures and functions, you now can create class libraries to reuse custom objects you create.

■ The need to access data from a variety of stored formats and platforms

Rather than convert data from one application format to another, it is easier to access it in its native format. Also, applications are increasingly using the client/server model to centrally store data.

■ The emergence of client/server database platforms

Client/server lets a user store data centrally and to perform any data manipulations on the server, reserving the processing power of the local machine to handle the user interface.

■ More emphasis on giving the user control

Today's users want to control which fields they enter and in which order they enter them, rather than be forced to enter data or perform tasks in a fixed sequence.

■ Procedural code applications often repeat the same code in multiple places, which makes maintenance difficult, and changes are likely to miss one of the occurrences.

All of these reasons have placed an enormous strain on traditional programming methods. Programmers are no longer in control; the users are. Therefore, the time has come to consider a new programming paradigm. That paradigm is object-oriented programming, otherwise known as OOP.

Although Visual FoxPro for Windows dives deeply and solidly into the world of OOP, it continues to respect your previous code investment by maintaining compatibility with your previous FoxPro applications. In fact, the capability to run previous applications in the current version of FoxPro is a major concern in its design. This capability gives you time to familiarize yourself with the new OOP programming techniques without having to abandon existing code. When you are ready, you can focus your efforts on using OOP tools with new applications or complete rewrites of existing ones. But before you can start, you need to learn basic OOP concepts. ■

# Objects and Classes

A good place to start understanding objects is to ask, "What is an object?" If you have experience developing applications in FoxPro, you have at least some familiarity with objects. In effect, an object is a thing. Thus, a window is an object. A field is an object. A command button is an object. You can list each of the "things" with which you are familiar from FoxPro's interface, and most of them are objects.

However, the treatment of objects in earlier versions of FoxPro was more limiting than Visual FoxPro's. Visual FoxPro extends the definition. An object has properties and methods. Think of properties as physical attributes of an object. For example, a command button on a form has attributes such as the following:

- Location on the form
- Width
- Height
- Color
- Text label of the button
- Font type, size, and style for the button's text
- Variable associated with the button

Each attribute describes the object and makes it unique. But objects do not have to be just physical "things" that you can see on-screen. You could just as easily define the animals in a zoo as objects. The attributes of an animal might include:

- Name
- Size
- Type of body covering
- Number of legs
- Where it lives

If the zoo you are describing is your company and an employee is the object, then some of its properties might be:

- employee number
- salary grade level
- current pay rate

As you can see, object properties identify physical attributes of things. But objects need more than these properties. They also need methods. *Methods* are actions that objects can perform. Two obvious methods for a form object are Open and Close. You would not create a form unless you intend to open it, at least sometime. And once you open it, you must close it. Therefore, forms have built-in code or default code that tells Visual FoxPro how to open and close them. Similarly, our zoo animals have methods. They sleep, eat, and occasionally work.

Let's see how Visual FoxPro deals with simple objects. From the Command window, enter the following commands, which create a window, using traditional FoxPro language as follows:

```
DEFINE WINDOW TestWind1 ;
    FROM 1,1 TO 20,30 ;
```

```
        CLOSE FLOAT GROW MINIMIZE ZOOM SYSTEM ;
        TITLE "Traditional Style Window"
ACTIVATE WINDOW TestWind1
```

**N O T E**  Visual FoxPro for Windows defaults to a half-height window title bar unless you use the SYSTEM or FONT clause when defining it. ■

The above code defines a form object using FoxPro 2.6 style code in VFP, even though it is not given a specific name with the NAME clause. You can still reference all the properties normally associated with a form object by using the indirect reference.

```
_Screen.ActiveForm
```

For example, to double its current height programmatically, enter:

```
_Screen.ActiveForm.Height = _Screen.ActiveForm.Height * 2
```

And now lets see how we create a form object in VFP using the new object language commands. The key function is CREATEOBJECT().

```
frmTestWind2 = CREATEOBJECT("FORM")
frmTestWind2.show
frmTestWind2.caption = "New Style Window"
```

**N O T E**  When used interactively, the SHOW method opens and activates the new window, changing focus to it. To return to the Command window after this command, press Ctrl+F2. ■

The first line of the code creates the object. It also returns a reference to the object, which it places in variable frmTestWind2. In fact, if you enter the command

```
DISPLAY MEMORY LIKE frmTestWind2
```

you see the following:

```
FRMTESTWIND2        Pub     O    FORM
```

This line tells you that frmTestWind2 is a public variable of type O (for object). Furthermore, the specific object type is a form.

You can also use the command DISPLAY OBJECTS to get a complete listing of all active objects, their properties, and their values and available methods and events.

The second line uses the form object SHOW method to display the form. This is similar to the old ACTIVATE WINDOW command; it makes the form both visible and active.

Finally, the third line changes the default window title from Form1 to New Style Window. The standard format for changing any property includes the name of the object, separated from the property name by a period. The OOP syntax is called *dot notation* and is formatted as follows:

```
<Control object name>.<Property>
```

**N O T E** Visual FoxPro assigns default object names based on the object type and a sequential number. The number is incremented sequentially during the current work session. Therefore, if you were to create a second form, its name would be Form2 until you rename it. Note that an object's name, such as a form's name, is how we reference that object's properties and methods. A form's caption, like its color, is just one of those properties. However, VFP defaults the form's caption to its name until you otherwise assign it. ■

**FIGURE 2.1**

These two windows may look similar, yet one is a traditional window, and the other is an object form.

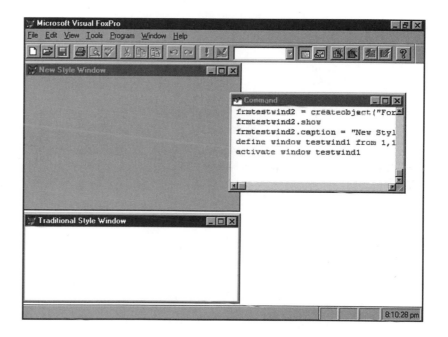

Figure 2.1 shows these two windows side-by-side.

Both windows look basically the same (except for size, position, title, and the fact that windows created from the form object have a gray background).

▶ **See** "Defining the Overall Form Properties," **p. 443**

## Base Classes

As you learned earlier, the function CREATEOBJECT creates an object from a class definition. In the New Style Window example, that object is created from the base class form.

Visual FoxPro provides 27 predefined base classes, from which you can create new objects. The following table lists Visual FoxPro's base classes:

| | | |
|---|---|---|
| Check Box | Form | OleContainerControl |
| Column | FormSet | OptionButton Group |
| Combo Box | Grid | Page |
| CommandButton | Header | PageFrame |
| CommandGroup | Image | Shape |
| Container | Label | Spinner |
| Control | Line | Text Box |
| Custom | List Box | Timer |
| Edit Box | OleBoundControl | ToolBar |
| OptionGroup | Separator | |

## Container Classes

Visual FoxPro further divides these base classes into container and control classes. A container class can hold other objects inside it. A form belongs to the container class, because you can put other objects—check boxes, edit boxes, text boxes, lines, and the like—inside it. Base container classes include:

- Column
- Command Button Group
- Form
- FormSet
- Grid
- Option Button Group
- Page
- PageFrame
- ToolBar

## Control Classes

Control classes cannot contain other objects. For example, you cannot put a line object in a text-box object. Once you place a control object in a container, any reference to the control object must go through the container. To reference a control property stored in a container, use this syntax:

```
<container object name>.<Control object name>.<Property>
```

This syntax identifies the property within a control object that itself is in a container object.

## Inheritance

Notice that in the traditional window-creation example, you have to include several clauses to tell Visual FoxPro to include a close box, minimize box, zoom box, and borders that stretch the window. Visual FoxPro includes these properties in the definition of the base class, Form. Observe also that you do not have to include a start position or size. Again, the base class assigns default values for these properties. In fact, all properties in a base class must have default values, even if they are empty strings.

When you create an object, VFP copies not only the properties, methods, and events from the parent class, but also the default values. It inherits this information. You will see later that you can create new classes from existing classes ad infinitum. At each step, the new class inherits everything known from its predecessor. In fact, some objects may have many levels of parents and inherit properties from all of them.

For example, if you want to use a form that has your company logo in the upper-left corner, a sky-blue background, and a close button in the lower-right corner on all forms you build, you have two ways to do this. You could use the old procedural method of building each form one at a time and adding these features to each form. Or you could build the form once and save it as a class. Then you could build each of your application's forms based on this first form. Each of the application's forms will inherit the characteristics of that first form including its blue background, its logo, and its close button. Now you can add any additional, unique features to the new form.

## Instance

The dictionary calls an *instance* a case or an example. The application forms referred to in the previous example based on a common form with a specific background color, logo, and close button are instances of that first form. Similarly, the code that created frmTestWind2 created a new object from a base class called Form. The new form is an example of that base form. The object frmTestWind2 is an instance of the base-class form. In general, any object created from another object is an instance of its parent object. The process of creating the object is, therefore, called *instantiation*. If you make another instance of the object, it will be exactly like the first one. The following commands create two instances of the class Form:

```
frmTestWind3 = CREATEOBJECT("FORM")
frmTestWind4 = CREATEOBJECT("FORM")
```

Part

I

Ch

2

```
frmTestWind3.Show
frmTestWind4.Show
```

# Properties

The only difference you might see if you look closely is that the title of the second window has a different sequence number than the first. Otherwise, both windows are exactly the same. In fact, they are actually on top of each other. However, you can type the following lines in the Command window to interactively change their size and position properties:

```
frmTestWind3.Left = 40
frmTestWind3.Width = 30
frmTestWind4.Top = 25
frmTestWind4.Left = 10
frmTestWind4.Height = 5
```

**N O T E**  By default, all the size properties of the form are measured in units of pixels (dots on the screen). However, we have the option of using coordinates more related to the size of a character called a foxel. One foxel in height is equivalent to the height of the current select font for the container. A foxel in width is equivalent to the average character width (for proportional character sets, each character can have a different width). To use foxels, add the command

```
<form name>.ScaleMode = 0
```

before entering any of the property values. To see the effect, enter this command then reenter the above commands via the Command window. ■

# Property Encapsulation

Even though these commands create two forms from the same base class, each form is independent of the other. An interesting fact is that although the forms are independent, the property names are exactly the same in each one. Note that the property Left was changed in both forms. The other properties used also appear in both forms.

Previous versions of FoxPro supported only two types of variables: public and private. However, neither would work for object properties. Objects require that variables for properties remain local to the instance, yet they can be referenced from outside the object definition. In effect, objects need to encapsulate the variables in them.

As a result, you can have the same property name in more than one object. To display any instance of a property, use the following command syntax:

```
? <Object name>.<property name>
```

Notice the dot between the object and property names. Visual FoxPro refers to this type of notation as *dot notation*. It connects properties to specific objects, because there could be several active objects with the same property. That is, in fact, the case with these two instances of a form. The following lines display some of the properties of the two windows.

```
? frmTestWind3.Top
? frmTestWind3.Height
? frmTestWind3.Left
? frmTestWind3.Width
? frmTestWind4.Caption
? frmTestWind4.Visible
```

If you try to print a property without using the object name, VFP thinks that you want the value of a table's field or a memory variable. If the current table has a field with that name, or if a memory variable exists, VFP prints that value. Otherwise, VFP prints this message:

```
Variable '<property name>' is not found.
```

# Objects

The preceding sections created new forms with the CREATEOBJECT function. In each case, we associated the form with a name. The name became the primary way to address the properties and methods of that object. But you need to remember that the object name is merely associated with the object; it is not the object itself.

## Assigning Multiple Alias Names to an Object

An object name merely contains a *pointer*—a reference to an area in memory that stores the real information about the object. Therefore, there is no reason why you cannot have more than one variable with the same pointer value. The following expression defines a second variable that points to the same form pointed to by frmTestWind3:

```
frmTestWind5 = frmTestWind3
```

We can prove this by printing and changing its Top property, as follows:

```
? frmTestWind3.Top
? frmTestWind5.Top
frmTestWind3.Top = 3
? frmTestWind5.Top
```

Understand that frmTestWind5 is not another instance of the form; it is just another name for frmTestWind3, an alias. We know this because we did not use the CREATEOBJECT function. In many ways it is not different than defining two variables "A" and "B" to be equal to a name as follows:

```
A = "Natasha"
B = A
? B
```

# Releasing Objects

At some point, you will get bored with "empty" forms and want to get rid of them. You can still remove windows created with DEFINE WINDOW by using traditional commands. Use RELEASE WINDOW <window name> to remove them individually or CLEAR WINDOWS to remove them all at once.

To release a form object, RELEASE WINDOW will not work unless you know the form's name, not its caption or the alias used as the object name. The following command displays the form's name:

```
? <object name>.Name
```

Therefore, you could type the following:

```
cNname = <object name>.Name
RELEASE WINDOW &cName
```

However, this would work only for forms, not for other object types. Therefore, there has to be another way to release objects in general. That way is to release the memory variable that points to the object, as shown here:

```
RELEASE frmTestWind3, frmTestWind4
```

Releasing an object's name also releases the object (usually). If you created multiple alias names for frmTestWind3, as suggested earlier, this RELEASE command removes only one of the two windows, because Visual FoxPro removes an object only if you release all references to it (alias names). As long as an alias still exists (frmTestWind5, in this case), the object must remain. Of course, you could include frmTestWind5 in the list of variables, or you could say:

```
RELEASE ALL LIKE frmTestWind*
```

The RELEASE ALL command is a quick way to clear all memory variables and arrays. With the addition of the LIKE clause, we can clear selected memory variables or through the use of wildcards like "?" for single characters and "*" for many characters clear groups of memory variables.

You might use CLEAR ALL. However, this command does not allow for the selective release of individual memory variables. Plus it also clears menu bars, menus, windows and closes tables, indexes, memo files, and external library functions. Obviously, this is more of a shotgun approach.

# Class Hierarchy

Because a container class can hold other control classes and even other container classes, you can see a hierarchy develop.

## Building Container Classes

The fun of creating empty forms eventually wears off. What you really want to do is add other objects to the form. Enter the lines below in the Command window to create a default form. Notice that it is similar to the prior form but then adds a command button labeled EXIT.

```
RELEASE ALL
frmTestWind3 = CREATEOBJECT("FORM")
frmTestWind3.ScaleMode = 0
frmTestWind3.Show
frmTestWind3.Caption = "Form with Button"
frmTestWind3.AddObject("MyFirstButton", "CommandButton")
cmdButton1 = frmTestWind3.MyFirstButton
cmdButton1.Visible = .T.
cmdButton1.Top = 2
cmdButton1.Left = 5
cmdButton1.Width = 10
cmdButton1.Height = 2
cmdButton1.Caption = "Exit"
```

N O T E    For the sake of entering this example interactively, the button was made visible before it was sized, positioned, and named. In an application, you probably want to keep objects invisible until you completely define their visual properties. ▪

Figure 2.2 shows the form created from this code.

**FIGURE 2.2**
A simple instance of a form shows a contained object: a command button.

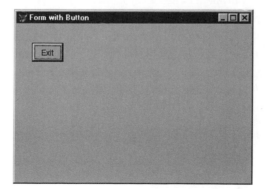

There are several interesting features in this small program. The first four lines create a basic form and give it a new title. The fifth line creates a new object in `frmTestWind3`, called `MyFirstButton`. The base class used to create this object is `CommandButton`. Notice that, like variable names, object classes cannot contain blanks. Also, the use of uppercase and lowercase letters in window and object names, although a matter of personal preference, might follow a standard naming convention. Visual FoxPro is completely case-insensitive.

▶ **See** "Naming Conventions," **p. 182**

# Referencing Objects in a Container

At this point, we could easily use the following notation to further define the form's properties:

```
frmTestWind3.MyFirstButton.Visible = .T.
frmTestWind3.MyFirstButton.Top = 2
frmTestWind3.MyFirstButton.Left = 5
etc.
```

The first line tells Visual FoxPro to change the visible property to logical true in the object `MyFirstButton`, which is an object in `frmTestWind3`. In effect, this line traces the hierarchy of objects from form to control to property. Although this notation is correct, it can be rather lengthy to enter and is susceptible to spelling errors. It is also more difficult to read.

However, as mentioned earlier, object names are not the objects themselves, but pointers to memory locations that store the object information. Think of properties in a control as nothing more than elements in an array (or list of values). To reference any element in an array, you need the array name and the element number. In this case, the object name is the equivalent of the array name, and the property name identifies the element. When you place one object in another, as in this case, you merely add another element to the first object's array to store a pointer to the new object. Therefore, `frmTestWind3.MyFirstButton.Visible` looks at "array" `frmTestWind3` for "element" `MyFirstButton`. There, it finds a pointer to the location of `MyFirstButton`. It then looks into "array" `MyFirstButton` to find "element" `Visible`. Why not just shortcut the process and store the reference to `Visible` in a separate variable?

That is exactly what you can do. Because object names are nothing more than pointers to the real object, you can have FoxPro trace the pointer tree to find the reference to the lowest-level object and store it separately. With this fact, you can understand how the following statement assigns the pointer to object `MyFirstButton` found in object `frmTestWind3` to cmdButton1:

```
cmdButton1 = FrmTestWind3.MyFirstButton
```

Subsequently, you can use the new, shorter alias to assign the balance of the properties to the command button, as originally shown.

# Using Code to Create Subclasses

The preceding example runs in the Command window. You also can save it as a program and run it later. But it is not the only way to create objects from base classes. In fact, there is a more flexible notation.

## Defining a Subclass

Suppose that you want to create a custom, consistent look to your application. Suppose further that this custom look requires windows with yellow backgrounds and red text (because you really like the Hot Dog Stand color scheme in Windows).

Begin by creating the form with the command DEFINE CLASS. DEFINE CLASS can create subclasses from any base class. A subclass is not an object; rather, think of it as a copy of a master pattern used to create objects. The following shows the full command syntax.

```
DEFINE CLASS ClassName1 AS cParentClass [OLEPUBLIC]
    [[PROTECTED|HIDDEN PropertyName1, PropertyName2 ...]
        [object.]PropertyName = eExpression
    [ADD OBJECT [PROTECTED] ObjectName AS ClassName [NOINIT]
        [WITH cPropertylist]]...
    [[PROTECTED|HIDDEN]FUNCTION|PROCEDURE Name
    [NODEFAULT]
        cStatements
    [ENDFUNC|ENDPROC]]...
ENDDEFINE
```

However, for many simple class definitions, you may only need the following subset of the DEFINE CLASS syntax, which allows for the definition of custom properties and a few simple methods:

```
DEFINE CLASS ClassName1 AS cParentClass
    PropertyName = eExpression
[FUNCTION|PROCEDURE Name
    cStatements
[ENDFUNC|ENDPROC]]...
ENDDEFINE
```

The simplest form of DEFINE CLASS creates a new class, also called a subclass, from one of the base classes. You use a subclass to create a custom object like the form previously mentioned with a sky-blue background, logo, and close button. The following statement is a complete, although simple, subclass definition:

```
DEFINE CLASS TestWind AS FORM
ENDDEFINE
```

The DEFINE CLASS command just used creates a new class based on the base class Form, and assigns it an alias name (TestWind). This new class is a subclass. However, if you type these statements by themselves, they don't appear to do anything. Like CREATEOBJECT, they define something in memory, but that is all. Again, use CREATEOBJECT to create an instance of the new class. Remember, it returns a pointer that you can assign to a variable name.

To create an object from the new class TestWind, call the function CREATEOBJECT. This time, however, the name of the class is that of the subclass TestWind, not the base class Form. The following two lines create and show a form based on subclass TestWind:

```
frmTestWind6 = CREATEOBJECT("TestWind")
frmTestWind6.Show
```

Finally, you can encapsulate information using a program to create a new class definition for a form as shown in Listing 2.1. Then every form created using this class inherits its properties, such as the very desirable hotdog stand colors.

**Listing 2.1    02PRG01.PRG—Program Example to Create a Form with a Command Button**

```
* Program 2.1
* Program example to create a form with a command button

TestWind6 = CREATEOBJECT("TestWind")
TestWind6.Show
? 'The colors that appear here are encapsulated in the class TestWind'
?
? 'Each instance of this class inherits them.'
WAIT WINDOW    && Added to keep form on screen

DEFINE CLASS TestWind AS FORM
    Top = 2
    Left = 10
    Height = 10
    Width = 80
    ScaleMode = 0
    BackColor = RGB(255, 255, 0)
    ForeColor = RGB(128, 0, 0)
ENDDEFINE
```

Specifying colors has become more complex over the years. Gone are the days when a relatively simple statement such as COLOR W/B would put white text on a blue background. Of course, there were only 16 colors to deal with then. Today, most monitors support 16, 64, 256, or even 16,777,216 colors. It would be hard enough to think of 256 color names, much less 16 million!

Therefore, Visual FoxPro takes a scientific approach and defines colors as a mixture of the three primary colors: red, green, and blue. Obviously, this is the origin of the term *RGB*. Each primary color has a value of 0 to 255, representing the amount of that color. The combination of all three values for each color determines the overall color.

For example, specifying all three values as 0 means that you do not want any of the primary colors. This absence of color creates black. Similarly, setting each primary color to their maximum value of 255 results in white. If this is confusing, think back to your school days, when the teacher used a prism to divide sunlight into a rainbow of colors. At night, of course, there is no light, so everything is black. If you keep all three color values equal as you increment them from 1 to 254, you get 254 shades of gray. Maybe that is why people always say that there are so many shades of gray in programming. Rather than keep you guessing, Table 2.1 shows the RGB values for the 16 common colors.

**Table 2.1   Common RGB and Color Values**

| Color | RGB Values | Color Value |
|---|---|---|
| White | 255, 255, 255 | 16777215 |
| Black | 0, 0, 0 | 0 |
| Gray | 192, 192, 192 | 12632256 |
| Dark Gray | 128, 128, 128, | 8421504 |
| Red | 255, 0, 0 | 255 |
| Dark Red | 128, 0, 0 | 128 |
| Yellow | 255, 255, 0 | 65535 |
| Dark Yellow | 128, 128, 0 | 32896 |
| Green | 0, 255, 0 | 65280 |
| Dark Green | 0, 128, 0 | 32768 |
| Cyan | 0, 255, 255 | 16776960 |
| Dark Cyan | 0, 128, 128 | 8421376 |
| Blue | 0, 0, 255 | 16711680 |
| Dark Blue | 0, 0, 128 | 8388608 |
| Magenta | 255, 0, 255 | 16711935 |
| Dark Magenta | 128, 0, 128 | 8388736 |

The table displays a third column that represents each color as an integer. You can specify colors by using this integer in place of the RGB function. To calculate this integer, use the following equation:

```
color value = B*256*256 + G*256 + R
```

where B is the value for blue from zero to 255

G is the value for green from zero to 255

R is the value of red from zero to 255

## Adding New Properties to a Class Definition

Visual FoxPro makes it easy to add new properties to a subclass. All you need is to include the property name immediately after the DEFINE CLASS statement and follow it with a default value. The class definition shown adds an Owner property to a form that defaults to Copyright 1996 MicMin Associates.

```
DEFINE CLASS TestWind AS FORM
  Top = 2
  Left = 10
  Height = 10
  Width = 80
  Owner = 'Copyright 1996 MicMin Associates'
ENDDEFINE
```

**N O T E**  Although you can initialize the default values of properties to any variable type (character, numeric, and so on), you cannot define the default value by using an expression. ■

There is no limit on the number of properties a class can have. As a general rule, unless you or VFP specifically do something with the property through a method, there is little reason for it to exist. The previous example constitutes one of the few exceptions. Another exception might be to include a version number with all of your custom controls. Because of inheritance, adding this Owner property early in the hierarchy brands all subsequent subclasses created from TestWind.

## Adding Controls to a Container

When you define a new class from an existing base class, you can add new properties to those that already exist. Suppose that you have a form with several basic controls that most users need. However, you also have advanced controls for expert users. You need a form that can expand on demand. You could do this with an Advanced or More>> button.

First, you need to add a control button to a form. Listing 2.2 uses the ADD OBJECT option of DEFINE CLASS to add a command button called SizeIt. It places the button at the top-left corner of the form initially.

**N O T E** Using the ADD OBJECT option incorporates the Control button into the definition of the subclass. Thus it can be inherited. If the example were to use

```
frmTestWind7.AddObject("SizeIt", "CommandButton")
```

instead, the button would become an object in the instance of the subclass, rather than part of the subclass itself. Therefore, which method you use depends on whether you want to inherit the added object as part of the subclass created with DEFINE CLASS. ■

**Listing 2.2  02PRG02.PRG—Program to Open a Form with a Single Command Button Object**

```
* Program 2.2
* Program to open a form with a single command button object

* Main Program
  TestWind7 = CREATEOBJECT("TestWind")
  TestWind7.Show(1)

* Define Classes
  DEFINE CLASS TestWind AS FORM
    Top = 2
    Left = 10
    Height = 7
    Width  = 40
    BackColor = RGB(255, 255, 0)
    ForeColor = RGB(0, 0, 0)
    ScaleMode = 0

  ADD OBJECT sizeit AS COMMANDBUTTON ;
    WITH caption = 'MORE>>', ;
      Top = 0, ;
      Left = 0, ;
      Height = 2, ;
      Width = 12

ENDDEFINE
```

You can click this button (as it has been defined) all day, if you like; it does not do a thing, because it has no method associated with the CLICK event yet. Therefore, Visual FoxPro does not know what to do when you click it, other than make it look depressed when clicked and then release it. To get the button to do something, you need to write a method for the event.

Part

I

Ch

2

# Events

Without events, the world of object programming would be pretty dull. Events make things happen. Clicking the mouse on a Command button is an event. Pressing a key is an event. Moving the mouse is an event. Even the process of opening a form triggers a series of events to initialize the form and its contained controls. Understanding all this object-oriented terminology will probably be a major personal event for many of you; it was for me. But seriously, events are predefined by VFP. You cannot define your own events for an object.

## Recognizing Events

Table 2.2 lists common events that Visual FoxPro recognizes. In most cases, the event name adequately sums up how FoxPro recognizes it. However, brief descriptions have also been provided.

**Table 2.2  Common Events and Their Descriptions**

| Event | Executes a Method... |
| --- | --- |
| Activate | When a container object receives focus. |
| Click | When you quickly press and release the left mouse button. |
| DblClick | When you quickly press and release the left mouse button twice in rapid succession. |
| Deactivate | When you deactivate a container object, such as a form. |
| Deleted | When you mark a record for deletion. |
| Destroy | When you release an instance of an object. |
| DownClick | When you click the down arrow on a control (combo box, list box, or spinner). |
| DragDrop | When you complete a drag-and-drop operation. |
| DragOver | When you drag a control over a potential target. |
| DropDown | When you click the arrow next to a combo or list box, but just before dropping down its list. Use this event to update selections before displaying them. |
| Error | When a method encounters a run-time error. |
| ErrorMessage | When a Valid event fails; used to return an error message. |
| GotFocus | When you move into a field or control; can also be triggered by the code. |

| Event | Executes a Method... |
|-------|---------------------|
| Init | When an object is created in memory, before it is shown. |
| Interactive Change | When you change a control's value. |
| KeyPress | When you press any key. |
| Load | When you create an object. If the method returns .F., the object is not created. |
| LostFocus | When you or the code move the focus off an object. |
| Message | When control gets focus; used to display a message in the status bar |
| MouseDown | When you press a mouse button. |
| MouseMove | When you move the mouse. |
| MouseUp | When you release a mouse button. |
| Moved | When you move a column to a new position in a grid. |
| Paint | When you repaint a form after it has been covered by other objects, resized, or moved |
| Programmatic Change | When the code changes a value of a control. |
| Resize | When you change the width of a column in a grid; occurs when a form changes size. |
| RightClick | When you press and release the right mouse button. |
| Scrolled | When you are scrolling through a grid control. |
| Timer | When a specified number of milliseconds have elapsed. |
| Unload | When releasing an object. |
| Valid | Before a control loses focus. If the method associated with this event returns .F., Visual FoxPro will not allow focus to leave this control. |
| When | Before a control gains focus. If the method associated with this event returns .F., Visual FoxPro will not give focus to the control. |

Part

I

Ch

2

Don't panic with all of these events. No object uses all of the events in this list. In fact, most objects only use a handful, and of these, only two or three are common in any one object. Furthermore, you cannot change or add to the events that an object recognizes. So you don't have to worry about any surprise events.

Actually, you may already be familiar with the last two events from previous versions of FoxPro. The When and Valid clauses have existed for some time. You probably use the When clause to determine whether the user can move into a field. Maybe you even use it to set up function keys for key value searches. Similarly, the Valid clause validates the user's input. If the input passes the validation tests, you allow the program to move to the next field. Otherwise, you keep the user in the current field or otherwise deal with the error. In Visual FoxPro, you can continue to use these two events in a similar way. However, there are other events you can trap and program for. One new event that you will find invaluable is the Click event. In fact, that is the one needed now.

## Attaching Methods to Events

In this example, when the user clicks the button, it should change the form's size, change the button's caption, and reposition the button to keep it in the lower-right corner. To define how the command button will respond when clicked, you place a Click procedure or method, in the DEFINE CLASS code segment.

Notice in Listing 2.3 that one modification to the previous program is a procedure named SizeIt.CLICK that appears in the class definition. When defining an event procedure, you must qualify the event name (CLICK) with the object name (SizeIt), just as when you reference properties. After all, you could have more than one Click event in a class belonging to different objects.

**Listing 2.3   02PRG03.PRG—Program Opens a Form with a Command Button to Change the Form Size**

```
* Program 2.3
* Program opens a form with a Command Button that expands and shrinks form
* This type of button is often used to 'hide' expert or advanced features.

* Main Program
  TestWind7 = CREATEOBJECT("TestWind")
  TestWind7.Show(1)

* Define Classes
  DEFINE CLASS TestWind AS FORM
     Scale = 1
     Top = 2
     Left = 10
     Height = 7
     Width  = 40
     Enabled = .T.
     BackColor = RGB(255, 255, 0)
     ForeColor = RGB(0, 0, 0)
     ScaleMode = 0

  ADD OBJECT sizeit AS COMMANDBUTTON ;
     WITH caption = 'MORE>>', ;
        Top = 0, ;
        Left = 0, ;
```

```
      Height = 2, ;
      Width = 15

  PROCEDURE Sizeit.INIT
  * Center button on resized form
    This.Left = This.Parent.Width - This.Width - 1
    This.Top = This.Parent.Height - This.Height - .5
  ENDPROC

  PROCEDURE sizeit.CLICK
    IF This.Parent.Scale = 1
      This.Parent.Scale = 2
      This.Parent.Height = This.Parent.Height * 2
      This.Parent.Width = This.Parent.Width * 2
      This.Caption = '<<SHRINK'
    ELSE
      This.Parent.Scale = 1
      This.Parent.Height = This.Parent.Height /2
      This.Parent.Width = This.Parent.Width /2
      This.Caption = 'MORE>>'
    ENDIF

  * Recenter button on resized form
    This.Left = This.Parent.Width - This.Width - 1
    This.Top = This.Parent.Height - This.Height - .5
  ENDPROC
ENDDEFINE
```

The first thing to notice about the code in this procedure is the use of This. and This.Parent. Actually, these are just two of several shortcut object reference keywords that you need when defining subclasses. They are called relative referencing rather than absolute referencing, which requires the actual object names. In fact, their use is essential to generalizing references in procedures that encapsulate a class definition, as was done in the last program. Table 2.3 shows the object reference keywords and their definitions.

**Table 2.3    Relative Referencing Shortcuts**

| Keyword | Reference |
| --- | --- |
| Parent | The immediate container of the current object |
| This | The current object, event, or procedure of the object |
| ThisForm | The form containing the current object |
| ThisFormSet | The form set containing the current object |

Thus, when the click procedure refers to property, This.Parent.Height, it refers to the form's height variable. Similarly, This.Caption refers to the command button's caption or text.

**N O T E**  In this case, `This.Parent` is synonymous with `ThisForm`. However, that may not always be the case, such as when you place a check box in a column grid. ■

Why not just put the form or command button names in the procedure? Because when Visual FoxPro runs this code, it creates an object based on the class definition. The name of the actual form object is not `TestWind`, which is a class name, but `frmTestWind7`, which is an object reference. If you used `TestWind` in the procedure, VFP would generate this run-time program error:

```
Alias 'TESTWIND' not found.
```

If, instead, you use `This.Parent.` and `This.`, Visual FoxPro replaces these names with the actual object name at runtime. In other words, it replaces `This.Parent` with `frmTestWind7` and `This` with `frmTestWind7.Sizeit` when you run the code. If it were not for such general referencing techniques, it would not be possible to create general class definitions that support inheritance.

Another feature included in this class definition is a new property, `Scale`, which can be used to track which window size is active. Even though this code creates class `TestWind` from the base class `Form`, and inherits all the properties, events, and methods from it, you can add new properties at any time. In this case, you simply include the following line in the property declaration section of the class definition:

```
Scale = 1
```

When that is done, you can reference and use the new property in any procedure or function, as done here to track the form's status.

**N O T E**  You can add properties and methods to an object, but you cannot add a new event. You cannot modify the types of events that Visual FoxPro recognizes for any control. ■

If you run this example, it initializes the button in the upper-left corner of the form. After you click the button, it repositions itself to the lower-right corner of the window. When you click it, the button moves between the two window sizes, but it always remains in the lower-right corner. To be consistent, the button should start in this corner, not the upper-left corner. To achieve this, simply add the procedure shown in Listing 2.4 to the bottom of the class definition.

**Listing 2.4    02PRG09.PRG—Procedure *SIZEIT_INIT***

```
PROCEDURE Sizeit.INIT
*  Position button on resized form in lower right corner
  This.Left = This.Parent.Width - This.Width - 1
  This.Top = This.Parent.Height - This.Height - .5
ENDPROC
```

When Visual FoxPro opens a form, it executes code assigned to the form INIT method or any of the contained object INIT methods. In this case, we use it to reposition a command button in the bottom-right corner of a form. Now, when you run the program, you should see the forms in Figures 2.3 and 2.4 as you click each of the buttons.

**FIGURE 2.3**
This image shows the original-size form with the MORE>> button ready to expand it.

**FIGURE 2.4**
This image shows the expanded form after the MORE>> button is clicked. Notice that the button caption changes to SHRINK.

The next example creates a small window to get a password from the user. The example creates a form called GetPass. Within the form, it adds a single text box called PassWord. The main event for this text box occurs when the user presses any key. Because you want the user to enter a password, you need to capture the keystrokes without displaying them on-screen.

VFP passes the procedure GetPass.KeyPress two parameters. The first is a keycode that is the ASCII code for the key. It also passes a second parameter that defines whether the Shift, Alt, or Ctrl key is also pressed with the primary key. You can ignore this second parameter for this example.

The program needs to build an internal string, cPassWord, containing the keystrokes that occur between the characters *A* and *z*. Because you need to access this string outside the object, this example initializes the variable in the main program. At the same time, it displays a mask character, *, on-screen. Other features include the capability to press Backspace to remove one character at a time and the capability to press Esc to clear the password and start over. Listing 2.5 shows the resulting code.

**Listing 2.5  02PRG05.PRG—Creating a Password Class**

```
*Program 2.5
* This program creates the base functionality of the password class

* Enter a login password, but don't display it
  CLEAR

* Create the form and change some of its properties
  frmKey = CREATEOBJECT("GetPass")
  WITH frmKey
      .Caption = 'ENTER PASSWORD'
      .ScaleMode = 0
      .Height  = 2
      .Width   = 35
  ENDWITH

* Display the form
  frmKey.Show

* Initialize the password variable so it can be retrieved.
  cPassWord = ''

* Initiate event monitoring
  READ EVENTS

* Check the value of the returned password
  IF EMPTY(cPassWord)
     = MESSAGEBOX("Sorry, you need a password to continue")
     CANCEL
  ENDIF
  ? 'Password entered was: ' + cPassWord

* Begin the form definition
  DEFINE CLASS GetPass AS FORM
  ADD OBJECT PassWord AS TEXTBOX

* Create a method to evaluate the keys pressed
  PROCEDURE PassWord.KeyPress
     PARAMETERS nKeyCode, nShiftAltCtrl

    * Do not echo the keys pressed back to the screen
      NODEFAULT

    * Determine which key was pressed.
      DO CASE
        CASE nKeyCode = 13     && Return key
          RELEASE THISFORM

        CASE nKeyCode = 27     && Escape key
          This.Value  = ''
          cPassWord   = ''

        CASE nKeyCode = 127    && Backspace key
          This.Value  = LEFT(This.Value, LEN(This.Value)-1)
```

```
        cPassWord    = LEFT(cPassWord, LEN(cPassWord)-1)

      OTHERWISE                && Check for character key
        IF BETWEEN(nKeyCode, 65, 122)  &&between 'A' and 'z'
          This.Value = ALLTRIM(This.Value) + '*'
          cPassWord  = cPassWord + CHR(nKeyCode)
        ENDIF
    ENDCASE
  ENDPROC

* Define a destroy event to clear event monitoring
  PROCEDURE DESTROY
    CLEAR EVENTS
  ENDPROC

ENDDEFINE
```

Part

I

Ch

2

> **N O T E**   Of course, a much more efficient way to accomplish the specific goal of hiding keystrokes would be to set the PasswordChar property of a text box to "*". However, by creating a custom class, you can add additional functionality such as password verification and encryption. ■

Several other changes have been made to this code's style. Notice that after creating the form, the program uses the WITH…ENDWITH structure to modify some of its properties. Notice that the object name appears after WITH. Each property then appears on a separate line and begins with a dot character. This simplifies defining a long list of properties for an object.

Second, after showing the form, the program executes a READ EVENTS command. This command turns on VFP's event processor, where it remains while monitoring for events until a CLEAR EVENTS is processed. At the end of the DEFINE CLASS block, you can see the CLEAR EVENTS command in a procedure called DESTROY. However, you might say, nothing calls this procedure. So how does the program end?

The KeyPress procedure checks for several special keys. The first one is the Return key, represented by ASCII value 13. When the procedure encounters this key, it releases the form that causes a Destroy event. That is how CLEAR EVENTS gets called to end VFP's event monitoring.

Another command in the KeyPress procedure is NODEFAULT. This command prevents VFP from executing the default method for this event, which would be to display the pressed character on-screen. Remember, you do not want to display the password as it is entered. Rather, you display This.Value, which contains the mask string. NODEFAULT prevents the actual key from being echoed to the screen.

If you understand this chapter so far, you may be starting to see some of the benefits that Visual FoxPro's object-oriented approach offers. Suppose that you have a large application that requires many forms. If you create one master form definition, defined as a new class with company logo, title, navigation buttons, and so on, you can use that class to create each new form. Furthermore, after you test the new class definition with a few simple forms, you never have to worry about that portion of the code again. Even better, if you need to change the company logo, add or modify a navigation button, or change the background color (because no one else likes Hot Dog Stand as much as you do), you can make that change in the class definition one time.

# Referencing Objects

There are many ways to reference objects. Previous examples use an alias name to reference them. You saw that an object can have more than one reference name. Also, when an object contains other objects, you can reference individual objects by using a hierarchy of object names, or you can assign a new alias to represent any portion of that hierarchy. This section looks at two new ways to reference objects: through arrays and through scope resolution.

## Using Arrays of Objects

Often, you define a form that has a group of related buttons or other controls. You could define each object as a separate object reference. However, you would also need a separate procedure for each event for each object. By combining objects into an array, you can use a single procedure for each common event and, through a CASE statement, define individual actions.

Listing 2.6 shows a simple example of a two-button form. Each button is a member of an array called Choices. FoxPro passes the index number of the control to events as a parameter. Thus, the click procedure for choices recognizes this parameter named MemIndex and uses it to determine which member method to run.

**Listing 2.6   02PRG06.PRG—A Two-Button Form**

```
* Program 2.6
* Program opens a form with a Command Button that expands and shrinks form

* Main Program
  Shipper = CREATEOBJECT('ShipForm')
  Shipper.Show(1)

* Define Classes
```

```
DEFINE CLASS ShipForm AS FORM
DIMENSION CHOICES[2]
  Caption = "Shippers"
  ScaleMode = 0
  Width  = 20
  Height = 8

  ADD OBJECT Choices[1] AS CommandButton ;
    WITH Top = 1, ;
         Height = 2, ;
         Caption = 'AirLorn', ;
         Left  = 2, ;
         Width = 15
  ADD OBJECT Choices[2] AS CommandButton ;
    WITH TOP = 5, ;
         Height = 2, ;
         Caption = 'Fed Excess', ;
         Left = 2, ;
         Width = 15

  PROCEDURE Choices.CLICK
  PARAMETER INDEX
  DO CASE
    CASE INDEX = 1
      = MESSAGEBOX("Sent via AirLorn")
    CASE INDEX = 2
      = MESSAGEBOX("Sent via Fed Excess")
  ENDCASE
  ENDPROC
ENDDEFINE
```

Part

I

Ch

2

Arrays of objects are similar to arrays of other variable types. For example, each member can hold a different object type. The first element could be a command button, the next a radio button, and so on. If you redimension the array, Visual FoxPro initializes added elements to .F.. If you reduce the array size, it releases objects referenced by deleted elements.

On the other hand, you cannot assign an object to an entire array with a single command, as you assign values to other arrays. Neither can you change any property common to all objects across the entire array with a single statement.

## Referencing Methods Using the Scope Resolution Operator

Inheritance can be very powerful. When you create subclasses, you inherit all the properties and methods from the preceding class. You can add new properties and methods in the subclass. You can even overwrite the method of a previous class. Sometimes, this is exactly what you want to do. At other times, you really want to augment or append to the method of a prior class. Look at Listing 2.7.

**Listing 2.7   02PRG07.PRG**

```
* Program 2.7

HierarchyForm2 = CREATEOBJECT("ParentForm")
= ACLASS(CLASSLIST, HierarchyForm2)
HierarchyForm2.Show(1)
DISPLAY MEMORY LIKE CLASSLIST

DEFINE CLASS GrandForm AS FORM
    Top = 2
    Left = 0
    Height = 7
    Width  = 40
    ScaleMode = 0
    BackColor = RGB(255, 255, 0)
    ForeColor = RGB(0, 0, 0)

  ADD OBJECT messageit AS COMMANDBUTTON ;
    WITH caption = 'PRESS ME', ;
      Top = 0, ;
      Left = 0, ;
      Height = 2, ;
      Width = 15


  PROCEDURE messageit.CLICK
    = MESSAGEBOX('This message comes from GrandForm')
  ENDPROC
ENDDEFINE

DEFINE CLASS ParentForm AS GrandForm
  BackColor = RGB(255, 255, 0)
  Left = 50

  PROCEDURE messageit.CLICK
    = MESSAGEBOX('This message comes from ParentForm')
    GrandForm.Messageit::Click
  ENDPROC
ENDDEFINE
```

This example creates a subclass of Form called GrandForm. It has a yellow background and a button labeled Press Me. The Click event associated with the button displays this message:

```
This message comes from GrandForm
```

The example then creates a subclass of GrandForm named ParentForm. This form overrides the background color, making it cyan, and moves it over to the right side of the screen. It also redefines the Click event to display this message:

```
This message comes from ParentForm
```

If you run this program, it creates a form from the second subclass, ParentForm. Notice that it inherits the command button from GrandForm, even through the DEFINE CLASS code for ParentForm never mentions a command button explicitly. Click the button, and the program displays the message from ParentForm. Just like color and position, the message in the subclass ParentForm overrides similar properties and methods in GrandForm.

What if you want also to execute the Click method from GrandForm? You could repeat the code in the subclass definition. Although this example would require that you repeat only a single line of code, other applications may have dozens of lines. Then, as in traditional programming, having duplicate copies of code leads to the possibility that changes may not occur consistently in all copies. A better solution references the code in GrandForm. Remove the asterisk from the third line from the end, and rerun the example.

This line uses a scope resolution operator (::) to refer to a method in a class higher in the inheritance hierarchy. Now, when you run the program, the message box from ParentForm is followed by the one from GrandForm.

Another way to reference the method in GrandForm is to simply remove the click procedure from ParentForm. In this case, the program automatically works back up the class hierarchy to look for the event code in the parent class. If no event code exists, Visual FoxPro ignores the event and moves on to the next event.

# Creating Custom Classes

You can create custom classes that have no visual elements. They consist entirely of properties and methods. Suppose that you need to track products at Al's Hardware. You might create an object called hardware to store information about each item. The code shown in Listing 2.8 creates a class called Hardware defined as a Custom class. Use the Custom base class for objects without visual components. The Custom class does not reserve space for events and methods that have no meaning for nonvisual objects. For example, there is no need for mouse events, drag-and-drop events, activate events, and so on.

**Listing 2.8  02PRG08.PRG**

```
* Program 2.8

* Add a hammer to Hardware
Hammer = CREATEOBJECT("Hardware")
Hammer.ProductId = 'A1265'
Hammer.ProductName = "Wooden Mallet"
Hammer.OnHandQty = 5
Hammer.UnitPrice = 8.95
Hammer.UnitCost = 3.95
```

*continues*

**Listing 2.8    Continued**

```
Hammer.InvCalc
CLEAR
? 'Inventory value for Hammer: ' + ;
  TRANSFORM(Hammer.InvValue, "$$$,$$$.99")

DISPLAY OBJECTS LIKE Hammer

DEFINE CLASS Hardware AS CUSTOM
    ProductId = ""
    ProductName = ""
    OnHandQty = 0
    OnOrderQty = 0
    UnitPrice=0.00
    UnitCost=0.00
    Taxable = .T.
    InvValue = 0.00

    PROCEDURE INVCALC
      This.InvValue = This.UnitCost * This.OnHandQty
    ENDPROC
ENDDEFINE
```

This program creates the nonvisual class called Hardware, which has several properties and a method called INVCALC. The main part of the program uses this class to create an object: a hammer. The class definition first assigns values to the class (which could come from a table) and then defines the INVCALC method to calculate the current cost of inventory.

This example also includes the DISPLAY OBJECTS command, which provides a quick way to see details about an object. It begins by displaying the name of the object. It then displays the class hierarchy used to create the object, followed by its properties, and finally its methods and events. DISPLAY OBJECTS, with no object name, displays all these details for any objects currently defined. It's an excellent way to document the current status of the system when an error occurs.

**TIP** Use DISPLAY OBJECTS to view the details of any class interactively. Just create a dummy object with CREATEOBJECT(); then use DISPLAY OBJECTS to see what it contains.

## TROUBLESHOOTING

**I've defined a memory variable in a procedure used as a method for a custom object. I even declared the variable to be PUBLIC. However, I still cannot access its value from other parts of the application.** This problem probably will be common as developers move into the world of objects. The reason why the supposedly public variable cannot be accessed from outside the object is that all variables defined and used within a class definition become encapsulated in it. That means that they do not exist anywhere except within that object. If you want to access a variable that gets defined in a class method, you must either initialize and scope the variable outside the object or make it a new object property that can be accessed through dot notation.

# Creating a Class Library

So far, this chapter has concentrated on creating objects each time they are needed. However, if the object is a visual object, you may want to take advantage of Visual FoxPro's capability to create a library of classes. You can then attach and use this common library in your applications.

To begin using a class library, you must create it, as follows:

```
CREATE CLASSLIB USEFOX
```

**N O T E**  This class library already exists on the CD, which you may have installed on your hard disk in directory \VFP5BOOK\DATA. Do not overwrite it. Rather, choose a different directory such as C:\TEMP to test this feature. ■

This statement creates a physical file with the extension .VCX in the current or default drive. You can provide a path name to create the file in any drive or directory. Also, you can specify an extension other than .VCX. However, Visual FoxPro assumes .VCX if an extension is not specified here or any other place that it uses the class library.

Next, you need to create a class for the new library. The following statement creates a command button called LISTALL:

```
CREATE CLASS LISTALL OF USEFOX AS 'COMMANDBUTTON'
```

**N O T E**  The class name must be enclosed in quotes; otherwise, you will get an error. ■

Notice that you can create a custom class by using any of the base classes supported by Visual FoxPro. You can also reference a custom class by including the FROM <ClassLibraryName> clause, telling VFP where to find it.

CREATE CLASS opens the Class Designer, shown in Figure 2.5.

**FIGURE 2.5**

The Class Designer can create individual object classes, such as this custom push button, or groups of objects, such as record-navigation buttons.

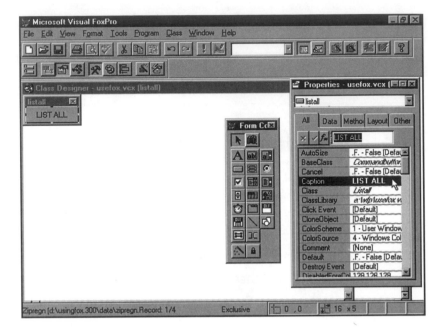

The Class Designer has a work area that contains a smaller window. This window has the title LIST ALL. Inside this window is a command button with the caption Command1. This is the appearance of the default command button. You may want to change this caption to LIST ALL.

On the right side of the screen is a window titled Properties (refer to Figure 2.5). (If this window does not automatically appear for you, simply right-click the command button that is being created to display a shortcut menu. Choose Properties... from this menu to display the Properties dialog box.)

This window contains the definitions for all properties, methods, and events associated with the object currently being designed. The center portion of this window contains a page frame with five pages. Each page shows a scrollable list of properties and their current values. Initially, VFP displays the ALL page. However, you may find it easier to use one of the other pages, which include only those properties related to data, methods, or layout.

You also may notice that Visual FoxPro displays some properties in italics, which indicates properties that you cannot edit. For example, you cannot change the class name at this time. You specified the name when creating the class, and Visual FoxPro will not allow you to change it now.

If you click any of the properties, Visual FoxPro not only highlights the property in the list, but also places its current value in the property edit box immediately above the list. You can use this box to edit the value directly.

When you select a property and change the value, Visual FoxPro displays that value as bold text in the property list. However, even if you manually change the value back to its default, VFP continues to display it as bold.

 Some properties add a down-arrow button next to the edit box. This button indicates properties that support a limited number of options. Furthermore, Visual FoxPro has predetermined what these options are and can display them in a list. Obviously, not all of properties have a fixed list of choices. You must enter properties such as Caption directly. However, if you select property FontName and then click the down-arrow button, VFP displays a list of all fonts known to your Windows installation.

These lists comes in handy for properties such as MousePointer. The mouse pointer supports 14 common mouse images. Without the list box to display a description of each value, it is unlikely that you will remember the difference between mouse pointer 6 and 7.

 Instead of displaying a down arrow, some properties display an ellipsis button (...). It often appears with color and picture properties. Clicking the button opens another dialog box. For example, if the current property you want to edit is BackColor, FontColor, or ForeColor, Visual FoxPro displays the Color dialog box. Similarly, properties such as Disabled Picture, DownPicture, DragIcon, and Picture display the Open dialog box. Because selecting pictures or icons based on just their names can be difficult, VFP expands this dialog box to include a picture preview area, as shown in Figure 2.6.

**FIGURE 2.6**
When you are using the Open dialog box to select a picture or icon for an object property, you can preview the image.

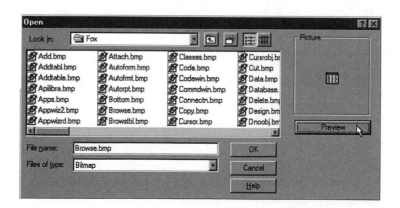

 The button immediately to the left of the property edit box has a scriptlike *fx*, representing *function*. This button calls up the Expression Builder dialog box. If you needed to create a complex expression for the status-bar text, you could open the Expression Builder to create it. However, not all properties can be set with expressions. For many, you must declare their properties with actual values.

 Suppose that you edit a property and later change your mind and want to return to the original value. Click the *X* button to the left of the property edit window. This button cancels the current change and restores the preceding value of the property as long as the user has not already accepted the change by pressing the Enter key or clicking the "check" button.

For most properties, even after you save a property change, you can right-click the property value and choose Reset to Default from the shortcut menu. This action returns the property value to its original value, not to its preceding value. Although you are free to change whatever properties you want, the only ones necessary for this example are:

| Caption | - | List All |
|---------|---|----------|
| Height  | - | 1.5      |
| Width   | - | 14.0     |

In addition, you want to provide code in the `Click` event to list the contents of a current table. Figure 2.7 shows the code window that opens when you double-click the Click event shown in the Methods list of the Property sheet. It displays the name of the current object and the procedure name. In this window, you enter the code that you want Visual FoxPro to execute when the Click event occurs. In this case, you want it to list the data in the current table or, if no table is open, to display an appropriate error message.

**FIGURE 2.7**

Add procedure code to the `Click` event of class LISTALL to list all records in the current table, if one is open.

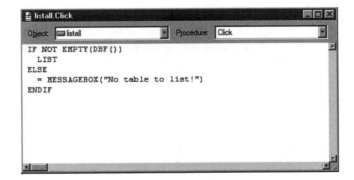

To save the procedure code, click the close box in the title bar. In the Properties list, the text next to Click Event changes from [Default] to [User Procedure]. This indicates that custom code has been added to this event.

Now it is time to save this new class. Simply click the close box in the Class Designer title bar. When you are prompted to save the changes made in the Class Designer, click Yes.

Of course, you can create other custom classes as needed and add them to the same class library. Like a procedure library, a class library has the capability to store multiple definitions in a single file.

## Using a Class Library

To use a class library, open it with the following command:

```
SET CLASSLIB TO \VFP5BOOK\DATA\USEFOX.VCX
```

 **TIP** It is always good practice to open a class library with its full path name. Never assume that the path or the default directory is set correctly.

If you open multiple class libraries, simply append the keyword ADDITIVE to the end of the command.

Next, create an object directly from any of the classes. To create an object using the LISTALL class, enter this command:

```
mybutton = CREATEOBJECT('LISTALL')
```

To show the use of class libraries in a program setting, consider the code shown in Listing 2.9.

---

**Listing 2.9   02PRG09.PRG—Class Libraries in a Program Setting**

```
* Program 2.9

* Open the class library
  SET CLASSLIB TO \VFP5BOOK\PROGRAMS\USEFOX.VCX

* Open table
  USE \VFP5BOOK\DATA\ZIPREGN

* Create form object to test button
  MyForm = CREATEOBJECT('Form1')
  MyForm.Caption = 'TEST LIST BUTTON'
  MyForm.Show(1)

* Release class library
  RELEASE CLASSLIB \VFP5BOOK\PROGRAMS\USEFOX

* Define a form with a button on it
  DEFINE CLASS form1 AS FORM
    Width = 70
    ScaleMode = 0

    ADD OBJECT MyButton AS LISTALL

    PROCEDURE MyButton.INIT
```

*continues*

**Listing 2.9 Continued**

```
* Positions button centered on form
   This.Left = (This.Parent.Width - This.Width) / 2
   This.Top  = (This.Parent.Height - This.Height) / 2
ENDPROC
ENDDEFINE
```

Notice that before closing, the program releases the class library from memory. Unless you intend to continue using the class library from the Command window, remember to close all libraries after using them. If your program has multiple procedures and only one procedure uses a class library, open the library at the beginning of the procedure, but close it before leaving the procedure. This practice ensures that Visual FoxPro has as much memory available as possible at all times to perform other tasks.

You also can remove all class libraries from memory by using the following code:

```
SET CLASSLIB TO
```

## TROUBLESHOOTING

**I tried to edit an existing class library created with an earlier version of Visual FoxPro, but an error message pops up, saying that the file was compiled in a previous version of FoxPro. How can I open it to recompile it?** Obviously, you need to recompile the code. Specifically, it is the code associated with the class methods. You cannot open the class with the Class Designer when the object code has been compiled with an earlier Visual FoxPro version.

The solution, fortunately, is simple. Enter the following command, replacing the text in brackets with the name of your class library. This should recompile the code and allow the Class Designer to open the library.

```
COMPILE CLASSLIB <library name>
```

If the preceding code does not work, you may need to look at the source code. Open the class library as a table with the USE command. Next, locate the records associated with the class. The record with the class name in the field OBJNAME is the container class. The other objects added to the container have the class name in the PARENT field. Next, look at the memo field METHODS. If an object has associated methods, the memo field appears as Memo (with the first letter in uppercase). Open the memo to review the source code for the method. Look for syntax errors or code that may not be valid in VFP 5.0. Make any needed changes, and close the memo field. Then try the COMPILE CLASSLIB command again.

## Modifying a Class Definition in a Library

Modifying an existing class definition in a class library is as easy as creating one. Simply use the following MODIFY CLASS command:

```
MODIFY CLASS LISTALL of \VFP5BOOK\DATA\USEFOX.VCX
```

> **NOTE** If you are not sure of the class name, but you know the class library, use the MODIFY CLASS command in the Command window to display the Open dialog box. This dialog box is similar to all the other Open dialog boxes, in that it allows you to select a file from any directory or drive. Because it recognizes that you want a class, not just the class library, however, it includes a list box that displays the class names within each class. Simply select a class library to display a list of all classes that it contains. To modify one, click it and choose the open button. ▪

## Removing a Class Definition from a Library

To remove an existing class definition from a class library, use the following REMOVE CLASS command:

```
REMOVE CLASS LISTALL of \VFP5BOOK\DATA\USEFOX.VCX
```

> **TIP** You can also display the class library in a Project Manager window, select the class, and click the Remove button.

## Moving a Class Definition from One Library to Another

The easiest way to move a class from one library to another is to open a project with both class libraries in it. This can be an existing class library or a new one, because classes can be assigned to more than one project. Figure 2.8 shows the copying of class LOGINPICTURE from class library LOGIN to ABOUT. As a result of this process, the class is stored in both libraries. Of course, you can delete the copied class from the original library to simulate a move.

If you need to move a class programmatically, you can use CREATE CLASS and REMOVE CLASS to accomplish this task without much trouble.

Suppose that you have a second class library, called USEFOX2.VCX. The following commands transfer LISTALL from USEFOX.VCX to USEFOX2.VCX:

```
CREATE CLASS LISTALL2 OF \VFP5BOOK\DATA\USEFOX2.VCX ;
    AS 'LISTALL' FROM \VFP5BOOK\DATA\USEFOX.VCX
REMOVE CLASS LISTALL OF \VFP5BOOK\DATA\USEFOX.VCX
```

**FIGURE 2.8**
Use a project to simplify copying or moving classes from one library to another.

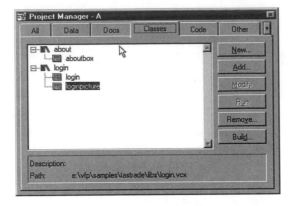

# Things You Have Learned About Object-Oriented Programming

- A class can create many objects. Using the CREATEOBJ command, you can create any number of objects from a class definition, as long as you make the reference name that is assigned to each one unique.

- Objects have properties that define the physical attributes of the object. They also have methods that define how the object relates to things around it and to events.

- You can have the same property and method names for different objects of the same class or a different class.

- All objects created from a class definition begin life as identical objects. Only after you assign new or modified properties and methods do they take on identities of their own.

- Changing the properties or methods of an object requires that you use dot notation to specify the object name and property name.

- You can create your subclasses, which initially inherit their properties, events, and methods from a parent class. You can change any or all properties and methods, however.

- You can create custom classes from scratch and then save them in a class library.

- Class libraries can contain any number of visual classes, which you can then use in your applications to create objects.

# From Here...

Although this chapter introduces the concepts and terms required to understand object-oriented programming, many later chapters expand upon the techniques that you learned here.

To learn more about how Visual FoxPro uses objects to create forms, refer to the following chapters:

- Chapter 11, "Building Applications with Simple Form Structures," covers the specifics of using objects in the creation of forms with the Form Designer.

- Chapter 12, "A Deeper Look at Object-Oriented Design," expands the concepts from this chapter to show how to take better advantage of inheritance, class libraries, and program control through event management

- Chapter 13, "Controls for Advanced Form Design," examines the more complex controls and their objects. Grids present an interesting new feature that embed lists, buttons, or even other grids in a grid cell.

- Bonus Chapter 07, "Extending Visual FoxPro with Third-Party Tools," shows how to use custom controls and libraries built as third-party products for Visual FoxPro and other object-oriented languages. This chapter is located on the CD.

# CHAPTER 3

# Defining Databases, Tables, and Indexes

*by Michael P. Antonovich and*
*Sandra Richardson-Lutzow*

Your next task when starting an application is to determine what data to collect and how to save it. You might determine this by examining samples of existing reports. Obviously, any data shown in a report must either be collected directly or derived from other collected data.

Next, you must organize this data into individual tables and define relations between the tables. In many ways, the basic structure of tables, indexes, and databases defines applications more than most programmers realize. Poor data design leads to inefficient code, frequent errors, longer development times, and many other problems.

The process of creating a database actually involves several steps:

- Defining the scope of the database
- Determining the fields required to support the database
- Dividing the fields into a set of normalized tables
- Establishing relations among the tables

**Creating free tables and their define fields**

It is important to properly structure tables and their fields in order to maintain your data efficiently and to avoid problems that could occur in the future with poorly defined tables.

**Modifying existing table structures**

Table structures very rarely exist exactly as defined at the start of development. You will need to take caution in modifying the structures to avoid problems such as loss of data.

**Defining the different index types and how to use them**

You can create indexes to serve many functions for your system if defined in the proper type and style.

**Creating a database of tables**

Take advantage of the database container's features and make the programmer's job simpler in ensuring data integrity.

**Defining some of a database's enhanced features**

The database container provides referential integrity, long, more descriptive table and field names, persistent relationships, validations and other features that aid in the relationships, validations, and other features.

Another way to state the first step is to answer the question, "What is the purpose of this application?" Your application may involve payroll, sales tracking, or inventory monitoring. Until you have a firm understanding of the purpose of your application, you cannot begin to define the data it requires. You need to ask questions such as these:

- What reports or other output must this application generate?

- Who needs this information?

- Who enters the information required for this output, and is it entered all at once by one person or in several steps by different people?

- Does another application already enter and store any of the information in the computer?

- How can a computer make collecting and reporting this information more timely and less expensive than current procedures?

# Creating Tables for an Application

Suppose that you want to track orders for a small business. After thinking about what information you collect when taking an order, you might create the following initial information list:

- Order date
- Customer name
- Customer address
- List of items purchased
- Quantity of each item purchased
- Unit price of each item purchased
- Tax on each item purchased
- Extended order amount
- Method of payment

This list uses at least four obvious data categories to store information about an order. The first category pertains to customer information. The second category tracks information common to orders, but not specific to individual items ordered. This category might contain the order date, the total order amount, the method of payment, and so on. The third category contains the order details. In this category, you can envision one record for each item purchased in each order. Finally, the fourth category stores details on each product, such as product identification, description, and price.

# Determining the Data Categories Needed

A logical question to ask at this point is exactly what information about the customer you need. Could you use more than a name and address? What happens if you need to back-order an item? Can you telephone the customer to pick up the order when you receive it? Does the customer have multiple shipping addresses but a central billing location? If so, which address do you enter? What are the customer's sales to date? Do you want to offer discounts to frequent customers? Have all the customer's outstanding bills been paid? Should you mail new orders to customers who have not paid their bills?

There may be even more questions, but the point is that now, during system and table design, is the time to ask these questions—not after the program has been created.

Suppose that after asking these questions (and for the sake of keeping this example fairly simple), you decide to track the following customer information:

- Company name
- Contact name
- Address
- Telephone number
- Fax number
- Outstanding bills total
- Purchases YTD (year to date)
- Standard payment method
- Credit card number
- Credit card expiration date
- Preferred shipper
- Date of last purchase

A review of the customer information, using the preceding list, could reveal several problems.

You have several orders from large corporate customers that have different shipping and billing locations. You further realize that simply storing the customer contact name may not be the easiest way to search the file if you know only a last name. Therefore, you need to break the name into first- and last-name fields. Similarly, an address consists of several components, including one or more street address lines, city, state or province, and postal code. Each of these components needs a separate field. Even a telephone number may not be sufficient detail for customers that have extension numbers.

What you are accomplishing is *atomizing* the customer's information. Each atom defines a single element that further defines the customer. The following list shows the results:

- ID (a unique identifier for a customer)
- Company name
- Contact first name
- Contact last name
- Billing street address
- Billing city
- Billing state/province
- Billing postal code
- Shipping street address
- Shipping city
- Shipping state/province
- Shipping postal code
- Telephone number
- Telephone extension number
- Fax number
- Outstanding bills total
- Purchases YTD
- Standard payment method
- Credit card number
- Credit card expiration date
- Preferred shipper
- Date of last purchase

In your customer system, you may require even more fields. However, these fields serve to show you how to create a table.

## Naming Each Data Fact

Now you need to define a field name for each data element. Traditionally, FoxPro limited field names to 10 characters. The first character was restricted to an alphabetic character; thereafter, FoxPro accepted any characters, with the exception of a space. However, with Visual FoxPro, you can define field names with up to 128 characters, but only if the field is in a table defined in a database. If you initially define a stand-alone table, called a *free table*, you must follow the 10-character limit.

Many field-naming conventions have been devised in previous versions of FoxPro to help make programs more readable. The conventions differentiate variables by type, by scope, and by whether they are memory or table variables. One common method defines fields in a table beginning with a two-character prefix followed by an underscore. This prefix identifies the table and is unique in the application. Using table identifiers, however, can become unacceptable in a couple of cases:

- If you plan to implement your own data dictionary, you will have fields that have common data descriptions and definitions between tables. In this case, you want to keep the same field name in each table.

- If you plan to transfer data between tables, using memory variables created with SCATTER, you cannot have table identifier prefixes in the field names for GATHER to replace the proper values. In the examples for this chapter, we will not use the table identifiers for these reasons.

Today, the generally recommended convention is to start each field name with a single character that identifies its field type.

▶ **See** "Naming Conventions," **p. 182**
▶ **See** "Designing Your Own Data Dictionary," **p. 734**

In this naming convention, memory variables also begin with two characters—the first represents its scope, and the second represents its type. The third character could be an underscore; however, the use of underscores is no longer encouraged. Table 3.1 shows possible character prefixes.

**Table 3.1 Memory Variable Naming Convention Prefix Parameters**

| 1st Character | 2nd Character |
|---|---|
| G (global) | C (character) |
| L (local) | D (date) |
| P (private) | L (logical) |
|  | N (numeric) |

## Assigning Data Types

Deciding what information to save in a table is only half of the battle in planning a new table structure. Next, you need to examine each data item and determine whether you should store it as character, numeric, date, or some other data type. Furthermore, for character and numeric fields, you need to determine the number of required characters.

You can begin by looking at the available data types provided by Visual FoxPro.

**Character**   Character is the most common data type in most tables. Character fields store 1 to 254 characters, consisting of printable characters such as letters, numbers, spaces, and punctuation marks. Certain characters, such as CHR(0), cannot appear in a regular character field. You must define fields that require more characters as memos.

Character fields have a fixed size. If you define a field such as Address with 35 characters, it consumes 35 characters in every record, even if Address equals 15 Main Street. Although this may sound trivial, the difference of 5 characters in a 300,000-record file is more than 1.4M. On the other hand, if Address requires more than 35 characters, Visual FoxPro stores only the first 35, truncating the rest.

You can even use character fields that consist entirely of numbers. For example, you should store ZIP codes, telephone numbers, and even customer IDs as character fields, for several reasons. First, numeric fields truncate leading zeros. Therefore, if you save a ZIP code such as 01995, Visual FoxPro would store it as 1995. Second, you may want to format a telephone number field as (215)084-1988. Finally, you may need to combine a field such as a customer ID with another field to form an index. Usually, you can combine fields into a single index expression only by concatenating character strings.

Perhaps a better way to determine whether to make a field character or numeric is to ask, "Will I ever perform calculations on this field?" If you answer yes, you may want to store it as numeric; otherwise, store it as a character. An exception is a numeric ID field. Even though you may need to increase the size of the ID field incrementally for new records, it works best as a right-justified character field with blank or zero padding to the left to fill the field. For example, you would zero-pad ZIP codes in a five-character field. You may also zero-pad customer ID numbers. Listing 3.1 shows one method of enlarging a zero-padded character customer ID.

**Listing 3.1   03PRG01.PRG**

```
SELECT CUSTOMER
APPEND BLANK
REPLACE cCustomerId WITH INCR_ID()

FUNCTION INCR_ID
*************************************************************
*
* FUNCTION INCR_ID Increments a character ID that contains
*                  only digits
*
```

```
* Designed specifically for CUSTOMER..cCustomerId
*
***********************************************************
LOCAL pnCurDec, pnCurRec, pcCurTag, pcNewId
* Capture current position in file, # of decimals, and tag
  pnCurDec = SYS(2001, 'DECIMAL')
  pnCurRec = RECNO()
  pcCurTag = TAG()
  SET DECIMALS TO 0

* Get last customer id used
  SET ORDER TO TAG CUSTID
  GOTO BOTTOM

* Calculate the next available ID
  pcNewId = PADL(VAL(cCustomerId)+1, 6, '0')

* Reset file position and tag, return next available id
  SET ORDER TO TAG (m.pcCurTag)
  SET DECIMAL TO EVAL(m.pnCurDec)
  GOTO pnCurRec
RETURN m.pcNewId
```

Enlarging an alphanumeric ID is more difficult, but Listing 3.2 finds the numeric portion of a field and expands it incrementally.

### Listing 3.2  03PRG02.PRG

```
USE CUSTOMER
APPEND BLANK
REPLACE cCustomerId WITH INCR_ID2()

FUNCTION INCR_ID2
***********************************************************
*
* FUNCTION INCR_ID2 finds the numeric portion of an id
*                     embedded in an alphanumeric field
*
* Designed specifically for CUSTOMER.cCustomerId
*
***********************************************************
LOCAL pnCurDec, pnCurRec, pnStartNum, pnEndNum, ;
      pnIdNum,  pcCurTag, pcNewId
* Capture current position in file and current tag
  pnCurDec = SYS(2001, 'DECIMAL')
  pnCurRec = RECNO()
  pcCurTag = TAG()
  SET DECIMALS TO 0
  STORE 0 TO pnStartNum, pnEndNum

* Get last customer id used
  SET ORDER TO TAG custid
  GOTO BOTTOM
```

*continues*

**Listing 3.2   Continued**

```
* Find start and end of numeric portion of field
  FOR i = 1 TO LEN(cCustomerId)
    IF ISDIGIT(SUBSTR(cCustomerId, i, 1)) AND ;
             pnStartNum = 0
pnStartNum = i
    ENDIF
    IF NOT ISDIGIT(SUBSTR(cust_id, i, 1)) AND ;
      pnStartNum>0 AND ;
      pnEndNum = 0
      pnEndNum = i
    ENDIF
  ENDFOR

* Check if there is a numeric portion
  IF m.pnStartNum = 0
    = MESSAGEBOX('There is no numeric portion to this id')
    RETURN cCustId
  ELSE
  * If no alpha suffix, fix end of number position
    IF m.pnEndNum = 0
      pnEndNum = LEN(cCustomerId) + 1
    ENDIF
  ENDIF

* Extract numeric portion of last id
  pnIdNum = SUBSTR(cCustomerId, m.pnStartNum, ;
           m.pnEndNum - m.pnStartNum)

* Calculate the next available customer id
  pcNewId = PADL(VAL(m.pnIdNum) + 1, ;
           m.pnEndNum - m.pnStartNum, '0')

* Reconstruct entire id
* Add alpha prefix
  IF m.pnStartNum = 1
    pcNewId = m.pcNewId
  ELSE
    pcNewId = SUBSTR(cCustomerId, 1, m.pnStartNum - 1) + ;
           m.pcNewId
  ENDIF
* Add alpha suffix
  IF m.pn_endnum <= LEN(cCustomerId)
    pcNewId = m.pcNewId + SUBSTR(cCustomerId, m.pnEndNum, ;
           LEN(cCustomerId) - m.pnEndNum + 1)
  ENDIF

* Reset file position and tag, return next available id
  SET ORDER TO TAG (m.pcCurTag)
  SET DECIMALS TO EVAL(m.pnCurDec)
  GOTO m.pnCurRec
RETURN m.pcNewId
```

**Currency**    To store dollar amounts, consider using a special numeric type called Currency. As a maximum amount, Currency can store a little more than $922 trillion. Currency defaults to a maximum of 4 decimal places and requires a fixed 8 bytes of storage in a table.

**N O T E**    For those who love details, currency values range from –922,337,203,685,477.5807 to 922,337,203,685,477.5807. ■

**Date and DateTime**    These two field types are similar in that they both store dates. Both types require 8 bytes to store a date in the form YYYYMMDD, regardless of whether SET CENTURY is ON or OFF. DateTime fields use an additional 6 bytes to store time stored as HHMMSS, with HH recorded by a 24-hour clock. If you convert a Date field to a DateTime field, the time defaults to 12:00:00AM.

**N O T E**    Dates range from 01/01/100 to 12/31/9999, and times range from 12:00:00 a.m. to 11:59:59 p.m. ■

 **T I P**    You can stamp a record that has a DateTime field with the current date and time by using the DATETIME() function.

**N O T E**    Just as you can add 1 to a Date field to increase it incrementally by one day, you can increase a DateTime field by seconds. Because there are 86,400 seconds in a day, you need to add 86,400 to a DateTime field to increase it by one day. ■

**Double**    Double fields are floating-point fields that store up to 18 digits in a compressed format that uses exactly 8 bytes. In fact, no matter how many digits you use, the number of bytes remains fixed at 8. The only decision that you make is the number of decimal places.

**N O T E**    Double values range from –4.94065648541247E–324 to 1.79769313486232E +308. ■

**Float and Numeric**    Both of these field types support up to 20 digits with a maximum of 19 decimal places, but each digit requires 1 storage byte. FoxPro treats both types identically, which results in the same degree of accuracy. However, providing both fields maintains compatibility with dBASE IV, which differentiates between them.

Unlike Double fields, Float and Numeric fields allow you to specify the number of bytes required, because FoxPro stores the ASCII code for each digit in a separate byte. Therefore, if a field value always uses integer values less than 100,000, a field width of 6 with

Part
I
Ch
3

zero decimal places suffices. To optimally size a numeric field, try to determine the largest and smallest values possible. Sizing a field too small for the values that are being stored forces FoxPro to store asterisks in the field.

**N O T E**   Float values range from −.9999999999E−19 to .9999999999E+20. ■

**T I P**   When sizing fields, remember that negative values need a character position to store the minus sign.

**CAUTION**

If you store a calculation result in a field that has a fixed number of decimal places, FoxPro truncates the value to match the field definition, which may adversely affect the precision of the value. Subsequent calculations that use this truncated field may lead to apparent rounding errors.

**General**   The most common use for General fields is to store graphics. A General field is a specialized Memo field. FoxPro stores a General field in the same .FPT file used by other Memo fields in the table, but you cannot use it the same way. It is primarily used to store references to bound OLE objects.

**Logical**   Logical fields store binary information in the form of .T. or .F.. Logical fields store information with only two states, such as taxable vs. nontaxable, male vs. female, and shipped versus back-ordered. Forms often use Logical fields as the source for check boxes.

**Memo**   Memo fields not only store large character strings (greater than 254 characters), but also provide a variable amount of storage per record, based on block size. A *block* is a fixed number of characters that FoxPro reserves for a memo. By default, FoxPro uses 64 bytes per block. This means that each group of 64 characters in a text string requires an additional block. If you have a string of 72 bytes, the extra 8 bytes require a second block of 64 characters.

**T I P**   From its 64 bytes, each block in a memo allocates 8 bytes to two 4-byte pointers. (These pointers tell Visual FoxPro how to find the preceding or following block.) Strictly speaking, the memo block has only 56 bytes.

You can change the block size by using the SET BLOCKSIZE command, which sets the number of bytes from 33 to 511 bytes. For larger blocks, use an integer from 1 to 32 to allocate blocks in multiples of 512 bytes. With the introduction of Visual FoxPro, you can also set block size to 0, which causes VFP to allocate space one byte at a time, resulting in no wasted space. However, performance will not be as good as when you use larger block sizes.

You must use SET BLOCKSIZE before adding the first record with a memo. When you add the first memo, FoxPro embeds the current block size in the memo file. To change the block size of an existing memo file, you must rewrite each Memo field. However, regardless of the block size, remember that the first block reserves 8 bytes for the pointers.

Why should you worry about the block size? The larger the block size, the more wasted space memos consume, if they vary greatly in length. On the other hand, the more blocks FoxPro needs to store a memo, the less efficiently it retrieves the memo. The practice sounds more like art than science, but in general, you want to define the block size as the most likely memo length.

**Part**

**I**

**Ch**

**3**

FoxPro stores memos in a file separate from the .DBF, with the extension .FPT. Whether you have one Memo field or several in a table, it stores all memos in this one .FPT file. In fact, if you have General fields, FoxPro stores them in the same file as memos. Pointers from the .DBF file keep track of what information belongs to each record and field.

Because memo pointers point only one way—from the .DBF to the .FPT—you need to ensure that .DBF and .FPT files never get separated. How can this happen? Perhaps you have a table that contains a Memo field on two or more machines. If you copy (by accident, it is assumed) the .DBF from one machine to another without also copying the .FPT file, the copy could be out of synchronization with the current .FPT. If this happens and you add records before realizing the problem, you may find that the memo text no longer corresponds with the proper records. It is almost impossible to fix this problem without manually resetting the pointers from the .DBF to the .FPT. Third-party tools are available to perform this very complex task.

▶ **See** "Handling Corruption in Files," **p. 634**

**N O T E** One solution stores the record key with the memo just in case the unthinkable happens. If you have more than one Memo field per record, also store the field name with the key. ▪

Don't worry about records without memos; FoxPro does not reserve additional storage space in the memo file for them. However, every memo in every record requires a 4-byte pointer in the .DBF file, even if it is blank.

The following are typical uses for Memo fields:

- Character fields that only occasionally contain text
- Character fields that vary greatly in length or whose length cannot be predicted
- Text files, such as résumés, letters, and historical archiving of program versions

# Using the Table Designer

Suppose that today is the start of a new project, and you want to use the Project Manager to organize your files. Therefore, you need to create a project first. As is true of most functions, FoxPro provides several methods of performing this task such as using VFP commands, menu-driven options, or the Project Wizard.

▶ **See** "Introducing the Project Manager," **p. 51**

Choose File, New from the main system menu. The New dialog box appears (see Figure 3.1).

**FIGURE 3.1**

Create a new project, using the New dialog box.

Choose Project as the file type, and click New File. Because FoxPro requires a name to identify any file, it first opens the Create dialog box to request a project file name (see Figure 3.2). FoxPro uses the same dialog box for all file-name requests.

The Create dialog displays the current or default directory. If you already have projects defined in this directory, they appear dimmed in the list box, so that you cannot select them. They serve as a reminder not to use the same project name twice. You can switch to another directory or drive to store the project, but after you select a directory, you must enter the new project file name manually.

If you prefer a more direct method when creating tables and don't mind typing, enter the file name in the Command window, as follows:

```
CREATE PROJECT PTOFSALE
```

Using a command is quicker, but you must learn basic command syntax, and you must already have a valid name and directory under which to store the project.

**FIGURE 3.2**

Name a new project file, using the Create dialog box.

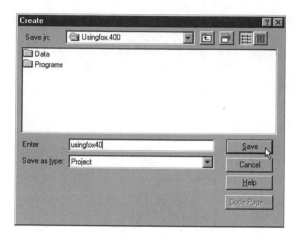

**NOTE** If you open a project and close it immediately, Visual FoxPro prompts you to delete the project file or retain it without adding any files. ■

Having created a project, FoxPro automatically opens it. Projects have *page frames*. Each frame represents a different file type, identified by a tab across the top of the page. To select a page, click its tab. To create a table, click the Data page. Currently, this project has no defined tables (see Figure 3.3). Create a free table by selecting Free Tables and clicking New. VFP will then give you the option of using a Wizard or the Table designer to create the table.

**FIGURE 3.3**

Create a new free table by selecting the Data page in Project Manager and clicking New.

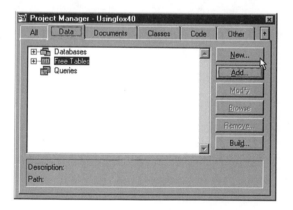

VFP next prompts you for a file name, this time for the table. For the example, call this table CUST.DBF.

Finally, FoxPro displays the Table Designer dialog box. This form has a page-frame object with three pages. The first page defines the table structure, the second one defines the indexes, and the third shows the status of the table. The table structure page should appear by default. If not, you need only click the Table page, as shown in Figure 3.4.

**FIGURE 3.4**
The Table Designer displays completed field definitions for CUST.DBF.

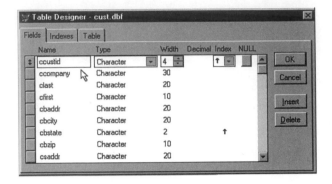

To define the table structure, enter the field information shown in Table 3.2, which includes field types, widths, and decimals. Notice that each customer is identified by a unique customer ID. Type the customer ID in the first field.

**Table 3.2  Suggested File Structure for Fields in CUST.DBF**

| 10-Character Field Names | Field Type | Field Width | Decimals |
|---|---|---|---|
| _cCUSTID | Character | 4 | |
| _cCOMPANY | Character | 30 | |
| _cFIRST | Character | 10 | |
| _cLAST | Character | 20 | |
| _cBADDR | Character | 20 | |
| _cBCITY | Character | 20 | |
| _cBSTATE | Character | 2 | |
| _cBZIP | Character | 10 | |
| _cSADDR | Character | 20 | |
| _cSCITY | Character | 20 | |
| _cSSTATE | Character | 2 | |
| _cSZIP | Character | 10 | |
| _cPHONE | Character | 13 | |
| _cEXTENSN | Character | 4 | |
| _cFAXPHON | Character | 13 | |
| _nBILLDUE | Numeric | 9 | 2 |
| _nYTDORDR | Numeric | 9 | 2 |

| 10-Character Field Names | Field Type | Field Width | Decimals |
|---|---|---|---|
| _cPAYMETH | Character | 2 | |
| _cCRDCARD | Character | 16 | |
| _dCCEXPIR | Date | 8 | |
| _cPRFSHIP | Character | 10 | |
| _dLASTPUR | Date | 8 | |

**N O T E** FoxPro does not require a file's unique field to appear first. However, some people prefer to list index fields—especially unique fields—first, because that practice makes browsing and listing the table easier. Also, if you use the file in a list box to select customers, you can define it more easily if the unique fields appear first in the file. ■

When you enter field names in a free table, FoxPro prevents you from entering more than 10 characters. If you attempt to enter a duplicate field name, FoxPro generates an error message. For now, use the structured 10-character field names listed in Table 3.2.

Pressing Tab moves you to the Type field, which defaults to Character. This field uses a drop-down list. If you click the down arrow to the right of the field, a drop-down list appears, showing possible values. For this example, accept the default type: Character.

Specify how many characters to reserve for this field. Character fields default to 10, but you can use the spinner to change that setting to any value from 1 to 254. Alternatively, you can edit the number directly. A nice feature of the spinner is that it starts slowly and picks up speed as you continue to click the arrow.

**N O T E** If you are not familiar with them, spinners allow users to click either an up or down arrow to increase or decrease the displayed value. Spinners modify only numeric fields. However, you can combine a spinner control with other controls to simulate spinning any variable type, such as dates or index field values. Narrow the spinner control until just the arrows without space between are displayed. Then add code to the Click event of the spinner to modify the value property of the non-numeric control. ■

Numeric fields use the decimal column to define the number of decimal places to reserve to the right of the decimal point. In fact, FoxPro activates this column only for numeric fields. For a numeric field such as nBillDue, you need two decimal places.

The next column displays the index direction, if an index exists, for the field.

The last column in the structure determines whether the current field allows null values. Null use is discussed later in this chapter, so you can skip this column for now.

Part

I

Ch

3

After you enter the structure of the CUST file, the Table Designer dialog box should match Figure 3.4. You can see only nine fields at a time, but by using the vertical scroll bar, you can move through all the table fields.

The buttons to the left of the field names allow you to rearrange the default field order when issuing a Browse or List command for the table. To make cFirst appear before cLast, click the button to the left of cFirst and drag the field up. While you hold down the mouse button, FoxPro displays a dotted box at the proposed new position of the field. When the field is in the desired position, simply release the mouse button; all subsequent fields adjust their positions.

When you have entered the complete table structure, click OK to exit the Table Designer and save the table. Because this table is new, FoxPro asks whether you want to input data records now. FoxPro assumes that because you created a table, you probably want to store data in it, but that is not always true. You may want to append data into a new table from an existing one, or you may want to add data by using a form. For now, click No and return to the Project Manager.

The name of the table that you just created now appears in Free Tables in Project Manager. To see it, click the plus sign to the left of the Free Tables line. The table has two symbols before it: a plus sign and a circle with a slash through it. In the Project Manager, the plus sign indicates additional levels that are currently hidden or rolled into the current line. If you click the plus sign next to a table name, Project Manager rolls out the table's fields. Notice that the plus sign changes to a minus sign. This change indicates that all levels are currently open. FoxPro uses the second symbol (the circle with the slash through it) during compilation to indicate that it should not include this file in the compilation. Your screen should look like Figure 3.5.

▶ **See** "Including and Excluding Files from Your .APPs and .EXEs," **p. 596**

**FIGURE 3.5**
The Project Manager shows the fields in CUST listed below the table name.

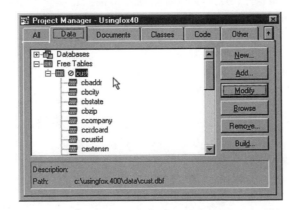

# Using Nulls

In earlier versions of FoxPro, you could not determine whether a user intentionally left a field blank or merely forgot it. FoxPro interprets an empty field as being an empty character string, a numeric zero, or a logical `False`, depending on the field type. Any of these values could be legitimate entries for the field. If an employee file contains a field for the employee's middle initial, for example, does a blank mean that the employee did not enter his middle initial or that he does not have one? With numeric data, would a year-to-date field with a value of zero indicate that the customer had no transactions or that the sum of purchases and returns exactly canceled each other? Finally, with logical fields, you cannot determine whether the user actually selected a false value or merely skipped the field. Suppose that John Smith missed the question "Are you married?" for which `False` represents NO? Mrs. Smith might have a question or two about that.

To use null tokens in a field (any field type), you must do two things. First, you must specify SET NULL ON in the Command window or in the program. Second, you must modify the structure and click the null column button for each field that allows nulls. If you do not do this, FoxPro displays an error when you append a record with APPEND FROM or INSERT SQL and do not include a value for this field. FoxPro places the token .NULL. in fields that allow nulls and contain no values.

**N O T E** If you use SET NULL ON and do not select the null check box for these fields, FoxPro will not allow nulls or blanks in primary or candidate key fields. (For more information, see "Primary and Candidate Keys" later in this chapter.) ■

**CAUTION**

FoxPro's default disallows nulls. If you enter SET NULL ON, you will not be able to skip a field without entering something in that field.

Remember the following rules when you use nulls:

- By default, APPEND BLANK does not trigger a null token in all fields of a new table record.
- When you are changing a character field from a non-null field to allow nulls, blank fields remain blank.
- When you are changing a numeric field from a non-null field to allow nulls, fields with values of zero remain zero.

- When you are changing a character field from a null field to disallow nulls, a blank string is placed in the field.

- When you are changing a numeric field from a null field to disallow nulls, a zero is placed in the field.

# Modifying Table Structures

At some point in every project's life, you can expect to modify a table's structure. The severity of a modification can be classified by how much it changes the table and index files.

Adding a field, for example, is a small change because it has no impact on existing fields—although it does require rewriting the entire .DBF. Renaming a field also requires only a minimal change; in fact, it usually does nothing more than modify the .DBF header. However, if you rename a field that appears in an index, that index or tag must also be updated. Deleting fields, as long as they are not part of an index or tag, requires rewriting the entire .DBF, but little else. On the other hand, modifying field sizes or the number of decimal places forces FoxPro to rewrite the entire .DBF and can result in the loss of data. When you are changing the field type, FoxPro attempts to automatically convert the data to the new type, but it can also automatically trash the data if it does not know what to do or if the conversion does not make sense.

The following section examines various changes that you can make to table structures and explains the effects of those changes.

> **CAUTION**
> Before making any table-structure changes, make a backup of the data file (.DBF) and all indexes.

## Adding Fields

Adding new fields to an existing table is one of the safest changes you can make. In fact, problems can occur only if you attempt to use the same field name twice. Even in that situation, FoxPro responds automatically.

FoxPro will not allow you to exit the name column if it is a duplicate of an existing field name. Rather, FoxPro displays an information box with the message `Invalid or duplicate field name` and allows you to edit it.

## Deleting Fields

At some point, one or more fields in a table may become obsolete. Rather than waste space, you may decide to remove them from the table. To delete a field, simply display the table in the Table Designer dialog box (refer to Figure 3.4), highlight the obsolete field, and click the <u>D</u>elete button.

> **CAUTION**
>
> After you delete a field and save the structure, it is gone forever, including any indexes that reference the deleted field. Make a backup copy of your .DBF before deleting a field.

Part
I
Ch
3

## Renaming Fields

Renaming fields may require only rewriting the .DBF header with the new field name. To change a field name, simply open the Table Designer dialog box, highlight the name, edit the name, and then save the structure.

As long as an open index does not reference the field, FoxPro renames the field when you save the structure. If the renamed field appears in an open index, FoxPro displays the warning shown in Figure 3.6.

**FIGURE 3.6**
This alert box appears when you are saving the modified structure and renaming a field used in an index.

When you click OK in this alert box, Visual FoxPro returns you to the Index page of the Table Designer to correct the index expression. You can redefine the expression by re-naming the field name in the index expression. VFP does not automatically rename the field in the index expression when you rename a field used in it. Why isn't FoxPro smart enough to simply substitute the new field name for the old one in all the tags? FoxPro probably doesn't know whether you really mean to rename a field or to replace it with a new field.

**TROUBLESHOOTING**

**I need to reverse the names of two fields in a single table, but issuing the modify structure command won't let me change the names.** The Table Designer does prohibit you from renaming

*continues*

*continued*

a table field with the name of another existing field in the table. However, you can accomplish this name switch by using an intermediate name, as described in the following steps:

1. Rename the first field to any name that is not currently being used.

2. Rename the second field to the first field's original name.

3. Rename the first field to the second field's original name.

## Redefining Fields

Redefining field types, widths, or decimal places can be simple or complex, depending on the change. For example, you can open the Table Designer dialog box, highlight a field, and increase the size of the field with no problem at all; FoxPro rewrites the .DBF to expand the field size. However, character fields merely get blanks appended to them, and numeric fields have more available digits to use. You can even change the size of an indexed field without any problems. Visual FoxPro regenerates the index when you close the Table Designer.

On the other hand, decreasing the size of the field or number of decimals can cause data loss. FoxPro accepts the change and asks whether you want to update the table structure when you leave the Table Designer dialog box. If you continue, FoxPro resizes the fields as requested. Character fields are shortened by truncating existing text to the new field size. Numeric data may lose decimal places or digits when it is shortened. Reducing the number of digits in the integer portion of the number may cause some values to be replaced by asterisks, thereby causing you to lose the entire number. On the other hand, VFP happily truncates decimal places.

Some changes in field types are more likely to cause disaster than others are. Changing a numeric field to a character field simply converts the number to a string, as though FoxPro used the STR function when it rewrote the table. Similarly, changing a string to a numeric field appears to use the VAL function. Converting strings with leading numbers results in the numbers being saved to a numeric field. FoxPro converts strings that begin with alpha characters (other than blanks) to zero when they are converted to numeric values.

Similarly, you can convert date fields to character strings by changing their type. FoxPro appears to transform the data by using the DTOC function. You can even change character-formatted dates back into true date fields.

Most other conversions result in a loss of data. Again, the need to make a backup copy of a table before making any structural change cannot be emphasized enough.

## Defining Order in a Table

No one would expect users to enter data in a sorted order (unless they key the entries in from a telephone book). Certainly, customers don't arrive at a business in alphabetical order or buy products sequentially by product ID. Wouldn't it be nice if they did? But because they don't, you must add records in random order, although you probably will want to view them sorted by one or more fields.

You can use the SORT command to reorder the records in a table. SORT takes an existing table and creates a new one sorted by a field or a combination of fields. The following command creates a new table called CUSTLIST, sorted by the customer's last name:

```
SORT TO CUSTLIST ON Last
```

A more complex SORT creates a new table called CURCUST, which contains customers (sorted in descending customer-ID order) who have made purchases this year. The following is the appropriate command to create the new table.

```
SORT TO CURCUST ON cCustId /D FOR Goods_Ytd>0
```

This method has two flaws. First, every new sort order duplicates the entire original table or filtered portion thereof. If you need several sort orders for a large table, you may quickly run out of disk space. Second (and more important), having more than one copy of a table inevitably leads to data inconsistencies. If you do not update all tables simultaneously, you soon will have several tables, each of which has some, but not all, of the recent updates.

Sorting does have its place. If you have a rarely changed table that has one preferred sort order, you may want to keep a sorted version of it. However, indexes provide a more effective way to allow users to view and retrieve data from a table in an orderly manner. Because a table can have more than one index, you can define different indexes for different views or reports.

 **TIP** Even with indexes, a table sorted by the same fields as the index performs just a bit faster.

## Examining Stand-Alone versus Structural and Nonstructural Indexes

When indexes were developed for database systems, they required a separate index for each index definition. To index the CUST table on both the customer number and their last name, for example, you would create two indexes, as shown in the following example:

```
USE CUST
INDEX ON cCustId TO CUSTID
INDEX ON cLast TO CUSTNAME
```

These statements would create two index files, named CUSTID.IDX and CUSTNAME.IDX. These files are now referred to as *stand-alone indexes*, because each index file contains a single index entry and is independent of the others. You can have any number of stand-alone indexes defined for a given table, limited only by the FILES statement in CONFIG.SYS. When you open the table, you might open all indexes, as in the following example:

```
USE CUST INDEX CUSTID, CUSTNAME
```

Alternatively, you can open the table with only a single index, as in this line:

```
USE CUST INDEX CUSTID
```

In both cases, the first index after the keyword INDEX controls the order in which FoxPro accesses the table records. In the first example, FoxPro updates and maintains both indexes if you add, delete, or modify records. In the second case, FoxPro maintains only CUSTID.IDX. In this case, FoxPro has no knowledge of CUSTNAME. If you make changes to CUST.DBF, CUSTNAME may lose synchronization with the table. In other words, the index may no longer point to the right records.

Finally, you can open each index separately by using the SET INDEX statement, as follows:

```
USE CUST
SET INDEX TO CUSTID
SET INDEX TO CUSTNAME ADDITIVE
```

Now FoxPro opens both indexes, and CUSTID controls the access order. Notice the keyword ADDITIVE in the second SET INDEX statement. If you did not include that keyword, FoxPro would close CUSTID before opening CUSTNAME.

The problems with stand-alone indexes should be obvious. Because the names usually have no relation to their .DBF, you can easily forget which indexes belong to each table. In fact, your directories may soon become littered with obsolete and forgotten indexes that you no longer need, and no one remembers to which tables the indexes belong.

Furthermore, if you do not open all the indexes when you edit the table, FoxPro does not update the missing indexes. The indexes may point to the wrong records or even beyond the end of the table after you pack deleted records.

With the introduction of FoxPro, you now have structural and nonstructural indexes, also called *compound indexes*. These files are special index files that can contain several index definitions in one physical file. Now you can store all index definitions for one .DBF in a single file. You no longer need to worry about forgetting to open an index file or encountering nonsynchronized index pointers.

You define a compound index as shown in the following example:

```
USE CUST
INDEX ON cCustId TAG CUSTID OF CUSTSORT
INDEX ON cLast TAG CUSTNAME OF CUSTSORT
USE CUST INDEX CUSTSORT
```

The USE statement opens the CUST table, along with a nonstructural index called CUSTSORT. FoxPro calls a compound index *nonstructural* when its base name differs from the .DBF—in this case, CUSTSORT versus CUST. You can make the index structural by giving it the same base name as the .DBF, as in the following example:

```
USE CUST
INDEX ON cCustId TAG CUSTID OF CUST
INDEX ON cLast TAG CUSTNAME OF CUST
USE CUST
```

 **TIP** Omitting the OF clause in INDEX ON automatically creates or adds the index definition to a structural index.

In this case, you did not include the INDEX clause of the USE statement, but the index—CUST.CDX—opens anyway. When the structural index exists, FoxPro automatically opens it when you open the table. There is no way to forget to open the indexes if you store index expressions as tags in a structural index. Structural indexes should never get out of synchronization, although that is possible; one way would be to accidentally copy a different version of the .DBF or .CDX to the current directory.

## Defining Normal and Unique Indexes

To create indexes for CUST.DBF, return to the Table Designer dialog box. Click the Index page to switch to the index definition page (see Figure 3.7).

**FIGURE 3.7**
The index definition screen displays four index definitions in the Table Designer.

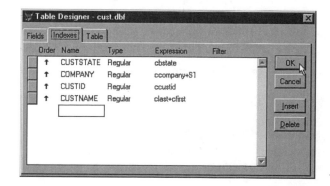

Four indexes are already defined. Index definitions begin with the tag name on the left, followed by the index type (accept the default, Regular), the tag expression, and a filter. Notice that FoxPro automatically assumes that you want to create a structural index. If you want to create a stand-alone index or a nonstructural index, you need to enter the syntax described in the preceding section into the Command window.

The arrows to the left of the names indicate whether the index is in ascending (up arrow) or descending (down arrow) order. To change the direction, select the row and click the button that appears with the arrow to toggle between ascending and descending.

A *Regular* index type means that FoxPro stores the value generated by the index expression for each table record in the index. If more than one record has the same expression, FoxPro stores the expression multiple times, with separate pointers to each record.

In the CUST table, the last name may not uniquely identify every record in the table. You may have customers Bill Jones and Kevin Jones. Therefore, an index on the last name has repeated values, but you can use it as a Regular index.

By clicking the down arrow next to Type, you can see another index type, called *Unique*. Unique includes only unique expressions in the index. If more than one record generates the same index expression value, Unique stores only the first one encountered. If you define a unique index on Last in the CUST table, you may not include every record in the index. Therefore, either Bill Jones or Kevin Jones would appear, but not both.

## Defining Candidate and Primary Keys

The third index type, called *Candidate*, creates a unique index, but it includes every record in the table. Candidate indexes prohibit duplicate expression values for any two records in the table. What if you decide to change an existing regular index to candidate? After making the change, VFP prompts you to save the structure modification. Also appearing in the dialog box is a check box for checking data against the index. Whether you choose to or not, if you currently have duplicate data corresponding to the index definition, VFP warns you of this uniqueness error and changes the index back to regular. Your data will have to be modified before making this change.

> **CAUTION**
>
> Records marked for deletion are not ignored when a primary or candidate index tests for duplicate values. Therefore, when you try to add a new record that has the value in a field used in a primary or candidate index definition, a uniqueness error occurs, and you will not be able to add the record until you pack the table.

A free table may have a candidate index, but only tables within a database container can have a primary index. CUSTOMER.DBF in the PTOFSALE database includes a field named cCustomerId; it's defined as a single field that uniquely identifies each record. Because indexing in this field generates a unique index that includes every record, it is a candidate index, but in this case, it is also the primary index. Occasionally, a single table may have more than one field that uniquely identifies each record. Each such index is a candidate index and qualifies as a potential primary key. However, any one table can only have one primary index. Primary keys often form relationships between multiple files and serve as lookup values in a referenced table.

## Indexing on Complex Expressions

FoxPro does not restrict index expressions to single fields. In fact, any combination of fields can serve as an index expression. Beware of making an expression overly complex just to make it a Candidate index. You might include Last_Name and First_Name to make a Candidate index. But what if you have customers Jim T. Kirk and Jim C. Kirk? You may want to add another field to the index for the customer's middle initial. But such an index does not guarantee uniqueness. Some programs attempt to combine portions of a customer's last name with the last four digits of their phone number plus their ZIP code (maybe even age, sex, and title of their favorite *Star Trek* movie). It's easier to just assign a sequential customer ID to a new customer.

To build a complex expression, click the button to the right of the Expression text box in the Table Designer dialog box. FoxPro displays the Expression Builder dialog box (see Figure 3.8).

**FIGURE 3.8**

Use the Expression Builder dialog box to create complex index expressions.

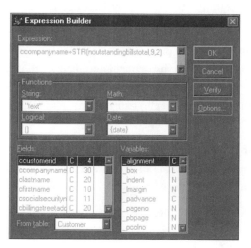

FoxPro uses the Expression Builder dialog box with many operations to help build complex expressions. The Functions section provides access to FoxPro's built-in functions, which are divided into four groups: Date, Logical, Math, and String. Click the arrow button to the right of a function field to display a drop-down list of functions. To select a function, highlight it and then press Enter or click it. FoxPro displays the selected function in the function list box and the expression text area. For a function, FoxPro automatically places the insert cursor inside the parentheses. Now you can enter the parameters.

Below the Expression list box, FoxPro lists the fields in the current table. You can choose a field to be added to the insert position of the expression; just highlight the field and press Enter. To select a field from a different table, click the arrow to the right of the From table text box. Only open tables that appear in this list. If you need to reference a table that is not currently open, exit the Expression Builder dialog box, open the table in a new work area, and then reenter the Expression Builder dialog box. You can create indexes on fields from other tables, although that practice is not recommended. However, you do need the capability to access other tables in other situations that use the Expression Builder.

Finally, the Variables list box contains the current memory and system variables. This feature generally does not apply to defining indexes, but remember that FoxPro uses the Expression Builder dialog box in many places.

Figure 3.8 shows an index that alphabetically displays companies that have outstanding bills, using cCompanyName and nOutstandingBillsTotal. Because cCompanyName is a character field and nOutstandingBillsTotal is numeric, you cannot simply combine them with a plus sign. To combine two or more fields of different data types, you must convert one or more of them to a common type—usually, Character. Use the STR function to convert nOutstandingBillsTotal to a string before concatenating it to cCompanyName.

Finally, before you click OK and accept an expression, FoxPro provides a utility to verify the syntax. The Verify button checks the syntax and displays an error message if it cannot interpret the expression. Common reasons for invalid expressions include mismatched parentheses or a missing comma. For valid expressions, a message appears in the status bar, telling you that the expression is valid.

**Including User-Defined Functions**    You can not only use FoxPro's predefined functions, but also define your own. A *user-defined function* is any group of statements stored as a separate file or as a separate procedure or function in a program.

Suppose that you want to create an index based on sales regions. First, you need a separate table that relates ZIP codes to regions. Then you create a small function, similar to the one shown in Listing 3.3, to find the region.

## Listing 3.3   03PRG03.PRG

```
FUNCTION GETREGION
LPARAMETER lcZipCode
************************************************
*
* This function uses file ZIPREGN with the
* following structure:
*
*    StartZip    C(10)
*    EndZip      C(10)
*    Region      C(10)
*
* All zip codes that fall in a zip code range
* defined by a record are assigned to that
* region. Otherwise, the region is left blank.
*
************************************************
LOCAL lcCurNear, lcCurArea, lcRtnRegion, lcA

* Use an inexact search
  lcCurNear = SYS(2001, 'NEAR')
  SET NEAR ON

* Store current work area - VFP supports 32767 work areas
  lcCurArea = SELECT()   &&Retrieves current work area number

* Check if ZIPREGN IS OPEN
  IF !USED('ZIPREGN.DBF')
     lcA = ('\VFP5BOOK\DATA\ZIPREGN.DBF')
     USE (lcA)
  ELSE
     SELECT ZIPREGN   &&selects work area where ZIPERGN is open
  ENDIF

* Check if controlling index is on STARTZIP
  IF !TAG() = 'STARTZIP'
     SET ORDER TO TAG STARTZIP
  ENDIF

  = SEEK(lcZipCode)
* Check if an exact match was found
  IF FOUND()
    lcRtnRegion = Region
  ELSE
  * Check if on last record
    IF EOF()
      GOTO BOTTOM
      lcRtnRegion = Region
    ELSE
      SKIP -1
      lcRtnRegion = Region
    ENDIF
```

*continues*

Part

I

Ch

3

**Listing 3.3    Continued**

```
  ENDIF

* Check if beyond last zip code in range
  IF lc_ZipCode > ZIPREGN.EndZip
    lcRtnRegion = SPACE(10)
  ENDIF

* RESET  environment and area
  SELECT (lcCurArea)
  SET NEAR &lcCurNear

RETURN lcRtnRegion

* END OF FUNCTION GETREGION
```

**N O T E**  SELECT and SELECT() perform a variety of tasks. SELECT as a command requires as a
parameter either a work-area number or a table alias name. SELECT 4, for example,
opens work area 4. On the other hand, SELECT 0 opens the first unused work area, beginning
with 1. However, you usually do not know the work area number of a table. Instead, you can use
the table alias to open its work area as in SELECT CUSTOMER.

By itself, SELECT() returns the number of the current work area. You can also include a parameter
of 0 to perform the same task. A parameter of 1 returns the highest numbered unused work area.
Thus, ? SELECT(1) tells you that VFP supports 32,767 work areas. By supplying the table alias
name as the parameter, as in SELECT('CUSTOMER'), you can get the work-area number for any
open table.  ■

To use the GETREGION function, simply place the following expression in the expression
box of the index:

```
GETREGION(CUSTOMER.cBillingPostalCode)
```

**Using Stored Procedures**    The major disadvantage of using a user-defined function in an
index expression is that FoxPro must be able to find the function to modify the index.
Because you cannot store the function with the index, it can be easily misplaced, deleted,
or forgotten when you transfer the table to another system. Thanks to the database
container, you do have an alternative.

If the table is bound to a database, user-defined functions can be stored in the database,
thus eliminating the search for a procedure or function.

**N O T E**  FoxPro searches for procedures and functions in a specific order. It first looks in the
current file. Next, it checks to see whether SET PROCEDURE TO defined a separate
procedure library, and it looks there. Then it checks any previously executed procedure files as
part of the same program. It searches the current directory for a file that has the same name as

the procedure or function. Finally, it searches in another directory defined with FoxPro's SET PATH statement for a file with the same name. As you might expect, the farther down in the search sequence you go, the slower the application performs. ▓

**Realizing Index Limitations** The limits of an index expression depend on the length of the index expression string, as well as its value. Index files reserve a limited amount of space for an index expression and its value.

For a stand-alone index, the index expression can consist of up to 220 characters. FoxPro limits the resulting index value to 100 characters. If you define the stand-alone index as a *compact stand-alone index* (a special case of stand-alone indexes that requires less total disk space), the index expression shares space with the FOR expression. The combined length of both expression strings cannot be more than 512 characters. The individual index value cannot exceed 240 characters. A similar requirement applies to compound indexes. Compound indexes are nothing more than compact indexes with repeated tags; thus, they have the same limitations.

> **N O T E** Short index expressions are more efficient than long ones. Also, choose fields that have short, meaningful values where possible. If complex long values appear to be the only way to define unique keys, create an "artificial" number, such as the customer ID field in CUSTOMER.DBF. ▓

Part
**I**

Ch
**3**

## Selecting an Active Index at Run Time

In applications that have stand-alone indexes, you can easily determine the active index. If a USE statement opens more than one index, FoxPro makes the first one in the list the active one by default. To change to a different index, use SET ORDER to change the controlling order. The following statements open CUSTOMER with two stand-alone indexes (CUSTID and CUSTNAME), and the SET ORDER statement changes the controlling index from CUSTID to CUSTNAME:

```
USE CUSTOMER INDEX CUSTID, CUSTNAME
SET ORDER TO 2
```

To be clearer, you can also specify the index name rather than its position number in the list.

If the USE statement does not open the index files, issue the SET INDEX command to both define the index list and set the controlling index, as follows:

```
USE CUSTOMER
SET INDEX TO CUSTID, CUSTNAME ORDER 2
```

These options continue to work in Visual FoxPro. However, with the introduction of compound indexes, in which each index has a tag name, you need to add a TAG argument such as the following:

```
USE CUSTOMER
SET ORDER TO TAG CUSTNAME
```

In this example, assume that CUSTOMER has a structural index with tags named CUSTID and CUSTNAME. Although FoxPro automatically opens a structural index, it does not automatically set a controlling index. You need to use a command such as SET ORDER to select a tag.

 **TIP** You also can use USE CUSTOMER TAG CUSTNAME.

The issue becomes more complex if you have both structural and stand-alone indexes. In the following statement, you again open CUSTOMER.DBF along with the structural index CUSTOMER.CDX, but FoxPro also opens a stand-alone index called CUSTZIP:

```
USE CUSTOMER INDEX CUSTZIP
```

Notice that you did not specify the structural index; FoxPro opens it automatically. Furthermore, CUSTZIP—not the structural index—has precedence in the index order over a stand-alone index. Therefore, CUSTZIP controls the record-viewing order in this case.

# Appending Records

You create tables to add records to them. In fact, FoxPro is so sure that you want to populate a table with records as soon as possible that it prompts you to add records immediately upon closing the table structure. Of course, this time may not always be the best time to add records. You may not even be the person to do the adding. But somewhere, sometime, someone (or some program) will add records to the table.

You can add records to a table in several ways. The following sections explore these options.

## Adding Records Through BROWSE or EDIT Screens

Many casual FoxPro users begin by opening an Append window. To do so yourself, simply open the table and type APPEND in the Command window such as the following:

```
USE CUSTOMER
APPEND
```

These commands open an edit window, add a blank record, and place the cursor in the first field, as shown in Figure 3.9. After you enter data in the fields of the first record, FoxPro automatically adds another blank record and places the cursor in it. This process continues until you close the window.

**FIGURE 3.9**
APPEND opens this simple edit window when you add records.

You also can open the edit window directly with the EDIT command or open a Browse window with BROWSE. In these windows, FoxPro assumes that you want to edit or view existing records. You cannot simply move the cursor to a record beyond the last one to start entering a new record. Rather, you must press Ctrl+Y or open the Table pull-down menu and choose Append New Record.

## Adding Records Programmatically

You can append records to a table from within a program in several ways, depending on the source of the records. The code that follows allows users to add a new table record and update the fields directly.

```
* Code appends record to table and updates fields directly
  SELECT <table>
  APPEND BLANK

* Call a previously created form that allows the user
* to enter fields
  DO FillForm
```

However, you may not always want to modify the table directly. Many programmers prefer to modify memory variables that represent each of the table's fields (although buffering techniques in VFP are preferred). The sample code shown as follows creates a set of memory variables from a table and, after entering values for the memory variables, saves them to the table on request.

Part
I

Ch
3

```
* Code creates a set of memory variables from table
  SELECT <table>
  SCATTER MEMVAR MEMO

* Call a previously created form that allows the user
* to enter fields
* Function returns .T. if user clicks the SAVE button to exit
  SaveIt = FillForm()

* If user clicks SAVE, append a blank record and
* gather the memory variable fields
  IF SaveIt
    APPEND BLANK
    GATHER MEMVAR MEMO
  ENDIF
```

The second example improves on the first, because it does not add a new record to the table until the user decides to save the data.

## Appending Data from Other Tables

Suppose that you want to append records to the current table from a second table. You could read through one record at a time, store the fields in memory variables, and then append these values to a record in the second table. The code in Listing 3.4 shows one implementation.

### Listing 3.4   03PRG04.PRG

```
SELECT EMPLOYEE
SCAN
  SCATTER MEMVAR
  SELECT EMPL9
  APPEND BLANK
  GATHER MEMVAR
  SELECT EMPLOYEE
ENDSCAN
```

Rather than scatter values to memory variables, use an array to store the field values from a single record. The following code illustrates this method.

▶ **See** "Creating Arrays" in Bonus Chapter 05 located on the CD

### Listing 3.5   03PRG05.PRG

```
SELECT EMPLOYEE
SCAN
  SCATTER TO EMPLOYEE
  SELECT EMPL9
  APPEND BLANK
```

```
    GATHER FROM EMPLOYEE
    SELECT EMPLOYEE
ENDSCAN
```

An alternative method allows you to copy all records from the first table into a two-dimensional array with a single command, eliminating the loop. This method works only if the table does not have too many records. How many is too many records? The number of records times the number of fields per record cannot exceed 65,000. The following code illustrates this method.

**Listing 3.6  03PRG06.PRG**

```
SELECT EMPLOYEE
IF RECCOUNT() * FCOUNT() < 65000
  COPY TO ARRAY aEmployee
  SELECT EMPL9
  APPEND FROM ARRAY aEmployee
ELSE
  SCAN
    SCATTER TO aEmployee
    SELECT EMPL9
    APPEND BLANK
    GATHER FROM aEmployee
    SELECT EMPLOYEE
  ENDSCAN
ENDIF
```

Part
I

Ch
3

You might want to get even more sophisticated and copy blocks of 65,000 elements from one table to another, as shown in Listing 3.7.

**Listing 3.7  03PRG07.PRG**

```
SELECT EMPL10
GO TOP
IF RECCOUNT() * FCOUNT() < 65000

* Records can be copied in a single block
  COPY TO ARRAY aEmployee
  SELECT EMPL9
  APPEND FROM ARRAY aEmployee
ELSE

* Determine the maximum number of records to copy at a time
  nRecBlk = INT(RECCOUNT()/FCOUNT())
  nRemain = RECCOUNT()

* Loop until all records are copied
  DO WHILE nRemain > 0

  * Copy next block of records
```

*continues*

---

**Listing 3.7 Continued**

```
    COPY TO ARRAY aEmployee NEXT nRecBlk
    SELECT EMPL9
    APPEND FROM ARRAY aEmployee
    SELECT EMPL10

  * Check if on last block
    nRemain = nRemain - nRecBlk
    nRecBlk = IIF(nRecBlk < nRemain, nRecBlk, nRemain)
  ENDDO
ENDIF
```

---

**CAUTION**

Any method that uses arrays works only if both tables have the same structure or if you use the FIELDS clause in the command to prearrange the order of the fields. Using an array eliminates the requirement that the fields have the same name in both files.

▶ **See** "Naming Conventions," **p. 182**

If you have the same table structure in both files, you can use a much simpler approach. The following command appends all records from CURPROD to PRODHIST:

```
    SELECT PRODHIST
    APPEND FROM CURPROD
```

If you want to append records from CURPROD only where field lInProduction equals .F., use the following program lines:

```
    SELECT PRODHIST
    APPEND FROM CURPROD FOR NOT lInProduction
```

You can even specify, with the FIELDS clause, which fields to append.

**CAUTION**

The FIELDS clause identifies fields in the table that you are appending data to, not appending from. Furthermore, appended fields must have the same name and definition in both files.

# Creating a Database

In Visual FoxPro, a *database* is a collection of tables. You can continue working with tables individually, as you would in the old FoxPro style. However, Visual FoxPro also provides several powerful enhancements for storing tables in databases. The balance of this chapter and the next chapter examine these enhanced properties.

First, create a database container to store the tables. The following command creates and names a new database in one step:

```
CREATE DATABASE SALES
```

You also can choose File, New, Database from the system menu, but as it does when you create tables, this method requires stepping through a series of dialog boxes.

One way to tell whether you have a database open is to look at the database list box in the toolbar. Normally, this box is empty. If one or more databases are open, the current one is displayed in the box, and the drop-down list allows you to change to another. In a program, you can return the name and path of the current database with DBC(), and you can change the current database with SET DATABASE. To determine the names and paths of all open databases, use the ADATABASES() function. The function creates a two-dimensional array, with the database name as one element and its path as another.

**Part**

**I**

**Ch**

**3**

To modify the contents of the current database interactively, use this command:

```
MODIFY DATABASE
```

This command opens the Database Designer. Figure 3.10 shows the Database Designer for the Tastrade application that comes with Visual FoxPro.

**FIGURE 3.10**

The Database Designer shows tables and relations for database TASTRADE.DBC.

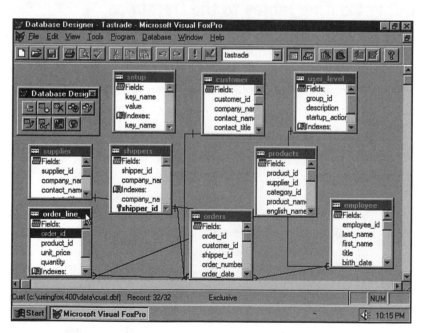

The Database Designer has its own toolbar. Figure 3.11 defines the buttons that it uses.

**FIGURE 3.11**
This figure shows the
database toolbar
buttons that are
available from within
Database Designer.

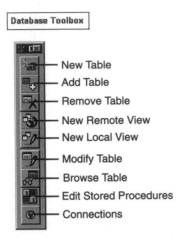

Database Toolbox

— New Table
— Add Table
— Remove Table
— New Remote View
— New Local View
— Modify Table
— Browse Table
— Edit Stored Procedures
— Connections

As you add tables to a database, they appear in the Database Designer window. Scroll bars appear as you add more tables. Each table lists the fields, followed by their indexes. A small key before an index name identifies the primary index. Relations between tables are shown with connecting lines. To browse a table, simply double-click it.

## Adding Existing Tables to the Database

 To add an existing table (such as CUSTOMER.DBF) to the current database, click the Add Table button in the Database Designer toolbar or choose Database, Add Table. When the table appears in the design window, it may overlap or cover existing tables. You treat table definitions as you do any other window, and you can drag and resize them as you please.

> **N O T E**  You can add any table to only one database. Any attempt to add a table to a second
> database results in the following error message:
>
>     File <filename> is part of a database ■

 To modify the contents of a table, right-click any part of it and then choose Modify from the shortcut menu. You also can left-click the table to select it and then click the Modify Table button in the Database Designer toolbar. This button opens the Table Designer dialog box, in which you can modify any of the table's characteristics.

**Long Field Names**   One of the first changes you may want to make is to rename the fields that use long field names. In a database, you can have up to 128 characters per field name. To change a field name, simply highlight it and enter a new name. Spaces are not allowed in field names (FoxPro would not know when a field ended). One solution uses the underscore where a blank would be used to create clearer, more descriptive field names. However, the new recommended naming convention frowns on underscores. Rather, it recommends that you can make the first letter of each significant word in the field name uppercase and the rest lowercase. Unfortunately, the Table Designer in Visual FoxPro does not support case. In fact, Visual FoxPro displays field names in different case in different parts of the system. Browse window column headers, for example, are all initial capital letters.

N O T E    Tables bound to databases can have 128-character table names. Use the Table Name text box in the Table Designer or a command like the following:

```
CREATE TABLE orddetl NAME order_details
```

In addition, the common naming convention for table fields includes a type prefix before the name. Figure 3.12 shows the first few fields of the CUSTOMER table with longer field names.

Part
I

Ch
3

**FIGURE 3.12**
This figure shows the enhanced features that are available after you add tables to a database.

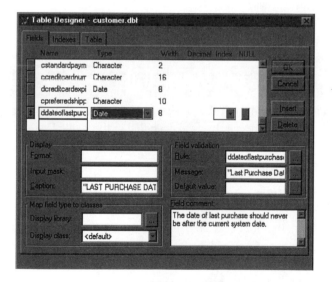

*continued*

field names to 10 characters.) If the truncation does not affect the first 10 characters, you do not have a problem. But remember—FoxPro may automatically replace the last character or two with sequential numbers to ensure that each field name within a table is unique.

**N O T E**   Many field lists used in Visual FoxPro—particularly those in wizards—display a limited number of characters. If you use table-identifying prefixes, or if you begin related fields with a common first word, you may not be able to distinguish the fields. You will not be able to distinguish the following two field names in many wizard field lists:

    CUST_BillingAddressLine1

    CUST_BillingAddressLine2 ■

**N O T E**   If you define long field names for a table, you must always use them. You cannot use either the shorter names stored in the .DBF or the truncated 10-character names described elsewhere in this section. ■

**Field Format and Input Mask**   You can store the field's preferred format and input mask for the field data in the database. The format and input mask options that you enter are the same as the available options in forms and reports. In fact, the purpose of storing them in the database comes into play when you are creating a field control in a form. When you create a field control in a form by dragging and dropping the field from the table to the form, the format that you specified in the Table Designer automatically sets the appropriate properties for the control.

▶ **See** "Adding Controls to a Form," **p. 447**

**Field-Level Validations**   You also can add field-level validation rules in the Table Designer dialog box (refer to Figure 3.12). To add a rule, enter it directly in the Field Properties Validation Rule text box, or click the Expression Builder button (the button to the immediate right of the field, with the ellipsis on it). You have seen the Expression Builder before, so you already know how to use it. For the date-of-last-purchase field, you want to ensure that the date never exceeds the current system date. If it does, you want to display the error message Last Purchase Date Cannot Be a Future Date.

You can use any logical expression when you define a validation rule. You can even call a function for tests that are too complex to express as a single statement. The only restriction is that the function must return .T. or .F.. Field validation rules trigger when you attempt to move off the field or when the value changes due to an INSERT or REPLACE statement.

**Field Default Values**    Although the date-of-last-purchase field in Figure 3.12 does not contain a default value, you can add a default value for any table field. To default to the current system date, for example, place DATE() in the Default Value text box. The expression added for the default value must result in the same data type as the field itself; otherwise, FoxPro generates an error. FoxPro places the default value in the table field whenever you add a new record with a command such as APPEND or interactively in a Browse or Edit window.

**Caption Values**    FoxPro uses caption values as column headings when you browse or edit the table. By default, FoxPro uses the field name as the caption value. However, the field name may not always be the best choice. After all, if you use table prefixes or any other naming convention in the field names, you would not want to display them as field headings in Browse or Edit windows. You can define the caption based on the contents of another field or other variable, but the most common choice is to enter a simple text string in the Caption text box. This value is also used to create a label for a control when you are using the drag-and-drop method of creating field controls in a form or when you use the Form Wizard.

**Field Comment**    A field comment is a note to help document the meaning or purpose of a field. FoxPro stores this element as a memo field; therefore, it can be as long you want. Figure 3.12 uses it as a reminder to use the current date to validate the input field. For other fields, a field comment could list possible values, tables used to validate an entry, and other information. You determine the use of a field comment; you can even ignore it. But the more information you store in the table definition, the easier it is to maintain it later.

This text appears after the label Description: when you highlight the field name in the Project Manager. This value is also used for the Comment property of a control when you are using the drag-and-drop method of creating field controls in a form.

# Using Primary and Candidate Keys

Click the Index page of the Table Designer, and open the Type drop-down list. From the earlier discussion about indexes, you remember that all four index types appear in this list. Remember that only an index that qualifies as a Candidate index can be named primary. This means that the index expression references every record in the table with a unique value. You use the primary index to form relations with other tables. An Order table, for example, includes a customer ID with every order. FoxPro can relate the customer ID in that table to the customer ID in the CUSTOMER table to retrieve any or all of the customer's information.

Part
I

Ch
3

Primary and candidate tests occur when VFP updates the record. Therefore, you may not get an immediate error if the key value is not unique until you move off the record.

## Changing Table Properties Programmatically

In the past, changing table properties while you were in a program was difficult. The task basically required the program to re-create a new copy of the table with the changes and then copy the data from the old table to the new one. With Visual FoxPro, this task has become easier, due to the addition of two commands: ALTER TABLE and ALTER COLUMN.

Suppose that you want to change the default value for a company name during data entry. You could use the following expression type:

```
ALTER TABLE customer ALTER COLUMN company SET DEFAULT 'Documation'
```

In fact, you can do almost anything that you want to do, as the ALTER TABLE syntax in Listing 3.8 shows. Be aware, however, that this capability applies only to tables that are part of a database.

**Listing 3.8   03PRG08.PRG**

```
[NULL¦NOT NULL]
    [CHECK Iexpression1 [ERROR cMessageText1]]
    [DEFAULT eExpression1]
    [PRIMARY KEY¦UNIQUE]
    [REFERENCES TableName2 [TAG TagName1]]
    [NOCPTRANS]
-Or-
ALTER TABLE TableName1
  ALTER [COLUMN] FieldName2
    [SET DEFAULT eExpression2]
    [SET CHECK Iexpression2 [ERROR cMessageText2]]
    [DROP DEFAULT]
    [DROP CHECK]
-Or-
ALTER TABLE TableName1
  [DROP [COLUMN] FieldName3]
  [SET CHECK Iexpression3 [ERROR cMessageText3]]
  [DROP CHECK]
  [ADD PRIMARY KEY eExpression3 TAG TagName2]
  [DROP PRIMARY KEY]
  [ADD UNIQUE eExpression4 [TAG TagName3]]
  [DROP UNIQUE TAG TagName4]
  [ADD FOREIGN KEY [eExpression5] TAG TagName4
    REFERENCES TableName2 [TAG TagName5]]
  [DROP FOREIGN KEY TAG TagName6 [SAVE]]
  [RENAME COLUMN FieldName4 TO FieldName5]
  [NOVALIDATE]
```

# Examining Compatibility Issues

After the release of any major product upgrade, there is always a transition period in which some users are using the old version while others use the new one. You may need to share data between these versions. Eventually, you will need to convert the old system to the new version. This section describes some of the issues to consider during this transition.

## Sharing Tables with FoxPro 2.x

In general, free tables can be shared between FoxPro 2.x and Visual FoxPro. However, FoxPro 2.x cannot share tables that have been included in a Visual FoxPro database. Attempting to use such a table in FoxPro 2.x results in the warning message Not a table/ DBF. This behavior results from Visual FoxPro's changing the first byte of the .DBF file that identifies it.

Another problem occurs when you create a table in VFP that uses a Memo field. In VFP, the Memo field pointer is stored in 4 bytes rather than 10, as it was in previous versions of FoxPro.

If you remove a table from your system, a reference to it still exists in the database. You can remove such references by opening the database like a table and deleting the appropriate records. Similarly, if a database is accidentally deleted from disk, references to the database remain in the tables that formerly were contained in the database. The FREE TABLE command removes the database reference from a table. Thereafter, you can add the table to a different database or use it from FoxPro 2.x.

If you need to share tables with applications written in FoxPro 2.x, you cannot take advantage of the features provided by databases. In addition to being restricted to using free tables, you cannot define fields with the types Currency, DateTime, Double, Character (binary), or Memo (binary). These field types do not exist in FoxPro 2.x. If you can live with these limitations, you can share tables and their indexes with FoxPro 2.x. If you cannot, you may need to use a remote connection to the 2.x table using ODBC.

▶ **See** "Views of Remote Data," **p. 380**

## Conversion from Visual FoxPro 3.0

When you open a project file created in VFP 3.0, VFP 5.0 has a built-in converter that converts all your files in that project. Actually, what FoxPro does at this point is rebuild your project, so if files have been moved, FoxPro prompts you to locate them.

Also, when you try to open a database container created in VFP 3.0, VFP prompts you that the database container was compiled in a previous version if the database container has stored procedures. To solve this problem, type the following command in the Command window:

```
COMPILE DATABASE DatabaseName
```

# Removing a Table from the Database

When it adds a table to a database, Visual FoxPro changes the first byte in the .DBF header and adds a relative reference to the .DBC, prohibiting you from using the table as a free table or from adding it to another database. However, you can run FREE TABLE as shown in the following example to reset the first byte in the DBF file and clear the back link:

```
FREE TABLE CUSTOMER
```

Current values for this first byte in the .DBF include:

| | |
|------|---------|
| 0x02 | FoxBASE |
| 0x03 | FoxPro, FoxBASE+, dBASE III PLUS, dBASE IV (no memo) |
| 0x30 | Visual FoxPro |
| 0x43 | dBASE IV SQL table file, no memo |
| 0x63 | dBASE IV SQL system file, no memo |
| 0x83 | FoxBASE+, dBASE III PLUS (with memo) |
| 0x8B | dBASE IV (with memo) |
| 0xCB | dBASE IV ASQL table file, with memo |
| 0xF5 | FoxPro 2.x (or earlier) (with memo) |
| 0xFB | FoxBASE |

 **TIP** One way to hide data from other users and applications that read .DBF files is to change the first byte to something that other applications do not recognize.

Then you can add the table to another database (which, of course, sets the first byte again). But you don't need to move tables. You can open more than one database at a time within an application by including multiple OPEN DATABASE commands, as in the following example:

```
OPEN DATABASE databas1
OPEN DATABASE databas2 ADDITIVE
OPEN DATABASE databas3 ADDITIVE
```

# From Here...

This chapter showed you how to create a free table and how to add free tables databases. Many of the features and capabilities discussed in this chapter are familiar (or nearly so) to users of earlier versions of FoxPro. By concentrating on these features, you will be comfortable enough to dive in deeper.

As you move forward, you will see that using databases, rather than free tables, offers substantial benefits. These benefits include longer and more descriptive field names, engine-driven field validation and captions, persistent relations between files, and client/server support.

To learn more, refer to these chapters:

- Chapter 4, "Advanced Database Management Concepts," teaches data structuring based on the concepts of data normalization.
- Chapter 10, "Programming Structures," explores in more detail the concepts of how to organize your data.
- Chapter 18, "Data Dictionary Issues," discusses the implementation of an efficient data dictionary for easy re-creation of your system.

Part
I

Ch
3

# Advanced Database Management Concepts

*by Michael Antonovich and
Sandra Richardson-Lutzow*

**N**o other single factor has a greater influence on the success of a database application than the design of the database itself. The way you organize individual data items in tables and then relate those tables with one another in a database forms the very foundation of the application. A poorly built foundation weakens the programs built on it by making them more difficult to write, more difficult to maintain, and more difficult to enhance as demands on the software grow. Furthermore, improper design may force the programmer to fall back on less efficient methods of coding, which thus require more time and are more susceptible to error.

Perhaps you learned programming from classroom courses that taught you good design methods right from the start. On the other hand, maybe you learned programming by doing it and learned good design methods by trial and error. In either case, this chapter should help you build on your existing skills to create better database designs. To do so, it examines several areas of database management. ■

**Normalize your tables for better relational operation**

By designing a good structure to store your data, you can eliminate many headaches in manipulating data.

**Use a variable- and field-naming convention to make your code clearer and to prevent naming and use conflicts**

When you choose a common naming convention, reading and analyzing code is more conclusive to the approach and process being performed.

**Use Visual FoxPro's table-level validation**

The database container can perform automatic validations on data as it is entered into your tables.

**Use the Referential Integrity Designer**

The database container stores procedures with your relationships that will act on child tables automatically when you are modifying data in a parent table.

**Use triggers to execute code whenever a record is added, changed, or deleted from a table**

The database container uses stored procedures that are executed when you are performing on a table action that may affect other data.

# Data Normalization

The most important thing that you can do when you start a new application is design the structure of your tables carefully. A poorly structured database results in very inefficient code at best; at worst, it makes some features nearly impossible to implement. On the plus side, a well-designed set of tables not only solves your current problem, but also provides the flexibility to answer questions that you don't yet anticipate. Perhaps even more important, you will write programs faster. You can take advantage of queries and SQL SELECT statements to retrieve and maintain data. Finally, reports that may have required awkward manual coding under a denormalized structure almost write themselves when you use the report generator.

In general, the data structure of an application, more than any other factor, makes or breaks the application's success. Visual FoxPro is based on the relational-database model proposed by E.F. Codd in 1970. Codd based his model on mathematical principles that govern relational set theory. By following only a few very specific rules defining the creation of sets, he proved that you can manipulate the data easily. His technique became known as *data normalization*.

All relational-database theory revolves around the concept of using key fields to define relations between flat file tables. The more tables you have, the more relations FoxPro requires to connect them. Set theory does not demand, or even expect, that each table be connected directly to every other table. However, because each table is connected to at least one other, all tables in the database have direct or indirect relations with one another.

To examine the concepts of normalization, this section examines the Tasmanian Trader example provided with Visual FoxPro. However, it takes a view close to the beginning of the application-development process—just after establishing the data requirements.

▶ **See** "Defining the Scope" in Bonus Chapter 01 located on the CD

## Functional Dependencies

Assuming that you have decided what data fields you need, the next step is to divide them into tables. (Of course, you could put all the fields in a single table.) Even without normalization rules, it should be obvious that you do not want to repeat all the information about employees, customers, products, suppliers, and shippers for each item ordered. The only way to determine which fields belong together in each table is through functional dependency analysis. (It's not the same thing as taking away a computer terminal from a programmer; that's a functionally dependent analyst.)

*Functional dependency* defines the relation between an attribute or a group of attributes in one table to another attribute or group of attributes in another. In this discussion, *attributes* refers to fields. Therefore, you need to see which fields depend on other fields. A person's last name, for example, depends on his Social Security number (not originally, but at least according to the U.S. government). For any given Social Security number (person), there is only one corresponding name—not necessarily a unique name, but still only one name.

On the other hand, a Social Security number does not depend on a name. Given only a person's last name, there may be dozens, if not hundreds, of Social Security numbers. Even if you add a first name to the last, it still might not uniquely identify a single Social Security number. Imagine how many Bob Smiths there are, for example.

Thus, you can conclude that a last name is functionally dependent on Social Security, but not the other way around. You might even go the Orwellian route of referring to a person by his Social Security number.

Next, you might want to find other attributes that are functionally dependent on a Social Security number. Having gone through all the fields, you might have a list like the one in Table 4.1.

**Table 4.1  Fields Functionally Dependent on a Social Security Number**

| | | | |
|---|---|---|---|
| Address | FirstName | Password | SalesRegion |
| BirthDate | GroupId | Photo | Ssn |
| Cty | HireDate | Position | StartSalary |
| Country | HomePhone | PostalCode | SystemUser |
| EmplId | LastName | Region | TaskDesc |
| Extension | LicenseNo | ReportsTo | Title |

▶ **See** "Summarizing the Data Mapping Process" in Bonus Chapter 01 located on the CD

As a first pass at designing tables, you might group these fields into one table. Then, following similar logic, you might determine the functional dependencies in the remaining fields. Continue to group those attributes that have the same dependency in the same table. In effect, the number of functional dependencies determines the number of tables required.

Actually, if you follow this method of grouping fields, the resulting table should be very close to a normalized form already. However, to guarantee that they are normalized, you should verify that they obey at least the first three rules of normalized data:

- **First normal form:** eliminates repeating fields and nonatomic values
- **Second normal form:** requires each column to be dependent on every part of the primary key
- **Third normal form:** requires that all nonprimary fields depend solely on the primary fields

## First Normal Form

The first normal form eliminates repeating fields and nonatomic values. What is an atomic value, and will it explode upon use? An *atomic value* means that the field represents a single thing, not a concatenation of values—just as an atom represents a single element.

In the early days of relational databases, there were some rather small limits on the number of fields allowed in a record. As a result, programmers concatenated fields so as to fit all the data into a single record. Thus, one field might contain something like the following:

```
12/03/9412/15/9401/05/95T
```

This value actually represents four fields: an order date, a start-production date, a completion date, and a flag to indicate whether the order was shipped.

Forming relations between fields, retrieving data, and performing other operations is not easy when a field contains multiple values. The need to perform substring searches and to parse the fields slows applications tremendously—not to mention adding extra complexity to the code. To bring this table into first normal form, you need to split this field into four separate fields: three Date fields and one Logical field.

Another common problem addressed by the first normal form is repeated fields. Again, it was not unusual for early database developers to hard-code the number of items that a customer could order. They did so by placing the ordered products' IDs in the same record as the general order information, as shown in the following table:

| OrderId | OrderDate | ProdId1 | ProdId2 | ProdId3 | ProdId4 | Net |
|---------|-----------|---------|---------|---------|---------|-------|
| 00006 | 08/04/94 | A3426 | B8483 | C398 | | 59.34 |

In this example, there is no problem as long as the customer never orders more than four items at a time. (Only three items were ordered in this example.) However, it would be difficult to search the database to determine how many units of each product have sold. The program has to check each product column and then sum the results. Reports that display a list of customers who order specific products are similarly difficult to produce. In fact, most reports need complex hand coding so that they can search each field. As a result, the reports tend to be more likely to generate errors and require more time to execute.

Of course, you could increase the number of possible products that a customer can buy. But how many is enough (5? 10? 20?)? If you select 20, what if most customers order only two or three items? The resulting database wastes a great deal of space. More important, depending on the way that the code reads these fields, it may spend a great deal of time processing empty fields.

One alternative is to define a database that has a variable number of fields. In fact, some database systems several years ago supported this feature; they even promoted it as the best solution, in their marketing department's opinion. Fortunately, FoxPro continued to support the true relational definition of tables and kept records fixed in length.

The first normal form replaces repeating fields with a single field. It then creates as many records as necessary (one per ordered item), as shown in the following table:

| OrderId | OrderDate | ProductId | OrderNet |
|---------|-----------|-----------|----------|
| 00006   | 08/04/94  | A3426     | 59.34    |
| 00006   | 08/04/94  | B8483     | 59.34    |
| 00006   | 08/04/94  | C398      | 59.34    |

**Part**

**I**

**Ch**

**4**

After performing this analysis on each table in the database, the preliminary relational model of the data is complete. This first normal form is called *structural* or *syntactic normalization*. However, it should never be your final goal. There can still be problems in the data that cause the code to be more complex than it needs to be.

Intuitively, you may not like the solution offered in the preceding example. For one thing, it repeats values—not within records, but across multiple records. And wherever repeated values occur, inconsistencies can occur. This problem is addressed in subsequent normal forms.

## Second Normal Form

The second normal form requires that each column be dependent on every part of the primary key. Look again at the table that results from the first normal form:

**ORDERS.DBF**

| OrderId | OrderDate | ProductId | OrderNet |
|---------|-----------|-----------|----------|
| 00006 | 08/04/94 | A3426 | 59.34 |
| 00006 | 08/04/94 | B8483 | 59.34 |
| 00006 | 08/04/94 | C398 | 59.34 |
| 00007 | 08/05/94 | B8483 | 9.18 |

Because of the transformation performed by the first normal form, OrderId is no longer unique; neither is any other single field. However, the combination of OrderId and ProductId may be unique. Using this as a working assumption, you next need to examine the other fields to see whether they depend on the new primary key.

OrderDate depends only on OrderId, not on the combination of OrderId and ProductId. The same is true of OrderNet. Therefore, according to the second normal form, you need to remove these fields and place them in a separate table, along with a copy of the field on which they depend: OrderId. This results in two tables. Name the one that uses OrderId as the primary key, ORDERS.DBF; name the other, which contains a primary key on OrderId and ProductId, ORDITEMS.DBF. These new tables are:

**ORDERS.DBF**

| OrderId | OrderDate | OrderNet |
|---------|-----------|----------|
| 00006 | 08/04/94 | 59.34 |
| 00007 | 08/05/94 | 9.18 |

**ORDITEMS.DBF**

| OrderId | ProductId | LineNo |
|---------|-----------|--------|
| 00006 | A3426 | 0001 |
| 00006 | B8483 | 0002 |
| 00006 | C398 | 0003 |
| 00007 | B8483 | 0001 |

Merely by following the rules of normalization, you have taken the original order data and derived a structure that consists of two tables: one table with information about the overall order and the other with details on each order. Notice that a new field has been added to ORDITEMS.DBF: LineNo. This additional field counts the number of items in the form. This field has a fixed size of four digits; thus, it allows for up to 9,999 items to appear in the same order.

To associate the information in ORDERS.DBF with ORDITEMS.DBF, you form a relation between them based on OrderId. This relation is a one-to-many relation, because for every order in ORDERS.DBF, there can be more than one record in ORDITEMS.DBF. In fact, there is no limit to the number of items that the customer can order—one item or a million. (Well, actually, you set an arbitrary limit of 9,999 via the size of the field LineNo, but you could always increase the size of this field.) The program, when it is written to use related files, handles both situations equally well.

## Third Normal Form

To reach the third normal form, the table must already be in first and second normal form. Then, you determine which field or combination of fields represents the primary key for the table. For the employee table, a logical choice would be either employees' Social Security numbers or their employee IDs. For the order table, OrderId makes a good choice.

For the order-items table, no single field uniquely defines a record. There can be more than one detail record for an order ID, and ProductId can occur many times, both in the same order and across orders. OrderId also can occur many times within a single order. LineNo repeats the same sequence, beginning with 1 for each order. However, the combination of OrderId and LineNo is unique. Even if the same item appears more than once in a single order, its line-item value will be different. Thus, this file requires a composite primary key.

To illustrate third normal form, another field—ProdName—has been added. Suppose that the order-detail table includes the following fields:

### ORDITEMS.DBF

| OrderId | LineNo | ProductId | ProdName |
|---------|--------|-----------|-------------|
| 00006 | 0001 | A3426 | Tape Drives |
| 00006 | 0002 | B8483 | Modems |
| 00006 | 0003 | C398 | Track Balls |
| 00007 | 0001 | B8483 | Modems |

To be in third normal form, all nonprimary fields must depend solely on the primary fields. First, determine whether ProductId depends solely on the key field combination OrderId and LineNo. The answer is yes, because there can be only one product ID for each combination of OrderId and LineNo.

Part

I

Ch

4

Does product ID depend on the product name? This is a trick question. In some ways, it does, but product names may not be unique. Some products could have multiple sizes, colors, or other attributes. Each product has its own unique product ID, but the same product name. Therefore, product ID does not depend solely on product name.

Does ProdName depend solely on the primary key fields? Not really. The product name is not a function of the order ID and line number; rather, it depends on the product ID. Remember that each product ID has one unique product name, although the product name may be assigned to more than one product ID. Therefore, this field fails the third normal form.

The solution in this case is to move the product name into a new file called PRODUCTS, in which ProductId is the primary key. You may have reached this conclusion independently from your analysis of functional dependencies. Remember that normalization rules just reinforce functional analysis and common sense. The new table structure appears as follows:

**ORDITEMS.DBF**

| OrderId | LineNo | ProductId |
| --- | --- | --- |
| 00006 | 0001 | A3426 |
| 00006 | 0002 | B8483 |
| 00006 | 0003 | C398 |
| 00007 | 0001 | B8483 |

**PRODUCTS.DBF**

| ProductId | ProdName |
| --- | --- |
| A3426 | Tape Drives |
| B8483 | Modems |
| C398 | Track Balls |
| B8483 | Modems |

Of course, you need to perform this same analysis on every table in the application. When the analysis is complete, you can say that the application is normalized. Although there are additional levels of normalization, the need for them is rare. If you practice creating tables in third normal form, you can avoid most data-structure problems. You usually do not want to include fields that can be derived from other fields in the same or related tables. For example, you may not want to include an order-total field in the order file if the detail file also contains the price of each item ordered—it is safer to sum the individual prices to arrive at the order total. Of course, the amount actually paid may go on the order to compare against the total due. Think of it this way: The customer typically pays against an order but is billed based on individual items.

Perhaps you feel overwhelmed by these rules. Actually, with practice, you will begin creating normalized files right from the start. Some wise person once said that true understanding comes only when you see it in your dreams. When you look at the data for a new application and immediately visualize multiple files in your head, you truly understand normalization.

## When to Break the Rules

Normalization rules are not laws; they are merely guidelines to help you avoid creating data structures that limit the flexibility of the application or reduce its efficiency. However, no one will knock on your door and arrest you for breaking normalization rules (except maybe your boss). The following examples are situations in which breaking normalization rules may make sense:

Part

I

Ch

4

- You need to write a library system that prevents any patron from checking out more than five books at one time. You could write the system by normalizing the file that tracks the books checked out; it would have to ensure that no more than five records exist for each patron. However, a single record with five fields—one for each book—may make this application easier to develop. (An alternative is to add to the main patron table a field that simply counts the number of books that the patron has currently borrowed.)

- An order ID actually consists of the concatenation of two digits that represent the year plus a five-digit sequential number. Because the order-date field also reflects the year, you could, in theory, extract it or use the date in combination with the sequence number. However, the ease of referencing a single field in this case probably outweighs the strict avoidance of repeating data that can be derived from other fields.

- You have accepted a project to build a database for the National Association of Twins. Would you create a separate record for the name of each twin, or would you include twins in the same record? After all, you know by definition that there will always be exactly two names.

The intent here is to emphasize that normalization is a desired goal, but every once in a while, it makes sense to be a little abnormal.

# Naming Conventions

Your first question may be, "Why do I need a naming convention? FoxPro does not require it." Although Visual FoxPro does not require a naming convention, using one makes code clearer. You may appreciate this benefit only when you have to return to code that you wrote months or years earlier and try to remember what the variables mean. You may encounter similar problems when you try to work with code written by someone else. It can take considerable time just to determine the type, scope, and origin of variables. Using a naming convention solves these problems, when you use the convention consistently and if you take into account the variable's type and scope. This practice can eliminate naming and scoping conflicts common in many large applications.

Attempts at implementing naming conventions in earlier versions of FoxPro met with limited success. FoxPro limited both table field and memory variable names to 10 characters. With so few characters available, using any of them detracted from a programmer's ability to assign meaningful names. Also, some proposed naming conventions limited users' capabilities to transfer data between tables easily, especially when they were using commands such as SCATTER and GATHER. Thus, the issue became a trade-off; programmers felt that they had to choose between two conflicting goals. They could adopt a naming convention that identified a variable's source and type, or they could use all 10 characters to make meaningful names.

Now, with Visual FoxPro's support of long field and variable names, you can have both naming conventions and significant names. The following sections recommend naming conventions for different categories of variables. The sections also mention some possible variations that you may consider. Each section uses a slightly different method, due to differences in the variables and objects that each variable attempts to name. However, implementing an overall naming convention for your applications will make supporting multiprogrammer development easier, resulting in fewer naming and scoping conflicts.

There is no one absolute naming convention. Rather, the one that you pick (or that your company standardizes on) becomes the right one. It is difficult, if not impossible, to switch to a new naming convention after you have worked with a product for some time. That is why the introduction of Visual FoxPro presents a rare opportunity to begin using a naming convention with your new applications, especially if you have never used one before.

## Naming Issues Within an Application

Developers of independent applications do not often see the immediate advantages of implementing naming conventions. After all, they are the only ones who are working on the code, and they know everything in it. Right? Well, put aside an application for a few months and try to come back to it. How much do you really remember? The larger the application, the bigger the problem. It is easy to forget which variables each procedure uses. And what about the program that failed because Bill and Beth developed separate routines that use the same variables? Both situations lead to naming conflicts. If you reuse the same variable name, the program may accidentally overwrite values that are needed elsewhere. Suddenly, the application no longer works, and users are on the phone, waiting patiently to politely inform you of a problem.

Visual FoxPro does not require that you adopt a naming convention. For many programmers, conforming to a convention may seem like wearing a straitjacket. Give it a try, however, as you start developing Visual FoxPro projects, and see whether things run more smoothly once you get used to the convention.

The following sections describe some proposed naming convention rules for different variable types. Feel free to adopt what you like and discard the rest. Add additional rules if you need them. But when you have something that you like, stick with it for at least the duration of your current project. Also, keep an eye on the industry as naming conventions become more commonly used and more standardized.

## Naming Memory Variables

You must follow some basic rules when naming a variable. A variable name:

- Must begin with a letter.
- Must contain only letters, numbers, and underscore characters. Spaces and special characters are not permitted, and underscores are frowned upon.
- Must not exceed 255 characters.
- Must not be a reserved word, or (if the variable is only four characters long) must not be the first four characters of a reserved word—the first four characters of any Visual FoxPro command.

**N O T E**   You probably think that the third rule is a misprint. It's not. A memory variable can have up to 255 characters. Using that many characters means:

- You like to type.
- You have trouble coming up with significant, unique names.
- You don't want other people to be able to read your code.
- You have a good story to tell, and you put it in each variable name.

Seriously, although 10 characters is too few, 255 characters is too many for most applications. ■

Microsoft's intent is to bring the object languages of its major products (such as Visual FoxPro, Access, Visual Basic, and C++) closer together. All these products support longer field names. Access currently supports up to 64 characters, and Visual Basic supports 40 characters. Other products that allow you to access their data via ODBC or OCX controls may have variable names of other lengths. If you intend to share data with one of these products, try to limit your variable-name sizes to match the smaller of them. In this way, you will eliminate potential name conflicts based on name size.

**Variable Scope** The first attribute to consider when naming variables is scope identification. A variable's *scope* defines where and when it is known in a program. For example, a program can reference a *public variable* (global in other languages) from any line in the application when it is defined. The simple program shown in Listing 4.1 illustrates this concept.

**Listing 4.1   04PRG01.PRG—Public Variables Can Be Referenced Anywhere in Your Program**

```
* Main program
  DO SUB1
  ? abc

PROCEDURE SUB1
PUBLIC ABC
  ABC = 5
  DO SUB2
RETURN

PROCEDURE SUB2
  ? ABC
RETURN
```

This example defines variable ABC as a public variable and initializes it in Procedure SUB1. Any lower procedure or function called directly or indirectly by SUB1 after defining ABC can use it. Similarly, any higher routine that calls SUB1 can also use ABC after calling SUB1. The capability to reference a variable value in both higher and lower procedures is the key distinguishing feature of *public variables*.

Many programmers use public variables extensively, so they do not have to worry about where they define or use those variables. They may even initialize every variable in the main program. Although this practice actually gives them a scope of private (meaning that the variables are known only to the current procedure and any called procedure), the fact that the variables have been defined in the initial procedure makes them available to all subsequent procedures. However, this type of coding often results in problems. Primarily, it is difficult to locate errors caused when a "new" variable in a lower subroutine has the same name as the public variable. The program simply appears to inexplicably change the variable's value.

> **CAUTION**
>
> If you use a variable in a program without declaring its scope first, you cannot later declare it public without generating an error.

**N O T E** Declaring variables at the start of a PRG makes them available throughout the PRG, but private only to the PRG. If the PRG is called by another program, these variables will not be known in the calling program. On the other hand, a variable declared public will be known in all PRGs involved in the application after it is declared and defined. ■

*Private variables* offer a more limited scope. When initialized, these variables are known to the current procedure and all procedures that it calls. However, they are not known to the procedure that calls it, to any other higher procedures, or to procedures that follow a different calling sequence. In other words, the scope travels in one direction only—down one branch of the procedure call stack.

 **T I P** If you need a variable to be known across multiple branches of the procedure call stack, declare it public.

**N O T E** Declaring a variable private in the main routine has almost the same effect as declaring it public. The difference is that the private variable is known only within the current PRG file. Of course, this makes a difference only when you have one PRG call another. ■

To see the scope of a private variable, change the line PUBLIC ABC to PRIVATE ABC in the preceding example. Although Visual FoxPro recognizes the variable ABC in routines SUB1 and SUB2, it is not known in the main program. In fact, FoxPro generates an error when it attempts to use that variable.

The manual states that declaring a variable private does not create a new variable—it merely hides any previous variable with the same name from the current module. When the program exits the current module, it reveals the hidden variables again.

A new scope introduced in Visual FoxPro is the *local variable*. A variable declared local is known only in the routine that declares and defines it; higher- or lower-level routines cannot use it. If you replace the PUBLIC ABC line in the example with LOCAL ABC, ABC exists only in SUB1; neither SUB2 nor the main program can reference it.

Although not specifically defined as a variable scope, variables defined in class definitions have unique status. First, like local variables, they exist only in the class that defines them.

Second, they retain their values between references to the class. This is different from a local variable, which must be redefined and initialized each time the program executes the routine that uses it. Other languages refer to variables with similar scope as *static variables*. Unfortunately, you cannot define static variables outside a class definition.

As programs grow, it becomes easier to forget or confuse the scope of each variable. A common naming convention identifies a variable's scope by adding a scope-prefix character to each variable's name. Table 4.2 lists the available scope levels and suggests appropriate prefixes.

**Table 4.2   Scope-Prefix Characters**

| Scope | Prefix | Example |
| --- | --- | --- |
| Local | l | llTaxableItem |
| Private | p | pnTotalDue |
| Public/Global | g | gcCurrentUser |
| Static (Class Variable) | s | snCounter |

**N O T E**  The need for a prefix in static variables that are used to define properties of a class or in event code is less obvious than for other variable scopes, because these variables cannot be used anywhere else anyway. This convention does not apply to property or method names—just to other variables used with event method code.

In Chapter 2, "Introducing Object-Oriented Programming," you learned how to store a reference to an object in a variable. Therefore, you might be tempted to use prefixes in these object reference variables. Strictly speaking, these variables may act like private variables in scope, but they are so different in use that they deserve their own naming convention. Those conventions are listed in Table 4.4 later in this chapter.

**N O T E**  Because naming conventions are optional, you may decide to use different prefix letters for scope. However, Visual FoxPro and Microsoft recommend these characters. Using them will help you read other programmers' code if those programmers follow the same recommended conventions.

**N O T E**  Some developers include naming conventions for windows, procedures, functions, menu pads, and other objects. Because these names cannot be used outside their very restricted context, there is less likelihood of confusion. However, the "Naming Objects" section later in this chapter provides possible guidelines for these objects as well.

**Variable Type**    The next attribute of the variable that you can identify is its *type*. Knowing a variable's type can help prevent errors caused by using the wrong variable type in an expression. Suppose that you want to use a variable named START. By itself, the variable gives no indication whether it stores a date, character string, or number. Suppose that you want to use START in an expression such as the following:

```
? 'List records from ' + start + ' TO ' + end
```

If START stores anything other than character-type data, Visual FoxPro quickly responds with the following error message:

```
Operator/operand type mismatch
```

On the other hand, using a prefix that identifies the variable type can immediately warn you of the need to convert the variable to a different type before you use it. The following line combines two variables that have the prefix gd with text strings. The prefix indicates that the variables are global variables of type Date. Notice that the variable-type information provided by the second character of the prefix alerts you to a potential problem. You cannot directly combine text with dates. Therefore, you know to use DTOC() before concatenating the variables with text as the following illustrates.

```
? 'List records from ' + DTOC(gdstart) + ;
        ' to ' + DTOC(gdend)
```

Table 4.3 lists the variable types in Visual FoxPro, along with suggested prefixes. These prefixes represent Microsoft's recommendations, based on internal representations of these variable types.

**Table 4.3    Type-Prefix Characters**

| Type | Prefix | Example |
|------|--------|---------|
| Array | a | gaMonthsInYear |
| Character | c | gcLastName |
| Currency | y | pyProductCost |
| Date | d | pdBirthDate |
| DateTime | t | ltRecordPackStamp |
| Double | b | lbAnnualRiceProduction |
| Float | f | lfMilesBetweenCities |
| General | g | lgSoundSample |
| Integer | I | liTries |
| Logical | l | llTaxable |

*continues*

**Table 4.3   Continued**

| Type | Prefix | Example |
|------|--------|---------|
| Memo | m | lmProductDescription |
| Numeric | n | gnAge |
| Picture | p | lpProductPicture |
| Unknown | u | luSampleData |

**CAUTION**

Using this naming convention requires that a variable have a two-character prefix. The first prefix character always denotes the scope; the second denotes the type. Although you could define these characters in reverse order, you should never switch the order of these characters after you start an application. If you do, the resulting confusion will make you wish that you never heard of naming conventions—and it will not make you popular with other programmers who need to read your code, if they follow the standard prefix order.

**Using Case to Make Variables Readable**   A variation on the preceding naming examples includes an underscore character between the prefix characters and the rest of the variable name. Often, underscores are included between individual words in the variable name. This personal preference of some developers is not part of the new Microsoft recommendation, but you may encounter it in the naming convention used by other applications. In fact, the recommended conventions proposed for Visual Basic, Access, and Visual FoxPro do not include the underscore anywhere in a variable name. The conventions rely on the fact that the first capitalized letter indicates the beginning of the unique portion of the variable name and the end of the prefix. Also, when the variable name consists of two or more words, the first letter of each word also begins with a capital letter. The rest of the characters are always lowercase.

The only time the recommended convention could conceivably pose a problem is if you use an external text editor that does not honor case. (That possibility is relatively remote these days.) On the other hand, Visual FoxPro does not yet completely honor the case of field names, which detracts from their readability.

**NOTE**   Because naming conventions are optional, many variations exist. To some extent, this situation is good, because experimentation sometimes discovers better methods. Many leading FoxPro developers have developed their own naming conventions over the years, some of which are better than others. At this writing, it is too early to determine whether these conventions will be abandoned for a common naming convention. Actually, global acceptance would be a surprise. Part of the problem is that the naming convention proposed for FoxPro is not completely consistent with other development languages yet. Another problem is that Visual FoxPro does not fully support cases in all the places where variables and field names appear. Finally, developers may use naming conventions for different purposes.

On the other hand, any naming convention probably is better than no naming convention, as long as it is strictly followed within the application. ■

Keep in mind that although you may enter variable names with the uppercase and lowercase rule as suggested earlier in this chapter, Visual FoxPro is case-ignorant. FoxPro really doesn't care whether the variable is called lsOrderEnter or lsorderenter—both variables represent the same data memory location. This means that the burden of following such a naming convention is solely on your shoulders. Visual FoxPro's Documenting Wizard not only supports all uppercase or all lowercase, but also uses the case of the first occurrence of a variable and matches all subsequent occurrences. Thus, it even supports mixed-case variable names. Using initial caps for each word in a variable name makes the variable easier to read.

Remember, FoxPro does not require that you use a naming convention. But following any naming convention (even one that you create yourself) generates the following benefits:

- It makes identifying the scope and type of a variable easier.
- It reduces syntax errors and undefined variable errors.
- It makes it easier for other programmers to identify the purpose of a variable when they look at your code.

Places where you may not want to use these prefixes in variable names include:

- Constants created with #DEFINE. (In fact, the recommended convention for these variable names is all uppercase.)
- Class names, properties, or methods.

## Naming Fields in Tables

If you need to use free tables in an application, Visual FoxPro continues to limit field names to 10 characters. Even in such cases, some developers have proposed using character prefixes. One three-character-prefix convention uses the first two characters of the prefix to uniquely identify the table. These characters can be the first two characters of the table name, but they don't have to be. The third character is an underscore to clearly separate the prefix from the rest of the field name.

If the same field appears in multiple tables, you can continue to use a table prefix. However, you should make the remaining seven characters exactly the same in each table in which the field appears. Suppose that you have a Style field in several databases. If style has the same meaning in each database, you might have:

| or_Style | for the style in the order file |
| pr_Style | for the style in the product file |
| in_Style | for the style in the inventory file |

However, if style means something different in each file, the seven characters should uniquely reflect this difference, as follows:

| or_CStyle | for customer style |
| pr_PStyle | for product style |
| in_ClStyle | for cloth style |

The recommended Visual FoxPro naming convention used with table fields uses only the first character of a field name to identify its type (refer to Table 4.2). The remaining nine characters uniquely identify the field. Because the same field name can appear in more than one table, you should always precede it with the file alias when you use it in code, as in the following example:

```
customer.cLastName
order.dOrderDate
```

> **CAUTION**
>
> Despite the recommendation that you use uppercase and lowercase, the Visual FoxPro Table Designer supports only lowercase. To make matters more confusing, commands such as DISPLAY STRUCTURE list field names in uppercase. The Browse and Edit commands label column headings by displaying field names with initial caps only. Thus, there is no way to differentiate case in a table name. This is another reason for some developers to use the underscore character after the prefix, or even between major words. Would the field C_RAP, for example, make more sense in a table that lists types of music, or would you prefer CRAP?

Never use just a letter to identify a work area, such as A.cLastName. Such a practice restricts programs to always opening tables in the same work area. When you write generalized code that more than one procedure can call, you cannot always guarantee a work area's availability for a table. Therefore, always reference fields by their table alias.

 **TIP** Even though Visual FoxPro may not honor case in field names, there is no reason not to use case when you are coding field names.

Applications rewritten with Visual FoxPro can take advantage of the enhanced table features of a database. (It is unlikely that anyone will modify existing FoxPro applications just to add long character names. As part of an application rewrite to take advantage of other VFP features, however, converting to longer character names makes sense.)

When you add a table to a database, you can define 128-character field names. As indicated earlier, 128 characters may be overkill. With this many available characters, there is no reason why you cannot adopt one of the naming conventions and still define significant names.

The trade-off in using a naming convention for table fields is the fact that some commands and procedures may not work with some conventions. Suppose that you include a table-prefix code in each field name. With 128 characters, you could include the entire table or alias name. But code that uses SCATTER and GATHER to transfer data between tables will not work, because the prefix names would be different. Furthermore, Visual FoxPro will not automatically identify relations between tables. On the other hand, if you limit the prefix to a single field-type character in all tables, SCATTER, GATHER, and other table commands continue to work well.

Finally, even if you adopt a naming convention for your table variables, using commands such as SCATTER can lead to unexpected problems. When you scatter table fields to memory variables, Visual FoxPro creates a memory variable with the exact name as the field. When you use that variable without an alias identifier, Visual FoxPro makes the following assumptions about whether you mean the table variable or the memory variable:

- Any variable used with STORE is assumed to be a memory variable.
- A variable that is assigned a value with a REPLACE statement is assumed to be a table variable.
- The variable on the left side of an equation is assumed to be a memory variable.
- Any variable on the right side of an equation is first assumed to be a table variable and then a memory variable.

 **TIP** You can override some of these assumptions by prefixing the variable with the table alias. If the variable is a memory variable, use m. as the prefix.

The following equation takes the table variable Quantity, adds sale quantity (SaleQty) to it, and then saves the sum in the memory variable Quantity:

```
Quantity = Quantity + SaleQty
```

If you have this statement in your code, you may wonder why Quantity never seems to increase. The following redefined statement, using the recommended naming convention, makes the assignment clearer:

```
m.nQuantity = m.nQuantity + m.lnSaleQty
```

This statement tells you that nQuantity is a numeric variable saved to a memory variable from a table (because the prefix has only a single character). It also clearly adds a local numeric memory variable, lnSaleQty, which represents the sales quantity.

# Naming Objects

When you create an instance of a class, you store a pointer to it in a reference variable. You may want to include a special prefix to identify its class type. When you are looking at a property reference such as the following, it can be difficult to guess what class was used to create this object:

? Customer.City.Value

You may guess that Value represents the name of the city; therefore, the object probably is a text box within a form. The form is referenced by the object-reference name Customer, and the text box has the object-reference name City. But it could just as easily be a list or a combo box. The point is that you cannot be really sure to which class this object belongs. Why is this important? Knowing the class of an object tells you what properties, events, and methods to expect from it. Notice how much more information you know about the object when it includes an object prefix. Immediately, you know that it is a text box in a form such as the following:

? frmCustomer.txtCity.Value

This modified expression defines the object hierarchy. It says that a form named Customer contains a text box named City and that it returns the object's value. The recommended prefixes for naming object references are listed in Table 4.4.

**Table 4.4    Object-Reference Name Prefixes**

| Object | Prefix | Example |
|---|---|---|
| Check Box | chk | chkCurrentYrOnly |
| Combo Box | cbo | cboShipMethod |
| Command Button | cmd | cmdRecordMove |
| Command Group | cmg | cgpReportOptions |
| Container | cnt | cntBitBucket |
| Control | ctl | ctlOrders |
| Custom | cst | cstDiscountCalculation |
| Edit Box | edt | edbBugDescription |
| Form | frm | frmCustomerAddress |
| Form Set | frs | fstCustomer |
| Grid | grd | grdProductMatrix |
| Grid Column | grc | grcProductPrice |
| Grid Column Header | grh | grhProductFieldName |

| Object | Prefix | Example |
|--------|--------|---------|
| Image | img | imgProductPicture |
| Label | lbl | lblCustomerLabel |
| Line | lin | linSeparator |
| List Box | lst | lstStatesList |
| Menu | mnu | mnuMainMenu |
| OLE Bound Control | olb | olbEmployeePicture |
| OLE | ole | oleExcelGraph |
| Option Button | opt | optPaymentMethod |
| Option Group | ogr | ogrPaymentDistribution |
| Page | pag | pagStoreConfiguration |
| Page Frame | pfr | pfrPointOfSaleOptions |
| Separator | sep | sepFirstGapShape |
| Shape | shp | shpTitleBox |
| Spinner | spn | spnReportCopies |
| Text Box | txt | txtLastName |
| Timer | tmr | tmrStartProcess |
| Toolbar | tbr | btnFileSelect |

This naming convention distinguishes object references by a three-character prefix.

Chapter 2, "Introducing Object-Oriented Programming," describes ways to use a reference variable to shorten the full object reference. Because the complete reference can be rather lengthy to type, consider assigning aliases to recurring objects, using the prefix for the lowest-level object, as follows:

```
txtCustCity = OrderForm.CustomerInfo.CityName
txtCustCity.Value = 'Redmond'
```

N O T E  The recommended convention does not prefix characters to object names. However, you can use prefixes on object references.  ■

## Naming Issues Across Related Applications

All the conventions in the preceding section apply whether you develop a single application or multiple applications. However, it is more common for problems to occur when different teams develop different modules of larger applications. There are more

Part

I

Ch

4

possibilities for naming, scoping, and typing inconsistencies. The following paragraphs describe a few of these possibilities:

■ Suppose that two developers create two separate tables that share several common fields, but they name the fields differently and assign them different sizes. (In variations on this scenario, the developers name the fields consistently but assign them different sizes, or assign the same sizes but different names.)

■ Now, suppose that you have the opposite situation: Two developers create fields in separate tables that have exactly the same name and definition. The problem is that the fields really represent two different things.

■ Suppose that two developers create modules, each using their own data-naming conventions. If both developers use entirely different conventions, it may be possible to bring one module into alignment with the other by using a few replace statements. The real problem is when the naming conventions used by the two developers have common prefixes that do not mean the same thing. Suppose that one developer puts field type first and scope second, and the other developer puts scope first and type second. In this case, does a variable labeled pl_thing represent a private logical or a local picture?

■ Suppose that two developers create two separate applications and use the same variable name for different purposes. Each developer defines the variable as a different type, therefore causing confusion. However, a most difficult obstacle to resolve occurs when the same variables from the two separate applications have a different definition but are of the same data type. It takes longer to realize that the variables are actually different. If the applications are truly separate, this situation may not pose more than an academic question. But if the applications form two modules in a system, at some point, a third developer may look at both applications and attempt to form a relation by using this field between the two tables.

Not many data dictionaries are products on the market yet, especially products that deal with cross-application development. But as Visual FoxPro begins to become more a corporate development tool than a department tool, the need for these tools will force their creation. In the meantime, you may want to consider assigning one person to be responsible for a list of field names and their definitions. Then, when anyone needs to create a new database, he must first consult this list to see whether the names that he wants are already in use, with the same or different meanings.

Another option is to create your own data dictionary. Our experience in developing and working with a data dictionary proved that it can quickly became an essential tool to your project.

▶ **See** "Designing Your Own Data Dictionary," **p. 734**

## Using Enterprisewide Naming Conventions

Enterprise issues expand on the cross-application issues, especially as development teams become separated over greater distances. In developing client/server applications, the focus on consistency switches to a central data repository. In some ways, this situation is a benefit, because it becomes easier for everyone to check what field names have already been used and how they have been defined. On the other hand, no system has the internal intelligence to prevent the types of situations mentioned earlier in this chapter.

One of the greatest potential areas for problems is development of applications in different departments of the same company, because there usually is little coordination between application developers in each department. As a result, the risk of naming inconsistencies increases dramatically. As long as each department operates independently of the other, these problems never surface. But as soon as two departments are required to work together on a common system, the naming inconsistencies create significant problems. A companywide naming convention will not eliminate all these problems, but it will reduce them.

# Other Advanced Features of Visual FoxPro's Database Container

Part

I

Ch

4

In Chapter 3, "Defining Databases, Tables, and Indexes," we mentioned a few of the advanced features that Visual FoxPro's data container offers at the field level, in addition to its capability to assign 128-character field names. Although this situation tremendously improves the 10-character limitation of free tables, it comes with a price: When you begin using 128-character field names, going back to 10-character names is difficult. All programs, forms, reports, and other files that reference the table will require changes to referenced, shortened field names.

## Using Record-Level Validations

You can define additional properties at table level by clicking the Table Properties button. Figure 4.1 shows the Table Properties dialog box, with its six additional fields.

**FIGURE 4.1**

The Table Properties dialog box shows a record-level validation rule.

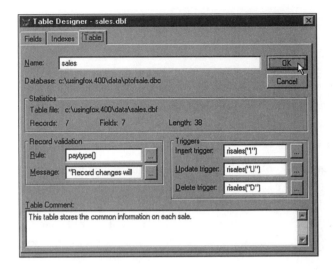

The validation rule in this dialog box is a record-level validation. Visual FoxPro triggers this rule when you change any value in the record and attempt to move to another record. When you are in a browse window, form, or other interface feature that allows scanning of records, you can move between records without triggering the validation only if you make no changes.

When you use record-level validation, the validation code cannot change any field in the current record or move the record pointer. It can, however, compare the values of one field with those of another, as follows:

```
(dHireDate - dBirthDate) > 18 * 365.25
```

The code can also perform a lookup validation against another file, as follows:

```
SEEK(cCustId, 'CUSTOMER')
```

In Figure 4.1, the record validation is more complex than a single expression. Therefore, a UDF (user-defined function) calls the validation code saved as a stored procedure in the database.

**N O T E**   Before you can enter a UDF for a validation rule, the stored procedure must exist. Otherwise, Visual FoxPro rejects the UDF reference. Therefore, choose Edit Stored Procedure from the Database pull-down menu before adding the validation clause to the table structure. You can also open the stored procedures anytime the database is open by typing **MODIFY PROCEDURE** in the Command window. ■

Any validation expression or function call must evaluate to a logical result. If the field validation returns .F., Visual FoxPro keeps the record pointer in the same record and does not save any changes made to it; it also displays the validation text. Following is the full text for the validation text that was cut off in Figure 4.1:

```
"Record changes will not be accepted!"
```

To validate the records, you need to use a new Visual FoxPro function called GETFLDSTATE. This function determines whether a field in a table or cursor has changed during the current command or whether the delete status has changed. The basic syntax of this command is:

```
GETFLDSTATE(cFieldName¦nFieldNumber [,cTableAlias¦nWorkArea])
```

**N O T E** Row or table buffering must be enabled with CURSORSETPROP() before GETFLDSTATE() can operate on local tables. ∎

If you include a field name or number, GETFLDSTATE returns one of the values listed in Table 4.5, indicating the status of that field. The preceding validation text uses GETFLDSTATE to determine which error message to display, based on whether the sales-total field has changed.

**Table 4.5    Return Values for GETFLDSTATE**

| Return Value | Edit/Delete Status |
| --- | --- |
| 1 | Field has not changed value, and deletion-status flag has not changed. |
| 2 | Either field or deletion-status flag has changed. |
| 3 | Field in appended record has not been changed, and its deletion status has not changed. |
| 4 | Field in appended record has changed, or the deletion-status flag has changed. |

**N O T E** Visual FoxPro returns this information only for tables in a database. ∎

You can also return the information about all fields in the current table with GETFLDSTATE(–1). This command returns a string. Its first value represents the deletion-status flag, which is followed by one return value for each field in the record.

Calling GETFLDSTATE() with an argument of 0 returns a single value that represents the status of the deletion flag.

> **CAUTION**
>
> When you are evaluating return values from GETFLDSTATE(), all options other than –1 return a numeric value. Option –1 returns a string.

▶ **See** "Detecting and Resolving Conflicts," **p. 696**

The code segment in Listing 4.2 shows the complete validation code associated with the record-validation function shown in Figure 4.2.

**Listing 4.2 04PRG02.PRG—A Record Validation Function Called by the Valid Event of the Total Order Amount Field**

```
FUNCTION PAYTYPE
* This function checks the payment type as a function
* of the total order amount to validate the record.
LOCAL llReturnCode, lnChangeCheck

* Check if any changes were made to either the sales total or
* the payment method.
* Check if customer attempts to pay < $10 by credit card.
  IF (MOD(GETFLDSTATE('nSalesTotal'),2) = 0 OR ;
      MOD(GETFLDSTATE('cPaymentMethod'),2) = 0) AND ;
      nSalesTotal < 10.00
    * Check for payment method of 'CA' - Cash
    IF cPaymentMethod # 'CA'
      = MESSAGEBOX('Orders of less than $10 must be cash')
      RETURN .F.
    ENDIF
  ENDIF

* If paid by credit card, Check if credit card was approved.
  IF (MOD(GETFLDSTATE('nSalesTotal'),2) = 0 OR ;
      MOD(GETFLDSTATE('cPaymentMethod'),2) = 0) AND ;
      cPaymentMethod # 'CA'
    * Ask if card was approved. If not reject record.
    IF MESSAGEBOX('Was card approved?', 36) = 7
      = MESSAGEBOX('Cannot accept a credit card ' + ;
        'order without approval')
      RETURN .F.
    ENDIF
  ENDIF

RETURN .T.
```

Notice that the function first checks to see whether the change that triggered the validation occurred to either the sales-total or payment-method field. Remember that a change to any field triggers the record validation. Therefore, you should determine whether to perform the validation. You certainly don't want to perform the validation for every field that changes.

**CAUTION**

While you are in the validation-rule code, do not attempt to move the record pointer for the current table. Any change could result in a series of recursive calls that could create more error conditions. For this reason, VFP prohibits changes to any field in the current table. Therefore, you cannot use the record validation to "correct" an error.

Even if you don't move off the current record, but instead attempt to close the browse or form after making a change to a field, Visual FoxPro still performs the record validation.

**CAUTION**

Visual FoxPro stores all validation code and text in the database. Freeing a table from a database removes the link to these definitions. The stored procedures remain in the database, but the links to the table are broken.

**TIP** You can add, modify, or delete a record validation with the CHECK or DROP CHECK clause in ALTER TABLE.

# Maintaining Referential Integrity

In general, *referential integrity* defines which operations are permissible between tables that are connected with relations. The basic premise is that a foreign key value in the parent table must have a corresponding lookup or primary key in another table (called the *child table*). Referential integrity treats records that do not meet these criteria as being invalid.

You can implement referential integrity in several ways. You need to decide what method best suits the data. Consider the basic relation between general order information and detailed order information, for example. The Tasmanian Trader example provided with Visual FoxPro represents these files as ORDERS.DBF and ORDITEMS.DBF, respectively.

The orders table contains information that is unique to the order as a whole. This information includes Order_Id, Order_Date, Customer_Id, and many other fields. The order detail table contains specifics on individual items ordered, such as Order_Id, Product_Id, Quantity, and Unit_Price. The relation that ties these two tables together is based on Order_Id.

When you add a record to ORDERS.DBF, you do so with the intent of adding details to ORDITEMS.DBF. After all, an order without details is not a complete order. Similarly, you would never think of adding details to ORDITEMS.DBF without also adding an order record to ORDERS.DBF. These files reference each other in a parent/child relation. ORDERS.DBF represents the parent, and ORDITEMS.DBF is the child. The analogy is that you can have a parent without a child, but you cannot have a child without a parent.

## Forming Persistent Relations

Persistent relations define relations between two tables and are stored in the Database Designer. Visual FoxPro automatically uses them each time the tables are subsequently opened. This feature is especially useful for automatically setting the relations between tables in SQL statements and for creating lookups, validations, and the data environment of forms and reports.

Persistent relations are sometimes called permanent relations, as opposed to temporary relations created with the SET RELATION command. The reason that SET relations are temporary is that FoxPro dissolves them when you exit FoxPro or issue the SET RELATION command by itself. Persistent relations remain in place between applications.

**Creating Relations Among Tables**   To create a relation between tables, return to the Database Designer window. Figure 4.2 shows two tables between which you need to define relations.

**FIGURE 4.2**
The Edit Relationship dialog box, used by the Database Designer, defines which fields connect the tables.

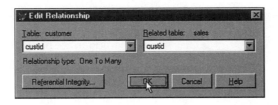

Create the following indexes, using the Table Designer dialog box, if you do not have them already:

In CUSTOMER.DBF:

| | | |
|---|---|---|
| TAG: CUSTID | PRIMARY | INDEX ON: cCustomerId |
| TAG: CUSTNAME | REGULAR | INDEX ON: cLastName + cFirstName |
| TAG: COMPANY | REGULAR | INDEX ON: cCompanyName + STR(cOutstandingBillsTotal, 9, 2) |

In SALES.DBF:

| | | |
|---|---|---|
| TAG: ORDERID | PRIMARY | INDEX ON: cOrderId |
| TAG: CUSTID | REGULAR | INDEX ON: cCustomerId |

TAG: SALESMAN     REGULAR     INDEX ON: cSalesmanId

TAG: SALES     CANDIDATE     INDEX ON: DTOC(dSaleDate)+cOrderId

In DETAILS.DBF:

TAG: ORDERID     REGULAR     INDEX ON: cOrderId

TAG: DETAILS     PRIMARY     INDEX ON: cOrderId+cItemId

Use the scroll bars of each table to display the index list at the bottom. To form a relation, simply click the index name in one of the tables and drag it to an index in another table. Suppose that you want to find the sales information for each customer. Click CUSTID in the CUSTOMER table, and drag it to CUSTID in the SALES table. FoxPro displays the Edit Relationship dialog box (refer to Figure 4.2).

Because you dragged the index from one table to another, FoxPro automatically fills in the customers' names. FoxPro also defines the relationship as one-to-many, because there can be many sales orders for each customer. Finally, to accept the relation, simply click OK.

FoxPro follows a few simple rules to define the relation type. First, it assumes that the start table, or from table, is on the "one" side and must be a candidate or primary index. (You cannot start a persistent relation from a unique or regular index.) If you then connect to a primary, or candidate, index in the related table, FoxPro knows that it must be a one-to-one relation, because these are unique indexes that include every record in the table. Connecting to any other index (regular or unique) allows for more than one record on the "to" side; therefore, FoxPro assumes a one-to-many relationship. Remember that a unique index does not prohibit multiple records that have the same index value—it merely keeps a pointer to only the first one.

Create a similar relation between ORDER_ID in SALES.DBF and ORDER_ID in DETAILS.DBF. The details side of this relation defines a many relation, because each order can contain many ordered items.

In the Database Designer window, you now see a connecting line between the indexes. FoxPro displays the "one" side of a relation, with a single line coming out of the table. The "many" side has three lines leading from the index.

**Breaking a Relation**    To break a relation that is no longer needed or defined incorrectly, merely click it and then press the Delete key. You can also right-click and then choose Remove Relationship from the shortcut menu.

**Creating Self-Referential Relations**    A *self-referential relation* relates one field in a table to another field in the same table. An example that illustrates this concept involves the relation between a supervisor and an employee. An employee table contains a record for each company employee, identified by an employee ID. Each record has one field that identifies the ID of the employee's supervisor. That ID is also the supervisor's employee number. Thus, by referencing the employee's number, you can get the supervisor's name, the name of that supervisor's supervisor, and so on.

Figure 4.3 shows the Database Designer after the formation of the relation between EMPL_ID, defined as the primary index, and SUPERVISOR, defined as a regular index.

**FIGURE 4.3**
This Database Designer view shows a self-referencing relation.

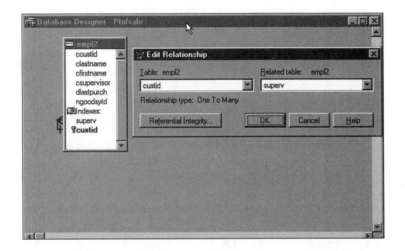

Although queries have not been discussed yet, following is a query that lists every employee and his or her supervisor's name, using the self-referencing relation in EMPL2:

```
SELECT A.EmplId, ;
    A.LastName AS EMPLOYEE_LAST_NAME, ;
    A.FirstName AS EMPLOYEE_FIRST_NAME, ;
    B.LastName AS SUPERVISOR_LAST_NAME ;
    B.FirstName AS SUPERVISOR_FIRST_NAME ;
    FROM EMPL2 A, EMPL2 B ;
    WHERE A.Supervisor = B.EmplId
```

▶ **See** "Creating Basic Queries," **p. 303**
▶ **See** "Advanced Queries and Views," **p. 347**

# Using the Referential Integrity Builder

Visual FoxPro adds a powerful new feature by providing engine-based referential integrity. To access the Referential Integrity (RI) Builder:

■ Open the database that contains the tables for which you want to define referential-integrity rules.

■ Right-click the persistent relation, or double-left-click the relation to display the Edit Relation box.

The first method displays a menu that contains the Referential Integrity option; the second method displays a command button. Choosing either option displays the builder shown in Figure 4.4.

**FIGURE 4.4**

Referential Integrity Builder opened for database \VFP\ SAMPLES\TASTRADE\ DATA\TASTRADE.DBC, showing all the table relations and their current RI rules.

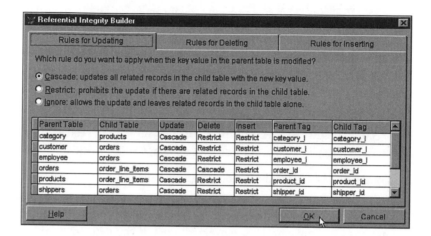

The bottom half of the builder lists each relation on a separate line or row. The columns across the row name the parent and child tables. Next are three columns for the Update, Delete, and Insert integrity rules. Initially, all these columns say Ignore. However, you can define rules for each relation and action. Finally, the last two columns define the parent and child tags involved in the relation.

Only the referential-rule columns can be modified. If you select any of these columns by clicking them, a drop-down-arrow button appears; that button when clicked, displays the referential options. These options are also defined in the page frame in the top half of the builder.

Each referential action has its own page, which lists the available options. The referential options available when you are updating the key value in a parent table include:

- **Cascade.** This option updates all child records with the new parent key value that had the same old parent key value.

- **Restrict.** This option checks to see whether any child records exist with the current parent key value. If so, FoxPro prohibits you from changing the parent key value.

- **Ignore.** This option performs no referential integrity and allows changes to the parent key without regard to any related child records.

As you can see, each of these options has an option (radio) button. Clicking the button changes the selected rule for the highlighted relation in the top half of the builder. Thus, you have two ways to select the referential rules.

Part

I

Ch

4

The rules for deleting parent records are similar to those for updating. The rules for inserting records, however, apply from the child side of the relation. The two possible rules provided here are:

- **Restrict.** This rule prevents the insertion of a child record if a parent record with the same key value does not exist.
- **Ignore.** This option performs no referential-integrity checks.

After you define the referential-integrity rules for each relation and action, click OK to exit the builder. You may want to cascade key updates made in the CUSTOMER table to the ORDERS table. On the other hand, you may want to restrict deletion of CUSTOMER records if ORDERS records exist. Finally, you want to restrict the entry of an ORDERS record if the customer key does not exist in CUSTOMER.

When you click OK, the builder displays a dialog box that asks you to save your changes, generates the RI code, and exits. This process creates a set of triggers and stored procedures in the database. If the database previously defined triggers or a stored procedure, it makes a backup copy before overwriting it. If you defined stored procedures for other features, such as validations, you need to manually copy them from the backup to the new stored procedures.

After the RI Builder completes this task, you can open the Table Designer and select Table Properties to view the added triggers. Alternatively, you can view the stored procedures by clicking the Edit Stored Procedure button in the Database Designer toolbar.

> **CAUTION**
>
> If you change any of the tables that are involved in referential integrity, their indexes (or persistent relations) rerun the RI Builder. This action revises the code as appropriate, due to the changes made.

Although the Referential Integrity Builder is a fast and easy way to adding common referential-integrity rules to your database relations, you define referential integrity in many ways. Some of these ways are discussed in the following section.

## Building Your Own Referential Integrity

On the CD

To illustrate some of these principles, the disk that comes with this book contains a database called PTOFSALE (for point-of-sale). This database is a modification of the Tastrade files, which show one way of implementing referential integrity.

The following section examines referential-integrity rules created for two files in the database: SALES.DBF and DETAILS.DBF. These files loosely resemble ORDERS.DBF and ORDITEMS.DBF, from Tasmanian Traders, but with fewer fields and records to help illustrate the points. By using separate files, you can experiment with triggers without worrying about potential damage to your Tasmanian Trader example. Table 4.6 displays the field structure for SALES.DBF, and Table 4.7 displays the field structures for DETAILS.DBF.

**Table 4.6    Field Structure for SALES.DBF**

| Field Name | Type | Width | Decimals | Null |
| --- | --- | --- | --- | --- |
| dSaleDate | Date | 8 | | No |
| cCustomerId | Character | 4 | | No |
| cSalesmanId | Character | 4 | | No |
| cOrderId | Character | 6 | | No |
| nSalesTotal | Numeric | 9 | 2 | No |
| cPaymentMethod | Character | 2 | | No |
| cShipperId | Character | 4 | | No |

**Table 4.7    Field Structure for DETAILS.DBF**

| Field Name | Type | Width | Decimals | Null |
| --- | --- | --- | --- | --- |
| cOrderId | Character | 6 | | No |
| cItemId | Character | 6 | | No |
| nQuantity | Numeric | 4 | 0 | No |
| nUnitPrice | Numeric | 8 | 2 | No |
| lTaxable | Logical | 1 | | No |

Part
I

Ch
4

**N O T E**  These two files use the standard recommended naming convention for table variables, which includes a single-character type prefix. The convention also uses initial caps for words within the field name where Visual FoxPro recognizes them, such as within code to help make reading the names easier. ■

## Using Triggers

The next three options after Record Validations in the Table Properties dialog box are called *triggers*. Visual FoxPro executes these triggers when you insert, update, or delete a record in the table. As is true of record-validation rules, you need to store the code for triggers as stored procedures in the database.

You can use triggers for additional calculations or validations when you perform any of these three operations. You could send an e-mail message to Purchasing when the inventory of any item falls below a predefined stock value, for example. You could also log all changes made to a table or create your own referential integrity rules. However, you cannot do several things with them. You can't do the following:

- Move the record pointer in the current work area
- Change the value of any field in the current record
- Close the current work area or open another file in the same work area

The most common use for triggers is to implement referential integrity.

**Initializing the Stored Procedures for Triggers**   In this section, you learn how to define the triggers. Figure 4.1 shows the extended options for triggers in SALES.DBF, defined as follows:

| | |
|---|---|
| Insert Trigger: | RISALES("I") |
| Update Trigger: | RISALES("U") |
| Delete Trigger: | RISALES("D") |

Next, define a similar set of triggers for DETAILS.DBF:

| | |
|---|---|
| Insert Trigger: | RIDETAILS("I") |
| Update Trigger: | RIDETAILS("U") |
| Delete Trigger: | RIDETAILS("D") |

Notice that in both cases, triggers for each table call the same function, merely passing it a different single-character parameter to identify the operation. The reason is that referential integrity requires some common additional support, or housekeeping tasks. These tasks are called from RIDETAILS and RISALES, so they do not have to be repeated. Each of these requirements is examined later in this chapter; the following section starts by examining RISALES().

**Defining Triggers for the Parent Table**   Whenever Visual FoxPro senses the insertion, updating, or deletion of a record, it checks to see whether a trigger for that event exists. If it does, as in this case, VFP executes the trigger. All triggers for the table SALES.DBF call function RISALES(), as shown in Listing 4.3.

---

**Listing 4.3    04PRG03.PRG—Referential Integrity Code Generated by the RI Builder Called on by VFP in the Event of a Delete, Insert, or Modify**

```
****************
FUNCTION RISALES
* This routine is called by the triggers in SALES.DBF
LPARAMETERS lcAction
LOCAL llReturnValue, Dummy

* Start Transaction
  Dummy         = IIF(TYPE("nLevel")<>"N" OR nLevel=0, ;
                    RISTART(), "")
  nLevel        = nLevel + 1
  llReturnValue = .F.

* Perform action
  DO CASE
    CASE TYPE('lcAction') # 'C' ;
         OR !UPPER(lcAction) $ 'DIU' ;
         OR LEN(lcAction)>1
      ERROR 'Invalid action code passed to RISALES'
    CASE UPPER(lcAction) == 'D'
      llReturnValue = SALEDEL()
    CASE UPPER(lcAction) == 'I'
      llReturnValue = SALEINS()
    CASE UPPER(lcAction) == 'U'
      llReturnValue = SALEMOD()
  ENDCASE

* End transaction
  nLevel = nLevel - 1
  Dummy  = IIF(nLevel = 0, RIEND(llReturnValue), 0)

RETURN llReturnValue
```

Notice that this routine begins by assigning the passed character to a local parameter (LPARAMETER) called lcAction. It then defines a local variable, which it uses to return a logical value to the trigger, llReturnValue.

This function itself has three parts. The first part initializes a transaction by checking the current value of variable nLevel. If you object that nLevel is not defined yet, you are correct. That is the purpose of the first conditional test in the IIF statement; it takes advantage of the way Visual FoxPro evaluates expressions. When a conditional statement has more than one expression, VFP evaluates them one at a time, from left to right. As soon as VFP can evaluate the expression, it stops, even if it does not evaluate all conditions.

Part

I

Ch

4

In this case, `IIF()` contains two conditions connected with OR. The logical result of this expression is true, as long as one or the other condition is true. Visual FoxPro knows this. It evaluates the first expression, and because nLevel is undefined, it returns a type of "U." Therefore, the first condition is true. Because this is all that FoxPro needs to evaluate the entire expression, it never checks to see whether nLevel is equal to zero. If nLevel were equal to zero, it would generate an error, because nLevel is undefined. Thus, FoxPro executes function `RISTART()` when the expression is true, as occurs at the start of the first trigger event.

**N O T E**   When defining conditional expressions, define the evaluation order so as to minimize the work that Visual FoxPro must do. Put the most critical condition first. This action saves VFP time; it also allows you to include in the second part of the test conditions that are not otherwise valid. ■

**T I P**   When you are connecting two expressions with OR, put the one that is most likely to pass first. When you are connecting two expressions with AND, put the one that is most likely to fail first.

This first section also increments the value of nLevel, which `RISTART()` initializes to zero. This variable tracks how many triggers have been set and which one is being processed. An nLevel value of 1 indicates that processing should execute code related to the primary trigger event. Higher values of nLevel evaluate cascade events.

The second portion of `RISALES()` uses a case statement to check whether the parameter passed is valid and then to branch to the correct function. Notice, again, that a compound test is used in the first CASE statement. If the TYPE of lcAction is not Character, Visual FoxPro ignores the rest of the conditions—which only makes sense, because lcAction should be Character.

Finally, the last section performs a cleanup. First, the section decreases the trigger level. If it has executed all the triggers (nLevel=0), it executes one final function: `RIEND()`.

Now examine RISTART, shown in Listing 4.4.

**Listing 4.4   04PRG04—The *RISTART* Code**

```
****************
FUNCTION RISTART
* Call this program when starting Referential Integrity.
* It initializes several variables.
  IF TYPE("nLevel") <> 'N'
    PUBLIC nLevel
    nLevel = 0
  ENDIF
```

```
    IF TYPE("cCursors") <> "C"
      PUBLIC cCursors
    ENDIF

    IF nLevel = 0
      BEGIN TRANSACTION
      PUBLIC cOldError, nError
      cCursors  = ""
      cOldError = ON("ERROR")
      nError    = 0
      ON ERROR nError = ERROR()
    ENDIF
  RETURN
```

As you can see, the routine initializes nLevel to zero and makes it a public variable. This routine also initializes two other variables. The first variable, cCursors, tracks the names of cursors opened by the code in the triggers. The second variable, cOldError, stores the current ON ERROR action.

The following statement is very important:

```
BEGIN TRANSACTION
```

This statement defines the beginning of a transaction and tells Visual FoxPro to buffer all record changes that are made until it executes an END TRANSACTION. END TRANSACTION writes the changes from the buffer permanently to the file. If you decide to cancel changes, you can use ROLLBACK or TABLEREVERT( ) to back out or discard changes. Function TABLEREVERT( ) has the following syntax:

```
TABLEREVERT([lAllRows][,cTableAlias¦nWorkArea]
```

The first parameter, when it is set to true, discards changes made to all records in the current table or in the table referenced by an alias or work-area number. When it is set to false, the parameter discards only changes made in the current record.

Up to this point in this chapter, the routines used have been fairly generic. In fact, you could use them in your own applications virtually unchanged, except for the functions called by the CASE statement in RISALES. The following section examines the first function that performs the real action of the trigger.

**Defining a Cascade Delete Trigger**   The SALEDEL( ) function defines the trigger action when Visual FoxPro senses the deletion of a record in SALES.DBF. The purpose of this routine is to cause a delete cascade to remove all order details associated with the deleted order record. After all, when the parent order record no longer exists, the child details are no longer valid. Listing 4.5 shows the code required to accomplish this task.

**Listing 4.5   04PRG05.PRG—Referential Integrity Code Generated by the RI Builder Called on the Event of a Delete**

```
****************
FUNCTION SALEDEL
* If deleting a sales record, delete all details
LOCAL  llReturnValue, lcOrderId, lnDetArea

  llReturnValue = .T.
  IF nLevel = 1
    lcOrderId     = cOrderId
    lnDetArea     = RIOPEN('DETAILS')
    SELECT (lnDetArea)
    SCAN FOR cOrderId = lcOrderId
      llReturnValue = RIDELETE()
    ENDSCAN
    SELECT sales
  ENDIF

RETURN llReturnValue
```

This relatively short routine starts by storing the order ID from the sales record in lcOrderId and then uses RIOPEN( ) to safely open a copy of DETAILS. The routine opens DETAILS.DBF without setting a tag, so that Rushmore can fully optimize the FOR clause. The code uses SCAN FOR to find all records with a matching order ID; then, it deletes each matching record by calling the RIDELETE( ) function.

The SALEDEL( ) function introduces two new functions, both of which are generalized functions that you can use in any referential-integrity situation. In fact, triggers from the DETAILS table also use them. The following section discusses RIOPEN( ).

**Using a Common Procedure to Open Cursors**   The RIOPEN( ) function supports two parameters: one for the table name and the other for an optional tag name. Listing 4.6 shows the RIOPEN( ) code.

**Listing 4.6   04PRG06.PRG—The *RIOPEN()* Code**

```
***************
FUNCTION RIOPEN
* This procedure opens cursors for use during Referential
* Integrity checks since operations that perform record
* pointer moves are not allowed directly.
LPARAMETERS lcTable, lcTag
LOCAL lnNewArea, nInUseArea

  nInUseArea = ATC(lcTable+"*", cCursors)

* Open reference table
  IF nInUseArea = 0
```

```
    SELECT 0
    lnNewArea = SELECT()
    IF EMPTY(lcTag)
      USE (lcTable) ;
          ALIAS ("RI_"+LTRIM(STR(lnNewArea))) ;
          AGAIN SHARE
    ELSE
      USE (lcTable) ;
          ORDER (lcTag) ;
          ALIAS ("RI_"+LTRIM(STR(lnNewArea))) ;
          AGAIN SHARE
    ENDIF
    cCursors = cCursors + UPPER(lcTable) + "?" + ;
               STR(lnNewArea,5)
  ELSE
  * Retrieve work area of referential integrity cursor
    nNewArea = VAL(SUBSTR(cCursors, ;
               nInUseArea + LEN(lcTable) + 1, 5))
    cCursors = STRTRAN(cCursors, ;
               UPPER(lcTable) + "*" + STR(nNewArea,5), ;
               UPPER(lcTable) + "?" + STR(nNewArea,5))
  ENDIF

RETURN (lnNewArea)
```

Part
I
Ch
4

This routine begins by checking variable cCursors to see whether the table has already been opened for use by the referential-integrity routines. Variable cCursors has the following structure:

- Table name
- Character to identify whether the table is in use for another trigger
- Work-area number where table is open

Actually, cCursors is a string that repeats the preceding structure for each open table. If the table is already open, all that the routine needs to do is retrieve the work area that it is in and change the in-use character flag from * to ?. Then, RIOPEN( ) returns the work-area number. This tracking is required to keep track of which tables are open and can have their record pointer moved. Remember that you cannot move the record pointer of tables that are directly involved in the current trigger.

If the table is not open, RIOPEN( ) selects the next available work area with SELECT 0 and opens the table with the AGAIN and SHARE clauses. The AGAIN clause creates a cursor, which allows you to open the table multiple times. The table could already be open, but referential integrity requires a separate copy, with its own tag and record pointer. Systems developed for use on a network require the SHARE clause so that multiple users can have the same file open at the same time.

▶ **See** "Network Data Sharing," **p. 681**

The last thing that RIOPEN( ) does is update variable cCursors with the following information:

- The name of the table
- The ? character, indicating that the file is in active use
- The work-area number

The other routine used by SALEDEL( ) is RIDELETE( ), which performs the actual deletion of records referenced by triggers. In this case, SALEDEL( has already changed the default work area to DETAILS.DBF and points to a record to delete. However, RIDELETE( ) cannot simply delete the record—it first checks to see whether it can get a record lock. If not, REDELETE( ) begins a rollback process by returning a false value in llReturnValue. This value eventually works its way back up to the trigger, which cancels the deletion of the parent record and any child records deleted for this parent since the trigger began.

Listing 4.7 shows the code for RIDELETE( ).

**Listing 4.7   04PRG07.PRG—The *RIDELETE* Code**

```
*****************
FUNCTION RIDELETE
* Delete the current record in the current area
LOCAL llReturnValue

llReturnValue = .T.
* Attempt to get a record lock
  IF (UPPER(SYS(2011))='RECORD LOCKED' and !DELETED()) OR !RLOCK()
    llReturnValue = .F.
  ELSE
  * If not deleted, delete it.
    IF !DELETED()
      DELETE
      nError = 0
      UNLOCK RECORD (RECNO())
      IF nError <> 0
        = TABLEREVERT()
        UNLOCK RECORD (RECNO())
        llReturnValue = .F.
      ENDIF
    ENDIF
  ENDIF
RETURN llReturnValue
```

When it obtains a record lock, RIDELETE( ) checks to see whether the record has already been deleted. (It hardly makes sense to delete it twice.) The function then deletes the current record in the current table. If an error occurs, it executes a function called

TABLEREVERT( ), which cancels the delete. RIDELETE( ) passes the llReturnValue back to the trigger to cancel any related deletions.

If everything deletes successfully, llReturnValue passes a value of true back to the trigger, and the event ends. Although the trigger on the SALES file can perform other actions, it is the programmer's responsibility to determine appropriate actions in each situation.

After a procedure is performed by means of a cursor, the procedure can close it. On the other hand, leaving it open until the end of the transaction allows other functions in the program to reuse it. The special character (?) after the table name in variable cCursors indicates that the cursor is currently in use. If so, subsequent functions cannot reuse the cursor, because another routine may need the current record-pointer position. (Remember that you cannot move the record-pointer position of a table that is currently involved in a trigger or validation.) When you are done with the cursor, change this character to a different character (*) in variable cCursors to tell the program that it can reuse the cursor. That is the purpose of RIREUSE( ); it changes the special character from a question mark (?) to an asterisk(*) to indicate that the cursor can be reused. The following listing illustrates the code to perform this action.

Part
I
Ch
4

**Listing 4.8   04PRG08.PRG—Referential Integrity Code Generated by the RI Builder Called at the End of Every Trigger**

```
* * * * * * * * * * * * * * * *
FUNCTION RIREUSE
* This routine allows reuse of exiting cursor
LPARAMETERS lcTable, lcArea
  cCursors = STRTRAN(cCursors, ;
             UPPER(lcTable) + "?" + STR(lcArea,5), ;
             UPPER(lcTable) + "*" + STR(lcArea,5))
RETURN .T.
```

**Triggers Performing No Action**   The insert trigger for SALES calls the SALEINS( ) function, which simply returns a value of true as shown in the following code. When you are adding a new sales order, there is no reason to check DETAILS.

```
* * * * * * * * * * * * * * * *
FUNCTION SALEINS
* No referential action required when adding a parent
RETURN .T.
```

N O T E   Actually, there may be a reason for adding code to the insert trigger of SALES. Visual FoxPro executes this trigger not only when you add a new record to the table, but also when you recall a deleted one. When a sales order is recalled, you may want to recall its details automatically. ■

**Performing a Cascade Modify**   The last trigger in SALES.DBF occurs when you change any field value in a record. This routine begins by initializing the return variable to true; then it checks to see whether it is in the first trigger level. This means that you are modifying a SALES record directly, not as a result of deleting DETAIL records for the same order ID.

Next, the routine stores the current order ID in a local variable, along with the "pre-change" order ID. When a transaction begins, think of Visual FoxPro as storing the changes to the current record in a buffer. You can access the changed values of any field by using the variable name directly. However, to access the original values of any field, you need to use the OLDVAL( ) function.

The SALEMOD( ) function retrieves both values to determine whether the relational fields (cOrderId, in this case) have changed. If they have not changed, the function exits with a return value of true. Otherwise, this function locates the matching records in DETAILS.DBF and updates the old key values to the new one. This portion of the routine is similar to SALEDEL( ), with the exception that it uses a REPLACE statement instead of a call to RIDELETE( ).

Listing 4.9 shows the code for SALEMOD( ).

> **Listing 4.9   04PRG09.PRG—Referential Integrity Called on a Modify to Modify All Related Records Automatically**

```
****************
FUNCTION SALEMOD
* If modifying a sales record, modify all details
LOCAL  llReturnValue, lcOrderId, lcOldValue, lnDetArea

  llReturnValue = .T.
  IF nLevel = 1
    lcOrderId    = cOrderId
    lcOldValue   = OLDVAL('cOrderId')

  * If key value changed, updated the child records
    IF lcOrderID <> lcOldValue
      lnDetArea = RIOPEN('DETAILS')
      SELECT (lnDetArea)
      SCAN FOR cOrderId = lcOldValue
        REPLACE cOrderId WITH lcOrderId
      ENDSCAN
      SELECT sales
    ENDIF
  ENDIF
RETURN llReturnValue
```

Another way to see whether the foreign key has changed uses the GETFLDSTATE() function. However, the function still needs OLDVAL() to find and replace the key value in the child records.

**Using Triggers for the Child Table**   DETAILS.DBF also has three triggers. Each trigger calls a single routine called RIDETAILS(), with a single-character parameter to identify the trigger. The code of RIDETAILS(), which appears in Listing 4.10, shows that except for the function calls in the case statement, it mirrors RISALES().

**Listing 4.10   04PRG10.PRG—Referential Integrity Code Generated by the RI Builder Called on a Modification to Update All Related Records**

```
********************
FUNCTION RIDETAILS
* This routine is called by the triggers in DETAILS.DBF
LPARAMETERS lcAction
LOCAL llReturnValue, Dummy

* Start Transaction
  Dummy         = IIF(TYPE("nLevel")<>"N" OR nLevel=0, ;
                  RISTART(), "")
  nLevel        = nLevel + 1
  llReturnValue = .F.

* Perform action
  DO CASE
    CASE TYPE('lcAction') # 'C' ;
         OR !UPPER(lcAction) $ 'DIU' ;
         OR LEN(lcAction)>1
      ERROR 'Invalid action code passed to RIDETAILS'
    CASE UPPER(lcAction) == 'D'
      llReturnValue = DETAILDEL()
    CASE UPPER(lcAction) == 'I'
      llReturnValue = DETAILINS()
    CASE UPPER(lcAction) == 'U'
      llReturnValue = DETAILMOD()
  ENDCASE

* End transaction
  nLevel = nLevel - 1
  Dummy  = IIF(nLevel = 0, RIEND(llReturnValue), 0)
RETURN llReturnValue
```

Part

**I**

Ch

**4**

**Using a Trigger to Delete Parent When Last Child Is Deleted**   When a user deletes an order detail record, you may want to know whether he deleted one of many detail records for the order, or the last one. In this case, you should delete the parent record if you delete the last or only child record. However, not every application should delete the parent record. Just because you delete all the employee's projects, for example, does not mean that you delete the employee as well. So the developer must take an active role in determining the expected functionality of each trigger. The code shown in Listing 4.11 implements a trigger that deletes the parent record when the last child is deleted.

### Listing 4.11  04PRG.11PRG—Code that Deletes the Parent Record When the Last Child Is Deleted

```
******************
FUNCTION DETAILDEL
* Check if all order details are deleted, then delete parent
LOCAL cnt, lcOrderId, lnCurrentArea, ;
      lnSalesArea, lnDetArea, llReturnValue

   llReturnValue    = .T.
   lcOrderId        = cOrderId
   lnCurrentArea    = SELECT()

   IF !EMPTY(lcOrderId)
     lnDetArea       = RIOPEN('DETAILS')
     cnt             = 0
     SELECT (lnDetArea)
     SCAN FOR cOrderId = lcOrderId AND !DELETED()
       cnt           = cnt + 1
     ENDSCAN

     IF cnt = 1 AND nLevel =1
       lnSaleArea   = RIOPEN('SALES', 'ORDERID')
       IF SEEK(lcOrderId)
         llReturnValue = RIDELETE()
       ENDIF
       = RIREUSE('SALES', lnSaleArea)
     ENDIF
     SELECT (lnCurrentArea)
   ENDIF
 RETURN llReturnValue
```

This routine first checks to see whether the OrderId exists before proceeding, so the user can delete a blank record without going through the rest of the validation. Then, the routine opens a second occurrence of DETAILS and counts the number of active records that have the same OrderId. If this number is greater than 1, and if the trigger sequence began by deleting details, it looks for and deletes the parent record.

Why check for a count greater than 1 if the conditional string contains the function NOT DELETED()? During a transaction, the record is not recognized as deleted until you commit the transaction.

The reason why you have to check the level is that SALEDEL() can also call DETAILDEL(). When SALEDEL() initiates a DETAIL record delete, the function does not have to go back to SALEDEL() a second time, which could potentially lead to an endless loop. But when the trigger initiates the detail delete, you do want to check SALEDEL() when you delete the last child.

**Using an Insert Trigger that Checks for a Parent Record** The second trigger for file DETAILS occurs when you add a record or recall a deleted one. Remember that the Visual FoxPro triggers the insert trigger when you add a new record, not after you fill in its fields. Therefore, FoxPro triggers for a new, but blank, record. Because you do not want to check for a blank foreign key in SALES.DBF, the DETAILINS() function tests for an empty OrderId. When that field is empty, the function simply skips the check.

On the other hand, a recalled record should have a corresponding parent. Therefore, when OrderId exists, the following routine uses it to search a copy of SALES.DBF. If the routine finds a matching order record, it completes the record recall; otherwise, the record remains deleted. When this happens, a message box appears, telling the user that there is No corresponding order for this detail.

**Listing 4.12  04PRG12.PRG—Referential Integrity Can Insert a Detail Record on the Insert of a Parent Record Automatically**

```
******************
FUNCTION DETAILINS
* Insert a detail record only if a sales record exists
LOCAL lcOrderId, lnSaleArea, llReturnValue, lnCurrentArea

  llReturnValue =  .T.
  lcOrderId     = cOrderId
  lnCurrentArea = SELECT()

  IF !EMPTY(lcOrderId)
    lnSaleArea    = RIOPEN('SALES', 'ORDERID')
    llReturnValue = SEEK(lcOrderId, lnSaleArea) AND ;
                    !DELETED(lnSaleArea)
    = RIREUSE('SALES', lnSaleArea)
    IF !llReturnValue
      = MESSAGEBOX('No corresponding order for this detail')
    ENDIF
    SELECT (lnCurrentArea)
  ENDIF
RETURN llReturnValue
```

Part
I

Ch
4

If triggers cannot guarantee that a new detail record has a corresponding sales record, how can you guarantee it? One method uses the VALID clause on the field cOrderId field, and it performs a SEEK against cOrderId in SALES. Barring that, consider checking for a SALES record in the update trigger of DETAILS. After all, filling in a blank field is still an update.

The following section examines the final trigger for DETAILS: the update trigger.

**Using a Modify Trigger that Also Checks for a Parent Record** The update trigger, named DETAILMOD( ), makes sure that cOrderId in DETAILS matches cOrderId in SALES. The trigger also checks to see whether any other detail records exist with the old cOrderId value. If not, it deletes the parent record that has the old ID.

Of course, there are other ways to handle an order ID modification. The first way is to change all records with matching order IDS in DETAILS to the new value. Also, you can change the order ID in the parent record. If a corresponding parent record does not exist for the new order ID, find the SALES record with the preceding order ID, and change it first. Then change all corresponding records in DETAILS to match the new order ID.

The code in Listing 4.13 shows the DETAILMOD() function.

> **Listing 4.13 04PRG13.PRG—Referential Integrity Can Check for a Matching Parent Key Value on the Modification of a Child Key Value and Delete the Child if the Child's Key Value Has No Match to a Parent**

```
******************
FUNCTION DETAILMOD
* Allow key value change if it matches another parent
* If no more child records for this parent, delete it
LOCAL cnt, lcOrderId, lcOldValue, ;
      lnSalesArea, llReturnValue, lnDetArea

  llReturnValue   = .T.

  IF nLevel=1
    lcOrderId      = cOrderId
    lcOldValue     = OLDVAL('cOrderId')

  * First check if new value is a valid parent key
    lnSaleArea     = RIOPEN('SALES', 'ORDERID')
    llReturnValue  = SEEK(lcOrderId, lnSaleArea) AND ;
                     !DELETED(lnSaleArea)
    IF !llReturnValue
      = MESSAGEBOX('No corresponding order for this detail')
    ENDIF

  * New order id is valid, check for other child records in old order
    IF llReturnValue
      cnt            = 0
      lnDetArea      = RIOPEN('DETAILS')
      SELECT (lnDetArea)
      SCAN FOR OLDVAL('cOrderId') = lcOldValue AND !DELETED()
        cnt = cnt + 1
      ENDSCAN
      = RIREUSE('DETAILS', lnDetArea)
```

```
        * If no other child records, delete the parent
          IF cnt = 1
            SELECT (lnSaleArea)
            IF SEEK(lcOldValue)
              llReturnValue = RIDELETE()
            ENDIF
          ENDIF
        ENDIF
        SELECT DETAILS
      ENDIF
      = RIREUSE('SALES', lnSaleArea)
   RETURN llReturnValue
```

Again, this routine first checks to see whether DETAILS.cOrderId exists in the parent file, SALES.DBF. If not, the routine displays a message and exits with a return value of false. However, if the order ID does exist, the routine first counts the number of active DETAIL records with the old order ID. If no others exist, the routine opens SALES.DBF and deletes the parent record.

**Using a Cleanup Routine**     Only one routine remains. When Visual FoxPro completes any of these six triggers, it returns to either RISALES() or RIDETAILS(). FoxPro then executes the RIEND() routine, which takes the return value from the trigger and determines whether to commit the transaction or roll it back. To commit the transaction, FoxPro executes END TRANSACTION.

You have a choice, however. You can use ROLLBACK, which discards every change made since the transaction began in the RISTART() function. Alternatively, you can roll back incrementally, using TABLEREVERT(). This command rolls back individual (or all) records in one table at a time. Listing 4.14 shows this code.

**Listing 4.14   04PRG14.PRG—Referential Integrity Can Call a Routine to Perform the Appropriate Action After a Check**

```
**************
FUNCTION RIEND
* Call this routine to exit the referential integrity check
* It saves changes or reverts to original values depending
* on the value passed to it.
LPARAMETER llSuccess
LOCAL lnXx

* Complete transaction or roll it back
  IF !llSuccess
    IF USED('SALES')
      = TABLEREVERT(.T., 'SALES')
    ENDIF
    IF USED('DETAILS')
      = TABLEREVERT(.T., 'DETAILS')
```

*continues*

**Listing 4.14   Continued**

```
    ENDIF
  ENDIF
  END TRANSACTION
* or use this code:
*   IF llSuccess
*     END TRANSACTION
*   ELSE
*     ROLLBACK
*   ENDIF

* Reset on error
  IF EMPTY(cOldError)
    ON ERROR
  ELSE
    ON ERROR (cOldError)
  ENDIF

* Remove cursors and reset variables that track them
  FOR lnXx = 1 TO OCCURS("?", cCursors)
    cFound = ATC('?', cCursors, lnXx) + 1
    USE IN (VAL(SUBSTR(cCursors, cFound, 5)))
  ENDFOR
  FOR lnXx = 1 TO OCCURS("*", cCursors)
    cFound = ATC('*', cCursors, lnXx) + 1
    USE IN (VAL(SUBSTR(cCursors, cFound, 5)))
  ENDFOR
  STORE "" TO cCursors
RETURN .T.
```

This routine reads cCursors to remove the cursors created by referential integrity, so that functions can move the record pointer.

In the past, you could easily have programmed these functions into forms. But you could not have done anything about users who directly edited the tables, using browse windows or other commands directly from the Command window. Now, by adding triggers to critical tables, you can protect referential integrity even from users who prefer to edit files directly rather than to use forms.

As you can see from these routines, writing your own referential-integrity rules is certainly possible—and even necessary, if you want to handle changes differently from the VFP defaults. If you can accept the rules defined by VFP's own Referential Integrity Builder, however, your task will be much easier and more error-proof.

# From Here...

This chapter covered a great many structural issues in designing tables and databases. Equally important are the issues of defining indexes and basic table properties.

To learn more about how Visual FoxPro builds and maintains tables, databases, and indexes, refer to the following chapters:

- Chapter 3, "Defining Databases, Tables, and Indexes," covers the basics required to build tables, add them to databases, and implement indexes for both sorting and Rushmore optimization.
- Chapter 10, "Programming Structures," discusses how to go from data requirements to table design.
- Chapter 18, "Data Dictionary Issues," discusses how to design a data dictionary to handle verification and possible re-creation of table definitions.

Part
I

Ch
4

# Using Wizards for Rapid Application Development

*by Michael Antonovich*

**W**izards do not totally replace programming. However, the framework that they create for forms, reports, and other components can save you countless hours when you are developing an application. Wizards also allow you to build working prototypes quickly. Use wizards to prototype applications to help identify program structure and logic problems before you spend time on extensive coding. ∎

**Using wizards to prototype and cut development time**

A wizard does not replace the need for hand-coding, but it could get most of your components off to a good start. The first part of this chapter explains where to find the wizards, how to open them, save their results, and then use those results in the more powerful designers to complete your design.

**Using wizards to help with every application component**

The balance of the chapter covers the features of each wizard to discover its strengths and reveal its weaknesses.

# Introducing the Wizards

The wizards provided with Visual FoxPro include:

- Crosstab Wizard
- Documenting Wizard*
- Form Wizard
- Graph Wizard
- Group/Total Report Wizard
- Import Wizard
- Label Wizard
- Local View Wizard
- Mail Merge Wizard

- One-To-Many Form Wizard
- One-To-Many Report Wizard
- Pivot Table Wizard
- Query Wizard
- Report Wizard
- Remote View Wizard
- Setup Wizard*
- Table Wizard
- Upsizing Wizard*

*\* Indicates wizards that are included only with the Professional version*

This chapter examines most of these wizards in detail. Several wizards, however (including the Setup and Upsizing Wizards), are covered in detail in later chapters.

▶ **See** "Building Visual FoxPro .APPs and .EXEs," **p. 593**

▶ **See** "Upsizing to SQL Server or Oracle" in Bonus Chapter 07 located on the CD

## Opening a Wizard

Visual FoxPro provides several ways to open a wizard. The first is to choose Tools, Wizards from the system menu. This command opens a submenu that lists the available wizards. This list groups the wizards into 11 basic types, plus All. Selecting a group type may directly execute a wizard or display a list of related wizards within that group. Select All, for example, to display a dialog box that displays all the wizards in a list box. Figure 5.1 shows a composite image of the Wizards menu and the Wizard Selection dialog box.

 The second way to open a wizard is to choose File, New from the main menu. This command opens the New dialog box, which you used previously to open databases and tables (see Figure 5.2). The dialog box also includes most other application components. If the component has a wizard available to help create it, Visual FoxPro activates the Wizard button. Click this button to start the wizard.

**FIGURE 5.1**
You can access 11 types of wizards by choosing Tools, Wizards.

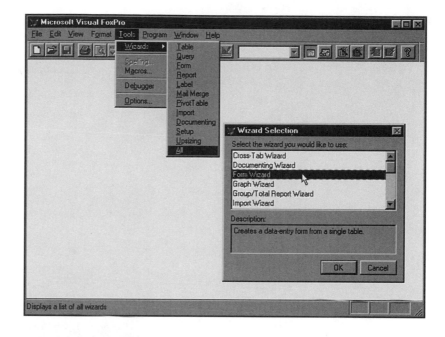

**FIGURE 5.2**
Use File, New to create a new file. If a wizard exists for the selected file type, the Wizard button is enabled.

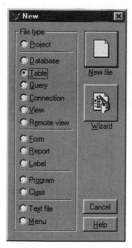

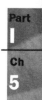

Part

I

Ch

5

A third way to create a new file with a wizard is to use the Project Manager. When you select a file type and click New, VFP gives you the option of using a wizard or the designer with a blank/empty object (see Figure 5.3).

**FIGURE 5.3**
Wizards are also
available when you
click the New button
in the Project
Manager.

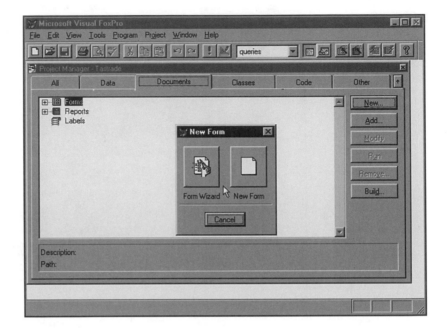

## Designing with Wizards

Don't hesitate to begin designing any object with a wizard. Although wizards are not perfect in that they do not include every possible feature for the objects that they create, they
do help create a solid foundation. In fact, one way to practice rapid prototyping is to design
all objects with the wizards. Then, after the overall design is complete, you can return to
the specific object designer to further customize your work.

## Saving Wizard Designs

Most wizards allow you to save your design when you complete it. In fact, you can save
the design at any point; simply jump to the last step and select one of the save options.
Wizards do not force you to complete all the steps before saving the design. Of course,
partially designed objects may not be functional. Also, a few wizards—such as the Import,
Documenting, and Setup Wizards—execute their respective tasks immediately after you
define their options.

**TIP**   If you started a wizard directly from the menu, remember to add the completed object to the
appropriate project file so that you can easily find and access it later.

Wizards that create and save a file usually give you three options when you save your results:

- Save the object and return to the Command window.
- Save the object and run it.
- Save the object and immediately open the appropriate designer to customize the object further.

## Modifying Results from Wizards

After you create an object with a wizard, you cannot return to the wizard and modify the object's design. Some wizards, such as the Form and Report Wizards, allow you to preview the results of your design. In these cases, you can return to the appropriate wizard step to modify the design and preview the new results without leaving the wizard. After you leave a wizard, you must use the designers to modify the object design further. Working with designers is the topic of many chapters throughout this book.

# Looking at the Wizards

Wizards provide a significant tool for developers who are practicing the concept of rapid application development or prototyping. Therefore, the following sections take a detailed look at the most common wizards. Because of the number of wizards, and because many wizards employ similar steps, the chapter usually covers only the first instance of similar steps. Subsequent wizards may refer you to previous wizard descriptions and figures.

Part

I

Ch

5

## The Table Wizard

The first step in project implementation usually involves creating the necessary tables. The Table Wizard helps you create new tables. You might ask, "How can a wizard make creating a table easier?" Well, it starts with more than 40 sample tables, each with recommended fields, type declarations, and sizes.

Suppose that you want to create a table containing information about your employees. Opening the Table Wizard displays a dialog box like the one shown in Figure 5.4.

The first field at the top of the wizard dialog box is a drop-down list containing the steps required to complete a table. If you open this list, you see the steps that the Table Wizard requires. Some steps may be dimmed, which means that you cannot directly select those steps yet. Often, steps are disabled until you supply other information that the step requires. For steps that are enabled, you can simply click the step to jump immediately to it.

**FIGURE 5.4**

Use the first page of the Table Wizard to select appropriate fields from the sample table Employees.

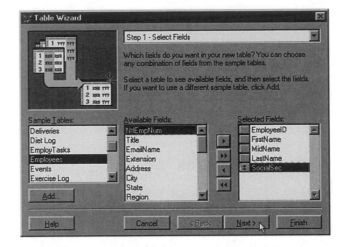

As you might expect, the first step in creating the table is to select fields for it. VFP provides more than 40 predefined tables, each of which contains typical fields used in that type of table. You can also use the _A_dd button to reference fields in one of your own tables. Find a table type that is similar to the one you need. In this case, scroll down until you see Employees.

As you select different table types, the list of available fields in the middle list box changes. These fields represent "typical" fields that are appropriate to the table type selected. If you want to create a table that contains all of these fields, click the double-right-arrow button. In any given situation, you may not need all of the fields, so you can select them individually by highlighting them and clicking the right-arrow button. You also can remove selected fields individually or in total by clicking the other arrow buttons. Also, double-clicking a field name moves the field from one list to the other.

You can select fields from more than one table. Select the first table and move the desired field from the available to the selected list; then select the second table and select more fields.

**T I P** If you need all but a few fields from a table, select them all and then remove the ones that you do not want from the selected list.

**N O T E** The wizard provides no obvious option for adding new fields that are not in the predefined table lists or in your own files. One way to trick the wizard is to add an extra field that you really don't want. Then, in the next step, change the field definition to match what you really need. ■

After you select all the fields that you need, click the <u>N</u>ext button at the bottom of the dialog box. This button takes you to the next step.

### Navigating Through the Wizards

There are four navigation buttons at the bottom of each wizard page:

- Cancel
- <u>B</u>ack
- <u>N</u>ext
- <u>F</u>inish

The first button allows you to cancel the wizard. The second and third buttons move backward and forward through the wizard one step at a time. Thus, you can always return to a previous step to change an option. The <u>F</u>inish button tells the wizard that you are finished and moves to the last step. Having a <u>F</u>inish button available in the first screen may seem strange, but you can stop the wizard and define the table or other object with only the information that you have entered so far. Also, because you can return to any step—especially in wizards that provide a <u>P</u>review button—you can jump back to the last step to exit the wizard when you preview your progress. In addition, each step now has a Help button to give you more information about the objects in any step.

In the second step, you define the properties of each field, including the field name, type, width, and decimals, and whether or not to allow nulls. If you concurrently have a database open, the wizard also allows you to edit the caption. (This feature is a database feature, not a table feature.) Figure 5.5 shows the field-settings screen.

**FIGURE 5.5**

The second page of the Table Wizard allows you to customize the field attributes, including attributes stored in databases.

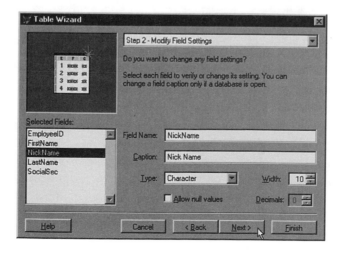

**N O T E**   If no database is open, the Table Wizard limits field names to 10 characters, because
it generates a free table definition, not a bound table. If a database is open, the wizard
automatically assumes that you want to bind the new table into the open database and allows
you to create long field names. The wizard also allows you to define captions and whether or not
to allow nulls. ■

**CAUTION**

If you do not want to bind a new table into an open database automatically, close all databases
before starting the Table Wizard. If you want a bound table, make sure that if multiple databases are
open, the current database is the one into which you want to bind the table.

The next step in this wizard allows you to define indexes. If a database is open, you can
specify a primary index. Simply click the arrow to the right of the Primary Key field to
display a drop-down list of fields. Select one of the fields as a primary key. The wizard
cannot create a multiple-field primary key.

If no database is open, the wizard does not allow you to create an index; you have to create
independent indexes through the Table Designer or through code. With an open database, the wizard generates a separate tag for each individual field checked. Therefore, if
you were to check the Employee ID and Social Security fields, the wizard would create
two index tags—one for each field. The wizard can create only single field indexes. To
create a compound field index, you need to modify the table with the Table Designer.
Figure 5.6 shows the index-definition step.

**FIGURE 5.6**

After defining indexes,
if a database is open,
you can select one to
use as the primary key
for the table.

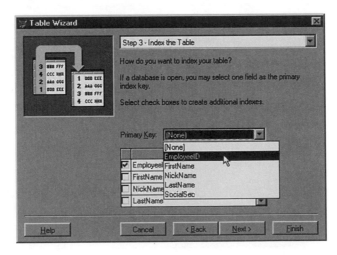

▶ **See** "Defining Normal and Unique Indexes," **p. 151**

▶ **See** "Indexing on Complex Expressions," **p. 153**

The final step in the Table Wizard defines what to do after saving the table. This step offers three choices:

- Save the table for later use.

- Save the table and browse it.

- Save the table and modify it in the Table Designer.

Figure 5.7 shows these choices.

**FIGURE 5.7**

To complete the Table Wizard, you must save the table.

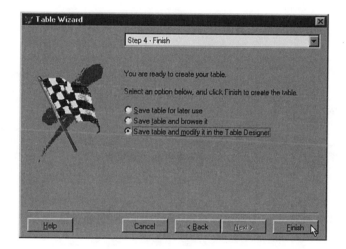

The first two save options are quite clear. But why would you want to go into the Table Designer immediately after creating a table with the wizard?

For a free table, the main reason would be to add more fields that were not part of the sample table definitions (assuming that you did not take advantage of the earlier note on adding "extra" fields). Also, you may want to define multiple-field index tags.

For a table bound into a database, the reasons for going directly into the Table Designer are more varied. The Table Wizard includes only a few features from the available database features: the field caption, the option to allow nulls, and the capability to set a primary key. As you know from Chapter 4, however, a bound table can also have field and table validations, defaults, error messages, and triggers.

Thus, if you need to further customize the table, select the last option to open the Table Designer. Remember that wizards provide a quick but functional design, not a complete design.

Part

I

Ch

5

# The Query Wizard Family

Another way to prepare data for a form or report uses a query to extract selected fields and records from one or more separate tables. Visual FoxPro actually provides several query types, depending on whether you intend to just view data or update it as well. You also can define queries on local as well as remote data. Special variations on standard queries are the crosstab and pivot table queries.

**The Basic Query Wizard**   The basic Query Wizard begins with a screen that is common to many of the wizards. Figure 5.8 shows the field-selection page of the Query Wizard dialog box.

**FIGURE 5.8**

For any query, the first step must be the selection of fields from one or more tables.

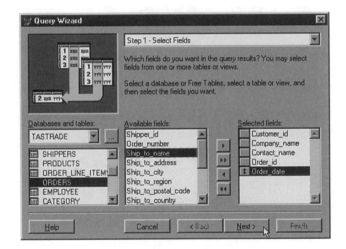

As you might expect, the first step in creating a query is to select the database, table, and fields. The wizard lists these steps in the area immediately below the field-selection drop-down list.

The first option below the label Databases and Tables displays the current database, if one is open; otherwise, it displays the words Free Tables. If a database is open, the names of the tables it contains appear in the scrollable list immediately beneath this field.

If more than one database is open, you can change to nother by opening the drop-down list and selecting the one you want. You can select fields from tables contained in multiple databases.

If the database is not open, or if you want to use a free table, click the ellipsis button (...). This button opens a dialog box that allows you to select any table or database on the system. This dialog box displays both free and bound tables because they share the extension .DB5. If the table that you select is bound to another database, you can still select it from the dialog box. The back link stored in bound tables identifies and opens the appropriate database. When the database is open, the wizard displays the names of other tables that are bound to it.

If you select a free table, that table name appears alone in the table list. While you are in the Open dialog box, you could also change the List Files of Type setting to Database to select the database first.

Back in the wizard, the list box to the immediate right of the table list displays fields from the selected table. If you select a database, moving through the table list automatically updates the field list. Notice that the fields appear in their natural table order.

For any query, you determine which fields from a table you want to use. You can use just one field or all of them. However, until you move one or more fields from the Available Fields list to the Selected Fields list, the query has no fields.

VFP provides several ways to move fields between these two lists.

The first method uses the buttons located between the two lists. The arrow directions indicate the move direction. A single-arrow button moves a single field; a double-arrow button moves all fields. To move a field from the available list, first choose it by clicking it or using the arrow keys to highlight it; then click the button that has the single right arrow. This button moves the highlighted field to the Selected Fields list. To select all the fields, click the double-right-arrow button. This method works even if you have already selected some of the fields; it will not duplicate fields, because as a field is selected, it is removed from the Available Fields list.

If you select the wrong field or change your mind, you can highlight it in the Selected Fields list and then click the left-arrow button. You can even start over by clicking the double-left-arrow button to deselect all fields.

Because a query can extract data from more than one table, you can return to the first column and select a different table. When the table is selected, you can select additional fields to include in the query. Keep in mind that for each additional table used in a query, you must eventually define a relation between it and at least one other selected table in the query. Failure to relate tables together causes the query to form a Cartesian product of the table's records—in other words, the query matches each record from one table with each record from the other table. Thus, two tables with 100 records each would create a result set of 10,000 records. This result probably is not what you want.

Figure 5.8 shows the fields selected from the table CUSTOMER in the TASTRADE database. If you specify fields from more than one table, the wizard can proceed to the next step. In fact, the next two steps, which define the relationships, have meaning only if the query includes fields from more than a single table. With fields from a single table, the wizard proceeds immediately to Step 4.

**N O T E**   The fields used in this query example are CUSTOMER.Customer_Id,
CUSTOMER.Company_Name, CUSTOMER.Contact_Name, ORDERS.Order_Id, and
ORDERS.Order_Date. ■

In Step 2 (see Figure 5.9), you must define relations among the tables from which you
selected fields. Fortunately, the wizard is smart enough not to allow you to advance to the
next step until you define relations among the tables. The wizard disables the Next button
until you do this.

**FIGURE 5.9**
To relate the CUS-
TOMER file to the
ORDER file, the most
appropriate field is
Customer_Id.

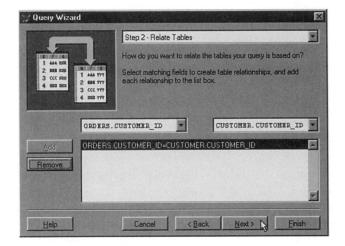

In addition to defining the field (or fields) from each table that defines the relation between two tables, you must specify the type of join. In earlier versions of Visual FoxPro,
the wizard did not provide this option; it automatically assumed that you wanted only
records from each table that had matching field values. As described in the later query
chapters, this type of join is called an inner join.

▶ **See** "Creating Inner Joins," **p. 357**

In this step, you can specify left outer joins (all records from the parent table and only
matching records from the child table), right outer joins (all records from the child table
and only matching records from the parent table), and full outer joins (all records from
both tables). A full outer join is not the same as a Cartesian product; rather, it includes all
matching records from the parent table without matches in the child table and records
from the child table without matches from the parent table. Figure 5.10 shows a join being
created.

**FIGURE 5.10**

Define the type of join for each relation in the query, or accept the default, an inner join.

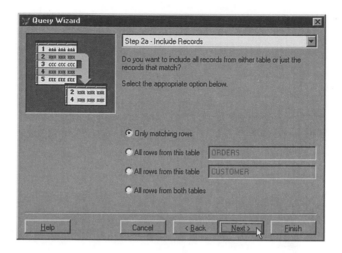

The third query step defines filters, which limit the records included in the query by creating selection criteria for records in the source tables. The fields used for this selection do not have be included in the query's selected fields. You might want all customers from the state of California, for example. The following filter condition selects customers from California, even though you do not include the field REGION in the query's selected fields:

```
CUSTOMER.REGION = 'CA'
```

## Filter Operators

Filtering supports nine operators:

- Equals
- Not Equals
- More Than
- Less Than
- Is Blank
- Is Null
- Contains
- In
- Between

Quotes around strings are optional. However, case is important if the operator is not Contains, which performs a case-insensitive test. Is Blank requires no operator. To use the operator In,

*continues*

Part
I
Ch
5

*continued*

separate the values in the list with commas, but do not add extra blanks. To get customers from California, Oregon, and Washington, for example, use the following:

    CA,OR,WA

Similarly, for Between, include the first and last values, separated by a comma, with no space.

If you define a second filter criteria, as shown in Figure 5.11, you must join it to the preceding one with an <u>A</u>nd or <u>O</u>r connector. The wizard, however, limits you to two filter conditions. In reality, you may need more. In such a situation, you want to save the query and immediately modify it in the Query Designer to add more filter conditions.

**FIGURE 5.11**
The Query Wizard limits you to two filters, but you can define more filters in the Query Designer.

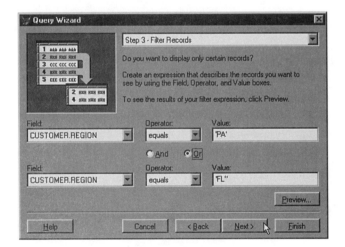

The fourth step allows you to create a sort order for the query result set. You can select any of the available fields. However, the order in which you select these fields determines their sort priority. You can change the sort priority by moving the relative positions of the selected fields, using the mover buttons to the left of the field names. Just click a mover button and drag it up or down to a new position. Furthermore, you can sort the data in either ascending or descending order. The sort direction applies to all fields that are used to sort, not just the current field. Figure 5.12 shows the sort-order step.

You can further limit the records returned by the query in the next step, which allows you to define either a fixed number of records or a percentage of records to be included in the query. By default, the query returns all records that match the relations and filters. Suppose that you wanted to see only the first five records. Perhaps the query returns a list of your customers, sorted from the customer with the largest order to the smallest. In that case, the query limit shown in Figure 5.13 displays your five largest-order customers.

**FIGURE 5.12**
When defining a sort order, you can use only selected fields from the query.

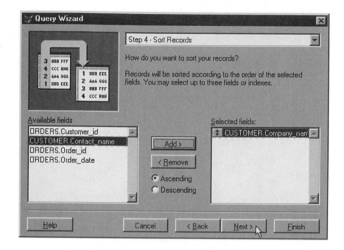

**FIGURE 5.13**
You can limit the records returned by the query, either by number of records or by percentage.

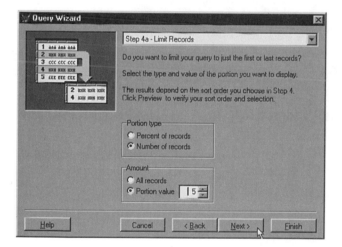

Part
I

Ch
5

Figure 5.14 shows the last wizard step, which saves the query. As in all wizards, you can save and exit, save and run, or save and modify the query. You also have a Preview button, which allows you to run the query while you are still in the wizard and view the results. If you do not get the expected records, you can use the Back button to return to any earlier step and change the query definition. You can move between the preview and any wizard step as often as you like. After you save the query, however, you can modify it further only by using the Query Designer.

**N O T E** The Preview button is present in earlier steps. Therefore, you can try different options, such as filters, and use Preview to check the results. ∎

**FIGURE 5.14**

Before you save the query, click Preview to ensure that the query returns the expected records.

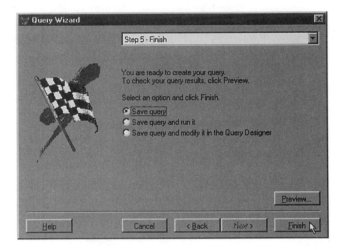

The query created from the selections, shown in the figures in this section, is on the disk that comes with this book as 05QRY01.QPR.

**The Local View Wizard**    The Local View Wizard performs the same steps as a query, but it saves the results in a view definition in a database rather than as a separate query file. Also, views are potentially updatable.

The first step requires you to select the tables and fields that you want to appear in the view. This dialog box is the same as the one shown in Figure 5.8. You can select fields from more than one table. If you do, you must define the relations between the tables in Step 2 (refer to Figure 5.9). You can also define the join type, as shown in Figure 5.10.

In the third step, you can filter the records. The filter clause is applied to all the records in the original table; therefore, it corresponds to the WHERE clause in an SQL SELECT statement. Figure 5.11 shows a similar dialog box used by the Query Wizard.

Next, you can define a sort order for the records. This sort order applies to all the records included in the query. The wizard limits you to a maximum three sort fields. This dialog box uses the same layout as the simple query in Figure 5.12.

Finally, you can save the resulting view, using a dialog box like the one in Figure 5.14. When you click the Finish button, the wizard prompts you for a view name. Remember that VFP stores views in a database. You also can modify the view directly by opening the View Designer. One reason to open the View Designer is that the wizard creates a static view; you cannot use it to update the data in the view. To create an updatable view, you must manually change the update criteria in the View Designer.

▶ **See** "Using Views and Updatable Queries," **p. 368**

**The Remote View Wizard**   You need to use a remote view to use any other data source other than a Visual FoxPro 3.0 or 4.0 database and free tables from earlier versions of FoxPro. The standard way to access a remote file is through ODBC drivers, which allow you to read data from any data source that supports an ODBC driver. These drivers may be loaded automatically by the application when it is installed. If the application does not include the drivers, you may need to contact the manufacturer to get them.

Microsoft provides several ODBC drivers (in both 16-bit and 32-bit versions) for FoxPro, Access, Paradox, dBASE, Oracle, and several other common systems. Also, companies such as InterSolv specialize in ODBC drivers.

The first screen in the Remote View Wizard allows you to select a data source as shown in Figure 5.15. Data sources come in two varieties: ODBC data sources and Connections. An ODBC driver is the basic driver definition created in the ODBC section of the Control Panel. You can also use a previously defined connection. Connections must be defined and stored in a database.

▶ **See** "Establishing a Remote Connection," **p. 380**

**FIGURE 5.15**
Before you can access a remote data file, you must select an ODBC data source or a previously defined connection.

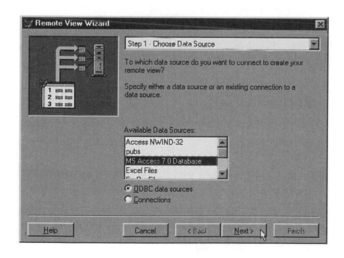

Part

I

Ch

5

From this point, the Remote View Wizard follows the same basic steps as a local view. These steps include:

- **Field selection:** to select tables and fields for the remote view
- **Relationship:** to define relations among tables, if more than table one is selected
- **Join type:** to define the type of relations among tables (inner, left outer, right outer, and full outer)
- **Filtering:** to select a subset of all possible records
- **Sort order:** to define the sort order of the displayed records

The Remote View Wizard, like the Local View Wizard, does not automatically allow for data updates. If you need to use the view to update data in the server, you must save the view and go into the View Designer to set the appropriate update criteria properties.

Also, each remote view can access only a single data source. If you need to relate records between a Paradox file and a Visual FoxPro file, you need to create separate Paradox and Visual FoxPro views. Then, assuming that you have fields that are compatible with a relation, you can relate the two views in the data environment of a form, a report, or even a third view.

## The CrossTab Wizard

A *crosstab* is a special query type that allows you to see how one data field in a table relates to other data fields in the same table. An example can make this definition clearer. A typical order file contains information on all purchase orders. Management wants to see a report of product sales by month. To be more specific, management wants to see one product per report line, with columns totaling sales for each month, as well as a yearly-total column. Such a report cannot be easily produced from the raw order data.

**N O T E**  You can create this type of report by using the IIF function in each column to determine whether or not to include the current record data in the current month. The following expression shows an example:

```
IIF(MONTH(orderdate)=1, unit_price*quantity, 0)
```

Furthermore, you need to group by product ID and show only a report summary, not the details. ■

A crosstab creates a special cursor that reorganizes the data from the original table. It has one field to define the rows (product ID, in the example) and a field for each unique column (months, in the example). You can easily use this cursor with the Report Wizard or Report Designer to create the required report without resorting to complex expressions within the report. More important, you can easily display the data in a form or even a grid.

Start the Crosstab Wizard by choosing File, New, Query or Tools, Wizard, Query. The first step in this wizard, shown in Figure 5.16, selects the database, table, and fields.

A crosstab requires three fields: one for the columns, one for the rows, and one for the calculated data. In fact, until you select at least three fields, you cannot move to the second step of this wizard.

As an example, use PRODUCTS.DBF from the database TASTRADE. Suppose that you want to determine the number of items in stock for each product category and product

ID. The Category_Id field serves as the columns, Product_Id serves as the rows, and Units_In_Stock serves as the data. The order in which you add these fields to the Selected Fields list does not matter.

**FIGURE 5.16**
In the first page of the Crosstab Wizard, select the fields that you want to use.

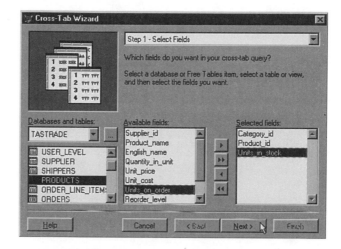

In the second page of this wizard, shown in Figure 5.17, you assign fields to their crosstab locations by dragging the field name to a location. Each field can be used only one time. If you drag a field to more than one location, the most recent location is the only one that the field appears in. There are three locations (Column, Row, and Data), and each location can have only one field assigned to it.

**FIGURE 5.17**
After selecting three fields to use in the crosstab, you need to assign each field to a specific location.

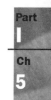

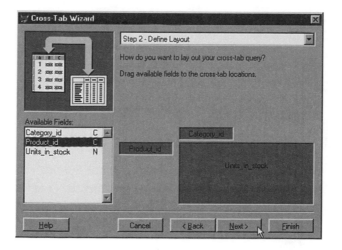

Part

I

Ch

5

**N O T E**   Even though you may be able to select more than three fields in the first step, you can
use only one field in each area of the crosstab. If you attempt to add a second field to
the data area, it actually replaces the field that was placed there. ∎

The basic purpose of the example crosstab at this point is to sum the number of units in
stock for each product ID and to display the total in the appropriate category ID column.
In addition to summing the data field, a crosstab can count the number of records that
contain values and calculate the average, minimum, or maximum value. You can find these
options in the Summary group shown in Figure 5.18.

**FIGURE 5.18**
You can specify other
row calculations in the
third step of the
Crosstab Wizard.

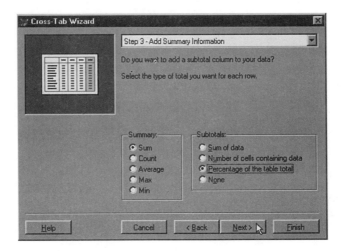

The crosstab can also perform additional calculations across a row. The third step of the
wizard defines these calculations in the Subtotals group. By default, the last column includes a sum of the data in each row; therefore, it would include the sum of all units in
stock for a specific product ID, regardless of its category. However, the wizard also can
count the number of cells that contain data or the percentage of the data in the entire table
represented by the current row. Finally, to turn off all row calculations, click None to
display only the crosstab values. These options are shown in the Add Summary Information step of the Crosstab Wizard (refer to Figure 5.18).

The last step saves the query. Then you can exit to the Command window, run the query
immediately, or open the Query Designer to customize the query further.

## The Pivot Table Wizard

Closely related to the Crosstab Wizard is the Pivot Table Wizard. If you think of a
crosstab as being a two-dimensional view of data, a pivot table is a three-dimensional view.

In a crosstab, you define the rows and columns of a data matrix, using fields from a table. In a pivot table, you can add a third axis.

Using the product table again, suppose that you want to look up the number of units in stock by product and category. In this simple form, this request requires only a crosstab. If you also want to see this comparison broken down by supplier rather than for the entire inventory, you need the third dimension in the pivot table.

You can display the data from only one slice of the pivot table at a time (one value of the third axis or one supplier, in this example). However, by changing this value, you can see different "slices" of the data (suppliers).

The first step in creating a pivot table selects the fields from an available table, as you saw in earlier wizards. This screen is virtually the same as Figure 5.16, with the addition of a fourth field. For this example, select the following four fields from PRODUCTS in TASTRADE:

Category_Id

Product_Id

Supplier_Id

Units_In_Stock

The second step assigns each of the fields to a location. The locations labeled Column, Row, and Data are the same as those used for a crosstab. However, because a crosstab can be thought of as a slice in a pivot table, the Page location defines the third axis. Figure 5.19 shows the just-mentioned fields assigned to their locations.

Part

I

Ch

5

**FIGURE 5.19**
A pivot table has three axes: Page, Column, and Row. The data displayed represent a single-value slice through the Page axis.

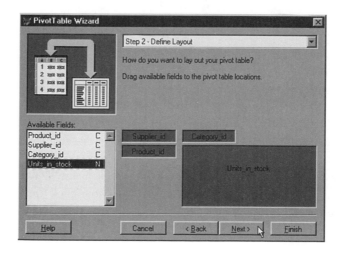

**N O T E** Even though you may be able to select more than four fields in this first step, you can
use only one field in each area of the pivot table. If you attempt to add a second field
to any data area, that field replaces the field that was placed there. ■

The last page of the Pivot Table Wizard allows you to save the pivot table. You can save it
as an Excel pivot table, or you can embed it in a form. In either case, you can choose
whether to create totals for columns or rows.

## The Form Wizard

The Form Wizard supports two form styles. The first style is a simple form based on a
single table. The second style creates a one-to-many form. This section looks first at the
simple data-entry form for a single table.

The first page of the Form Wizard is set up for field selection, as shown in Figure 5.20.

**FIGURE 5.20**

As it does when
creating queries, the
Form Wizard starts by
selecting bound or free
tables, followed by
selecting fields from
those tables.

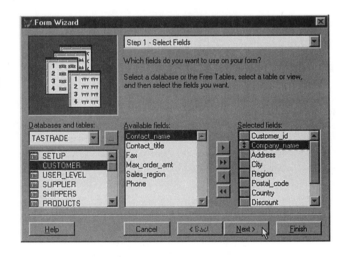

**N O T E** The order of the selected fields determines the order in which the wizard places the
fields in the form, as well as the default tab order for the form. If you intend to
customize the form generated by the wizard, the default order may not matter to you. Otherwise,
carefully order the Selected Fields list before moving on to the next step. ■

A faster way to move fields from one list to another is to simply double-click the field
name. When you complete the first page, you can either click the Next button at the bottom of the dialog box or click the Step button and select the next step.

The second page of the Form Wizard defines the overall form style. Visual FoxPro provides five basic styles:

- Standard
- Chiseled
- Shadowed
- Boxed
- Embossed

As you select any style, the image in the upper-left corner of the dialog box shows a small sample of that style. Figure 5.21 shows this step.

**FIGURE 5.21**
After selecting the fields to include in a form, you need to select a style.

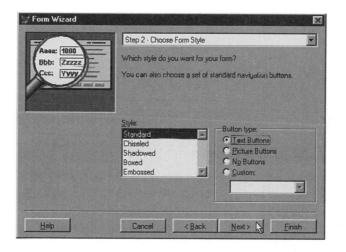

Part
I

Ch

5

The Style list includes four button options, which refer to the buttons that are automatically added to the bottom of the form for navigation and editing. You can display these buttons with either text or picture icons to identify them. You also can choose to not include buttons in the form. In such a case, you must supply your own method of navigating among records in the table. One way to provide your own buttons is to choose the Custom option.

Table 5.1 documents the methods associated with VFP's predefined buttons. Some buttons are *polymorphic*, which means that they have two different definitions, depending on the current state of the form. Add and Save is one such combination; Revert and Edit is another.

**Table 5.1   Default Button Controls Added to Wizard-Generated Forms**

| Button | Description |
| --- | --- |
| Top | Moves to the first table record |
| Prev | Moves to the preceding table record |
| Next | Moves to the following table record |
| Bottom | Moves to the last table record |
| Find | Locates a record |
| Print | Prints the records in the table |
| Add | Adds a new record |
| Edit | Edits the current record |
| Delete | Deletes the current record |
| Save | Saves the changes to the current record (replaces Add when you are editing a record) |
| Revert | Throws out changes to current record and rereads original field contents (replaces Edit when you are editing a record) |
| Exit | Leaves the form |

**N O T E**   This button group comes from class Txtbtns in the custom class library WIZSTYLE.VCX. If you create a form with this wizard and later want to add another field, open this class library to use the same style control. ■

The third page of the Form Wizard (see Figure 5.22) defines a sort order for the records. Because forms save the data environment, you can define a sorted view of the selected table fields in the first page of the wizard. If you don't select a sort order, the form selects records from the table in their natural order. (This order relates to the Top, Prev, Next, and Bottom buttons, described in Table 5.1.) You also can define the sort order as ascending or descending. However, this choice applies to the entire sort, not to individual fields in the sort.

**T I P**   Although you can define a sort on any field or combination of fields, forms perform best if the sort definition matches an index tag.

Figure 5.23 shows the final page of the Form Wizard. In this page, you merely supply the form title. This text appears in the title bar of the completed form.

**FIGURE 5.22**

The third page of the Form Wizard defines a sort order for displaying the records.

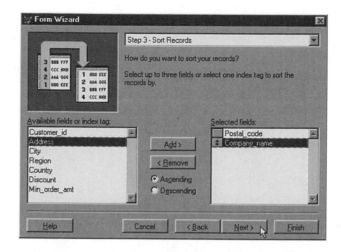

**FIGURE 5.23**

The title you assign to a form in the last page of the Form Wizard appears in the form's window header.

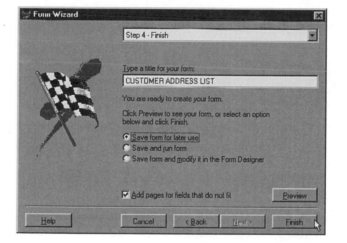

Part
I
Ch
5

You also have three save options. The first option saves the form for later use and then returns you to wherever you were when you started the wizard. The second option saves the form and immediately runs it. The final option saves the form and immediately opens the Form Designer with the new form, allowing further customization.

As in the Query Wizard, a Preview button appears in the bottom-left corner of this last page. If you click this button, Visual FoxPro creates the form based on the definitions provided and displays it. Figure 5.24 shows an example of this preview. The form is only partially functional in this mode, as you can tell from the dimmed buttons at the bottom. You can move through the records in the table (to verify the sort order), but the other options are not available until you generate the form.

**FIGURE 5.24**

The Preview button allows you to verify your form design before you save it and exit the wizard.

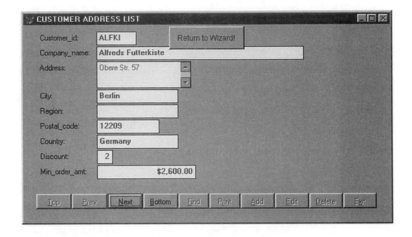

Notice that a big Return to Wizard! command button appears in the top center of the form. In case you were worried, this button appears only while you are in the wizard; it is not a permanent addition to your form. Clicking this button returns you to the last page of the wizard. If you see something in the form design that you do not like, return to the specific step used in its design, and change it. You can move between the steps and this preview mode as many times as you like, as long as you do not leave the wizard. You might use this feature to test-view different styles, for example.

One option in the final page that you may want to check out is the check box at the bottom. When selected, this option tells VFP to use a multiple-page page frame to display the fields. If all the selected fields fit on a single page screen, VFP ignores this option. On the other hand, if you do not check this box, and you have more fields than can fit on the screen, VFP ignores the extra fields. In creating the page frame, VFP creates as many pages as are needed while trying to balance the space used on each page so that no page looks overly crowded or empty. Figure 5.25 shows an example of a page frame created with this option in Preview mode.

When you click the Finish button, the wizard prompts you for a file name and saves the form. If you later discover that you want to change the form, you must make the changes through the Form Designer, not the wizard. You cannot re-enter the wizard for an existing form.

▶ **See** "Defining the Overall Form Properties," **p. 443**

## The One-To-Many Form Wizard

The One-To-Many Form Wizard is related to the simple Form Wizard. The primary difference is that it uses two tables to create forms. Specifically, it creates a form to display individual parent records and all of their children. The parent record fields typically appear in the top half of the form, using individual controls. The child records generally appear in a scrollable grid in the bottom half of the form. In the past, this form type has been one of the hardest for many developers to create and get working. The One-To-Many Wizard allows you to create this form in six easy steps.

**FIGURE 5.25**
VFP can create a multiple-page pageframe form when you have more fields than can fit on a single screen.

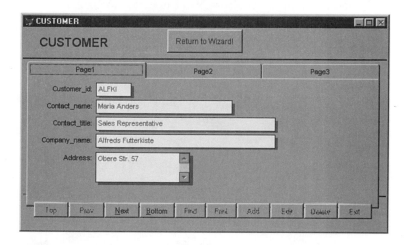

The first step selects the fields from the main, or parent, table. This step resembles the first step of the regular Form Wizard (refer to Figure 5.20) or the Query Wizard (refer to Figure 5.8). As with a form, you begin by selecting a database or table to use as the parent table. From the Available Fields list, select the fields that you want to include in this form.

**NOTE** If you have more fields in the parent table than can fit in a form, you may need to customize the top area of the form later, using the Form Designer. Use the One-To-Many Form Wizard to create the basic form structure, especially to define the relation between the parent and child portions. ■

Notice the small red arrow pointing to the top half of the form in the form-image area in the upper-left corner. This arrow reminds you where the main data appears in the form.

The second page looks very much like the first, except that this page prompts you for the fields from the related, or child, table. Again, you must select a table and fields from the table. Notice that the arrow in the form image shifts to the bottom half of the screen. Remember that all child records appear in a browse-like control. Therefore, all fields must fit horizontally across the form. If you select more fields than will fit horizontally, the wizard adds a horizontal scroll bar that enables you to view them.

 Avoid selecting so many related table fields that a horizontal scroll bar becomes necessary. If a scroll bar is needed, at least try to order the fields so that the most important ones appear first (that is, without requiring you to scroll to see them).

When you are creating a One-To-Many form, the most important fields are the ones that define the relation between the parent and child. That field in this example—Order_Id—appears in both ORDERS and ORDITEMS, the two files that define customer orders. In fact, the wizard sets this relation in Step 3 automatically when a persistent relation exists between the two files. Otherwise, you can easily establish the relation by using the drop-down field lists from both files.

▶ **See** "Forming Persistent Relations," **p. 200**

Figure 5.26 shows the relation formed between parent and child tables.

**FIGURE 5.26**

The third step of the One-To-Many Form Wizard defines the relation between the parent and child file.

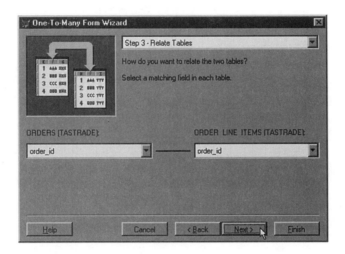

In a relation, the selected fields must match type and size; they do not have to have the same names. The important consideration in this regard is that each child record must have one and only one parent record.

The fourth page of this wizard defines the form's style. The style options are the same as the Form Wizard's form styles, which are listed in the preceding section and shown in Figure 5.21.

The next page of the wizard defines the sort order used to display records in the main or parent table. You can include any of the fields selected from the main table to define the order by double-clicking them in the Available Fields list. You can also highlight them and click the Add button. This step is the same as the one for the Form Wizard, as shown in Figure 5.22.

Notice that the order of the fields in the Selected Fields list determines the sort hierarchy. You can also select one of the radio buttons to determine whether to sort the fields in ascending or descending order. However, this option applies to the entire sort, not to individual fields.

The last screen asks for a form title. Then you can save the form and exit, save, and run it, or save and immediately go to the Form Designer. You can also preview the form by clicking the Preview button. Remember that after returning from the preview, you can revisit any of the earlier steps to make corrections or changes as necessary before you save the form. After you save the form and exit the wizard, you cannot return to the wizard to make changes; you must use the Form Designer to make all subsequent changes.

## The Label Wizard

The Label Wizard helps you create routines that print labels. Suppose that you want to print mailing labels to send a catalog to your customers. Opening the Label Wizard displays the screen shown in Figure 5.27.

**FIGURE 5.27**
To start a label, you need only select the table or view.

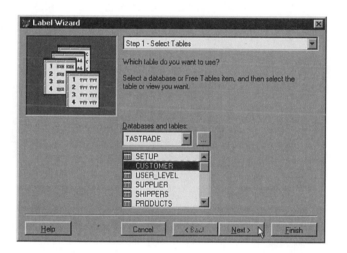

The first step in creating a mailing label is selecting the table or database. As you can with forms, you can select a free table or a database. If you click the ellipsis button (...), you can select the table or database in the Open dialog box. If the table happens to belong to a database, the back link automatically opens the associated database. This example uses the CUSTOMER table from the TASTRADE database.

After selecting a table, you must select a label type. Figure 5.28 shows the second screen of the Label Wizard, with a few of the possible labels displayed in the list box. Visual FoxPro comes with more than 80 predefined English and metric labels. All label definitions come from the Avery standard labels. When you buy labels from your stationery store, if they are not Avery labels, they usually have the equivalent Avery label number on them.

**FIGURE 5.28**

VFP supports a wide range of standard label formats in both English and metric units.

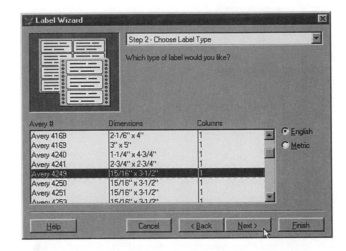

After selecting a label type, you need to define the field layout. Step 3, shown in Figure 5.29, shows this screen.

**FIGURE 5.29**

Step 3 of the Label Wizard allows you to define the contents and appearance of the label by selecting fields from the selected table.

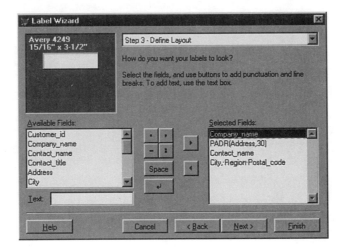

This page of the wizard helps you build a label definition line by line. From the available fields, select the first field for the first line, and click the right-arrow button. This button moves the field into the Selected Fields list.

If you attempt to select another field and move it to the Selected Fields list, the wizard merely appends the second field to the first. To end a line and move to the next line, you must click the Return button. (The Return button shows an angled arrow that points to the left.)

If you need to have multiple fields in a line, you can select the fields one after the other. Remember to include a space between the fields; otherwise, the characters in the fields could run into each other. To add a space, click the button labeled Space. Above this button are other punctuation buttons (period, comma, hyphen, and colon).

You can also include text for functions by using the Text box at the bottom of the option area. If you try to include the customer address, for example, it is too long and extends beyond the width of the label. You might try to define a function like the following in the text box:

```
PADR(Address,30)
```

After entering the expression, click the right-arrow button, just as you do in selecting a field. The wizard adds the content of the text box to the label definition; however, it adds the content as though it were a text string. In this case, you want to save your wizard output and go directly to the appropriate designer. You will have to use the Label Designer to remove the surrounding quotes before Visual FoxPro evaluates the expression, but this method is still faster than adding the expression from scratch in the designer. You can use the Text box, of course, to place any fixed text string on a label.

**TIP**
If you forget to include a line, simply go to the end of the line just before the line where you want to add one, and click the Return button again. This button adds a blank line to the label; then you can select one of the available fields.

To delete a line from the label, select it and then click the left-arrow button. Each click removes one element from the line—the most recent one. If you have only a single element on the line, this button leaves the line blank. If you click the left-arrow button while a blank label line is selected, the wizard removes the blank line and moves the other lines up.

As the next step in creating a label, you can define a sort order. You can skip this step and allow the labels to print in their natural order. However, the postal system often provides a discount for mail sorted by postal code. Therefore, defining a sort order may be worth the few seconds that it takes.

Figure 5.30 shows three fields used for the sort order. As in any Selected Fields list, the order of the fields determines the sort hierarchy. Because Postal_Code appears first, it defines the primary sort. Within each postal code, the wizard sorts by company and then by contact name.

Notice the Ascending and Descending option buttons. Unfortunately, these options operate on the entire index, not on individual fields. Therefore, you cannot define a sort order that sorts Postal_Code in ascending order and Company_Name in descending order.

Part
I

Ch
5

**FIGURE 5.30**
You can choose to sort the label by using any field from the selected table, not just those fields that are displayed on the label.

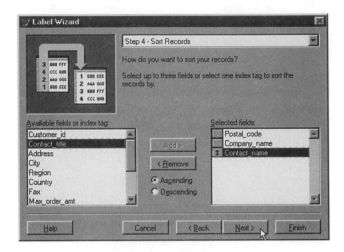

The final step of the Label Wizard allows you to preview your label design and save it. When you save the label definition, you must supply a name and path. You can either save the label and exit to the Command window, or you can go immediately into the Label Designer to customize the label further.

The wizard does not provide an option that allows you to determine the flow of labels in multiple-column label forms. In other words, when a label form has two or more labels horizontally, you may first want to select whether the sort order flows down each column before going to the next column, or whether the sort order flows across each column in the same row before dropping down to the next column.

You can define the print order in the Page Setup dialog box. First, save the label definition. Then, when you are ready to print, open the Label Designer with the new label definition, and choose File, Page Setup. In the Page Setup dialog box, click the print order that you prefer. Figure 5.31 shows a two-up label printed row-wise.

After defining the page setup, you can click the Print Setup button or choose File, Print to print your labels from the open label definition.

---

### Syntax of the LABEL Command

You can use the LABEL command to print your labels directly from the Command window. The command's syntax is:

```
LABEL [FORM FileName1|FORM ?]
    [ENVIRONMENT]
    [Scope]
    [FOR Iexpression1]
    [WHILE Iexpression2]
    [NOCONSOLE]
```

```
[NOOPTIMIZE]
[PDSETUP]
[PREVIEW]
[SAMPLE]
[TO PRINTER [PROMPT] |TO FILE FileName2]
```

If you do this, make sure that you set your Page Setup properties before issuing this command.

**FIGURE 5.31**
When defining the page setup, you can control whether to print the labels column-wise or row-wise.

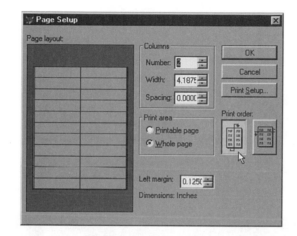

> **CAUTION**
> When you preview the label, the text on the edges may appear to be cut off. This situation could be a function of your printer. Open the Printer Setup dialog box, and review the settings for the Print Area and Left Margin options. Remember that most laser printers have an unprintable margin, whereas dot-matrix printers often can print right up to the edge of the page. Avery has different form numbers for laser labels that account for this margin. Be sure to select the correct one.

## The Import Wizard

The Import Wizard helps translate data files from other applications, such as Excel and Lotus, into Visual FoxPro 5.0 tables. The Import Wizard converts files from the following systems:

- Text files
- Excel spreadsheets 2.0, 3.0, 4.0, and 5.0
- Framework II (only from the File, Import option)
- Multiplan 4.1
- Lotus 1.2.3 1-A, 2.x, and 3.x

- Symphony 1.01 and 1.10
- Paradox 3.5, 4.0, and 4.5
- Rapidfile

Figure 5.32 shows the first screen of the Import Wizard. The first text box allows you to select the file type of the source data. The drop-down list displays the types shown in the preceding list.

**FIGURE 5.32**

To import a file, you must know the source file's type and location; then you can create a new table with it or append it to an existing table.

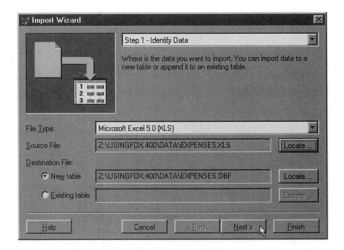

The next text box must be filled; it specifies the fully qualified name of the source file. If the destination file is a new file, its name is automatically made the same as the source file, but with the .DBF extension. If you want to store the destination file elsewhere or give it a different name, click the button with the three dots to its right. This displays the Save As dialog box and allows you to save the file with any name on any drive or directory.

You can also append the data from the source file to an existing table. However, use this option with care. Remember that the columns must line up with the appropriate fields for the resulting table to still have meaning.

As shown in Figure 5.33, the second page of the wizard reads your source file and attempts to interpret it in a column format. Depending on the type of source file, this preview may appear different. The vertical and horizontal scroll bars allow you to view additional columns and rows of data, if not all of them fit. Figure 5.34 shows the additional options that you can set from this step to help import your file.

The next step allows you to select each data column and define a field name, type, and size for the resulting table, if the destination is a new table. Figure 5.35 shows this screen with a definition for the first column.

**FIGURE 5.33**
VFP's first job in the Import Wizard is to interpret the imported data; in this case, it reads the spreadsheet rows as records and columns as fields.

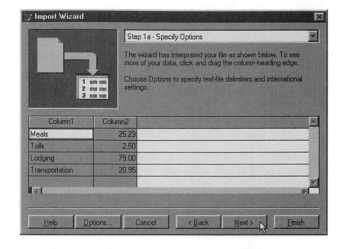

**FIGURE 5.34**
In some cases, you need to help VFP by using the Options dialog box, which is available from the preceding step.

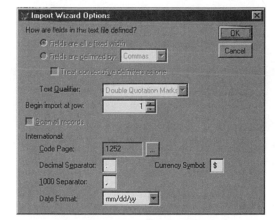

Part
I

Ch
5

**FIGURE 5.35**
In Step 2 of the Import Wizard, you can define the name, type, and size of each imported field.

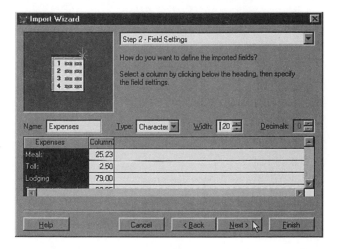

When you are appending data to an existing file, you still must assign a name to each data column. This time, however, you must pick the name from the list of existing field names in the existing table. First, select the column that you want to assign; then open the drop-down list to select a name. If the existing table does not have an appropriate field, you can select Unassigned Field. This option tells the wizard to ignore that data column when it appends the data.

Also notice that you cannot change the field type or size definitions. Basically, all you need to remember is that when you are appending data, you cannot change the structure of the table to which you are appending. As each field in the existing table is assigned to a data column, its background becomes gray, and it cannot be selected for any other data column. After all, you cannot assign two values from the same record to the same field.

This step completes the import definition. In the final step, you need only to click the Finish button to begin the import. Because this wizard does not create a file, as the Form and Query Wizards do, there are no additional options or designers to further refine the definition.

## The Report Wizard Family

Visual FoxPro has three types of report wizards:

- The general Report Wizard formats a single-table report.
- The One-To-Many Report Wizard, like the One-To-Many Form Wizard, uses a parent–child relation between two tables to create a report.
- Finally, the Group/Total Report Wizard creates reports that total numeric fields, based on a grouping of records.

**The Basic Report Wizard**   The first step in the basic Report Wizard, like the first step in the Form Wizard, is selecting fields. This dialog box is the same as the one for the Query and Form Wizards. You select the database, the table, and then the individual fields that you want to include in the report. Figure 5.36 shows several fields selected from CUSTOMER.DBF in TASTRADE.

 **TIP** If you need fields from more than one table, create a view and save it in the database first.

In the second step, shown in Figure 5.37, you can select one of three standard report styles:

- Executive
- Ledger
- Presentation

As you click each of these styles, the icon in the upper-left corner changes to show a small representation of the style.

**FIGURE 5.36**
When you are using the general Report Wizard, you select fields from a single table.

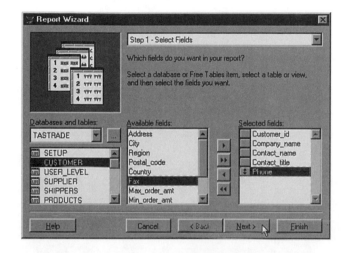

**FIGURE 5.37**
Select one of the three styles for your report.

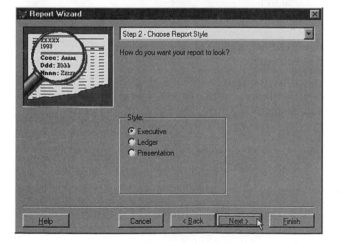

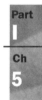

The third step of this wizard defines the overall layout of the report. The first option defines the field layout. The two options are Colu̲mns and R̲ows. If you have only a few fields that fit across the page horizontally, you may want to consider the column-style report, because it fits more records on a page. If you have many fields in each record to display, you may have to consider a row-style layout.

Almost all paper has a width different from its height. A Portrait-style report means that the print goes across the narrower paper dimension. This is the default mode. To show more columns in a report, consider rotating the output with Landscape mode.

The number of columns determines the number of columns of repeated data that can appear across a page. If you use a row-style field layout, for example, the data may not extend beyond the middle of the page. In this case, consider having two columns on the page to double the amount of information printed on each page. You also can use columns for column-style filed layouts.

Figure 5.38 shows these options.

**FIGURE 5.38**

The report layout step identifies how to display rows and columns in the report.

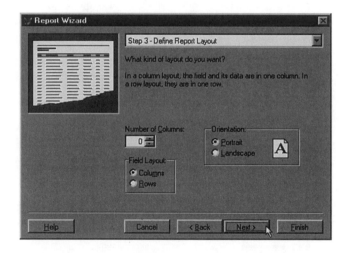

Figure 5.39 shows the fourth step, which defines the sort order of the records. You can select any of the fields used in the report. The order in which the fields appear in the Selected Fields list determines the sort level. The sort direction can be Ascending or Descending.

 **TIP** To sort with more than three fields, you must modify the report in the Report Designer.

The last step allows you to define a title for the report and to save the report. You also have the option to wrap fields to continuation lines if they do not fit in the desired column widths. An important button in the last screen is the Preview button. Remember to preview your report before you save and exit. After previewing the report, you can return to earlier steps in the wizard by clicking the Back button. After you save the report, however, you must make any subsequent modifications through the Report Designer.

**FIGURE 5.39**
VFP limits the sort to three fields when you are using the wizard.

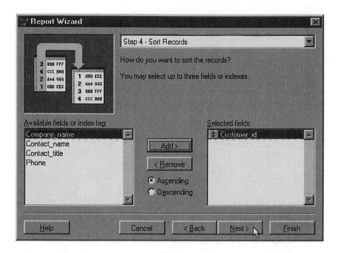

## Syntax of the REPORT Command

You can use the REPORT command to print your report directly from the Command window. The command's syntax is:

```
REPORT FORM FileName1|?
    [ENVIRONMENT]
    [Scope]
    [FOR Iexpression1]
    [WHILE Iexpression2]
    [HEADING cHeadingText]
    [NOEJECT]
    [NOCONSOLE]
    [NOOPTIMIZE]
    [PDSETUP]
    [PLAIN]
    [PREVIEW [NOWAIT]]
    [TO PRINTER [PROMPT] |TO FILE FileName2 [ASCII]]
    [NAME]
    [SUMMARY]
```

**Part**

**I**

**Ch**

**5**

**The One-To-Many Report Wizard**   The One-To-Many Report Wizard starts with two steps, in which you select the table and fields to be used for the main table and the related table. These two steps mirror the steps in the One-to-Many Form Wizard.

The third step is also familiar. Because you have two tables in a parent–child relation, you need to identify the field that connects the two tables. This field should be the primary key (or at least a candidate key) in the child file.

The fourth step defines the sort order of the output records. The sort is only on fields in the main table; the wizard has no provision for sorting the child records within the parent. To do so, you must create an appropriate view outside the wizard and use it in your report definition.

The fifth step defines the layout options, as shown in Figure 5.40.

**FIGURE 5.40**

Layout options in the
One-To-Many Report
Wizard do not include
the field and column
options of the general
Report Wizard.

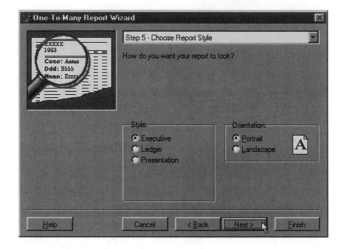

This step does not support as many options as a simple form does. You can choose among only three styles:

- Executive
- Ledger
- Presentation

You also can select paper orientation.

The final step allows you to enter a report title, wrap fields, and preview the report. Be sure to preview the report, because the style sample does not do justice to the actual generated report.

**The Group/Total Report Wizard**   The first two report types merely print the data in the tables; they perform no totaling and do not group the records by specific fields. If you select a field to sort on, the report does not include any header or footer lines to separate one group from the next. If this is the type of report that you want and need, use the Group/Total Report Wizard.

This wizard starts the same way that the two other report wizards do, because it also has to get the table and fields needed for the report. Suppose that you select the following CUSTOMER fields:

Customer_Id

Company_Name

Contact_Name

Contact_Title

Discount

Sales_Region

The first difference occurs in the second step, as shown in Figure 5.41. You can select up to three grouping levels.

**FIGURE 5.41**

The second step of the Group/Total Report Wizard forms the heart of this wizard. This step defines the fields used to group the records and determines whether to total or subtotal numeric fields.

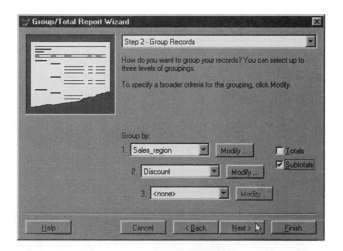

**N O T E** In the context of reports, *grouping* refers to the additional report bands added to a report to allow for subtotaling and totaling of numeric fields for constant values of the group field. This is not to be confused with grouping in queries, which combines records that have a similar group field value. ■

In the report, you want to group the customers by sales region and then, within the sales region, by discount. Therefore, Figure 5.41 defines the first group on the Sales_Region field and the second group on Discount. You also can select the Total and Subtotal options, which operate only on numeric fields. Total sums the numeric fields of records and prints the total at the end of the report. Subtotal also sums numeric fields, but it places subtotals at the end of each group value and then begins summing again with the next group value.

The third step determines a sort order. This sort order is within a group, however; do not include the sort order required by the groups themselves. Actually, you cannot make this mistake because the wizard does not include the group fields in the Available Fields list. Thus, you can have up to three additional sort levels within each group. In this case, you could sort all the records by company name that have the same discount in a sales region. To create this sort, select the fields Sales_Region, Discount, and Company_Name, respectively.

Part

I

Ch

5

The fourth step includes the same style and layout options shown in Figure 5.40 for the One-To-Many Report Wizard. Finally, you can assign a report title in the last step and allow fields to wrap. Remember to preview your report before you save it.

## The Documenting Wizard

When you start the Documenting Wizard, the first step identifies the file or project that you want to document. If you use the Project Manager to develop applications, the best way to document your system is to select the project. If you use the Project Manager merely to organize a collection of separate programs, the appropriate source code to document is the file.

Figure 5.42 shows the initial screen of the Documenting Wizard.

**FIGURE 5.42**

You can document an entire project or individual files by using the Document-ing Wizard, which calls an updated version of FoxDoc that is specifically designed for Visual FoxPro features.

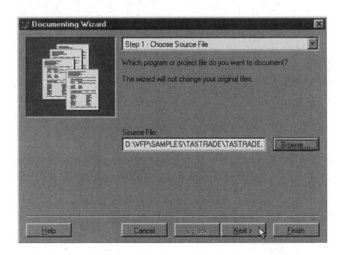

By default, the wizard assumes that you want to document the currently open project. Notice that the Tastrade project is currently open in the background of this figure. If you click the Browse button next to the entry field in Figure 5.42, you can select any file or project in any directory.

Step two of the wizard defines the capitalization to be used for keywords and variables. For keywords, the wizard provides four options. The default setting is MixedCase, which corresponds to the recommended use of case for object properties.

▶ **See** "Naming Conventions," **p. 182**

The wizard also supports four capitalization options for symbols (variables). The default matches the first occurrence of a variable. Thus, if the first occurrence is UPPERCASE, the wizard changes all subsequent occurrences to UPPERCASE. If the first occurrence is mixed-case, as in gcSupplierName, the wizard uses this mix of uppercase and lowercase in all subsequent occurrences. Figure 5.43 shows this step.

**FIGURE 5.43**
The Documenting Wizard allows you to establish consistent case for keywords and variables.

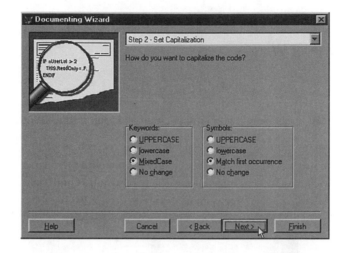

The third screen defines how and where to indent text, as shown in Figure 5.44.

**FIGURE 5.44**
Indenting text makes it easier to read and to identify blocks of code. This step adds consistent indentation.

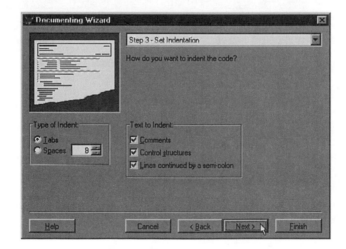

Part
I
Ch
5

The first indentation option allows you to choose between Tabs and Spaces. If you choose to use tabs, the number of equivalent character spaces must be set in the Edit tab of the Options dialog box (choose Tools, Options). If you choose spaces, you can set the number of spaces used in this step.

The second set of options identifies where to indent text. FoxDoc installs three types of code:

Comments

Control structures

Lines broken by a semi-colon (;)

The fourth step, shown in Figure 5.45, identifies where to add header comments.

**FIGURE 5.45**

The Documenting Wizard can add comment-block headers to several code structures.

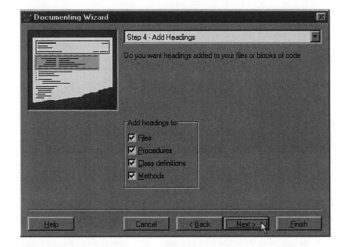

You can add four types of header comments to the code:

- File headings
- Procedure headings
- Class-definition headings
- Method headings

Figure 5.46 shows the reports step. In this step, you select reports from the list on the left and move them to the list on the right. Available Reports include:

- Source Code Listing
- Action Diagram
- Cross Reference
- File Listing
- Tree Diagram

**FIGURE 5.46**

You can generate several reports with the Documenting Wizard, including several code listings and a variable cross-reference.

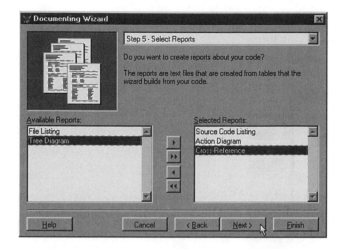

**FIGURE 5.47**

Files created with the Documenting Wizard can replace existing files or be stored in a separate directory.

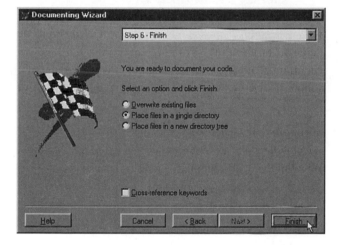

Part
I

Ch
5

The final step asks where to place the files created by the wizard (see Figure 5.47). You can overwrite existing files or place them in a new directory, or even in a new directory tree. Finally, you can opt to build a cross-reference of keywords used in the application or program.

# From Here...

This chapter examined the features of the major Visual FoxPro wizards. As you learn more about the Visual FoxPro language and features, you will see that the wizards do not provide the total solution; however, they provide a jump-start on creating most features. Therefore, you should give serious consideration to using the wizards to build prototypes of new applications quickly. You can work interactively with your endusers or clients, developing the application's basic structure right in front of them.

Following are some chapters that you may want to look at or return to after you see what wizards can do:

- Chapter 3, "Defining Databases, Tables, and Indexes," covers the basics of manually creating both free and bound tables with the Table Designer.
- Chapter 7, "Creating Basic Queries," shows you how to create simple queries with the Query Designer.
- Chapter 11, "Building Applications with Simple Form Structures," describes how to use the Form Designer to create forms.
- Chapter 14, "Custom Report Generation," teaches you how to generate reports and labels with the Report Designer and Label Designer.

# Turning Data into Information

# Selecting, Viewing, and Ordering Data

*by Michael Antonovich*

**A** fundamental operation of any data-management system is opening tables and viewing the data that they contain. With Visual FoxPro 5.0, the way that you open and view data is determined by how you store data. In this new release, you have the capability to store tables of information either as free tables or as part of an associated group of tables called a database. Although a database offers many new data-management options that previously were unavailable to FoxPro users, you may find yourself supporting many existing applications that still use the stand-alone table model. Fortunately, working with tables bound into databases is not much more difficult than working with free tables. In fact, databases provide additional features, such as persistent relations, that make working with them easier.

Critical to the viewing of data is the effective use of indexes. The use (and misuse) of indexes greatly affects the way that you retrieve and view data from a table. Visual FoxPro 5.0 supports three major types of indexes: independent single-index files, structural compound indexes, and non-structural compound indexes. Indexes serve two primary purposes.

**Open free tables and tables bound to a database**

Learn how to open any table, whether a free or bound table.

**Use LIST and DISPLAY to output data to the screen and printer**

Learn how to use LIST and DISPLAY to quickly retrieve selected records from your tables and display them to the screen or printer

**Locate specific records by using conditional clauses with LOCATE and SEEK**

Discover when to use LOCATE versus SEEK when retrieving data from your tables. Also learn how to use the FOR and WHEN clauses individually and together to retrieve groups of records.

**Sort data with simple and compound indexes**

See how to define different sort orders for your data using any of three different index styles.

**Define indexes for use with Rushmore optimization**

Uncover the secrets of Rushmore's blinding speed in retrieving selected records from your tables.

You use some indexes primarily to form relations between tables; you use others to help retrieve data and to improve the performance of queries and reports. ■

# Opening Tables in Work Areas

Before you view data that is stored in a table or work with table data in any other way, you need to open it in a work area. Visual FoxPro 5.0 supports 32,767 work areas. Each work area can hold one table and its related indexes, both independent and compound. It is unlikely that you will ever need to use all 32,767 areas—at least, not at the same time. Other system restrictions typically restrict most users to fewer than 256 files.

## Opening Free Tables

How do you open a table to look at it? If the table is a free table, select one of the 32,767 areas and issue a USE command, as shown in this example:

```
SELECT 2
USE CUST   && Found in \VFP5BOOK\DATA of this book's CD
```

**N O T E**   CUST.DBF, located on the CD provided with this book, is the same as CUSTOMER.DBF, except that it is a free table with field names limited to 10 characters. ■

The first command tells Visual FoxPro 5.0 to use the second work area. The second command tries to open CUST.DBF from the current directory. If CUST.DBF is not there, Visual FoxPro 5.0 displays the following message, which includes the current drive and directory:

```
File '<current directory>\CUST.DBF' does not exist
```

You can also retrieve the current drive and directory with this command:

```
? SYS(5)+SYS(2003)
```

A safer way to open a file is to first test if it exists before issuing the USE command. You can do this with the FILE function as shown in Listing 6.1.

### Listing 6.1   06PRG01.PRG—The File Function

```
* Program 6.1 - Testing if a file exists before using it
SELECT 2
IF FILE('CUST.DBF')
     USE CUST
ELSE
     = MESSAGEBOX('File CUST.DBF does not exist in ' ;
      + SYS(5) + SYS(2003))
ENDIF
```

Of course, you can include a drive and directory with the table's name to open it, as follows:

```
USE C:\VFP5BOOK\DATA\CUST
```

The preceding examples select the second work area without first checking to see whether another file is open there. Visual FoxPro 5.0 automatically closes any file that is open in the selected area when you issue a USE command, whether the command succeeds or not. This means that even if the file being opened is not in the current directory or if VFP cannot open it, VFP closes the file that was open in the selected area. Therefore, you should find out whether the work area contains a file before you use it. Use the ALIAS function, which returns the alias name of a file when present, to test whether a work area is empty, as in Listing 6.2.

### Listing 6.2  06PRG02.PRG—The ALIAS Function

```
* Program 6.2 - Use ALIAS to see if table is already open
* Check if work area 2 is available (empty)
  IF EMPTY(ALIAS(2)) && Returns .T. If no file is open in area 2
      SELECT 2
  ELSE
      = MESSAGEBOX('Work area 2 is in use')
  ENDIF
```

Of course, you should test successive work areas to find an empty one. Although you could write the code to perform such an iteration, there is a faster way. If you use SELECT 0, rather than open a specific work area, Visual FoxPro 5.0 begins with work area 1 and continues searching until it finds the first empty one. You do not really need to know what work area VFP opens a file in. Always reference files by their alias names after opening them instead of using their work-area numbers.

You don't even need a separate SELECT statement to open a table. Select the work area and open the table at the same time by adding the IN clause to the USE statement. But before I show you the modified code that you use to open a file this way, consider an additional enhancement. If the file is not in the current or specified directory, open a dialog box to allow the user to locate the file. The GETFILE function, shown in Listing 6.3, provides this capability.

**Part**

**II**

**Ch**

**6**

### Listing 6.3  06PRG03.PRG—The GETFILE Function

```
* Program 6.3 - Use ALIAS and FILE to open table in next
*               available work area.
*
* Open CUST.DBF in the next available work area
```

*continues*

**Listing 6.3 Continued**

```
IF FILE('CUST.DBF')
    USE CUST IN 0
ELSE
    = MESSAGEBOX('File CUST.DBF does not exist in ' ;
     + SYS(5) + SYS(2003))
    lcNewFile = GETFILE('DBF', 'Pick table:', 'Select', 1)
    IF !EMPTY(lcNewFile)
        USE (lcNewFile) IN 0
    ENDIF
ENDIF
```

Notice that GETFILE() allows you to select a table from any drive or directory and returns the fully qualified path name to the variable lcNewFile. Use this variable in USE to open the file. The parentheses in this statement tell Visual FoxPro 5.0 to use the contents of the variable pcNewFile, rather than the name pcNewFile itself.

What if the file that you want to open is already open in a different work area? By default, Visual FoxPro 5.0 considers this situation to be an error and displays the message File is in use.

Test for this condition with the USED() function, which requires the file alias as its parameter. As shown in Listing 6.4, the function checks to see whether the file alias exists in any work area.

**Listing 6.4 06PRG04.PRG—USED() Function**

```
* Program 06PRG04.PRG
  CLOSE DATABASES
  CLEAR

* Test if CUST is already in use
  IF USED("CUST")
    = MESSAGEBOX("File CUST.DBF is already in use.")
    SELECT CUST
  ELSE
  * If file CUST.DBF exists, open it
    cCurDirectory = CURDIR()
    CD \VFP5BOOK\DATA
    IF FILE("CUST.DBF")
      USE CUST.DBF IN 0
      = MESSAGEBOX("File CUST.DBF successfully opened.")
    ELSE

    * File CUST.DBF is not in default drive,
    * ask user to locate it
      = MESSAGEBOX("File CUST.DBF does not exist in ";
       + SYS(5) + SYS(2003))
      lcNewFile = GETFILE("DBF", "Select a table:", "Select", 1)
```

```
      lcFileName = SUBSTR(lcNewFile, RAT("\", lcNewFile) + 1)
      lcRootName = LEFT(lcFileName, LEN(lcFileName) - 4)

    * Check if used selected file is already open.  If not, open it
      IF !EMPTY(lcNewFile)
        IF USED(lcRootName)
          = MESSAGEBOX("File " + lcNewFile + " is already in use.")
          SELECT(lcRootName)
        ELSE
          USE (lcNewFile) IN 0
          = MESSAGEBOX("File CUST.DBF successfully opened.")
        ENDIF
      ENDIF
    ENDIF
    CD &cCurDirectory
  ENDIF
```

Notice that you have to extract the file name from the value returned by GETFILE before you can use USED() to test for it.

### TROUBLESHOOTING

**I try to open a table in an empty work area, but VFP keeps telling me that the file is in use. Yet when I use the View window to look at the work areas, I don't see it listed.** Remember that USED() looks for files based on their alias names. If you open the file CUST.DBF and assign an alias of BUYERS to it, USED('CUST') returns false, even though any attempt to open CUST.DBF a second time in a different work area fails, with a File is in use error message. If you open tables with alias names other than their file names, document this information in the program so that other programmers can find it.

## Opening Tables More Than Once

At times, you may want to open a file twice, such as when you perform a recursive reference on a file. Chapter 3, "Defining Databases, Tables, and Indexes," includes an example of a self-referencing relation that finds the supervisor of every employee. That example used a query and the relation to find each supervisor's name. Now you can achieve the same result by opening the file in two different work areas, using the AGAIN clause of USE. AGAIN allows you to open a file more than once. The advantage is that you can use different indexes and move the record pointer independently in each work area. The following two lines show how to open a table a second time.

```
USE empl1 IN 1
USE empl1 IN 2 AGAIN
```

▶ **See** "Creating Self-Referential Relations," **p. 201**

Although Visual FoxPro 5.0 allows you to open a file multiple times by including the AGAIN clause in USE, remember that it is really the same file. You can even turn an index on in one area and set a relation to it from the other. The record pointer is independent in each work area. Therefore, you can step through the first file to read the employee information, including supervisor IDs; then you could switch to the second work area to search for the employee who has the first employee's supervisor ID and report their name. Listing 6.5 shows this technique.

**Listing 6.5   06PRG05.PRG**

```
* Program 06PRG05.PRG
  CLOSE DATABASES
  CLEAR

* Open EMPL1.DBF in two work areas
  SELECT 1
  USE \VFP5BOOK\DATA\EMPL1
  SELECT 2
  USE \VFP5BOOK\DATA\EMPL1 AGAIN ;
      ALIAS SUPERVISOR ;
      ORDER EMPLOYEEID

* Step through the first area
  SELECT 1
  SCAN
    ? EmplID, ;
      LastName FONT "Foxfont", 10, ;
      FirstName FONT "Foxfont", 10, ;
      Supervisor FONT "Foxfont", 10
  * Now find the employee corresponding to the supervisor id
    IF SEEK(Supervisor, 'SUPERVISOR')
      ?? supervisor.LastName FONT "Foxfont", 10, ;
         supervisor.FirstName FONT "Foxfont", 10
    ENDIF
  ENDSCAN
```

# Opening Tables Bound to a Database

If you try to open a table that is bound to a database without first opening the database, VFP uses a back link to identify and open the corresponding database automatically.

VFP stores this back link or reference in the table to identify its parent database. It stores this information at the end of the field list in the table header. The reference includes the name of the database and a relative path to the database from the table. If you open the table with a full path name, VFP bases its relative path search for the database on that path name rather than the current directory.

◆ **TROUBLESHOOTING**

**I attempt to open a table, and VFP displays an error message, saying that it cannot locate the database.** One of two things happened. You either moved the table relative to the database, or you moved the database relative to the table.

Suppose that you begin with the database PTOFSALE and table CUSTOMER (installed by the CD-ROM included with this book) in the same directory. In this case, the back link in CUSTOMER simply is PTOFSALE.DBC. In other words, VFP looks in the same directory as the table for the database.

On the other hand, suppose that you store the database as \app1\PTOFSALE.DBC and the table as \app1\data\CUSTOMER.DBF. Now the back link is ..\PTOFSALE. In this case, the double dot at the beginning of the back link means to return to the parent directory of the current directory.

Similarly, suppose that you store the database as \app1\database\PTOFSALE.DBC and the table as \app1\data\CUSTOMER.DBF. Now the back link becomes ..\database\PTOFSALE. In this case, the back link returns first to the parent directory and then goes down a different branch: the \database subdirectory.

Following this logic, you can see that moving the entire tree structure that contains the database and table continues to work, because the relative paths remain the same. You can even move the tree to a different directory or drive without a problem. You cannot move the tables relative to the database, however.

To be more explicit in your coding, precede commands that open a bound table with a command that opens the database, as in the following example:

```
OPEN DATABASE C:\VFP5BOOK\DATA\PTOFSALE
USE C:\VFP5BOOK\DATA\CUSTOMER
```

VFP requires the database to be open because bound tables may use long table names, validation rules, triggers, or other database enhancements. Visual FoxPro would know nothing about these new features unless it opened the database first.

Part
II

Ch
6

# Listing Data to the Screen or Printer

Visual FoxPro has two commands—DISPLAY and LIST—that create simple data listings. Following is the syntax for both commands:

```
DISPLAY
    [[FIELDS] FieldList]
    [Scope][FOR IExpression1][WHILE Iexpression2]
    [OFF]
    [TO PRINTER [PROMPT]¦TO FILE FileName]
    [NOCONSOLE]
```

```
        [NOOPTIMIZE]
LIST
        [FIELDS FieldList]
        [Scope][FOR IExpression1][WHILE Iexpression2]
        [OFF]
        [TO PRINTER [PROMPT]¦TO FILE FileName]
        [NOCONSOLE]
        [NOOPTIMIZE]
```

In addition to listing the contents of tables, Table 6.1 lists other clauses that are available with LIST and DISPLAY.

**Table 6.1    Clauses of LIST and DISPLAY**

| Clause | What It Lists |
| --- | --- |
| CONNECTIONS | Information on named connections to external data sources, such as SQL SERVER, Access, dBASE, and Paradox |
| DATABASE | Information about the current database |
| FIELDS | Contents of table fields |
| FILES | File names |
| MEMORY | Contents of memory variables |
| OBJECTS | Information about objects |
| PROCEDURES | Information on stored procedures |
| STATUS | System status |
| STRUCTURE | File structures |
| TABLES | Tables in an open database |
| VIEWS | Information on SQL views |

DISPLAY, with no additional clauses, shows the current record of the current table. On the other hand, LIST shows all the current records from the current table, beginning with the first one. You can modify the scope of either command with ALL, NEXT, RECORD, or REST. Table 6.2 defines these modifiers.

**Table 6.2    Record Scope Modifiers**

| Scope | What It Includes |
| --- | --- |
| ALL | Every record in the table |
| NEXT *n* | The next *n* records, where *n* can be any integer, beginning with the current record |

| Scope | What It Includes |
|---|---|
| RECORD *n* | The *n*th record in the table (based on physical record numbers, not logical orders defined by a sort) |
| REST | All records from the current one to the end of the table |

You can also specify a subset of fields by using the FIELDS clause for both commands. You need to list only the fields; the keyword FIELDS is optional. Following are the various syntax forms for these two commands:

```
USE C:\VFP5BOOK\DATA\CUST IN 1
DISPLAY            && Displays the first record only
LIST               && Lists all records, scrolling if necessary
DISPLAY NEXT 4     && Displays the next four records
DISPLAY REST       && Display the rest of the record in the table
                   && from the current record pointer position
DISPLAY ALL        && Display all the records in the table
LIST cLast, cFirst      && List the last and first names of
                        && every record in the table
```

Another difference between these two commands appears when you are displaying more records than will fit on-screen. When LIST reaches the bottom of the screen, it does not stop; it simply clears the screen and begins again from the top without pausing. DISPLAY pauses when it reaches the bottom of the screen and waits until you press a key to continue. Therefore, you may want to use LIST with the TO PRINTER clause to redirect output to the printer, so that Visual FoxPro 5.0 does not pause. On the other hand, when you are viewing records on-screen, use DISPLAY to see each record. You can also list records to a file by using the TO FILE clause.

To display records on-screen, use the following:

```
DISPLAY ALL cCustId, cCompany
```

To list records to the printer, use the following:

```
LIST cCustId, cCompany TO PRINTER
```

To list records to a file, use the following:

```
LIST cCustId, cCompany TO FILE CUSTOMER.TXT
```

## TROUBLESHOOTING

**When I issue a list REST, I don't get all the records that I expected to get.** Both of the scope modifiers REST and NEXT begin retrieving records from the current record pointer. If you move the record pointer before issuing these commands, you may not get the records that you expect.

Part
II

Ch
6

# Finding Records with LOCATE

If you have only a few records in a table, listing or displaying all records in a table to find the one that you want may not seem to be a bad idea. As tables grow to hundreds or thousands of records, however, LIST and DISPLAY by themselves become impractical. You need to jump immediately to the record or records that match the desired condition.

LOCATE helps you find records for a specific condition, even if the records are scattered throughout the table. Suppose that you want to see records for customers who have outstanding bills. Unless you have a really bad collection history, you really do not want to see every record. The following statement jumps to the first record that matches the search condition:

```
SELECT CUST
LOCATE FOR cBillDue > 0
```

LOCATE always begins at the first record in a file and checks records sequentially until it finds the first one that passes the condition test. To see more information about this customer, use DISPLAY by itself to print to the screen all fields for the current record. You can also use LIST NEXT 1.

But suppose you suspect that more customers have outstanding bills. If you reissue the LOCATE command, Visual FoxPro 5.0 merely displays the same record, because it always begins its search from the top of the file. If you use CONTINUE instead, the search begins at the record immediately after the current one and finds the next record that matches the condition. In fact, you can continue issuing CONTINUE until VFP reaches the end of the file. The code segment in Listing 6.6 shows you how to use these commands to view all customers who have outstanding bills.

**Listing 6.6   06PRG06.PRG**

```
* Program 06PRG06.PRG
* View customers with outstanding bills
USE CUST
LOCATE FOR cBillDue > 0
DISPLAY OFF cCustId, cBillDue
DO WHILE !EOF()
  CONTINUE
  IF NOT EOF()
    DISPLAY OFF cCustId, cBillDue
  ENDIF
ENDDO
```

**TIP** When you are using LOCATE or CONTINUE, EOF() remains .F. until the search fails to find additional records that match the condition. Alternatively, you can use FOUND(), which returns .T. as long as records are found.

The advantage with LOCATE is that you can define a condition on any field or portion of a field in the table; it does not need an index. To find all customers who have the word CONSULTANTS in their company names, use the commands in Listing 6.7.

### Listing 6.7  06PRG07.PRG

```
* Program 06PRG07.PRG
* Locate all customers who are consultants
USE CUST
LOCATE FOR 'CONSULTANTS' $ UPPER(cCompany)
LIST OFF cCompany
DO WHILE !EOF()
  CONTINUE
  IF FOUND()
    LIST OFF cCompany
  ENDIF
ENDDO
```

 **TIP** When you compare strings, convert both sides of the string to all uppercase or all lowercase before comparing them, to make comparisons independent of case. To avoid the case issue entirely, use the SET COLLATE TO GENERAL feature when you define the index.

You can even use LOCATE with a condition that combines several fields. Although LOCATE does not require an index, if one exists that matches the form of the condition, LOCATE automatically uses Rushmore to optimize the search for matching records. What this means to you is improved performance with almost instantaneous response, even in tables that have thousands of records.

## Seeking Records on Index Values

Another command that you can use to find selected records in a table is SEEK. Unlike LOCATE, SEEK requires the use of an index. Furthermore, if the index is a compound one, or if you open multiple simple indexes, SEEK works only with the current one. Therefore, first SET ORDER TO the index that you want SEEK to use. SEEK has a simple syntax. Simply follow SEEK with the value that you want it to find. To find CUSTOMER 0025, enter the code in Listing 6.8.

Part
II

Ch
6

**Listing 6.8   06PRG08.PRG**

```
* Program 06PRG08.PRG
* Locate customer '0025'
USE CUST
SET ORDER TO TAG custid
SEEK '0025'
IF FOUND()
  DISPLAY
ELSE
  = MESSAGEBOX('CUSTOMER 0025 was not found')
ENDIF
```

SEEK requires a value of the same data type as the current index. A seek expression does not always have to match the index value exactly, however. If SET EXACT is OFF, it needs to match character-for-character for only as many characters as are in the seek value. Suppose that you want to search CUST.DBF for a company whose name begins with *Laser*. Use the following code:

```
USE C:\VFP5BOOK\DATA\CUST
SET ORDER TO TAG company
SEEK 'Laser'
```

If SET EXACT is OFF, Visual FoxPro 5.0 finds the record. If SET EXACT is ON, the seek value must match the index value exactly, in total number of characters as well as each individual character. Thus, if you index CUSTOMER.DBF by company and perform the following SEEK with SET EXACT OFF, VFP places the record pointer at the first company whose name begins with *L*:

```
SET EXACT OFF
SEEK 'L'
```

The SET EXACT command also works for other conditional tests, such as in the FOR clause, described earlier in this chapter. In these cases, however, an inexact search matches characters from left to right until a mismatch is found or until the expression on the right side of the = operator ends. You can temporarily override inexact comparisons for a single conditional test by using the == operator. Therefore, the following two LOCATEs are equivalent:

```
SET EXACT ON
LOCATE FOR cFirst = 'NATASHA    '
```

and

```
SET EXACT OFF
LOCATE FOR cFirst == 'NATASHA    '
```

Normally, when a LOCATE or SEEK fails, Visual FoxPro 5.0 leaves the record pointer at the end of the table. In some cases, however, you may not know exactly what value to search for, so you guess. You want the pointer to stop at the next record after the position of the search value, if that value exists.

Suppose that you don't know the exact name of the company, but you think that it's Golf Heaven, so you write the code shown in Listing 6.9. If no company name in CUST.DBF has this exact spelling, the record pointer moves to the end of the file. If you first enter the command SET NEAR ON, however, VFP stops at the first company name that alphabetically follows Golf Heaven: Goofer's Arcade Heaven, in table CUST.DBF.

Table 6.3 might help clarify interpreting a SEEK with SET NEAR ON and SET EXACT OFF.

**Table 6.3   Results of SEEK with SET NEAR ON and SET EXACT OFF**

| EOF() | FOUND() | Search Result |
|-------|---------|---------------|
| .F. | .T. | Exact match of search string found |
| .F. | .F. | No exact match found, but record pointer is on the next record alphabetically |
| .T. | .F. | No exact match found; search string is beyond the last value in the table |

**Listing 6.9   06PRG09.PRG**

```
* Program 06PRG09.PRG
* Locate customer data for GOLF HEAVEN
* Open table and set tag to COMPANY
  USE C:\VFP5BOOK\DATA\CUST
  SET ORDER TO TAG company

* Save current setting of NEAR, and turn NEAR ON
  curnear = SYS(2001, 'NEAR')
  SET NEAR ON

* Find record closest to 'GOLF HEAVEN'
  SEEK 'GOLF HEAVEN'

* If search goes beyond last records, display last record.
  IF EOF()
    GOTO BOTTOM
  ENDIF
  DISPLAY

* Reset NEAR to original value
  SET NEAR &curnear
```

Part

II

Ch

6

**N O T E**   Use SET EXACT ON only if you search or compare with strings of the same length as the index or comparison field. Otherwise, SET EXACT OFF allows you to search by entering a substring. If you know that the substring that you want to search with matches character for character a field in the table, you can SET NEAR OFF. Otherwise, SET NEAR ON finds the next record alphabetically after the substring. ■

**N O T E**   Whenever you use a SET command in a program, consider capturing the current state of the SET parameter by using SYS(2001, '<parameter>'). Remember to restore the parameter to its original value when you leave the program. Always begin programs with a common SET definition. Then program by exception only those SET parameters that must change from this default. ■

If you are not sure that an entered value will exactly match a value in the table, use SET NEAR ON to find the next record alphabetically. Use this technique when you are setting ranges for parameters in reports. On the other hand, if you need to create a relation between customer ID in the order file and in the customer file, you want an exact match and should use both SET EXACT ON and SET NEAR OFF.

## Selecting Groups of Records

Many operations call for a subset of the table that is being used. Perhaps you want to see only the customers in Pennsylvania or those customers in California who have outstanding bills. In either case, define a filter condition, using the SET FILTER TO command followed by LIST or DISPLAY, as follows:

```
USE C:\VFP5BOOK\DATA\CUST
SET FILTER TO cBState = 'PA'
LIST
```

 **T I P**   Even though it does not use a FOR clause, SET FILTER is Rushmore-optimizable.

You have the same capability to filter records directly from within both LIST and DISPLAY. The FOR clause allows you to define a condition that selects records from the table. To select records for Pennsylvania customers, for example, use an expression like the following:

```
FOR cBState = 'PA'
```

Use the following expression to DISPLAY the results:

```
DISPLAY ALL cCustId, cCompany FOR cBState = 'PA'
```

This command steps through the records sequentially from the first record and displays only those that match the condition of the FOR expression. The potential problem with this method is apparent if you envision that the customer records will be sorted but not indexed by state. Visual FoxPro reads more records than it needs to. When the records are sorted, Visual FoxPro 5.0 physically groups the records for Pennsylvania customers. But without an index, when Visual FoxPro reads the table using a FOR clause, it tests each record to find the Pennsylvania ones. Furthermore, even after VFP displays the last record for Pennsylvania customers, it continues reading records until it reaches the end of the file. The FOR clause makes no assumptions about sort orders; it is a brute-force way of processing all records that match the condition.

**NOTE** If the FOR expression is Rushmore-optimizable, performance is greatly improved. If the FOR expression is not optimized, it can be extremely slow, because it reads every record in the table. The programmer has the responsibility of ensuring that the FOR expression is Rushmore-optimizable. ■

## Processing Records with WHILE

An alternative method of finding records that match an expression uses the WHILE clause. To begin, open a table and an index that uses the same order as the search condition. Next, find the first record that matches the search condition. To do so, use LOCATE or SEEK. If EOF() returns .T. or FOUND() returns .F., no records match the search condition. Having found the first record that matches the condition, you know that all additional matching records in the table follow it sequentially. Read these records one at a time, using a simple loop such as DO WHILE or SCAN, until the search condition fails. Then you can ignore the rest of the table without searching it, because you know that no other records will match.

Listing 6.10 shows a variation on the preceding search. It requires a nonoptimizable search, because it uses a substring expression to find a customer whose name begins with the letter *M*:

**Listing 6.10  06PRG10.PRG**

```
* Program 06PRG10.PRG
  SELECT CUST
  SET ORDER TO TAG COMPANY
  LOCATE FOR LEFT(cCompany,1) =  'M'
  SCAN WHILE LEFT(cCompany,1) =  'M'
    ? cCustId, cCompany
  ENDSCAN
```

Part II
Ch 6

**N O T E** If you need to retrieve records based on an expression that does not have a corresponding index, you probably need to use a nonoptimized FOR. Because such
expressions are slow, you may want to consider creating a separate index for this situation if it
occurs frequently. ■

Sometimes, using SEEK with a DO WHILE block can provide performance that is as good
as—or better than—that of a Rushmore-optimized FOR expression.

One additional enhancement can be added to this example. SEEK has an equivalent function call that returns .T. when it finds a match. You can place this function directly in the
DO WHILE statement, as in Listing 6.11:

**Listing 6.11    06PRG11.PRG**

```
* Program 06PRG11.PRG
SELECT CUST
SET ORDER TO TAG CUSTSTATE
IF SEEK('PA')    && Execute the code block on if PA is found
  DISPLAY REST cCustId, cCompany ;
        WHILE cBState = 'PA'
ENDIF
```

**TROUBLESHOOTING**

**I have a *DISPLAY* command with both a *FOR* and a *WHILE* expression, yet it does not return
all the records that match the *FOR* condition.** When you combine a FOR and WHILE expression
in the same statement, the WHILE expression has primary control. To return any records at all,
the WHILE expression must evaluate to .T. for the current record. If not, the statement returns
nothing. If the WHILE expression evaluates to .T., the record is passed to the FOR expression,
and only if the FOR expression also evaluates to .T. does VFP display that record. The result is that
the WHILE clause retrieves records beginning with the first one as long as the WHILE expression
remains true. Of these records, only those that pass the FOR condition are displayed. Notice that
because the WHILE clause has priority, it eliminates much of the benefit of Rushmore-enhanced
performance in the FOR clause.

# Sorting Data in the Table

You can sort data in a table in two fundamental ways. The first is a *physical sort,* also called
a *permanent sort.* To create a physical sort, you need to rewrite the table in the desired
sort order. The advantage of this method is that you need no additional file other than the
data file itself. The disadvantage is that the sort order is difficult to maintain if users make

frequent updates to the data. A physical sort requires more code to maintain or requires frequent re-sorting.

The second type of sort uses a second file called an index. An index stores values for the indexed field and pointers to the location of that value in the database. The pointer is a record number. Visual FoxPro 5.0 stores the indexed field values in a b-tree (binary search) structure that it can search quickly.

## Creating Permanent Sortings

As mentioned earlier in this chapter, you are unlikely to add records to the table in a sorted order. But if you do, what happens if you need more than one sort order? You certainly cannot have two physical sort orders in one table. The alternative—maintaining two or more separate copies of the data in tables with different sort orders—is a major nightmare. Yet at times, you want to store data in sorted order. Other than entering the records that way, how can you create a sorted table?

The SORT command creates another copy of the table and allows you to sort on any field or combination of fields. SORT's syntax is rather rich, as follows:

```
SORT TO TableName
     ON FieldName1 [/A][/D][/C]
     [FieldName2 [/A][/D][/C]...]
     [ASCENDING¦DESCENDING]
     [Scope][FOR Iexpression1][WHILE Iexpression2]
     [FIELDS FieldNameList¦FIELDS LIKE Skeleton
     ¦FIELDS EXCEPT Skeleton]
     [NOOPTIMIZE]
```

SORT's primary advantage is that it allows you to define a sort direction—ascending [/A] or descending [/D]—for individual fields. You can even sort a field and make it case-insensitive [/C]! When you create an index, you define the sort direction for the entire index expression, not for individual fields in the index expression.

Suppose that you need to generate a report that lists customers alphabetically by state, and within each state, you want to list customers with the largest annual purchases first and continue to the smallest. You need an ascending sort on state and a descending sort on purchases. SORT can create this file with the following statement:

```
USE \VFP5BOOK\DATA\CUSTOMER
SORT TO STATSALE ON cBillingStateProvince /A/C + ;
          nPurchasesYearToDate /D
```

Part
II

Ch
6

**CAUTION**

SORT creates a free table. Therefore, it truncates the long field names defined in the original table of the example to 10-character fields.

**TIP** You can sometimes trick Visual FoxPro into sorting fields in different directions, as follows:

```
INDEX ON cState + STR(999999.99-nPurchases,9,2)
```

Another disadvantage of using SORT is the quick obsolescence of the data. As soon as you create the table, it begins to become obsolete. Someone else may immediately add, delete, or modify a record. As a snapshot of the table for report purposes, SORT serves a valuable purpose, but keeping tables created with SORT around for very long is not recommended, even though the sort order is "permanently" defined by the records themselves. Perhaps the problem is that sorted tables are permanent and cannot adapt to changes.

▶ **See** "Using Query Designer versus Manually Created SQL SELECT Statements," **p. 326**

In Chapter 7, "Creating Basic Queries," you learn to create CURSORS with the SQL SELECT command. Cursors provide the same advantages as SORT (sort directions by field). In addition, Visual FoxPro 5.0 automatically deletes cursors when you exit VFP or open another table in the same work area.

## Creating Virtual Sorts with Index

Indexes provide the best way to provide different sort orders for data. Visual FoxPro 5.0 can create, use, and maintain three types of indexes:

- Independent indexes (IDX)
- Compound structural indexes (CDX)
- Compound non-structural indexes (CDX)

    ▶ **See** "Examining Stand-alone versus Structural and Non-structural Indexes," **p. 149**

Indexes are not permanent in the same way that tables created with SORT are. Rather, indexes are dynamic. Indexes adapt automatically to added, deleted, and modified records, as long as you keep them open.

```
INDEX ON eExpression ;
    TO IDXFileName¦TAG TagName [OF CDXFileName]
    [FOR lExpression]
    [COMPACT]
    [ASCENDING¦DESCENDING]
    [UNIQUE¦CANDIDATE]
    [ADDITIVE]
```

Chapter 3, "Defining Databases, Tables, and Indexes," discusses how to create compound structural indexes by using the index page of the Table Designer. You can create and use any of the three indexes directly from the Command window or from within a program, however.

**Simple Independent Indexes**  Independent indexes on a single expression were the first indexes used by FoxBase, the predecessor of FoxPro. They are also called independent indexes. For each index expression, create a separate index file with its own name. The root names of the table (.DBF) and index (.IDX) do not have to be the same. In fact, if you have more than one simple index, it is not possible for all of the indexes to have the same root name. Many programmers developed the habit of naming the primary index with the same root name as the table. The following lines use the INDEX command to create an independent index on customer_ID in CUST.DBF, which has 10-character field names:

```
USE CUST
INDEX ON cCustId TO CUSTID.IDX
```

At this point, the table and index are open. But in most programs, you need to specifically open previously created indexes with the table, as in the following command:

```
USE CUST INDEX CUSTID
```

If you have more than one index for a table, open the indexes at the same time if you plan to make modifications to the records, as follows:

```
USE CUST INDEX CUSTID, COMPANY, ZIPCODE
```

If you do not open each index, VFP cannot maintain the indexes that are not open if you add, delete, or modify records. (Because the indexes can have any name, how would FoxPro know about them?) If you attempt to use the table with one of these indexes later, VFP may display records out of order or even point outside the table, due to deleted records.

On the plus side, individual indexes can be more efficient than large compound ones that have several index definitions, especially when you only need to read them. Visual FoxPro 5.0 can read more of the index into memory, and memory access is significantly faster than disk access.

N O T E   To get the best performance, use the COMPACT option with single indexes. Except for backward compatibility, continued use of independent indexes is not recommended. It is too easy for the indexes to get out of sync, and they are much slower than compact indexes. The exception is when you need to use an index temporarily and will delete it when the task is complete. ■

**CAUTION**

Compact independent indexes are not compatible with older versions of FoxBase.

**Compound Indexes**  Although independent indexes work, compound indexes are a better alternative for most indexing needs. These indexes allow an unlimited number of

Part

II

Ch

6

separate index expressions in one file. You cannot lose files or forget the names of all the index files that belong to one table. If you assign the same root name to the index files used by the table, you do not even have to worry about opening the index file; Visual FoxPro 5.0 opens that file automatically when it opens the table. These compound indexes have a special name: *structural indexes.*

When you are working with compound indexes, you need to know not only how to set a tag, but also which tag is current, the names of the defined tags associated with a table, and their index expressions. You saw earlier that SET ORDER TO sets the current index when you are using standalone index files, and SET ORDER TO TAG sets the current tag for compound tags. But how can you determine which indexes are associated with a table?

Unfortunately, no functions like ADATABASE() (which captures the names of all open databases and their paths, and puts them in an array) that stores a list of indexes associated with a table. Furthermore, no relation exists between a table and its independent indexes or non-structural indexes. The only index that you can automatically associate with a table is its structural index, when present. Even in the context of a program that opens independent and non-structural indexes with their table, you cannot be sure that you have opened all the indexes.

You can examine the indexes opened with a table, however, by using several functions. The NDX() function returns the names of any open IDX files. (Originally, index files had an .NDX extension, and they still do in dBASE. Therefore, the function to list them became NDX(). The name NDX() remained the same in Visual FoxPro 5.0, even though its indexes have an .IDX extension to provide compatibility.)

To find the names of open compound indexes, use the CDX() or MDX() function. These two functions perform the same task. At minimum, each function requires a numeric parameter. A value of 1 returns the name of the structural index, if present. Subsequent values return the names of other compound indexes, in the order in which they are opened. These two functions, along with NDX(), return an empty string when the index number exceeds the number of open indexes. Therefore, test for this condition so as to know when to stop.

**N O T E**  Both the CDX() and MDX() functions support a second parameter that allows you to determine the index names associated with tables in another work area. Enter the second parameter as the work-area number or the file alias, as in the following example:

```
? CDX(1,'customer')
```

When you know the names of the compound indexes, find their tag names. The TAG() function returns the name of each tag in the current compound index, as in the following example:

```
i = 1
DO WHILE !EMPTY(TAG(i))
      ? TAG(i)
      i = i + 1
ENDDO
```

You also can include arguments to specify the compound-index name, as well as the table name or work area.

Although the preceding functions help you define the index files and tag names that are associated with an open table, they do not tell you which index or tag currently controls the order. Two SYS functions provide this information. SYS(21) returns the controlling index number, and SYS(22) returns the controlling index tag or index name.

To use SYS(21), you need to know how Visual FoxPro 5.0 assigns index numbers. Suppose that you have the following command line:

```
USE product INDEX prodid.idx, prodname.idx, prodpric.idx
```

VFP would number these indexes sequentially, in the order listed from 1 to 3. But consider what happens when you throw a compound index into the command, as follows:

```
USE product INDEX prodid.idx, prod1.cdx, prodpric.idx
```

In this case, PRODID.IDX is still 1. VFP skips to PRODPRICE.IDX, however, making it 2; then VFP returns to PROD1.CDX and numbers its tags sequentially. To make matters somewhat confusing at first glance, if you add the structural index, PRODUCT.CDX, VFP automatically opens it and numbers its tags after PRODPRIC.IDX but before the tags in PROD1.CDX. Actually, if you read the line carefully, you will discover the pattern. VFP always uses independent indexes first, followed by structured indexes, and finally by nonstructured indexes. Within any index type, such as independent indexes, VFP uses indexes from left to right in the order in which they are declared.

Finally, use the SYS(14,$n$) function to return the index expressions. The value of $n$ represents the index number assigned by Visual FoxPro 5.0. You can cycle through the index expressions until you encounter a null value, which indicates the end. You can also obtain the index expression more easily with the KEY() function, which allows both a CDX file name and an index number relative to that file.

Listing 6.12 provides a routine that documents the tables and indexes that are currently open in an application.

**Listing 6.12  06PRG12.PRG**

```
* Program 06PRG12.PRG
  LOCAL lnCurArea, lnHighestArea, lnIwork, lnIndx, lnIcdx, lnItag
  CLEAR
```

*continues*

**Listing 6.12   Continued**

```
* Current information on open tables
* Save the current work area
  lnCurArea = SELECT()

* Find the highest work area in use
  SELECT 0
  lnHighestArea = SELECT(0) - 1

* Loop through the work areas
  FOR lnWork = 1 to lnHighestArea
    WAIT WINDOW "Examining workarea: "+STR(m.lnWork,5) NOWAIT
    SELECT (lnWork)
    IF EMPTY(DBF())
      LOOP
    ENDIF
    ? 'Work area ' + STR(m.lnWork,5) + ': '
    ? '  Table: ' + DBF()

  * Next scan for simple indexes
    ? '  Simple Indexes'
    FOR lnIdx = 1 to 256
      IF EMPTY(NDX(lnIdx))
        IF lnIdx = 1
          ? '      NONE'
        ENDIF
        EXIT
      ENDIF
      ? '    Index: ' + NDX(lnIdx)
      ? '      Expression: ' + TAG(lnIdx)

    * Check if this IDX is the master index
      IF ORDER(ALIAS(),1) = NDX(lnIdx)
        ? '      This is the MASTER index'
      ENDIF

    ENDFOR

  * Scan for compound indexes
    ? '  Compound Indexes'
    FOR lnCdx = 1 to 256
      IF EMPTY(CDX(lnCdx))
        IF lnCdx = 1
          ? '      NONE'
        ENDIF
        EXIT
      ENDIF
      ? '    Index: ' + CDX(lnCdx)

    * Check if this CDX holds the master index
      IF ORDER(ALIAS(),1) = CDX(lnCdx)
        ? '        MASTER index:      ' + SYS(22)
        ? '            expression: ' + TAG(VAL(SYS(21)))
      ENDIF
```

```
    * Loop for each tag in the compound index
    FOR lnTag = 1 TO 256
      IF EMPTY(TAG(CDX(lnCdx),lnTag))
        EXIT
      ENDIF
      ? '       Tag Name:       ' + TAG(CDX(lnCdx),lnTag)
      ? '              Expression: ' + KEY(CDX(lnCdx),lnTag)
    ENDFOR
    ?
  ENDFOR
ENDFOR

* Return to original area
  SELECT (lnCurArea)
```

**N O T E**    Under some conditions, Visual FoxPro 5.0 retains the old tags in a CDX file after reindexing it. This arrangement causes the CDX file to grow. To prevent this growth, delete the CDX and re-create the tags. How can you do this in a program? Use the concepts from the preceding program to save the tag names and expressions for your selected CDX in an array; then delete the CDX and re-create the tags from the array. ■

# Planning Indexes for Rushmore

Indexing is more than just sorting records for views or reports. Indexes have a more direct impact on the application's performance than ever before. Since the release of FoxPro 2.0, when Microsoft introduced Rushmore, this optimization technique has dramatically improved the performance of applications by locating records in large tables. Rushmore achieves this task through the use of indexes. It uses any index type—IDX files, compact IDXs, or CDXs. In fact, it is common today to define indexes that you never intend to use for retrieving or viewing data; rather, these indexes exist solely to enhance the performance of SEEKs and REPORTs. Developers have reported search improvements 100 to 1,000 times faster when they use an optimizable Rushmore expression, compared with a nonoptimized expression. The greatest improvements come from using compact IDX or CDX files, principally because VFP can read more of the index into memory at one time.

To see the benefit of Rushmore yourself, the CD that comes with this book contains a file called ZIPCODE.DBF in the directory \VFP5BOOK\DATA\ that contains U.S. ZIP codes. Although this table has only 42,818 records, rather than millions, it serves to illustrate Rushmore's power.

**N O T E**    To quickly inflate the number of records in ZIPCODE.DBF, so as to provide a more
dramatic demonstration of Rushmore, perform the following steps:

```
CLOSE DATABASES

USE C:\VFP5BOOK\DATA\ZIPCODE in 1

COPY TO C:\VFP5BOOK\DATA\ADDZIP.DBF

FOR i = 1 to 11  && or as many times as you like

APPEND FROM C:\VFP5BOOK\DATA\ADDZIP.DBF

ENDFOR
```

This program creates a file that has slightly more than a half-million records. You may need to
take a coffee break while it runs.  ■

The table, as supplied, contains an index, but you can test a nonoptimized search on this
file by first issuing SET OPTIMIZE OFF. Listing 6.13 times how long it takes to count the
number of ZIP codes in Pennsylvania.

### Listing 6.13    06PRG13.PRG

```
* Program 06PRG13.PRG
  CLOSE ALL
  CLEAR

  SET OPTIMIZE OFF
  ? "Counting the number of zip codes in Pennsylvania."
  USE \VFP5BOOK\DATA\ZIPCODE
  nStart = SECONDS()
  COUNT FOR (STATE == 'PA') TO nZipCnt
  nEnd   = SECONDS()
  ? '       COUNT WAS: ' + STR(nZipCnt, 12, 0)
  ? 'ELAPSED TIME WAS: ' + STR(nEnd - nStart, 8, 2)
  SET OPTIMIZE ON
```

On a test system, it took 4.61 seconds to find 2,217 records out of 42,818. Elapse time on
your system will vary, depending on the processor speed, drive speed, physical sector
allocation, and other factors. If you remove both SET OPTIMIZE statements, the required
time drops to 0.16 second. Although this figure is an increase of only 29 times, the sample
table is small; improvements become more dramatic as the number of records grows.
The difference can easily extend into minutes and even hours for large tables that have
millions of records.

How can Rushmore provide such improved performance? First, by reading an index, it
quickly locates the first record reference required by the condition and then reads the
index only until the condition changes. Second, it reads only the index, rather than the
table; it does not have to use the record pointer to read the actual table data. In the

ZIP-code table, Rushmore reads the index tag STATE that contains an entry for each record in the table. This entry contains the state name and a pointer to the table record. There is no reason to go to the table. Because Rushmore can directly read the state name stored in the index, it can simply count the number of times that the state *PA* occurs.

**N O T E** Rushmore must compare the index expression with a memory variable or constant. In other words, you can compare the index expression with a string, number, or date value, or store a value in a constant and use it. But Rushmore cannot optimize an expression that compares an index expression with another variable in the table. Suppose that you have a table that includes birth dates and hire dates. Rushmore cannot optimize an expression such as the following, which lists records for people 16-years old or older:

```
LIST FOR dHire_Date > GOMONTH(dBirth_Date, 16*12)
```

To use Rushmore, you don't need to know the details of how it works internally, any more than you need to know the details of how an internal-combustion engine works to drive a car. But obviously, you need to know how to define indexes that Rushmore can optimize. More important, you need to know what Rushmore likes and dislikes.

This chapter has already mentioned a few rules that you must obey to use Rushmore successfully. Another rule is that Rushmore can optimize only expressions based on regular, primary, and candidate indexes. These indexes (as mentioned in Chapter 3, "Defining Databases, Tables, and Indexes") contain a reference for every record in the table, even if the index value is not unique. If you think about it, how else would Rushmore count the number of ZIP codes in a state if you defined the state index as unique? You would never get a value other than 0 or 1.

▶ **See** "Defining Normal and Unique Indexes," **p. 151**

Rushmore also requires that any search or query exactly match the index key. This statement led many developers to believe that they needed a separate index tag for every field in their tables. Then the developers realized that they also need more complex index expressions for reports or other activities, so they created additional indexes. Before long, the total number of indexes grew out of control, and the size of the .CDX file rivaled or exceeded that of the data itself. Performance degrades not just because of the size of the .CDX, but because Visual FoxPro 5.0 has more indexes to maintain every time you add, delete, or modify a record.

Often, you can delete many of these indexes without seriously affecting the application's performance. Returning to the customer file, suppose that you have the following set of indexes (using short field names in CUST.DBF):

```
INDEX ON UPPER(cLast) TAG LASTNAME
INDEX ON UPPER(cFirst) TAG FIRSTNAME
```

```
INDEX ON UPPER(cCompany) TAG COMPANY
INDEX ON UPPER(cLast)+UPPER(cFirst) TAG STAFF
INDEX ON UPPER(cCompany) + UPPER(cLast) +  ;
        UPPER(cFirst) TAG EMPLOYEES
```

Although these tags appear to cover every contingency, they affect performance when you add, delete, or modify records, because VFP must change more information in more tags. An alternative method takes advantage of the fact that Rushmore can optimize concatenated indexes. If you use SET EXACT OFF, you do not need to supply every field in the index.

If you wanted to search on the company field, for example, you could use either the COMPANY or EMPLOYEES tag, as follows:

```
LOCATE FOR cCompany = 'RENARD CONSULTANTS'
```

Alternatively, you could use the following:

```
SET EXACT OFF
LOCATE FOR cCompany + cLast + cFirst = ;
           'RENARD CONSULTANTS'
```

In the first LOCATE, Rushmore looks at the index expression on the left and decides to use the COMPANY tag. In the second, LOCATE uses the EMPLOYEES tag. The second expression is only slightly slower than the first. The only consideration is that you must include the entire index expression on the left side.

A similar argument applies when you are searching for names and choosing between tags STAFF and LASTNAME. The only individual field tag that you may still need is FIRSTNAME. Therefore, you can eliminate at least two of these five indexes and maybe more, depending on what the application really needs to do.

> **CAUTION**
>
> Although Rushmore can optimize an expression that matches only a portion of the concatenated fields, as in SET EXACT OFF, the shorter string must be on the right side of the expression. Also, there is no way to skip a field in a multiple-field index so as to search only for later components.

Notice that if you eliminate tags LASTNAME and COMPANY, Rushmore does not optimize a search like the following, because the index expression no longer exactly matches an index tag:

```
LOCATE FOR cCompany = 'RENARD CONSULTANTS'
```

Other things that Rushmore does not like and will not handle include index expressions that contain NOT or !. Surprisingly, you can include NOT or ! in the FOR expression and have Rushmore optimize it. Therefore, remove all negative expressions from indexes and move them into FOR expressions. Do not create an index like the following:

```
INDEX ON cState FOR NOT (cState = 'PA')
DISPLAY ALL
```

Rather, move the NOT (!) into the FOR clause, as follows:

```
INDEX ON cState
DISPLAY ALL FOR !(cState = 'PA')
```

Rushmore optimizes expressions that contain exactly equal relational operators (==), but not the contained-in operator ($), AT(), ATC(), or RAT(). It will not use indexes that include FOR conditions.

On the other hand, you can build compound FOR expressions that Rushmore can optimize (or at least partially optimize). A compound expression joins two or more simple expressions with an AND or an OR. In this case, each expression may reference a different index expression. When it is looking at compound expressions two at a time, Rushmore optimizes the entire expression only if it can optimize both individual expressions. If it can only optimize one of the expressions, and you join the expressions with AND, Rushmore executes the part that it can optimize first. Then Rushmore takes this intermediate result set and performs the nonoptimizable portion on it, rather than on the entire database. This arrangement usually results in some improvement over a completely nonoptimizable expression.

Visual FoxPro 5.0 cannot optimize a compound expression that contains one optimizable expression and one nonoptimizable expression joined with an OR, because it still must read the entire table to evaluate the nonoptimizable expression. Finally, if both individual expressions are nonoptimizable, Rushmore cannot optimize any part of the expression.

Table 6.4 displays possible combinations of expressions and their results.

**Table 6.4    Combining Optimizable Expressions**

| First Expression | Connection | Second Expression | Result |
|---|---|---|---|
| Optimizable | AND | Optimizable | Optimizable |
| Optimizable | OR | Optimizable | Optimizable |
| Optimizable | AND | Nonoptimizable | Partial |
| Optimizable | OR | Nonoptimizable | Nonoptimizable |
| Nonoptimizable | AND | Nonoptimizable | Nonoptimizable |
| Nonoptimizable | OR | Nonoptimizable | Non-optimizable |

Part
II

Ch
6

Potentially, Rushmore can optimize every VFP command that supports a FOR clause. You must work with a single table, however, and follow the rules described earlier in this section. The following list shows the commands that Rushmore supports:

| | | |
|---|---|---|
| AVERAGE | DISPLAY | REPORT FORM |
| BROWSE | EDIT | SCAN |
| CALCULATE | EXPORT | SET FILTER TO |
| CHANGE | LABEL | SORT |
| COPY TO | LIST | SQL SELECT |
| COPY TO ARRAY | LOCATE | SUM |
| COUNT | RECALL | TOTAL |
| DELETE | REPLACE | |

Remember that Rushmore works with these commands only if you use them with a single table. To query or gather data from multiple tables, use SQL SELECT. Only the SQL SELECT command supports Rushmore optimization across multiple tables.

**N O T E**   If you have a simple SQL SELECT on a single table with no special functions, groups, or sort orders, Visual FoxPro 5.0 uses Rushmore to create a filter on the database that returns the result set extremely fast. VFP does use Rushmore on multiple-table queries, but only if you use SQL SELECT.  ■

**N O T E**   With the introduction of Rushmore, traditional accessing of files with deleted records exhibited a performance degradation. A simple solution exists, however: Merely add a tag to the structured index, using the function DELETED( ), but do not name it DELETED, which is a restricted keyword. Now Rushmore can use the index to determine whether to include a record, rather than having to check the deleted flag in the table.  ■

## Turning Rushmore Off

At the beginning of this section, you learned that SET OPTIMIZE OFF can turn Rushmore off. Why turn off a tool that usually results in better performance? You typically don't want to turn Rushmore off when you are using expressions that it can optimize. When you are using nonoptimizable expressions, however, leaving it on actually lowers performance. In such cases, Rushmore needs extra machine cycles just to know that it is not needed. Therefore, turn optimization off by using the SET OPTIMIZE statement or by adding the clause NOOPTIMIZE after the FOR expression, as follows:

```
LOCATE FOR cFirst = 'NATASHA' NOOPTIMIZE
```

Another reason for turning off optimization involves the way that Rushmore stores information on networks. The first time that Rushmore executes an optimizable FOR expression, it reads the entire table and makes a memory map of those records that match the selection criteria. If you issue a command with the same FOR expression, Rushmore checks to see whether the memory map still exists and uses it, if possible. During this time, someone else on the network may have made changes in the file that would change the records selected. Rushmore has no way of knowing this, however, so it may use the wrong records in the second command.

## Helping Rushmore Along

You can improve the performance of Rushmore by deselecting any default index or tag before executing a command that Rushmore can optimize. The following command leaves the index file open but turns off its active use:

```
SET ORDER TO 0
```

Rushmore wastes time examining the current index expression and deciding whether it can use it. If you set order to 0, Rushmore skips this first step and immediately proceeds with selecting the proper index, based on the FOR expression.

 **TIP** As a general rule, you add as many indexes as necessary to search for and display data. You should periodically review whether you require all of them, however.

When an application's performance slows due to index overload, you need to identify indexes that you use only occasionally. You should delete those index tags and allow the program to re-create them as needed.

 **TIP** To delete a tag, open the table and use the command DELETE TAG <tagname>.

You may even want to create temporary indexes on a local rather than a network drive or (even better) a RAM drive. You may even gain some performance by creating a cursor with an SQL SELECT statement to gather and sort the data for a report. Listing 6.14 shows a method that may appear to be awkward at first, yet yields quite respectable performance when the selected records are widely scattered and need to be reused. The routine begins by creating a temporary index; then it uses a Rushmore-assisted SEEK to find the first record. The routine processes the desired records, using a DO WHILE clause; generates a report with the same index; and, finally, deletes the temporary index.

Part
**II**

Ch
**6**

**Listing 6.14   06PRG14.PRG**

```
* Program 06PRG14.PRG
  CLOSE DATABASES
  CLEAR
```

*continues*

**Listing 6.14   Continued**

```
* Open the customer table (free table)
  USE \VFP5BOOK\DATA\cust

* Set NEAR ON to find first customer with more than
* $200 of outstanding bills
  cCurNear   = SYS(2001, 'NEAR')
  cCurExact  = SYS(2001, 'EXACT')
  cCurSafety = SYS(2001, 'SAFETY')
  SET NEAR   ON
  SET EXACT  OFF
  SET SAFETY OFF

* Create a temporary index on outstanding bills
* This assumes that you have previously created a directory
* with the name C:\TEMP
  INDEX ON nBillDue TO C:\TEMP\BILLS.IDX

* Find records and change default billing method to cash 'CA'
  SEEK 200
  SCAN WHILE nBillDue >= 200
    REPLACE cPayMeth WITH 'CA'
  ENDSCAN

* Create a report for sales representative of customer that
* must pay cash
  REPORT FORM \VFP5BOOK\PROGRAMS\BillMeth ;
    FOR nBillDue => 200

* Reset environment
  SET NEAR   &cCurNear
  SET EXACT  &cCurExact
  SET SAFETY &cCurSafety

* Delete temporary index
  USE
  ERASE C:\temp\bills.idx
RETURN
```

In this example, SEEK takes advantage of Rushmore to find the first record, but SCAN WHILE does not use Rushmore. In fact, any command that supports the WHILE clause will not invoke Rushmore when you are WHILE. A SEEK combined with SCAN WHILE structure almost always executes as fast as Rushmore and may even be faster in a few cases. Also notice the use of SET NEAR ON to find the first record above a specific value, just in case no records have a value of exactly 200.

The best indexing method varies from one situation to the next. Your choice depends on the specific task that you want to accomplish, the current organization of the data, the specific commands that you use, and (probably) the phase of the moon.

The BROWSE command illustrates this point. Reopen ZIPCODE.DBF and turn off the index, as follows:

```
USE C:\VFP5BOOK\DATA\ZIPCODE
SET ORDER TO
```

The natural order of this data is city within state. Thus, all the ZIP codes for Alaska appear first, and all the ZIP codes for Wyoming appear at the end of the file. Now try the following simple BROWSEs:

```
BROWSE FOR cBState = 'AK'
BROWSE FOR cBState = 'WY'
```

The first BROWSE comes up almost immediately. The second BROWSE opens a window immediately but takes several seconds to display the first screen of data. BROWSE displays the first screen of data as soon as it has enough records to populate it. Thus, the second command pauses with a blank window, while BROWSE searches through the file until it finds *Wyoming*.

Suppose you know that the selected data either appears very near the beginning of the file or that it encompasses the majority of the data (such as BROWSE FOR !DELETED()). A simple BROWSE statement without an index may appear to be as quick as one with an index using Rushmore, because BROWSE does not need to find every record that matches the criteria—only enough to display a screen of records. That explanation may be stretching the point just a little, but you should try several alternatives before you assume that Rushmore and another index tag provide the best performance.

# From Here...

In this chapter, you learned to be aware of the number of open files in your system, as well as the work areas in which they are used. You learned that opening tables bound to databases is almost as simple as opening a free table, thanks to the embedded backlink to the database, but if moved, you must move the database and the tables together.

Next, you saw ways to list and display data to the screen, printer, and file. You learned how to search for specific records with and without an index and various ways to loop through the table for all records that match a criteria.

Finally, you saw how Rushmore uses indexes to optimize many commands that support FOR expressions. To use Rushmore effectively, you must exercise caution when you define both the index expressions and the FOR expressions. Rushmore cannot optimize every valid expression, but when it can optimize one, it provides dramatic performance gains. Sometimes Rushmore can get in the way and needs to be turned off.

Part
II

Ch
6

To learn more, refer to the following chapters:

- Chapter 3, "Defining Databases, Tables, and Indexes," teaches you the basics of creating databases, tables, and indexes.

- Chapter 7, "Creating Basic Queries," shows you how to use the Query Designer and how to manually create simple SQL SELECT statements to extract data from multiple tables.

- Chapter 8, "Advanced Queries and Views," takes query generation to a higher level with joins, cross-tabs, and views.

- Chapter 9, "Using BROWSE to View Data," examines the new BROWSE features that go beyond the simple viewing of data.

# Creating Basic Queries

*by Michael Antonovich
and Richard Curtis*

**A**ccording to the American Heritage Dictionary, a *query* is a question, an inquiry. So when you query a database, you are asking it questions about data. Using a sales file, for example, you might ask the following questions:

> What is the total value of all sales for last week? Last month? Last year?
>
> Are sales increasing?
>
> Which products sell the greatest quantity?
>
> Which products produce the most sales dollars?
>
> Which products are losing sales?
>
> How many sales are made to repeat customers?
>
> How are sales distributed by state?

With a little effort, we're sure that you can come up with infinitely more questions. Although you might write programs to answer many of those questions, there is no way to anticipate them all. ■

**Use the Query Designer to visually create queries**

Learn to create queries with visual tools.

**Use the queries created by the Query Designer in program code**

Learn to integrate query code into programs and forms.

**Route query results to the screen, tables, reports, graphs, and labels**

Learn to send query results to multiple locations.

**Manually define queries to answer questions**

Learn to use SQL SELECT to retrieve information.

# Selecting Tables for a Query

Before starting a query, open the database that contains the needed tables; you do not have to open the tables themselves. Next, open the Query Designer by choosing File, New from the system menu or by clicking the New button in the toolbar. Choose the Query option in the New dialog box, and click the New File button, as shown in Figure 7.1.

**FIGURE 7.1**
Use the New dialog box to start a new query.

## Adding a Table or View from a Database

**TIP** You also can start a new query from the Command window by using the CREATE QUERY or MODIFY QUERY command.

A query requires at least one table. However, Visual FoxPro does not assume that you want to query the table in the current work area; rather, it immediately opens a window displaying the Open Table dialog box and allows you to select the first table. Actually, VFP can open two windows, depending on whether a database is open. Figure 7.2 shows the Add Table or View dialog box, which lists tables in an open database. If more than one database is open, you can pull down the database combo list and change the current one.

For this set of examples, open the Tastrade database that comes with Visual FoxPro. In the Select area, you can choose either Tables or Views to use in the query. Tastrade has both tables and some predefined views. To start a new query definition, select from the available tables. Notice that the list of tables in this dialog box includes only tables that are defined in the Tastrade database.

**FIGURE 7.2**

The Add Table or View dialog box appears when you create a new query, allowing you to select a table.

 **TIP**  Keep in mind that the methods discussed in this chapter apply to views as well.

## Adding a Free Table

To use a free table, either start the Query Designer without first opening a database, or click the Other button in the Add Table or View dialog box (see Figure 7.2). VFP displays the standard Open dialog box, shown in Figure 7.3. This dialog box allows you to select a table from any directory or drive, including network drives. If the selected table really is bound to a database, Visual FoxPro automatically opens the database, too.

**FIGURE 7.3**

The Open dialog box allows you to select free tables or tables from databases that are not open.

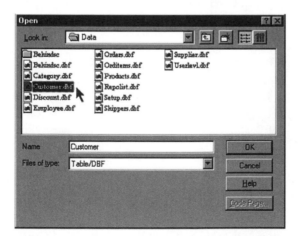

To begin the first query, return to the Add Table or View dialog box, and select the PRODUCTS table from the Tastrade database. A small window in the table view area (the top half) of the Query Designer displays the table's field names. The name of the selected tables always appears in the window header. Figure 7.4 shows the Query Designer at this point.

Part

II

Ch

7

**FIGURE 7.4**
The Query Designer, with two tables from the Tastrade database is open in the table view area.

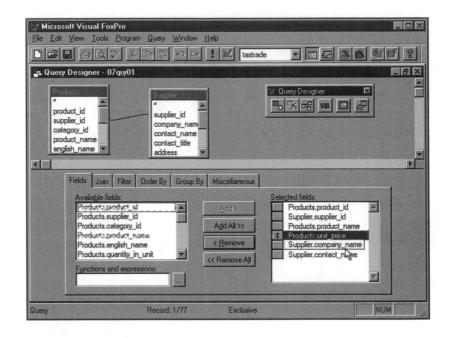

When the Query Designer opens, it also opens a toolbar (see Figure 7.5). The toolbar's six buttons perform functions that are specific to queries.

**FIGURE 7.5**
The Query Designer toolbox has six buttons that provide fast access to some of the most common functions.

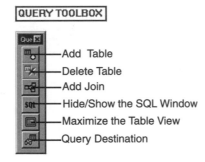

QUERY TOOLBOX

- Add Table
- Delete Table
- Add Join
- Hide/Show the SQL Window
- Maximize the Table View
- Query Destination

 Suppose that you want to list products by suppliers. The PRODUCTS file has a supplier ID associated with every product. But the SUPPLIER table stores the details about each supplier, such as name and address. Therefore, you need to open both files. To add a second table, click the Add Table button in the query toolbar. VFP displays the View dialog box. Select the SUPPLIER table, and click ADD.

In Figure 7.6, notice that when Query Designer adds the SUPPLIER table to the table view area, it also draws a line between PRODUCTS and SUPPLIER. To be more specific, it draws the line between the field PRODUCTS.Supply_Id and SUPPLIER.Supply_Id.

This line indicates that these two files share a field that relates records from one table to another. FoxPro knew to draw this line because of the persistent relation defined between these two files, created with the Table Designer and stored in the database. VFP also displays this *join condition* on the Join page in the bottom half of the Query Designer window.

**FIGURE 7.6**
The Query Designer is shown with two open tables.

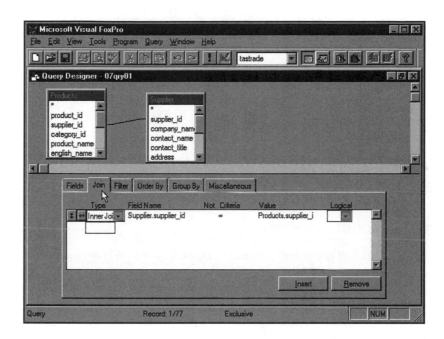

Perhaps you wonder what the two buttons to the left of the field name in the Join page do. The leftmost button, which points up and down, allows you to change the order of the selection expressions (if you have more than one). The second button, which points left and right, appears only when the criteria define the link between tables and allow modification to the type of join condition. Click this second button to display the dialog box shown in Figure 7.7. You can also open this dialog box by clicking the Add Join button in the toolbar or by double-clicking the line that links the two tables in the table view area.

The Join page enables you to customize the join condition. You can select the type of join from the Type drop-down list, open the drop-down list for either field, and select fields to define the join relation. You can also change the connection criteria and reverse the logic by clicking the Not button. Join supports five criteria:

- Equal
- Like

- Exactly Like
- More Than
- Less Than

▶ **See** "Forming Persistent Relations," **p. 200**

**FIGURE 7.7**
Define the join criteria by using the Join Condition dialog box.

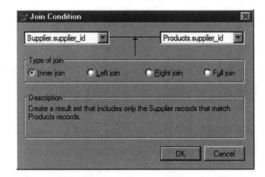

**TROUBLESHOOTING**

**When I try to modify the join condition, the drop-down lists are disabled.** Join conditions that are established as the result of a persistent relationship between tables cannot be modified. You must remove the join condition and then set it again from the Join page. Removing the join condition from the Join page does not affect the persistent relationships between tables.

The Join Condition dialog box enables you to select the type of join and describes each condition. The four types of joins are:

- *Inner* join, which includes records from both tables that match the join condition.
- Left *outer* join, which includes records that match the join condition *and* records from the table to the left of the join (the parent table) that do *not* match the join condition.
- Right *outer* join, which includes records that match the join condition *and* records from the table to the right of the join (the child table) that do *not* match the join condition.
- Full *outer* join, which includes records that match *and* do *not* match the join condition. For records without corresponding matches, the unmatched fields are blank.

### Additional Filter Criteria

Record filters support three additional criteria, BETWEEN, IN, and IS NULL. BETWEEN defines an inclusive range of values. The following would include employees between 0100 and 0199, inclusive:

```
Employee_Id BETWEEN '0100' AND '0199'
```

On the other hand, IN defines a list of independent values. The following statement tells the query to include only records for these three employees:

```
Employee_Id IN ('0100', '0133', '0175')
```

You also can use Is NULL to find any records that do not have an employee ID entered. In this case, no Example value is necessary.

### Criteria Comparison

The preceding sidebar shows the selection example as it appears in the resulting SQL statement. However, when you are entering the example for a criteria comparison, follow these rules:

- Do not enclose character strings in quotation marks. The Query Designer automatically adds the necessary quotes. If your comparison string contains multiple words that are separated by blanks, you may want to use the quotation marks for your own clarity. You also need to enclose the string in quotation marks if the text is the same as the name of a field in a table used by the query.

- If the example is the name of a field used by the query, the Query Designer treats it as such.

- Do not enclose dates in braces or use CTOD(). Simply enter the date in this format: 08/04/95.

- If the example is a logical value, include the periods before and after the value (.T.).

The Equal criterion performs exactly like a simple equal sign between the strings on either side of the join. Thus, whether trailing blanks are considered in the comparison depends on the current setting of SET ANSI. If SET ANSI is ON, it pads the shorter string before comparing the strings, character for character, for their entire length. If SET ANSI is OFF, the strings are compared only until the end of the shorter string is reached.

The Like criterion performs a comparison equivalent to that of SET EXACT OFF. FoxPro compares the expression on the left, character by character, with the one on the right for as many characters as the expression has.

Part
II

Ch
7

The Exactly Like criterion creates a more restrictive comparison. It first pads the shorter of the two expressions with blanks, to make them equal in length; then it compares them character for character to see whether they match. It includes only those records whose criteria match exactly.

The More Than and Less Than criteria perform simple less-than or greater-than comparisons of the expression values. You can ask for product records with product unit prices more than $10, for example. In that case, only records whose product unit price is greater than $10 appear in the result set.

Because this example compares two fields in separate tables, each representing supplier ID defined the same way, choosing Like or Exactly Like generates the same results. Additional criteria in the form of record filters, however, might use these alternative comparison criteria.

Another option when you are defining the comparison criteria is the Not button. Clicking this button reverses the criteria's logic. Choose Not with Exactly Like to create Not Exactly Like; choose it with More Than to create Less Than Or Equal To.

Finally, you can ignore the case of character strings by clicking the button on the right that appears below the Case heading. You might use it in record-selection criteria to ignore inconsistent case in field values.

# Selecting Fields to Include in the Query

Having defined the relation between the two tables, you next define which fields to include in the results. Clicking the Fields tab in the Query Designer displays two lists: Available Fields and Selected Fields. Initially, all fields in all selected tables appear in the Available Fields list, and the Selected Output list is empty.

To include all fields in the Selected Fields list, click the Add All button. (You also can double-click the asterisk in the table's field list or drag the asterisk to the Selected Fields list.) However, you seldom need to see all fields when viewing data. To select individual fields, click them in the Available Fields list. Each time you click an available field, the Add button becomes enabled. Click this button to move the field to the Selected Fields list. You may find double-clicking a field to be a faster way to select and move it.

Other ways to move a field from the Available Fields list to the Selected Fields list include:

- Drag the field from the Available list to the Selected list.
- Click the field name in the table field list in the table view of Query Designer and drag it to the selected list.

- Double-click the field name in the table field list in the table view of Query Designer.

- Hold the Ctrl key down and click on multiple fields and choose the Add button.

- Drag or double-click the asterisk in the table field list in the table view to include all the table's fields.

 **N O T E** Selected Output fields initially appear in the order in which they are added. You can rearrange the order by dragging the mover button to the left of each field. The order of the selected fields determines the column order of the output view or file. ■

To remove all the Selected Fields, placing them back in the Available Fields list, click Remove All. You also can remove fields one at a time by double-clicking a field in the Selected Fields list or by clicking to a field and then clicking Remove.

**TIP** If you want to add more than half of the fields from the Available Fields list, the quickest way is to click Add All to move them to the Selected Fields list. Then select the individual fields that you don't want to use and send them back by clicking the Remove button.

The No Duplicates check box, in the Miscellaneous page, checks to see whether the value of every selected field remains the same from one record to the next. If so, VFP does not include the record. If at least one value in one field differs from record to record, VFP includes the record.

# Ordering the Results

To see products alphabetically by description for each supplier, click the Order By tab. This tab, shown in Figure 7.8, provides options to customize the sort order of the results.

This page displays two list boxes that contain fields. The left box contains only the Selected fields. After all, you cannot sort on a field that is not included in the results. To begin the sort with the supplier's company name, click it and then click Add. As with adding fields, this action moves the selected field to the right list box. Notice that a small up arrow appears next to the field name in the Ordering Criteria list. This arrow indicates that the current sort order for this field is ascending. Change the field sort order to descending by selecting the field and then clicking the Descending option in the Order Options area. You can also select the order option before moving the fields to the Ordering Criteria list.

**FIGURE 7.8**
Define the sort order of the query results by dragging fields to the Ordering Criteria list in the order in which you want to sort the query results.

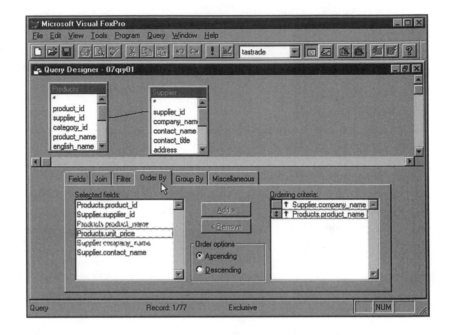

 To see products alphabetically for each supplier, double-click Product_Name. The order in which you select fields for the ordering criteria determines their sort order. If you use the mover button to put Product_Name before Company_Name, the query would sort the records first by product name. Then, if the product has more than one supplier, the query would list them alphabetically.

# Miscellaneous Tab Options

This tab provides options for additional record-selection criteria:

- No Duplicates allows you to show or to exclude duplicate records from your selection.

- Cross-Tabulate outputs the result set into a cross-tabular format. It also automatically selects the Group and Order By fields.

- Top allows you to select all records, several records, or a percentage of records to be returned. If you want to show the top 10 sales items, a query ordered by the units sold and limited to 10 records would provide your top 10 items. Changing the order option from ascending to descending provides the bottom 10 sales items.

# Viewing the Results

To see the results of a query using the current query definition, click the Run button (the button with an exclamation point on it) in the toolbar. Visual FoxPro runs the query; gathers the records from the tables, based on the selection criteria; selects fields to display; and sorts the records. VFP then displays the results in Browse mode, as shown in Figure 7.9.

**FIGURE 7.9**
Display a view of query results in Browse mode at any time by clicking the Run button in the standard toolbar.

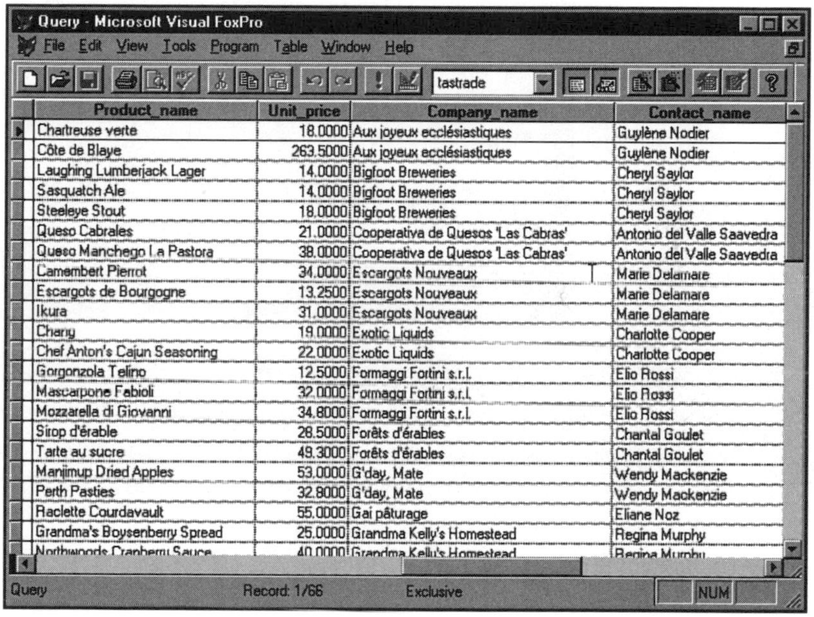


| Product_name | Unit_price | Company_name | Contact_name |
|---|---|---|---|
| Chartreuse verte | 18.0000 | Aux joyeux ecclésiastiques | Guylène Nodier |
| Côte de Blaye | 263.5000 | Aux joyeux ecclésiastiques | Guylène Nodier |
| Laughing Lumberjack Lager | 14.0000 | Bigfoot Breweries | Cheryl Saylor |
| Sasquatch Ale | 14.0000 | Bigfoot Breweries | Cheryl Saylor |
| Steeleye Stout | 18.0000 | Bigfoot Breweries | Cheryl Saylor |
| Queso Cabrales | 21.0000 | Cooperativa de Quesos 'Las Cabras' | Antonio del Valle Saavedra |
| Queso Manchego La Pastora | 38.0000 | Cooperativa de Quesos 'Las Cabras' | Antonio del Valle Saavedra |
| Camembert Pierrot | 34.0000 | Escargots Nouveaux | Marie Delamare |
| Escargots de Bourgogne | 13.2500 | Escargots Nouveaux | Marie Delamare |
| Ikura | 31.0000 | Escargots Nouveaux | Marie Delamare |
| Chang | 19.0000 | Exotic Liquids | Charlotte Cooper |
| Chef Anton's Cajun Seasoning | 22.0000 | Exotic Liquids | Charlotte Cooper |
| Gorgonzola Telino | 12.5000 | Formaggi Fortini s.r.l. | Elio Rossi |
| Mascarpone Fabioli | 32.0000 | Formaggi Fortini s.r.l. | Elio Rossi |
| Mozzarella di Giovanni | 34.8000 | Formaggi Fortini s.r.l. | Elio Rossi |
| Sirop d'érable | 28.5000 | Forêts d'érables | Chantal Goulet |
| Tarte au sucre | 49.3000 | Forêts d'érables | Chantal Goulet |
| Manjimup Dried Apples | 53.0000 | G'day, Mate | Wendy Mackenzie |
| Perth Pasties | 32.8000 | G'day, Mate | Wendy Mackenzie |
| Raclette Courdavault | 55.0000 | Gai pâturage | Eliane Noz |
| Grandma's Boysenberry Spread | 25.0000 | Grandma Kelly's Homestead | Regina Murphy |
| Northwoods Cranberry Sauce | 40.0000 | Grandma Kelly's Homestead | Regina Murphy |

▶ **See** "Browsing Related Tables," **p. 405**

Notice that columns in the result set appear in the order in which you selected the fields. If you do not like this order, you can change it. Click the column heading, and drag it left or right. As you move the mouse, the column heading follows. Simply release the mouse button when you are satisfied with the new position.

You also can adjust column widths to view more columns at one time. Place the mouse pointer over any vertical bar that separates two column headings. The mouse pointer changes to a thick vertical bar with a left and right arrow (see Figure 7.10). Click and drag this separator to resize the column. If you make the column smaller than necessary to display its values, VFP truncates the displayed values, not the actual data.

**FIGURE 7.10**

A split query window, with the Product Name column being resized.

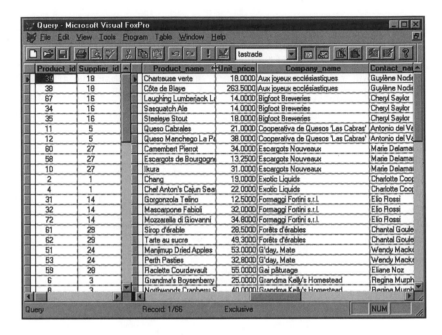

Because query results appear in an actual Browse window, they have a few additional features. Perhaps you have noticed that when you press Tab or use the scroll bars to view additional columns, that columns on the other side of the screen scroll out of view. Often, the first few columns include fields (such as ID or name fields) that identify the rows. Sometimes, a query has so many columns that by the time you scroll to the ones that you need, you forget which row you are in. Although you could manually move these columns together (or redefine the query with the columns closer together), you may need to view so many columns that moving them would simply not be practical.

**N O T E** Clicking the arrows at the end of the horizontal scroll bars moves the view one field to the left or right. Clicking the arrows at the top and bottom of the vertical scroll bar moves up or down one record. ■

To view all the columns that you need to view, no matter how far apart they are, split the Browse window by using the browse splitter. Initially, the browse splitter appears as a thin black box in the lower-left corner of the window. To split the window, click the splitter and drag it horizontally. Immediately, the query window splits into two partitions, each with its own set of scroll bars (refer to Figure 7.10).

After splitting the window, use the scroll bars to move through records or columns in either window. When you move between fields by pressing the Tab key or by using the horizontal scroll bar, the fields scroll horizontally in one window but remain unaffected in the other. Using this method, you can keep key fields displayed in one window to identify the record while you view the remaining fields in the other one.

Initially, moving between rows in one window automatically moves the corresponding record pointer in the other window and also scrolls both windows, if necessary, because Visual FoxPro maintains a link between the two windows. To break this link, deselect the Link Partitions option in the Table menu. Now VFP still moves the pointer in both windows, but it no longer scrolls the other window as you move between records. This feature helps you view records that are scattered throughout the table. If you later turn Link Partitions back on, VFP resynchronizes the two windows to match the selected record in the active partition.

You can also change the view from browse style to edit style for the entire window or just one partition. To change a partition to edit view, click the desired partition and then choose View, Edit.

You cannot modify the results in either the browse or edit style view.

To remove the partitioned window, simply drag the splitter bar back to the far-left side of the main Query window. Whatever view mode exists in the partition on the right side of the window remains in effect.

# Using Multiple-Condition Filters

In this section, you return to the Query Designer and add a second condition to the filter criteria. Rather than view all products from a supplier, limit the view to products on order. To do so, click the Filter tab, pull down the Field Name list, and click the Units_On_Order field to select it.

**TIP** Fields used for Filter criteria do not have to appear in the results.

To limit selected records to those that have products on order, you want to find records that have a Units_On_Order value greater than zero. Therefore, select > (More Than) as a Criteria and enter **0** in the Example field.

Suppose that you also want to see items that sell for less than 25 percent above cost. First, move down to a new Filter Criteria line and click the Field Name text area. At the bottom of the drop-down field list is an item called <Expression...>. This item opens the Expression Builder dialog box, in which you can create any valid FoxPro expression. Figure 7.11 shows the Expression Builder dialog box with the completed expression for profit margin.

Part
II

Ch
7

To complete these criteria, you want records that evaluate to < (Less Than) .25, because the profit-margin expression generates a fraction, not a percentage.

**N O T E** If .25 returns zero records in your record set, increase the fraction to .45. ■

**FIGURE 7.11**

Calculate the profit margin of a product by building an expression with the Expression Builder.

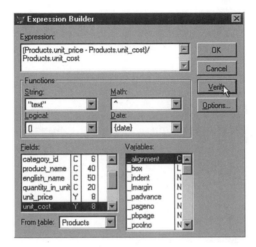

Because the profit-margin expression includes division by one of the fields, you should eliminate records in which UNIT_COST is zero. You cannot lose money on a product that costs nothing unless you have to pay someone to take it. But more important, you cannot divide by zero. You accomplish this task with a separate filter criterion that selects only those records in which UNIT_COST is greater than zero. To get VFP to evaluate this expression before the profit-margin expression, place it before the profit-margin expression.

Notice that VFP evaluates criteria sequentially. If a potential result record fails an intermediate criterion, VFP does not evaluate the remaining criteria. Thus, check to see whether the unit cost is zero before you use it as a divisor in a later expression.

Figure 7.12 shows the completed Filter page. This query now has four selection criteria, one join on the Join tab, and three filter conditions on the Filter tab. VFP automatically joins these elements with AND. Therefore, all four selection criteria must evaluate to true before VFP will include the record in the results table.

**N O T E** Place expressions that are most likely to eliminate records near the beginning (top) of the selection criteria list, so that FoxPro does not waste time going through the other criteria. In this example, test for a zero value of UNIT_COST before performing the profitability calculation. ■

**FIGURE 7.12**

The completed Filter tab shows several criteria for selecting records.

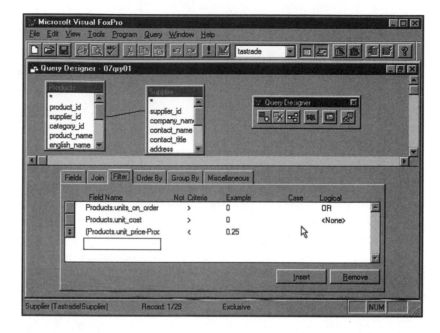

Running this query results in six selected records. This result means that of the items on order, six of them have profit margins of less than 25 percent. Looking at the query results, the store manager may decide to discontinue stocking these items.

But what if you wanted to know how many items from the entire inventory had profit margins of less than 25 percent or were on reorder? To find out, you need to connect the last two expressions with OR instead of AND. Click the Logical drop-down list for the first Field Name—Products.units_on_order—and select OR. Rerunning the query retrieves 17 records.

It's important to remember that the Query Designer merely checks the syntax of the criteria; it has no knowledge of what makes sense. You can easily define a meaningless set of conditions or a set that eliminates all records. You control the criteria's meaning.

> **CAUTION**
>
> Although it is easy to define a query that uses legal FoxPro syntax, the query may be meaningless. FoxPro allows users to create any query, no matter how ridiculous, as long as it has valid syntax.

Part
II

Ch
7

> **CAUTION**
>
> Adding OR in the middle of a series of conditions automatically groups the expressions that come before and after it. Only then does VFP compare the logical results of the groups. As long as one of the groups on either side of the OR evaluates to true, the query includes the record. This grouping ignores clauses that are used to join files.

Finally, the Insert and Remove buttons permit you to add or remove expressions from the Join tab and Filter tab criteria lists. To add a criterion to the bottom of the list, just use the empty Field Name box provided by the Query Designer. To insert a criterion between existing criteria, select the lower criterion and click the Insert button. Insert adds a blank line above the selected criterion. Alternatively, you could always add the criterion to the bottom of the list and move it up with the mover button.

# Routing the Query Results

 So far, all the examples in this chapter have written the query results to a Browse or Edit window on-screen. You may want to keep some query results around a little longer, perhaps saving them or using them in a report. To change the query destination from on-screen to a file or printer, click the Query Destination button in the Query toolbar.

FoxPro displays the Query Destination dialog box (see Figure 7.13), which includes the options shown in Table 7.1.

**FIGURE 7.13**
The Query Destination dialog box provides seven ways to display the query results.

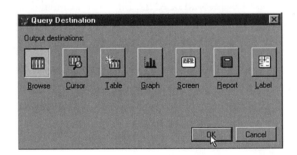

**Table 7.1    Query Destination Options**

| Destination | Definition |
|---|---|
| Browse | View query results in a Browse window only |
| Cursor | Create a temporary table or cursor with query results |
| Table | Create a permanent table |
| Graph | Use query results to produce a graph with Microsoft Graph |
| Screen | Display results to screen only |
| Report | Use query results as data source for a report |
| Label | Use query results as data source for labels |

By default, the Browse button is selected. When you generate results to a Browse window, FoxPro creates a temporary table that contains the query results (usually, in memory), opens the Browse window, and displays the table. As soon as you close the Browse window, Visual FoxPro erases the temporary table. If you need only a quick view of data that matches certain conditions, sending the query results to a Browse window is fine, and it saves a tree. You don't need to define anything else with this option, because it is VFP's default and needs no special parameters.

## Output to a Cursor

The next output-destination option creates a cursor. *Cursors* are also temporary files, but they remain open and active for as long as you choose. When cursors are closed, however, Visual FoxPro deletes them. Other than in the actual process of creating a cursor, you cannot write to one created as output from a query. After a cursor is created, you cannot replace values or add or delete records.

Cursors have only one additional, required attribute: Despite their temporary status, cursors must have names. The Query Destination dialog box provides a suggested cursor name, based on the query name. You can accept the name or provide your own name. The assigned name then serves as an alias, allowing you to reference it from within a program or other command lines.

**N O T E**  In a networked environment, consider directing smaller cursors to a local drive or a RAM drive. This arrangement not only improves performance, but also prevents potential problems with file-name conflicts. Although cursors exist in memory when enough memory exists, Visual FoxPro writes them to a physical medium as they grow. ■

## Output to a Table

Sending query results to a table is similar to sending them to a cursor, with one major exception: A table, by definition, has a physical existence on your disk and, therefore, can exist after the current Visual FoxPro session. You can close and reopen tables. You can add, delete, and modify records in a table. When you select Table in the Query Destination dialog box, you can directly enter a table name or click the button containing an ellipsis (…). This button opens the Open dialog box, which allows you to select tables from any directory and drive. This causes the query results to overwrite existing tables. You may want to open the directory to ensure that the table name that you enter does not already exist.

**N O T E**   In a networked environment, try not to hard-code table names; rather, use the SYS(3) function to assign random names. After you create a table, immediately rename it with an alias. There is no problem with each user having his or her own separate table with a common alias name, as long as the physical file name is different. This technique allows the program code to reference separate tables with the common alias name. The following sample code shows how easy it is to do this:

```
myfile = SYS(3)              && Obtain a unique name.
SELECT * FROM <anyfile> INTO TABLE &myfile
USE DBF() ALIAS MYALIAS      && Assign a common alias reference
SELECT MYALIAS ▓
```

### TROUBLESHOOTING

**When I store multiple file names to variables, using the SYS(3) function, the names are not always unique.** On a fast computer, selecting multiple file names in succession by using SYS(3) may not provide unique names. Use SUBSTR(SYS(2015), 3, 10) to ensure a unique name.

## Output to a Graph

To show the output, the query was changed (see Figure 7.14) to select only three fields from the Product file: Product_Id, Unit_Cost, and Unit_Price. Open the Query Destination dialog box, and select Graph. Finally, run the query.

When the query runs, it opens the Graph Wizard to help define the graph. The query skips the first step of this wizard, because the fields have already been selected in the query; it begins with the layout step. In this step, you assign fields to desired locations on a graph. In this example, you want to use Product_Id as the axis variable. You also have two data series to plot: Unit_Cost and Unit_Price. Your Graph Wizard dialog box should look like Figure 7.15 after you make these selections.

**FIGURE 7.14**
This query on just the Product table extracts product information to display as a graph.

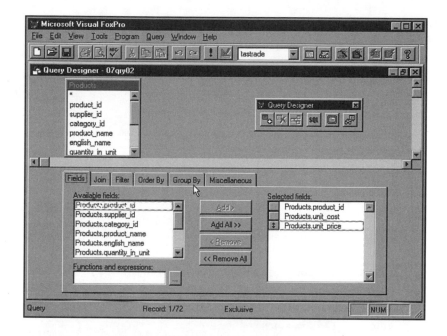

**FIGURE 7.15**
Use the layout step of the Graph Wizard to assign fields to various graph locations.

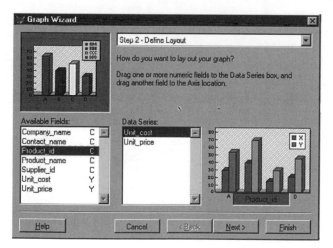

Move to the next step by clicking <u>N</u>ext or by choosing Step 3 from the step drop-down list. In this step, you can choose any of 12 predefined graph styles, as shown in Figure 7.16. To select a style, click the button that displays a picture of the style that you want to use.

Part
II

Ch
7

**FIGURE 7.16**

Choose one of the 12 available graph styles.

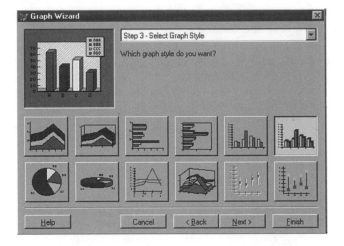

The last step of the Graph Wizard allows you to display null values, add a legend to the graph, and Preview the graph before you click Finish. The legend identifies the data series with the field name. You also can enter a title to display at the top of the graph. Figure 7.17 shows these options.

**FIGURE 7.17**

The last step of the Graph Wizard allows you to include a legend and graph title before saving the graph.

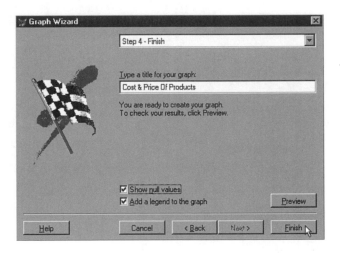

When you click Finish, the Graph Wizard prompts you for a table name under which to save the graph. After you save the graph, the Graph Wizard displays the result.

Before completing Step 4 - Finish, you can click the Back button to change the features of your graph and then click the Preview option to see the results. This way, you can preview several graph styles before committing to a final one.

## Output to the Screen

Figure 7.18 shows the options that are available when you output query results to the screen.

**FIGURE 7.18**
The Query Destination dialog box displays options for outputting query results to the screen.

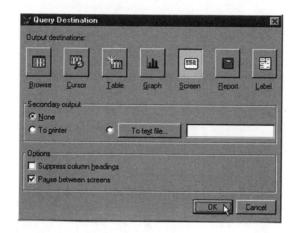

First, you can define a secondary output destination. Why? Because FoxPro does not retain the query results after writing them to the screen. Therefore, use a secondary output destination to create a more permanent copy by selecting To Printer or To Text File. When you are outputting to a printer, be aware that fields within a record wrap across multiple lines if they do not all fit on one line. When you select To Text File, you must also supply a file name, using the Open dialog box. If you know the fully qualified text-file name, you can enter it directly in the text box. Notice that you cannot choose both the printer and a text file as a secondary output destination.

Additional options include the capability to Suppress Column Headings and Pause Between Screens. To view the data, be sure to check the Pause Between Screens check box; otherwise, the data scrolls past faster than you can read it.

> **CAUTION**
> During pauses between screens, output directed to a secondary source repeats the column headings every time Visual FoxPro starts a new screen.

## Output to a Report

When you are outputting to a report, Visual FoxPro provides a wide selection of options, as shown in Figure 7.19.

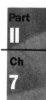

**FIGURE 7.19**

The Query Destination dialog box lists the options for sending query results to a report.

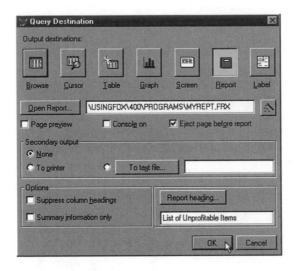

▶ **See** "Custom Report Generation," **p. 555**

To use an existing report definition with the new query results, click the Open Report button, and select an existing report in the Open dialog box that appears. You can also use the Open dialog box to ensure that the report name that you supply does not currently exist if you intend to create a new report. If you know the report's file name without opening the Open dialog box, enter it directly in the text box.

The button on the right side of the dialog box that looks like a magic wand opens the Report Wizard. Use this wizard to create a new report in seconds.

▶ **See** "The Report Wizard Family," **p. 258**

If you click Page Preview, VFP outputs the report in a window for review. Notice that if you select Page Preview, you cannot simultaneously output the report to a secondary destination This feature is best used for the following purposes:

- To test reports during development
- To view reports when the user needs to see a few results and does not keep a hard copy
- To review reports when you don't want to walk up three flights of stairs and down four halls to retrieve the report output from the only network printer
- To view reports when you do not have access to a printer, either because it temporarily does not work or is busy printing past-due notices to clients

Console On echoes the report output to the current window, and Eject Page Before Report sends a page-eject command to the printer before beginning a report to ensure that the report starts at the top of the form.

**TROUBLESHOOTING**

**When I print a report, the last line, or perhaps even the last page, does not print.** Some printers store one or more lines of output in a buffer. This arrangement prevents the printer from printing the last page or at least the last line until another print job starts. If that print job does not use a page eject at the beginning, it most likely appends to the end of the report. One solution to this problem is to use the Report Designer to add a page eject after the report as well.

As you can when you send output to the screen, you can define a secondary output destination. (The primary destination for a report is the screen.) Choose <u>N</u>one, To <u>P</u>rinter, or To Te<u>x</u>t File. When you choose the latter option, Visual FoxPro displays the Open dialog box, allowing you to enter or choose a file. If you select a file that already exists and SAFETY is OFF, VFP overwrites the old file automatically. When SAFETY is ON, VFP displays a warning and allows you to decide whether to overwrite the file. You can also enter a text-file name in the edit box next to the To Te<u>x</u>t File button.

In the Options area, you can Suppress Column <u>H</u>eadings or create a report with Summary <u>I</u>nformation Only. When you choose Summary <u>I</u>nformation Only, Visual FoxPro suppresses all detail lines and prints only Title, Group, Page, and Summary bands.

Finally, you can add a separate Report Hea<u>d</u>ing that appears at the top of each page, in addition to any heading that is already in the Page Header band of the report. Clicking this button opens the Expression Builder dialog box. Use this dialog box to define a heading that includes memory variables, table fields, and calculated results.

## Output to a Label

Outputting options for labels are similar to those for reports, as shown in Figure 7.20.

**FIGURE 7.20**
The Query Destination dialog box lists the options for sending query results to a label.

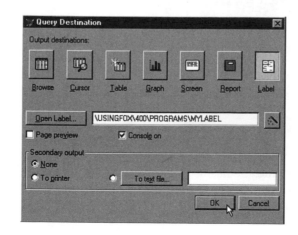

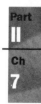

Part

II

Ch

7

To use an existing label definition with the new query results, click the Open Label button and select an existing label from the Open dialog box. You also can use the Open dialog box to ensure that the label name that you supply does not currently exist, if you intend to create a new label. If you know the label's file name without opening the Open dialog box, enter it in the text box.

When Page Preview is selected, Visual FoxPro outputs the label in a window for review. Notice that when you select Page Preview, you cannot simultaneously output the label to any other destination. This feature is best used for the following purposes:

- To test labels during development
- To ensure that the labels are correct before rerunning the query and sending the output to a printer

The Console On option echoes the label output to the screen when the label output is created.

▶ **See** "Creating Label Objects," **p. 556**

As you can for reports, you can define a secondary output destination. (The primary destination for a label is the screen.) Choose None, To Printer, or To Text File. If you choose the latter option, Visual FoxPro displays the Open dialog box, which allows you to enter or choose a file. If you select a file that already exists and SAFETY is OFF, VFP overwrites the old file automatically. When SAFETY is ON, VFP displays a warning and allows you to decide whether to overwrite the file. You also can enter a text-file name directly in the edit box next to the To Text File button.

# Using Query Designer versus Manually Created SQL SELECT Statements

By now, you have seen how easily you can query data by using the Query Designer. You may not realize that you have been creating SQL SELECT statements throughout this entire chapter. If you have been hesitant to write your own SQL statements because you thought they were too complex, continue reading to explore the world of SQL SELECT statements.

The simplest query grabs every field and every record from a single table, and displays them in a Browse window. The following code shows this query command used in the CUSTOMER.DBF table (in the Tastrade example provided with Visual FoxPro):

```
USE \VFP\SAMPLES\ DATA\CUSTOMER
SELECT * FROM TASTRADE!CUSTOMER
```

**N O T E** If the table is part of an open database but is not open, VFP uses the information in the database to open it. If the table is a free table, VFP opens the Open dialog box to allow you to select it. ■

The asterisk immediately after the SELECT keyword tells Visual FoxPro to get all fields in the table referenced by the FROM clause. If you do not want to see all the fields, list the ones that you do want to see, as in the following:

```
SELECT Customer_Id, Company_Name FROM TASTRADE!CUSTOMER
```

Notice that commas separate the field names. To see the companies that begin with the letter *A*, add a WHERE clause, as shown in the following command (which assumes that SET ANSI is OFF):

```
SELECT Customer_Id, Company_Name FROM TASTRADE!CUSTOMER ;
    WHERE Company_Name = 'A'
```

To perform an exact search, use the == operator.

With that introduction, let's return to the SQL SELECT statements that were generated by FoxPro while using the Query Designer that we created earlier.

 Any time while you are in the Query Designer, you can view the SQL that Visual FoxPro continuously builds in the background. Simply click the SQL button in the SQL toolbar. Actually, this button alternately shows and hides the SQL window. After you click it, the button stays down until you click it again or use the Window menu to switch the active window.

**T I P** Add a comment to your SQL SELECT statement by choosing Query, Comments and entering text in the dialog box that appears.

When you started the first query in this chapter, you selected two tables: PRODUCTS and SUPPLIER. A persistent relation on the field Supplier_Id joined those tables. You also selected several fields to display: PRODUCTS.Product_Id, PRODUCTS.Supplier_Id, PRODUCTS.Product_Name, and SUPPLIER.Company_Name. This information defines a simple query. If you click the Run button, a Browse window pops up and displays the query results. But what SQL SELECT statement did FoxPro actually run to produce this output? If you click the SQL button in the toolbar, you should see something similar to Figure 7.21.

Part
II

Ch
7

**FIGURE 7.21**

Here is the SQL SELECT statement in which the INNER JOIN keywords replace the WHERE statement.

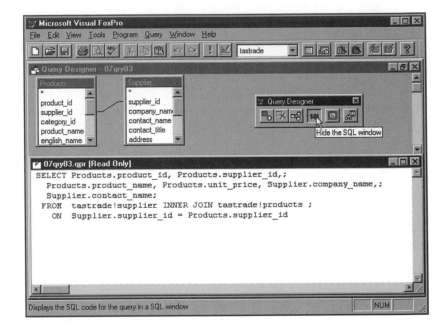

SQL SELECT commands begin with the SELECT keyword. You immediately follow SELECT with a list of fields to include in the results. Notice that Visual FoxPro qualifies each field with the name of the database. Strictly speaking, you do not need to qualify every field—only those fields that exist in both tables, such as SUPPLY_Id. Qualifying every field, however, helps you document the table to which the field belongs. When you are writing an SQL SELECT that uses a single table, you do not need to qualify the fields.

**N O T E** The examples used in this chapter prefix fields with their table name. You can also equate a field name to a simple alias, even using a single character. Although this method makes the SQL a little more difficult to read, it may make entering it a little easier by reducing the amount of typing. The following simple example shows you how to assign a one-letter alias:

```
SELECT A.Customer_Id, B.Customer_Id ;
FROM TASTRADE!ORDERS A, TASTRADE!CUSTOMER B ■
```

The field list, as well as the entire SQL SELECT statement, can extend over multiple lines. Just remember to end each line (except the last) with a semicolon. The field order in the SQL SELECT statement determines the field output order in the results table.

The SQL SELECT statement requires the FROM clause to identify the table or tables containing the fields. Notice that when a table belongs to a database, its name is preceded by the database name, separated by an exclamation point.

**CAUTION**

Because the SQL SELECT statement includes the name of the table and database, Visual FoxPro can execute the statement even if you do not first open the database or tables, if they reside in the current directory.

 **T I P** When you are creating an SQL SELECT statement in the Command window or a program, precede the database name with its full path so that the query will work from any directory.

Finally, you need a WHERE clause. SQL requires this clause to join tables when you use two or more tables. In fact, you need a minimum of *n*-1 WHERE clauses when you use *n* tables, just to define the relations between the tables. In Figure 7.21 the SELECT statement says that you want records in the results table where Supply_Id in PRODUCTS matches Supply_Id in SUPPLIER. A WHERE clause can be expressed as a JOIN condition and counts as one of n-1 WHERE clauses.

After you define it, use the SQL SELECT statement in the Command window or embed it in a program. No matter where you use it, the statement creates the same results as it does when you use it from the Query Designer.

**N O T E** Use the Query Designer to create SQL SELECT commands visually. Then copy the commands from the SQL window to the Command window or the program's Edit window, where you can customize them further or run them as they are. Alternatively, save the query and run the QPR file, using DO. ▪

Figure 7.22 expands the SELECT statement to include more fields and conditions. First, notice the DISTINCT clause added after SELECT. This clause, which corresponds to the No Duplicates check box in the Miscellaneous tab, appears only at the beginning of the field list but applies to all fields. The clause means that if all selected fields have the same value as they did in the preceding record, the current record is not included in the results.

A second condition is added to the WHERE clause in Figure 7.22. This expression examines the value of the field Units_On_Order in the PRODUCTS table and includes records only if this value is greater than zero. By default, Visual FoxPro connects all criteria with AND. This means that the records must pass all the criteria before they are added to the result set. In this example, VFP would create a result set of unprofitable products that are also on order. However, suppose that you want to see all the products that are on order, or the unprofitable products. To do so, you need to add an OR criterion. In other words, you want to see records for those products that have outstanding orders and for those that are unprofitable.

Part
II

Ch
7

**FIGURE 7.22**

Add conditions to the
SQL SELECT statement
to filter and sort
results.

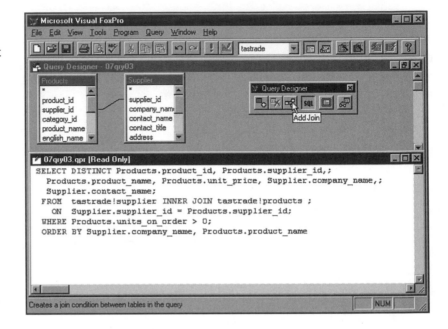

Finally, the ORDER BY clause defines a sort order for the results. In this case, you want to sort records first by company and then by product name. Each field in the ORDER BY clause can have a different sort direction. By default, the sort order is ascending. However, you can follow the field name with DESC to define a descending sort or ASC to ensure an ascending sort.

Now look at the SQL SELECT statement generated at the end of the Query Designer session (see Figure 7.23).

This expression adds additional filter clauses to limit the on-order product list to products that have low profit margins. Notice that with the OR condition between the second and third condition, Visual FoxPro groups the last two expressions together, using parentheses. This is exactly what you want, because you should perform the profitability calculation only for records that have a unit cost greater than zero.

By default, VFP sends all queries to a Browse window. The INTO clause specifies where to redirect the query results. In Figure 7.23, the results are output to a cursor named UNPROFIT. However, you can select several other destinations, including the following:

- An array (INTO ARRAY <arrayname>)
- A different cursor (INTO CURSOR <cursorname>)
- A table or DBF file (INTO TABLE <dbfname>)
- A printer (TO PRINTER)

- The screen (TO SCREEN)
- A file (TO FILE <filename>)

**FIGURE 7.23**

This is the final SQL SELECT created to select items with profit margins less than 25 percent.

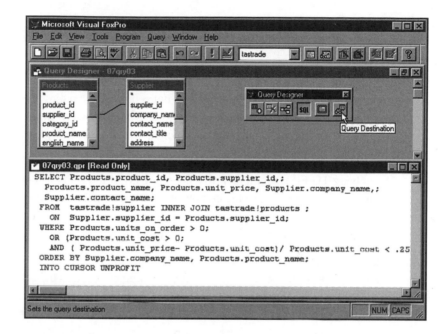

The array option, which is not available from the Query Designer, adds the query results to a memory variable array. VFP does not create the array if the query does not return at least one record. Therefore, before you attempt to use the array variable, test how many records the query returned by checking the value of _TALLY. This system memory variable records the number of records processed by the most recent table command. The variable also works with the following commands:

| | |
|---|---|
| APPEND FROM | PACK |
| AVERAGE | REINDEX |
| CALCULATE | REPLACE |
| COPY TO | SELECT - SQL |
| COUNT | SORT |
| DELETE | SUM |
| INDEX | TOTAL |
| JOIN | UPDATE |

If _TALLY equals 0, the query found no records.

When storing the query results to a cursor or table, VFP prompts you before overwriting existing tables with the same name if SET SAFETY is ON. The Alert dialog box displays the following text:

```
<filename>

This file already exists

Replace existing file?
```

Click the Yes or No button to replace or not replace the existing file. When SET SAFETY is OFF, Visual FoxPro overwrites existing files automatically. In most programming environments, unless the user specifies the file name, you probably want SET SAFETY OFF to overwrite existing files.

Specifying TO FILE together with a file name is not the same as creating a cursor or table. Sending query results to a file creates an ASCII text file, not a table. You can print this file directly to the printer or screen from DOS, using the TYPE command. You can also append the file to other documents that read text files.

Another option, NOCONSOLE, suppresses echoing the query results to the screen, which is especially useful when you are directing output to a file or printer. Sending query results to a cursor or table never echoes the results to the screen; therefore, this command is not needed. PLAIN removes the column headings from the output. Use this option if you intend to send the query results to a file and later use that file as input to another program.

We hope that by seeing how the Query Designer sessions result in SELECT statements, you will not think of SQL statements as being difficult. Just remember to break the SELECT into individual clauses when you try to understand it.

# Grouping Records to Summarize Data

Before leaving this introductory chapter on queries and SQL, return to the Query Designer one more time to see how to group records to provide summary information.

This example requires three tables from the Tastrade database: ORDERS, ORDER_LINE_ITEMS, and PRODUCTS. Using the previously defined persistent relations, notice that ORDERS relates to ORDER_LINE_ITEMS through the Order_Id field. Similarly, ORDER_LINE_ITEMS relates to PRODUCTS through the Product_Id field. Figure 7.24 shows the inner joins and the persistent relations. A separate filter that limits the result set to orders taken in 1994 has been set in the Filter tab.

**FIGURE 7.24**

The inner joins used in the Query Designer to join ORDERS, PRODUCTS, and ORDER_LINE_ITEMS.

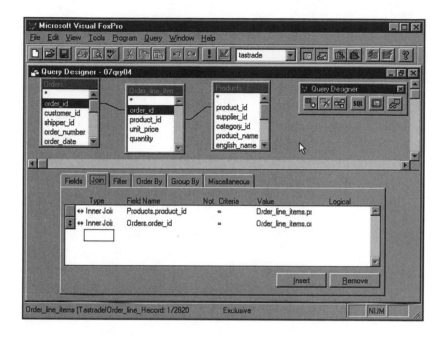

This report requires as output the product name, the quantity sold, and a price analysis. In fact, you want to see only one record for each product—a record that sums the number of units sold for that product. In a report, you would group the output records by product ID or product name, sum the quantity field for each detail record, and print the resulting sum after the last record for that product.

In the Query Designer, you accomplish something similar by using options in the Group By tab. Move the Product_Id field from the Available Fields list to the Grouped Fields list. This tells the Query Designer to output only a single record for each product ID. Figure 7.25 shows the Group By definition in the Query Designer.

When you are looking at the field values for a group of records for the same Product ID, some values change, and others remain constant. If, as in this case, Product ID identifies the group, the ID value remains constant, but so do other fields, such as description. Do not worry about these fields. In the quantity field, however, each detail record represents a different transaction. Because you need to include this field in the query, you must tell Visual FoxPro what to do with it. Otherwise, VFP outputs to the results table the values in the last record that it processes for each group.

In this query, you want to sum the quantity sold in each transaction. Going to the Fields tab, click the button to the right of the Functions and Expressions field. This button displays the Expression Builder. The grouping functions are listed in the Math drop-down list; Table 7.2 defines them.

Part

II

Ch

7

**FIGURE 7.25**
Group selected
records by Product_Id,
using the Group By tab
of the Query Designer.

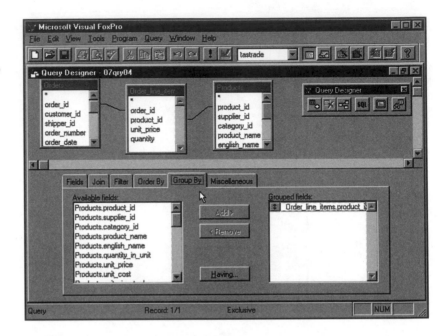

## Table 7.2 Grouping Functions

| Grouping Function | Description |
| --- | --- |
| COUNT( ) | Counts number of records in group |
| SUM( ) | Sums field value for records in group |
| AVG( ) | Averages field value for records in group |
| MIN( ) | Minimum field value for records in group |
| MAX( ) | Maximum field value for records in group |
| COUNT(DISTINCT) | Counts distinct records in group |
| SUM(DISTINCT) | Sums field value for distinct records in group |
| AVG(DISTINCT) | Averages field value for distinct records in group |

Click SUM( ) to calculate the total quantity of a numeric field. Visual FoxPro immediately displays "SUM(expN)" in the Expression text area. Select Order_line_items from the From Table drop-down list. Then select ORDER_LINE_ITEMS.Quantity in the Fields list (see Figure 7.26). The required expression appears in the text area. Clicking OK adds the expression to the Functions and expression field. Finally, select the new function and add it to the Fields list by clicking the Add button.

**FIGURE 7.26**
Open the Fields tab of the Expression Builder to define a calculation method and a field for a query.

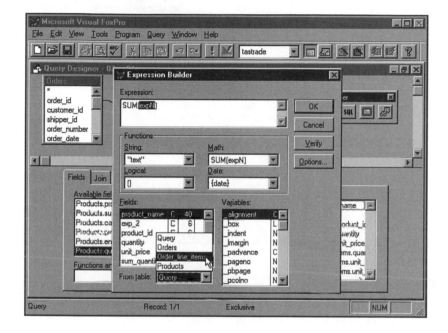

Because the selected data spans a year, you expect that prices will change at least for some products. Thus, although Unit_Price (stored in PRODUCTS) represents the current price, it may not equal the price for previous orders. Because the program saves the Unit_Price with each order in the order details file (ORDER_LINE_ITEMS), however, you can determine the minimum, maximum, and average price throughout the year. To retrieve these other prices for the report, use the Fields page of the Expression Builder. The new calculated fields for this query include:

- SUM(ORDER_LINE_ITEMS.quantity)
- MIN(ORDER_LINE_ITEMS.unit_price)
- MAX(ORDER_LINE_ITEMS.unit_price)
- AVG(ORDER_LINE_ITEMS.unit_price)

Figure 7.27 shows the SQL SELECT statement for the completed query.

Part

II

Ch

7

**FIGURE 7.27**

Here is the complete query to analyze Tastrade product prices.

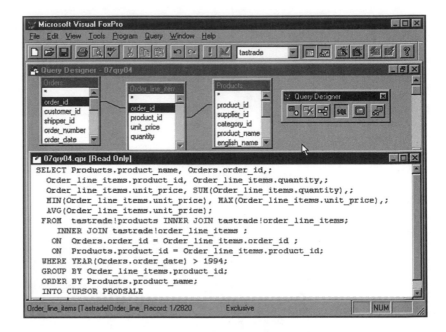

```
SELECT Products.product_name, Orders.order_id,;
    Order_line_items.product_id, Order_line_items.quantity,;
    Order_line_items.unit_price, SUM(Order_line_items.quantity),;
    MIN(Order_line_items.unit_price), MAX(Order_line_items.unit_price),;
    AVG(Order_line_items.unit_price);
  FROM  tastrade!products INNER JOIN tastrade!order_line_items;
    INNER JOIN tastrade!order_line_items ;
    ON  Orders.order_id = Order_line_items.order_id ;
    ON  Products.product_id = Order_line_items.product_id;
  WHERE YEAR(Orders.order_date) > 1994;
  GROUP BY Order_line_items.product_id;
  ORDER BY Products.product_name;
  INTO CURSOR PRODSALE
```

# Using Queries in Programs and Forms

When you are using the Query Designer to create a query that you later want to use in a program or form, remember to save the query after testing it. Visual FoxPro saves the SQL SELECT statement in a file with the extension .QPR. You can execute the SQL directly from the Command window, program, or form with a simple DO command, such as the following:

```
DO SALBYPRD.QPR
```

Because the Query Designer does not automatically include drive or path prefixes for databases or tables, you must do one of the following things:

- Run the query from the directory that contains the databases or tables.

- Add a SET DEFAULT TO command to change to the directory that contains the data.

- Modify the query manually to contain the drive and path information.

The following SELECT statement shows a simple example:

```
SELECT * ;
    FROM C:\VFP\SAMPLES\ \DATA\TASTRADE!CUSTOMER
```

From within a form control, simply attach a DO statement like the preceding one to the click event. Visual FoxPro executes the query whenever someone clicks the control.

# Editing the Generated SQL SELECT Statement

The .QPR file is a text file. just like a .PRG. Therefore, you can edit it with either of the following commands.

```
MODIFY COMMAND SELBYPRD.QPR
MODIFY FILE SELBYPRD.QPR
```

Both commands open an Edit window and load SELBYPRD.QPR into it. Some additional reasons why you might edit the SQL SELECT statement directly, as opposed to using the Query Designer, are:

- Faster editing of minor changes, such as adding or deleting a field or changing a condition test value.

- Creating more complex queries. After all, the Query Designer is still an enduser's tool and lacks the robustness available with direct creation of SQL SELECT statements.

# Creating Complex Queries

The first part of this chapter concentrated on using the Query Designer to create the SQL SELECT statements. The Query Designer has enough power for many basic queries, and it helps teach you query design in an interactive environment in which you can concentrate on what you want to do, not on how to do it. If you plan to write your own SQL SELECT statements from scratch, you need to know the syntax. The following shows the complete syntax for creating SQL SELECT statements.

```
SELECT [ALL ¦ DISTINCT] [TOP nExpr [PERCENT]]
 [Alias.] Select_Item [AS Column_Name]
 [, [Alias.] Select_Item [AS Column_Name] ...]
FROM [FORCE] [DatabaseName!]Table [LocalAlias]
 [[INNER ¦ LEFT [OUTER] ¦ RIGHT [OUTER] ¦ FULL [OUTER] JOIN]
[, [DatabaseName!]Table [Local_Alias]
 [[INNER ¦ LEFT [OUTER] ¦ RIGHT [OUTER] ¦ FULL [OUTER] JOIN] ...]
 [ON [DatabaseName!]Table [Local Alias] .Column_Name =
 [DatabaseName!]Table [Local_Alias] .Column_Name]

[[INTO Destination]
 ¦ [TO FILE FileName [ADDITIVE] ¦ TO PRINTER [PROMPT]
 ¦ TO SCREEN]]
[PREFERENCE PreferenceName]
[NOCONSOLE]
[PLAIN]
[NOWAIT]
[WHERE JoinCondition [AND JoinCondition ...]
 [AND ¦ OR FilterCondition [AND ¦ OR FilterCondition ...]]]
[GROUP BY GroupColumn [, GroupColumn ...]]
```

Part

II

Ch

7

```
[HAVING FilterCondition]
[UNION [ALL] SELECTCommand]
[ORDER BY Order_Item [ASC ¦ DESC] [, Order_Item [ASC ¦ DESC] ...]]
```

Many of these clauses are described earlier in this chapter. As you can quickly tell, not all of these clauses appear in the Query Designer. Two primary clauses that are not included are the use of subqueries and UNIONs. The balance of this chapter is devoted to subqueries. Chapter 8, "Advanced Queries and Views," picks up with a discussion of UNIONs (not the AFL-CIO or the autoworkers' union).

▶ **See** "Joining the Results of Multiple Queries," **p. 348**

# Using a BETWEEN Clause to Filter a Range of Values

The BETWEEN clause allows you to define a value range for a field by using a single condition statement, rather than two. However, there seems to be very little difference in performance whether you use the BETWEEN clause or two separate conditions. Suppose that you want a list of order details for products that have product IDs between 10 and 19. You could write a two-condition SELECT, as follows:

```
SET ANSI ON
SELECT * ;
  FROM order_line_items ;
  WHERE ALLTRIM(Product_Id) >= '10' AND ALLTRIM(Product_Id) <= '19'
```

### Set ANSI and SQL

SET ANSI determines the way that SQL commands compare strings connected with the = operator. The default is OFF, in which case SQL compares strings character for character until reaching the end of the shorter string. The following table provides examples of how SET ANSI affects comparisons:

| SET ANSI | OFF | ON |
|----------|------|-------|
| '10' = '1' | True | False |
| '1' = '10' | True | False |
| '' = '1' | True | False |
| '1' = '' | True | False |
| '10' = '10' | True | True |
| '10' == '101' | False | False |
| '10' == '1' | False | False |
| '10 ' == '10' | True | True |
| '10' == '10 ' | True | True |

With SET ANSI OFF, a single character matches any field value that begins with that character, and empty fields match everything. Although you can use == in place of the = operator to force an exact comparison, you cannot replace >= with >==. In these situations, you must exercise extra caution. One solution changes SET ANSI to ON, as shown in the preceding table. To see the effect with real data, run the preceding SELECT with SET ANSI OFF, and compare the results table to the one generated with SET ANSI ON.

---

**CAUTION**

When you are comparing a field (such as CAT_ID) to a character string, be aware of whether the field is left- or right-justified when the comparison values do not have to use all character positions. Use ALLTRIM on the field to prevent problems, or pad the comparison value to the full field size.

---

Combining these two conditions with BETWEEN results in the following statement:

```
SET ANSI ON
SELECT * ;
  FROM order_line_items ;
 WHERE ALLTRIM(Product_Id) BETWEEN '10' AND '19'
```

There is little difference between the times that it takes these two statements to find 31,280 records out of 225,840 (in a modified version of the ORDER_LINE_ITEMS table). In fact, the first statement ran only slightly faster on the test machine, requiring 44.00 seconds, compared with 44.87 seconds for the second statement. Perhaps the difference is that the first statement eliminates some records that have only a single comparison expression. The difference is minimal, however.

---

### SQL Performance Testing

The timings of different SELECT versions probably will vary on your system. Many factors affect the overall SELECT speed, including the system CPU, the storage medium that is being used for the file, the access rate for that storage medium, the controller card, and the transfer method for that storage medium. However, the basic overall pattern of which method is fastest should remain the same.

Visual FoxPro attempts to keep Rushmore-related information about a completed SELECT in memory. Therefore, if you repeat the same or similar SELECT, the relative times decrease. One sure way to ensure that no residual Rushmore information exists in memory is to exit Visual FoxPro between tests.

For many of the SQL examples used in this section, the files from Tastrade were artificially bloated to create files with more records. This procedure involved first copying a file to a new file name and then opening the new file and repeatedly appending the original table to it. This technique works for SQL tests that require extracting a subset of records based on a field value that extracts records based on a product ID range. If you need to test an SQL statement that joins two files, however, this technique may lead to unexpected and incorrect results, with multiple "matches" between the files.

Part
II

Ch
7

Because the field used in this condition contains only digits, you could also write the condition as follows:

```
SET ANSI ON
SELECT * ;
  FROM products ;
 WHERE VAL(Product_Id) BETWEEN 10 AND 19
```

The performance of this query is significantly slower than that of the first two. Perhaps this fact reflects on the inefficiency of converting the string to a numeric value first before performing the comparison. This SELECT requires 47.35 seconds on the test system. The problem in each case is that the field criteria do not match a index definition. The index on product ID uses no special functions. Therefore, the only way to obtain better performance from a query is to eliminate all functions used in the WHERE clauses. The following example, which carefully formats the test values as right-justified six-character fields, executes in 31.47 seconds (still a long time, but the query is retrieving 32,180 records out of 225,840):

```
SELECT * ;
  FROM order_line_items ;
  WHERE product_id >= '    10' AND product_id <= '    19'
```

This procedure also averts any potential problems caused by having SET ANSI ON or OFF.

**N O T E**   The preceding SELECT statement was tested after setting the order to the tag based on Product_Id. This is a common mistake of many developers who think that they can help SELECT work faster by presetting the "correct" tag. In this case, the query required 32.35 seconds—almost a second longer, just because a tag was set. ∎

## Using an IN Clause to Filter Selected Values

The IN clause allows you to specify a discrete set of values that do not constitute an inclusive range. Suppose that you want to see only the customers from Canada, Mexico, the United Kingdom, and the United States. CUSTOMER.DBF has a Country field that you can use, but it would be awkward to test for each country separately, as in the following example:

```
SELECT Company_Name ;
  FROM CUSTOMER ;
 WHERE UPPER(Country) = 'CANADA' OR ;
       UPPER(Country) = 'MEXICO' OR ;
       UPPER(Country) = 'UK' OR ;
       UPPER(Country) = 'USA' ;
 ORDER BY Country, Company_Name
```

You can perform the same query faster by using an IN clause that lists the possible values, as follows:

```
SELECT Company_Name ;
  FROM CUSTOMER ;
 WHERE UPPER(Country) IN ('CANADA', 'MEXICO', 'UK', 'USA') ;
 ORDER BY Country, Company_Name
```

This second expression required less time than the first: 4.67 seconds for the first versus 4.07 seconds for the second to find 1,540 records out of 5,005. (An inflated version of CUSTOMER was used.) The performance difference becomes even greater the more values that Visual FoxPro needs to compare. This fact implies that if you need to compare a field with several values, using the IN clause is more efficient.

> **N O T E** Another feature of this second query is that it includes Country in the sort order, even though it does not output this field in the results. SQL SELECT allows this sorting. ■

## Defining Subqueries

The filter conditions used in; queries earlier in this chapter had this basic structure:

```
<field expression> <operator> <field expression or value>
```

You can create more complex conditions that use a subquery to limit the values. A *subquery* is simply a query within a query. You use subqueries primarily for two reasons:

■ To define a set of values, of which a field must be a member, before including the record in the result table

■ To determine whether a field value exists in another table

Suppose that you want to produce a list of customers who did not make any purchases during a given year, such as 1994. Producing a list of customers who did make purchases is easy. Simply enter the following command:

```
SELECT DISTINCT CUSTOMER.Company_Name ;
  FROM CUSTOMER, ORDERS ;
 WHERE CUSTOMER.Customer_Id = ORDERS.Customer_Id AND ;
       YEAR(ORDERS.Order_Date) = 1994
```

Notice that the DISTINCT clause prevents the company name from appearing more than one time. On a test system using Tastrade data, this query took 1.15 seconds to retrieve 87 records out of 91. To get those 87 records, the query had to examine 929 order records.

You can also write this query using a subquery. The subquery creates a list of customer IDs that placed orders in 1994. The main query retrieves the company name for customer

Part
II

Ch
7

IDs in the subquery list, as follows:

```
SELECT Company_Name ;
  FROM CUSTOMER ;
 WHERE Customer_Id IN (SELECT Customer_Id ;
                         FROM ORDERS ;
                        WHERE YEAR(Order_Date) = 1994)
```

This complex query retrieves the same data as the preceding one, but it requires 5.11 seconds. Notice that a complex query takes more time than a simple one does. In almost all cases, a simple query outperforms a complex query.

The problem is that neither command answered the real question: What are the names of the customers that did not place orders? You would have trouble attempting to modify the first query to answer this request. You can modify the second query, however, by adding a single word, as follows:

```
SELECT Company_Name ;
  FROM CUSTOMER ;
 WHERE Customer_Id NOT IN (SELECT Customer_Id ;
                             FROM ORDERS ;
                            WHERE YEAR(Order_Date) = 1994)
```

Adding NOT before IN changes the meaning of the query to answer the question correctly. In case you are interested, this query ran in 5.27 seconds and returned the names of the 4 customers who did not buy anything in 1994.

Sometimes, it is just not convenient to write a single SQL, because SQL generates a results table with duplicated fields. Suppose that you want to retrieve only orders from outside the United States. You might write the following command:

```
SELECT * ;
  FROM ORDERS, CUSTOMER ;
 WHERE CUSTOMER.Customer_Id = ORDERS.Customer_Id AND ;
       UPPER(CUSTOMER.Country) # 'USA'
```

A problem occurs when SQL sees the potential for duplicated field names; it renames both fields by appending an underscore and letter to them. You could manually list each field that you want to be prefixed by its table name, thereby averting duplicate references, but for tables that have a large number of fields, this method requires a great deal of extra work.

**N O T E**   One way to get around the problem of duplicate field names is to use the AS clause. You could rename a field for the query by using the following clause:

```
SELECT id AS customer_id, name AS cust_name ...
```

You can even add "new" or calculated fields, such as the calculated tax amount based on the sales total and a tax rate, as follows:

```
SELECT order_amt, order_amt*.07 AS sales_tax, ;
   order_amt*1.07 AS sale_total, ... ■
```

Another solution splits the query into two pieces. The inner query creates a list of customers that are not from the United States. The outer one retrieves records from ORDERS only if the inner query returns any records.

```
SELECT * ;
  FROM ORDERS ;
  WHERE EXISTS (SELECT Customer_Id FROM CUSTOMER ;
                  WHERE CUSTOMER.Customer_Id = ORDERS.Customer_Id AND ;
                  UPPER(CUSTOMER.Country) # 'USA')
```

The second query takes longer than the first simple one (2.20 seconds, compared with 1.65 seconds, for 931 records out of 1,080), but it has no problem with renamed fields.

This type of complex query is called an *existence* or *correlated query*. When executed, the inner query must reference a field from the outer query (ORDERS.CUSTOMER_ID, in this case). As a result, VFP performs the inner query for each record in the outer query, which slows performance.

Because EXIST merely checks to see whether any records exist, it doesn't matter what fields it returns. EXIST can even return all fields with an asterisk (*), although using a single field results in slightly better performance.

A better subquery than the preceding method uses IN. IN does not require re-executing the query for each row in the outer query. Because it uses a subquery, however, it does take longer (2.14 seconds) than a simple query.

```
SELECT * ;
  FROM ORDERS ;
  WHERE Customer_Id IN (SELECT Customer_Id FROM CUSTOMER ;
                  WHERE UPPER(Country) # 'USA')
```

The ALL clause compared a value in one SELECT against all values in another SELECT. Suppose that you want to find out which products, if any, have not been purchased since the last price increase posted in PRODUCTS.DBF. In this case, use an inner SQL SELECT to create a list of all product prices for orders by Product_Id. Then, using the outer SELECT, check to see whether the current unit price in PRODUCTS is greater than all values in the first list. The following query result displays the product name and ID of any such products:

```
SELECT DISTINCT PRODUCTS.Product_Name, PRODUCTS.Product_Id ;
   FROM PRODUCTS, ORDER_LINE_ITEMS ;
  WHERE PRODUCTS.Product_Id = ORDER_LINE_ITEMS.product_id AND ;
        PRODUCTS.Unit_Price > IN (SELECT DISTINCT Unit_Price ;
            FROM ORDER_LINE_ITEMS ;
          WHERE ORDER_LINE_ITEMS.Product_Id = PRODUCTS.product_id);
  ORDER BY PRODUCTS.Product_Id
```

Part
**II**

Ch
**7**

Finally, use SOME or ANY to compare the value of a field in the outer query with at least one or more of the values selected by the inner query. Suppose that you want to know whether any products have a current price that is more than 50 percent greater than that of their first order. Modify the preceding query by using SOME, as follows:

```
SELECT DISTINCT PRODUCTS.Product_Name, PRODUCTS.Product_Id ;
   FROM PRODUCTS, ORDER_LINE_ITEMS ;
   WHERE PRODUCTS.Product_Id = ORDER_LINE_ITEMS.Product_Id AND ;
         PRODUCTS.Unit_Price/1.5 > SOME (SELECT DISTINCT Unit_Price ;
               FROM ORDER_LINE_ITEMS ;
               WHERE ORDER_LINE_ITEMS.Product_Id = PRODUCTS.Product_Id);
   ORDER BY PRODUCTS.Product_Id
```

The point of all these examples was not only to show you some of the other clauses that SQL SELECT supports, but also to show you that different ways of expressing a query can lead to different query times. A method that may provide the best performance for small tables in which the selected records are relatively concentrated may not be the best when the tables become large and the data more scattered. The best advice is to experiment with various ways of writing the SQL SELECT to find out which method yields the best performance.

# From Here...

This chapter introduced queries created with the Query Designer, a powerful tool that creates basic queries through a visual interface. Because Visual FoxPro creates an SQL SELECT statement in the background, you can use it to learn the query syntax.

The more you learn about creating queries, the more you realize that the Query Designer has limits. To break beyond those limits, you must expand the SQL SELECT statements that the Query Designer creates with additional clauses. Some of these clauses add capabilities that do not exist in the visual query designer. The last section of this chapter explores the use of subqueries to answer questions that simple queries may not be capable of answering.

In many cases, there is more than one way to write an SQL statement to answer a question. Sometimes, the only way to determine which solution provides the best performance is to try several. In general, you want to keep SQL commands as simple as possible while still answering the question.

To learn more, refer to these chapters:

- Chapter 3, "Defining Databases, Tables, and Indexes," covers the creation of persistent relations for tables managed by a database.

- Chapter 5, "Using Wizards for Rapid Application Development," discusses the use of the Query Wizard.

- Chapter 8, "Advanced Queries and Views," shows you how to take the knowledge gained in this chapter and expand your capability to query data by joining multiple queries, creating cross-tab queries, and using updatable queries and views.

Part
II

Ch
7

# Advanced Queries and Views

*by Michael Antonovich and Richard Curtis*

The preceding chapter examined basic query creation with the Query Designer. It also examined the syntax needed to manually create the same queries in the Command window. This chapter expands on these concepts to create advanced queries, cross-tabs, and updatable queries. ■

**Join the results of multiple queries**

Learn to combine the data from different SQL statements.

**Create outer joins**

Learn to find parent records with children.

**Create self-joins**

Learn to form relationships between fields in the same table.

**Create cross-tabs**

Learn to use the power of a cross-tab query to present data.

**Create updatable views**

Learn to update and remove data with views.

**Access remote data through ODBC connections**

Learn to access information with different data structures.

# Joining the Results of Multiple Queries

Several examples in Chapter 7, "Creating Basic Queries," used subqueries to define subsets of data from which to draw records in the main SELECT statement. However, what if you need to combine the results of two separate SELECT statements?

Suppose that it is time to send out invitations to the Tasmanian Annual Appreciation Picnic. You want to send invitations to all current customers (ones who bought something this year), suppliers, and employees.

## Retrieving Current Customer Records

You have customer information stored in table CUSTOMER.DBF of the database TASTRADE.DBC. Table 8.1 shows the appropriate customer fields.

| Table 8.1   Customer Mailing Information Fields | | |
| --- | --- | --- |
| **Field** | **Type** | **Size** |
| Customer_Id | Character | 6 |
| Contact_Name | Character | 30 |
| Company_Name | Character | 40 |
| Address | Character | 60 |
| City | Character | 15 |
| Region | Character | 15 |
| Postal_Code | Character | 10 |
| Country | Character | 15 |

 **TIP** To maintain SQL SELECT compatibility with earlier versions of FoxPro, replace the JOIN condition with a WHERE statement.

Because you only want customers who made purchases in the current year, you need to also use ORDERS.DBF to identify records for current year purchases. Then match the customer ID field, Customer_Id, with a record in CUSTOMER.DBF. Assuming that all necessary tables are open, either of the SQL SELECT statements in the following example extracts the needed records.

```
SELECT Customer.contact_name, Customer.company_name, Customer.address,;
  Customer.city, Customer.region, Customer.postal_code, Customer.country;
 FROM  tastrade!customer INNER JOIN tastrade!orders ;
   ON  Customer.customer_id = Orders.customer_id;
WHERE YEAR(Orders.order_date) = 1995

SELECT A.Contact_Name, A.Company_Name, A.Address, A.City, ;
       A.Region, A.Postal_Code, A.Country ;
  FROM \VFP\SAMPLES\MAINSAMP\DATA\TASTRADE!CUSTOMER A, ;
       \VFP\SAMPLES\MAINSAMP\DATA\TASTRADE!ORDERS B ;
 WHERE A.Customer_Id = B.Customer_Id AND ;
       YEAR(B.Order_Date) = 1995
```

Both of the preceding SQL SELECT statements will work with Visual FoxPro 5.0. With version 5.0, however, join conditions have been added to the SELECT-SQL command, and if you need to maintain compatibility with version 3.0, you must replace the JOIN condition with a WHERE statement.

By fully qualifying the table names, you can successfully run SELECTs from any directory.

A query that includes only records that exactly match the criteria from both tables is an *inner join*.

These commands create a cursor and display the records in a browse window. The first thing to observe is the use of an alias name, as defined in the database, rather than the table name when specifying the fields. Instead of repeating the table name with each field, you can use a local alias to reduce the amount of typing and the spelling errors associated with typing SQL SELECT statements. Note that this alias is independent of the work-area alias.

Observe also that the selected records do not appear in any particular order. If you want to see the customers in order by name, you need to add the following clause to the SELECT statement:

```
ORDER BY A.Contact_Name
```

## Using DISTINCT versus GROUP BY

After putting the records in order, you see that many customers occur several times. This happens because the SELECT statement includes a record for each customer order in ORDERS.DBF during 1995. Adding the DISTINCT clause at the beginning of the field list includes each customer one time only. The SELECT now looks like the following:

```
SELECT DISTINCT Customer.contact_name, Customer.company_name,
➥Customer.address,;
  Customer.city, Customer.region, Customer.postal_code, Customer.country;
 FROM  tastrade!customer INNER JOIN tastrade!orders ;
   ON  Customer.customer_id = Orders.customer_id;
 WHERE YEAR(Orders.order_date) = 1995;
 ORDER BY Customer.contact_name
```

This command generates a list of all active customers in 1995, listed alphabetically by contact name. However, the ORDER BY clause is no longer needed. When you include DISTINCT, SELECT automatically orders the records alphabetically based on the field sequence. As long as you place the fields in order beginning with the first one you want to sort on, you do not need a separate ORDER BY clause.

There is another way to perform the same SELECT with improved performance. Rather than use SELECT DISTINCT, select all the records and then include a GROUP BY clause. When SELECT uses DISTINCT, it checks all the fields in the added record to see if anything has changed. On the other hand, GROUP BY works with the result table and combines records with the same selected group field or fields. In this case, group on CONTACT_NAME. The resulting SELECT, shown in the following example, executes faster:

```
SELECT Customer.contact_name, Customer.company_name, Customer.address,;
  Customer.city, Customer.region, Customer.postal_code, Customer.country;
 FROM  tastrade!customer INNER JOIN tastrade!orders ;
   ON  Customer.customer_id = Orders.customer_id;
 WHERE YEAR(Orders.order_date) = 1995;
 GROUP BY Customer.contact_name
```

## Retrieving Supplier Records Corresponding to Purchases

Using similar logic, you can retrieve records of suppliers from which you purchased product during the year. Table 8.2 shows the appropriate Supplier fields.

**Table 8.2    Supplier Mailing Information Fields**

| Field | Type | Size |
| --- | --- | --- |
| Supplier_Id | Character | 6 |
| Contact_Name | Character | 30 |
| Company_Name | Character | 40 |
| Address | Character | 60 |
| City | Character | 15 |

| Field | Type | Size |
|-------|------|------|
| Region | Character | 15 |
| Postal_Code | Character | 10 |
| Country | Character | 15 |

The required SELECT statement to retrieve supplier names and addresses selects suppliers based on which products Tasmanian Traders sold during the year. Product-supplier information appears in the Products file. Therefore, you need to work from ORDERS, through ORDER_LINE_ITEMS, and then Products to identify the current suppliers. The following SELECT captures this information:

```
SELECT Supplier.contact_name, Supplier.company_name, Supplier.address,;
   Supplier.city, Supplier.region, Supplier.postal_code, Supplier.country;
  FROM  tastrade!supplier INNER JOIN tastrade!products;
    INNER JOIN tastrade!order_line_items;
    INNER JOIN tastrade!order_line_items ;
   ON  Orders.order_id = Order_line_items.order_id ;
   ON  Products.product_id = Order_line_items.product_id ;
   ON  Supplier.supplier_id = Products.supplier_id;
  WHERE YEAR( Orders.order_date) = 1995;
  GROUP BY Supplier.contact_name
```

This SELECT is similar to the customer SELECT, except that it requires several files to determine which suppliers to invite. Both SELECT statements use fields in tables to select records for the result table, even though those fields do not appear in the result. This is not a problem. Selection criteria looks at the source tables, not the result table.

## Retrieving Employee Records

Finally, you need an employee list. Table 8.3 shows the appropriate Employee fields. Unfortunately, the Employee table includes only a hire date; there is no termination date. Perhaps everyone is so happy working for Tasmanian Traders that no one ever leaves, and all of the employees are model employees.

**Table 8.3   Employee Mailing Information Fields**

| Field | Type | Size |
|-------|------|------|
| LAST_NAME | Character | 20 |
| FIRST_NAME | Character | 10 |
| ADDRESS | Character | 60 |

*continues*

| Table 8.3 Continued | | |
|---|---|---|
| **Field** | **Type** | **Size** |
| CITY | Character | 15 |
| REGION | Character | 15 |
| POSTAL_CODE | Character | 10 |
| COUNTRY | Character | 15 |

This SELECT is the simplest of the three:

```
SELECT Employee.last_name, Employee.first_name, Employee.address,;
  Employee.city, Employee.region, Employee.postal_code, Employee.country;
  FROM tastrade!employee;
  GROUP BY Employee.last_name, Employee.first_name
```

You could now run each of these three SELECT statements and obtain three separate mailing lists. However, what you really want is a single list. That is where the UNION clause helps.

## Using UNION to Join SELECT Results

UNION combines information from two or more separate SELECT statements in a single cursor or table.

To use UNION to combine the result sets of multiple SELECT commands, you must follow some rules.

- You can combine any number of SELECT results, connecting each to the preceding one with a UNION clause. The important thing to remember is that the result set created by the first SELECT determines the required structure of the rest.

- The order, number, size, and type of fields in the first SELECT define the structure required in all subsequent SELECTs. Visual FoxPro 5.0 does not require that the corresponding fields in each SELECT have the same names. However, the first SELECT does define the field name used in the result set. It uses the field order to determine how to combine two or more SELECTs. This means that if you accidentally switch the order of two fields, Visual FoxPro appends the data that way. If this results in the wrong field type, Visual FoxPro generates the vague error: SELECTs are not UNION-compatible. (Could *SELECTs* be a synonym for *management?*)

Observe that the SELECTs for CUSTOMER and SUPPLIER have a contact name of 30 characters, which includes both the first and last names. On the other hand, Employee uses a separate field for first and last names, although the sum of their lengths is also 30. Another difference is that customers and suppliers have a company field; employees do not.

To combine these result sets, you must reconcile these differences. Listing 8.1 combines the three SELECTs to create a single result table.

---

**Listing 8.1   08PRG01.PRG**

```
* PROGRAM 8.1
*
* Creates a annual picnic invitation list from customers,
* suppliers, and employees for Tasmanian Traders
  CLOSE ALL
  CLEAR

* Create mailing list of employees, suppliers and customers
SELECT Customer.contact_name, Customer.company_name, Customer.address,;
  Customer.city, Customer.region, Customer.postal_code, Customer.country;
 FROM  tastrade!customer INNER JOIN tastrade!orders;
   ON  Customer.customer_id = Orders.customer_id;
 WHERE YEAR(Orders.order_date) = 1995;
 UNION ;
 SELECT SPACE(40)AS Company_Name, ;
   ALLTRIM(Employee.first_name) + ' ' + ALLTRIM(Employee.last_name)AS Contact,;
   Employee.address, Employee.city, Employee.region, Employee.postal_code,;
   Employee.country;
 FROM tastrade!employee;
 UNION ;
 SELECT Supplier.contact_name, Supplier.company_name, Supplier.address,;
  Supplier.city, Supplier.region, Supplier.postal_code, Supplier.country;
 FROM  tastrade!supplier INNER JOIN tastrade!products;
    INNER JOIN tastrade!order_line_items;
    INNER JOIN tastrade!order_line_items ;
   ON  Orders.order_id = Order_line_items.order_id ;
   ON  Products.product_id = Order_line_items.product_id ;
   ON  Supplier.supplier_id = Products.supplier_id ;
 WHERE YEAR(Orders.order_date) = 1995
```

---

Notice the use of the following clause:

```
SPACE(40) as Company
```

This expression is a placeholder that corresponds to the company field in the CUSTOMER and SUPPLIER files. This clause fills the company field in the combined result table with blanks, because the EMPLOYEE file has no company field. Without it, Visual FoxPro would not place the rest of the Employee fields in the correct columns.

You can put a placeholder in any SELECT statement. You can put it in the first SELECT statement of a group to reserve space for a field that exists only in later SELECTs. Alternatively, as in this example, you can include it in a later SELECT to match the columns of the first or master SELECT.

To ensure that employees are not confused with customers or suppliers, you could replace the preceding clause with the following:

```
"Tastrade" AS Company_Name
```

**TIP** You can use placeholders in single SELECTs. Then you can use the "new" fields to add to the cursor information that does not exist in the cursor, perhaps through a form or calculation.

Next, the SELECT statement concatenates the employee first- and last-name fields to match the contact names in CUSTOMER and SUPPLIER. It uses ALLTRIM with the employee's first name to remove trailing blanks. However, a blank must then be added to separate it from the employee's last name. The employee first name can store up to 10 characters, and the last name can have 20 characters, according to the Employee table structure. Thus, it is possible that with the addition of a blank between these two fields, the total field size may exceed the 30-character limit of CONTACT. In that case, Visual FoxPro truncates the last character.

### TROUBLESHOOTING

**I combined the three individual SELECTs, with Employee first, followed by Customer and Supplier. However, the program failed.** Although you can insert placeholders into the field list of the first or master SELECT, you cannot place calculated fields there. Thus, you cannot use Employee as the first SELECT, because you need to concatenate the first and last names. If you try it, FoxPro displays an error message, telling you that SELECTs are not UNION-compatible.

You can define placeholders for variables of other types as well. Some examples include:

```
.T. AS InStock
000.00 AS UnitPrice
00000 AS OnHand
{//} AS OrderDate
```

Observe that in the case of numeric values, the picture used determines the size of the field and number of decimal places.

Sometimes, a field exists in all SELECTs combined with UNIONs, but the field sizes differ. Suppose, for the sake of this example, that the Employee files use a 30-character address field. The ADDRESS field in CUSTOMER and SUPPLIER has 60 characters. Although you do not have to do anything when subsequent fields are smaller, you could pad the employee address in the third SELECT with 30 trailing blanks, as follows:

```
AEmployee.Address + SPACE(30) AS Address
```

 **TIP** Make sure that field definition in the first SELECT is large enough for its associated fields in the other SELECTs. If it is not, Visual FoxPro truncates the data.

**N O T E** An error anywhere within a set of SELECTs connected with UNION causes the entire statement to fail. Often, you cannot easily determine which SELECT caused the failure. Therefore, consider testing each SELECT individually before combining them with UNIONs. ■

Some other considerations in combining SELECTs with UNION are:

- Because ORDER BY and INTO clauses work with the final result set, they can appear only in the final SELECT. After all, it would not make sense to UNION result sets sorted by different fields or output to different files or devices.

- On the other hand, GROUP BY and HAVING work with the selected records in creating the final result set. Because each SELECT creates an intermediate result set before UNION combines them, these clauses can appear in each SELECT. They affect only records from the SELECT that they are in.

> **CAUTION**
> Surprisingly, you can put a single ORDER BY or INTO clause in any of the SELECT statements, and Visual FoxPro uses it appropriately for the entire result table. However, if more than one SELECT has an ORDER BY or INTO clause, Visual FoxPro displays the nonspecific error message `Unrecognized phrase/keyword in command`.

 **TROUBLESHOOTING**

**To sort the output of the company picnic list, I included the clause ORDER BY Company_Name. However, the program failed.** In individual SELECT statements, you can sort the result table by adding an ORDER BY clause, followed by the name of the field, as follows:

```
ORDER BY Company_Name
```

*continues*

*continued*

However, when combining SELECT results with UNION, you must refer to the relative field position of the column to sort on, as in

```
ORDER BY 2
```

to sort on one field or

```
ORDER BY 6, 2
```

to sort on more than multiple fields. Attempts to reference a field by its name in one of the original tables result in the error SQL Invalid ORDER BY.

Perhaps you also noticed that the records in the result set were already sorted by contact name. Whenever you create a UNION between two or more SELECTs, and if you do not specify a sort order, Visual FoxPro automatically sorts them, using the selected field order to define a default sort. Thus, the Tasmanian Trader picnic SELECT sorts by contact.

Unlike the basic SELECT statement, which automatically includes duplicate records as long as they match the selection criteria, UNION performs an automatic DISTINCT. This means that it checks each record added to the result table to ensure that no other records in the result table match it exactly, field for field. Obviously, this takes additional time. To help, VFP places the records in a default sorted order if the code does not specify an order.

If you know that the SELECT statements do not duplicate records, you can replace UNION with UNION ALL. Adding ALL eliminates the test for duplicates, thus reducing the overall execution time.

Visual FoxPro uses UNIONs only between queries, not subqueries. Suppose that you want to see the name of all employees who do not live in a country where you have suppliers or customers. (Pink-slip time!) You might want to perform the following query:

```
SELECT A.First_Name, A.Last_Name ;
  FROM \VFP\SAMPLES\MAINSAMP\DATA\TASTRADE!EMPLOYEE A ;
WHERE Country NOT IN (SELECT customer.Country ;
        FROM \VFP\SAMPLES\MAINSAMP\DATA\TASTRADE!CUSTOMER, ;
        UNION ;
        SELECT supplier.Country
          FROM \VFP\SAMPLES\MAINSAMP\DATA\TASTRADE!SUPPLIER)
```

Visual FoxPro does not support this use of UNION. In fact, it generates the error SQL Invalid use of union in subquery. Rather, you need to ask the following:

```
SELECT A.First_Name, A.Last_Name ;
  FROM EMPLOYEE A ;
WHERE Country NOT IN (SELECT customer.Country) ;
        FROM \VFP\SAMPLES\MAINSAMP\DATA\TASTRADE!CUSTOMER) ;
        OR Country NOT IN (SELECT supplier.Country ;
        FROM \VFP\SAMPLES\MAINSAMP\DATA\TASTRADE!SUPPLIER)
```

Following is a summary of Visual FoxPro's UNION rules:

- Any field included in the first field list must be represented by a field or placeholder in subsequent field lists.

- Any field from a subsequent field list that is not part of the first field list must be represented by a placeholder in the first field list.

- No calculated fields can appear in the first field list.

- ORDER BY and INTO clauses can appear in any SELECT in the UNION, but only one time, and they apply to the entire result.

- ORDER BY must reference the column by numeric position rather than by name.

- If no ORDER BY clause exists, Visual FoxPro uses the field order as the default order.

- GROUP BY and HAVING clauses can appear in each SELECT in the UNION, and they apply to only the partial results generated by that SELECT.

- UNION cannot combine the results of subqueries (SELECTs used within the WHERE clause of other SELECTs).

## Creating Inner Joins

Actually, you have been creating inner joins for the past chapter and a half. An *inner join* includes all records from each table that match a join condition. Thus, you create an inner join whenever you include a WHERE condition in a SELECT, as in the following example:

```
SELECT A.Contact_Name, A.Company_Name, A.Address, A.City, ;
       A.Region, A.Postal_Code, A.Country ;
  FROM \VFP\SAMPLES\MAINSAMP\DATA\TASTRADE!CUSTOMER A, ;
       \VFP\SAMPLES\MAINSAMP\DATA\TASTRADE!ORDERS B ;
 WHERE A.Customer_Id = B.Customer_Id
```

The following SELECT - SQL Command from Visual FoxPro 5.0 shows the syntax that supports the JOIN argument:

```
SELECT Customer.contact_name, Customer.company_name, Customer.address,;
   Customer.city, Customer.region, Customer.postal_code, Customer.country;
 FROM  tastrade!customer INNER JOIN tastrade!orders;
   ON Customer.customer_id = Orders.customer_id
```

These SELECTs include records for customer ID that exist in both CUSTOMER.DBF and ORDERS.DBF.

## Creating Outer Joins

Normally, when Visual FoxPro joins records in a SQL SELECT, it looks from the records in the child table to find records in the parent. If the tables follow referential-integrity rules, there should never be a child record without a corresponding parent record. However, in some cases, there may be parent records without corresponding children. A SELECT does not include those records.

Suppose that you want to create an SQL SELECT that sums the quantity of each product sold by Tasmanian Traders. The following SELECT counts the sales, using ORDER_LINE_ITEMS:

```
SELECT A.Product_ID, SUM(A.Quantity) AS Total_Sales, ;
       B.Product_Name ;
  FROM \VFP\SAMPLES\MAINSAMP\DATA\TASTRADE!ORDER_LINE_ITEMS A, ;
       \VFP\SAMPLES\MAINSAMP\DATA\TASTRADE!PRODUCTS B ;
 WHERE A.Product_ID = B.Product_ID ;
 GROUP BY A.Product_ID
```

The problem with this SELECT is that it includes only records for items with sales. There may be products without sales. To include them, you need a left outer join.

A *left outer join* includes all records from the parent file (the "one" side of the relation), whether or not they have corresponding child records. The way to implement a left outer join is to perform two SELECTs: one for all records with children and one with all records without children. Then combine the results of these two SELECTs with a UNION. Listing 8.2 creates the necessary list.

**N O T E**  To show that this example really does include products without sales, modify the PRODUCTS.DBF table in \VFP\SAMPLES\DATA before running this program. Add a few records with new PRODUCT_ID values. Include at least a product name (for example, Discontinued Product #1) to help you identify the ones that were added. ■

**Listing 8.2   08PRG02.PRG**

```
* PROGRAM 8.2
* Creates an outer-join to list all products and their sales.
  CLOSE ALL
  CLEAR

  SELECT A.Product_ID, SUM(A.Quantity) AS TotalSales, ;
         B.Product_Name ;
    FROM \VFP\SAMPLES\MAINSAMP\DATA\TASTRADE!ORDER_LINE_ITEMS A, ;
         \VFP\SAMPLES\MAINSAMP\DATA\TASTRADE!PRODUCTS B ;
   WHERE A.Product_ID = B.Product_ID ;
   GROUP BY A.Product_ID ;
 UNION ALL ;
  SELECT B.Product_ID, 0, B.Product_Name ;
    FROM \VFP\SAMPLES\MAINSAMP\DATA\TASTRADE!PRODUCTS B ;
   WHERE Product_ID NOT IN (SELECT DISTINCT Product_ID ;
         FROM \VFP\SAMPLES\MAINSAMP\DATA\TASTRADE!ORDER_LINE_ITEMS)
```

```
*/Visual FoxPro 5.0

SELECT Products.product_id,;
  SUM(Order_line_items.quantity) AS totalsales, Products.product_name;
  FROM  tastrade!products LEFT OUTER JOIN tastrade!order_line_items ;
   ON  Products.product_id = Order_line_items.product_id;
  GROUP BY Products.product_id
```

**Part**

**II**

**Ch**

**8**

---

**TIP** For a left outer join, there should never be an overlap of records. Therefore, use UNION ALL to optimize performance when combining the two record sets.

---

**NOTE** A *right outer join* combines all the records that satisfy the relational criteria, as well as all child records without parent records. However, if you have implemented referential integrity through the database for your tables, you should never need a right outer join. ■

## Creating a Self-Join

A *self-join* is a query that needs to form a relation between two fields in the same table. See "Creating Self-Referencing Relations" in Chapter 4, which uses a self-join in an employee file to find the names of each employee's supervisor. Listing 8.3 shows the necessary SELECT statement to generate the required result.

**Listing 8.3  08PRG03.PRG**

```
* PROGRAM 8.3
* Creates a self-join to find the suppliers
* of both products 16 and 17.
  CLOSE ALL
  CLEAR

  SELECT A.cCustId, ;
         A.cLastName AS Employee_Last_Name, ;
         A.cFirstName AS Employee_First_Name, ;
         B.cLastName AS Supervisor_Last_Name, ;
         B.cFirstName AS Supervisor_First_Name ;
     FROM \USINGFOX.300\DATA\PTOFSALE!EMPL2 A, ;
          \USINGFOX.300\DATA\PTOFSALE!EMPL2 B ;
    WHERE A.cSupervisor = B.cCustId
```

Observe that to form a self-join, you must open the table more than once, with a different alias for each occurrence. This example opens the file EMPL2.DBF, using the simple character aliases A and B. It then forms a relation between the supervisor ID in one instance and the employee ID in the other.

Another situation that calls for a self-join occurs when you need to find records that match two or more occurrences of the same field. Suppose that you want to know which Tasmanian Traders supplier, if any, provides both product ID 16 and 17. Because this request requires comparing products across multiple records, a simple query will not solve it. Listing 8.4 opens PRODUCT.DBF twice, once to find each product. If the supplier ID for both is the same, it retrieves the name of the supplier for the result table.

**Listing 8.4   08PRG04.PRG**

```
* PROGRAM 8.4
* Creates a self-join to find the suppliers of both products 16 and 18.
* Ensure the Products.Supplier_Id for both products 16 and 18 are the same.
  CLOSE ALL
  CLEAR

  SELECT A.Product_Name, B.Product_Name, ;
         C.Company_Name, A.Product_ID, B.Product_id ;
    FROM TASTRADE!PRODUCTS A,;
         TASTRADE!PRODUCTS B,;
         TASTRADE!SUPPLIER C ;
   WHERE A.Product_ID = '    16' AND ;
         B.Product_ID = '    18' AND ;
         A.Supplier_ID = B.Supplier_ID AND ;
         A.Supplier_ID = C.Supplier_ID

* Visual FoxPro 5.0
CLOSE ALL
SELECT 0
USE products ALIAS products
SELECT 0
USE products ALIAS products_a AGAIN
SELECT 0
USE supplier
SELECT Products.product_name, Products_a.product_name, ;
  Supplier.company_name, Products.product_id, Products_a.product_id;
 FROM  tastrade!products INNER JOIN tastrade!supplier;
   INNER JOIN tastrade!products Products_a ;
  ON  Products.supplier_id ==Supplier.supplier_id ;
  ON  Products.supplier_id == Products_a.supplier_id;
 WHERE Products.product_id == '    16';
   AND (Products_a.product_id == '    18');
 ORDER BY Products.product_id
```

# Optimizing Query Generation

A poorly designed query can require minutes or even hours to return a result set that a properly designed query can do in seconds. This section examines techniques that improve the performance time of queries.

# Basic Rules for Using Rushmore

Rushmore can improve the performance of most queries when used properly. However, many developers don't understand how Rushmore really works; therefore, they create queries that do not perform at their optimal level.

First, Rushmore uses existing indexes whenever possible to process a query. If an existing index does not exist, it creates a "virtual" index in memory for the request. However, creating an index takes more time than using an existing one.

Many developers, knowing that Rushmore uses indexes, try to "help" it along by setting the order of the tables before running the query. In commands that use the Rushmore optimizable FOR clauses, such as BROWSE, LIST, and SCAN, this practice slows the command. It does not turn Rushmore off, however. Rushmore finds the records that match the criteria; then it has to go back to the index to determine the order in which to display them.

When you create queries using SELECT, Visual FoxPro ignores any established order for selected tables. Therefore, you do not need to go back and turn indexes off to benefit from Rushmore. But setting them doesn't help either. You still have to phrase all WHERE clause criteria, using Rushmore-optimizable clauses, for the best performance.

The main criterion in determining whether a clause is Rushmore-optimizable is whether it exactly matches a current index or tag expression. If it does, Rushmore optimizes the expression. For this reason, many developers create a separate index tag on each field in the table. For example:

```
INDEX ON Company_Name TAG company
INDEX ON Employee_ID TAG employee
```

This means Visual FoxPro must update each index every time it adds, changes, or deletes a record. Alternatively, you can define a concatenated index like the following:

```
INDEX ON Company_Name + Employee_Id TAG employee
```

This index performs searches only slightly slower than indexes on individual fields. It reduces the total number of indexes that Visual FoxPro must maintain, however. If you look at your applications, you usually don't need indexes on every field. In fact, only a few indexes may really be necessary to form relations and queries. A good goal is to minimize the total number of indexes while providing an index for every defined need.

On the other hand, if you need individual indexes on Company and Employee ID, don't create a third index on the concatenation of the two; this actually slows Rushmore.

Even a seemingly minor change to the index expression can turn off Rushmore. Using the preceding index expression on Company_Name, for example, Rushmore will not optimize the following expression:

```
UPPER(Company_Name) = 'FRANS'
```

The function UPPER() invalidates the use of Rushmore. On the other hand, if you know that the application stores all company names in uppercase, Rushmore will optimize the following expression:

```
Company_Name = UPPER('frans')
```

 **TIP** Don't control case in conditional statements. Use PICTURE or FUNCTION clauses in GET statements or object fields to control case.

If the WHERE clause contains several conditions connected with AND, Rushmore optimizes each condition separately. However, if you connect conditions with OR, Rushmore will not optimize the SELECT if either expression is not optimizable.

Unless you want to display all records in the table regardless of their delete status, you should create an index on DELETED(). Rushmore uses this index to determine which records it can use when SET DELETED ON is set. If Rushmore has to read the table to determine the delete flag on each record, the SELECT cannot be fully optimized.

**N O T E** You may not have realized that deleted records can cause a problem for Rushmore. Just because the SELECT does not include a !DELETED() clause does not mean that VFP does not look at the delete flag. Remember that the command SET DELETED ON could be set elsewhere in the current program, a previous program, the FoxPro CONFIG.FPW file, or even interactively. If you want to skip deleted records and want optimal performance from Rushmore, you must have a tag defined on the DELETED() function. ∎

Rushmore will not use indexes that contain NOT or FOR when optimizing an expression. However, you can use NOT in the condition. For example, you can have a SELECT like the following:

```
SELECT Company_Name FROM customer WHERE NOT (State='TX')
```

As long as an index exists on the field STATE, Rushmore will optimize the expression.

Sometimes, you can benefit from previous Rushmore optimization. Suppose that you begin by searching the ORDERS table for all orders in 1995, as follows:

```
BROWSE FOR YEAR(Order_Date) = 1995
```

Next, suppose that you need only orders from customer 'FRANS' in 1995:

```
BROWSE FOR YEAR(Order_Date) = 1995 AND Customer_ID = 'FRANS'
```

Assuming that the following indexes exist:

```
INDEX ON YEAR(Order_Date) TAG year
INDEX ON Customer_ID TAG customer
```

Rushmore optimizes the first expression, finding all orders for 1995. When it begins the second browse, it recognizes that it already has information about orders in 1995. Therefore, it examines those records only for customer 'FRANS'.

Another problem that few developers consider is index fragmentation. Structural indexes usually contain more than one tag. As you modify the table, the index blocks become interwoven, causing Visual FoxPro to spend more time looking for the next block. Because disk access rates are relatively slow, this affects performance. This situation is similar to file fragmentation on a hard disk. The answer is to periodically REINDEX the file—the equivalent of defragmenting a disk. Of course, the safest way to reindex erases the current index and re-creates it from individual tag definitions.

The biggest potential danger with Rushmore is that it creates a solution set for any given optimizable expression only once. If you use a SCAN FOR clause, Rushmore determines which records to process the first time it executes the FOR. In a shared environment, another user could make a change that would affect Rushmore's solution set while SCAN is processing. However, because Rushmore does not check for changes, you may process the wrong records. For the average application, the benefits of Rushmore outweigh this remote but possible problem. However, you should be aware of it if you have very-high-transaction-rate tables. If you decide that the potential danger is too great, turn optimization off before the SELECT with the following statement:

```
SET OPTIMIZE OFF
```

**TIP** You can turn Rushmore optimization ON and OFF globally with the SET OPTIMIZE Command or use the NOOPTOMIZE clause to disable it for a command.

Suppose that you need to reference selected records from a single table and need no special column functions, groups, or orders. SELECT creates a special cursor that effectively reopens the table in a different work area and applies a filter to it. It performs this activity almost instantaneously. Therefore, rather than use this code,

```
SELECT orders
SCAN FOR Customer_Name = 'TAZMAN'
  << commands that process each selected order >>
ENDSCAN
```

you might instead use this code:

```
SELECT * FROM orders WHERE Customer_Name = 'TAZMAN'
SCAN
  << commands that process each selected order >>
ENDSCAN
```

## Minimizing Fields in a Query

All too often, it seems easier to just include the * character in a SELECT statement to include all the fields in a table. However, you should include only the fields that you absolutely need. If you want only DISTINCT records, SELECT compares every field in every record to determine if the new record is distinct. This consumes time. Reducing the number of fields in the SELECT reduces the number of comparisons. However, a better solution is to use the GROUP BY clause wherever possible.

Another trap is the assumption that it is easier to form relations between SELECT results and other existing tables than to include all the fields in the SELECT. Actually, the most likely reason for doing this is reluctance to include all of the field references. It is true that large multiple-table SELECTs consume a great deal of memory and often need to be stored partially on disk. Further, the more fields included in the SELECT, the more memory it needs or the more disk access time it requires. Of course, any disk access slows a SELECT considerably. You might be tempted to include only those fields that are necessary to uniquely identify the records in the SELECT and then form relations to other physical tables. This generally is not a good solution. The main reason is that accessing all the other physical tables to form and access the relations definitely involves slower disk access.

# Creating Cross-Tabs

*Cross-tabs* are a special type of query in which you define column and row headings of a table and calculate results for the intersecting cells. Suppose that you want to create a monthly sales summary, by customer, for Tasmanian Traders. This report needs to display 12 column headings, each one representing a different month. Each row represents a different customer. You probably would not normally store a table with a structure like the following:

```
CustomerId       Character       8
JanuarySales     Numeric         8    2
FebruarySales    Numeric         8    2
MarchSales       Numeric         8    2
AprilSales       Numeric         8    2
MaySales         Numeric         8    2
```

| JuneSales | Numeric | 8 | 2 |
|---|---|---|---|
| JulySales | Numeric | 8 | 2 |
| AugustSales | Numeric | 8 | 2 |
| SeptemberSales | Numeric | 8 | 2 |
| OctoberSales | Numeric | 8 | 2 |
| NovemberSales | Numeric | 8 | 2 |
| DecemberSales | Numeric | 8 | 2 |

Instead, the data file looks like this:

| CustomerId | Character | 8 | |
|---|---|---|---|
| SalesDate | Date | 8 | |
| SalesAmt | Numeric | 8 | 2 |

How do you get from the second form to the first? Visual FoxPro includes a special program called VFPXTAB, which converts a SELECT cursor that contains the necessary information to a cross-tab table. To gather the necessary information for the cross-tab, you first need a cursor with three fields:

- The row headings
- The column headings
- The row–column intersection values

The first SELECT statement in Listing 8.5 gathers the required data for 1994 and stores it in a table named MyTab. The second SELECT creates the cross-tab, using the data from MyTab to provide the row, column, and data. Function SYS(2015) generates a unique name for the cursor.

## Listing 8.5  08PRG05.PRG

```
* PROGRAM 8.5
* Creates a cross-tab
  CLOSE ALL
  CLEAR

*/ Create the source information for row, column, and data
  SELECT A.Customer_id, C.Monthid, ;
         (B.Unit_Price*B.Quantity) AS Order_Net ;
    FROM TASTRADE!ORDERS A, ;
         TASTRADE!ORDER_LINE_ITEMS B, ;
         PERIOD C ;
   WHERE YEAR(A.Order_Date) = 1994 AND ;
         MONTH(A.Order_Date) = C.MonthId AND ;
         A.Order_Id = B.Order_Id ;
   GROUP BY A.Customer_Id, C.MonthId ;
    INTO TABLE MyTab
```

*continues*

---

**Listing 8.5    Continued**

```
*/ Create the cross-tab
SELECT MyTab.customer_i, MyTab.monthid, SUM(MyTab.order_net);
FROM MyTab;
GROUP BY MyTab.customer_i, MyTab.monthid;
ORDER BY MyTab.customer_i, MyTab.monthid;
INTO CURSOR SYS(2015)
DO (_GENXTAB)
BROWSE NOMODIFY
```

---

This SELECT requires a special table that is not included with the Tasmanian Trader example. You can quickly create this table, based on the structure shown in Table 8.4. Table 8.5 shows the contents of all 12 records. Place this table in directory \USINGFOX.500\DATA.

**Table 8.4    Table Structure for PERIOD.DBF Used in the Cross-Tab**

| Field | Type | Size |
|---|---|---|
| MonthID | Numeric | 2 |
| MonthName | Character | 10 |

**Table 8.5    Records in PERIOD.DBF**

| Record # | MonthID | MonthName |
|---|---|---|
| 1 | 1 | January |
| 2 | 2 | February |
| 3 | 3 | March |
| 4 | 4 | April |
| 5 | 5 | May |
| 6 | 6 | June |
| 7 | 7 | July |
| 8 | 8 | August |
| 9 | 9 | September |
| 10 | 10 | October |
| 11 | 11 | November |
| 12 | 12 | December |

The SELECT in Listing 8.5 creates a cursor with one record for each customer–month combination. It first has to link ORDERS with ORDER_LINE_ITEMS to calculate the product of the Unit_Price and Quantity. It stores this product in the result set field ORDER_NET. The GROUP BY clause then sums ORDER_NET if the customer ordered more than one item in any month.

The result table from this SELECT is not a cross tabulation. However, you could create a cross-tab report with it if you sort and group by customer ID. First, you need to define report variables such as the following:

```
JanSales = IIF(MonthName = 'JANUARY', Order_Net, 0)
```

This expression totals sales for January. You need to create 11 similar expressions, defining total sales for other months. Then add these report variables to the customer ID group footer and set the calculation method to SUM. This report does not need detail lines—only group footers.

This solution works for a report. However, it would not be as easy to display the information in a form, use the results with another table, or generate a graph. That is why you need to use VFPXTAB.

VFPXTAB reads the cursor created by the preceding SELECT and determines the number of distinct columns. Next, it creates a new table with the same first column (Customer_Id, in this case), and columns for each distinct value in the cursor's second field. Then it creates one record for each customer and puts the corresponding total sales in the correct column. The net result is a cross-tab table with 13 columns and 1 row for each customer. Now you can directly use this table to generate reports or graphs.

To execute VFPXTAB, you can call it directly, as follows:

```
DO \VFP\VFPXTAB
```

This statement assumes that the root directory for Visual FoxPro is \VFP\. If your root directory is different, adjust this statement appropriately. If you have never run VFPXTAB before, Visual FoxPro must first compile it.

VFPXTAB uses, as input, the table in the current work area. Therefore, the table does not have to be named in the command that executes VFPXTAB. However, VFPXTAB has nine other possible parameters. All of these parameters have default values and can be omitted. The parameters are:

| Parm1 | Output file/cursor name (default: XTAB.DBF) |
|-------|----------------------------------------------|
| Parm2 | Cursor only (creates only a cursor) (default: .F.) |
| Parm3 | Closes input table after use (default: .T.) |

| Parm4 | Shows progress thermometer (default: .T.) |
|---|---|
| Parm5 | Row field (field number to use as row) (default: 1) |
| Parm6 | Column field (field number to use as column) (default: 2) |
| Parm7 | Data field (field number to use as data) (default: 3) |
| Parm8 | Total rows (calculate row total) (default: .F.) |
| Parm9 | Totaling options (0-sum, 1-count, 2-% of total) |

You also can assign the fully qualified file name to the system variable, _genxtab, if it is not already defined. You also can assign this variable in CONFIG.FPW, using the following command:

```
_GENXTAB=""
```

To use the system variable and create the cross-tab, use this command:

```
DO (_genxtab)
```

The following command creates a cross-tab with one row per customer; then it sums all the customer's sales by month and displays one column per month:

```
DO \VFP\VFPXTAB WITH 'CUSTSALE.DBF', .F., .F., .T., 1, 2, 3, .T.
```

The eighth parameter has been set to .T.; thus, it creates an additional column at the end to total all of the sales for the previous columns. In this case, because the SELECT limited records to a single year, this column represents the annual sales to each customer.

When you add 2 as the ninth parameter, the cross-tab calculates the percentage of total sales attributed to each customer during the year. Then you could sort the resulting cross-tab table to display the customers in order of total sales percentage, as follows:

```
DO \VFP\VFPXTAB WITH 'CUSTSALE.DBF', .F., .F., .T., 1, 2, 3, .T., 2
```

**CAUTION**

A maximum of 254 unique values are allowed for the "columns" side of the cross-tab.

▶ **See** "The CrossTab Wizard," **p. 240**

# Using Views and Updatable Queries

Views and queries are almost the same thing. The principal difference is that you can use views to update data in the source tables. Also, Visual FoxPro stores views in the database, not as separate QPR files; as a result, you can access them only while the database is open. Because you can update data in a view, views provide an excellent way to access and edit data stored in multiple related files. They also provide access to remote data on the same machine or on a remote server. When you are working with server data, you do not have to download all the records to your local machine to accomplish a change. The view can retrieve a subset of data, process it, and return it.

## Views of Local Data

This section starts by showing you how to create views of local data. Creating a view is very similar to creating a query. You can create a view in two primary ways:

- Choose File, New, View from the system menu.
- Type **CREATE VIEW** in the Command window.

Both methods open the View Designer. This feature is similar to the Query Designer, with the addition of an Update Criteria Page. Suppose that you want to create a view between tables CUSTOMER and ORDERS in TASMANIAN TRADERS. Figure 8.1 shows the opening screen of the View Designer, with the Add Table or View dialog box open and ready to add the second table.

**FIGURE 8.1**

To begin a view, open the Add Table or View dialog box, and add the tables or views from the database used in the view.

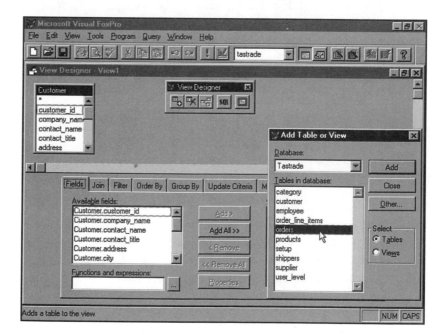

The first five pages and the last page in the page frame provide the same options as queries. For further information about how to use these pages, refer to Chapter 7, "Creating Basic Queries."

The first page, shown in Figure 8.2, displays a list of selected fields.

**FIGURE 8.2**

The Fields page of the View Designer allows you to select fields from the available tables and to rearrange their order.

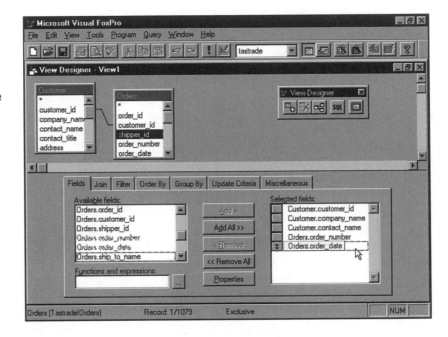

You can add or remove fields from this list by doing the following things:

- Double-clicking the field name in the Table View area. Double-clicking the asterisk at the top of each table copies all fields to the output list.

- Dragging the selected fields from the Table View area to the Selected Fields list.

- Double-clicking the field names in the Available Fields list and Selected Fields list, or clicking the buttons that are positioned between the lists.

The order in which you select fields becomes the fields' default order in the selected output list. You can easily change this order by clicking and dragging the button to the left of each field name, moving it up or down in the list. Defining the field order is important, because it defines the field order in the result set.

Figure 8.3 shows the Properties dialog box that appears when you click the Properties button in the Fields page. In this dialog box, you can specify validation, display, and mapping options, as well as enter a comment for each field in the view.

**FIGURE 8.3**
The View Field
Properties dialog box
provides field-property
options.

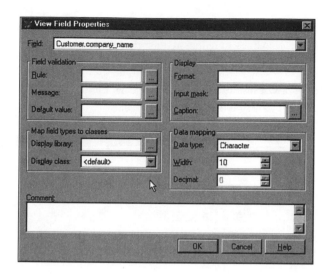

The Join page allows you to set up inner, left, right, and full joins when a view or query has more than one table (see Figure 8.4).

**FIGURE 8.4**
The Join page displays
the join condition(s)
for the tables in the
top pane of the
designer.

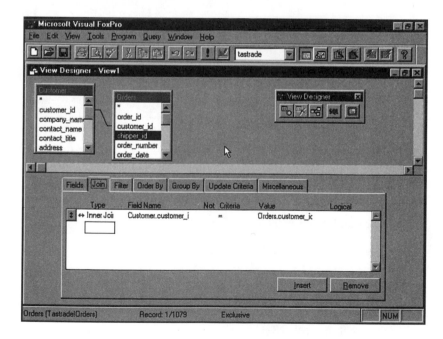

The two check boxes below the Selected Fields list create a DISTINCT result set (No Duplicates) or a Cross Tabulate result set. Thus, you can use the Query or View Designer to create the necessary intermediate table for GENXTAB, described in the preceding section. This check box is disabled if you do not initialize the memory variable _GENXTAB. You also have to select at least three fields.

The Filter page is where you enter the conditions that are expressed in the WHERE clause of the SELECT statement (see Figure 8.5). Fields do not have to be included in the Selected Fields list to be used in filter conditions.

**FIGURE 8.5**

Exclude records from the view by selecting filter conditions.

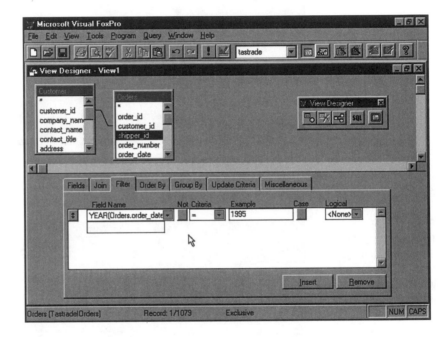

The Order By page (see Figure 8.6) determines a sort order for the fields. Order criteria allow you to establish a sort order based on selected fields and expressions. You can sort each selected field in ascending or descending order. The order of the fields in the Ordering Criteria list determines the sort hierarchy. To change the sort hierarchy, simply click and drag the button to the left of each field name.

The Group By page (see Figure 8.7) provides an alternative to using No Duplicates.

The section "Using DISTINCT versus GROUP BY" earlier in this chapter describes the advantage of using GROUP BY over the DISTINCT clause in SQL statements. The Group By page also allows you to add a HAVING clause by clicking the Having button. Remember that the HAVING clause operates on the selected records in the result set. Therefore, you can use GROUP BY to collect and sum records by customer ID. Then you can select customers who made total purchases of more than $1,000 by using a HAVING clause such as the following:

```
HAVING TotalPurchases > 1000
```

**FIGURE 8.6**
Define the order of the records in the result set by selecting fields in the Order By page of the View Designer.

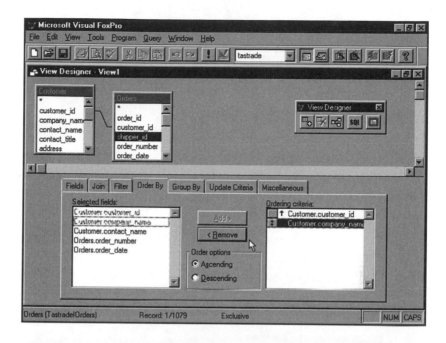

**FIGURE 8.7**
Use the Group By Page of the View Designer to sum records by one or more of the selected fields.

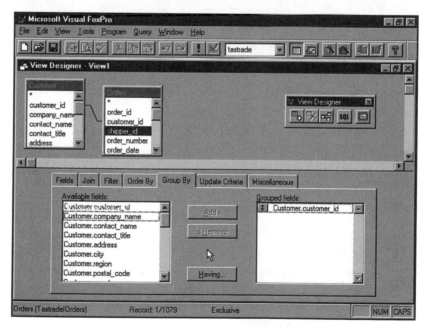

**NOTE** Visual FoxPro can create an updatable view of local data, but the data is only buffered. The features that update the original tables are in the Update Criteria page of the View Designer. ■

For a local table view, Visual FoxPro supports only buffering. By default, buffering is turned off. By using the CURSORSETPROP() function, however, you can set buffering to one of the following values:

> 1 - Row and table buffering off
>
> 2 - Pessimistic row buffering on
>
> 3 - Optimistic row buffering on
>
> 4 - Pessimistic table buffering on
>
> 5 - Optimistic table buffering on

To use buffering, you must first turn on MULTILOCKS. Then, using the CURSORSETPROP() function, you can select one of the buffering methods. The following code would turn on optimistic table buffering for the CUSTOMER table:

```
SET MULTILOCKS ON
= CURSORSETPROP('BUFFERING', 5, 'CUSTOMER')
```

Notice that this function requires three parameters. The first is BUFFERING for all local tables. The second is a numeric value to identify the buffering method. Finally, the last parameter identifies the table.

**N O T E**   The Miscellaneous page has check boxes for the duplicate-records and cross-tabulate options. The cross-tabulate option is enabled when you select three fields. These fields must represent the X axis, the Y axis, and data for the cross-tab. Record selections include all records, a specified number of records, or a percentage of the records that meet the selection criteria. (See Figure 8.8.) ■

## Remote View Update Options

The Update Criteria page of the View Designer page frame contains options that are specifically related to the capability of views to update the remote data that they represent. Figure 8.9 shows the options on this page.

Within a view, you can control which tables and fields the user can update and how Visual FoxPro performs the updates. By default, Visual FoxPro prohibits all field updates in the view. To allow updates, first select the table to which the field belongs, using the table combo box in the upper-left corner of this page. You can select individual tables or all tables involved in the view. When you select a table, Visual FoxPro displays its fields in the center list box. Observe that it does not display all the fields from the table—just those that are  included in the output set.

**FIGURE 8.8**

The Miscellaneous page of the View Designer specifies duplicate records, cross-tabular format, and how records are selected for the result set.

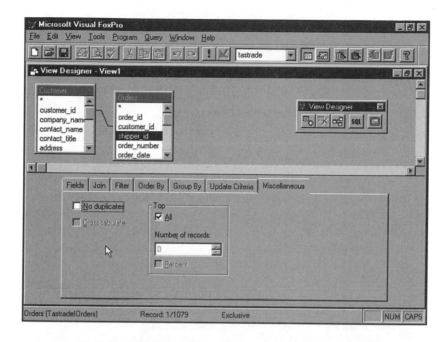

**FIGURE 8.9**

The Update Criteria page of the View Designer defines how Visual FoxPro updates the remote tables when changes are made to the view result set.

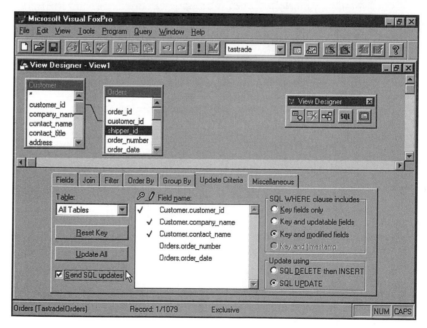

If a table has a primary key, and if that field appears in the output set, a check mark appears in the first column, below the key symbol. You can change the field(s) used to uniquely identify records in the original table. However, you should select only the primary-key field or a candidate-key field. These fields must appear in the selected fields.

The Reset Key button immediately below the table combo box returns the key-field status to the original setting used by the source table.

The Update All button places check marks in the second column of the field list, below the pencil icon. This column determines which fields VFP will update. You can select individual fields for updating by clicking the button in this column next to the field name. Conversely, you can click the Update All button and turn off individual fields that you do not want to update.

By default, the Update All button does not select the key field as an updatable field. Although you can mark the key field as updatable by manually clicking its second column, you normally do not want to update the key field. Before allowing updates to a key field, you should define referential-integrity rules by using the RI Builder or by using the append, delete, and update triggers. Then you should allow updates only from the primary table field.

▶ **See** "Maintaining Referential Integrity," **p. 199**

Even if you mark fields as updatable, SQL does not send the updates back to the original files unless you also select the Send SQL Updates option. When you allow updates, you must also select one of the four update options shown in Table 8.6.

**Table 8.6   Update Options for the SQL WHERE Clause**

| Option | Description |
| --- | --- |
| Key Fields Only | This option tells Visual FoxPro to proceed with the update as long as the key field in the original table has not changed. |
| Key and Updatable Fields | This option causes the update to fail if the key field or any of the updatable fields changed in the original table. Notice that this option does not care whether you actually modified the updatable field. |
| Key and Modified Fields | This option checks if the key field or if the field corresponding to a locally modified field has changed in the source table. If so, the update fails. |

| Option | Description |
|---|---|
| Key and Timestamp | This option causes the update to fail if the key value or the time stamp in the original table has changed. (Not all remote tables support a time stamp.) |

Observe that the most severe test in this sequence is the last one, but it is also the safest. It can cause an update to fail even if the only field in the original table to change is one that is not selected as updatable in the current view.

The next-most-severe test checks the key and updatable fields. Usually, this test does not cause a problem, because views cannot update nonupdatable fields. Therefore, changes made by other users are safe.

The option that checks only modified fields leaves open the possibility of overwriting changes to updatable fields in the original table. This occurs if you do not change an updatable field that someone else changes before you send the update back.

A similar problem occurs if you check only whether the key field has changed—the least severe test. Another user could change one of the other updatable fields, and you could easily overwrite these changes. However, if other users have only add or delete rights to a file, this less restrictive update test performs better, because it has fewer fields to check for changes.

The last two options in the Update Criteria page determine which technique to use when the original data is updated. SQL can either delete the original records first and then insert the new ones or simply update the existing record. The first method guarantees that there are no intervening changes to any field in the table during the view. This option creates SQL DELETE and SQL INSERT commands to update the data.

Updating the existing record creates a SQL UPDATE command to update the source table. This option preserves changes to fields that are not used in the SQL WHERE clause.

N O T E   Although you can include a memo field in a view, it is not updatable. ■

### Creating an SQL View in Code

You also can create a view directly within your program code by first opening the database and then using the CREATE SQL VIEW command, as follows:

*continues*

*continued*

```
OPEN DATABASE \VFP\SAMPLES\MAINSAMP\DATA\TASTRADE
CREATE SQL VIEW CustInfo_View AS ;
SELECT Customer.customer_id, Customer.company_name,;
 Customer.contact_name, Orders.order_number, Orders.order_date;
FROM  tastrade!customer INNER JOIN tastrade!orders ;
ON  Customer.customer_id = Orders.customer_id;
WHERE YEAR(Orders.order_date) = 1995;
GROUP BY Customer.customer_id;
ORDER BY Customer.customer_id
```

To make this view updatable, you must set table properties with the DBSETPROP() function. It is easier to create the view ahead of time and then just open the database and USE the view. This method has the added advantage of allowing you to define the table properties more easily.

## Using Memory Variables in Selection Criteria

In all the examples so far, the selection criteria used to limit the selected records used actual values in the example portion of the criteria. Unfortunately, this limits the query to extracting only a fixed set of records each time the query is run, unless you modify the query. You might perform the following query, using the field Region to select records from the table CUSTOMER of TASTRADE:

```
SELECT CUSTOMER.Customer_Id, CUSTOMER.Company_Name, ;
       CUSTOMER.Region, CUSTOMER.Max_Order_Amt ;
   FROM TASTRADE!Customer ;
  WHERE CUSTOMER.Region = "PA"
```

This WHERE clause returns those records for customers from Pennsylvania (PA). Every time you run the query, however, it returns the same records. To change the records that are returned, you have to modify the statement.

This may be fine for users who are familiar and comfortable with working in interactive mode. But suppose that you need to put the query in a program. Further suppose that you want the user to still be able to select which state to retrieve records from.

One solution involves the use of memory variables. You must define a memory variable to hold the state code. Then you need to create a way to allow the user to enter a state code in this variable. The easiest way is to give the user a simple form that asks for the state. Alternatively, you can give the user a list from which he or she can pick valid state codes.

In either case, the next step is to redefine the SELECT statement with a memory variable that holds the selection for the criteria's example, rather than use a fixed value. The following statement shows the new SELECT, assuming that the user enters the state code in the lcGetState variable:

```
SELECT CUSTOMER.Customer_Id, CUSTOMER.Company_Name, ;
       CUSTOMER.Region, CUSTOMER.Max_Order_Amt ;
  FROM TASTRADE!Customer ;
 WHERE CUSTOMER.Region = lcGetState
```

You can try this example interactively simply by assigning lcGetState a value through the Command window before executing the SELECT. In a program, this technique allows the user to customize the records returned by the SELECT.

This method works for both queries and views. However, views support another way to obtain a value from the user.

## Parameterized Query Criteria

It is not always possible, or even desirable, to fix the record-selection criteria at design time. Neither do you necessarily want to create a separate form just to prompt for criteria values. Yet you still want the user to determine the condition. This is relatively easy to do in a view.

First, you need to define a view parameter by choosing Query, View Parameters. In the View Parameters dialog box, you can enter any valid variable name, along with its type. Then click OK to save it. In Figure 8.10, the parameter GroupDiscount has been defined as numeric.

**FIGURE 8.10**
To allow the user to control the criteria value used in the selection criteria of a view, you must define the criteria with a view parameter.

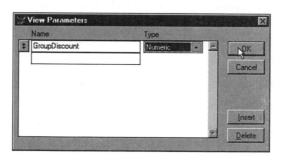

After defining the parameter, place the view parameter in the Example box of the appropriate selection criteria. To tell Visual FoxPro that this parameter is a view parameter and not a variable, precede it with a question mark. There is no space between the question mark and the parameter. The GroupDiscount parameter is entered as:

```
?GroupDiscount
```

When the view runs, a dialog box appears, asking the user to enter a value of the view parameter. VFP then uses the entered value to select records for the view. If you run the view and respond with a value of 2, VFP creates a view of customers who have a 2 percent discount.

**N O T E**   The option of defining a view parameter exists only when you are creating a view; it does not exist for simple queries. However, remember that you can create a view in which none of the fields is updatable, thus simulating a query. ■

# Views of Remote Data

The capability to access remote data depends on the use of ODBC (Open Database Connectivity) and SQL (Structured Query Language). SQL, which resulted from IBM relation database research in the 1970s, allows applications to delete, insert, read, and update data. The American National Standards Institute (ANSI) and the International Standards Organization (ISO) have adopted SQL for relation database access. Many companies have included SQL commands in their languages.

Unfortunately, most of these companies have "adapted" the commands to their own specific languages' features and syntax. Therefore, each implementation can have slight differences in syntax, preventing easy connections between different products. Recognizing this problem, many of the manufacturers joined Microsoft to develop a solution. This solution is called *CLI* (Common Language Interface). Microsoft, along with the other companies, has committed to including CLI in all Windows products. The resulting interface, which allows access to databases from other products, has been called ODBC.

ODBC uses drivers to translate the SQL syntax from one product to another. As a result, drivers exist to share data with many other products, including Access, Microsoft SQL Server, Sybase SQL Server, DB2, Oracle, Rdb, dBASE, and Paradox. To access data from another product, you must first establish a connection to it.

**Establishing a Remote Connection**   It is easy to create a remote connection to other databases on your computer that support ODBC connections. Suppose that you have dBASE, Paradox, and Access files. Each of these systems supports ODBC connections; therefore, Visual FoxPro can use them directly.

The first step in making a connection is opening the Control Panel and clicking the ODBC icon to check which data sources are available. ODBC support is installed by Visual FoxPro if you perform a complete installation or a custom installation with ODBC selected. You can access any ODBC data source with its registered driver installed on your computer. Microsoft supplies a separate package called ODBC 2.0 Driver Pack, which includes both 16-bit and 32-bit drivers for the following applications:

- Access 1.x and 2.0
- FoxPro 2.x
- Excel 3, 4, and 5

■ dBASE III and IV

■ MS SQL Server

The package also includes 16-bit drivers for the following:

■ Oracle 6 and Oracle 7

■ Btrieve

If the drivers that you need did not come with the application, contact the software manufacturer to see whether a driver is available.

Many times, the database manufacturer supplies its own ODBC driver and includes a program that registers it in the Windows file ODBC.INI. Figure 8.11 shows a typical list of data sources. The list on your computer will depend on what data sources you have installed.

**FIGURE 8.11**

To see which ODBC drivers are available on your system, open the ODBC Administrator icon in your Microsoft Visual FoxPro Group, or open the Windows Control Panel and click ODBC.

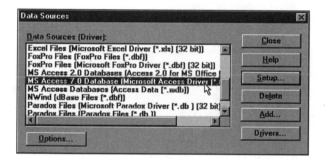

**TROUBLESHOOTING**

**I try to connect to a remote data source that I know exists, but VFP does not show the connection.** If you think that a data source should exist, but it does not appear in the list, you may have skipped that option when you installed the application. Return to the original distribution disks for that application, and follow the install instructions to reinstall it. If the ODBC driver exists as a separate file, you may be able to install it directly by clicking the Drivers button, followed by Add. Then you will be prompted to insert the ODBC driver disk or to locate the file in another directory or drive to install it.

 Rather than convert FoxPro 2.x files to 5.0 format, consider using an ODBC driver to connect to them. This method may help you share data with users who still work with FoxPro 2.x applications.

All drivers have setup screens in which you can specify additional information such as versions, directories, and tables. If your driver lists several versions, such as the

FoxPro ODBC driver, you should set up a separate data source definition for each version that you use. Similarly, some drivers require that you select a specific directory or access the current one (current directory while the application runs). The MS Access ODBC driver goes a step further and allows you to select a specific database. If you leave any of these options blank, the driver has Visual FoxPro display a directory during runtime to allow you to specify the database or file and its directory.

Next, start Visual FoxPro and open a database. Visual FoxPro stores information about connections and remote views in DBC files. This example uses the database PTOFSALE in \USINGFOX.500\DATA. Next, choose File, New, Connection, as shown in Figure 8.12.

**FIGURE 8.12**

Remote access to data begins by defining a connection to the remote source.

Starting a new remote connection opens the Connection Designer, shown in Figure 8.13.

**FIGURE 8.13**

The Connection Designer sets options for accessing the remote data, as well as for processing and time-out intervals.

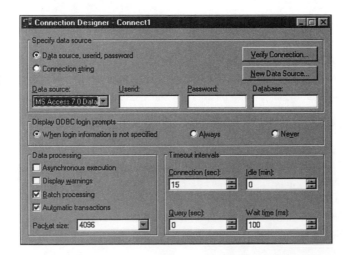

The Connection Designer supports many options that identify the data source and may enable you to define a username and password. For an Access database, as shown in Figure 8.13, the Connection Designer includes the name of the data source, but not the user ID or password. Because the When Login Info Is Not Specified option is selected, however, Visual FoxPro will display a prompt for this information if the Access database requires it.

The following check boxes (in the Data Processing group) control the way that SQL accesses the server data.

- *Asynchronous Execution.* This option determines whether control returns to your application immediately after sending a SQL pass-through statement. In synchronous operation, control does not return until the entire result set is returned. With asynchronous execution, your application can do other things while it waits for the SQL to complete.
- *Display Warnings.* The Display Warnings option determines whether to display error messages during the processing of a remote SQL pass-through.
- *Batch Processing.* This option determines how to retrieve multiple result sets.
- *Automatic Transactions.* This option determines whether SQL transactions are handled automatically by Visual FoxPro or whether the application must include its own SQLCOMMIT() and SQLROLLBACK() functions.

Another area that you should review before accepting the connection definition is the Timeout Interval values, which determine how long Visual FoxPro waits for the server to perform various actions. Consider the following:

- *Connection.* This parameter limits the number of seconds that Visual FoxPro waits after requesting a connection with a server. If it receives no response within the specified time, VFP returns an error.
- *Idle.* Idle determines the number of minutes that Visual FoxPro remains connected to the server after being connected and before receiving a request. Even if it exceeds the idle time, however, VFP automatically reconnects when a request is made.
- *Query.* The Query interval determines the number of seconds to wait for the server to return a result set. If the server takes longer than the number of seconds specified, an error results.

**TIP** You can use the query interval to stop a "runaway" query by limiting the execution time.

■ *Wait Time.* This interval defines the time to wait after receiving the results of a request from the server to confirm that it is complete. If the specified number of seconds expires, VFP assumes that the request is complete.

To close the Connection Designer, click the close box. Visual FoxPro then prompts you for a connection name. The connection name can be any text string and can include blank characters.

The connection that you just defined should appear below the Connections heading of Data, Databases in the Project Manager that includes the database Ptofsale. (A PTOFSALE project is included in \USINGFOX.500\DATA\, but it does not come with predefined connections. You can add new connections, modify existing ones, or remove existing ones from within the Project Manager. Remember that you can define as many connections as you have data sources, directories, or tables, as the case may be. Each connection can then support views of remote data, and you can include these views in forms, queries, and reports.

Figure 8.14 shows the Project Manager.

**FIGURE 8.14**
You can add, modify, and remove connections while you are in the Project Manager.

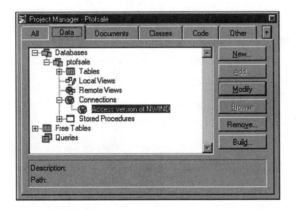

**Creating a View of a Remote Table**   Next, to create a remote view, choose File, New, Remote View from the menu system. Alternatively, you can click Remote Views, then New in any Project Manager that uses the database to which the connection was added. You can use a wizard to create the view, or you can create it manually. Click the New View button to create the view manually. This button displays the Select Connection or Available Datasource option, shown in Figure 8.15.

▶ **See** "The Remote View Wizard," **p. 239**

The list box displays the connections defined in the current database if the Select button is Connections. You can also choose among Available Datasources by clicking this

Select option. Continue the example by selecting the Access version of the NWIND connection and clicking the OK button.

**FIGURE 8.15**

The first step in creating a remote view is selecting a connection or data source.

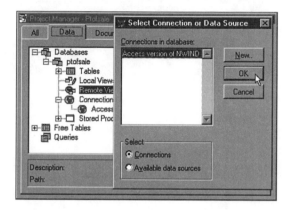

Suppose that you defined a general Access connection that did not specify a database. In that case, a dialog box would appear at run time, asking you to select one. If the connection did not specify a directory either, you could browse through the directories and drives to find the database. Figure 8.16 shows the Select Database dialog box that appears in this case. Notice that the List Files of Type box displays Access Databases.

**FIGURE 8.16**

If the connection does not specify a database, VFP displays a dialog box that allows you to select it from any directory or drive to which you have access.

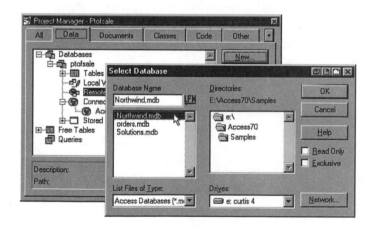

After you select the Access database (or if the connection already defined the database), Visual FoxPro reads its header. Because Access databases, like Visual FoxPro databases, consist of multiple tables, VFP displays a dialog box like the one shown in Figure 8.17. Observe that when you select a table, it appears in the View Designer's table view area. You can select additional tables as necessary by clicking the Add Table button in the View Designer toolbar.

**FIGURE 8.17**

After you select an Access database, Visual FoxPro reads the header to determine the names of the tables that it contains.

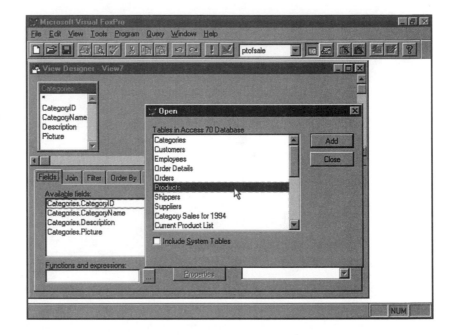

You can add other tables to the view, but you must define relations among them. If you don't, Visual FoxPro attempts to join every record in one table to every record in every other table. This situation can quickly result in a tremendously large file of junk, also called a *Cartesian product*. Then you can add further selection criteria. The one thing that you cannot do within a single view is link the tables from one remote connection to another. Having established a view, however, you can create a query or form that uses data from multiple sources.

> **CAUTION**
>
> Visual FoxPro does not attempt to validate the syntax of selection criteria expressions entered into the view. It has no way of knowing what functions or expressions the server database supports. Therefore, it passes the string unparsed. Your server application may generate an error if it cannot understand the criteria. Please refer to the manuals that come with the server database for assistance on building valid expressions.

Some options that you can change appear in the Advanced Options dialog box, which appears when you choose Query, Advanced Options from the main menu. Figure 8.18 shows this dialog box.

**FIGURE 8.18**

The Advanced Options dialog box defines whether the connection can be shared over multiple views and how data is fetched from the remote file.

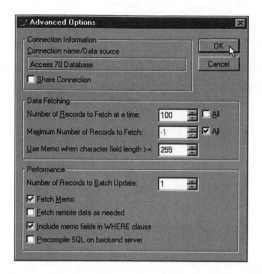

**NOTE** If possible, use a single connection for multiple remote views. A shared connection helps by:

- Reducing the resource requirements on your system

- Reducing the number of connections that the server must support

- Reducing the cost of your server application, if you pay for it on a per-connection basis ■

This dialog box defines how Visual FoxPro retrieves records from the remote database. The Share Connection check box below the connection name determines whether Visual FoxPro allows you to create multiple views with the same connection.

There are three Data Fetching options. The first determines the number of records that VFP gets from the ODBC connection at one time. The default is 100 records. If the table has fewer than 100 records, VFP retrieves them all; otherwise, it retrieves just the first 100. As you step through the table, VFP reads blocks of 100 records.

The second option limits the total number of records that a view can retrieve. Typically, you would want to retrieve all records that match the selection criteria. However, during testing, you may want to retrieve a smaller subset.

The option titled Use Memo When Character Field Length >= determines the maximum number of characters that Visual FoxPro retrieves as a Character field before it switches to a Memo field. This option determines how the local cursor stores the data, not how the source file stores it. Remember that the largest Character field in FoxPro is 254 characters.

The last section includes the five Performance options. The first option determines the number of records that Visual FoxPro can update as a batch process.

Fetch Memo tells Visual FoxPro to fetch Memo-field data only when the user attempts to open a field that contains a memo. This option limits the data traffic across the ODBC connection; therefore, you usually want to select it.

The third option allows Visual FoxPro to fetch data as needed. The fourth determines whether Memo fields can be used in WHERE clauses. The fifth option precompiles SQL on the server.

After selecting the tables that you want to use in the remote view, define the selection criteria, fields, sort orders, groupings, or update criteria, just as you would for a local view. Then save the view. After the view is saved, you can use it to create a form or report. You can even add it to a data environment of a form to create a more complex data structure.

**Connecting to a Remote Table Manually**   An alternative way to connect to a remote table uses some of the new SQL commands that have been added to Visual FoxPro specifically to access remote data. The following method assumes that the connection to the remote data source has already been defined as CONNECT1. The connection is to an Access table.

The first command needed to establish the remote connection is SQLCONNECT. Its syntax is:

```
SQLCONNECT([DataSourceName, cUserID, cPassword¦cConnectionName])
```

To connect to an ODBC-compliant Access database that does not use a password, you can simply enter the following:

```
lnSqlHandle = SQLCONNECT('Access version of NWIND')
```

This command opens the connection. Because CONNECT1 does not have a default database associated with it, Visual FoxPro displays a dialog box that allows you to select one (refer to Figure 8.14).

SQLCONNECT returns a handle used to reference the SQL connection. This numerical value serves the same purpose as handles in low-level functions. Because you can have more than one SQL connection open at one time, you need a way to reference each one. The preceding command uses the variable lnSqlHandle to store the returned handle for use in later SQL statements.

Suppose that you want to reference the CUSTOMERS table from the database NWIND.MDB, which is included with Access. Assuming that you selected NWIND.MDB when you were prompted during the SQLCONNECT command, you can enter the following command.

```
lnSqlError = SQLEXEC(lnSqlHandle, 'SELECT * FROM CUSTOMERS', ;
                     'CUSTLIST')
```

This command sends the SELECT statement to the ODBC driver, telling it to retrieve all the records from the customer database. Furthermore, the third parameter, CUSTLIST, defines an alias name for the result cursor (which otherwise is merely called SQLRESULT). If you press Ctrl+V to open the View dialog box, you see this cursor in one of the work areas. Browse the work area to see the data. Observe that if any field name consists of more than one word separated with a blank, the cursor automatically replaces the blank with an underscore. This is a way around the "blanks in field names" problem.

You can generate as many cursors as you want from a single connection. Without closing the preceding cursor, you can enter the following command:

```
lnSqlError = SQLEXEC(lnSqlHandle, 'SELECT * FROM ORDERS', ;
                     'ORDERS')
```

Looking at the View dialog box again, you should see both cursors. Accessing remote data on your local machine via ODBC works the same way as accessing server data on SQL Server, Oracle, or any of the other popular server databases. Appendix B, "The Resource File," explores this topic in greater depth.

▶ **See** "Accessing Client/Server Data from Visual FoxPro" in Bonus Chapter 08 located on the CD

To close a connection, simply enter the following command:

```
= SQLDISCONNECT(lnSqlHandle)
```

**N O T E**  To remove a connection from a database, use the following command:

```
DELETE CONNECTION ConnectName
```

Alternatively, open a project that contains the database; open the Data page frame; choose the Databases, Connections, Access version of NWIND; and click the Remove button. ■

### TROUBLESHOOTING

**I open the remote database successfully with SQLCONNECT and create a cursor with SQLEXEC, but the changes that I make to the table do not get written back to the original data.** Remember that a cursor is just a copy of the data in the original table, not the table itself. Therefore, although you can make changes to the data, these changes are made to the copy only.

# From Here...

This chapter explored some of the powerful capabilities of queries. But perhaps more powerful was its introduction of updatable views, especially updatable remote views. Now you can use Visual FoxPro to directly access data from other applications without having to translate it or make duplicate copies. This capability, of course, leads to true client/ server computing.

To learn more about how Visual FoxPro works with client/server files and remote SQL statements, refer to the following chapter:

■ Bonus Chapter 08, "Time for Client/Server," drills deeper into the world of client/ server computing with Visual FoxPro, using the new SQL command support. This chapter is located on the CD.

# Using BROWSE to View Data

*by Monte Mitzelfelt and Arthur Young*

**I**n the world of Xbase programming, one command has truly stood the test of time. The BROWSE command continues to be one of the most-used utilities. Although the grid control may be the object of choice in OOP-style applications, BROWSE is still the tool of choice for day-to-day database management activities. ∎

**Open and navigate a BROWSE window**

View the contents of free and database tables with BROWSE.

**Configure a BROWSE window**

Create reusable BROWSE configurations for all situations.

**Add, modify, and delete data from a BROWSE window**

Perform database management duties with BROWSE.

**Use the optional BROWSE clauses from the Command window**

Extend BROWSE by using the optional clauses.

**BROWSE related tables**

View parent-child relationships with multiple BROWSE windows.

# Opening and Navigating a BROWSE Window

Opening a BROWSE window can be as simple as issuing a single command or selecting an item from the Visual FoxPro menu system. In many settings, BROWSE is the only tool that you'll need on a daily basis to access and maintain your tables. The user-friendly, spreadsheet-like interface provides familiar navigational keystrokes, while in the background, Visual FoxPro's underlying database technology provides superior speed and lookup capabilities. Speed and lookup superiority, however, have a price: Your data must be much more structured in a BROWSE window than in a spreadsheet.

To get a good feel for browsing a table, BROWSE one of the sample tables included with the Tasmanian Trader application. (For the purposes of this chapter, we will assume that the path for the sample data is \VFP4\SAMPLES\TASTRADE\DATA.) Follow these steps:

1.  From the Command window, set your default directory to the Tasmanian Trader data directory by entering the following:

    ```
    CD \VFP4\SAMPLES\TASTRADE\DATA
    ```

2.  Click the Open button, or choose File, Open.

3.  Choose Table (*.DBF) from the List Files of Type drop-down list.

4.  Select EMPLOYEE.DBF.

5.  Choose OK.

6.  Choose View, BROWSE, "Employee."

As you can see in Figure 9.1, the BROWSE window displays several columns and rows of data. Each column represents a field in the Employee table, and each row is one record of data.

**FIGURE 9.1**

Explore vast quantities of your data rapidly in a BROWSE window.

| Employee_id | Last_name | First_name | Title |
|---|---|---|---|
| 1 | Buchanan | Steven | Sales Manager |
| 2 | Suyama | Michael | Sales Representative |
| 3 | King | Robert | Sales Representative |
| 4 | Callahan | Laura | Inside Sales Coordinator |
| 5 | Dodsworth | Anne | Sales Representative |
| 6 | Hellstern | Albert | Business Manager |
| 7 | Smith | Tim | Mail Clerk |
| 8 | Patterson | Caroline | Receptionist |
| 9 | Brid | Justin | Marketing Director |
| 10 | Martin | Xavier | Marketing Associate |
| 11 | Pereira | Laurent | Advertising Specialist |
| 12 | Davolio | Nancy | Applications Developer |
| 13 | Fuller | Andrew | Entry Clerk |
| 14 | Leverling | Janet | Applications Developer |
| 15 | Peacock | Margaret | Sales Manager |

If you prefer to see the entire record, try choosing <u>V</u>iew, <u>E</u>dit to edit the records, as shown in Figure 9.2.

▶ **See** "View Menu Options," **p. 30**

Part

II

Ch

9

**FIGURE 9.2**
Use edit mode to focus on single records.

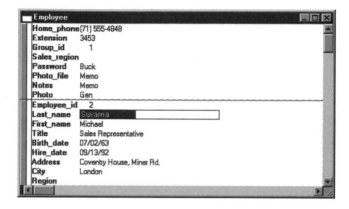

## Navigating with the Keyboard and the Mouse

Table 9.1 describes the navigational keys that are common to both BROWSE and edit modes.

**Table 9.1    Navigational Keystrokes for BROWSE and Edit Modes**

| Key | Description |
| --- | --- |
| Tab | Move to the next cell. |
| Enter | Move to the next cell. |
| Shift+Tab | Move to the preceding cell. |
| Up arrow | Move up one cell. |
| Down arrow | Move down one cell. |
| Left arrow | If the entire cell is selected, move to the preceding cell; otherwise, move left one character. |
| Right arrow | If the entire cell is selected, move to the next cell; otherwise, move right one character. |
| Home | Go to the start of the current cell or, if you are at the start, select the entire preceding cell. |
| End | Go to the end of the current cell or, if you are at the end, select the entire next cell. |

*continues*

**Table 9.1 Continued**

| Key | Description |
|-----|-------------|
| Page Up | *Browse mode*—If the current cell is at the top of the window, go up one page; otherwise, go to the top of the window. *Edit mode*—Move up one record. |
| Page Down | *Browse mode*—If the current cell is at the bottom of the window, go down one page; otherwise; go to the bottom of the window. *Edit mode*—Move down one record. |
| Esc | Abort changes to current cell and close the window. |
| Ctrl+End | Close the window and save all changes. |

In addition to navigating with the keyboard, you can use the mouse and the scroll bars to point and click your way around. The scroll box in the vertical scroll bar can be moved up or down to display additional records. Use the horizontal scroll bar to reveal additional columns. To select and activate a record, simply click one of the fields in the desired record.

## Navigating from the Table Menu

You also can navigate by choosing Top, Bottom, Next, Previous, Record #, or Locate from the Table, Go to Record submenu. Top and Bottom send you to their respective ends of the table, based on the current table order. Next and Previous are also influenced by the active index. The Record # option displays the dialog box pictured in Figure 9.3. This value corresponds to the value returned by the RECNO() function for a given record and is not dependent on the current index.

**FIGURE 9.3**

Jump to a specific record number from the Record Number option.

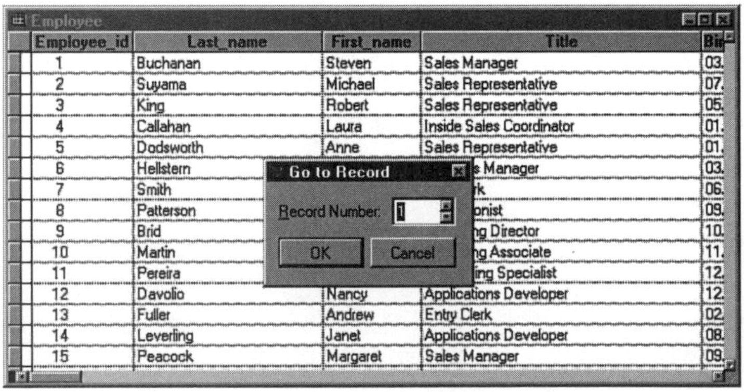

The Locate option is a little more complicated, but much more useful. The following steps should simplify it for you.

1. Choose Table, Go to Record, Locate.

2. Click the For button on the Locate dialog that appears.

3. Double-click Country in the Fields listbox. Notice it adds Employee.country to the edit box above.

4. Type = **[France]**, as shown in Figure 9.4.

**FIGURE 9.4**

FOR expressions provide infinite flexibility for looking up records in your tables.

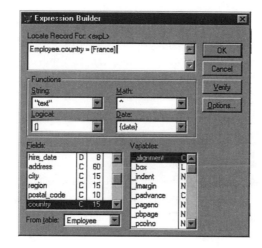

5. Choose OK.

6. Choose Locate from the Locate dialog. The first record from France is selected, as shown in Figure 9.5.

**FIGURE 9.5**

Viewing the record after a locate.

| Employee_id | Last_name | First_name | Title |
|---|---|---|---|
| 1 | Buchanan | Steven | Sales Manager |
| 2 | Suyama | Michael | Sales Representative |
| 3 | King | Robert | Sales Representative |
| 4 | Callahan | Laura | Inside Sales Coordinator |
| 5 | Dodsworth | Anne | Sales Representative |
| 6 | Hellstern | Albert | Business Manager |
| 7 | Smith | Tim | Mail Clerk |
| 8 | Patterson | Caroline | Receptionist |
| 9 | Brid | Justin | Marketing Director |
| 10 | Martin | Xavier | Marketing Associate |
| 11 | Pereira | Laurent | Advertising Specialist |
| 12 | Davolio | Nancy | Applications Developer |
| 13 | Fuller | Andrew | Entry Clerk |
| 14 | Leverling | Janet | Applications Developer |
| 15 | Peacock | Margaret | Sales Manager |

**TIP** For quick searches on small tables, you can also choose Edit, Find and then search just as you would in a text file.

# Configuring a BROWSE Window

When you launch a BROWSE window, the fields are displayed in the order they appear in the table. For most tables, this is sufficient, but sometimes the default display could use some customization.  Fields that are on opposite ends might be more useful if they were side-by-side. A column might be easier to view if it were wider or narrower. A BROWSE window can be modified in several ways from the Visual FoxPro interface. These modifications enable you to resize column widths to fit more columns on-screen at the same time, reorganize the fields for easier data entry, and partition the BROWSE window to access different parts of the table at the same time.

## Resizing Column Widths

In today's graphical user interfaces, fonts provide a great deal of flexibility in the presentation of data. A BROWSE window enables you to set its font, as well as the widths of the columns in the window. (The width setting doesn't affect the field width in the table.) Using these two capabilities, you can fit as much or as little data on the screen as you like. Follow these steps:

1. Choose Table, Font. This brings up the Font dialog
2. Type **Arial**, press Tab twice, and type **6** or, select Arial in the Font combo box and select 6 in Size combo box.
3. Click OK. Visual FoxPro shrinks all the text in the BROWSE window to the specified size.

**TIP** When invoked from a program or the Command window, the BROWSE command supports an optional FONT for setting the base font and size and an optional STYLE clause for setting the font style.

4. Position the mouse pointer between the last_name and first_name column headers. The east-west column sizing cursor should appear. Drag the column border to the left until the white space in the first column is mostly gone.

   You could also perform this step by choosing Table, Size Field and then pressing the left- and right-arrow keys.
5. Repeat the procedure for all columns.

When you're done, the BROWSE window should look somewhat like Figure 9.6.

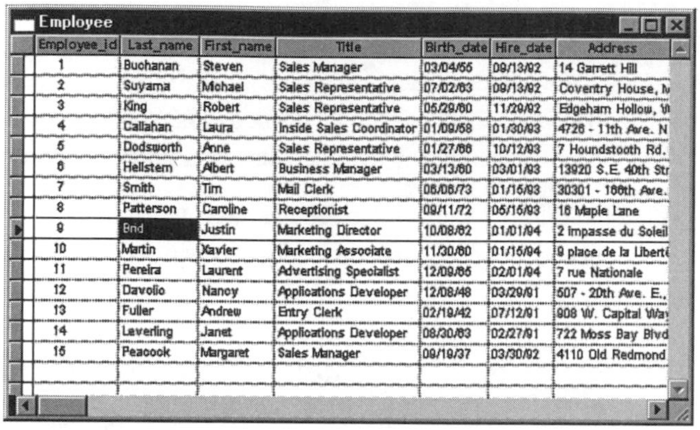

Employee

| Employee_id | Last_name | First_name | Title | Birth_date | Hire_date | Address |
|---|---|---|---|---|---|---|
| 1 | Buchanan | Steven | Sales Manager | 03/04/55 | 09/13/92 | 14 Garrett Hill |
| 2 | Suyama | Michael | Sales Representative | 07/02/63 | 09/13/92 | Coventry House, M |
| 3 | King | Robert | Sales Representative | 05/29/60 | 11/29/92 | Edgeham Hollow, W |
| 4 | Callahan | Laura | Inside Sales Coordinator | 01/09/58 | 01/30/93 | 4726 - 11th Ave. N |
| 5 | Dodsworth | Anne | Sales Representative | 01/27/66 | 10/12/93 | 7 Houndstooth Rd. |
| 6 | Hellstern | Albert | Business Manager | 03/13/60 | 03/01/93 | 13920 S.E. 40th Str |
| 7 | Smith | Tim | Mail Clerk | 06/06/73 | 01/15/93 | 30301 - 166th Ave. |
| 8 | Patterson | Caroline | Receptionist | 09/11/72 | 05/15/93 | 16 Maple Lane |
| 9 | Brid | Justin | Marketing Director | 10/08/62 | 01/01/94 | 2 impasse du Soleil |
| 10 | Martin | Xavier | Marketing Associate | 11/30/60 | 01/15/94 | 9 place de la Liberté |
| 11 | Pereira | Laurent | Advertising Specialist | 12/09/65 | 02/01/94 | 7 rue Nationale |
| 12 | Davolio | Nancy | Applications Developer | 12/08/48 | 03/29/91 | 507 - 20th Ave. E., |
| 13 | Fuller | Andrew | Entry Clerk | 02/19/42 | 07/12/91 | 908 W. Capital Way |
| 14 | Leverling | Janet | Applications Developer | 08/30/63 | 02/27/91 | 722 Moss Bay Blvd |
| 15 | Peacock | Margaret | Sales Manager | 09/19/37 | 03/30/92 | 4110 Old Redmond |

**FIGURE 9.6**
Adjust font and column widths to maximize your use of screen real estate.

## Reorganizing BROWSE Columns

Many times, the order in which the fields are defined in the table is not always the ideal order for BROWSE columns. The BROWSE columns can be organized independently of the table definition, which means that you can reorganize your BROWSE columns without fear of changing your table. Follow these steps:

1. Position the mouse pointer on the first_name column header. The mouse pointer turns into a down arrow.
2. Click and drag the column to the left, before last_name.

You also can choose Table, Move Field and then press the arrow keys to arrange the fields. As shown in Figure 9.7, the fields are now in a more familiar order.

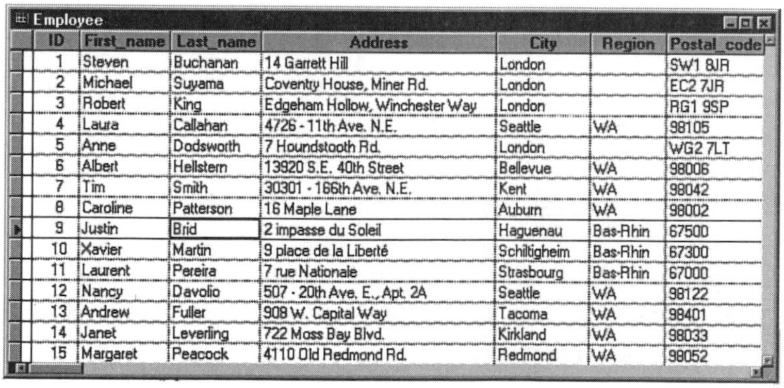

Employee

| ID | First_name | Last_name | Address | City | Region | Postal_code |
|---|---|---|---|---|---|---|
| 1 | Steven | Buchanan | 14 Garrett Hill | London | | SW1 8JR |
| 2 | Michael | Suyama | Coventry House, Miner Rd. | London | | EC2 7JR |
| 3 | Robert | King | Edgeham Hollow, Winchester Way | London | | RG1 9SP |
| 4 | Laura | Callahan | 4726 - 11th Ave. N.E. | Seattle | WA | 98105 |
| 5 | Anne | Dodsworth | 7 Houndstooth Rd. | London | | WG2 7LT |
| 6 | Albert | Hellstern | 13920 S.E. 40th Street | Bellevue | WA | 98006 |
| 7 | Tim | Smith | 30301 - 166th Ave. N.E. | Kent | WA | 98042 |
| 8 | Caroline | Patterson | 16 Maple Lane | Auburn | WA | 98002 |
| 9 | Justin | Brid | 2 impasse du Soleil | Haguenau | Bas-Rhin | 67500 |
| 10 | Xavier | Martin | 9 place de la Liberté | Schiltigheim | Bas-Rhin | 67300 |
| 11 | Laurent | Pereira | 7 rue Nationale | Strasbourg | Bas-Rhin | 67000 |
| 12 | Nancy | Davolio | 507 - 20th Ave. E., Apt. 2A | Seattle | WA | 98122 |
| 13 | Andrew | Fuller | 908 W. Capital Way | Tacoma | WA | 98401 |
| 14 | Janet | Leverling | 722 Moss Bay Blvd. | Kirkland | WA | 98033 |
| 15 | Margaret | Peacock | 4110 Old Redmond Rd. | Redmond | WA | 98052 |

**FIGURE 9.7**
Rearrange the columns for smoother data entry.

**NOTE** In edit mode, you can drag the field names up and down instead of dragging the column headers left and right. ■

## Partitioning the BROWSE Window

Occasionally, you may want to view two records at the same time or copy data from one record to another. Visual FoxPro can partition a BROWSE window into two separate panes. By unlinking the partitions, you can scroll to different records in the table.

You can create partitions by dragging the partition mark, pictured in Figure 9.8, in the bottom center of the BROWSE window or by choosing Table, Resize Partitions and pressing the arrow keys.

**FIGURE 9.8**

Use one partition to browse and scroll the key fields; use the other to edit all the details.

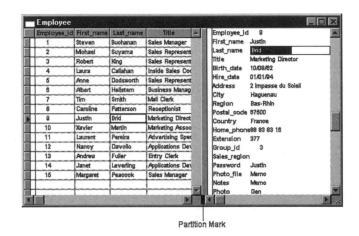

Partition Mark

# Adding, Modifying, and Deleting Data

Adding and modifying data are what BROWSE is all about. You can use BROWSE to add records one at a time or in bulk. BROWSE is also a great place to view and modify existing records.

To add a single blank record to the bottom of the table, you can choose Table, Append New Record or press Ctrl+Y. Visual FoxPro automatically selects the first cell of the new record. Simply begin typing, pressing Tab or Enter after each field. To add records *en masse*, simply choose View, Append Mode. In this mode, you continue to add new records until you close the BROWSE window. If you are in BROWSE mode, press the down-arrow key after completing a record. In edit mode, simply press Tab or Enter after the last field to append another record.

**N O T E** The SET CARRY command can simplify data entry. By copying data down to new records in append mode, SET CARRY reduces keying. Issue SET CARRY ON from the Command window, or issue SET CARRY TO *field_list* to carry only certain fields. ∎

To modify a record, use the navigation keys or the mouse and scroll bars to locate the field that you want to change. If the field is highlighted, and you want to replace the entire field, begin typing to overwrite the existing data. If you just want to edit the existing data, use the mouse, or press Home or End, to deselect the field and access the insertion point. Finally, press Ctrl+Home to modify a selected Memo or General field, or double-click the Memo or General field that you want to edit.

To delete a record, just click the deletion-mark box, shown in Figure 9.9 to the left of the Employee_Id field, or choose Table, Toggle Deletion Mark. A filled-in deletion mark indicates that the record will be purged during the next PACK or when Table, Remove Deleted Records is chosen. Repeat the toggle command or click the deletion mark to undelete (recall) a record.

> **N O T E** If the table you are browsing is a member of a database container, then any changes must pass all referential integrity rules before they are saved. For instance, if a parent-child relationship is defined in the DBC, then no records can be deleted from the parent table if it would create orphaned records in the child table. ■

**FIGURE 9.9**
The deletion mark flags a record for purging during a PACK command.

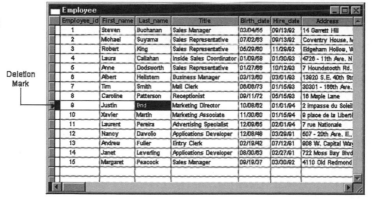

Deletion Mark

**CAUTION**
After you use PACK on a table, those records marked for deletion cannot be retrieved. Visual FoxPro literally rebuilds all the records associated with the table and leaves out the marked records.

# Using the BROWSE Clause from the Command Window

Although the Visual FoxPro interface invokes a BROWSE window from a variety of menus and managers, you can harness the full power of BROWSE only via the Command window or a program. The BROWSE command supports more than 30 clauses that you can use to control the appearance and behavior of each and every aspect of a BROWSE window. This section covers the essential clauses for everyday BROWSE use.

Listing 9.1 shows the syntax for BROWSE with all the available clauses and options.

**Listing 9.1 The BROWSE Syntax**

```
BROWSE
  [FIELDS FieldList]
  [FONT cFontName [, nFontSize]]
  [STYLE cFontStyle]
  [FOR lExpression1 [REST]]
  [FORMAT]
  [FREEZE FieldName]
  [KEY eExpression1 [, eExpression2]]
  [LAST ¦ NOINIT]
  [LOCK nNumberOfFields]
  [LPARTITION]
  [NAME ObjectName]
  [NOAPPEND]
  [NOCLEAR]
  [NODELETE]
  [NOEDIT ¦ NOMODIFY]
  [NOLGRID] [NORGRID]
  [NOLINK]
  [NOMENU]
  [NOOPTIMIZE]
  [NOREFRESH]
  [NORMAL]
  [NOWAIT]
  [PARTITION nColumnNumber [LEDIT] [REDIT]]
  [PREFERENCE PreferenceName]
  [SAVE]
  [TIMEOUT nSeconds]
  [TITLE cTitleText]
  [VALID [:F] lExpression2 [ERROR cMessageText]]
  [WHEN lExpression3]
  [WIDTH nFieldWidth]
  [[WINDOW WindowName1]
  [IN [WINDOW] WindowName2 ¦ IN SCREEN ¦ IN MACDESKTOP]]
  [COLOR SCHEME nSchemeNumber
  ¦ COLOR ColorPairList]
```

# Using a FIELD List

The FIELD clause of the BROWSE command enables you to choose only specific fields and to set various properties for each of the chosen fields. The FIELD clause accepts a list of fields, which can be modified by field modifiers and separated by commas. Table 9.2 describes the field modifiers.

Part

II

Ch

9

**Table 9.2   FIELD Lixst Modifiers**

| Syntax | Description |
| --- | --- |
| *:numeric1* | A colon (:) followed by a numeric expression in a field list specifies the column width. |
| *:P=character1* | *character1* is a picture string and defines a field template exactly like a PICTURE clause in an @ SAY or @ GET or the format codes in the TRANSFORM( ) function. |
| :R | This modifier makes the field read-only. |
| *:H=character2* | *character2* is a character string used for the column heading. |
| *:W=logical* | Evaluated before entering the field, *logical* determines whether the field can be edited. Use this modifier like the WHEN event of a control object. |
| *:B=lower, upper* [:F] | *lower* defines the lowest acceptable value for the field; *upper* defines the highest acceptable value. The optional :F forces bounds checking on, leaving the field whether the value changed or not. |
| *:V=expression* [:F] | *expression* is an expression that evaluates to either true (.T.) or false (.F.) and tells Visual FoxPro whether or not the field value is valid. If not valid, VFP keeps focus in this field. If *expression* is zero (.NULL.), Visual FoxPro does not permit the changes, but does not display an error message either. :F here, as with the preceding modifier, forces validation. |
| *:E=errormsg* | If the current field value is invalid and the :E modifier is in use, *errormsg* replaces the standard Visual FoxPro error message. |

**TIP**  If you include a user-defined function as part of the :W=*logical* or :V=*expression*, the user-defined function, along with the :W and :V, can be treated as events within your BROWSE environment.

Additionally, a field list can contain a calculated field. Calculated fields appear in the list as calcname=*expression* and are also subject to the field modifiers. Listing 9.2 demonstrates the use and syntax of a BROWSE command with a field list and field modifiers.

**Listing 9.2 BROWFIEL.PRG**

```
*BROWFIEL.PRG

USE employee IN (SELECT("employee"))

SELECT employee

BROWSE FIELDS;
    name_title=ALLTRIM( last_name ) + ", " + ;
                ALLTRIM( first_name ) :20,;
    address :30,;
    city :17,;
    region :12 :H="State/Region" :P="@!",;
    postal_code :H="ZIP/Postal Code" :R,;
    country :V=ALLTRIM( country ) $ "USA,Canada,Mexico" ;
            :F;
            :E="This table is for North American addresses only"
```

Listing 9.2 first ensures that EMPLOYEE.DBF is open. The routine then invokes a BROWSE window with a calculated *last_name, first_name* field, adjusts the widths of various columns, sets a few headings, and ensures that all the addresses in your table are from North American nations. Figure 9.10 shows the BROWSE window rejecting an address outside of North America.

▶ **See** "Field-Level Validations," **p. 166**

**FIGURE 9.10**
Enforce table rules with the :V modifier.

| City | State/Reg | ZIP/Postal Code | Country | |
|------|-----------|-----------------|---------|---|
| London | | SW1 8JR | UK | |
| London | | EC2 7JR | UK | |
| London | | RG1 9SP | UK | |
| Seattle | WA | 98105 | UK | |
| London | | WG2 7LT | UK | |
| Bellevue | WA | 98006 | USA | |
| Kent | WA | 98042 | USA | |
| Auburn | WA | 98002 | USA | |
| Haguenau | BAS-RHIN | 67500 | France | |
| Schiltigheim | BAS-RHIN | 67300 | France | |
| Strasbourg | BAS-RHIN | 67000 | France | |
| Seattle | WA | 98122 | USA | |
| Tacoma | WA | 98401 | USA | |
| Kirkland | WA | 98033 | USA | |

# Using FOR and KEY to BROWSE Subsets of Tables

The FOR and KEY clauses allow you to filter the data that appears in the BROWSE window. The FOR clause filters data, using a logical expression such as, country = "France." The KEY clause specifies a range of records, using the current active index. Listing 9.3 uses a FOR clause and then a KEY clause to perform the same filter operation.

**Listing 9.3    BROWCRIT.PRG**

```
*BROWCRIT.PRG

USE employee IN (SELECT("employee"))

SELECT employee

BROWSE;
    TITLE "Employee - BROWSE FOR";
    FOR group_id = space( 5 ) + [2]

SET ORDER TO group_id
BROWSE;
    TITLE "Employee - BROWSE KEY";
    KEY space( 5 ) + [2]
```

 The FOR clause uses Visual FoxPro's Rushmore technology, which is hampered if you have an active index. If the active index coincides with the desired viewing criteria, the KEY clause performs faster.

▶ **See** "Selecting an Active Index at Run Time," **p. 157**

▶ **See** "Selecting Groups of Records," **p. 284**

## Using LAST

The LAST clause of a BROWSE command tells Visual FoxPro to look into the system resource file and look for a previous BROWSE configuration associated with the current table. If one is found, the BROWSE window "remembers" its previous state, including such settings as font, column widths, memo and general windows, and column order. To use the preceding BROWSE configuration, enter the following:

```
BROWSE LAST
```

## Using PREFERENCE

The PREFERENCE clause is identical to the LAST clause in its capability to recall previous resizings and rearrangements with one major difference. PREFERENCE enables you to name a particular configuration. (By default, LAST uses the table name as the preference name.) Thus, you can have many preferences for a given table, as opposed to only one last setting. To name a BROWSE configuration, enter the following:

```
BROWSE PREFERENCE pref_name
```

### TROUBLESHOOTING

**I issue BROWSE LAST or give my BROWSE a name, and Visual FoxPro doesn't remember my settings.** Because the LAST and PREFERENCE commands use the resource file to store information, you must have the same resource file active when you recall that information. SET RESOURCE ON activates FOXUSER.DBF, the default resource file. If you have any question about which resource file is active, print SYS(2005). Also, be sure not to confuse the NAME clause with the PREFERENCE clause. The NAME clause defines the name of an object variable and treats a BROWSE window as though it were a grid control. The PREFERENCE clause specifies an identifier in your resource file associated with a given record.

> **N O T E**   BROWSE LAST and BROWSE PREFERENCE do not interact directly. If, for instance, you open a BROWSE window and specify a preference, and then reopen the BROWSE with BROWSE LAST, the BROWSE window does not use the changes from the PREFERENCE session. The LAST clause is really a PREFERENCE that uses the table name as its resource file identifier. ■

## Using WHEN, VALID, and ERROR

The WHEN and VALID clauses of a BROWSE command operate at the record level much as :W and :V act at the field level. Every time you shift the focus from one record to another, the WHEN expression is evaluated. If changes have been made to a record, the VALID expression is evaluated, too. Also like the :V field modifier, the VALID clause accepts the :F force evaluation directive. If you include :F in a VALID clause, the VALID expression is tested regardless of whether or not changes were made.

The WHEN and VALID clauses behave exactly as their field-level counterparts do. If the associated expressions return true (.T.), then all is well. If a WHEN expression evaluates to false (.F.), the current record becomes read-only. If a VALID expression is false (.F.), an error message (which you can set with the ERROR clause) is generated. Also, focus remains in that record until you correct the condition that caused the validation to fail. The expression associated with a VALID clause can also return a zero. In that case, VFP suppresses the error message and places the burden on the programmer to notify the user of the error. Either a false (.F.) or a zero prevents you from changing the currently selected record until the VALID expression returns true.

The syntax of a BROWSE command with the WHEN and VALID clauses is

```
BROWSE WHEN expression1 VALID expression2 :F ERROR error_string
```

▶ **See** "Using Record-Level Validations," **p. 195**

# Browsing Related Tables

In keeping with the rest of Visual FoxPro, the BROWSE command fully supports the relational paradigm. Using SET RELATION TO and SET SKIP TO, BROWSE can help you easily look up and navigate in the parent table data while updating and editing the child table. SET RELATION TO links the record-pointer movement in two tables based on the parent table. SET SKIP TO enhances SET RELATION TO by allowing the child table to drive.

**N O T E** The relations created with SET RELATION TO are not exactly the same as the relations in a database container. The relations in the database container are permanent relations. SET RELATION TO relations are temporary for as long as the BROWSE is active. The SET RELATION TO command synchronizes the record-pointer movement between tables. The database-container relations are passive and ensure the data integrity. ■

## Browsing One-to-One Relations

There are two steps to browse fields from tables in a one-to-one relation. First, establish the relation with the SET RELATION TO command. Next, issue a BROWSE command with a field list, including fields from the child table using the table alias-dot notation as shown in Listing 9.4.

---

**Listing 9.4    ONE2ONE.PRG**

```
*ONE2ONE.PRG

m.resource = SYS(2005)

SET RESOURCE TO (LOCFILE("vfp09.dbf","dbf","Where is VFP09.DBF"))

USE employee IN (SELECT("employee"))
USE orders IN (SELECT("orders")) ORDER employee_i

SELECT employee
SET RELATION TO employee_id INTO orders

BROWSE;
    FIELDS      employee_name = ALLTRIM( last_name ) + ;
                ", " + ALLTRIM( first_name),;
                orders.order_number, orders.order_date,;
                orders.discount, orders.ship_to_name,;
                max_dev_days = orders.deliver_by - ;
                            orders.order_date;
    PREFERENCE one2one


SET RESOURCE TO (m.resource)
```

Part II
Ch 9

The relation and the BROWSE window weld the two tables together so that they appear as one table, as shown in Figure 9.11.

**FIGURE 9.11**
Hide confusing ID
fields with SET
RELATION and
BROWSE.

| Order_number | Order_date | Discount | Ship_to_name | Name | Max_dev_days |
|---|---|---|---|---|---|
| 39 | 07/11/92 | 10 | Old World Delicatessen | Buchanan, Steven | 28 |
| 12 | 05/28/92 | 10 | Wellington Importadora | Suyama, Michael | 28 |
| 9 | 05/22/92 | 10 | Furia Bacalhau e Frutos do Mar | King, Robert | 28 |
| 19 | 06/09/92 | 10 | Rattlesnake Canyon Grocery | Callahan, Laura | 28 |
| 1 | 05/09/92 | 10 | B's Beverages | Dodsworth, Anne | 28 |
| 3 | 05/13/92 | 10 | Folk och fä HB | Hellstern, Albert | 28 |
| 4 | 05/14/92 | 10 | Simons bistro | Smith, Tim | 28 |
| 6 | 05/19/92 | 5 | Wartian Herkku | Patterson, Caroline | 28 |
| 8 | 05/21/92 | 10 | Morgenstern Gesundkost | Brid, Justin | 28 |
| 2 | 05/12/92 | 10 | Mère Paillarde | Martin, Xavier | 1854 |

## Browsing One-to-Many Relations

One-to-one relations are not common. More often, tables have a one-to-many relation, such as tables with many orders for one customer or many parts that can be purchased from one supplier. The BROWSE command natively supports one-to-many functionality in two ways.

**Browsing Related Tables in Separate Windows**    After you establish a relation between two tables by using SET RELATION or its equivalent, BROWSE automatically supports the relation if you open a BROWSE window for each table. After a chance to refresh, the child BROWSE window displays only those records that are related to the currently selected record in the parent table. Run Listing 9.5 to see related BROWSE windows in action.

**Listing 9.5   SEPARATE.PRG**

```
*SEPARATE.PRG

m.resource = SYS(2005)

SET RESOURCE TO (LOCFILE("vfp09.dbf","dbf","Where is VFP09.DBF"))


USE employee IN (SELECT("employee"))
USE orders IN (SELECT("orders")) ORDER employee_i

SELECT employee
BROWSE TITLE "employee before relation";
     PREFERENCE custseper SAVE
SELECT orders
BROWSE TITLE "Orders before relation";
     PREFERENCE ordseper SAVE
```

```
SELECT employee
SET RELATION TO employee_id INTO orders

SELECT orders
BROWSE TITLE "Orders after relation";
     PREFERENCE ordseper NOWAIT SAVE
SELECT employee
BROWSE TITLE "employee after relation";
     PREFERENCE custseper NOWAIT SAVE

SET RESOURCE TO (m.resource)
```

Figure 9.12 shows how the two windows appear before the relation is set, and Figure 9.13 shows the child BROWSE window respecting the newly established relation.

**FIGURE 9.12**

Before SET RELATION, the two BROWSE windows operate independently.

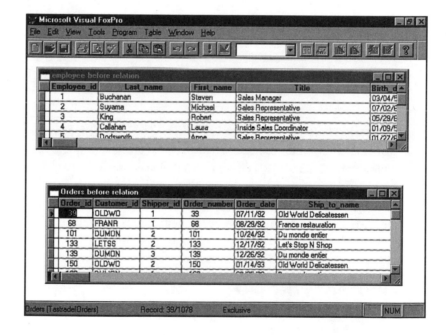

**N O T E** The relations that you create with SET RELATION TO are not the same as the relations in the database container. Like classes, the relations in a database container are the blueprints—a conceptual model. The SET RELATION TO relations and SQL Select joins are the actual instances of these relations. ■

**FIGURE 9.13**

After SET RELATION, the child BROWSE window displays only records that are related to the selected parent record.

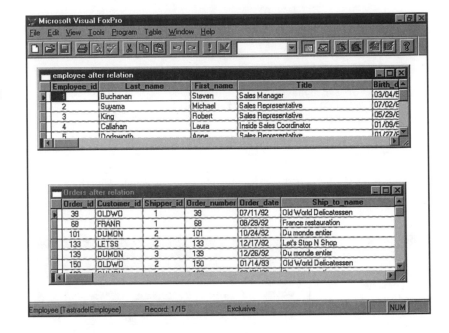

**Browsing Related Tables with SET SKIP**    The BROWSE command's support of SET SKIP allows you to view one-to-many related tables in a single BROWSE window. (See Figure 9.14.) SET SKIP accomplishes that task by moving the record pointer in the child table and by moving the record pointer in the parent table only when someone else's child record is pointed to. Effectively, the BROWSE emulates a one-to-one relation, and the BROWSE command handles one-to-one relations and relations with SET SKIP active identically. Listing 9.6 browses the same one-to-many relation that you saw in Listing 9.5.

**Listing 9.6   SETSKIP.PRG**

```
*SETSKIP.PRG

m.resource = SYS(2005)

SET RESOURCE TO (LOCFILE("vfp09.dbf","dbf","Where is VFP09.DBF"))

USE employee IN (SELECT("employee"))
USE orders IN (SELECT("orders")) ORDER employee_i

SELECT employee
SET RELATION TO employee_id INTO orders
SET SKIP TO orders
BROWSE TITLE "Employee/Orders with SET SKIP";
     FIELDS     employee_name = ALLTRIM( last_name ) + ;
                ", " + ALLTRIM( first_name),;
                orders.order_number, orders.order_date,;
```

```
                orders.discount, orders.ship_to_name,;
                max_dev_days = orders.deliver_by - ;
                            orders.order_date;
        PREFERENCE one2one NOWAIT SAVE

SET RESOURCE TO (m.resource)
```

**FIGURE 9.14**

Make two tables browse as one with SET SKIP.

Employee/Orders with SET SKIP

| Order_number | Order_date | Discount | Ship_to_name | Employee_name | Max_dev_days |
|---|---|---|---|---|---|
| 39 | 07/11/92 | 10 | Old World Delicatessen | Buchanan, Steven | 28 |
| 68 | 08/29/92 | 5 | France restauration | Buchanan, Steven | 28 |
| 101 | 10/24/92 | 10 | Du monde entier | Buchanan, Steven | 28 |
| 133 | 12/17/92 | 10 | Let's Stop N Shop | Buchanan, Steven | 28 |
| 139 | 12/26/92 | 5 | Du monde entier | Buchanan, Steven | 28 |
| 150 | 01/14/93 | 10 | Old World Delicatessen | Buchanan, Steven | 28 |
| 183 | 03/05/93 | 5 | Du monde entier | Buchanan, Steven | 42 |
| 204 | 04/01/93 | 10 | Du monde entier | Buchanan, Steven | 42 |
| 272 | 06/25/93 | 0 | Split Rail Beer & Ale | Buchanan, Steven | 28 |
| 306 | 08/07/93 | 10 | Old World Delicatessen | Buchanan, Steven | 28 |

**N O T E** The BROWSE window, in most cases, refreshes itself after the REPLACE, DELETE, or APPEND command. Keeping the BROWSE window open while you issue commands is an excellent way to view the results of a particular FOR clause. ■

# From Here...

This chapter introduced a Visual FoxPro database administrator's best friend: the BROWSE command. Its quick but comprehensive interface to your data makes BROWSE a tool that you'll use on a daily basis. The command's fluid nature allows it to be anything that a power user needs it to be in a matter of seconds. Additionally, the BROWSE command can be a fertile spawning ground for ideas. Tasks that you perform often in a BROWSE window may suggest new forms, programs, or queries that can improve your Visual FoxPro systems.

To learn about related topics, refer to these chapters:

- Chapter 6, "Selecting, Viewing, and Ordering Data," helps you understand the basics of working with tables.
- Chapter 7, "Creating Basic Queries," explores using Visual FoxPro's SELECT statement to analyze and filter your data.
- Chapter 13, "Advanced Form Design Controls," contains a large section on grid controls, which are the object version of BROWSE windows.

# Building Applications the Object Way

# Programming Structures

*by Michael P. Antonovich and Monte Mitzelfelt*

Programming structures provide the framework on which you hang your Visual FoxPro code. Much as an architect creates space and flow with two-by-fours and drywall, the Visual FoxPro programmer creates statement blocks and program execution sequences with programming structures. Although the architectural concepts of space and flow depend on some innate aesthetic principles, programming structures depend on the use of logical expressions to control how the program flows from one block of statements to the next.

Despite their internal rigidity, programming structures provide the basis for coding flexible, adaptable programs. By bracketing any block of Visual FoxPro code, programming structures can execute those processes as many times as necessary or even skip them.

In this chapter, you will learn how to use Visual FoxPro's two primary programming structures—conditional structures and looping structures—and how to call external code. ■

## Using conditional structures

A conditional structure uses a logical expression to determine which block of code to execute, if any. In any case, the structure executes that code block one time. Conditional structures include IF...ENDIF, IIF( ), and DO CASE...ENDCASE.

## Using looping structures

A looping structure uses a logical expression to determine how many times to execute a code block. Looping structures include DO WHILE...ENDDO, FOR...ENDFOR, and SCAN...ENDSCAN.

## Executing external programs

An external program is any procedure or function that is not stored in the current code block. External programs, because they can be called from any code block, open the possibility of code reusability. This situation allows you to develop, test, and debug code one time and reuse it multiple times, thereby enhancing your productivity.

# Building a Logical Expression

Unlike character or numeric values, whose domains are so vast that you couldn't hope to see all the strings of numbers that Visual FoxPro can store and represent in your lifetime, you can examine all the logical values in one sentence. True (.T., in Visual FoxPro parlance) and false (.F.) are the only real values in the logical domain. All the logical values that you encounter come from one of four sources:

- A Logical field in a table
- A logical memory or system variable
- A comparison of two values
- The return value from a function call

Although logical values may appear in a loop expression, using any of these four ways of defining a logical value, the most common is the comparison of two values.

## Comparing Two Values

While you are programming, the most plentiful source of logical values is the comparison of two other values. Almost all these comparisons take the following form:

```
value1 <<comparison_operator>> value2
```

value1 and value2 are both the same data type (such as Character or Numeric), and <<comparison_operator>> is one of the familiar comparisons listed in Table 10.1. These comparison operators are also known as *relational operators* because they can define the relationship between two values.

**Table 10.1  Visual FoxPro's Comparison Operators**

| Operator | Description |
|---|---|
| = | Equal to; character string matching depends on SET EXACT |
| == | Equal to; character strings match in total length as well as character for character, regardless of SET EXACT |
| < | Less than |
| <= | Less than or equal to |
| > | Greater than |
| >= | Greater than or equal to |
| != | Not equal to |

| Operator | Description |
|----------|-------------|
| < > | Not equal to |
| # | Not equal to |

**T I P** Objects are the primary exception to the use of comparison operators. To see whether or not two objects are identical, use the COMPOBJ() function.

**Understanding SET EXACT and String Comparisons**   The status of SET EXACT determines how Visual FoxPro compares two strings of unequal length. If SET EXACT is OFF (the default), Visual FoxPro compares the two character values up to the last character value in the string on the right side of the equal sign (=). The values must match character for character up to this length, including any trailing blank characters. If SET EXACT is ON, VFP pads the shorter string with trailing blanks to make both strings the same length. SET EXACT then compares the two strings character by character for a match, including the blanks.

If you use the == operator rather than the = operator, VFP does not pad the shorter string. However, VFP does check to see that both strings have the same length and exactly the same characters before returning a value of .T..

Listing 10.1 demonstrates the effect of SET EXACT on string comparisons, as well as how the == operator works.

**Listing 10.1   10PRG01.PRG**

```
*
CLEAR
SET EXACT OFF
? "SET EXACT OFF"
? '"NAT" = "NATASHA"      ', "NAT" = "NATASHA"
? '"NAT     " = "NATASHA"', "NAT     " = "NATASHA"
? '"NATASHA" = "NAT"      ', "NATASHA" = "NAT"
? '"NATASHA" = "NAT     "', "NATASHA" = "NAT     "
? '"TASHA" = "TASHA     "', "TASHA" = "TASHA     "
? '"TASHA     " = "TASHA"', "TASHA     " = "TASHA"
?
SET EXACT ON
? "SET EXACT ON"
? '"NAT" = "NATASHA"      ', "NAT" = "NATASHA"
? '"NAT     " = "NATASHA"', "NAT     " = "NATASHA"
? '"NATASHA" = "NAT"      ', "NATASHA" = "NAT"
? '"NATASHA" = "NAT     "', "NATASHA" = "NAT     "
? '"TASHA" = "TASHA     "', "TASHA" = "TASHA     "
? '"TASHA     " = "TASHA"', "TASHA     " = "TASHA"
```

*continues*

---

**Listing 10.1  Continued**

```
?
? '"NAT" == "NATASHA"    ', "NAT" == "NATASHA"
? '"NAT     " == "NATASHA"', "NAT     " == "NATASHA"
? '"NATASHA" == "NAT"     ', "NATASHA" == "NAT"
? '"NATASHA" == "NAT     "', "NATASHA" == "NAT     "
? '"NATASHA" == "NATASHA"', "NATASHA" == "NATASHA"
? '"TASHA" == "TASHA     "', "TASHA" == "TASHA     "
? '"TASHA     " == "TASHA"', "TASHA     " == "TASHA"
```

---

In Figure 10.1, you can see two things. When SET EXACT is OFF, Visual FoxPro believes that `"Natasha" = "Nat"` is true (`.T.`), but not that `"NaT" = "Natasha"`. Also note that the `==` comparison operator counts blanks when determining whether or not two string values are equal.

**FIGURE 10.1**

SET EXACT OFF facilitates searching for records that start with a certain letter or sequence of letters.

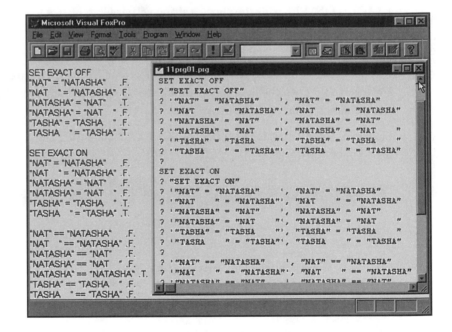

**N O T E**  The operation of the SEEK command also depends on SET EXACT's status. Normally, Visual FoxPro does partial SEEKs, because SET EXACT is usually off. If you SET EXACT ON, Visual FoxPro requires you to enter the entire index value to successfully SEEK it. So most of the time, it is better to leave SET EXACT OFF and deal with the ambiguities by padding your strings to equal length or to use the `==` operator when necessary. It may help to think of the SEEK value as being on the right side of the equivalent logical expression. ■

**Understanding SET COLLATE and String Comparisons**   SET COLLATE is one of the mechanisms by which Visual FoxPro aids the international developer. SET COLLATE determines how strings are compared with relation to a given language. SET COLLATE defaults to "MACHINE," which compares strings based on the ASCII code page. The "MACHINE" collation total ignores the uppercase/lowercase issue.

Listing 10.2 demonstrates using the "GENERAL" collation sequence, which deals with the uppercase/lowercase issue. Most major language groups have their own collation sequence to accommodate accents or other special characters.

**Listing 10.2   10PRG02.PRG**

```
PRIVATE collate

CLEAR
?
? PROGRAM() + ".PRG from Using Visual FoxPro 5.0 Special Edition"
?

m.collate = SET("COLLATE")

SET COLLATE TO "MACHINE"
? "SET COLLATE TO", ["] + SET("COLLATE") + ["]
? "a" = "A"

SET COLLATE TO "GENERAL"
? "SET COLLATE TO", ["] + SET("COLLATE") + ["]
? "a" = "A"

SET COLLATE TO m.collate
```

In Figure 10.2, the "MACHINE" collation compares strings by the ASCII values of each of their member characters. In the "GENERAL" collation, strings are compared by their alphabetic values rather than their ASCII values.

**N O T E**   Unlike SET EXACT, the SEEK command does not depend on the current SET COLLATE. Indexes have a built-in collation sequence, based on the SET COLLATE value when they were built. In fact, you can use a different collate sequence for each tag. The following code creates two indexes, one case-sensitive and the other case-insensitive:

```
USE \VFP5BOOK\DATA\CUST.DBF
* Create case sensitive index
SET COLLATE TO 'MACHINE'
INDEX ON cCompany TAG co1
* Create case insensitive index
SET COLLATE TO 'GENERAL'
INDEX ON cCompany TAG co2
```

Part **III**

Ch **10**

**FIGURE 10.2**

Forget the UPPER() function in your indexes; use SET COLLATE TO "GENERAL".

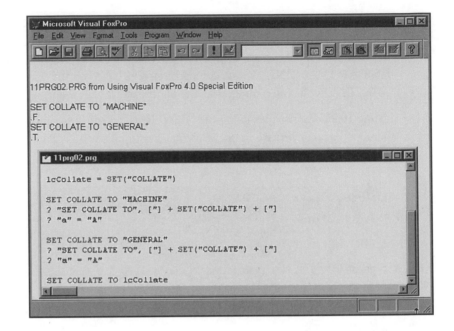

## Creating Compound Logical Expressions

Logical values can be combined into complex expressions by means of the three logical operators: AND, OR, and NOT. After you have compared two values or used a naturally occurring logical value, you may need to combine it with other logical values to determine what your course of action should be. Listing 10.3 demonstrates the effect of the three logical operators.

**Listing 10.3   10PRG03.PRG**

```
CLEAR
?
? PROGRAM() + ".PRG from Using Visual FoxPro 5.0 Special Edition" ;
            FONT "Courier", 10
? "Demonstration of Logical Expressions" FONT "Courier", 10
?
?
? "Logical AND"
? "       TRUE  FALSE" FONT "Courier", 10
? "TRUE     "  FONT "Courier", 10
?? (.T. AND .T.) FONT "Courier", 10
?? SPACE(3) FONT "Courier", 10
?? (.T. AND .F.) FONT "Courier", 10
? "FALSE    " FONT "Courier", 10
?? (.F. AND .T.) FONT "Courier", 10
?? SPACE(3) FONT "Courier", 10
```

```
?? (.F. AND .F.) FONT "Courier", 10
?
?
? "Logical OR"
? "          TRUE  FALSE" FONT "Courier", 10
? "TRUE      " FONT "Courier", 10
?? (.T. OR .T.) FONT "Courier", 10
?? SPACE(3) FONT "Courier", 10
?? (.T. OR .F.) FONT "Courier", 10
? "FALSE     " FONT "Courier", 10
?? (.F. OR .T.) FONT "Courier", 10
?? SPACE(3) FONT "Courier", 10
?? (.F. OR .F.) FONT "Courier", 10
?
?
? "Logical NOT"
? "          TRUE  FALSE" FONT "Courier", 10
? "NOT       " FONT "Courier", 10
?? (NOT .T.) FONT "Courier", 10
?? SPACE(3) FONT "Courier", 10
?? (NOT .F.) FONT "Courier", 10
```

As you can see in Figure 10.3, AND combines two logical values and tells you whether both are true (.T.), OR provides a way to tell whether at least one of two logical values is true (.T.), and NOT simply tells you the opposite of a single logical value. These three operators provide a palette of tools that are rich enough to handle any situation involving logical variables.

**FIGURE 10.3**

Combine logical values into complex expressions to implement business rules and the like.

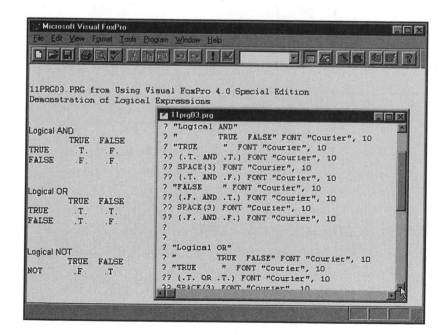

Visual FoxPro also recognizes the ! operator as a shorthand version of NOT. Many other languages, however, do not support this operator; you may want to avoid it for compatibility's sake.

Some languages require periods around the logical operators, as in .AND., .OR., and .NOT.. VFP optionally uses these forms as well as those without periods. On the other hand, the periods around .T. and .F. are absolutely required. You may want to define constants for these logical values at the beginning of your application, as follows:

```
#DEFINE TRUE .T.
#DEFINE FALSE .F.
```

▶ **See** "Preprocessor Directives" in Bonus Chapter 10 located on the CD

## Grouping Logical Expressions

Although the logical operators have a natural order of operation (first NOT, then AND, and finally OR), this order can be difficult to decipher in your code when your logical expressions start to become complex. Logical expressions can be grouped with parentheses, much like numeric expressions. In fact, NOT has the same precedence as the unary operator, AND has the same precedence as the multiplication operator (*), and OR has the same precedence as the addition operator (+). Listing 10.4 demonstrates the use of parentheses in logical expressions.

**Listing 10.4   10PRG04.PRG**

```
CLEAR
?
? PROGRAM() + ".PRG from Using Visual FoxPro 5.0 Special Edition"
?
? "#1: .F. AND .T. OR .T. = ", .F. AND .T. OR .T.
? "#2: .F. AND ( .T. OR .T. ) = ", .F. AND ( .T. OR .T. )
? "#3: ( .F. AND .T. ) OR .T. = ", ( .F. AND .T. ) OR .T.
```

The fact is not immediately apparent, but in Figure 10.4, expression 1 is the same as expression 3. In expression 2, the parentheses are used to override the natural precedence exactly as you would in a numeric expression.

## Short-Circuiting Logical Expressions

Visual FoxPro short-circuits logical expressions to speed program execution. Because Visual FoxPro knows that AND requires both of the logical values that it operates on to be true (.T.) for AND to return true (.T.), it stops if the first one is false. (You can verify this fact in the output of the program shown in Listing 10.3.) Similarly, Visual FoxPro knows that OR requires only one true (.т.) for OR to return true (.т.). So if Visual FoxPro sees a true (.т.) value and then an OR, it stops right there. You can use this situation to your advantage by placing the expression that is mostly likely to short-circuit first.

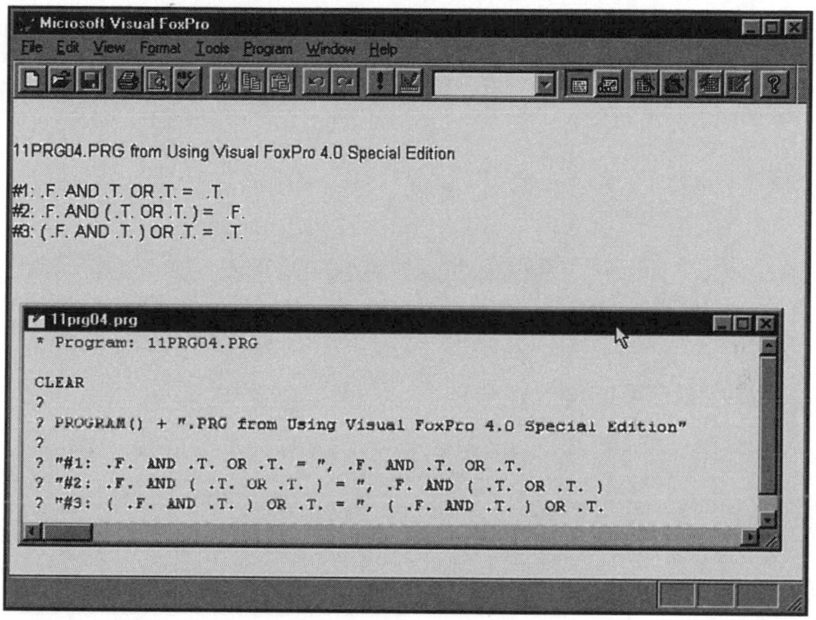

**FIGURE 10.4**

Always use parentheses to prevent confusion in complex expressions.

Listing 10.5 demonstrates another use of short-circuiting.

**Listing 10.5   10PRG05.PRG**

```
CLEAR
?
? PROGRAM() + ".PRG from Using Visual FoxPro 5.0 Special Edition"
?

ON ERROR DO trap WITH MESSAGE(), MESSAGE(1)

RELEASE ALL LIKE testme
? TYPE("m.testme") = "C" AND m.testme = "Testing..."? m.testme = "Testing..."

ON ERROR
PROCEDURE trap
PARAMETERS err, badline
 ? "Error", m.err, "in line", m.badline
RETURN
```

The first ? statement prints .F. to the screen, but the second statement generates a Variable 'TESTME' not found error, as shown in Figure 10.5. In the first case, the

TYPE("m.testme") = "C" comparison detected that the m.testme variable was not a character value and short-circuited the logical expression before the m.testme = "Testing..." comparison could be checked.

**FIGURE 10.5**
Short-circuit "dangerous" or slow logical evaluations by rearranging your expression.

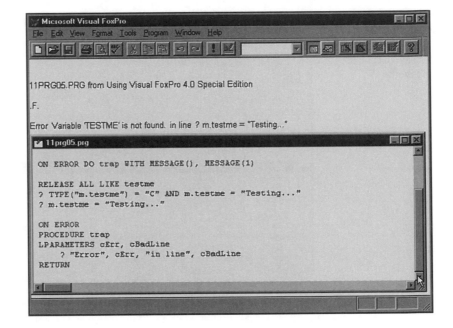

## Using Conditional Structures

The IF...ENDIF construct allows you to design code that executes based on the value of a logical expression. Being the simplest construct, IF...ENDIF also serves nicely as the head of the family of conditional programming structures. Look at Listing 10.6 before you proceed.

**Listing 10.6   10PRG06.PRG**

```
SET PATH TO (HOME())
#INCLUDE FOXPRO.H

IF MESSAGEBOX( "Is it raining?", MB_ICONQUESTION + MB_YESNO ) = IDYES
     WAIT WINDOW "Please take your umbrella." TIMEOUT 10
ENDIF
```

TIP   FOXPRO.H is a file that comes with Visual FoxPro. The file defines names for some of the esoteric function input and return values.

Listing 10.6 uses the IF...ENDIF construct, the MESSAGEBOX() function, and WAIT WIN-
DOW to give you some sound advice on meteorological fashions (see Figure 10.6). *Only
if* you choose Yes in the message dialog box and indicate that it is indeed raining outside
will Visual FoxPro advise you to take your umbrella. This capability to run blocks of program code based on logical expressions is the underlying principle of all the conditional
programming structures discussed in this chapter.

**FIGURE 10.6**

The MESSAGEBOX()
function creates
instant screens for
use in your logical
expressions.

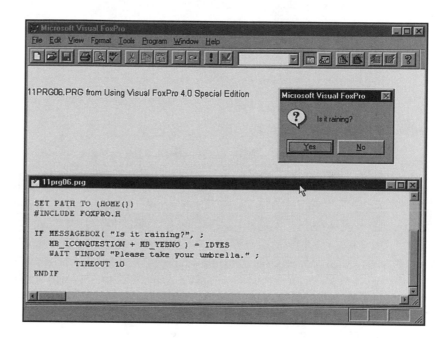

The syntax of the IF...ENDIF construct is:

```
IF logical_expression [comments]
     ... statement_block1 ...
[ ELSE [comments]
     ... statement_block2 ...
] ENDIF [comments]
```

Simply put, the IF...ENDIF construct evaluates logical_expression. If that expression is
true (.T.), the code in statement_block1 is executed. If the logical_expression is not true
(.F.) and there is an ELSE, the code in statement_block2 is run. Listing 10.7 demonstrates the optional ELSE clause.

**Listing 10.7   10PRG07.PRG**

```
SET PATH TO (HOME())
#INCLUDE FOXPRO.H
```

*continues*

**Listing 10.7   Continued**

```
IF MESSAGEBOX( "Is the sun shining?", ;
   MB_ICONQUESTION + MB_YESNO ) = IDYES

      WAIT WINDOW "Please take your sunglasses." ;
               TIMEOUT 10
   ELSE
      IF MESSAGEBOX( "Is it raining?", ;
         MB_ICONQUESTION + MB_YESNO ) = IDYES
         ___WAIT WINDOW "Please take your umbrella." ;
         TIMEOUT 10
      ENDIF
ENDIF
```

## TROUBLESHOOTING

**I can't seem to get my IF...ENDIF to evaluate all of the logical expression.** There are two likely causes. The first possibility is that your evaluation is short-circuiting. The section "Short-Circuiting Logical Expressions" earlier in this chapter discusses this behavior and demonstrates why it is useful. If a function call must execute, assign its return value to a memory variable in a separate statement, and compare the memory variable in the IF...ENDIF.

The second possibility deals with the fact that all Visual FoxPro programming constructs support structural comments such as those shown in Listing 10.7. Visual FoxPro allows you to place comments after the logical expression on the IF and DO WHILE lines, as well as the other structural elements, such as ELSE, ENDIF, and ENDDO. Make sure that all your ANDs and ORs are spelled correctly. If you spell them incorrectly, Visual FoxPro may believe that the logical expression has terminated and the comments have begun.

Some languages allow you to build simple IF statements in a single line, as follows:

```
IF MESSAGEBOX("Is it sunny?", ;
   MB_ICONQUESTION + MB_YESNO) = IDYES THEN ;
   PRINT "Use sun block!"
```

Unfortunately, VFP does not support this structure type, but it does support a similar function, IIF(). This function requires three arguments. The first is the logical expression to be tested. The second expression is returned if the logical expression evaluates to true. Otherwise, the third expression is returned. The following code shows how a teacher might use it to assign grades.

```
cGrade = IIF(nScore > 69, "PASS", "FAIL")
```

In this example, if the score is 70 or higher, the person passes the exam; otherwise, the person fails. Of course, the teacher may need a more complex scoring algorithm. The following example shows a series of nested IIF() calls:

```
CGrade = IIF(nScore > 89, 'A', ;
             IIF(nScore > 79, 'B', ;
             IIF(nScore > 69, 'C', ;
             IIF(nScore > 59, 'D', 'F'))))
```

# Extending an IF...ENDIF into a DO CASE...ENDCASE

IF...ENDIF executes code based on logical expressions and by using nesting techniques such as the one shown in Listing 10.7. With nesting, you can build elaborate program execution trees. The nesting of IF...ENDIFs has a limit (up to 385 levels), but more important, reading the logic gets difficult quickly. Therefore, nesting IF...ENDIFs generally is not naturally suited to handling more than two cases. The DO CASE...ENDCASE structure extends the principle of mutual exclusion from two possibilities to many cases, as shown in Listing 10.8.

**Listing 10.8  10PRG08.PRG**

```
SET PATH TO (HOME())
#INCLUDE FOXPRO.H

DO CASE
    CASE MESSAGEBOX( "Is the sun shining?", MB_ICONQUESTION + MB_YESNO ) =
    ➡IDYES

        WAIT WINDOW "Please take your sunglasses." TIMEOUT 10
    CASE MESSAGEBOX( "Is it raining?", MB_ICONQUESTION + MB_YESNO ) = IDYES

        WAIT WINDOW "Please take your umbrella." TIMEOUT 10
    CASE MESSAGEBOX( "Is it snowing?", MB_ICONQUESTION + MB_YESNO ) = IDYES

        WAIT WINDOW "Please wear your snow boots." TIMEOUT 10
    OTHERWISE
        WAIT WINDOW "Have a nice day." TIMEOUT 10
ENDCASE
```

Rather than force you to use mutually exclusive logical expressions, Visual FoxPro allows you to add any logical expression that you desire for each case. Visual FoxPro evaluates the expressions in order and executes the code associated with the first true (.T.) expression (and only the first). By enforcing mutual exclusion in this way, Visual FoxPro provides a great deal of flexibility in the nature and design of each case. Given this fact, the order of the cases is very important when the logical expressions are unrelated. If you know that several logical expressions are naturally exclusive, you can place the expression that is faster or more likely to evaluate to true (.T.) higher in the DO CASE...ENDCASE structure.

Much like the ELSE clause, the statement block associated with the optional OTHER-WISE clause executes only if none of the CASEs has a true (.T.) logical expression associated with it.

## Deciding When to Use an IF...ENDIF or CASE...ENDCASE

As a general rule, an IF...ENDIF structure is perfect when you need the program to execute two different blocks of code depending on a single condition. You can include additional IF...ENDIF structures within either of these two code blocks to further define other criteria.

A CASE...ENDCASE statement is perfect when you need the program to execute more than two different blocks of code depending on a single condition, such as different product colors. However, remember that each code block is mutually exclusive of all others in the CASE structure.

The challenge occurs when you need additional levels of conditional code within either structure. Obviously, each nested IF statement can have its own IF expression completely independent of the IF expression at any other level. What is not as obvious is that each block in a CASE structure can have a different expression. You could have something like the following pseudocode:

```
DO CASE
        CASE YEAR = "1997"
               . . .
        CASE MODEL = "Jag Z947"
               . . .
        CASE COLOR = "Burgundy"
               . . .
ENDCASE
```

This is completely different from saying:

```
IF YEAR = "1997"
        IF MODEL = "Jag Z947"
               IF COLOR = "Burgundy"
                       . . .
               ENDIF
               . . .
        ENDIF
        . . .
    ENDIF
```

In the CASE example, each expression is evaluated independently, and the first one that returns a value of true executes the corresponding code block. In the second example, the nested IF statements imply a hierarchy of properties.

# Creating a Simple Looping Structure

The easiest looping structure to understand is the DO WHILE...ENDDO. The following syntax shows the basic structure of this loop type:

```
DO WHILE Expression
   <<Commands>>
   [LOOP]
   [EXIT]
ENDDO
```

The key to using this structure is to define a logical expression that initially evaluates to .T.. Furthermore, you want to continue looping until this expression evaluates to .F.. This practice implies that the commands in the loop somehow cause the expression to eventually turn false. The loop shown in Listing 10.9, for example, never ends, because variable Z never changes inside the loop.

### Listing 10.9    10PRG09.PRG

```
x = 0
z = 1
DO WHILE z = 1
  x = x + 1
ENDDO
```

**TIP** An *infinite loop* is one that never terminates. If you are testing your loop and are concerned about whether or not it is infinite, make sure that you SET ESCAPE ON, so that you can interrupt the code by pressing the Esc key. Otherwise, you may have to reboot your computer to stop the program.

One way to break out of a loop is to create an expression that eventually becomes false, as in Listing 10.10.

### Listing 10.10    10PRG10.PRG

```
x = 0
DO WHILE x < 10
  ? x
  x = x + 1
ENDDO
```

In this example, the program remains in the loop until the value of x is 10 or greater and the value of x is incremented with each pass through the loop. If you run this program, you should see the numbers from 0 to 9.

You can also use the EXIT command to break out of a loop, as shown in Listing 10.11. When a program encounters an EXIT in a looping structure, it immediately shifts control to the statement following the ENDDO.

```
x = 0
DO WHILE .T.
  x = x + 1
  IF x > 10
    EXIT
  ENDIF
ENDDO
```

Another special keyword used with looping structures is LOOP. This command tells Visual FoxPro to return to the top of the loop and begin again. You can effectively use LOOP to skip selected instances within a loop. Be careful where you place the LOOP command, however; you do not want to accidentally create an endless loop.

The example shown in Listing 10.12 prints only odd numbers between 0 and 20.

```
x = 0
DO WHILE x < 20
  x = x + 1
  IF MOD(x,2) = 0
    LOOP
  ENDIF
  ? x
ENDDO
```

Notice that the LOOP statement occurs after the variable used in the logical expression is incremented. If the statement had tested the LOOP value to see whether or not it should loop before incrementing it, an endless loop would result.

## Deciding When to Use a DO WHILE...ENDDO Structure

DO WHILE...ENDDO is a great structure when you don't know the number of times you want to execute a loop, but you do know a condition that changes to indicate that you are done.

## Deciding When to Use a FOR...ENDFOR Structure

Sometimes, however, you know exactly the number of loops that you need before you enter the structure. Listing 10.13 shows a user-defined function that returns a string of 5 random numbers between 1 and 40 (anyone for a lottery ticket?).

### Listing 10.13  10PRG13.PRG

```
nStr = GETNBRS(5,40)
? nStr

FUNCTION GETNBRS
LPARAMETERS lnCount, lnMax, lnNbr, GetNbrs
GetNbrs = ""
FOR i = 1 TO lnCount
  lnNbr = INT(RAND() * lnMax + 1)
  GetNbrs = GetNbrs + STR(lnNbr, 2) + " "
ENDFOR
RETURN GetNbrs
```

Part

III

Ch

10

Another situation in which you know ahead of time the exact number of passes through a loop is when you read a table. You could use code similar to Listing 10.14 to step through a table to show a price increase of five percent.

### Listing 10.14  10PRG14.PRG

```
* Program: 11PRG14.PRG
CLEAR
CLOSE TABLES ALL
SELECT 0
USE E:\VFP\SAMPLES\DATA\PRODUCTS.DBF

lnRecCnt = RECCOUNT()
FOR i = 1 TO lnRecCnt
  ? prod_name + "Old Price: " + STR(Unit_Price,7,2) + ;
           "   New Price: " + STR(Unit_Price * 1.05,7,2) ;
    FONT "Courier New", 10
  SKIP 1
ENDFOR
```

### Minimizing Calculations in the LOOP Expression

Notice the use of a memory variable to store the number of records in the table returned by the RECCOUNT() function. We could have written the first line of the FOR...ENDFOR loop as follows:

```
    FOR i = 1 TO RECCOUNT()
```

*continues*

*continued*

Had we used that line, Visual FoxPro would have had to reevaluate the function with each pass through the loop. Because the number of records is unlikely to change while we are working with the loop, this extra file access degrades performance.

Call functions one time and store the result in a memory variable to improve the performance of FOR...ENDFOR loops. This technique applies to all looping structures. It also applies to any statements within a loop that are executed with each pass through the loop but that always return the same value.

The FOR loop has another feature that may be useful in some situations. First, the start value can be any value, not just 1. Visual FoxPro assumes that you want to increment the counter value by 1 with each pass unless you tell it otherwise. Use the STEP clause to provide a different increment value. To increment by 0.5, for example, use the following:

```
FOR i = 1 to 100 STEP .5
```

You can also use negative values for the increment value, but then the start value must be greater than the ending value. Otherwise, VFP will not execute the code within the loop.

## Deciding When to Use a SCAN...ENDSCAN Structure

The biggest problem with a FOR...ENDFOR structure when you are reading through a table is that if you forget the SKIP statement, the program goes into an endless loop, re-reading the same record. To prevent this problem, use the SCAN...ENDSCAN loop.

This structure is specifically designed for stepping through a file; it automatically advances the record pointer at the end of each loop pass. The following uses SCAN...ENDSCAN to perform the same price-increase function discussed earlier in the chapter:

```
SCAN
  REPLACE nPrice WITH nPrice * 1.05
ENDSCAN
```

A SCAN...ENDSCAN loop obviously needs far less code. Notice that there is no need for a separate variable to get the size of the table, no need to move the record pointer to the top, and no need to advance the record pointer with each loop pass.

SCAN...ENDSCAN has other options. Following is the syntax of the SCAN command:

```
SCAN [NOOPTIMIZE]
   [Scope] [FOR Expression1] [WHILE Expression2]
      [Commands]
   [LOOP]
   [EXIT]
ENDSCAN
```

SCAN also supports a FOR and WHEN clause, which allows you to conditionally process records at the same time that you loop. You can also use the scope clauses (REST, ALL, NEXT n) to determine where to start and how many records to process.

**TIP** In addition to being specifically designed for looping through tables, SCAN...ENDSCAN takes advantage of Rushmore optimization to speed processing.

# Executing External Program References

Nobody likes to code the same thing twice. Visual FoxPro's new object-oriented programming is designed to promote reusable code. Long before the advent of objects in Visual FoxPro, Visual FoxPro readily supported the ideal of reusable code by providing ways to call other programs and ways to load libraries of FoxPro or C functions and procedures.

In its simplest form, a procedure was always a reusable code block. The purpose of a procedure was to isolate a code segment and store it in such a way that it could be called from multiple locations in the same program. The concept of procedures, however, also included breaking large code blocks into smaller segments so that each segment represented a single task. This process made understanding, testing, debugging, and maintaining the code easier. It was even possible for each procedure to be stored as a separate file. FoxPro was smart enough to know to look for a file with the same name as the procedure if that procedure was not found in the current code block. With a separate file being used, it was theoretically possible for more than one application to use the same procedure.

Storing each procedure as a separate file may sound at first like a great solution, but for large applications, the number of procedures quickly becomes unmanageable. Therefore, FoxPro implemented the concept of a procedure library, which could hold multiple procedures. To call a procedure in such a library, the program first had to open the library with a command like the following:

```
SET PROCEDURE TO <library name>
```

Most FoxPro developers are familiar with the use of procedure libraries. FoxPro also allows applications to connect to compiled C programs stored as .FLLs. These libraries, too, must be opened before being used. The following command is used to open these libraries:

```
SET LIBRARY TO <library name>
```

In Visual FoxPro, this concept is extended to class libraries, which are opened with the following command:

```
SET CLASSLIB TO <class library>
```

**Part**
**III**

**Ch**
**10**

In all of these cases, the point is to develop code or objects that can be used in multiple places within an application and across applications.

## Executing External Programs with DO

The simplest way to create reusable code is to simply DO a program from within your program, exactly as you would from the Command window. The program shown in Listing 10.15 demonstrates a call to Listing 10.16.

### Listing 10.15   10PRG15.PRG

```
*11PRG15.PRG

CLEAR
?
? PROGRAM() + ".PRG from Using Visual FoxPro 5.0 Special Edition"
?

? "DOing 11PRG16.PRG ..."
DO 11PRG16.PRG

? "Back in " + PROGRAM()+ ".PRG"
```

### Listing 10.16   10PRG16.PRG

```
*11PRG16.PRG

?
? PROGRAM() + ".PRG from Using Visual FoxPro 5.0 Special Edition"
?
```

The PROGRAM() function, without any parameters, returns the name of the currently executing program. After running Listing 10.15 from Listing 10.16, you see in Figure 10.7 that the return value from PROGRAM() changes. Finally, after Listing 10.16 is done, the control returns to Listing 10.15 when you see Back in 11PRG15.PRG.

You can run other program files from within your code by using the IN clause of the DO command. And you can also run specific procedures in other files, as you can see by executing Listing 10.17 and Listing 10.18.

**FIGURE 10.7**
Nest programs with
the DO command.

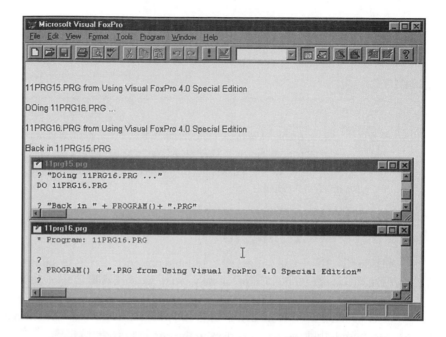

## Listing 10.17   10PRG17.PRG

```
*11PRG17.PRG

CLEAR
?
? PROGRAM() + ".PRG from Using Visual FoxPro 5.0 Special Edition"
?

? "DOing subproc IN 11PRG18.PRG ..."
DO subproc IN 11PRG18.PRG

? "Back in " + PROGRAM()+ ".PRG"
```

## Listing 10.18   10PRG18.PRG

```
*11PRG18.PRG

?
? PROGRAM() + ".PRG from Using Visual FoxPro 5.0 Special Edition"
?

PROCEDURE subproc

?
```

*continues*

Part III  Ch 10

---

**Listing 10.18   Continued**

```
? SYS(16) + " from Using Visual FoxPro 5.0 Special Edition"
?

ENDPROC
```

---

**N O T E**   All the examples in this chapter assume that the program files are in the current directory or at least in the VFP search path, as defined by the Search Path option in Tools, Options, File Locations. If this is not true, you can still reference the program if you include the full path for VFP to find it. ■

## Using SET PROCEDURE TO

Using the IN clause of the DO command provides access to subprocedures in any Visual FoxPro program file. Unfortunately, when you are calling user-defined functions, you have no similar capability. SET PROCEDURE TO makes up for this deficiency by allowing files that contain user-defined functions and procedures to be loaded into memory and treated as though they were procedures in the current program file.

Listing 10.19 SETs PROCEDURE TO 10PRG20.PRG (shown in Listing 10.20) and calls a user-defined function and a procedure from it.

---

**Listing 10.19   10PRG19.PRG**

```
*11PRG19.PRG

CLEAR
?
? PROGRAM() + ".PRG from Using Visual FoxPro 5.0 Special Edition"
?

SET PROCEDURE TO 11PRG20.PRG

? "DOing subproc IN 11PRG20.PRG ..."
DO subproc

? "Back in " + PROGRAM()+ ".PRG"

?
? UDF() + " from Using Visual FoxPro 5.0 Special Edition"
?
? "Back in " + PROGRAM()+ ".PRG"

SET PROCEDURE TO
```

---

**Listing 10.20   10PRG20.PRG**

```
*11PRG20.PRG

PROCEDURE subproc

?
? SYS(16) + " from Using Visual FoxPro 5.0 Special Edition"
?

ENDPROC

FUNCTION udf
RETURN SYS(16)
```

Because SET PROCEDURE TO loads the file into memory, it has speed advantages over DO...IN, but the memory overhead can be costly. You can also use SET PROCEDURE TO to load program files that contain nonvisual object classes into memory.

 **TIP** You can SET PROCEDURE TO a list of files separated by commas, or you can use the ADDITIVE keyword to SET PROCEDURE TO additional procedure files without unloading the existing procedure files.

## Using SET LIBRARY TO

SET LIBRARY TO is exactly like SET PROCEDURE TO, but it loads libraries of functions (FoxPro Link Libraries, or .FLLs) written in C, using the Visual FoxPro Application Programmer's Interface instead of Visual FoxPro code. These functions are integrated into Visual FoxPro and appear to the casual programmer to be system functions. The functions usually are small libraries that access operating system services directly and add to Visual FoxPro's capabilities.

# From Here...

This chapter introduced the two basic types of programming structures—conditionals and loops—implemented in Visual FoxPro, as well as some of the core ideas necessary to use them (such as comparison operators and logical expressions). The chapter also covered various ways to call external program files.

To learn about some related but more advanced topics, refer to these chapters:

- Chapter 2, "Introducing Object-Oriented Programming," teaches you about Visual FoxPro's newest programming constructs: objects.

Part **III**

Ch **10**

- Chapter 6, "Selecting, Viewing, and Ordering Data," addresses the database command scope, the FOR clause, and the WHILE clause.

- Bonus Chapter 07, "Extending Visual FoxPro with Third-Party Tools," provides information about FoxPro Link Libraries and other Visual FoxPro tools.

# Building Applications with Simple Form Structures

*by Michael Antonovich and Sandra Richardson-Lutzow*

Almost every application has at least one form. Some forms only display information to the user. However, most forms need some degree of user interaction. Over the years, the standard programming paradigm has changed from one in which the program controlled what the user could do. Now users expect to be in control of the application. Object-oriented programming meets this need.

Visual FoxPro has incorporated objects into form definition completely. In this chapter, you learn how to develop basic forms using common object types. Later chapters expand on these concepts to show you how to make forms more powerful than ever before. ■

## Define simple forms, using the object-oriented paradigm

With Visual FoxPro, you enter a new world of form creation involving objects, events, methods, and properties of the form.

## Add controls to the form, both manually (with drag-and-drop) and with the Builders

With different methods to add controls to forms, you have the choice to let VFP do most of the work for you.

## Gain an understanding of the basic form-control properties

Properties hold various values that control how your forms behave and look.

## Relate READ clauses from earlier versions of FoxPro to the new form and to object events and methods

You can control READ behavior directly from the form without additional code by using form properties and methods.

## Work with multiple forms and multiple instances of the same form

Using private data sessions, you can structure your form to run multiple instances and act on multiple records at the same time.

# Introducing the Form Object Paradigm

Object-oriented programs use two basic types of visual objects: a container and a control. A *container* is any object in which you can place other objects. Thus, a form is a container because it holds controls such as text boxes, labels, check boxes, and many other control types.

Some developers may think of a form as just another name for a window under previous FoxPro versions. Although its basic visual appearance is that of a window, its use of properties, events, and methods makes it more than a window. In fact, forms have over 60 properties and can respond to more than 40 events.

One other interesting feature of forms is that because they are objects, you can create new forms from existing ones. With object inheritance, you can create a basic form definition and then use it to create all subsequent forms for an application.

For example, you might want to define overall appearance, color, fonts, and other properties. Then simply save this form as a visual class and use it as a template for all new forms.

There are several ways to begin a new form:

■ Select File, New, Form from the System menu.

■ Enter the command **CREATE FORM** in the Command menu.

■ Enter the commands:

```
NewForm = CREATEOBJECT("FORM")

MODIFY FORM "NewForm"
```

■ Use the Form Wizard

Chapter 5, "Using Wizards for Rapid Application Development," discusses how to use the Form wizard. Although wizards help create a basic object like a form, you often need to modify and enhance what they create.

Figure 11.1 shows a blank form. It shows the open Form Designer work area in which you can build a visual representation of the form.

To add objects to the form, VFP uses the controls toolbar, which consists of three sections. The first and last sections have two buttons each and are fixed members of the toolbar. However, the middle section changes, depending on the current class library in use.

**FIGURE 11.1**

When creating a new form, two important additional windows to keep open are the Controls toolbar and the Properties window.

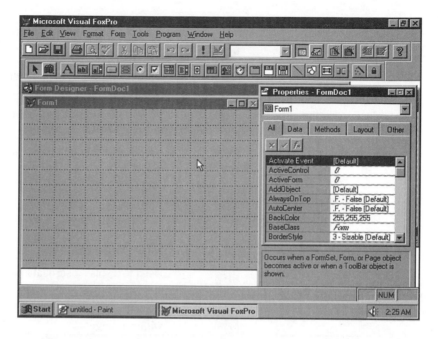

Later in this chapter we discuss selecting different class libraries for this middle section. Table 11.1 defines the Controls toolbar icons.

**Table 11.1    Form Control Toolbar Icons**

| Control | Icon | Description |
|---------|------|-------------|
| Select Pointer | | Resizes and moves controls. |
| View Classes | | Allows you to display registered class libraries or to open new class libraries. |
| Label | | Used to display fixed text. |
| Text Box | | Used to display single lines of text. |
| Command Button | | Used to create a button that the user can choose to execute a command. |

*continues*

**Table 11.1    Continued**

| Control | Icon | Description |
|---|---|---|
| Command Group | | Used to create a group of buttons that the user can choose to execute a command. |
| Option Button | | Used to display multiple options Group from which the user can select only one. |
| Check Box | | Used to indicate whether something is selected or not, true or false, or to display multiple choices when the user can select more than one. |
| Combo Box | | Used to create a drop-down list to let the user select one of a list of items. Also used to create a drop-down combo box to let the user select from a list or enter a new value. |
| List Box | | Used to display a scrollable list of items. |
| Spinner | | Used to increment or decrement an integer value within a range. |
| Grid | | Used to create a browse control. |
| Image | | Used to display a graphic image. |
| Timer | | Used to time events and to set intervals between them. |
| PageFrame | | Used to display multiple pages of a control in a single form. |
| OLE Container | | Used to provide object linking and embedding (OLE) from an OLE server. |
| OLE Bound | | Used to provide object linking and embedding (OLE) in the general field of a table. |
| Line | | Used to draw a variety of line styles on your form. |
| Shape | | Used to draw rectangles, squares, circles, and ovals. |
| Separator | | Used when creating a custom toolbar to separate tools into groups. |

| Control | Icon | Description |
|---------|------|-------------|
| Builder Lock | 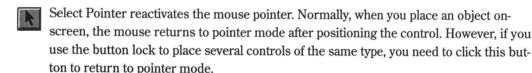 | Used to open builders for controls as they are selected. |
| Button Lock | | Used to add multiple controls of the same type without having to click the control button on the toolbar again. |

Select Pointer reactivates the mouse pointer. Normally, when you place an object on-screen, the mouse returns to pointer mode after positioning the control. However, if you use the button lock to place several controls of the same type, you need to click this button to return to pointer mode.

View Classes enables you to view other control classes saved as VCX files. Before using this button, you can register and select your custom class libraries using Tools, Options, Controls. You can also register a custom class library by pressing the View Classes button in the toolbar and selecting the Add option. This displays the Open dialog box, which enables you to select the library from any directory. Selecting the library opens and registers it at the same time.

▶ **See** "Creating a Class Library," **p. 119**

After you register them, the names of these custom class libraries appear when you select the View Classes button. When you select a custom library, the buttons in the middle section of this toolbar change to represent the new controls. If the custom classes in the selected library do not have their own icon, they display a generic tool icon as shown in the margin. Figure 11.2 shows the changed toolbar after you load the BUTTONS.VCX custom class library.

At any time, you can return to the default controls by selecting Standard from the View Classes list.

Builder Lock turns on the builder mode. Builders help define properties for an object by using a series of input screens prompting for the control's major properties. Builders are a good way to learn how to use a control's major properties.

Button Lock enables you to add multiple instances of the same base object without having to return to the Controls toolbar and reselect it. Click the button once to press it and then select the control you want to use. Add as many instances of the selected control as you want without returning to the toolbar. You can even change to a different control by clicking a different control button in the toolbar.

**FIGURE 11.2**

When you open a custom control library, the default icons provide little clue about the specific controls to which they refer.

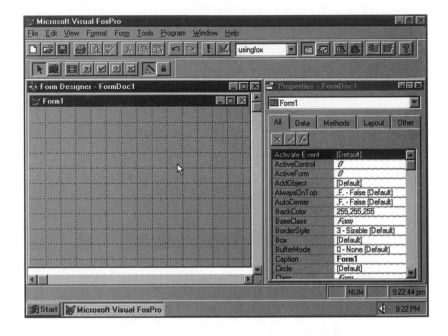

 **TIP** First, use Button Lock to "paint" the entire form with all the controls. Then return to pointer mode to select individual controls and customize them.

The properties windows may not open automatically with new forms. To open it, select View, Properties. In fact, this section of the View pull-down menu has five additional support windows for designing forms. Table 11.2 briefly describes each one.

**Table 11.2   Additional Support Windows for Form Designer**

| Window | Description |
|---|---|
| Properties | Displays the properties and events window. |
| Code | Displays the code associated with events in the current form or control. Drop-down list boxes let you select code from different events and objects. |
| Form Controls toolbar | Displays the Control toolbar with the standard or default controls. |
| Layout toolbar | The Layout toolbar contains 13 lucky buttons to align objects, either by an edge or by a center line. It can also change the relative stacking order of overlapping objects. Finally, it can resize all controls in a group, making them the same size. |
| Color Palette toolbar | Changes the foreground and background colors of forms and controls. |

Use the <u>V</u>iew pull-down menu to toggle these additional windows on and off. A check mark on the left of the option in the pull-down menu indicates that it is active. If you do not see it, it may be covered by other windows or the Form Designer itself. Deselect it and then reselect it to redisplay it on top.

Another way to get to the Properties window is to right-click anywhere on the form or object. Figure 11.3 shows the options that result from right-clicking anywhere on a form and Table 11.3 describes them.

**FIGURE 11.3**
Right-clicking anywhere on a form gives you various options for and shortcuts to other areas relating to the form.

**Table 11.3    Shortcut Menu for Forms**

| Option | Description |
|--------|-------------|
| <u>R</u>un Form | Saves any changes and runs the form. After it runs, returns to modify form mode. |
| <u>P</u>aste | Enabled when the Clipboard is not empty. |
| Data <u>E</u>nvironment | Displays Data Environment window. |
| Proper<u>t</u>ies | Displays Properties window. |
| <u>B</u>uilder | Runs Forms Builder. |
| <u>C</u>ode | Opens events and methods for the form in alphabetical order, starting with the first containing code. |
| <u>H</u>elp | Displays Help window for Form Object. |

The options available when you right-click an object of the form displays the options: Undo, Cut, Copy, Properties, Builder, Code, and Help.

# Defining the Overall Form Properties

The first step in creating a form is to define its overall properties. Because all properties have default values, you only specify the properties you want to change. This technique is sometimes called *programming by exception*. Fortunately, most of the time, only a few properties need to change (out of more than 60). The most obvious of these include:

- Size - Properties: Height, Width

- Position on-screen - Properties: Left, Top

- Title - Property: Name

- Foreground and background colors - Properties: ForeColor, BackColor

Open the properties window to see the current settings. VFP divides object properties into five page frames: All, Data, Methods, Layout, and Other. To change the physical appearance of the form, display the Layout page as shown in Figure 11.4.

**FIGURE 11.4**

The Layout properties of the form object contain physical attributes of the form such as the caption used as the form title.

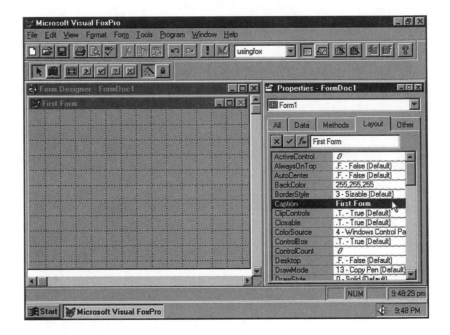

This figure shows the first several Layout properties. To change one, click it to select it or highlight it with the arrow keys. VFP places the current value in the edit box at the top of the box.

Figure 11.4 highlights the Caption property. The default value of Form1 was changed to First Form. Notice that VFP immediately reflects the change in the actual form's title bar once the user has pressed the Enter key.

Observe the three buttons to the left of the edit box. An <u>X</u> labels the first one. It cancels changes to the property, at least until you press Enter or select another property, or you can press the Esc key to cancel the change.

 The second button displays a check mark. Click it to verify the property value. It checks for syntax errors in equations used for property expressions. Some properties have limited values consisting of logical values or values selected from defined lists (as in border style). For these properties, the check button merely accepts the new value—much like pressing Enter or clicking a different property.

 The third button opens the Expression Builder dialog box. Use this button for properties that accept calculated values such as Top, Left, Height, or Width.

In addition to these buttons, additional buttons may appear on the right side of the edit box such as a down arrow indicating a drop-down list. Many properties like Border Style, Draw Style, Font, every logical property, and many others display a drop-down list. Clicking this button displays the possible values for the property. You cannot enter values not in this list.

For example, Border Style displays four styles numbered 0 through 3. The property edit box rejects any other values or characters. (Obviously, it would not know what to do with other values.) Thus, unlike manual code writing where you can easily specify an incorrect value, the property edit box often limits entry to valid values.

**N O T E**  Some properties such as font size also use a variation on the drop-down list called a *drop-down combo*. A drop-down combo accepts values not in the list. For example, if font sizes include 14, 16, 18, and 20, you can specify a font size of 17. With TrueType fonts, Windows sizes the selected font accordingly. ■

 A few properties such as ForeColor and BackColor display a button with three dots—an ellipsis (...). This button indicates that another dialog box exists with options for this property. In this case, clicking the button opens the Color dialog box, which displays a grid of 48 predefined colors. It also enables you to define up to 16 custom colors.

Four properties define the position and size of almost all visual objects, including forms. The Top and Left properties position the object's upper-left corner. As a default, VFP places a new form in the upper-left corner of the screen (Top = 0 and Left = 0).

Part
III

Ch
11

However, you can either change this position using these two properties or you can physically move the window in the Form Designer. You can even use the AutoCenter property to automatically center the form. Similarly, the Height and Width properties define the form's size.

Perhaps you only want to center the form in one dimension, horizontally or vertically. There is no button or property option to do this. Just set the Top or Left property as appropriate to one of the following equations:

```
Top:  =(_Screen.Height - This.Height) / 2
```

or

```
Left: =(_Screen.Width - This.Width) / 2
```

These equations rely on the ability to reference any object's properties. The FoxPro desktop always has the object name _SCREEN, and has the same position and size properties as a form. The equations use the relative reference keyword, *This*, to reference the current object's Width and Height properties. *This* refers to the form being designed.

**N O T E**   As you change any property value, VFP displays the new value in **bold** in the property list. You cannot change properties displayed in *italic*. ■

At the bottom of the properties window, a short description appears. In most cases, the property name and this description tell you the purpose of the property. However, the Language Reference provides additional details about each property or for quick help on any property or event, select it and right-click and choose Help. You could also choose "Zoom" for a code window (where appropriate), "Reset to Default" where appropriate, or "Expression Builder."

# Using the Data Environment

Almost every form needs to reference data from one or more tables. To include the required tables in the definition of the form, open View, Data Environment. This opens a window titled Data Environment. If your data environment is empty, the Add Table or View window is also displayed. The Data Environment window resembles the Table View area of the Database Designer.

To initially add tables to the data environment work area, simply highlight a table or view of an opened database from the Add Table or View list box and click Add or double-click on the table. To add other tables at another time to the data environment work area, open the Data Environment pull-down menu, which appears in the System menu after selecting the property. Note that you can either open multiple tables and define their relations in the form, or you can use a predefined view of multiple tables.

**TIP** When you use the Data Environment, opening tables is much faster than executing USE, SET ORDER, and SET RELATION commands in the form's load event because the Data Environment uses low-level calls.

To make a relation between two tables, click the linking field in the parent table and drag it to the child table to complete the relation. The data environment draws a line between the parent table field and the appropriate index in the child table, as shown in Figure 11.5. Note, however, that an appropriate index must exist beforehand.

As in previous versions of FoxPro, you can use the form to create and save a definition of which tables it needs to open, along with their relations.

**FIGURE 11.5**
Create a link between two tables in the data environment by dragging a field from the master table to the lookup table.

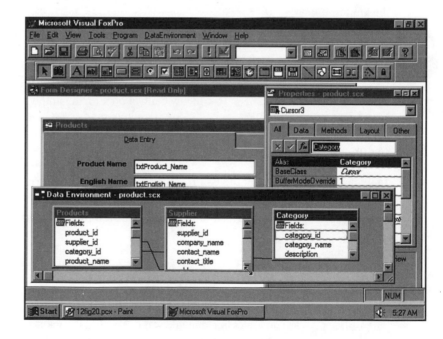

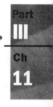

## Adding Controls to a Form

After you define the data environment, the next step adds controls to the form. VFP uses several types of controls. Some controls, once defined, need no user interaction. These include lines, shapes, and labels. You must bind other controls to specific fields in tables or views set in the data environment.

Finally, some controls tie VFP to other files or applications. The image control displays a bitmap image created by another application and stored separately as a BMP file. The OLE controls allow VFP to work with and include documents from other applications.

To add a control to a form, you need to open the Form Controls Toolbar if it is not already open. It can be found in the View pull-down menu.

All toolbars float. Therefore, you can pick one up and place it in a convenient location on-screen. When placed against an edge of the screen, it automatically changes to a vertical or a horizontal line, as appropriate. But because some toolbars have so many controls, placing it vertically along the side of the screen hides many controls from view.

Placing a toolbar against a screen edge is called *docking*. I guess if you think of the toolbar as a boat floating out on Lake Screen, moving the toolbar against any edge corresponds to docking that boat.

**TIP**   All toolbars float, even the Standard toolbar. When it is floating, you can "squash and stretch it" further by changing its border sizes.

**Adding Controls Manually**   To add any control on a form, simply click its icon and then click in the form. VFP displays the control in a default size defined by the base class. Of course, for some controls such as the text or edit box, you will want to define the size as you place it.

In this case, after selecting the control, click the mouse in the form and drag to form a rectangle representing the control size. When you release the mouse button, VFP sets the control's size to this rectangle. You usually save a step by placing and sizing the control in one step.

 **Using the Builder to Add Controls**   If you place controls on the form as described previously, you have to define all the properties for that control manually. However, VFP provides a tool called a Builder to help set major properties of each control.

The Builder Lock icon looks like a magic wand. You must click it first before selecting the control you want to add. Once clicked, it remains selected until you click it again. An alternative method is to place the control on the form, right-click on it, and choose Builder from the shortcut menu.

Suppose you want to use the Builder to add a group of option (radio) buttons. First click the Builder Lock, and then click the option button. Place the button group on the form by clicking once, or click and drag to size it.

VFP displays the Option Group Builder. It has three pages, the first of which is shown in Figure 11.6.

**FIGURE 11.6**

The first page of the Option Group Builder defines the number of buttons, their caption, and their graphics.

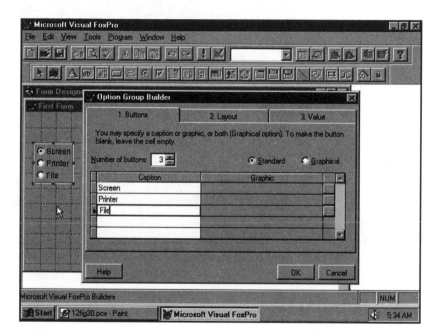

This page defines the number of buttons, their caption, and their graphics. In this case, three buttons have been defined as standard buttons with the captions: Screen, Printer, and File. As you enter the caption names or change the number of buttons, you can see your changes immediately in the form itself (if the builder does not cover it).

The second page of the Builder defines the layout by using three options. First, you can place the buttons vertically or horizontally. Unless you only have a few buttons, the most common choice is vertical. Second, you can change the spacing between buttons in units of pixels.

And, finally, you can define the border style around the button group. This means either displaying a single line border box or having no border at all. Figure 11.7 shows these options.

Part
III

Ch
**11**

**FIGURE 11.7**

The second page of the Option Group Builder defines the button-layout orientation, spacing between buttons, and border style.

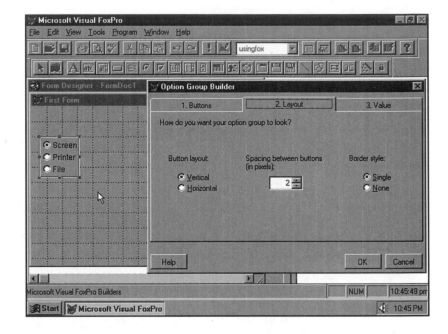

The final page of this Builder asks where to store the value that identifies which button the user selects. Typically, this is a field in a table or view, but it could also be a memory variable. To select the table or view, click the button with the three dots. This displays the Open dialog box. However, if you already have a table in the Data Environment, clicking the drop-down list will reveal all of the available fields.

After you select a table, clicking the down arrow of the drop-down list displays the fields in the table or view. Select the field from this list or directly enter a memory variable name. Figure 11.8 shows this page of the Option Group Builder.

Each Builder helps to define different properties for its associated control. Some builders, like the ComboBox or List Builder, need as many as four page frames to fully define the control. Others need one or two.

In any case, a Builder helps define enough of the properties to create a functional control. You can always return to the full Properties dialog box to set additional attributes for the control such as colors or fonts.

**Adding Controls with Drag and Drop**   Another method of adding controls to your form is drag and drop. From the Project Manager, Data Environment, or Database View, you can drag and drop a field or multiple fields, depending on the control desired, onto your form. When you use this method, VFP automatically creates a control for the field corresponding to the defaults you set for that data type in Tools Options Field Mapping.

**FIGURE 11.8**

The third page of the Option Group Builder defines where to find the value that defines which option button the user selected.

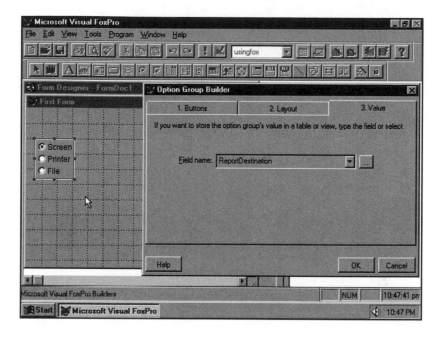

This is the most efficient method when you have taken full advantage of the database container's field properties. For instance, the field properties comment, input mask, and format correspond to the same control properties; the field name is copied to the end of the control name after the control prefix; the width of the control matches the field size; and the field is automatically assumed to be the control source for the control. In addition, the Form Designer creates a label using the field caption.

## Using Typical Properties of Controls

Every control, even the Timer, has position and size properties. VFP positions controls using their upper-left corner. Therefore, the appropriate property names are Top and Left. To define their size, each control also has a Height and Width. Keep in mind that Height is measured downward from the top.

Position and size measurements are based on the unit of measure defined in the form property ScaleMode. There are two possibilities: foxels or pixels. *Pixels* are the easiest to understand.

The basic screen resolution of a VGA monitor is 640 pixels wide by 480 pixels high. Each pixel represents one dot of color on the screen. When you use pixels, positioning text does not depend on the font size or other font characteristics. It is simply a matter of counting pixels.

On the other hand, VFP defines a *foxel* as the average size of a character. For nonproportional character sets like Courier, the average character width is the same as the width of every character.

But when proportional character sets are used, the average size of a foxel does not exactly match any one character. Furthermore, sizing and positioning of objects become more complex because any random set of five characters does not necessarily fit in a text box defined with a width of 5 foxels.

In fact, it is even more specific than that. Objects placed on a form using a ScaleMode of foxels use the font characteristics of the default form font to set their position and size. Within an object, you can use an entirely different font.

So if you were to size the object based on the form-font characteristics alone, you would be wrong. Likewise, if you size the object based on the object-font characteristics alone, you are also wrong. You need to ratio the font characteristics of both.

Fortunately, VFP provides functions such as FONTMETRIC( ) and WFONT( ) that help determine font characteristics.

## Adding New Properties or Methods

You can add new properties to a form any time the form is open. First, select the form and open the Form pull-down menu. The first menu option adds a new property and the second adds a new method. Selecting the New Property option displays the dialog box shown in Figure 11.9.

Observe that you can only specify the property name and description here. After you enter this information and click OK, VFP adds the property in the Property dialog box at the end of the All or Other page.

Notice that the default property value is .F. You can change this to any value by clicking it and entering a default value in the property-value edit box. Also, while you have the new property highlighted, the description previously entered appears in the description area at the bottom of the Properties dialog box.

The option Form, Edit Property/Method…lets you change the description of a property but not the spelling. If you make a mistake and need to change the spelling of an added property or method, you must remove it and add it again.

When might you want to add your own properties to a control or form? Many times you need to share values between methods or events. For example, in the click event of a command button, you calculate the total of an item sold for the month. Another method uses this value to project the supply of this item needed on hand for next month.

**FIGURE 11.9**
Use the New Property dialog box to add new properties to any of VFP's form objects. VFP has no limit on the number of new properties you can add to an object.

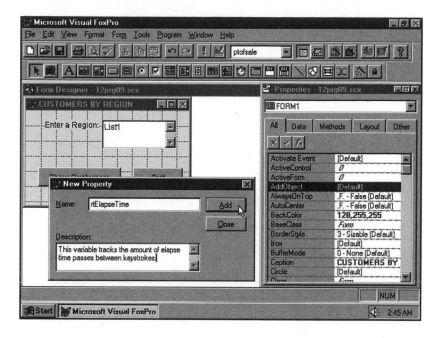

You can create a new property of the form, `rnItemsSold`, to store this value. The value can then be used by any other event, control, or form. You can think of this as an alternative to using global variables. Use code like the following in the click event of the command button after doing the calculation:

```
ThisForm.rnItemsSold = lnResultingValue
```

 **TIP**  It is helpful to use naming conventions for properties and methods also. User-defined properties are commonly prefixed with "r," followed by the data type prefix, and user-defined methods are commonly prefixed with "m."

If you add a method, it appears at the bottom of the methods page in the Properties dialog box. You can also open the code associated with the method by double-clicking it or by selecting View, Code.

## Defining Methods

You've probably heard the term *event-driven*, maybe even in respect to object-oriented programming. Event-driven programming means the user controls the program to act on a user action such as a key press or mouse click, or on an operating system reaction such as an error.

In effect, the program just sits there and waits for the user to do something. That something can be a key press or a mouse click. These events initiate an activity in VFP and in your applications.

Once an event starts, it may run a single method, or it may execute several. For example, clicking a mouse button initiates three sequential events: MouseDown, MouseUp, and Click. The Click event may cause the program to load a form.

Then there are a series of events associated with loading forms such as INIT and ACTIVATE for both the form and its objects. The sequence of these events starts with the innermost object to the outermost containers with the form being the outermost. Following is a breakdown of this sequence when you first load a form:

1. LOAD (only on initial load)
2. INIT (only on initial load)
3. ACTIVATE (only in same application)
4. GOTFOCUS

In Chapter 2, you saw that simply adding a button does not do anything more than display the button on the form and allow the user to press it. It performs no action by itself. In that case, you had to add code to the CLICK event to perform an action.

The same is still true when you want to define an action for a form object. Let's take an already existing form that prompts for a customer region. The form then uses that selected value to show a list of customers in that region.

On the CD

You can find this form on the samples disc with the name 11PRG09.SCX. Figure 11.10 shows the open form.

This form consists of four objects: one label, one list box, and two command buttons. "Basic Form Controls" in this chapter covers labels and command buttons and "Using List Boxes" in Chapter 13 covers list boxes. For now, concentrate on how this example assigns methods to various events.

The first method occurs in the form itself. When the form opens, you want it to open the TasTrade database so it can access the Customer table. You could do this with the Data Environment, but for the sake of showing some event code, it appears in the Load event of the form.

**FIGURE 11.10**

This form prompts the user for a region before displaying a list of customers from that region.

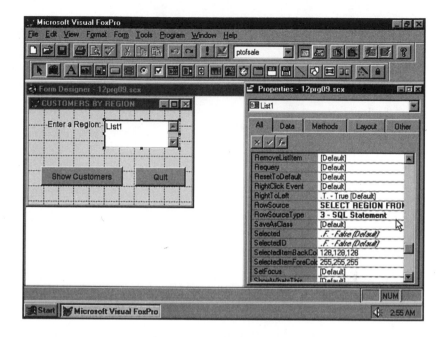

To open the code, double-click the Load event from the Methods list of the Properties dialog box for object Form1. You can also right-click anywhere on the form itself (not over another object) and select Code from the quick menu.

Figure 11.11 shows the dialog box that appears. It has two list boxes at the top and a large blank text area. The Object list box lets you select any object currently part of the form, including the form itself. The Procedure list box displays the available procedures or methods defined for that object.

In this case, make sure that the Object box shows Form1 and that the Procedure is Load. See the following code:

```
* Open the TasTrade database and select table Customer.
  CLOSE DATABASES
  OPEN DATABASE \VFP\SAMPLES\TASTRADE\DATA\TASTRADE
  USE CUSTOMER
```

This is all the code needed to open the customer table for this simple application. It is also the only code entered into the Form1 object.

Part
III

Ch
11

**FIGURE 11.11**

The code dialog box lets you switch between any procedure of any object without having to first return to the Form Designer.

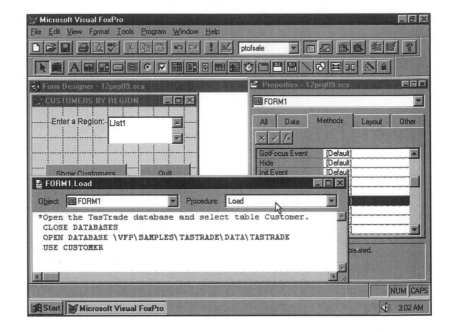

Now comes the part of this example that might appear to be done with lights and mirrors. The key to selecting a region is in the data properties of the list box. Without stealing the thunder from Chapter 13, all you need to know for now is that the list box identifies an SQL statement as its RowSourceType.

In fact, you have a choice of nine ways to populate a list box. Then an SQL statement is placed in the RowSource property to retrieve the region list. It uses a GROUP BY clause to eliminate duplicates and to sort the list. Finally, the ControlSource identifies the property rcState in Form1 as the place to store the region selected. rcState was added as a form property to illustrate one way of making variable values available to different objects on a form.

Switch to the code in the object Command1. Notice that the selected procedure immediately switches to Click. This dialog box moves to the first procedure with code when you select a different object.

The procedure uses the value of Form1.rcState selected in the list box using a relative reference, ThisForm.rcState. It first tests for a nonblank value and prints a message if it is blank. Then it creates a browse window displaying the customer ID and company names for customers in the selected state.

```
* Check if a region was selected
  IF EMPTY(ThisForm.rcState)
    = MESSAGEBOX('No state selected yet')
  ELSE
    BROWSE FIELDS Customer_Id, Company_Name ;
       FOR Region = ThisForm.rcState
  ENDIF
```

**N O T E**  Because this program did not define a separate window to display the browse, it uses the form windows as a default. If you don't like this, you can define a separate window using the DEFINE WINDOW command and add a WINDOW clause to the BROWSE. ▓

The second command button, Command2, also has a single method defined as procedure Click. In this case, it merely closes all data files and releases the form.

```
* Close all data files (Close the current database)
  CLOSE DATABASES

* Release the form
  ThisForm.Release
```

This relatively simple example defined three methods for a form and two objects. You would follow a similar procedure to define additional methods for other objects.

## Aligning Controls

Even if you turn on Snap to Grid from the Format menu pull-down, you may still not be happy with the alignment of the objects on the form. To realign everything, open the Layout toolbar found in the View pull-down menu. It contains 13 options for aligning objects. Table 11.5 describes them.

Part
III

Ch
11

### Table 11.5  Layout Toolbar Icons

| Control | Icon | Description |
| --- | --- | --- |
| Align Left Sides | | Aligns selected controls on the leftmost edge. |
| Align Right Sides | | Aligns selected controls on the rightmost edge. |
| Align Top Edges | | Aligns selected controls on the topmost edge. |
| Align Bottom Edges | | Aligns selected controls on the bottommost edge. |

*continues*

**Table 11.5   Continued**

| Control | Icon | Description |
| --- | --- | --- |
| Align Vertical Centers | | Aligns the selected control's centers on a vertical axis. |
| Align Horizontal Centers | | Aligns the selected control's centers on a horizontal axis. |
| Same Width | | Adjusts the width of the selected controls to the widest control. |
| Same Height | | Adjusts the height of the selected controls to the tallest control. |
| Same Size | | Adjusts the size of the selected controls to the largest control. |
| Center Horizontally | | Aligns the selected control's center on a vertical axis in the middle of the form. |
| Center Vertically | | Aligns the selected control's center on a horizontal axis in the middle of the form. |
| Bring to Front | | Positions the selected controls in front of all other controls. |
| Send to Back | | Positions the selected controls in back of all other controls. |

Before selecting an alignment style, select the controls you want to align. You can align them based on any edge or center line. You also can center objects horizontally or vertically on the form.

**CAUTION**

If you select a vertical set of controls, do not try to center them vertically in the form. VFP centers each object individually. The result is that VFP stacks the objects on top of each other.

Similar concerns apply to horizontally arranged controls. Do not try to align horizontal centers.

You also can resize a group of controls to force them to have the same width, height, or both.

Finally, if objects overlap (such as lines and shapes with other fields), you can change the stacking order with the Send To Back and Bring to Front options. These last two options are also on the Format pull-down menu.

Use the Layout toolbar to clean up a form after you have added all the objects on it. A form with evenly sized controls and alignment along one edge looks more appealing than one where each object appears to be randomly offset from those around it.

## Defining the Tab Order

Using a mouse to move from one field to the next is not always the most convenient way to move between fields. If users must enter data into most fields, they don't want to move their hands off the keyboard after each entry just to select the next field. Instead, they want to press Enter or Tab to tell VFP that they are done with the current field and are ready to move to the next.

By default, VFP defines the tab order by the sequence in which you add the fields to the form. But you may not define the fields in any particular order. Furthermore, you may add fields later that did not exist in the original form.

Most users expect the cursor to follow fields either vertically, horizontally, or in a logical combination of both, as though you were reading a book. If pressing Tab makes the cursor jump from one side of the form to another, the user wastes time finding the blinking cursor for the next entry field.

There are two methods for changing the tab order: interactively and by list. You can select the method you like by choosing Tools, Options, Forms. Then open the Tab Ordering pull-down list and select the method you want.

If you choose to *interactively* set the tab order, select View, Tab Order. This puts a small box in the upper-left corner of each object. Inside each box is a number representing the tab sequence order.

To change the tab sequence, click in the box of the object you want to change. This removes the number and renumbers all of the following objects. If you click the same box a second time, it places that object at the end of the list.

The easy way is to decide which will be the first object in the tab order, double-click it, and then single-click the remaining objects in the Tab order that you'd like them to have. When you are done, click View Tab Order again to set the new order.

Another way to set the tab order is by *list*. Now when you select View, Tab Order, the dialog box shown in Figure 11.12 appears.

**FIGURE 11.12**
If you set the object tab order by list, you physically arrange the order of the objects shown in a list by using the objects' mover buttons.

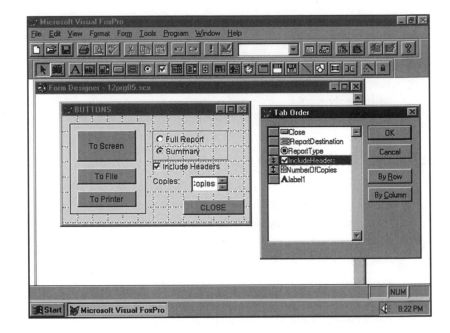

Every object in the form appears in the scrollable list on the left. By clicking and dragging the mover buttons to the left of the object name, you can customize the tab order.

Observe that VFP even gives you a small icon, representing the object type, to help identify the objects. You also can click the By Row or By Column buttons to quickly define default field orders. However, for many complex screens, this may not give you the desired results. When you have a tab order you like, click OK.

# Utilizing Basic Form Controls

VFP provides 21 basic visual form controls that you can use to create a form. This section highlights the basic properties of the most commonly used controls—it does not attempt to describe every property or event.

Many objects, however, share events and properties. Therefore, knowing how they work in one object gives you an idea of how they work in others. Chapter 13 continues discussing some of the other, more powerful controls.

As an alternative to listing all of the properties and methods for each control in the section describing it, Tables 11.7 through 11.10 summarize the properties. Table 11.6 provides a key to the column numbers used in the first four tables. Please note that the properties marked with an asterisk are new properties from VFP 3.0.

| Table 11.6 Key for Control Properties in Tables 11.7 Through 11.10 | |
|---|---|
| **Control Number** | **Control Name** |
| 1 | Label |
| 2 | Text Box |
| 3 | Edit Box |
| 4 | Command Button |
| 5 | Command Group |
| 6 | Option Button |
| 7 | Option Group |
| 8 | Check Box |
| 9 | Combo Box |
| 10 | List Box |
| 11 | Spinner |
| 12 | Grid |
| 13 | Image |
| 14 | Timer |
| 15 | Page Frame |
| 16 | Page |
| 17 | OLE Container Control |
| 18 | OLE Bound Control |
| 19 | Line |
| 20 | Shape |
| 21 | Container |
| 22 | Cursor |

Part
III

Ch
11

**Table 11.7 Data Properties of Standard Form Controls**

| Window | 1 | 2 | 3 | 4 | 5 | 6 | 7 | 8 | 9 | 10 | 11 | 12 | 13 | 14 | 15 | 16 | 17 | 18 | 19 | 20 | 21 | 22 |
|---|---|---|---|---|---|---|---|---|---|---|---|---|---|---|---|---|---|---|---|---|---|---|
| ActiveColumn | | | | | | | | | | | | | X | | | | | | | | | |
| ActivePage | | | | | | | | | | | | | | | X | | | | | | | |
| ActiveRow | | | | | | | | | | | | | X | | | | | | | | | |
| BoundColumn | | | | | | | | | X | X | | | | | | | | | | | | |
| BoundTo * | | | | | | | | | X | X | | | | | | | | | | | | |
| BufferModeOverride | | | | | | | | | | | | | | | | | | | | | X | |
| ChildOrder | | | | | | | | | | | | | X | | | | | | | | | |
| Comment | X | X | X | X | X | X | X | X | X | X | X | | X | X | X | X | X | X | X | X | X | |
| Controls | | | | | | | | | | | | | | | | | | | | | X | |
| ControlSource | | | | | X | X | X | X | X | X | X | | | | | X | X | X | | | | |
| CursorSource | | | | | | | | | | | | | | | | | | | | | | X |
| Database | | | | | | | | | | | | | | | | | | | | | | X |
| DisplayValue | | | | | | | | | X | X | | | | | | | | | | | | |
| Exclusive | | | | | | | | | | | | | | | | | | | | | | X |
| Filter | | | | | | | | | | | | | | | | | | | | | | X |
| FirstElement | | | | | | | | | X | X | | | | | | | | | | | | |
| Format | | X | X | | | | | | X | X | X | | | | | | | | | | | |
| Increment | | | | | | | | | | | X | | | | | | | | | | | |
| InputMask | | | | X | | | | | X | | X | | | | | | | | | | | |
| ItemData | | | | | | | | | X | X | | | | | | | | | | | | |
| ItemIDData | | | | | | | | | X | X | | | | | | | | | | | | |
| KeyboardHighValue | | | | | | | | | | X | | | | | | | | | | | | |
| KeyboardLowValue | | | | | | | | | | | X | | | | | | | | | | | |

| Window | 1 | 2 | 3 | 4 | 5 | 6 | 7 | 8 | 9 | 10 | 11 | 12 | 13 | 14 | 15 | 16 | 17 | 18 | 19 | 20 | 21 | 22 |
|---|---|---|---|---|---|---|---|---|---|---|---|---|---|---|---|---|---|---|---|---|---|---|
| LinkMaster List | | | | | | | | | X | X | | | | | | | | | | | | |
| ListItem | | | | | | | | | X | X | | | | | | | | | | | | |
| Margin | | X | X | | | | | | X | X | | | | | | | | | | | | |
| MaxLength | | | X | | | | | | | | | | | | | | | | | | | |
| MemoWindow | | X | | | | | | | | | | | | | | | | | | | | |
| NoDataOnLoad | | | | | | | | | | | | | | | | | | | | | X | |
| XNullDisplay * | | X | X | | | | | | X | X | X | | | | | | | | | | | |
| NumberOfElements | | | | | | | | | X | X | | | | | | | | | | | | |
| Objects * | | | | | | | | | | | | | | | | | | | X | | | |
| OpenWindow | | X | | | | | | | | | | | | | | | | | | | | |
| Order | | | | | | | | | | | | | | | | | | | | | X | |
| ReadOnly | | X | X | | | | | | X | | X | X | | | | | | | | | | |
| RecordSource | | | | | | | | | | | | | X | | | | | | | | | |
| RecordSourceType | | | | | | | | | | | | | X | | | | | | | | | |
| RelationalExpr | | | | | | | | | | | | | X | | | | | | | | | |
| RowSource | | | | | | | | | X | X | | | | | | | | | | | | |
| RowSourceType | | | | | | | | | X | X | | | | | | | | | | | | |
| Sorted | | | | | | | | | X | X | | | | | | | | | | | | |
| SpinnerHighValue | | | | | | | | | | X | | | | | | | | | | | | |
| SpinnerLowValue | | | | | | | | | | X | | | | | | | | | | | | |
| Tag | X | X | X | X | X | X | X | X | X | X | X | X | | | X | X | X | | | | | |
| TerminateRead | X | X | X | X | X | X | X | X | X | X | X | X | | | | | | | | | | |
| Value | X | X | X | X | X | X | X | X | X | X | X | X | | | | | | | | | | |

**Table 11.8  Methods of Standard Form Controls**

| Window | 1 | 2 | 3 | 4 | 5 | 6 | 7 | 8 | 9 | 10 | 11 | 12 | 13 | 14 | 15 | 16 | 17 | 18 | 19 | 20 | 21 |
|---|---|---|---|---|---|---|---|---|---|---|---|---|---|---|---|---|---|---|---|---|---|
| Activate | | | | | | | | | | | | | | | | X | | | | | |
| ActivateCell | | | | | | | | | | | | X | | | | | | | | | |
| AddColumn | | | | | | | | | | | | X | | | | | | | | | |
| AddItem | | | | | | | | | X | X | | | | | | | | | | | |
| AddListItem | | | | | | | | | X | X | | | | | | | | | | | |
| AddObject | | | | | X | | X | | | | | X | | X | X | | | | | | |
| AfterRowColChange | | | | | | | | | | | | X | | | | | | | | | |
| BeforeRowColChange | | | | | | | | | | | | X | | | | | | | | | |
| Clear | | | | | | | | | X | X | | | | | | | | | | | |
| Click Event | | X | X | X | X | X | X | X | X | X | X | X | X | X | X | X | | X | X | X | X |
| DblClick Event | | X | X | | X | X | X | X | X | X | X | X | X | X | X | X | | X | X | X | X |
| Deactivate | | | | | | | | | | | | | | | | X | | | | | |
| DeleteColumn | | | | | | | | | | | | X | | | | | | | | | |
| Delete | | | | | | | | | | | | X | | | | | | | | | |
| Destroy Event | X | X | X | X | X | X | X | X | X | X | X | X | X | X | X | X | X | X | X | X | X |
| DoScroll | | | | | | | | | | | | X | | | | | | | | | |
| DoVerb | | | | | | | | | | | | | | | | | X | X | | | |
| DownClick Event | | | | | | | | | X | | X | | | | | | | | | | |
| Drag | X | X | X | X | X | X | X | X | X | X | X | X | X | X | X | X | X | X | X | X | X |
| DragDrop Event | X | X | X | X | X | X | X | X | X | X | X | X | X | X | X | X | X | X | X | X | X |
| DragOver Event | X | X | X | X | X | X | X | X | X | X | X | X | X | X | X | X | X | X | X | X | X |
| DropDown Event | | | | | | | | | X | | | | | | | | | | | | |

| Window | 1 | 2 | 3 | 4 | 5 | 6 | 7 | 8 | 9 | 10 | 11 | 12 | 13 | 14 | 15 | 16 | 17 | 18 | 19 | 20 | 21 |
|---|---|---|---|---|---|---|---|---|---|---|---|---|---|---|---|---|---|---|---|---|---|
| Draw | | | | | | | | | | | | | | | | | | | | | X |
| Error | X | X | X | X | X | X | X | X | X | X | X | X | X | X | X | X | X | X | X | X | X |
| ErrorMessage | | X | X | X | X | X | X | X | X | X | | | | | | | | | | | |
| GotFocus Event | | X | X | X | | X | | X | X | X | X | | | | | X | X | | X | | |
| IndexToItemId | | | | | | | | | X | X | | | | | | | | | | | |
| Init | X | X | X | X | X | X | X | X | X | X | X | X | X | X | X | X | X | X | X | X | X |
| InteractiveChange | | X | X | | X | | X | X | X | X | X | | | | | | | | | | |
| ItemIdToIndex | | | | | | | | | X | X | | | | | | | | | | | |
| KeyPress Event | | X | X | | | X | | X | X | X | X | | | | | | | | | | |
| LostFocus Event | | X | X | X | | X | | X | X | X | X | | | | | | | X | X | | |
| Message Event | | X | X | X | X | X | X | X | X | X | X | | | | | | | | | | |
| MiddleClick * | X | X | X | X | X | X | X | X | X | X | X | X | X | X | | X | | X | X | X | X |
| MouseDown Event | X | X | X | X | X | X | X | X | X | X | X | X | X | X | X | X | X | X | X | X | X |
| MouseMove Event | X | X | X | X | X | X | X | X | X | X | X | X | X | X | X | X | X | X | X | X | X |
| MouseUp Event | X | X | X | X | X | X | X | X | X | X | X | X | X | X | X | X | X | X | X | X | X |
| Move | X | X | X | X | X | X | X | X | X | X | X | X | X | X | | X | X | X | X | X | X |
| Moved | | | | | | | | | | | | X | | | X | X | | X | | | X |
| ProgrammaticChange | X | X | | | X | | X | X | X | X | X | | | | | | | | | | |
| RangeHigh Event | X | | | | | | | | X | X | | | | | | | | | | | |
| RangeLow Event | X | | | | | | | | X | X | | | | | | | | | | | |
| ReadExpression * | X | X | X | X | X | X | X | X | X | X | X | X | X | X | X | X | X | X | X | X | X |
| ReadMethod * | X | X | X | X | X | X | X | X | X | X | X | X | X | X | X | X | X | X | X | X | X |

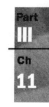

Part
III

Ch
11

*continues*

**Table 11.8  Continued**

| Window | 1 | 2 | 3 | 4 | 5 | 6 | 7 | 8 | 9 | 10 | 11 | 12 | 13 | 14 | 15 | 16 | 17 | 18 | 19 | 20 | 21 |
|---|---|---|---|---|---|---|---|---|---|---|---|---|---|---|---|---|---|---|---|---|---|
| Refresh | | X | X | X | X | X | X | X | X | X | X | X | X | | X | X | X | X | | | X |
| RemoveItem | | | | | | | | | X | X | | | | | | | | | | | |
| RemoveListItem | | | | | | | | | X | X | | | | | | | | | | | |
| RemoveObject | | | | | X | | X | | | | | X | | | X | X | | | | | X |
| Requery | | | | | X | | | | X | X | | | | | | | | | | | |
| Reset | | | | | | | | | | | | | | X | | | | | | | |
| ResetToDefault * | X | X | X | X | X | X | X | X | X | X | X | X | X | X | X | | X | X | X | | X |
| Resize | | | | | | | | | | | X | X | X | X | X | X | X | X | | X | X |
| RightClick Event | X | X | X | X | X | X | X | X | X | X | X | X | X | X | X | X | X | X | X | X | |
| SaveAsClass | X | X | X | X | X | X | X | X | X | X | X | X | X | X | X | X | X | X | X | X | X |
| Scrolled | | | | | | | | | | | | X | | | | | | | | | |
| SetAll | | | | | X | | X | | | | | X | | | X | X | | | | | X |
| SetFocus | | X | X | X | | X | | X | X | X | X | X | | | X | X | X | | | | |
| ShowWhatsThis * | X | X | X | X | X | X | X | X | X | X | X | X | X | X | X | X | X | X | | | X |
| Timer | | | | | | | | | | | | | X | | | | | | | | |
| UIEnable Event | X | X | X | X | X | X | X | X | X | X | X | X | X | | X | | X | X | X | X | X |
| UpClick Event | | | | | | | | | X | X | | | | | | | | | | | |
| Valid Event | | X | X | X | X | X | X | X | X | X | X | X | | | | | | | | | |
| When Event | | X | X | X | X | X | X | X | X | X | X | X | | | | | | | | | |
| WriteExpression * | X | X | X | X | X | X | X | X | X | X | X | X | X | X | X | X | X | X | X | X | X |
| WriteMethod * | X | X | X | X | X | X | X | X | X | X | X | X | X | X | X | X | X | X | X | X | X |
| ZOrder | X | X | X | X | X | X | X | X | X | X | X | X | X | X | X | X | X | X | X | X | X |

**Table 11.9 Layout Properties of Standard Form Controls**

| Window | 1 | 2 | 3 | 4 | 5 | 6 | 7 | 8 | 9 | 10 | 11 | 12 | 13 | 14 | 15 | 16 | 17 | 18 | 19 | 20 | 21 |
|---|---|---|---|---|---|---|---|---|---|---|---|---|---|---|---|---|---|---|---|---|---|
| ActiveControl | | | | | | | | | | | | | | | | X | | | | | X |
| Alignment | | X | X | | | X | X | X | X | X | | | | | | | | | | | |
| AutoActivate | | | | | | | | | | | | | | | | | X | X | | | |
| AllowAddNew * | | | | | | | | | | | | X | | | | | | | | | |
| AllowHeaderSizing * | | | | | | | | | | | | X | | | | | | | | | |
| AllowRowSizing * | | | | | | | | | | | | X | | | | | | | | | |
| AutoSize | X | | | X | X | X | X | X | | | | | | | | | X | X | | | |
| BackColor | | X | X | X | X | X | X | X | X | X | X | | X | | | X | | | X | X | X |
| BackStyle | | X | X | X | X | X | X | X | | | | | X | | | X | | | X | X | X |
| BorderColor | | X | X | | X | X | X | | X | X | | | X | X | X | | | | X | X | X |
| BorderStyle | | X | X | | X | X | X | | | | | | X | | | | | | X | X | X |
| BorderWidth | | | | | | | | | | | | | | | X | | | | X | X | X |
| ButtonCount | | | | | X | | X | | | | | | | | | | | | | | |
| Caption | X | | | X | | X | | X | | | | | | | | X | | | | | |
| Century * | | X | | | | | | | | | | | | | | | | | | | |
| ColorScheme | | X | X | X | | X | | X | X | X | X | | | | | X | | | | | |
| ColorSource | | X | X | X | X | X | X | X | X | X | | | X | | X | | | | X | X | X |
| ColumnCount | | | | | | | | | X | | X | X | | | | | | | | | |
| ColumnLines | | | | | | | | | X | X | | | | | | | | | | | |
| ColumnWidths | | | | | | | | | X | X | | | | | | | | | | | |

*continues*

Part
III

Ch
11

**Table 11.9   Continued**

| Window | 1 | 2 | 3 | 4 | 5 | 6 | 7 | 8 | 9 | 10 | 11 | 12 | 13 | 14 | 15 | 16 | 17 | 18 | 19 | 20 | 21 |
|---|---|---|---|---|---|---|---|---|---|---|---|---|---|---|---|---|---|---|---|---|---|
| ControlCount | | | | | | | | | | | | | | | | X | | | | | X |
| Curvature | | | | | | | | | | | | | | | | | | | | | X |
| DateFormat * | | X | | | | | | | | | | | | | | | | | | | |
| DateMark * | | X | | | | | | | | | | | | | | | | | | | |
| Delete Mark | | | | | | | | | | | | X | | | | | | | | | |
| DisabledBackColor | X | X | X | | | X | | X | X | X | X | | | | | | | | | | |
| DisabledForeColor | X | X | X | X | | X | | X | X | X | X | | | | | | | | | | |
| DisabledItemBackColor | | | | | | | | | X | X | | | | | | | | | | | |
| DisabledItemForeColor | | | | | | | | | X | X | | | | | | | | | | | |
| DisabledPicture | | | | X | | X | | X | | | | | | | | | | | | | |
| Down Picture | | | | X | | X | | X | | | | | | | | | | | | | |
| DragIcon | X | X | X | X | X | X | X | X | X | X | X | X | X | | | X | X | X | X | X | X |
| DrawMode | | | | | | | | | | | | | | | | | | X | X | | |
| FillColor | | | | | | | | | | | | | | | | | | | | X | |
| FillStyle | | | | | | | | | | | | | | | | | | | | X | |
| FontBold | X | X | X | X | | X | X | X | X | X | X | X | | | | X | | | | | |
| FontCondense * | X | X | X | X | | X | X | X | X | X | X | X | | | | X | | | | | |
| FontExtend * | X | X | X | X | | X | X | X | X | X | X | X | | | | X | | | | | |
| FontItalic | X | X | X | X | | X | X | X | X | X | X | X | | | | X | | | | | |
| FontName | X | X | X | X | | X | X | X | X | X | X | X | | | | X | | | | | |
| FontOutline | X | X | X | X | | X | X | X | X | X | X | X | | | | X | | | | | |
| FontShadow | X | X | X | X | | X | X | X | X | X | X | X | | | | X | | | | | |

| Window | 1 | 2 | 3 | 4 | 5 | 6 | 7 | 8 | 9 | 10 | 11 | 12 | 13 | 14 | 15 | 16 | 17 | 18 | 19 | 20 | 21 |
|---|---|---|---|---|---|---|---|---|---|---|---|---|---|---|---|---|---|---|---|---|---|
| FontSize | | X | X | X | | X | | X | X | X | X | X | | | | X | | | | | |
| FontStrikethru | | X | X | X | | X | | X | X | X | X | X | | | | X | | | | | |
| FontUnderline | | X | X | X | | X | | X | X | X | X | X | | | | X | | | | | |
| ForeColor | | X | X | X | | X | | X | X | | X | X | | | | X | | | | | X |
| GridLineColor | | | | | | | | | | | | X | | | | | | | | | |
| GridLineWidth | | | | | | | | | | | | X | | | | | | | | | |
| GridLines | | | | | | | | | | | | X | | | | | | | | | |
| HeaderHeight | | | | | | | | | | | | X | | | | | | | | | |
| HeaderWordWrap * | | | | | | | | | | | | X | | | | | | | | | |
| Height | X | X | X | X | X | X | X | X | X | X | X | X | X | X | X | | X | X | X | X | X |
| Highlight | | | | | | | | | | | | X | | | | | | | | | |
| HighlightRow * | | | | | | | | | | | | X | | | | | | | | | |
| Hours * | | X | | | | | | | | | | | | | | | | | | | |
| IntegralHeight * | | | X | | | | | | | X | | | | | | | | | | | |
| ItemBackColor | | | | | | | | X | X | | | | | | | | | | | | |
| ItemForeColor | | | | | | | | X | X | | | | | | | | | | | | |
| ItemTips * | | | | | | | | X | X | | | | | | | | | | | | |
| Left | X | X | X | X | X | X | X | X | X | X | X | X | X | X | X | X | X | X | X | X | |
| LeftColumn | | | | | | | | | | | | X | | | | | | | | | |
| LineSlant | | | | | | | | | | | | | | | | | | | | X | X |

Part
III

Ch
11

*continues*

**Table 11.9   Continued**

| Window | 1 | 2 | 3 | 4 | 5 | 6 | 7 | 8 | 9 | 10 | 11 | 12 | 13 | 14 | 15 | 16 | 17 | 18 | 19 | 20 | 21 |
|---|---|---|---|---|---|---|---|---|---|---|---|---|---|---|---|---|---|---|---|---|---|
| MouseIcon * | X | X | X | X | X | X | X | X | X | X | X | X | X |  | X | X | X | X | X | X | X |
| MousePointer | X | X | X | X | X | X | X | X | X | X | X | X | X |  |  | X | X | X | X | X | X |
| MoverBars |  |  |  |  |  |  |  |  |  | X |  |  |  |  |  |  |  |  |  |  |  |
| NewIndex |  |  |  |  |  |  |  |  | X | X |  |  |  |  |  |  |  |  |  |  |  |
| NewItemId |  |  |  |  |  |  |  |  | X | X |  |  |  |  |  |  |  |  |  |  |  |
| OLETypeAllowed |  |  |  |  |  |  |  |  |  |  |  |  |  |  |  |  | X |  | X |  |  |
| PageCount |  |  |  |  |  |  |  |  |  |  |  |  |  |  | X |  |  |  |  |  |  |
| PageHeight |  |  |  |  |  |  |  |  |  |  |  |  |  |  | X |  |  |  |  |  |  |
| PageWidth |  |  |  |  |  |  |  |  |  |  |  |  |  |  | X |  |  |  |  |  |  |
| Panel |  |  |  |  |  |  |  |  |  |  | X |  |  |  |  |  |  |  |  |  |  |
| PanelLink |  |  |  |  |  |  |  |  |  |  | X |  |  |  |  |  |  |  |  |  |  |
| Partition |  |  |  |  |  |  |  |  |  |  | X |  |  |  |  |  |  |  |  |  |  |
| PasswordChar |  | X | X |  |  |  |  |  |  |  |  |  |  |  |  |  |  |  |  |  |  |
| Picture |  |  |  | X |  | X |  | X | X | X |  |  | X |  | X |  |  |  | X |  |  |
| RecordMark |  |  |  |  |  |  |  |  |  |  | X |  |  |  |  |  |  |  |  |  |  |
| RelativeColumn |  |  |  |  |  |  |  |  |  |  | X |  |  |  |  |  |  |  |  |  |  |
| RelativeRow |  |  |  |  |  |  |  |  |  |  | X |  |  |  |  |  |  |  |  |  |  |
| RightToLeft * | X | X | X | X |  | X |  |  | X | X | X | X | X |  | X |  |  |  |  |  |  |
| RowHeight |  |  |  |  |  |  |  |  |  |  | X |  |  |  |  |  |  |  |  |  |  |
| ScrollBars |  |  | X |  |  |  |  |  |  |  | X |  |  |  |  |  |  |  |  |  |  |
| Seconds * |  | X |  |  |  |  |  |  |  |  |  |  |  |  |  |  |  |  |  |  |  |

| Window | 1 | 2 | 3 | 4 | 5 | 6 | 7 | 8 | 9 | 10 | 11 | 12 | 13 | 14 | 15 | 16 | 17 | 18 | 19 | 20 | 21 |
|---|---|---|---|---|---|---|---|---|---|---|---|---|---|---|---|---|---|---|---|---|---|
| SelLength | | X | X | | | | | | X | X | X | | | | | | | | | | |
| SelStart | | X | X | | | | | | X | X | X | | | | | | | | | | |
| SelText | | X | X | | | | | | X | X | X | | | | | | | | | | |
| Selected | | | | | | | | | X | X | | | | | | | | | | | |
| SelectedBackColor | | X | X | | | | | | X | X | X | | | | | | | | | | |
| SelectedForeColor | | X | X | | | | | | X | X | X | | | | | | | | | | |
| SelectedId * | | | | | | | | | X | X | | | | | | | | | | | |
| SelectedItemBackColor | | | | | | | | | X | X | | | | | | | | | | | |
| SelectedItemForeColor | | | | | | | | | X | X | | | | | | | | | | | |
| SelectOnEntry * | | X | X | | | | | | X | X | | | | | | | | | | | |
| Sizable | | | | | | | | | | | | | | | | | X | X | | | |
| SpecialEffect | | X | X | X | X | X | X | X | X | X | X | | | | X | | | | X | X | |
| SplitBar * | | | | | | | | | | | | X | | | | | | | | | |
| StatusBarText | | X | X | | | X | | X | X | X | X | | | | | | | | | | |
| Stretch | | | | | | | | | | | | | X | | | | X | X | | | |
| StrictDateEntry * | | X | | | | | | | | | | | | | | | | | | | |
| Style | | X | | X | | X | | X | X | | | | | | | | | | | | |
| TabStretch | | | | | | | | | | | | | | | X | | | | | | |
| Tabs | | | | | | | | | | | | | | | X | | | | | | |
| TabStyle * | | | | | | | | | | | | | | | X | | | | | | |
| Text * | | X | X | | | | | | X | X | | | | | | | | | | | |

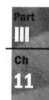

Part III

Ch 11

*continues*

**Table 11.9   Continued**

| Window | 1 | 2 | 3 | 4 | 5 | 6 | 7 | 8 | 9 | 10 | 11 | 12 | 13 | 14 | 15 | 16 | 17 | 18 | 19 | 20 | 21 |
|---|---|---|---|---|---|---|---|---|---|---|---|---|---|---|---|---|---|---|---|---|---|
| ToolTipText | X | X | X | X |  | X |  | X | X | X | X | X |  |  |  | X |  |  |  | X |  |
| Top | X | X | X | X | X | X | X | X | X | X | X | X | X |  |  |  | X | X | X | X | X |
| TopIndex |  |  |  |  |  |  |  |  | X | X |  |  |  |  |  |  |  |  |  |  |  |
| TopItemId |  |  |  |  |  |  |  | X | X | X |  |  |  |  |  |  |  |  |  |  |  |
| View |  |  |  |  |  |  |  |  |  |  | X |  |  |  |  |  |  |  |  |  |  |
| Visible | X | X | X | X | X | X | X | X | X | X | X | X |  | X |  | X | X | X | X | X | X |
| Width | X | X | X | X | X | X | X | X | X | X | X | X | X | X | X | X | X | X | X | X | X |
| WordWrap | X |  |  | X |  |  |  |  |  |  |  |  |  |  |  |  |  |  |  |  |  |

**Table 11.10   Other Properties of Standard Form Controls**

| Window | 1 | 2 | 3 | 4 | 5 | 6 | 7 | 8 | 9 | 10 | 11 | 12 | 13 | 14 | 15 | 16 | 17 | 18 | 19 | 20 | 21 |
|---|---|---|---|---|---|---|---|---|---|---|---|---|---|---|---|---|---|---|---|---|---|
| AllowSelect * |  |  |  |  |  |  |  |  |  |  |  | X |  |  |  |  |  |  |  |  |  |
| Allow Tabs |  |  | X |  |  |  |  |  |  |  |  |  |  |  |  |  |  |  |  |  |  |
| AutoVerbMenu * |  |  |  |  |  |  |  |  |  |  |  |  |  |  |  |  | X |  |  |  |  |
| BaseClass | X | X | X | X | X | X | X | X | X | X | X | X | X | X | X | X | X | X | X | X | X |
| Buttons |  |  |  |  | X |  | X |  |  |  |  |  |  |  |  |  |  |  |  |  |  |
| Cancel |  |  |  | X |  |  |  |  |  |  |  |  |  |  |  |  |  |  |  |  |  |
| Class | X | X | X | X | X | X | X | X | X | X | X | X | X | X | X | X | X | X | X | X | X |
| ClassLibrary | X | X | X | X | X | X | X | X | X | X | X | X | X | X | X | X | X | X | X | X | X |
| Columns |  |  |  |  |  |  |  |  |  |  |  | X |  |  |  |  |  |  |  |  |  |
| Default |  |  |  | X |  |  |  |  |  |  |  |  |  |  |  |  |  |  |  |  |  |

| Window | 1 | 2 | 3 | 4 | 5 | 6 | 7 | 8 | 9 | 10 | 11 | 12 | 13 | 14 | 15 | 16 | 17 | 18 | 19 | 20 | 21 |
|---|---|---|---|---|---|---|---|---|---|---|---|---|---|---|---|---|---|---|---|---|---|
| DocumentFile | | | | | | | | | | | | | | | | | X | X | | | |
| DragMode | | X | X | X | X | X | X | X | X | X | X | X | X | X | X | X | X | X | X | X | X |
| Enabled | | X | X | X | X | X | X | X | X | X | X | X | X | X | X | X | X | X | X | X | |
| HelpContextID | | X | X | X | X | X | X | X | X | X | X | X | X | X | X | X | X | X | X | | |
| HideSelection | | X | X | | | | | | | | X | | | | | | | | | | |
| HostName | | | | | | | | | | | | | | | | X | X | | | | |
| IMEMode * | | X | X | | | | | | X | | | | | | | | | | | | |
| IncrementalSearch | | | | | | | | X | X | | | | | | | | | | | | |
| Interval | | | | | | | | | | | | | X | | | | | | | | |
| ListCount | | | | | | | | X | X | X | | | | | | | | | | | |
| ListIndex | | | | | | | | X | X | | | | | | | | | | | | |
| ListItemId | | | | | | | | X | X | | | | | | | | | | | | |
| MultiSelect | | | | | | | | | X | | | | | | | | | | | | |
| Name | X | X | X | X | X | X | X | X | X | X | X | X | X | X | X | X | X | X | X | X | X |
| OleClass | | | | | | | | | | | | | | | | X | X | | | | |
| OleLCID * | | | | | | | | | | | | | | | | X | X | | | | |
| PageOrder | | | | | | | | | | | | | | | X | | | | | | |
| Pages | | | | | | | | | | | | | | X | | | | | | | |
| Parent | X | X | X | X | X | X | X | | X | | X | X | X | X | X | X | X | X | X | X | X |
| ParentClass | X | X | X | X | X | X | X | X | X | X | X | X | X | X | X | X | X | X | X | X | |
| TabIndex | X | X | X | X | X | X | X | X | X | X | X | X | X | X | X | | | | | | |

continues

Part III

Ch 11

**Table 11.10  Continued**

| Window | 1 | 2 | 3 | 4 | 5 | 6 | 7 | 8 | 9 | 10 | 11 | 12 | 13 | 14 | 15 | 16 | 17 | 18 | 19 | 20 | 21 |
|---|---|---|---|---|---|---|---|---|---|---|---|---|---|---|---|---|---|---|---|---|---|
| TabStop | | X | X | X | X | X | | X | X | X | X | X | | | X | X | X | | | | |
| WhatsThisHelpIDX | X | X | X | X | X | X | X | X | X | X | X | X | X | X | | X | X | X | X | X | X |

## Line Controls

 The Line control enables you to draw straight lines between any two points on the form. To draw a line, select the control and position the mouse where you want the line to begin. Then click and drag the mouse to the end point.

You see a box as you drag the mouse, representing an imaginary rectangle that surrounds the line. This is sort of like resizing a window. The line connects opposite corners.

When you release the mouse button, VFP displays a line from the upper-left corner to the lower-right corner of this box. But what if you want the line to go from the upper-right corner to the lower-left?

With the line still selected (represented by the small squares, called *handles*, along the sides and corners of the imaginary rectangle), open the Layout page of Properties. Next, select the LineSlant property and change its value from \ to /. Note that the angle of the slash determines the line slant.

You also can change the line width by changing the BorderWidth property (not the Width property, which changes the width of the imaginary box). Width value represents the number of pixels wide to draw the line.

An additional interesting property is the BorderStyle. It has seven different line styles, with the default being a solid line. It also has 16 different pen styles or draw modes. Some of these help display lines that cross other objects, even graphics. Figure 11.13 shows several different line styles.

 **TIP**

Only lines 1 pixel thick allow border styles other than solid.

 **On the CD**

Form 11PRG01.SCX on the samples disc illustrates various styles of lines.

 **TIP**

If you want to draw a vertical or horizontal line using Line control, make the line as narrow or flat as possible. If it doesn't look right, make the appropriate property (Height or Width) 0.00.

**FIGURE 11.13**

This set of line objects shows some of the possible variations on line styles.

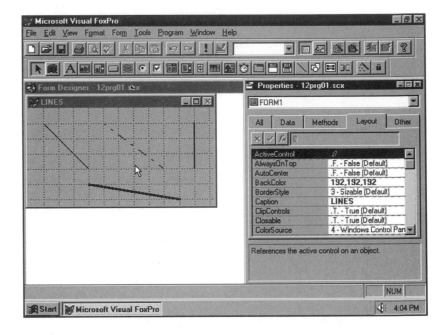

## Shape Controls

 The Shapes tool allows you to create squares, rectangles, ovals, and circles. The basic procedure to create shapes is like that used for lines but with a few enhancements. Figure 11.14 shows a variety of shapes.

**FIGURE 11.14**

The shape object ranges from squares and rectangles to circles and ovals by varying the amount of the Curvature property.

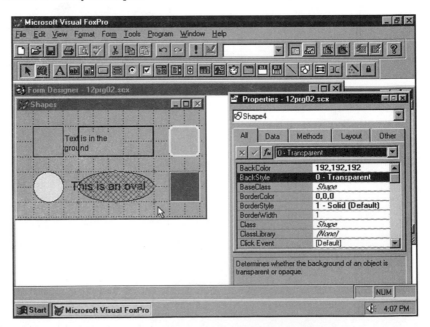

On the CD

Form 11PRG02.SCX on the samples disc shows various styles of rectangles and ovals.

**Rectangles and Squares**    The default shape is a rectangle. A square, of course, is just a special case of a rectangle with four equal-length sides. Similarly, ovals and circles are also derived from rectangles with increasingly rounded corners.

> **N O T E**    Actually, most monitors are 33 percent wider than they are high. That is why display images are 640×480, 800×600, and 1,024×768. Still, that does not mean that if you define the height and width properties as the same that the rectangle will look like a square.
>
> Remember that it is not the pixel count alone that determines the apparent shape of the rectangle but also the physical size of the monitor output. If the physical image is also in a ratio of 4 to 3 (width to height), then an equal number of pixels will look square or circular. ■

Shapes also have shading, which by default is transparent. A transparent object can have a color associated with it. But because it is transparent, it does not appear to have any color at all.

In fact, you see whatever is behind it, whether it is the plain background screen, text, or other objects. To see the color associated with an object, change the FillStyle from transparent to one of eight other fill patterns.

A solid fill (FillStyle = 0) paints the entire area with the selected FillColor. However, if you need to print a form, first test how your printer displays different colors. Some printers handle colors poorly, and you may want to use different fill patterns (the FillStyle property) rather than colors.

A feature of fill patterns is that they can be made opaque to other objects in the background by using the BackStyle property. With fills, VFP uses the BackColor property to define the background of the fill pattern and uses FillColor for the lines in the pattern. But if you set BackStyle to Transparent, VFP ignores the BackColor property and shows any overlapped object.

Part
**III**

Ch
**11**

---

### Head TK

Many colors are created by *dithering*, mixing different colored pixels rather than by using pure pixel colors. Unfortunately, Windows cannot use a dithered color pattern in all places. So it stores the dithered pattern as the Color and a single pixel color as the Solid definition of the color.

As a result, your selected color may have a different Color and Solid appearance. To see this, open the Color dialog box and click the Define Custom Colors button. This may explain why the actual displayed color does not always look like the color selected from the color picker.

If you use a pattern fill rather than a color fill for a shape, you might expect to see traces of any object overlayed by the shape. Unfortunately, you will not. If BackStyle is Opaque, you cannot see through the pattern, and VFP instead fills the background with BackColor.

---

One last special feature of shapes is the SpecialEffect property. Set this property to 0 to give the border a three-dimensional effect. Unfortunately, there is no control over the direction of the light source or the width of the shadowing.

The default is an engraved border with the light source coming from the upper-left corner of the screen. However, the effect is very subtle, and it only works with rectangles and squares with no corner rounding (the curvature = 0 and the BorderWidth = 1).

**Circles and Ovals**   A circle or oval is nothing more than a square or rectangle with severe corner curvature. In fact, you can use the Curvature property to control how much to round the corners of a rectangle. A perfect rectangle has zero curvature. On the other hand, a perfect oval has a curvature value of 99. Values in between represent various degrees of corner curvature.

## Container Controls

You can create a container for a group of related controls. The properties for the container also affect the controls in it.  You can add objects, remove objects, and set the active control with the container properties.

One common use is to keep a label control as a caption to a a textbox control, grouping them together in one container. This allows the container to be enabled/disabled, which does the same for all objects in the container through the SetAll method.

If you right-click a container, VFP adds another option to your choices: Edit. Edit enables you to click an object in the container to edit it. Another method of choosing an object in a container is by pressing Ctrl+PgUp and Ctrl+PgDn, which moves you from object to object in the hierarchical structure of the container.

## Label Controls

 *Labels* are simple text strings added to a form to identify fields or to display fixed character information to the user. A label can be a single line or, with WordWrap set to .T., it can span several lines.

The most common label properties include the capability to change the font, size, and style. You also can define a background color or make the background transparent to show anything beneath it. A simple box border can also surround the text. Figure 11.15 shows several label examples.

**FIGURE 11.15**
Labels define fixed
text strings on forms.

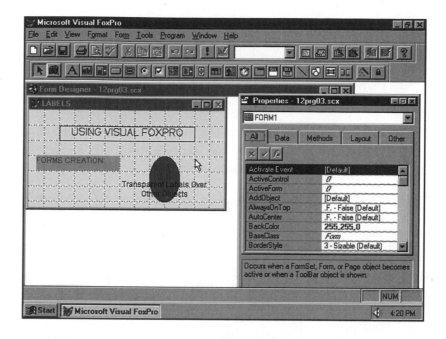

On the CD

Forms 11PRG02.SCX and 11PRG03.SCX on the samples disc show various styles of labels.

Labels do not have a data source. You enter the text directly into its caption property.
When the form is run, the user cannot edit or tab into a label.

Many objects have a Visible property. If you set this property to .F. when you define the
form, the object does not appear when you run the form. It is still there, just not visible.
This feature makes it possible to customize forms to display only those objects needed for
a specific process.

You can change the label Caption property dynamically, depending on certain conditions.
Suppose that you want to use the same form to enter both customer and employee address information. You want to display a label that says Employee Address when you edit
employee data and Customer Address when you edit customer data. You could define the
label Caption in the INIT method of the form this way:

```
IF plEditingCustomer      && logical to identify type of address
   AddressForm.AddressLabel.Caption = "Customer Address"

ELSE
  AddressForm.AddressLabel.Caption = "Employee Address"

ENDIF
```

# Text Box Controls

The primary difference between a label and a text box is their respective data source. For a label, the text is fixed in the Caption property for the object. A table field, on the other hand, often supplies the source for a text box. But it could also have its source defined by a memory variable.

The most common properties modified for a text box include those related to the color, font, size, and position of the text box—and, of course, the data source. Figure 11.16 shows an example of a text box labeled Text1.

**FIGURE 11.16**

Both text boxes and edit boxes display character strings, but edit boxes allow strings of more than 2 billion characters.

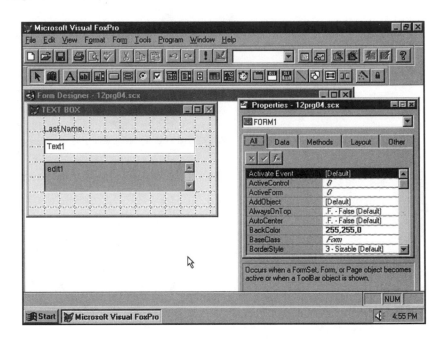

Form 11PRG04.SCX on the samples disc shows a typical text box.

In addition to the Visible property discussed with labels, text boxes (and other objects with data sources) have an Enabled property. When Enabled is .T., the user can move into the object. Of course, code associated with a When method may throw the user back out again. But if Enabled is set to .F., the When method never even executes.

In fact, you can visually display a disabled field differently from an enabled field by using different colors for the foreground and background. (See the previous discussions of the DisabledBackColor and the DisabledForeColor properties.) Using these properties rather than the Visible property lets the user know that the field or option exists, but that it cannot currently be selected.

> **TIP** To disable objects with the Enabled property, define different disabled foreground and back-
> ground colors, or make the object invisible. Don't confuse users by displaying disabled fields with
> the same colors as normal fields.

Another option when using controls with data sources is to make them Read Only. Use the Read Only property to let users view text without allowing them to change it. Text automatically continues on subsequent lines if the text box has enough height for more than one line.

Still, when it runs out of space, a text box must stop displaying the text. The maximum length of a character field defined in the Data page is 255 characters. For character data longer than this, use the edit box.

While it is possible to define a separate memo window to display memos bound to text fields, you may want to consider using the edit box controls.

## Edit Box Controls

The edit box enhances the capabilities of the text box. Primarily, it adds a vertical scroll bar, which enables the user to move through longer text faster by scrolling entire lines at a time.

Considering that an edit box allows up to 2,147,483,647 characters, scroll bars can be very important. Figure 11.16, earlier in this chapter, shows an edit box in the bottom half of the form. It uses most of the same features found in the text box.

A special property is Allow Tabs, which determines whether the user can use tabs in the text of the edit box. If you turn this option on, the user must press Ctrl+Tab to move to the next control (instead of Tab). Thus, if you allow tabs, be sure to indicate on the form that the user must press Ctrl+Tab to exit the field.

## Command Button Controls

 A command button on forms appears as a three-dimensional rectangle with text or a graphic, or both, inside it. Forms frequently use command buttons to make selections between sets of options. One of the more popular uses of command buttons is for navigating through a table. Typically, four buttons move the record pointer to the top, previous, next, or bottom of the file, respectively.

Other uses of command buttons include closing a form, quitting the application, or printing a report. In all cases, the primary event associated with a command button is Click. Clicking a button typically performs an action like moving to another record or exiting a form.

Part
**III**

Ch
**11**

However, command buttons have many other events, as listed in Table 11.8 earlier in this chapter. It is even possible to associate the value of a control button with a data source. Thus, you could theoretically use events such as When and Valid.

Figure 11.17 shows a CLOSE command button along with several other objects.

**FIGURE 11.17**

Buttons come in a variety of forms, including command buttons, option buttons, and button groups.

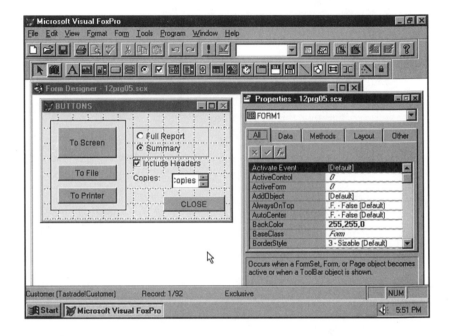

On the CD

Form 11PRG05.SCX on the samples disc shows various styles of command and option buttons, spinners, and check boxes.

Unlike many objects that enable you to control both the foreground and the background color, command buttons only allow you to set the foreground (the text). The Windows color set defines background color. But you can use different enabled and disabled foreground colors.

Another interesting feature of command buttons is their capability to display a bitmap image using the Picture, DisabledPicture, and DownPicture properties. All three properties enable you to select a BMP or DIB file to display in the button.

The Picture property defines the image to use when the button is "up." The DownPicture defines an image when the user clicks the button. Finally, the DisabledPicture defines an image when the button is disabled. A common image for the disabled picture is the "up" image with a red circle and slash over it.

Although any BMP image can be used, it must be small enough to fit in the command button without scaling. Otherwise, VFP truncates the portion that it cannot display. VFP does not scale the image. The To Screen button shown in Figure 11.17 shows an example of a bitmap on a command button.

## Command Group Controls

 You may want to define related command buttons as a group. The main advantage to using a group is that it enables you to place common code into a single method in the group. Refer again to Figure 11.17 and notice the three buttons in the box in the Buttons window. This box represents the border of a command group, not a rectangular shape.

The three buttons perform a similar action. They each route a report to a different destination. Rather than repeating the code necessary to generate the report in each button, it makes sense to combine them into a single object. The click event of the command group uses its Value property to determine which button the user pressed. The following code segment shows this:

```
DO CASE
  CASE This.Value = 1
    = MESSAGEBOX('REPORT SENT TO SCREEN')
  CASE This.Value = 2
    = MESSAGEBOX('REPORT SENT TO FILE')
  CASE This.Value = 3
    = MESSAGEBOX('REPORT SENT TO PRINTER')
ENDCASE
```

The Value property contains the number of the button clicked. VFP numbers buttons sequentially as you add them to a command group. The ButtonCount property must also be set to the number of buttons in the group.

To make one of the command buttons the default action (when the user presses Enter), change its Default property to .T. However, only one button on a form can serve as a default. You cannot set separate default buttons in a command group and an independent button, or set the buttons in two or more command groups.

## Option Group (Radio Button) Controls

 Radio buttons never appear alone. In fact, a single radio button does not make much sense—it would be like having only one button on your car radio. (Or like getting your car back from the mechanic only to find that all the radio buttons have been set to a single station: Car Talk—All Day, Every Day.)

The whole point of a set of radio buttons is to provide a series of choices from which the user must select one. Unlike a command group that a user can ignore, a group of radio buttons always has one button, and only one, selected.

Therefore, the most important property of a radio button (which VFP calls an *option group*) is ButtonCount. You must define this property before you can begin to label individual buttons. But before moving to the individual buttons, you may also want to define the default button.

By default, the first button becomes the default, but you can change the Value property in the option group to make any button the default. To make the second button the default, change the Value property to 2. This also sets the Value properties of each individual button. They have values of 0 (deselected) or 1 (selected).

Once you define the number of buttons in the option group, you can define their captions. Open the drop-down list at the top of the Properties dialog box. The individual radio buttons appear immediately beneath the option group. Figure 11.18 shows this list.

**FIGURE 11.18**

To access the properties of individual radio (option) buttons, open the object list in the Properties dialog box and select the option button you want.

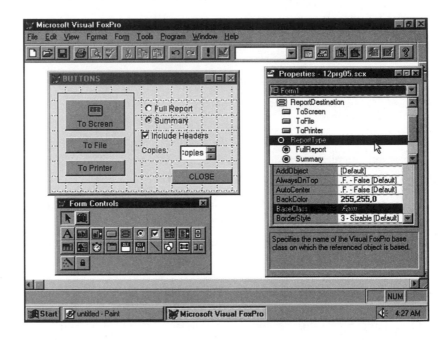

**N O T E**   By default, VFP assigns unique names to each object, beginning with the base class name and followed by a sequential number; that is unless you used the drag-and-drop method of adding controls to a form. The default sequential naming convention can be confusing, especially when you have several objects of the same base class. A better practice assigns individual names to each object.

A good choice is to base the name on the field name or label (see Figure 11.18). Next prefix the base name with one of the prefixes defined in Table 11.4 earlier in this chapter. An option group defining the report type might become cmgReportType. ■

As with command buttons, it is possible to use a picture with an option button but only if you first change the Style property to Graphical. Of course, this also makes the option button look like a command button. Also, with option buttons, it is possible to display text and graphics at the same time.

Remember, the key difference is that an option button always has a value selected. The selected option button remains pressed when selected.

Both command and option groups can display a border. Figure 11.18 shows the command group with the border on; the option group has the border off. Whereas the BorderStyle property determines whether a single line border exists, the BackStyle property determines whether to display it. With BackStyle set to transparent, VFP does not display the border and background color.

## Check Box Controls

 The next object displayed in Figure 11.18 is a check box. Check boxes usually represent individual logical fields or variables. An empty box traditionally means that the option is not selected. When the user selects a box, a check appears in the box.

Unlike command or option groups, check boxes work independently of each other. Thus, you can have any number of check boxes on a form. Furthermore, the user can select any, all, or none of them.

As with option buttons, it is possible to display a check box as a graphical button using the Style property. When displayed this way, it contains a bitmap image, as well as the caption.

If the button appears up, the option is not selected (has a value of 0 or .F.). If the button appears down, the value equals 1 or .T.. VFP determines whether to return a numeric or logical value, depending on the type of data source bound to the control.

Check boxes, however, can also have a value of 2. This state represents a .NULL. value, neither checked nor unchecked. In some applications, you may want to initialize check boxes to this value to determine whether the user made a selection or merely skipped it entirely. Visually, a check box with a .NULL. value appears as a shaded box.

## Spinner Controls

 The last control shown in Figure 11.18 is a *spinner,* which must have a numeric value as its ControlSource for the number of copies. The arrows to the right of the spinner allow the user to increment or decrement the spinner value. By default, the increment is 1.00, but you can change the Increment property to any value, including fractional values.

In addition to an Increment property, spinners have a range limit determined by the KeyboardHighValue, KeyboardLowValue, SpinnerHighValue, and SpinnerLowValue properties. Normally, the corresponding keyboard and spinner properties have the same value. The user cannot directly enter a value outside of this range or use the spinner arrow keys to go beyond it.

---

### Masking a Spinner Value

If you change the Increment property to a fraction such as 0.5 but you do not change the InputMask from something like ###, which represents a three-digit integer, the spinner does not increment properly. In fact, it does the increment but then rounds the result. And 1.5 rounds down to 1.0. So the spinner never goes anywhere.

Because spinners have a high and low value settings, the InputMask property must also accommodate these values or the spinner truncates the leading or trailing characters accordingly. This truncation is not just visual but physical as well.

For example, if you define SpinnerHighValue as 100 but define InputMask as ##, a 2-digit integer, the spinner never reaches 100. Every time it increments beyond 99, it exceeds the mask. It briefly displays ** but then it continues incrementing from 1 to 99.

---

## Image Controls

 *Images* consist of bitmaps saved as separate files. You can use them as logos on forms and reports. You cannot edit them; you can only display them. Figure 11.19 shows a form image using WINLOGO.BMP from the \WINDOWS directory.

 Form 11PRG06.SCX on the samples disc shows a bitmap of the Windows logo.

When VFP first inserts an image on a form, it defaults to the full size of the original bitmap. Of course, this may cause the image to overlap existing objects. You can either drag the other objects to a new position to make room for the image, or you can change the way VFP displays the image using the Stretch property.

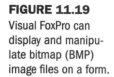

**FIGURE 11.19**
Visual FoxPro can display and manipulate bitmap (BMP) image files on a form.

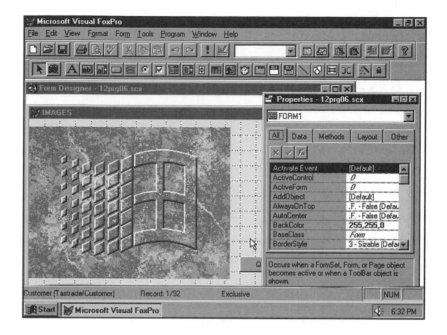

The Stretch property for an image identifies three ways to display an image:

0   Clip

1   Isometric

2   Stretch

If you select Clip, VFP clips the image as you reduce its size from its original. No matter which handle you use to resize the image, VFP always repositions the image, based on the new upper-left corner. Therefore, if it must clip the image, it clips the right and bottom sides as necessary, even if you moved the upper-left corner handle.

The second option is Isometric, which maintains the relative proportion of the height and width dimensions. So if you change the image area by cutting the width in half, Isometric automatically reduces the height by half, thus preserving the relative proportions of the original object.

The Stretch option changes the image display to fit the new object size. This technique distorts the relative dimensions of the image but does not clip it. Any dimension not changed remains the same size.

Therefore, resizing an image using the top- or bottom-center handles appears to "squash" the image. Use this method if you must resize an image to fit a very specific area and you don't care if its relative proportions change.

Part

III

Ch

11

# Examining Methods Associated with a READ Form

For all those developers who never really understood foundation READs, the good news is that they are no longer needed. READs are built into the new Form and Menu Designer. In fact, once you create a form, you only need to call the form with a DO FORM statement.

So where did all the options associated with a READ go? They simply became methods of the form. This section compares and contrasts the events associated with the new form definition and the clauses previously used with READ.

**N O T E**  The READ command remains in FoxPro for backward compatibility. It can be used with the new object form paradigm. Its basic syntax is:

```
READ
[CYCLE]
   [ACTIVATE IExpression1]
   [DEACTIVATE IExpression2]
   [MODAL]
   [WITH WindowTitleList]
   [SHOW IEexpression3]
   [VALID IExpression4¦nExpression]
   [WHEN IExpression5]
   [OBJECT nObjectNumber]
   [TIMEOUT nSeconds]
   [SAVE]
   [NOMOUSE]
   [LOCK¦NOLOCK]
   [COLOR SCHEME nSchemeNumber]
   [COLOR ColorPairList] ■
```

**N O T E**  An additional READ EVENTS command is a new command in VFP; it starts event processing. VFP then remains on the READ, watching for events and processing them until it encounters a CLEAR EVENTS command. Processing then continues on the line after READ EVENTS. ■

The following paragraphs show how the new form object uses each of the old READ clauses.

**CYCLE:** This clause allows the user to tab past the last object and return to the first object on the form. Similarly, Shift+Tab moves the user from the first form object to the last one. With the event paradigm, control automatically cycles through all objects until it encounters a CLEAR EVENTS or a TerminateRead property set to .T.

**ACTIVATE:** VFP executes this clause when it changes the current window. Form objects have an Activate event that performs a similar function. Code attached to this event can determine which form is active, and can hide or deactivate selected objects before READ begins monitoring events.

Visual FoxPro ignores any value returned by the Activate clause. As a result, you cannot control whether a form is activated with the ACTIVATE event. Rather, it defines code that executes when VFP activates the form. Users activate forms either by clicking the form object or by calling the SHOW method of the form.

 **TIP** The Init event not only provides a place for code that executes when you first create the form; it also returns a .T. or .F., determining whether to create the form or not.

**DEACTIVATE:** VFP executes the deactivate clause when you change the current window. You could call a user-defined function that perhaps performs a form-level validation. In any case, it must return a logical value. The READ terminates if the function returns a value of .T..

The new form object also has a Deactivate Event. However, it only triggers when the user moves from one window to another within the same application. To deactivate a form—removing it from the screen and memory—call the form's RELEASE method.

Alternatively, you can simply call the Hide method, which sets the form's Visible property to .F.. In this case, the form still exists in memory. Changing its Visible property to .T. redisplays it.

> **CAUTION**
>
> If you have two VFP applications running at the same time, the Activate and Deactivate event does not trigger if you switch between windows in different applications. It only triggers when the switch occurs between windows in the same application.

**MODAL and WITH:** These two commands work together to control which windows the user can activate. For example, if the program opens a single window with Modal, users cannot switch to another window by clicking it. They must exit the current window using whatever predefined close or quit method the window has. If the program needs to have two or more windows open, the windows must be listed using the WITH clause.

VFP uses the Show method both to open the form and to determine whether it is modeless or modal. The following command displays the modeless form—meaning that while the form opens, execution of the code continues:

```
Form1.Show(0)
```

Part

**III**

Ch

**11**

Listing 11.1 shows an example of this command.

**Listing 11.1   11PRG01.PRG**

```
MyWindow = CREATEOBJ('TestWind')
MyWindow.Caption = 'This window is MODELESS'
MyWindow.Show(0)
= MessageBox('Test program complete!')

DEFINE CLASS TestWind AS FORM
  ADD OBJECT Quit AS COMMANDBUTTON ;
    WITH Caption = 'QUIT', ;
         Top = 5, ;
         Left = 10, ;
         Height = 2, ;
         Width = 10
  PROCEDURE Quit.CLICK
    ThisForm.Release
  ENDPROC
    ENDDEFINE
```

The following command opens the modal form:

```
Form1.Show(1)
```

It prevents the user from switching to another window or letting the program continue executing until the form is closed. Listing 11.2 illustrates this point.

**Listing 11.2   11PRG02.PRG**

```
MyWindow = CREATEOBJ('TestWind')
MyWindow.Caption = 'This window is MODAL'
MyWindow.Show(1)
= MessageBox('Test program complete!')

DEFINE CLASS TestWind AS FORM
  ADD OBJECT Quit AS COMMANDBUTTON ;
    WITH Caption = 'QUIT', ;
         Top = 5, ;
         Left = 10, ;
         Height = 2, ;
         Width = 10
  PROCEDURE Quit.CLICK
    ThisForm.Release
  ENDPROC
    ENDDEFINE
```

If you do not include a parameter with Show, VFP uses the value in the WindowType property.

**N O T E** The parameter with Show overrides a form's WindowType. Similarly, a Form Set's WindowType overrides the individual form's WindowType property settings.

In a Form Set, a value of 2 for WindowType makes VFP work like READ. A value of 3 makes the forms in the Form Set behave as if they were activated with the older READ MODAL command. ■

**SHOW:** Previous versions of FoxPro used the READ SHOW clause to execute a command or user-defined function whenever it executed the SHOW GETS command. VFP's Show method for a form displays the form; instead, use the Refresh method. When you call the form's Refresh method, it refreshes the form and all the controls in it, as follows:

```
Form1.Refresh
```

This means repainting the form and its controls as well as updating their values.

But suppose only one object's value has changed. Repainting the entire form takes too much time. A faster method calls the Refresh method for the object only, as in:

```
Form1.TotalDue.Refresh
```

**VALID and WHEN:** Prior to VFP 3.0 the WHEN clause was used to determine whether to execute the READ. Thus, it expected a logical return value from an expression or user-defined function. If it got an .F. value, the READ would not execute. Similarly, VALID also used an expression or UDF to determine if it could exit the READ.

VFP forms do not allow a WHEN or VALID form level. Consider using an Activate method in place of a WHEN clause. To cancel the form, you can put a `Form.Release` command in the Activate code.

**OBJECT:** The old READ used the OBJECT clause to determine which object first received focus. Similarly, you could use a command such as the following to move focus to any object on-screen:

```
_CurObj = OBJNUM(LastName)
```

In the object world of VFP, the SetFocus Method serves this same purpose. Every object that allows user interaction allows this method. To deviate from the default tab order, simply issue a command like the following:

```
ThisForm.Spinner1.SetFocus
```

This command moves focus to an object named Spinner1. (Of course, you have to supply your own object names.)

**TIMEOUT:** The Timeout clause limits the amount of time that a READ remains in effect without a key being pressed. After that time elapses, FoxPro terminates the READ.

There is no direct equivalent to this command in VFP (unless you continue to use the old READ command). Yet VFP has a Timer control. It is possible to use this control to simulate the effect of TIMEOUT.

Part

**III**

Ch

**11**

## Create a Timeout for a Form

For you really dedicated developers who just have to know how to create a TIMEOUT for a form, follow these steps:

1. Create the form with all the objects you need on it.

2. Open the properties for the form. Then, using For<u>m</u>, New <u>P</u>roperty, add the ElapseTime and TimeOut properties. These appear at the bottom of the property list with a default value of .F.. Assign a value of 0.00 to ElapseTime and the number of seconds for your time-out in TimeOut.

3. Add a Timer object anywhere on the form. It is invisible during run time, so its position and size do not matter.

4. Set the Timer Interval property to 500. The timer interval can range from 0 to 2,147,483,647 ms. Because VFP actually uses the system clock, which only allows approximately 18 ticks per second, the real interval limit is about every 55.5 ms.

   Keep in mind the trade-off between interval checking and processing speed. If you do not really need more accuracy than every half second, use an interval of about half that or 250. For the purpose of a time-out, a value of 500 is fine.

5. Modify the Timer Event to include the following code:

   ```
   ThisForm.ElapseTime = ThisForm.ElapseTime + 0.5
   IF ThisForm.ElapseTime > ThisForm.TimeOut
           ThisForm.Release
   ENDIF
   ```

6. Add the following code to the Timer Reset Event:

   ```
   ThisForm.ElapseTime = 0.0
   ```

7. Select the form and modify the Keypress event by adding the following line:

   ```
   ThisForm.Timer1.Reset
   ```

Without the call to reset after every keypress, the time-out may expire before the user completes the entire form. This way, you can keep the time-out value smaller without interrupting normal work.

Also change the KeyPreview property to .T. so that the form keyboard event has priority. Observe that by putting the time reset in the form's Keypress event, you save the extra work of putting it in every object's Keypress event.

As an additional enhancement, you might display a message and play a .WAV file after the time-out interval expires. Reset the time-out. If the user still does not respond, close the form, hide it, or otherwise disable the system. You could even develop a password-protection routine using a modal window when the interval expires.

**NOMOUSE:** In previous versions of FoxPro, this clause prevented the user from using the mouse to move between fields. Its primary purpose was to force users to enter data and make selections in a sequential fashion. Because object-oriented programming strives to let users control how they run the program, this option has no equivalent.

**SAVE:** As with NOMOUSE, there is no equivalent for this clause in VFP.

**LOCK:** This clause tries to place locks on every record used by the edit fields in the screen. Visual FoxPro extends this concept with the BufferMode property. This property determines when to lock records, as defined in Table 11.11.

| Table 11.11 | BufferMode Record Locking |
|---|---|
| **Setting** | **Method** |
| 0 | None: Records are locked and fields are written when edited. |
| 1 | Pessimistic: Records are locked as soon as you begin editing any field. Fields are written back when the pointer moves. |
| 2 | Optimistic: Records are locked only when you try to write field data back. |

▶ **See** "Locking in Buffers," **p. 692**

**COLOR SCHEME and COLOR:** The properties for a Form do not allow the specification of a color scheme. However, they do allow you to set the foreground, background, and fill colors. On the other hand, individual objects allow foreground and background colors, as well as a color scheme and color source.

Setting the ColorScheme property to 0 tells VFP to use other standard color properties (ForeColor and BackColor). It also allows values from 1 to 24 to provide backward compatibility with FoxPro 2.x color schemes. To set a color scheme, you must use the SET COLOR SET command, which looks for the color set in the current resource file.

The ColorSource property has six possible values, as shown in Table 11.12.

| Table 11.12 | Color Source Property Values |
|---|---|
| **Source** | **Uses** |
| 0 | Uses object's color properties (BackColor and ForeColor). |
| 1 | Uses color properties of object's parent. |
| 2 | Uses object's color scheme. |
| 3 | Uses object's defaults from color scheme. |
| 4 | Uses Windows Control Panel 3-D colors. |
| 5 | Uses Windows Control Panel window colors. |

# Using Multiple Instances of a Single Form

VFP can work with multiple copies of the same form that is open at the same time. For example, you may need this capability if you want to interrupt data entry of one form instance because of missing information. Instead of losing data already entered or saving an incomplete record, you can leave the partially complete form open and open another.

VFP comes with a good example of multiple instance forms. To see it, select Sample Applications from the Help option of the main menu and run the Solutions Samples. Scroll down through the example list until you find, under Forms, Run Multiple Instances of a Form. Then click the Run Sample button; then press the Run Form button two or three times.

Figure 11.20 shows three separate instances of the form open at one time.

**FIGURE 11.20**
Running multiple instances of a form may allow users to work on several different entries.

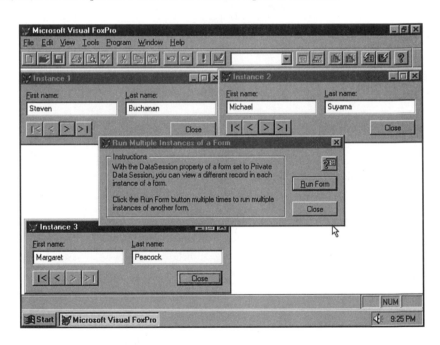

The controlling form is called LAUNCH.SCX. You can access it through the Sample Applications by choosing Open. It begins by defining a new array property in the form (similar to the way the time-out example created a new property). This array holds each instance of the form.

By using an array, you do not need to preplan or limit the number of instances created. Initialize the property aForms[1] to .NULL.. This creates the space in the array for the first instance but does not store anything yet.

The key code used to open multiple instances of the LAUNCH.SCX form appears in the Run Form command button. The click event contains the following code:

```
#define INSTANCE_LOC "Instance "
LOCAL nFormLeft, nFormTop, cFormCaption
nInstance = ALEN(THISFORM.aForms)


*Set the Top and Left Properties to Cascade the new Forms
IF nInstance > 1 AND TYPE('THISFORM.aForms[nInstance -1]') = 'O'
     nFormTop = THISFORM.aForms[nInstance -1].Top + 1
     nFormLeft = THISFORM.aForms[nInstance -1].Left + 1
ELSE
     nFormTop = 1
     nFormLeft = 1
ENDIF

*Set the caption to reflect the instance number
cFormCaption = INSTANCE_LOC + ALLTRIM(STR(nInstance))


* Run the form and assign the object variable to the array element
* The Linked keyword indicates that all instances will be released when
* the array is released. Without 'LINKED', the multiple instance forms
* would persist after the array is released
DO FORM Multi NAME THISFORM.aForms[nInstance] WITH ;
     nFormTop, nFormLeft, cFormCaption LINKED

*Redimension the array so that more instances of the form can be launched
DIMENSION THISFORM.aforms[nInstance + 1]
```

Part
III

Ch
11

Also in this form, the Close button's Click option defines code to release all forms. On the surface, it looks as if the Close button code merely releases the current form.

However, releasing a form also releases all of its properties. Because you linked the instances of the form MULTI.SCX to the array with the LINKED clause, this also releases all of its instances.

```
RELEASE ThisForm
```

Next, open the form that you want to create multiple instances of. First, change the DataSession property to 2—Private Data Session. This option tells VFP to open a separate data environment for each instance of the form. In the case of multiple instances, you cannot access the same files in the same data session simultaneously.

The rest of the form uses standard controls. There are two text boxes for the first and last names. The EMPLOYEE.DBF file is the control source for these. The four buttons that allow movement through the table come from the BUTTONS.VCX custom class. Finally, the OK button releases the form when clicked.

The net result is the ability to open multiple instances of a form, each with its own data environment. You can close each instance individually by clicking its OK button or close them all by clicking the main form's Quit button.

To reference the property of any instance, you can use the array. For example, the following line returns the last_name field in the second instance of the form:

```
Launch.aForms[2].LastName.Value
```

Notice that you have to reference the controlling form name because it holds the property that defines the object references to the instances.

# Working with Multiple Active Forms

You can work with multiple active forms by grouping them into a group control called a *form set*. The advantages of using Form Sets over calling separate forms with independent DO FORM statements include:

- It synchronizes the record pointers used by each form when you define the data environment at the Form Set level.

- You can Show and Hide all forms at one time.

- You can visually arrange multiple forms on-screen rather than use trial and error testing of positions.

To begin a Form Set, open or create the first form to include in the set. It does not matter if you need to create a new form. Once the Form Designer is active, it adds the Form pull-down menu in the main menu. One of the options in this menu is Create Form Set.

Selecting Form, Create Form Set automatically adds the current form to the set. To add additional forms, choose Add New Form from the Form menu. This opens a blank form. You cannot add a second existing form to a Form Set directly.

---

### Adding an Existing Form to a Form Set

Actually, there is a way to trick a Form Set into adding an existing form into a Form Set. Follow these steps:

1. Open the form you want to add in a normal Form Designer window.

2. Select Save As Class from the File menu. Assign a name to the form. This saves the form as a Class library with a VCX extension.

3. Select Tools, Options and display the Forms PageFrame. In the lower half, you can specify a default template for forms and Form Sets. Temporarily define the Form

---

template with the name of the class library you just created. Don't forget to first use the Controls page to register the class library.

4. Now return to the Form Set. Select Add New Form from the Form menu. Rather than giving you a blank form, VFP uses a copy of the existing form.

If you use this method to add an existing form to a Form Set, you must continue to maintain the original form and class library or make all changes to the form in the Form Set. Furthermore, if you delete or move the class library, the Form Set will fail!

## Referencing Objects in Other Forms of a Form Set

You can set the property of an object in a current form from another form by using a statement like the following:

```
ThisForm.Label1.Caption = ThisFormSet.Form2.Text3.Value
```

This expression takes the Value property from a text box named Text3 in a form named Form2 in the current Form Set. It then assigns it to the Caption property of a label named Label1 in the current form.

Similarly, you can set the property of an object in a different form of a Form Set using statements like the following:

```
ThisFormSet.Form2.Label2.Caption = 'Employee'
```

or

```
ThisFormSet.Form2.Label2.Caption = ThisForm.Text3.Value
```

The first of these two expressions assigns a fixed string to a label caption property in the form, Form2, of the current Form Set. The second expression uses a value from a text box named Text3 in the current form to update the same label caption.

It is easy to transfer data from one form to another in a Form Set as long as you remember the naming hierarchy needed to get to each object.

## Passing Control Between Windows

When you run a Form Set, VFP uses the order of the objects as defined in each individual form as the default tab sequence. It also uses the order in which the forms were added to the Form Set to define the tab order between separate forms.

When the user completes the objects in the first form, VFP smoothly moves focus into the next form, and so on. When the user reaches the last object of the last form, focus cycles back to the first object again.

Part
III
Ch
11

This process continues indefinitely unless one of the objects in one of the forms has the TerminateRead property set to .T. (only if WindowType is 2 or 3) or if it encounters a command like:

```
ThisFormSet.Release
```

This command releases all forms in the Form Set.

## Managing Windows

The WindowType property of Form Set can have one of four possible values, as shown in Table 11.13.

**Table 11.13  WindowType Values for Form Sets**

| Source | Uses |
| --- | --- |
| 0 | Modeless. Users can select any object in any form in the Form Set. They can also select from the menu or from other currently active forms. This option gives the user the most control. |
| 1 | Modal. Users can select any object in any form in the Form Set only. They cannot select from the menu or any other forms currently active. |
| 2 | Read. Execution stops on the command that activates the Form Set. The program only continues when the user closes the Form Set. |
| 3 | Read Modal. Execution stops on the command that activates the Form Set, but only those objects included in the WindowList property can be selected. Other objects in the Form Set and the menu cannot be accessed. |

**N O T E**  The last two options in WindowType (options 2 and 3) are included for backward compatibility but cannot be selected through the property list when you are using the Form Designer. ■

The ideal choice is either 0 or 1 for new application development. You want to give the user as much flexibility as possible in performing a task. You can control access to individual objects within a form by using the Enabled Property or even Hide.

Within the above limits defined by WindowType, the user can move to any object in any form by using the mouse—or the user can move programmatically with the SetFocus command.

# From Here...

Although this chapter covers the basics of creating a form, there are other form controls not covered here. Furthermore, you need to have a firm handle on object-oriented topics to help you understand how the new object-oriented forms work.

To learn more about how VFP builds and maintains forms, see the following chapters:

- Chapter 2, "Introducing Object-Oriented Programming," for an introduction of the concepts of object-oriented programming and its terms.

- Chapter 5, "Using Wizards for Rapid Application Development," to learn how to use Wizards to build basic functional application modules that you can later customize.

- Chapter 12, "A Deeper Look at Object-Oriented Design," for an examination of object-oriented concepts as they relate to form design, creation of custom classes, and control of applications through events.

- Chapter 13, "Advanced Form Design Controls," for a description of ways to use the more advanced custom controls available in VFP, including list boxes, combo boxes, page frames, and grids.

Part
III

Ch
11

# A Deeper Look at Object-Oriented Design

*by Rod Paddock and Michael P. Antonovich*

**V**isual FoxPro introduces FoxPro developers like you to the world of object-oriented programming. In Chapter 2, "Introducing Object-Oriented Programming," you learned how to begin implementing object-oriented techniques in code. Chapter 11, "Building Applications with Simple Form Structures," discussed ways to use the Form Designer tool, and how to begin using event-driven programming techniques. It's time to combine the capabilities of both of these tools into a basic framework from which you can begin developing your applications.

This chapter explores techniques used in developing object-oriented, event-driven architectures. Your first exploration begins with FoxPro's Visual Class Designer. The Visual Class Designer combines ease-of-use, found in the Form Designer, with the power of object-oriented programming. You will explore the abilities of the Visual Class Designer and learn how you can begin using its abilities now.

**Migration from the form designer to the visual class designer**

Because the interface for designing visual classes is the same as designing forms, the techniques that you learned in Chapter 11 apply here as well.

**How to develop an application framework**

Developing an application framework means building a set of classes in one or more libraries that can be used and reused not only in one application, but across all your applications.

**Techniques for using the Class Browser to maintain your class libraries**

The Class Browser allows you to examine the classes within a class library and to make modifications, deletions, and subclasses. You can also use it to copy classes from one library to another and to view the code behind any class, including forms.

**Techniques for trapping and understanding FoxPro's event model**

Visual FoxPro's event model is crucial to getting your application to do what you want when you want it. This section shows how to determine the event sequence for your forms.

Any chapter on object-oriented programming would be incomplete without a discussion of event-driven programming. Object-oriented programming and event-driven programming are often used synonymously. Objects receive messages to which they respond. This, in itself, is one of the principles of object-oriented programming. The latter parts of this chapter explore the use of event-driven programming techniques in FoxPro applications. ▪

# Making the Most of Inheritance

To discuss object-oriented programming, we first need to review some terms. Object-oriented programming can be compared to a cookbook that has lists of recipes. In object-oriented programming terminology, these recipes are defined as classes, and the cookbook is known as a class library. From these recipes (classes), you cook meals. In OOP terminology, these meals are known as objects or instances of objects.

Suppose that you have a section in your cookbook known as shrimp. You can have recipes for dozens of varieties of shrimp: popcorn, pineapple, garlic, and so on. These shrimp (class) recipes are known as subclasses. In a cookbook, each recipe has its own set of ingredients and a set of instructions for preparing the meal. The ingredients are known as properties, and the instructions are known as methods.

From these recipes and recipe books, you can begin building applications (meals). However, object-oriented programming adds a new capability to your recipes (classes). Any time you make a change to your recipes (classes), all the meals prepared from that recipe (objects) are instantly changed. This is known as inheritance.

The real power of object-oriented programming is found in its capability to reuse components. Rather than write specific programs for each aspect of an application, you can focus your time on creating a set of reusable components, which provide the foundation of an application.

# Using the Visual Class Designer

There are two components to object-oriented programming architecture. The first is a business object component. These types of objects are commonly developed using DEFINE CLASS and related object-oriented construction commands. The basics of this technique are covered in Chapter 2. The other component is a visual one. FoxPro provides a tool, known as the Visual Class Designer, that you can use to create the visual components of your application architecture.

Chapter 11, "Building Applications with Simple Form Structures," discusses using the Form Designer as a tool for designing data-input screens. However, the Form Designer has another hidden capability—that of providing FoxPro to you with a bridge into the object-oriented programming world. The FoxPro Form Designer has the capability to save any form or controls placed on a form as a class.

Sometimes you may start a form with specific controls with the intent to convert them into a custom class. Other times, you may be deep into the development of an application's form when you realize that a control you've added could, with a few changes, be reusable on other forms. In either case, creating a custom class with the Form Designer is a snap. Simply select an individual or a set of controls from a form and choose File, Save As Class (see Figure 12.1).

**FIGURE 12.1**

To save a text-box object as a visual class, use Save As Class, from the File menu.

After you choose File, Save As Class, FoxPro displays a dialog box requiring information for the class to be saved, as shown in Figure 12.2.

**FIGURE 12.2**

This dialog box enables you to save any combination of visual controls as a class.

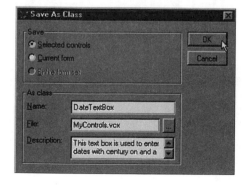

Part
III

Ch
12

The Save As Class dialog box provides the option of saving any of the following information: the selected controls, the entire form, or the entire formset. Upon choosing which portion of the form you want to save, you need to provide the Save As Class dialog box with a few more items. These items are:

- The name of the class you want it saved as.
- The name of the visual class library you want to save this class in. This library will normally end with a .VCX extension.
- A description of the class you are about to save.

**N O T E**   If you specify the name of an existing class name, VFP prompts you with this error:

```
Class '<classname>' already exists. Do you want to replace it?
```

On the other hand, if you specify the file name of a class library that does not exist, VFP assumes you want to create a new library. It does not display a message. Therefore, if you misspell the class file name, you create a new class library. ■

### TROUBLESHOOTING

**I created a new class in an existing class library, but when I went back to use it, it was not there.** You probably misspelled either the file name or the path. To correct this problem, open both class libraries in the Project Manager and drag the class name from one library to the other. You can keep or toss the original copy. If you keep both, changes made to one after the copy will not be reflected in the other. These are not shared definitions, like referencing the same file from multiple projects, but individual instances.

# Techniques for Developing an Application Framework

OOP's power lies in its capability to reuse components through inheritance. Through the power of inheritance, it is possible to make changes at the lowest possible level of applications and have these changes flow to all areas of the program.

When you are developing an application framework, it is desirable for inheritance to happen at the most primitive components possible. The most primitive components of FoxPro are the FoxPro base classes. Many of these base classes are found in the form designer. This is where a FoxPro foundation usually begins.

You begin a FoxPro framework by subclassing all the Visual FoxPro form controls. You begin this process by opening the Visual FoxPro Form Designer and placing one of each type of control onto the form. Then select each control individually and choose File, Save As Class from the FoxPro menu (as shown in Figure 12.2). After you do this, you must provide the required information to save each component to be subclassed.

After subclassing each control, you can use the visual class designer to extend the capabilities of the framework.

## Exploring the Visual Class Designer

After you create the necessary base classes with the form designer, you can modify them with the Visual Class Designer. Modifying classes begins with the MODIFY CLASS command. When you issue the MODIFY CLASS command in the Command window, VFP presents a dialog box prompting you to select the class to modify (see Figure 12.3).

**FIGURE 12.3**
The Open dialog is activated upon typing MODIFY CLASS in the command window, but defaults to show visual class libraries.

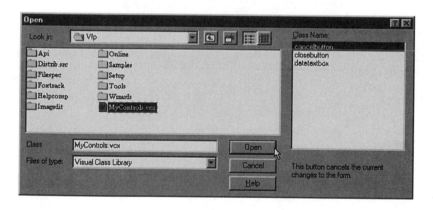

To select the class to modify, first select the appropriate class library, then select the class to modify and either double-click it or select Open from the dialog box. After selecting the class to modify, FoxPro activates the Visual Class Designer, which enables you to add new properties and methods to a class, as well as specify and include a file for a class. It also enables you to specify icons and other descriptive information to be presented when the visual class is used in the FoxPro Form Designer.

## Adding Debug Code to Controls

Because an object-oriented framework provides the foundation of all development processes, it should aid in the development process as much as possible. Developers spend a large part of their development process debugging code. With the use of object-oriented techniques, you can provide extended debugging abilities to the development process at the most basic level, yet not add greatly to development efforts.

One of the new enhancements to Visual FoxPro is its capability to use Include files, which enables you to define constants that will have their values substituted into a FoxPro program when it is compiled. The biggest advantage of Include files is that you can change code and the values of variables at the most primitive level, and have the benefits of these changes occur through a simple recompile of an application.

▶ **See** "Using Error Events in Objects," **p. 675**

## Including External Files in Objects

The Visual Class Designer enables you to specify an Include file for a visual class. Upon subclassing each FoxPro control, you should then specify an include file for each of them. You can specify an Include file by choosing Class, Include File. You then specify the name of the file to be included in the visual class (see Figure 12.4).

**FIGURE 12.4**
The Include File dialog box specifies the FRAMWORK.H header file.

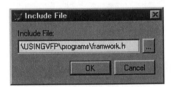

FoxPro Include files (usually ending with an .H extension) can contain only #DEFINE and #IF statements. #DEFINE statements enable you to define a constant variable that will have its value substituted into the compiled program. The syntax for #DEFINE is as follows:

```
#DEFINE CCLANGUAGE "ENGLISH"
```

During compile time, whenever FoxPro encounters the string CCLANGUAGE, it substitutes that string with the character value "ENGLISH" in the compiled program. One feature of this technique is its capability to add and remove programming code at compile time.

A common debugging technique is to have code that executes only during the development cycle, debug code. With the use of an Include file, you can add debugging code to your framework that can be removed when you compile and send this application to your customers. The code in Listing 12.1 demonstrates how to add and remove code at compile time using the header in Listing 12.2.

**Listing 12.1  12PRG01.PRG**

```
**-- 12PRG01.PRG
#INCLUDE FRAMWORK.H

SET ASSERT ASSERTMODE

ASSERTCMD "You are in TEST.PRG"
```

**Listing 12.2  FRAMWORK.H**

```
**-- FRAMWORK.H
**-- OOP Framework header file

*-- Uncomment this line to insert assert function
*-- calls into program files
#DEFINE DEBUGMODE = .T.

*-- Uncomment this line to remove assert calls
*#DEFINE DEBUGMODE = .F.

*-- Set debug mode options
#IF DEBUGMODE
   #DEFINE ASSERTMODE ON
   #DEFINE ASSERTCMD ASSERT .F. MESSAGE
#ELSE
   #DEFINE ASSERTMODE OFF
   #DEFINE ASSERTCMD *
#ENDIF
```

Part III
Ch
12

This example uses the new ASSERT command, which has this syntax:

```
ASSERT iExpression MESSAGE cMessageText
```

Normally, you would use the iExpression value to determine whether the message that follows is displayed in a message box. As unusual as it sounds, iExpression must return a logical value of .F. for the message to display. You must also set ASSERT on to activate the ASSERT commands.

In this example, the sole purpose of the define statements is to turn the ASSERT commands on or off, depending on the value of the constant debugmode. The point is that you can switch from debug mode to normal run mode by changing one line in the Include file and recompiling the application.

# Extending the Framework with Properties and Methods

Another feature in the visual class designer is its capability to add new properties and methods to visual classes. You can add new properties or methods to a visual class by choosing Class, New Property or Class, New Method.

Choosing Class, New Property or Class, New Method brings up the New Property or New Method dialog box, respectively (see Figures 12.5 and 12.6).

**FIGURE 12.5**
The New Property
dialog box defines the
Master Table property.

**FIGURE 12.6**
The New Method
dialog box defines the
Add Customer
method.

These dialog boxes require the following information to be filled in:

- The name of the property/method to be added to the class.
- An optional description of the property to be added. For properties, this description appears at the bottom of the property sheet whenever the custom property is selected.
- A check box that enables you to protect this property/method from modification from the external environment.

The name of the property is limited to 32 characters. The Visual FoxPro naming standard for a custom property states that the first letter of the property should specify its data type. The naming convention for a custom method states that the first character of its name should begin with the data type of that method's return value. For example, cFormMasterTable specifies a property that is a character data type; lAddCustomer() specifies a method that returns a logical value.

# Protecting Properties and Methods

One of the benefits of object-oriented programming is its capability to encapsulate data. The best method of encapsulation comes in the form of protected properties and methods, which prevent themselves from being accessed by code outside of the respective object. You can begin using protected properties and methods by checking the protected option in the New Property and New Method dialog boxes. After checking this option, the new property/method is accessible only from methods found inside the defined class. These properties are protected from modification from external objects or code.

Why would you want to protect properties or methods? A common set of properties you may want to protect are system user IDs and system access levels. Protecting properties and methods protects objects from intrusions by external code, thereby preventing bugs. Protecting properties and methods also enables you to completely change the way a property is initialized and accessed without causing a complete rewrite of system code.

A technique used for accessing and changing protected properties is known as GET/SET programming, which means there is a method defined for initializing (setting) a property and a method for retrieving (getting) a property. The code in Listing 12.2 illustrates a global password class using this GET/SET technique.

**Listing 12.2   12PRG02.PRG**

```
* Program 12PRG02.PRG
* Getting and Setting Protected Properties

go_globals = CREATEOBJECT("PROTECTED_GLOBALS")
go_globals.setuserid("TASHA")
? go_globals.getuserid()

DEFINE CLASS PROTECTED_GLOBALS AS CUSTOM
   PROTECTED cUserid

   *-- Returns the user ID
   FUNCTION getuserid
      RETURN this.cUserid
   ENDFUNC

   *-- Sets the user ID
   FUNCTION setuserid
   LPARAMETER cNewPassWord
      this.cUserid = cNewPassWord
      RETURN
   ENDFUNC
ENDDEFINE
```

Part
III

Ch
12

# Developing Objects Using Generalized Code

Upon establishing the base controls for a framework, more specialized components will be developed. To develop specialized components, you need to write them so they are generic, yet useful enough for the development process. The code technique used for these types of components is known as generalized coding.

# Referencing Objects Using FoxPro Access Variables

Visual FoxPro provides some very useful system variables that can be used to write generalized code, called object reference variables. The object reference variables commonly used to develop generalized components are THIS, THISFORM, and THISFORMSET.

When developing an application framework, the bulk of coding effort is spent coding the base classes from which applications are developed. Because these base classes are going to be instantiated into objects, it is not possible to know the names of the objects that are created. Therefore, you need to write code that addresses an object in a general manner, which is why object reference variables become crucial in the process of writing generic objects.

To create generic objects, you need to understand how objects can be referenced in FoxPro. The first object reference variable that you will explore is the THIS object reference, which provides a self-reference to an object.

A pseudocode example would say:

This text box's background color is GREEN.

The Visual FoxPro code for this command would be:

```
THIS.BACKCOLOR = RGB(0,255,0).
```

The THISFORM and THISFORMSET object references deal with a concept known as containership. Buttons, text boxes, check boxes, and other form objects cannot exist outside a form—they are contained within a container. From time to time, you want to address properties or methods found from a parent container, and THISFORM and THISFORMSET object references provide this access. The following code illustrates a common type of control (a next record button) that uses a property of the parent form. The property that it references is the cpTableName property. It is common to assign a property to a parent class so you don't have to provide that property for each component of a container.

```
SELECT (THISFORM.cpTableName)
SKIP 1
IF EOF()
      WAIT WINDOW "Last Record Reached" NOWAIT
      GO BOTTOM
ENDIF
THISFORM.REFRESH()
```

The following example illustrates ways to access both a property and a method from a container object. The SELECT (THISFORM.cpTableName) command accesses the cpTableName property of this control's form. The THISFORM.REFRESH() line accesses the REFRESH() method for the base form. If this form were a member of a formset, you would use syntax that referenced the object with a THISFORMSET.FORMNAME object reference variable.

```
SELECT (THISFORM.cpTableName)
SKIP 1
IF EOF()
      WAIT WINDOW "Last Record Reached" NOWAIT
      GO BOTTOM
ENDIF
THISFORM.REFRESH()
```

# Setting Class Information

When a class definition is complete, it is possible to specify a few more items of information. Choosing the Class, Class Info options from the FoxPro menu presents the Class Info dialog box, as shown in Figure 12.7.

**FIGURE 12.7**
The Class Info dialog box is used for defining icons associated with a new class, the OLE type, scale units, and a description.

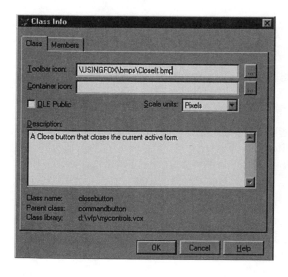

The Class Info dialog box is a Windows-tabbed dialog box that enables you to define additional parameters for your class library. There are two pages: a Class page and a Members page. The Class page, shown in Figure 12.7, enables you to specify the name, description, and graphical parameters for a particular class definition.

The Class page lets you define many of the graphical aspects of a visual class. Each visual class is a member of a class library. In the framework you developed, all the FoxPro controls were subclassed into a new library. During the development process, these controls are used in the form designer (see next section).

Visual FoxPro enables you to specify the Toolbar icon for each control. This icon can be specified in the Class Info dialog box. When you enter a value in the Toolbar Icon field, that icon is used when your class library is selected in the form designer. The other properties that you can specify are:

- Class Name: the name of the class
- Container Icon: icon used by the Visual Class Browser provided with Visual FoxPro
- OLE Public: specifies this class as a custom OLE server that can be accessed by an Automation client. It adds the OLEPUBLIC keyword to the DEFINE CLASS statement.
- Scale Units: the units of scale for the control (Pixels or Foxels)
- Description: a description of the class

The Members page protects the methods and properties of a defined class and controls the behavior of custom classes (see Figure 12.8).

**FIGURE 12.8**

The Class Info Members page for the command button base class shows all members (properties and methods), their visibility, and whether the class Init method is executed for subclasses.

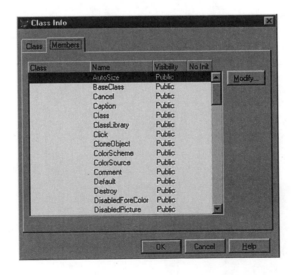

The Members page enables you to further modify some of the encapsulation and inheritance features of a defined class. In this page, you can control two attributes of the components of this class by clicking the Modify button to display the dialog box shown in Figure 12.9.

**FIGURE 12.9**
Use the Modify button of the Class Info dialog to change the Visibility of the property or method or set the Init function.

The first attribute defines the visibility of a method/property. The three options here are public, protected, or hidden. By default, all properties are public and can be seen by any code that can see the object itself. If the property is protected, its value cannot be seen or changed from outside the class or subclass. Finally, there are hidden or private properties. These are properties that can be accessed only by the methods of the class itself. Even subclasses cannot reference these properties with their methods.

The second and more interesting attribute is the No Init property. Whenever an object is instantiated, its Init() method is called. If the Init() method returns false, that object and its container object are not instantiated. You can prevent the Init() method of class from being called by checking the No Init clause. Commonly, the Init method of an object initializes variables and opens files that might be used by an object. When you subclass an object, you might want to control the initialization of properties or open files in one place. This is where it would be useful to override an Init() method.

# Extending the FoxPro Development Environment

The most significant aspect of the framework is that you subclassed all of FoxPro's controls. Now you can begin using this class library in the FoxPro form designer.

There are several ways to activate your class library in Visual FoxPro. The first is to select the View Classes option from the Form Controls toolbar (see Figure 12.10).

**FIGURE 12.10**

This pop-up menu opened by right-clicking the View Classes button shows one way to add a class library to the FoxPro development environment.

## Specifying Default Class Libraries

Initially, the class library is not included in the list of available class libraries. To include it in the list, select the Add option from the pop-up menu. This option displays the File Open dialog box, in which you can specify the class library you want to open.

Upon opening a class library, the Form Controls Toolbar items are replaced with the components of the specified development library. If icons were specified for a class, they are displayed in the toolbar. Otherwise, the Standard Control icon displays for each control. By default, FoxPro does not load your class libraries to the list of available libraries—this needs to be specified through Options. To specify which libraries to load, go into the Tools, Options, Controls page and add libraries into the dialog box (see Figure 12.11).

**FIGURE 12.11**

The Controls tab of the Options dialog box enables users to specify default class libraries.

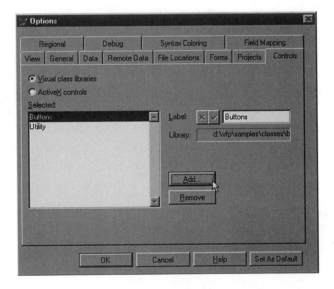

To make these options permanent, click the Set as Default button at the bottom of the Options screen.

## Specifying a Template Form

Visual FoxPro enables you to specify a template form from which all new forms are inherited. To specify this base form, go into the Tools, Options, Forms page, as shown in Figure 12.12. This page enables you to specify a template class.

**FIGURE 12.12**
The Forms tab of the Options dialog box enables users to specify a default form.

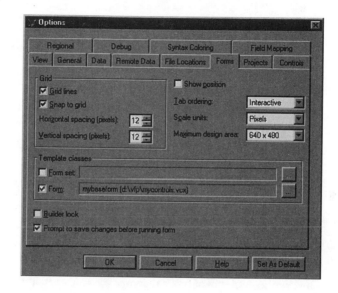

After selecting the form or formset option, you need to select a form class from one of your specified libraries.

# Using the Class Browser

Because of the complexity associated with developing robust class libraries, Visual FoxPro provides a visual tool for maintaining class libraries, the Class Browser (shown in Figure 12.13). It enables you to view, add, and modify contents of their class libraries. By using the Class Browser, you can subclass classes, delete classes, and rename classes. You can also select classes you want to view by specifying wildcard names of the classes.

The class browser is invoked by typing DO \VFP\BROWSER.APP from the command line or by choosing Tools, Class Browser. Upon invoking the Class Browser, you then specify which class library you want to browse. Then, select a class from the library. Upon your selecting a class, the Visual Class Designer's wide range of features becomes available to you.

**FIGURE 12.13**

The Class Browser dialog box shows the class library BUTTONS.VCX supplied in \VFP\SAMPLES\ CLASSES.

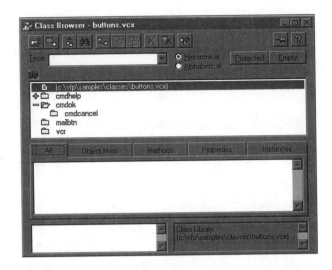

When you first open the Class Browser, the selected library appears in the scrollable list box on the left. The Open button in the toolbar enables you to open any class library to which you have access. When you use the Open button, the Class Browser automatically closes any previously opened class library. If you want to see the classes in more than one class library at a time, use the View Additional File button.

While you can view the contents of more than one class library at a time using a single instance of the Class Browser, you cannot copy a class from one library to the other using this method. You can, however, open a second instance of the Class Browser and then open a different class library in each instance. Now you can drag and drop classes between the two Class Browsers.

With more than one class library selected, the Class Browser displays the class library names first followed by an alphabetical list of the names from all open libraries. If an object itself contains addition subclasses, they appear as indented items. In Figure 12.14, cmdcancel is a subclass of cmdok. To create a subclass of an object, simply click the New Class button and enter a name for the new class as shown in Figure 12.14.

When you create a new class, VFP immediately opens the Class Designer to allow changes to the new class. You can, however, always enter the Class Designer for any existing class by simply double-clicking it.

**FIGURE 12.14**

Use the Class Browser to subclass the Help command button and define an Index button.

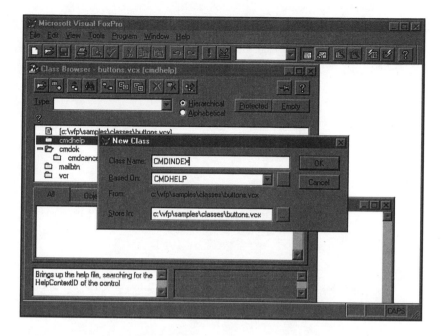

The Find option enables you to search the class names, class descriptions, property/method names, and their descriptions to find a specific text string. For example, you could search for the objects that contain the word ADD in their class names or property/method names.

To delete a class, simply highlight it and click the Remove button. Because the class library information is stored as a table, you need to occasionally pack the table with the Clean Up Class Library button. Until you pack the library to do this, you cannot add a new class with the same name as one that was removed.

You can also rename an object or redefined parent class of the selected class. As you build increasingly complex class libraries, the Redefine feature may be a valuable way to move a subclass to a different level. However, one of the more interesting things to do is to look at the code for the object.

To view the code, click the View Class Code button. This opens a window in which the Class Browser displays the code that defines the class as shown in Figure 12.15 for the VCR class. If you defined the class visually, you probably needed to set only a few properties and maybe add a few lines of code for a method or two. You can, however, define all classes with code, if you prefer. As one means of learning how to define your own classes, you can first visually design a class and then view the code required for the class with this button.

Part
III

Ch
12

**FIGURE 12.15**

Use the Class Browser to view the code associated with any class.

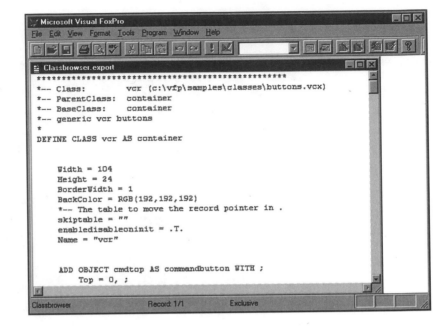

Although the capability to generate the equivalent code for a visually designed class is cool, the code is only viewable. You cannot edit the code and save the changes. You can, however, select it, copy it to the Clipboard, and then paste it into a program file. If you do this, you can use the class without referencing the original class library. Obviously, if you do this, changes made to the class library are not reflected in the copied code later.

As interesting as this may be, there is still another trick up the Class Browser's sleeve. You can use it to view the code for a screen. In FoxPro 2.x, you needed to generate code from the screen definitions that the Screen Designer created. FoxPro 2.x compiled the generated code. It did not read the screen definition tables. This created problems. You would use the Screen Designer to create the initial screen code and then make modifications to the screen code rather than go back into the Screen Designer. This was Okay as long as no one ever needed to go back into the Screen Designer; but, the moment someone did and regenerated code from the Screen Designer, the changes, added directly to the screen code, would be overwritten.

To solve that problem, Visual FoxPro compiles directly out of the screen definition tables. It does not need to generate a separate screen code file first. For those of us just learning object-oriented programming, it is nice to be able to see some of the code needed. The Class Browser lets us see the code for any object. Simply click the Open or View Additional File buttons, as shown in Figure 12.16, and select Form in the Files of type combo box of the Open dialog box.

**FIGURE 12.16**
Use the Class Browser to view the code required to create a form with all its objects, properties, and methods.

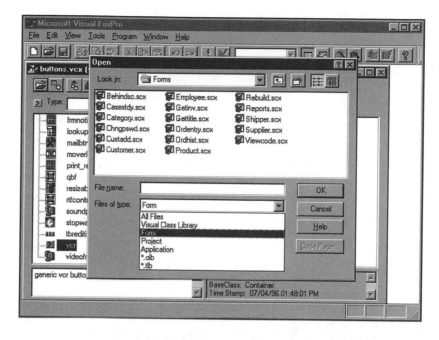

Now select a form from your system and click OK. (The forms shown in this figure are from the Tastrade example.) Then, simply select the form in the class list and click the View Class Code button. Figure 12.17 shows the beginning of the code generated for the customer form of the Tastrade example.

**FIGURE 12.17**
The Class Browser can generate and display code for any form.

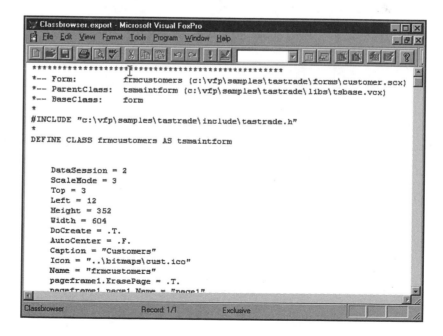

Back in the Class Browser, you may have noticed the frame at the right of the Class Browser. The  Class Browser uses this frame to display the names of custom properties and methods for the selected class. If the current class is defined as a set of objects, such as the VCR buttons class, this frame lists the objects that define the class. If the currently selected class has none of these characteristics, the frame appears empty.

The two edit boxes at the bottom of the dialog box provide descriptive information. The box on the left displays the Class Description for the selected class. This text field is user-editable. On the other hand, the Member Description box on the right can be edited only for methods and properties. The rest of the time, this box is used to display information for the library itself, its classes, its object members, and instances and cannot be changed here.

# Building Your Own OLE Server

As mentioned earlier, one of the properties of a class is the OLE Public option in the Class Info dialog box. When this option is set, VFP places the clause OLEPUBLIC at the end of class DEFINE statement. The code example in Listing 12.3 is the code created for a class named SPLITFILENAME. This class dissects a file name passed to one of its properties. It splits the file name into drive, directory, file, and extension components.

**Listing 12.3   12PRG03.PRG**

```
* Program 12PRG03
*****************************************************
*-- Class:        splitfilename (c:\vfp\spltname.vcx)
*-- ParentClass:  custom
*-- BaseClass:    custom
*-- This object splits a file name into its components
*
DEFINE CLASS splitfilename AS custom OLEPUBLIC

      *-- Full Filename passed to object by user
      fullname = ""
      *-- Drive Letter of the passed filename
      filedrive = ""
      *-- Path of the file passed to this object
      filepath = ""
      *-- Filename of the file passed
      filename = ""
      *-- Extension of the file passed
      fileextension = ""
      Name = "splitfilename"

        *-- Splits the fullname into its components
```

```
PROCEDURE splitname
    LOCAL lcFileTemp, lnSlash, lnDot

    lcFileTemp = This.FullName
    IF EMPTY(lcFileTemp)
      MESSAGEBOX("No filename has been set yet", 64, ;
          "Missing Filename")
    ELSE
      IF NOT (":" $ lcFileTemp)
        This.FileDrive = SYS(5)
      ELSE
        IF NOT (AT(":", lcFileTemp)=2)
          MESSAGEBOX("Filename Format Unknown", 64, ;
              "Bad Format")
          RETURN
        ELSE
          This.FileDrive = LEFT(lcFileTemp,2)
          lcFileTemp = SUBSTR(This.FullName,3)
        ENDIF
      ENDIF

      lnSlash = RAT("\", lcFileTemp)
      IF lnSlash = 0
        This.FilePath = ""
      ELSE
        This.FilePath = LEFT(lcFileTemp, lnSlash)
        lcFileTemp = SUBSTR(lcFileTemp, lnSlash+1)
      ENDIF

      This.FileName = lcFileTemp
        lnDot = AT(".", lcFileTemp)
      IF lnDot = 0
        This.FileExtension = ""
      ELSE
        This.FileExtension = SUBSTR(lcFileTemp, lnDot+1)
      ENDIF
    ENDIF

    RETURN
ENDPROC


PROCEDURE Init
    This.FileDrive = ""
    This.FilePath = ""
    This.FileName = ""
    This.FileExtension = ""
    This.FullName = ""
ENDPROC


ENDDEFINE
*
*-- EndDefine: splitfilename
**************************************************
```

By itself, this class definition does not automatically work as an OLE Server. However, you could call it directly as a custom class with the code in Listing 12.4.

---

**Listing 12.4    12PRG04.PRG**

```
close all
clear all
clear

SET CLASSLIB TO "\VFP5BOOK\PROGRAMS\CHAP12\SPLTNAME.VCX"

myfile = CREATEOBJECT("SPLTNAME.SPLITFILENAME")
myfile.FullName = "\VFP\JOB.DBF"
myfile.SPLITNAME
? myfile.FullName
? myfile.FileDrive
? myfile.FilePath
? myfile.FileName
? myfile.FileExtension
```

---

To make it an OLE Server, you must compile the class library into a DLL that FoxPro recognizes. The additional steps you must take are:

1.  Create a project for the class library.

2.  Add a dummy main program to the project—for example, a program with this line:

    ```
    MESSAGEBOX("My Special Utilities")
    ```

    It does not matter what is in the main program; the code does not execute when you use it as an OLE Server. The compiler, however, expects a main program, and the class library itself cannot serve as the main program.

3.  Select Project Build to open the Build Options dialog box.

4.  Select Build OLE DLL and click OK to create the DLL file. This step creates a file with the extension of DLL and one with the extension REG.

5.  From the Windows Explorer, run the registration file (REG) to register the OLE Server.

6.  In your code, use CREATEOBJECT or GETOBJECT with the following syntax:

    ```
    MyObject = CREATEOBJECT("<DLLNAME>.<CLASSNAME>")
    ```

The code in Listing 12.5 shows an example of using the class defined earlier to split a file name into its components.

**Listing 12.5   12PRG05.PRG**

```
* Program 12PRG05.PRG
* Using a OLE Server created from a FoxPro class
close all
clear all
clear

myfile = CREATEOBJECT("datadict.SPLITFILENAME")
myfile.FullName = "\VFP\JOB.DBF"
myfile.SPLITNAME
? myfile.FullName
? myfile.FileDrive
? myfile.FilePath
? myfile.FileName
? myfile.FileExtension
```

When you use the CREATEOBJECT or GETOBJECT function, the order in which VFP searches for the object definition is:

1. The Visual FoxPro base classes

2. Class definitions in memory in the order loaded

3. Class definitions in the current program

4. Class definitions in the .VCX class libraries opened with SET CLASSLIB

5. Class definitions in procedure files opened with SET PROCEDURE

6. Class definitions in the Visual FoxPro program execution chain

7. The OLE Registry

To use the OLE Registry, Visual FoxPro must first load OLE support. This reduces performance but must be done only once because it reduces the available memory for the current application, as well as any concurrent ones. Note also that the example assumes that the DLL is in the same directory as the program. Otherwise, you must include the full path for the DLL in the CREATEOBJECT statement.

Part
III

Ch
12

# Extending the Framework into the World of Events

Because Visual FoxPro exists in an event-driven world, you must be aware of the sequence and types of events that affect their object design. This section defines ways to use events within the context of object design and illustrates some techniques you can use to extend the capabilities of your object framework.

## Determining Common Control Events and Their Order

The most important aspect of event-driven programming is understanding the order of events and what caused events to fire. Each control in the FoxPro environment has literally dozens of events you can code for. Only a small percentage of these events, however, is used in actual applications. There is no immediate formula for determining which events are most common. This is dependent on the applications you develop. If your application uses the drag-and-drop capabilities of Visual FoxPro, this presents a different set of events than if your application is heavily push-button-driven.

The easiest way to determine the order in which events are triggered when your application runs is to create a simple form. Place on the form only those controls for which you want to determine an event sequence.

## Using Event Tracking

Open the Debugger, and select the file for which you want to track the events. Select Tools, Event Tracking to display the Event Tracking dialog box, as shown in Figure 12.18.

**FIGURE 12.18**
The Event Tracking dialog box allows you to determine which events you want to echo statements from in the Debug Output window.

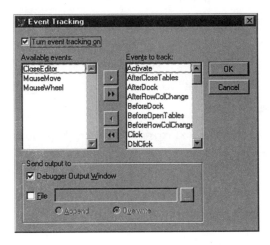

You select which events you want to track. By default, all events are preselected, but event tracking is not enabled. Click the check box at the top of the dialog box to enable Event Tracking. To move an event from one list to the other, select it; then click one of the buttons between the two lists. You can also double-click an event to move it from one list to the other.

The second half of the dialog box determines where VFP sends the output from event tracking. By default, VFP send messages to the Debug Output window of the Debugger. For large programs, however, this list can get rather large, and you may want to send it to a file and use the FoxPro Editor to search for specific event occurrences. Figure 12.19 shows an example of the Debug Output window with several event-tracking messages.

**FIGURE 12.19**

The Debug Output window shows an example of the output from the event-tracking feature of the Debugger.

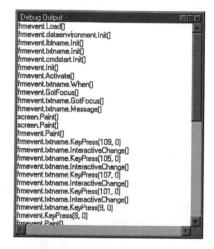

```
Debug Output
frmevent.Load()
frmevent.dataenvironment.Init()
frmevent.lblname.Init()
frmevent.txtname.Init()
frmevent.cmdstart.Init()
frmevent.Init()
frmevent.Activate()
frmevent.txtname.When()
frmevent.GotFocus()
frmevent.txtname.GotFocus()
frmevent.txtname.Message()
screen.Paint()
screen.Paint()
frmevent.Paint()
frmevent.txtname.KeyPress(109, 0)
frmevent.txtname.InteractiveChange()
frmevent.txtname.KeyPress(105, 0)
frmevent.txtname.InteractiveChange()
frmevent.txtname.KeyPress(107, 0)
frmevent.txtname.InteractiveChange()
frmevent.txtname.KeyPress(101, 0)
frmevent.txtname.InteractiveChange()
frmevent.txtname.KeyPress(9, 0)
frmevent.KeyPress(9, 0)
frmevent.Paint()
```

By studying the output from the event-tracking option, you can determine the order in which various events fire between objects. Use this knowledge to help determine where to place your code. The example consists of a single form with just three controls: one label, one text box, and one command button. Following are some observations that you can make from the event-tracking output:

The form Load event occurs before anything else.

The DataEnvironment initialization occurs after loading the form, but before the form is initialized, or the initialization of any other control on the form. This is absolutely necessary to ensure that the data is available for the controls that are bound to tables.

Before the form is initialized, all the controls on the form are initialized. If any of the controls returns a value of .F. (false) in their INIT( ) code, the rest of the controls and the form itself are not initialized; nor is the destroy event called.

Next, the form Initializations occurs. During this event, you can include code that requires knowledge of actual data in the tables. You can also set the record pointer of the tables opened in the DataEnvironment or the form Load events. If the form initialization event returns a value of .F. (false), the form is not activated, and the destroy event is not called.

Assuming that all initializations are successful, the form itself can be activated. This is followed immediately by the WHEN( ) event of the first control. If the WHEN( ) event is successful, the form received focus, followed by the control. If the WHEN( ) event returns .F. (false), VFP tests the WHEN( ) event of the next control. If none of the controls can receive focus, the form itself cannot receive focus.

After a control gets focus, other events can occur, such as KeyPress( ) and mouse-related events.

Each time the user presses a key in a text field, the KeyPress event occurs first and passes two parameters. The first is the Key value, which identifies the key pressed; the second parameter determines whether the key was pressed along with the Alt or Ctrl key. After each KeyPress, VFP executes the Interactive Change event. If you want the program to do something after the user changes the value in a field, you might at first glance try to put the code in the Interactive Change event. If the user has to enter only a single keystroke, that would be Okay. If, however, they have to enter an entire word or phrase, remember that the Interactive Change event fires after each character, not at the end of the phrase.

One way around this problem of where to put code is to check the first parameter returned by KeyPress( ) for the Tab and Enter keys. This, however, is not foolproof either, because the user could change focus to another control by using the mouse. A better method is to use the Valid or Lost Focus method. Observe that the Valid() method is called each time the user attempts to leave a field. If there are validations on the field value, you can place these in the VALID( ) method and return a value of .F. (false) if they fail. This keeps the user in the current field. Only when VALID( ) returns .T. (true) is the user able to leave the field; only then is the LostFocus( ) event fired. Therefore, it is here that you may want to place code that you want to execute only after the user successfully enters a new value in the field.

Another important event sequence is that of the command button. It begins with a call to WHEN( ). If there is no code here, or if the code returns .T. (True), the command button can receive focus. (Placing code in this event is a way to prevent the user from actually being able to click the button without disabling it.)

Actually, clicking the button causes a MouseDown( ) and a MouseUp( ) event to occur before the Click( ) event itself. Most programmers think of only the Click( ) event itself; however, the MouseDown( ) and MouseUp( ) events can be used to implement some of the features of drag-and-drop. (This requires the coordination of other events as well.) Finally, a Valid( ) event occurs.

When you click the close button to close the form, there is a sequence of events just like those when the form is opened. It begins with a QueryUnload for the form, followed by the form's Destroy() event. Next, the Destroy() event of each control is fired. Finally, if all the destroy events are successful, the form Unload() event fires. Last, the DataEnvironment closes the tables and fires the AfterCloseTables() event, followed by the Destroy() event of the DataEnvironment.

## Understanding the Event Hierarchy

In the preceding section, you saw how easy it is to determine the event sequence for a program in Visual FoxPro 5.0. This sequence is known as the *event hierarchy* and is crucial when it comes to developing your applications.

The point is that if you understand the sequence in which the various events fire, you can determine the optimal place to put any code. With the Event Tracking mode of the Debugger, you can easily create a sample form and test the order in which events fire without having to write complex code to print information out of each event.

# From Here...

The basis of any good object-oriented development effort comes in the development of a good framework. It was the goal of this chapter to provide the tools and techniques for implementing a successful framework.

For additional information related to object-oriented programming, refer to the following chapters:

- Chapter 2, "Introducing Object-Oriented Programming," provides a review of object-oriented principles.
- Chapter 11, "Building Applications with Simple Form Structures," discusses the form designer.
- Chapter 13, "Advanced Form Design Controls," discusses advanced form development.

Part
III

Ch
12

# Advanced Form Design Controls

*by Michael Antonovich and*
*Sandra Richardson-Lutzow*

In Chapter 11, "Building Applications with Simple Form Structures," you discovered the basics of form creation and design using Visual FoxPro 5.0. Now you can explore some of the more advanced form design controls: List boxes, combo boxes, page frames, and grids. These controls all have one thing in common: They allow you to determine how the user interfaces with your form. ■

**Create and use a list box**

List boxes serve as great tools to display data in forms with versatility in adding and removing items.

**Create and use a combo box**

A combo box is a combination list box and text box that limits the values that a user can enter, but gives the user the option to type an item that is not in the list.

**Create a page frame**

Page frames serve as a powerful tool for a form with multiple pages without using form sets.

**Define and use a grid**

Grids can display multiple records of a table, as BROWSE can, but with a control or object in each column.

# Using List Boxes

 A *list box* is a control that creates a scrollable list from which the user makes a selection. The List Box control on the Forms Control toolbar enables you to create a list box on your form. In earlier versions of FoxPro, a list box was called a pop-up. Visual FoxPro includes a List Box Builder to simplify creating a list box, but you also can add or change controls manually in the Properties window. Frequently used List Box properties, methods, and events are listed in Table 13.1. All of these elements are explained later in this chapter.

**TIP**  A builder is a FoxPro tool that helps you define properties and create expressions for a control such as a list box, combo box, or grid.

**N O T E**  It's important to understand the meanings of the terms *property, method,* and *event* before you work with list boxes and the other controls described in this chapter. An *event* is an action that an object recognizes and that responds to code—an action that occurs when a user double-clicks a specific form object, for example. A *property* is a definable control attribute—the width of a column, the color of specific text, and so on. A *method* is an action that an object performs, such as a list box that enables a user to add items to the list. Methods contain the code to run in response to an event. Programmers cannot add their own events or redefine them but can add their own properties and methods. ■

**Table 13.1   Frequently Used List Box Properties, Methods, and Events**

| Properties, Methods, and Events | Description |
|---|---|
| AddItem | Adds a new item to the list, optionally enabling you to specify the index position. RowSource must be 0-None or 1-Value. |
| AddListItem | Adds a new item to the list, enabling you to specify the items ID. RowSource must be 0-None or 1-Value. |
| BoundColumn | Determines which column of a multicolumn list is bound to the Value property and data source. |
| BoundTo | Determines whether bound to numeric data or not. |
| Click Event | Causes something to happen when you click the mouse. |
| ColumnCount | Specifies the number of columns in the object. |
| ColumnWidths | Sets the widths of columns. |
| ControlSource | Indicates the source of the data to which that object is bound. |
| DblClick Event | Causes something to happen when you double-click the mouse. |

| Properties, Methods, and Events | Description |
|---|---|
| DisplayValue | Displays the contents of the first column of the selected item. |
| KeyPressEvent | Causes something to happen when you press and release a key. |
| IncrementalSearch | Determines whether an object supports incremental searches. |
| ListCount | Counts the number of items in a list. |
| ListIndex | Determines the index of the selected item. |
| ListItemID | Determines the ID number of the selected item. |
| NewIndex | Determines the index of the most recently added item. |
| NewIndexID | Determines the ID of the most recently added item. |
| MultiSelect | Determines whether you can make multiple selections in a list box. |
| Requery | Populates a list or combo box according to the row source in which they are bound. |
| RemoveItem | Removes an item from the list with specified index of the item. |
| RemoveListItem | Removes an item from the list with specified ID of the item. |
| RowSource | Lists the source of the values in the list box. |
| Sorted | Keeps list sorted alphabetically, chronologically, or numerically, depending on the data type. |

▶ **See** "Attaching Methods to Events," **p. 108**

To see examples of controls such as list boxes, combo boxes, grids, and page frames, look at the Samples Application from the Help option in the main menu and run the solutions application, illustrated in Figure 13.1.

**FIGURE. 13.1**
Visual FoxPro
Solutions illustrates
the use of many of
Visual FoxPro's more
advanced controls: list
and combo boxes,
page frames, and
grids.

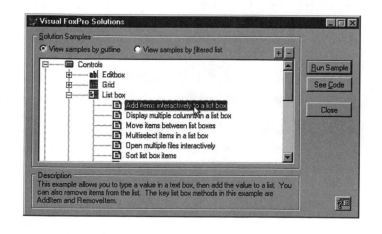

## Using the List Box Builder to Create a List Box

To create a list box using the Builder, follow these steps:

1. In the Form Designer, select the List Box control in the Form Controls toolbar.

2. Draw a box on the form where you want your list box to be.

  **T I P**  To open the Builder automatically any time you place a new control on your form, select the Builder Lock button on the Form Controls toolbar.

3. Right-click your list box to open the shortcut menu, and select Builder to open the List Box Builder, as shown in Figure 13.2.

**FIGURE 13.2**
The List Box Builder guides you step by step through creating a list box.

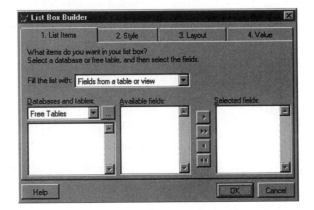

**N O T E**  A *free table* refers to a table that doesn't belong to a database. Any pre-existing tables from versions of FoxPro 2.x are free tables. ■

4. The first tab, List Items, helps you select the fields you want in your list box. The Fill the List With box offers three choices: Fields from a Table or View, Data Entered by Hand, and Values from an Array. For this example, choose Fields from a Table or View.

5. Select a database or table from the Databases/Tables list box, or click the ... button to open the Open dialog box, if you want to select a table in another directory.

**N O T E**  You can move all your fields at the same time by clicking the double-left-arrow button to move them to the Selected Fields list or by clicking the double-right-arrow button to move them back to the Available Fields list. Double-clicking a field also moves it to the other list. ■

6. Highlight your first desired field in the Available Fields list, and click the left-arrow button to move it to the Selected Fields list. You can remove a field from Selected Fields by highlighting it and clicking the right-arrow button.

7. Select the Style tab, illustrated in Figure 13.3, to continue.

**FIGURE 13.3**

You can determine the number of rows you want to display and enable incremental searching in the Style tab.

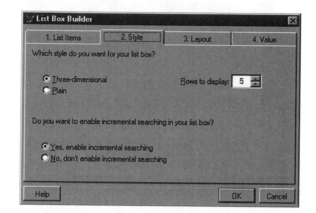

8. The Style tab of the List Box Builder offers you two choices for a style type: Three-Dimensional and Plain. For this example, choose Three-Dimensional, which the default.

9. Next, select how many rows to display. This setting depends on how large you want your list box to be.

**N O T E** Incremental searching enables you to search through lists of data one letter at a time. If you wanted to find the last name *Smith*, for example, you could enter **S** to reach all the last names beginning with *S*, then enter **M** to continue to last names beginning with *SM*, and so on. If incremental searching wasn't enabled, you would move to the last names beginning with *M* once you entered that letter. ■

10. Indicate whether you want to enable incremental searching.

 You can hide a column by double-clicking its heading.

11. Select the third tab, Layout. This tab, shown in Figure 13.4, enables you to adjust and select your columns.

**FIGURE 13.4**

The Layout tab helps you adjust your columns.

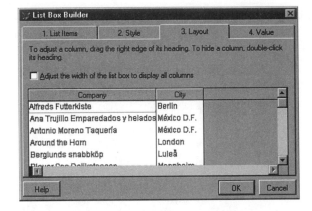

12. To adjust a column, drag the right edge of its heading to make that column wider or narrower.

13. Select the check box next to Adjust the width of the list box to display all columns if you would like to do this.

14. Select the Value tab, shown in Figure 13.5.

**FIGURE 13.5**

The Value tab lets you store a field value in another table.

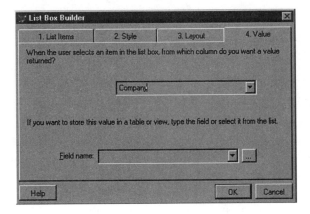

15. If your list box contains more than one field, you need to choose the column from which you want a value returned. Select this field from the list box.

16. If you want to store this value in another table, click the ... button to choose the table from the Open dialog box.

17. Select the field in which you want to store your selection from the Field Name list.

18. Click OK when you are finished to return to the Form Designer.

NOTE  You can also store the value in a variable or a user-defined form property by placing the name of the variable or property in the ControlSource property of the properties window. ■

Your list box may look the same as it did before you used the Builder, but if you open the Properties windows (right-click the list box and select Properties from the shortcut menu), you can see the changes to particular properties. ControlSource and RowSource, for example, now include field names. You can change these properties directly in the Properties window, but it's usually easier to start with the Builder. The properties affected will be in bold in the properties window.

▶ **See** "Naming Fields in Tables," **p. 189**

Notice that the first list box you create is automatically named list1. Although Visual FoxPro does name the objects on your form for you (List1, Combo1, and so on), it's a good idea to use proper naming conventions with your first FoxPro application—for example, lstCustomer or cboCustomer for a list box or combo box that lists a customer name field. Using naming conventions standardizes your objects, makes them easier to refer to in other parts of your application, and also makes it easier for someone else to understand the logic of your application.

## Using List Boxes to Limit Values

List boxes can simplify data entry by enabling the user to choose values from a list rather than manually entering each value. Manually entering values not only wastes time, but also increases the chance of data entry or spelling errors. Using list boxes can ensure that data is entered in a uniform way, to your specifications.

## Accessing List Items

When creating your first list boxes, you may experience some frustration regarding when to use methods such as AddItem versus AddListItem. Actually, for a single-column list you may not notice the difference, but when you start creating multicolumn lists, you need to know the difference. This section helps you understand these differences when you are accessing the items in a list.

Lists have two ways of pointing to specific data: Index and ID. When the list's Sorted property is set to .T., VFP determines the index of an item by the sorted order in which it falls. In other words, the index of an item is the displayed order of the item, with each row considered as 1, whether the list is single or multicolumn. In a sorted list, the first row of the list may have an ID of 5 because it was the fifth row initially added, but the index is 1.

Part
III

Ch
13

The index of an item changes when rows are added and removed; however, the ID never changes. Two properties, List and ListItem, are used to access items of lists. If you want to access an item by the index, you would use the List property. In a multicolumn list, you need to specify the index, or row, in addition to the column. The ListIndex property retrieves the index of a selected item. On the other hand, to access an item by the unique ID, you would use the ListItem property. To retrieve the unique ID of a selected item, you would use ListItemID property. Table 13.2 lists similar properties and methods that access the same items.

**Table 13.2   Similar List Properties Using Index Versus ID**

| Index | ID | Purpose |
| --- | --- | --- |
| AddItem | AddListItem | Adds a new item to the list |
| List | ListItem | Accesses an item |
| ListIndex | ListItemID | Specifies a selected item |
| RemoveItem | RemoveListItem | Removes an item from the list |
| Selected | SelectedID | Specifies whether an item is selected |

## Allowing Users to Add to Lists

In addition to simply selecting items from a list, you can enable users to interactively add items to a list by adding a user procedure to the KeyPress Event. The user can then enter text in a text box and press Enter to move the data to a list box, clearing the text box for another potential entry.

▶ **See** "Attaching Methods to Events," **p. 108**

For an example of how this works, run the Samples Application from the Help option in the main menu and run the Solutions application. Select List and Combo Boxes, and choose Add Items Interactively to a List Box under List Box in the outline. Select the Run Sample button to view the Adding and Removing List Items form, shown in Figure 13.6. Enter some text in the text box, and press Enter to add it to the list. The text moves to the list box. Select OK to return to the main form.

**FIGURE 13.6**
Users can easily add
or remove list items
interactively.

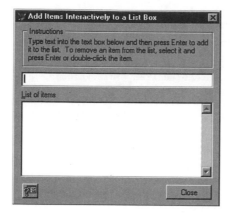

To view this form's design, illustrated in Figure 13.7, select the See Code button, which
enables you to modify the form.

**FIGURE 13.7**
Modify a form's
properties in the Form
Designer.

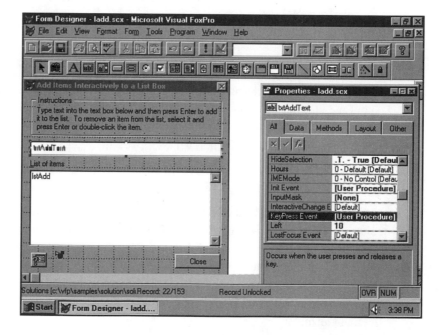

Open the Properties window for the text box named txtAddText, and look at the KeyPress
Event method. A KeyPress Event, you will recall, causes something to happen when you
release a key. Double-clicking this method opens the following User Procedure:

▶ **See** "Using Conditional Structures," **p. 422**

```
LPARAMETERS nKeyCode, nShiftCtrlAlt
IF nKeyCode = 13 && 13 is the Enter Key
     IF !EMPTY(THIS.Value)
          *add the value to the list box
          *----------------------------
          THISFORM.lstAdd.AddItem (THIS.Value)
     ENDIF

     *Set the text box value to an empty string
     *----------------------------
     THIS.Value = ""

     *Set the property to .F. so that Valid event will
     *return 0, keeping the focus on the textbox
     *----------------------------
     THISFORM.OkToLeave = .F.
ENDIF
```

Now open the Properties window for the list box named lstAdd and view the User Procedure for the DoubleClick Event method:

```
IF THIS.ListIndex > 0
     THISFORM.txtAddText.Value = THIS.List(THIS.ListIndex)
     THIS.RemoveItem (THIS.ListIndex)
ENDIF
```

Both of these user procedures include code, or subroutines, which cause the event to occur when the key is released. The first procedure is well documented to describe in plain English what the code does. Even if you don't plan to share your applications with others, it's a good idea to document all code clearly so that in the future you will remember what each procedure does and why.

## Displaying Multi-Column Lists

Visual FoxPro also enables you to create forms in which users can choose how many columns to display. To see an example of this, again run the Samples Application from the Help option in the main menu and then run the solutions application and choose Display Multiple Columns in the Samples list. Selecting the Run Sample button enables you to view the Multi-column List Box form, displayed in Figure 13.8. Adjust the number of columns using the spinner to see how columns are added or removed. Select OK to return to the main form.

**FIGURE 13.8**

You can provide the user with the option of displaying one or more columns.

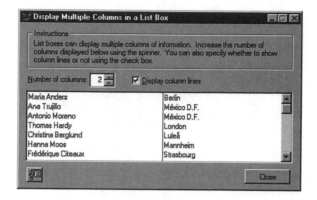

To view this form's design, select See Code in the Using Visual FoxPro Controls form. Select the spinner, SpnColumns, and view its properties. Look at the User Procedure in the Interactive Change event, listed here:

```
THISFORM.LockScreen = .T.
DO CASE
    CASE This.Value = 1
            THISFORM.lstDemo.ColumnCount = 1
            THISFORM.lstDemo.ColumnWidths =
THISFORM.CalcColumnWidths(THISFORM.lstDemo, 1)
            THISFORM.lstDemo.RowSource = "contact"
    CASE This.Value = 2
            THISFORM.lstDemo.ColumnCount = 2
            THISFORM.lstDemo.ColumnWidths =
THISFORM.CalcColumnWidths(THISFORM.lstDemo, 2)
            THISFORM.lstDemo.RowSource = "contact,city"
    CASE This.Value = 3
            THISFORM.lstDemo.ColumnCount = 3
            THISFORM.lstDemo.ColumnWidths =
THISFORM.CalcColumnWidths(THISFORM.lstDemo, 3)
            THISFORM.lstDemo.RowSource = "contact,city,country"
    CASE This.Value = 4
            THISFORM.lstDemo.ColumnCount = 4
            THISFORM.lstDemo.ColumnWidths =
THISFORM.CalcColumnWidths(THISFORM.lstDemo, 4)
            THISFORM.lstDemo.RowSource = "cust_id,contact,city,country"
ENDCASE
THISFORM.LockScreen = .F.
```

## Selecting Multiple Items in a List

The following example enables you to select multiple items in a list box. Again, run Solutions Application from the Sample Applications option in the Help menu item and run the example Multiselect Items In A List Box under Controls.

Part
**III**

Ch
**13**

This opens the form in Figure 13.9, MultiSelect Items in a List Box. In this form you have three main controls: A list box listing the user's choices, a text box that lists the number of selected items, and a combo box that stores the user's selections.

**FIGURE 13.9**

Users can select more than one item in a list using a form such as this.

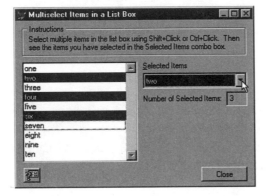

Return to the main controls form and select See Code. Open the Properties window for the list box, called lstMulti, and you see that the MultiSelect property has been set to true (.T.). The procedure that displays the number of records selected in the text box and the selected items in the combo box is located in the InteractiveChange event. Double-click this event to view the following procedure:

```
nNoSelected = 0
THISFORM.cboSelected.Clear
FOR i = 1 TO THIS.ListCount
    IF THIS.Selected(i)
        nNoSelected = nNoSelected + 1
        THISFORM.cboSelected.Additem (THIS.List(i))
    ENDIF
ENDFOR
THISFORM.txtNoSelected.Value = nNoSelected
THISFORM.cboSelected.Value = 1
```

To copy the items you selected to an array, or to use them in another part of your application, you can create conditional statements and loops using Visual FoxPro's programming language.

▶ **See** "Creating a Simple Looping Structure," **p. 427**

▶ **See** "Using Conditional Structures," **p. 422**

# Using Combo Boxes

A combo box lets you either enter a value or select an item from a list. It is a combination of a text box and a list box. Visual FoxPro also offers a Combo Box Builder that is very similar to the List Box Builder. The most frequently used combo box properties, methods, and events, all discussed later in this section, are listed in Table 13.3. Visual FoxPro provides you with a choice of two types of combo boxes: drop-down combo, and drop-down list. Drop-down combo is the default style. A drop-down list looks like a combo box, in that it conserves space, but it functions like a list box, in that it won't allow you to enter your own data. Figure 13.10 graphically illustrates the difference between drop-down combos, drop-down lists, and list boxes.

▶ **See** "Text Box Controls," **p. 480**

**FIGURE 13.10**
This sample form displays the three basic box types: Drop-down combos, drop-down lists, and list boxes.

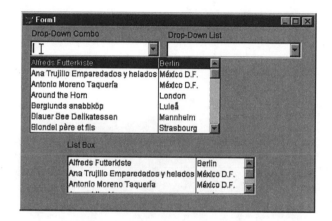

To create a combo box using the Builder, follow these steps:

1. In the Form Designer, select the Combo Box control in the Form Controls toolbar.
2. Draw a box on the form where you want your combo box to be.
3. The Combo Box Builder, shown in Figure 13.11, opens automatically, if you already selected the Builder Lock button. Otherwise, right-click your combo box to open the shortcut menu and select Builder.
4. The first tab, List Items, helps you select the fields you want in your combo box. The Fill the List With box offers three choices: Fields from a Table or View, Data Entered by Hand, or Values from an Array. In this example, choose Fields from a Table or View.
5. Select a database or table from the Databases/Tables list box or select the ... button to open the Open dialog box if you want to select a table in another directory.
6. Highlight your first desired field in the Available Fields list and click the left arrow button to move it to the Selected Fields list. You can remove a field from Selected Fields by highlighting it and clicking the right arrow button. Use the double-arrow buttons to move all fields from one list to the other.

Part
III

Ch
13

**FIGURE 13.11**

The Combo Box Builder simplifies creating complicated combo boxes.

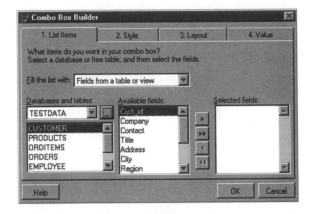

7. Select the Style tab, shown in Figure 13.12, to determine the style of your combo box.

**FIGURE 13.12**

Determine whether you want a drop-down combo or a drop-down list in this tab.

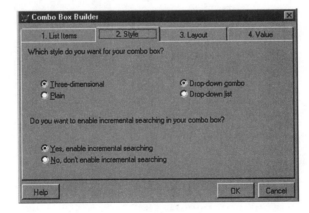

8. The Style tab on the Combo Box Builder offers you two choices for a style type: Three-Dimensional or Plain. In this example, select Three-Dimensional, the default.

**N O T E**  Using a drop-down list instead of a list box conserves form space by illustrating only the current selection rather than a long list of potential selections. ■

9. Next determine whether you want a Drop-down Combo or Drop-down List.

10. Select whether or not you want to enable incremental searching.

11. Select the third tab, Layout. This tab enables you to adjust and select your columns.

12. To adjust a column, drag the right edge of its heading to make that column wider or narrower. You also can hide a column by double-clicking its heading.

13. Select the check box next to <u>A</u>djust the width of the list box to display all columns, if you would like to do this.

14. Select the Value tab.

15. If your combo box contains more than one field, you need to choose the column from which you want a value returned. Select this field from the drop-down list.

16. If you want to store this value in another table, select the ... button to choose the table from the Open dialog box.

17. Select the field in which you want to store your selection from the <u>F</u>ield Name list.

18. Click OK when you are finished to return to the Form Designer.

Again, you can view the Properties window to see the changes the Builder made to the combo box. Some properties to look at include ControlSource, RowSource, Style, and IncrementalSearch.

### TROUBLESHOOTING

**I can't enter data into my list box.** List boxes only enable you to choose items from a pre-determined list. If you want the option to either select data from a list or enter your own data, choose a combo box.

**I don't know which type of combo box I need.** If you want to allow the user to enter data, choose a drop-down combo style combo box. If you want to conserve screen space and don't want to allow user entries, create a drop-down list style combo box. Of course, if you want a larger, scrollable list, choose a list box.

**I want to save the value entered in a Drop-Down Combo to the list.** When you enter a value into a combo box that isn't in the list, the Value property has an empty string for the value. You can add code to the valid event to compare the DisplayValue property to the Value property and if they don't match, add the DisplayValue to the list using the AddItem property.

**I want to see a value in a combo box upon initially running a form but without a control source, the combo box value is blank.** In the INIT() of the form set the value of the combo box equal to List(1). This will display the first item of the list.

**My combo box is bound to a numeric field in my table and the stored value is never right.** You need to set the BoundTo property to .T.. If BoundTo is .F., the value stored is the index of the item not the item itself.

**Is it possible for a date field to be the control source of my combo box?** The only data types that a list or combo box recognizes are character and numeric. You cannot use a control source for other types of data. There is, however, a way you can trick VFP into saving other data types. To use another data type, you have to first convert the data to character or numeric in the INIT() of

*continues*

*continued*

the list or combo box and manually add the items. If the data is bound to a field, you need to convert it back to the proper type in the InteractiveChange event before storing the value back to the field. VFP's data conversion functions include:

```
DTOC() - Date to Character
CTOD() - Character to Date
TTOC() - Time to Character
CTOT() - Character to Time
```

# Using Page Frames

A *page frame* is a container object (object that can contain other objects) that holds pages. Each page of a page frame, indicated by a tab, can hold individual controls. Page frames are useful when you want a form to take a user through several steps without creating independent forms for each step. The Builders you looked at earlier in this chapter are examples of how page frames can be used.

To create a page frame, follow these steps:

1. In the Form Designer, select the Page Frame control on the Form Controls toolbar.
2. Draw a box on your form to place your page frame.
3. Right-click the page frame and select Properties from the submenu to open the Properties window.
4. Select the PageCount property and enter your desired number of pages. The default will be 2. In this example, enter 4.

 **TIP** To remove a specific frame, but not the entire page frame, select that frame and press the Delete key.

Now that you have defined your basic page frame, shown in Figure 13.13, you can edit each individual tab. To edit each tab, right-click it and select Edit from the submenu to activate it. The tab of the active frame moves to the front so you can always tell which frame you are working with. You can now add controls to each tab.

**FIGURE 13.13**

Page frames simplify complicated user-interface forms.

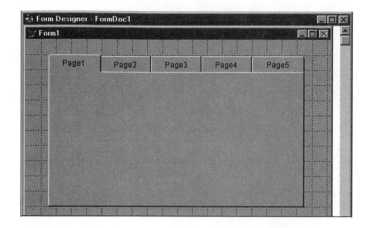

To change the caption of each tab, select it and then view its Properties window. Enter your preferred name in the Caption property. You have two properties, TabStretch and TabStyle, which effect the appearance of the caption. TabStretch gives you two options, 0-Multiple Rows or 1-Single Row (Default). If you use long tab captions you will want to use Multiple Rows because using Single Row may cut your captions off if you have many pages in your page frame. TabStyle also gives you two options, 0-Justified (Default) and 1-Nonjustified. Justified is the most common. It justifies the tabs to the page frame (refer to Figure 13.13).

---

### Hiding Pages

If you ever have the need to hide a page, or pages, dynamically in your page frame, there is an easy way to do that. It involves the page frame's property Pagecount and the pages' property PageOrder. For example, your page frame has 4 pages. You want to dynamically hide the second page on certain conditions; use security level. In the load of the form, test for the security level and if the level restricts the second page, set PageCount to 3 and PageOrder of the second page to 4. Following is sample code to perform this action on a page frame with 4 pages:

```
IF THISFORM.rnSecurity = 1

THISFORM.pfrFrame1.pagPage2.PageOrder = 4

    THISFORM.pfrFrame1.PageCount = 3

ENDIF
```

---

# Defining a Grid

A grid is a control that lets you display data in a tabular format, similar to a spreadsheet with rows and columns. It is often used in a one-to-many form in which text boxes display the data of a parent table (the one) and the grid displays the data in the child table (the many). Figure 13.14 displays a sample use of a grid, found in the Tasmanian Traders project in the Sample Applications from the Help option in the main menu.

**FIGURE 13.14**

A grid enables you to relate parent and child tables in one form.

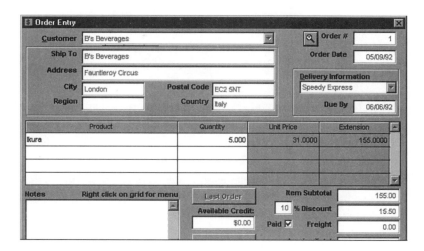

You can define a grid using the Grid Builder or you can manually set the grid's properties. Table 13.3 contains a list of common grid properties.

**Table 13.3  Frequently Used Grid Properties**

| Properties | Description |
| --- | --- |
| ColumnCount | Determines the number of columns displayed |
| ColumnOrder | Sets the order of columns in a grid |
| RowHeight | Indicates the height of each row |
| ChildOrder | Lists the key of the child table that is joined to the parent table |
| LinkMaster | Lists the master, or parent, table |
| RecordSource | Names the table that is the source of data for that grid |

To define a grid, follow these steps:

1. In the Form Designer, select the Grid control in the Form Controls toolbar.

2. Draw a box on the form where you want to place your grid.

3. The Grid Builder, shown in Figure 13.15, will open automatically if you already selected the Builder Lock button. Otherwise, right-click your grid to open the shortcut menu and select Builder.

**FIGURE 13.15**
Create a grid quickly using the Grid Builder.

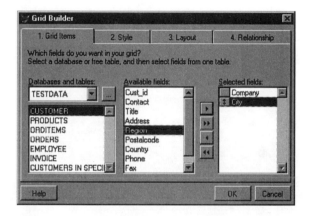

4. The first tab, Grid Items, helps you select the fields you want in your grid. Select a database or table from the Databases/Tables list box or select the ... button to open the Open dialog box if you want to select a table in another directory.

5. Highlight your first desired field in the Available Fields list and click the left arrow button to move it to the Selected Fields list. You can remove a field from Selected Fields by highlighting it and clicking the right arrow button. Use the double-arrow buttons to move all fields from one list to the other. Double-clicking also moves a field.

6. Select the Style tab to determine your grid's style as shown in Figure 13.16.

7. The Style tab on the Grid Builder offers you five choices for a style type: <Preserve current style>, Professional, Standard, Embossed, or Ledger. Experiment with each style type until you find what you like.

8. Select the third tab, Layout. This tab, shown in Figure 13.17, enables you to adjust and select your columns.

Part
III

Ch
13

**FIGURE 13.16**
Choose among a variety of grid styles—Professional, Standard, Embossed, and Ledger—in this tab.

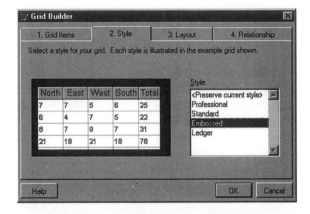

**FIGURE 13.17**
Adjust your columns in the Layout tab.

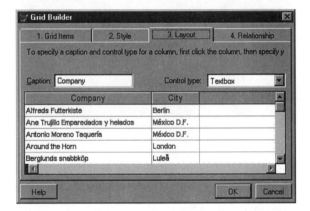

9. To adjust a column, drag the right edge of its heading to make that column wider or narrower.

10. If you want to change a column's caption, select the column and enter a new name in the Caption field.

11. To change a column's control type, select the column and choose a new type from the Control Type list Textbox, Editbox, Spinner, Checkbox, or OLEBoundControl.

12. Select the Relationship tab, illustrated in Figure 13.18.

13. If you want to create a one-to-many form, complete the Key field in parent table and Related index in child table boxes.

**FIGURE 13.18**
The Relationship tab in the Grid Builder enables you to relate a field in the grid to another field in the form.

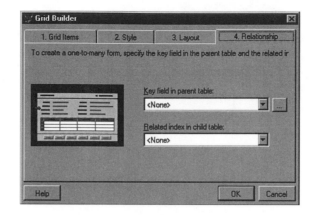

## Using Controls in a Grid Column

So far, you have seen only field data displayed in the sample grids. A grid can also contain controls.

To see an example of a control in a grid, run the Solutions Application from the Sample Applications in the Help option of the main menu and then run the Display Controls in Grid Columns example. In this form, shown in Figure 13.19, you can make each column either visible or invisible by selecting check boxes. To view the code behind this form, click the See Code box in the Using Visual FoxPro Controls form.

▶ See "Spinner Controls," **p. 486**
▶ See "Check Box Controls," **p. 485**

**FIGURE 13.19**
This form enables a user to display or hide columns.

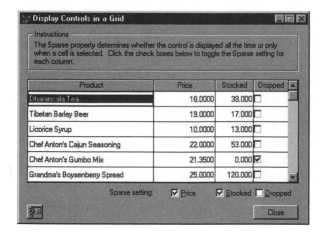

Part
**III**

Ch
**13**

Select the grid and view the Properties window. The Init method contains a user procedure that creates spinners in the second and third columns and a check box in the fourth. The check boxes at the lower left of the form enable the user to determine whether these controls are visible or not. The code for this procedure follows:

```
THIS.colPrice.AddObject('spnUnitPrice', 'SPINNER')
THIS.colStocked.AddObject('spnStocked', 'SPINNER')
THIS.colDropped.AddObject('chkDropped', 'CHECKBOX')

THIS.colPrice.CurrentControl = 'spnUnitPrice'
THIS.colStocked.CurrentControl = 'spnStocked'
THIS.colDropped.CurrentControl = 'chkDropped'

THIS.colDropped.chkDropped.Visible = .T.
THIS.colDropped.chkDropped.Caption = ""


THIS.colPrice.spnUnitPrice.Visible = .T.
THIS.colPrice.spnUnitPrice.FontSize = 8

THIS.colStocked.spnStocked.Visible = .T.
THIS.colStocked.spnStocked.FontSize = 8
```

## Setting Common Grid Properties

In many cases you may want to make changes to your grid after you (or a Form Wizard) have created it. You can change a grid's column and row properties as well as redefine its data source.

**Setting the Column Properties**   To change the number of columns in a grid, open the Properties window, shown in Figure 13.20, and select the ColumnCount property. Enter the new number of columns and select Enter.

You also can adjust the width of your grid columns by selecting the grid and right-clicking to open the shortcut menu. Select Edit from this menu to enable you to edit your grid. Then point to the header of the column you want to adjust. The mouse pointer changes to a bar with arrows, and you can adjust the width of your column by clicking and dragging.

To change the order of a column, select that column, open the Properties window, and enter the new order number in the ColumnOrder property.

**FIGURE 13.20**

You can edit your grid's properties in the Properties window.

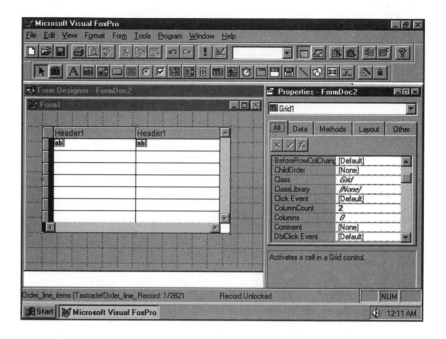

**Setting Row Properties**    To change the height of a row, select the grid, open the Properties window, and enter the new row height in the RowHeight property.

**Defining the Data Source**    In general, the data source for your grid will be set when you create a grid using either the One-to-Many Form Wizard or the Grid Builder. However, you can change the data source by editing the RecordSource property in the Properties window.

## Creating a One-To-Many Form in a Grid

A common use for a grid is to display the child records that relate to a parent record displayed in a text box or boxes on the same form. To see an example of this, run the Samples Application from the Help option in the main menu and then run the solutions application. Run the Display Child Records from a Relationship grid sample under Controls to view the One-to-Many-to-Many form. In this form, the parent table Customer is linked to two child tables: Orders, and Orditems. Note that when you change the customer name by using the arrow keys at the bottom of the form, displayed in Figure 13.21, you also change the data in the Orders and Items grids.

▶ **See** "The Form Wizard," **p. 244**

Part

**III**

Ch

**13**

**FIGURE 14.21**

A grid is commonly used to display a one-to-many relationship.

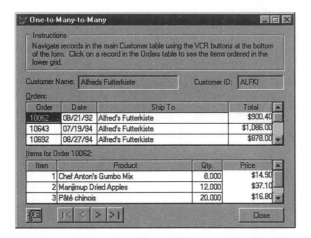

The One-to-Many Form Wizard makes creating a one-to-many grid a simple task. To use this wizard, choose File, New. Choose the Form radio button in the New dialog box and then select the Wizard button. Select the One-to-Many Form Wizard from the list and you can create a form that links parent and child records.

If necessary, you also can set up one-to-many relationships manually by setting these relationships in the Properties window. View the design of the Display A One-to-Many-to-Many Form by selecting See Example in the Using Visual FoxPro Controls form.

Note that the Control Source for both text boxes, txtCustomerName and txtCustomerID, is set to the parent table fields, customer.company and customer.cust_id. In the Orders grid, grdOrders, the RecordSource property is set to the name of the related table, in this case, orders. LinkMaster is set to the name of the parent table, customer. And ChildOrder is set to cust_ID, the name of the primary key in the parent table. The Items grid, grdItems, has the same properties.

## TROUBLESHOOTING

**I want to change the order of my columns in a grid, but I can't find the ColumnOrder property in the Properties window.** If you can't find the ColumnOrder property, you are probably viewing the properties of the entire grid, not that specific column. Select the proper column from the Object list in the Properties window.

**When I disable a grid control, I am still able to use the mouse to select the control.** This is normal for grids because the grid must change the record pointer before it can query columns or column controls for Enabled = .T.. Once the record pointer is changed, the grid can't go back because the grid does not save a previous record pointer. To resolve this issue include code in the AfterRowColChange event to handle it. Following is sample code:

```
_  Check which column you are in

IF nColIndex = 1

This.ActiveCell(This.RelativeRow, 2)

          ENDIF
```

**When using a check box in a cell of my grid I want to move to the next column automatically after clicking the check box.** In the Valid event of the check box add code to determine the current column and then move to the next column with the SetFocus method.

# From Here...

In this chapter, you learned how advanced form design controls, such as list boxes, combo boxes, page frames, and grids, can help you to create sophisticated, yet user-friendly applications. To take full advantage of what these controls can offer, however, you need a firm understanding of how Visual FoxPro uses object-oriented programming.

The chapters in the following list help take you to this next level and offer some suggestions for review if you want to strengthen your understanding of basic form design first.

- Chapter 2, "Introducing Object-Oriented Programming," overviews the basics of object-oriented design including properties, methods, and events.
- Chapter 4, "Advanced Database Management Concepts," discusses naming conventions in detail.
- Chapter 5, "Using Wizards for Rapid Application Development," gives more details on using the Report Wizard.
- Chapter 11, "Programming Structures," provides an overview of programming concepts such as conditional statements and loops.
- Chapter 12, "Building Applications with Simple Form Structures," introduces you to form creation and controls.

Part
**III**

Ch
**13**

# Custom Report Generation

*by Richard Curtis*

The capability to retrieve meaningful information from an information warehouse can be crucial to businesses as well as individuals. Whether you need to complete address labels for your Christmas cards or run an updated product inventory, getting information from a database quickly and in a usable format is essential. Visual FoxPro's report writing capabilities combined with the data access of queries and views can be a powerful tool in achieving this goal. ■

**Design a report**

Identify the issues to address in creating a report.

**Create a report template**

Leverage time by creating a reusable template.

**Use expressions and variables in reports**

Increase the flexibility of the report process.

**Use the template to build a report**

The mechanics of building reports from a base template.

**Use a program to initiate your report**

Automate running reports and allow user selections.

# Understanding Report Design

Before you begin planning your data extraction and how to present it, there are a few things you need to determine.

First, who is the audience for the report? If this is a working report that you are using as part of the development process, it does not need the refinement and eye appeal of one that is sent to corporate officers, clients, shareholders, and so on.

Next, who is responsible for running the report, and how often is it processed? Do you need a user interface from which to run it? Does it need a time stamp or reference number? If someone asks for a change in the report, can you easily identify it from all the other reports that are in the system?

Can you save time and money in the design of the report? Should an invoice be sent in a dual-window envelope, or should you print addresses on labels for envelopes you receive from a printer, with the company's logo and return address?

Once these and similar questions are determined, it is time to take a paper and pencil and rough out your report layout. What is the best way to present the data for its intended audience—portrait or landscape, standard or legal size, extra left margin for binding?

The idea is to have a solid design in mind before you write a query or type **CREATE REPORT**.

Table 14.1 provides a quick reference on the report controls and Designer toolbars.

| **Button** | **Name** | **Description** |
|---|---|---|
| Table 14.1 | **The Report Controls and Designer Toolbars** | |
| | Select Objects | Pointer to select objects |
| | Label | Creates a label object |
| | Field | Creates a field object |
| | Line | Draws a line object |
| | Rectangle | Draws a rectangle object |
| | Rounded Rectangle | Draws a rounded rectangle |

| Button | Name | Description |
|---|---|---|
| | Picture/OLE Bound | Inserts a picture or Control OLE object |
| | Lock Button | Locks down the selected control button |
| | Report Controls Toolbar | Opens the Report Control toolbar |
| | Color Palette Toolbar | Opens the Color Palette toolbar |
| | Layout Toolbar | Opens the Layout toolbar |
| | Data Environment | Opens the Data Environment |

# Creating a Report Template

 **T I P** You can open the Report Designer by entering **CREATE REPORT** in the Command window.

Suppose that after considering the issues in the preceding section, you have determined the following report criteria:

- The report's audience is customers outside the company.
- There will be a suite of similar reports, and a report indicator is required.
- The report is used by multiple queries and views, so no field alias is to be included.
- The report will be run numerous times during the day, and a reference number is required to ensure that earlier versions of the report are not confused with later versions.
- A logo is to be displayed on the first page of all reports.

Now that the report criteria have been determined, you can take the following steps to meet them. (These steps are by no means the only way to do it, but they should stimulate your imagination.)

Part
III

Ch
14

First, because the report is going outside of the company and will contain both alpha and numeric information, the Arial font (a standard Windows 95 font) will be used. Courier New is the default font, so this change requires a change to the template.

Second, the reason for a template is that there will be a suite of reports with a similar look. With a template, you do not have to make the same changes each time you start a new report.

With a large number of similar-looking reports, you need to be able to tell them apart. To do this, you will add to the template a report name, in 8-point text, in the bottom-right corner of the footer. This format is similar to the use of form numbers for preprinted forms.

These reports will not include an alias in the field names. Although an alias might ensure that a report is not used on the wrong data source, not using one allows a report to be used for multiple data sources. When to use one is a judgment call for the developer.

The next-to-last criterion is a reference number to differentiate reports that were created on the same date. A date/time stamp would serve the same purpose, but the reference number exposes you to two Visual FoxPro functions: SECONDS() and SYS(2). Both of these functions return the seconds since midnight; however, SECONDS() returns a numeric value, and SYS(2) returns a character string. To perform properly, each function must be stored in a memory variable; otherwise, each time the function is printed on a page of the report, the displayed value would be different. The two statements look like this:

```
cMyRefNo = ALLTRIM(STR(SECONDS()))
cMyRefNo = ALLTRIM(SYS(2))
```

Finally, the last criterion is a logo for the report. I selected a computer graphic that is a good approximation of a company logo (see Figure 14.5 in the following section).

# Using Expressions and Variables in Reports

The first expression to build for the report is the date expression. You accomplish this task by combining a text string with two date functions, as follows:

```
"Date: " + MDY(DATE())
```

Use SET CENTURY ON to display the year as four digits. Figure 14.1 illustrates this expression.

**FIGURE 14.1**

Use the Expression Builder's Verify button to ensure that the expression's syntax is correct.

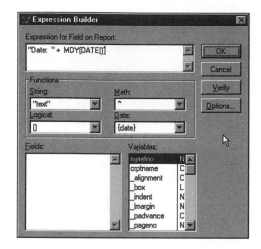

The reference-number variable, MyRefNo, is a report variable created from the Report and Variables menu items. MyRefNo receives its value from a memory variable, MyRefNumber, which is initialized just before the report is run. (This technique is detailed in the section on using a program to initiate your report.) Applying either of the seconds-since-midnight functions directly to MyRefNo results in a different reference number for each page of the report. (See Figure 14.2)

**N O T E** You could use MyRefNumber directly in the report; however, this example exposes you to one way of providing input to a report variable. ■

**FIGURE 14.2**

The report variable MyRefNo and other initialized and system variables appear in the Variables list box.

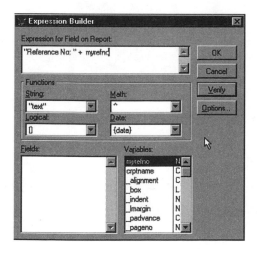

The expression for the page number (Figure 14.3) uses the system memory variable _pageno, a numeric value.

**FIGURE 14.3**

Combine the `ALLTRIM( )` and `STR( )` functions to turn the `_pageno` variable into a character string.

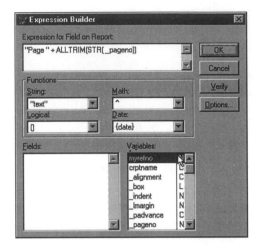

The `cRptName` variable shown in Figure 14.4 is declared in the Command window for developing the report. During production it is initialized in code (see Listing 14.1) and used in the REPORT FORM command.

```
cRptName = "Employees"
```

**FIGURE 14.4**

The Variables list box shows available variables and their data types.

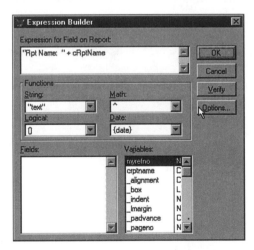

Figure 14.5 shows the completed form template with the four variables, a bitmap, and a company name and address. When the template is complete, you can use the MODIFY REPORT RptTemplate command to call it. Choose File, Save As; save the report under a new file name; and then design your new report. If you design the report and then save it, you will overwrite the template.

**FIGURE 14.5**

Depending on the complexity of a report template, you can save 30 minutes to several hours in setting up a series of similar reports.

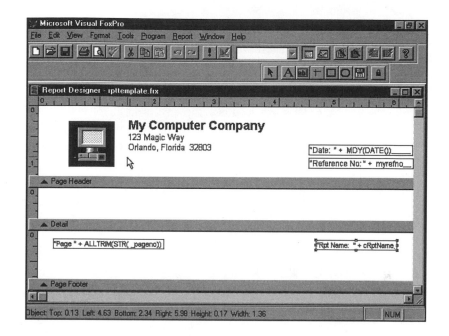

 **TIP** Keep several backups of your templates. Sooner or later, you will get interrupted or distracted and overwrite the template.

**NOTE** To use Print Preview in the Report Designer, you must have variables initialized and a table in the Data Environment. You don't have to place any fields in the report, and after you develop the report template, you can remove the table from the Data Environment. ■

 **TIP** Choose Show Position from the Report Designer's View menu. This command displays the selected object's Top, Left, Bottom, Right, Height, and Width.

# Using the Template to Build a Report

With the form template complete and backup copies created, it is time to create the first report. First, place a copy of the template in Visual FoxPro's default directory or path.

The report is a list of employees from TESTDATA.DBC, which is included with Visual FoxPro's sample data. This report is based on the following SELECT SQL statement:

Part
**III**

Ch
**14**

```
SELECT *;
 FROM testdata!employee;
 WHERE YEAR(Employee.hire_date) > 1993;
 GROUP BY Employee.emp_id;
 ORDER BY Employee.last_name ;
 INTO CURSOR MyEmployees
```

The SELECT statement results in three records, all for employees living in France. Included in the report are the Character fields LAST_NAME, FIRST_NAME, TITLE, ADDRESS, CITY, REGION, and COUNTRY; the General field PHOTO; and the Memo field NOTES. The SELECT statement is for employees hired after 1993. Records are grouped by the primary key, EMP_ID, and ordered by LAST_NAME. The data is stored in the MyEmployees cursor, which must be in the selected work area.

The next step is to start the template. In the Visual FoxPro Command window, type the following:

### MODIFY REPORT RptTemplate

When the template appears in the Report Designer, choose File, Save As, and save the report as Employees.

**N O T E** If you type **MODIFY REPORT RptTemplate** and a blank report appears, the template is not in Visual FoxPro's default directory or path. Close the report without saving it, and type **MODIFY REPORT ?** in the Command window. When the Open dialog box appears, navigate to the proper folder and open RptTemplate. ■

The group-by criterion for the MyEmployees cursor is the primary key, and it results in each record being a group. This grouping allows an easy way to break between each employee's information.

Right-click the Report Designer to activate the pop-up menu, and choose Data Grouping… to display the Data Grouping dialog box. In the Group Expressions box, type the field **EMP_ID**, and click OK to display the Group Header and Footer. Next, drag the Detail band flush below the Group Header band (see Figure 14.6).

The finished report layout has Character field information in the group header. The General field PHOTO and the Memo field NOTES are in the group footer.

Figure 14.7 displays the basic layout of the report fields.

**FIGURE 14.6**

The Data Grouping dialog box and Group Header and Detail band positions.

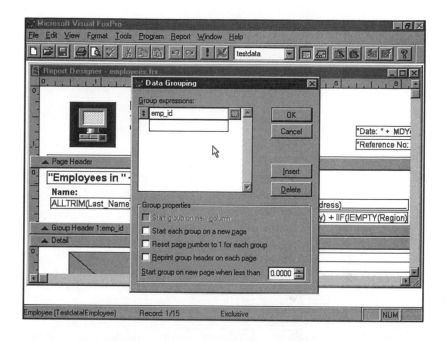

**FIGURE 14.7**

The completed report layout in Report Designer, with Show Position activated in the status bar.

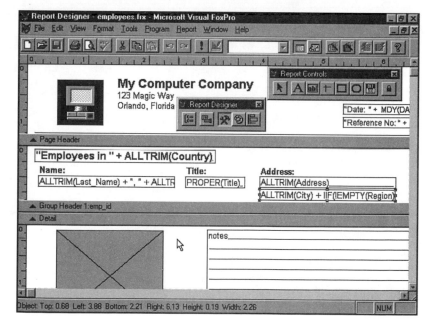

Part

**III**

Ch

**14**

Three of the Group Header fields have attributes that are worth reviewing.

The field "Employees in " + ALLTRIM(COUNTRY) is a straightforward combination of a character string and a Character field. It's located in the group header and results in the field printing for each employee. The desired print display is at the start of each page and when the country changes. To achieve this display, double-click the field to display the Report Expression dialog box. Click the Print When button to display the Print When dialog box (see Figure 14.8).

**FIGURE 14.8**

The Print When dialog box provides options for controlling when values are printed.

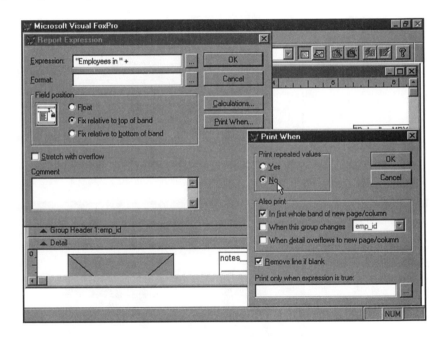

In the Print When dialog box, choose the following options:

- No (in the Print Repeated Values section)
- In First Whole Band of New Page/Column (in the Also Print section)
- Remove Line if Blank check box

The PROPER(Title) file has a width of 30 characters. With the design layout, this field is wider than the allotted space. The solution is to allow the field to Stretch with Overflow (see Figure 14.9).

**FIGURE 14.9**

The Report Expression dialog box provides field position options; a comment section; and access to the Expression Builder, Format, Calculations, and Print When dialog boxes.

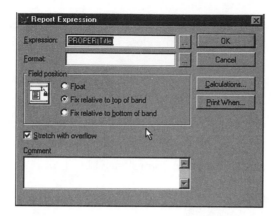

Select the Report Expression dialog box for PROPER(Title) and select:

- Fix Relative to Top of Band (in the Field Position section)
- Stretch with Overflow check box

ALLTRIM(City) + IIF(!EMPTY(Region),", ","") + ALLTRIM(Region) is the third field to review (see Figure 14.10).

**FIGURE 14.10**

The Expression Builder dialog box provides an interface to create complex expressions and verify them.

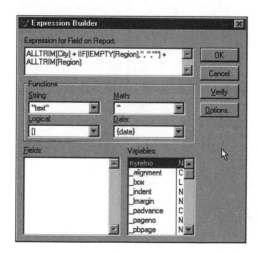

When two fields are combined and separated by a comma, there is the possibility of the *dreaded dangling comma* if the second field is empty. The imbedded IIF() statement is inserted to resolve this problem, as follows:

```
IIF(Logical Condition = True or False, True Condition Display, False
➥Condition Display)
```

Part
III

Ch
14

If the Region field contains data, then a comma, followed by a space, is printed in the report. Otherwise, *nothing* (signified by the closed quotation marks) is printed after the city name.

 **TIP**   During development, even the best programs can create system errors that result in computer lockup. Save your work frequently during the design to safeguard it against loss.

The final fields are PHOTO and NOTES, which are added in the group footer. The photo is added with the Picture/OLE Bound Control (see Figure 14.11).

**FIGURE 14.11**

Use the Picture/OLE Bound Control in the Report Controls toolbar to add pictures.

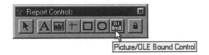

When the Picture/OLE Bound Control is dropped into the report, the Report Picture dialog box appears (see Figure 14.12).

**FIGURE 14.12**

The Report Picture dialog box provides file and field selections, picture and frame options, relative position options, check box for centering the picture, a comment, and access to the Print When dialog box.

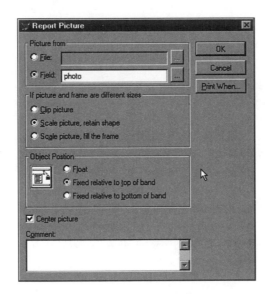

Choose the following options:

- Field (in the Picture From section), and enter PHOTO in the text box
- Scale Picture, Retain Shape (in the If Picture and Frame Are Different Sizes section)

- Fixed Relative to Top of Band (in the Object Position section)
- Center Picture check box

Finally, click the OK button in the dialog box, and position the PHOTO field on the left side of the group footer, as shown in Figure 14.12.

The last field in the report is the Memo field NOTES. The Field control in the Report Controls toolbar displays the Report Expression dialog box (see Figure 14.13).

**FIGURE 14.13**

The Report Expression dialog box, with selected options for the NOTES Memo field.

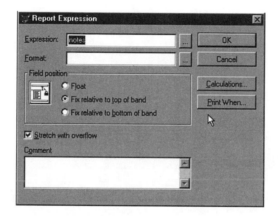

Choose the following options:

- Expression (type **NOTES** in the text box)
- Fix Relative to Top of Band (in the Field Position section)
- Stretch with Overflow check box

When both the PHOTO and NOTES fields have been added to the group footer, all that remains to do is size them. Use the Show Position option to set the Top to 0.05 and the Height to 1.52 for both objects. These options set the top of the picture and the first line of the Memo field to the same line in the report.

The final additions to the report are lines to provide visual breaks between the header, footer, and body of the report. With Show Position on, use the Line control in the Report Controls toolbar to draw two identical lines: one at the bottom of the page header and the other at the top of the page footer.

Save the report and preview your results. See Figure 14.14.

**N O T E** The look and feel of a report viewed in the Report Designer's preview window is different from the look and feel of a printed report. You should make your final evaluation of a report in the medium in which the report will be distributed. ■

**FIGURE 14.14**

The final report, viewed in the Report Designer's preview window with the Print Preview toolbar.

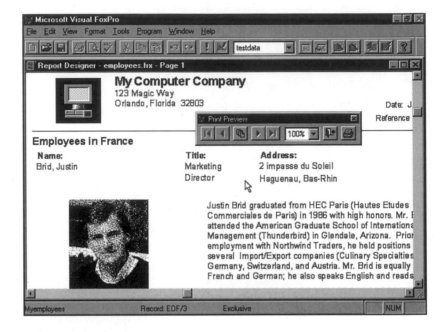

After you complete each report, review the report template's performance, as follows:

- Did it have all the necessary features?
- Were all the fields in the correct positions?
- Were the top, bottom, left, and right margins correct?
- Were all the field formats and alignments correct?

The lines that provide a visual break between the page header, body, and footer certainly are candidates for additions to the template. The report template is designed to save time and provide consistency to reports; change it or create a new one as necessary.

# Using a Program to Initiate the Report

Developing an interface for users to select and run reports is an essential part of creating a complete custom report package. Program 14PRG01 shown in Listing 14.1 shows a variety of options that you can use to develop your report interface. The program starts by declaring the two public variables needed for the report: cMyRefNumber and cRptName. Two additional LOCAL variables are declared: nToPrinter, to store the user's choice of options; and cMessageText, which will be used with the MESSAGEBOX() function to display information to the user.

Notice the way that the variable cRptName is used in the following lines of code:

```
cMessageText = "Send report " + cRptName + " to print ?"
REPORT FORM (cRptName) TO PRINTER NOCONSOLE
```

In the first instance, cRptName is used in the LOCAL cMessageText variable to provide the report name to the interface. In the second instance, the variable is enclosed in parentheses to call the report in the REPORT FORM command.

### YEAR 2000!!!

Having the correct century in your reports is always nice. The SET CENTURY command provides options to display date variables and functions. The command is scoped to the current data session. The code segment

```
SET CENTURY ON
SET CENTURY TO 19 ROLLOVER 60
```

results in dates displayed as follows:

{06/18/96} displays as 06/18/1996

{06/18/60} displays as 06/18/1960

{06/18/99} displays as 06/18/1999

{06/18/00} displays as 06/18/2000

{06/18/59} displays as 06/18/2059

As a result of this SET command, the years between 0 and 59 (inclusive) are displayed as 20??, and the years from 60 to 99 are displayed as 19??. SET CENTURY ON specifies a four-digit year display.

These set commands do not resolve all of the programming problems that can result with the arrival of the year 2000. For situations that cover large data ranges such as inventories of historical items or ages that may span more than 100 years, data storage must be structured to accommodate correct storage and retrieval of date information. *A careful analysis of the year 2000's impact on the data model should be accomplished during an applications specification and design phase.*

---

**Listing 14.1    14PRG01.PRG**

```
*/Program 14PRG01.PRG
PUBLIC cMyRefNumber, cRptName
LOCAL nToPrinter, cMessageText

*/Ensure the correct date is printed on the report.
SET CENTURY ON
SET CENTURY TO 19 ROLLOVER 60
```

Part
III

Ch
14

*continues*

**Listing 14.1   Continued**

```
*/Initialize variables
cMyRefNumber = SYS(2)
cRptName = "Employees"
nToPrinter = 0
cMessageText = "Send report " + cRptName + " to print ?"

*/Set the location to the report
SET PATH TO C:\VFP50\REPORTS

*/Close any open database and open TESTDATA.DBC
CLOSE DATABASE
OPEN DATABASE C:\VFP50\DATA\TESTDATA.DBC

*/Extract the desired report information
SELECT *;
 FROM testdata!employee;
 WHERE YEAR(Employee.hire_date) > 1993;
 GROUP BY Employee.emp_id;
 ORDER BY Employee.last_name ;
 INTO CURSOR MyEmployees


*/Check to ensure there are records available for the report
*/using the system variable _Tally
*/To verify the following IF..THEN..ENDIF set _Tally = 0
*/on the line before the IF statement.
IF _Tally < 1 THEN
     MESSAGEBOX ("No records were selected based " + chr(13) + ;
                    " the report selection criteria.",;
                    0 + 16 + 0, "Alert")
     */At this point in a report interface you could give the user the
     */option of providing a different data source or parameter.
     */If the interface was running a batch reporting system information
     */could be written to a log for review later.

     */Close the cursor, database, and release the public variables
     USE
     CLOSE DATABASE
     RELEASE cMyRefNumber, cRptName
     RETURN
ENDIF

*/Ensure the correct datasource is selected
SELECT MyEmployees

*/Give the user print options
*/Yes will print the report
*/No will send the report to preview
*/Cancel continues with printing or previewing the report
nToPrinter = MessageBox(cMessageText,3 + 32 + 256, "Print Report")
DO CASE
     CASE nToPrinter = 6
           REPORT FORM (cRptName) TO PRINTER NOCONSOLE      && YES BUTTON
```

```
      CASE nToPrinter = 7
           REPORT FORM (cRptName) PREVIEW                      && NO BUTTON
      OTHERWISE
      */ CANCEL BUTTON - NOTHING TO DO
ENDCASE

*/Close the cursor, database, and release the public variables
USE
CLOSE DATABASE
RELEASE cMyRefNumber, cRptName

RETURN
```

The next two steps in Listing 14.1 set a path to the reports and open the database that contains the necessary tables for the report.

To extract the information, a SELECT statement is included in the program. Another option is to use a query or parameterized view to provide a data source.

The next section of code checks for at least one record in the data source by evaluating the system memory variable _TALLY (see Figure 14.15). In the event that _TALLY is less than 1, no records are selected. Then the user can be prompted for a new parameter. Alternatively, information detailing why the report was terminated can be provided to the user or written to a log. Follow this step with a graceful termination of the print routine and return control to the user or system.

**FIGURE 14.15**

The Alert message box and the positioning of the code line "_TALLY = 0" to test the IF..THEN.. statement.

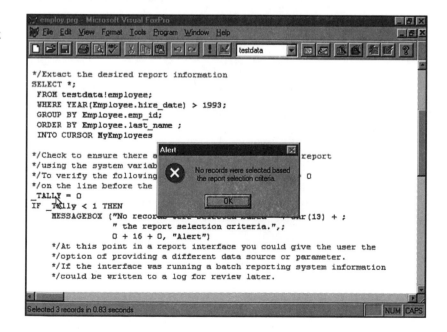

The statement SELECT MyEmployees is there as insurance that the proper data source is selected before running the report. It should be the current one but you can take a milli-second to be sure.

The MESSAGEBOX( ) function provides a quick way to demonstrate the user selection inter-face (see Figure 14.16). The options are:

- YES sends the report to the printer
- NO previews the report in a Report Designer window
- CANCEL continues to close and release commands

**FIGURE 14.16**

The Print Report message box, with the DO CASE statement. The default selection is the No button and results in the REPORT FORM (cRptName) PREVIEW being selected.

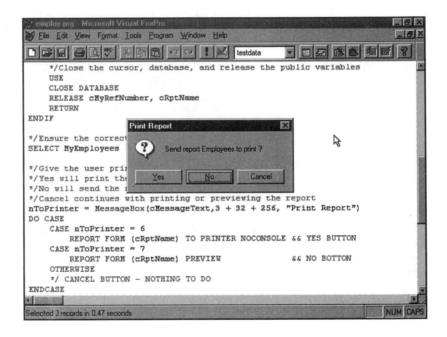

```
                */Close the cursor, database, and release the public variables
                USE
                CLOSE DATABASE
                RELEASE cMyRefNumber, cRptName
                RETURN
        ENDIF

        */Ensure the correct
        SELECT MyEmployees

        */Give the user pri
        */Yes will print the
        */No will send the
        */Cancel continues with printing or previewing the report
        nToPrinter = MessageBox(cMessageText,3 + 32 + 256, "Print Report")
        DO CASE
            CASE nToPrinter = 6
                REPORT FORM (cRptName) TO PRINTER NOCONSOLE && YES BUTTON
            CASE nToPrinter = 7
                REPORT FORM (cRptName) PREVIEW            && NO BOTTON
            OTHERWISE
                */ CANCEL BUTTON - NOTHING TO DO
        ENDCASE
```

The last lines of the program close the cursor, close the database, release the public variables, and then return control to the calling program.

Taking the next step! Using the techniques covered in this section, you now have the basic skills that you need to create a report interface form or class.

# From Here...

In this chapter, you learned how to identify and analyze design issues for a report, build reusable templates and methods, use expressions and variables in a report, and automate a user interface for reports.

For more details on the information in this chapter, or to learn how to create reports and labels with Wizards, refer to the following chapters:

- Chapter 1, "Quick Review of Visual FoxPro's Interfaces," provides an overview of FoxPro basics: toolbars, menus, and windows.

- Chapter 5, "Using Wizards for Rapid Application Development," contains more details on using the Report Wizard.

- Chapter 7, "Creating Basic Queries," provides an overview of query creation.

- Chapter 8, "Advanced Queries and Views," provides details on advanced querying techniques, such as cross-tabs.

- Chapter 11, "Building Applications with Simple Form Structures," provides details on creating forms for user interfaces.

- Chapter 13, "Advanced Form Design Controls," provides details on techniques for designing form controls.

Part
III

Ch
14

# Organizing Components of an Application into a Project

*by Monte Mitzefelt and*
*Sandra Richardson-Lutzow*

The Project Manager is Visual FoxPro's new command center. Even if you are a diehard fan of the old Command window, you will find yourself relying more and more on the Project Manager. Prior to Visual FoxPro 3.0 and many other developments, environments developed Project Managers to serve as a container of files, lacking functionality. A variety of files were pulled together and listed either alphabetically, or by the order in which they were added to the Project Manager. In the meantime, the size of Project Manager increased with files that weren't utilized anymore, taking up space and adding confusion. With such a system, it becomes hard to remember what is used and what isn't because of the inefficient organization of files. While something useful usually came out of the project management process, the process itself was not very pleasant.

## Find your way around the Project Manager

Visual FoxPro uses an outline control to display the files that make up your project.

## Use the Project Manager as an application interface

The Project Manager gives you the opportunity to run, preview, modify, and move or copy project elements.

## Use the Project Information dialog box

You can give your applications background information such as author, date stamps, and home directories, in addition to the use of debug encryption.

## Build Visual FoxPro .APPs and .EXEs

When you are building your application or stand-alone executable file, you have the option to exclude files from compilation.

## Build setup disks to distribute your application

You can give your application a professional look with setup disks for distribution.

## Use SourceSafe for Version Control and Tracking

SourceSafe is a version control application that works hand in hand with your team development project to control track your source code.

Visual FoxPro's Project Manager has retained the simplicity of its forebears while providing some much needed usability and structure. The Project Manager's enhanced interface makes it well suited to endusers who simply want to keep track of personal files, while its extensive leverage of drag-and-drop technology provides developers with many well-deserved shortcuts. If you fall anywhere in between these two groups, you will want to begin any major task by creating a project file. ■

# Finding Your Way Around the Project Manager

At first glance, the Project Manager appears to bristle with strange names and buttons, whose purposes mysteriously change, and tiny indecipherable icons. But once you learn to use the Project Manager's interface and take advantage of its organizational skills, you will wonder how you ever got along without it. In this section, you start by learning how to use each aspect of the Program Manager's interface.

## Using the Outline Control

The outline control is the heart of the Project Manager. You must master this control to effectively use the Project Manager. Fortunately, after you get used to it, the outline control is fairly simple. A plus icon indicates that there are additional hidden items that can be uncovered with a click. Clicking a minus icon hides all subordinate levels. This might sound complicated right now, but it will become second nature as you continue to explore the Project Manager.

Designed to demonstrate a comprehensive business application, TASTRADE.PJX is a great place to explore the world of possibilities within Visual FoxPro. First you'll open the TASTRADE.PJX project, and then you'll use the outline control. Follow these steps:

1. Type **CD (HOME() + "samples\tastrade")** in the Command window. Visual FoxPro changes to the directory where TASTRADE.PJX is located.

---

 **TIP** Visual FoxPro supports the DOS directory commands CD, RD, and MD.

---

2. Choose the Open icon from the Standard toolbar; choose File, Open (Ctrl+O); or enter the following in the Command window: **MODIFY PROJECT TASTRADE.PJX**.

3. If you initially installed Visual FoxPro in a directory other than the default, a dialog box similar to the one in Figure 15.1 appears. Choose Yes to register the directory change in the project.

**FIGURE 15.1**
Automatically updating a project's home directory with the new home directory dialog box is easy in Visual FoxPro.

4. Select each window individually from the Window menu and close them, except for the Project Manager - Tastrade window.

5. Choose Window, Arrange All. The Project Manager - Tastrade window should now look like Figure 15.2.

**FIGURE 15.2**
You can resize the Project Manager and outline control to take up as little or as much space as you need.

6. Click the plus icons beside the Data, Documents, Class Libraries, Code, and Other categories in the outline control. These categories expand and reveal several subcategories each. Figure 15.3 shows the Project Manager - Tastrade window with all categories open.

> **N O T E** The outline control is an OLE object, so you can use it in your own Visual FoxPro applications. It can be very useful for representing a company's organizational structure or to give an executive reporting system broad regional summaries and local details in one unified package. ■

▶ **See** "Using OCXs in Visual FoxPro" in Bonus Chapter 06 located on the CD

## Creating New Files and Adding Files to a Project

The task of building a project can be daunting if you have a lot of files already created. If you're starting from scratch, you should use the Project Manager to organize your application as you build it rather than creating each file individually and then trying to remember to add each one into the project. The Project Manager can help you much more effectively if you go through it—and not around it. To demonstrate how to do this, create a text file and automatically associate it with TASTRADE.PJX. (The process of creating a file elsewhere and adding it later is similar, but less natural.) Follow these steps:

**FIGURE 15.3**

The Project Manager provides organization by file type, freeing you to use the entire file name for richer descriptions.

1. From the Project Manager, highlight the Text subheading under the Other category.

2. Choose New from the right side of the Project Manager.

3. Type **This is a great place for program documentation and .H include files!**

4. Close the text editing window.

5. Choose Yes from the Save Changes dialog box.

6. Select the Save Document As field, enter **MYDOCS.TXT**, and choose Save (see Figure 15.4).

   You now see your new file beside the Text subcategory.

Notice the Code Page button on the Save As dialog box pictured in Figure 15.4. The Project Manager supports independent code pages for each text file. This enables developers to easily create #include files for international applications (see Appendix B for more information). As you can see in Figure 15.5, support for other versions of Windows such as Greek or Russian is already in the box.

To help keep track of files, after creating a new file, choose Project, Edit Description. You can provide a descriptive note about the project element that shows up on the bottom of the Project Manager whenever the element is highlighted.

**FIGURE 15.4**

You can access the Code Page dialog box for text files from the Save As dialog box.

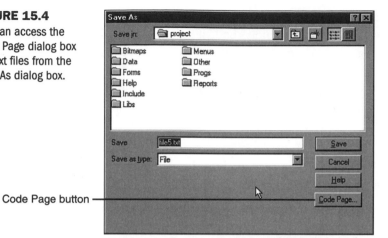

Code Page button

**FIGURE 15.5**

Ease international development with the Code Page dialog box.

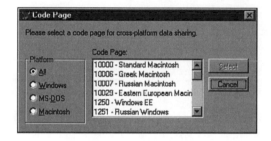

Adding a single file or project element would have been just as easy as creating a new one. Simply highlight the subcategory of interest and choose Add. Use the Open dialog box to locate your file. The file is now associated with your project.

You probably noticed that you used the standard file Open and Save As dialog boxes as you created MYDOCS.TXT. That's because in Visual FoxPro, unlike some other databases such as Microsoft Access, all of your project elements reside in separate files. This approach has a number of advantages. First, it allows your project elements to be easily associated with more than one project. Your projects know where to find a given file, but they don't really care if some other project knows, too. Second, if you do use the same project element in several projects, all modifications are realized by each of the projects. You don't have to worry about cutting and pasting changes later.

## Removing Files

If you've ever used other project managers, you've probably been frustrated by the two-step process needed to clean up and maintain projects. First, you would remove the project element from the project and then delete the project element's file from the disk. At your discretion, Visual FoxPro handles both of these tasks at once for you. The list that follows steps through the process of removing a file from the project.

 **TIP** The cross-reference reports from FoxDoc, the Documenting Wizard, might help you weed out old unused files in your project.

1. Highlight the MYDOCS project element under the Text subheading.

2. Choose the Remove button.

3. Choose Delete from the Remove dialog box, shown in Figure 15.6.

4. Click the minus icon beside the Text subheading to roll up the text file list.

**FIGURE 15.6**
Clean up your project and your disk with the Remove dialog box.

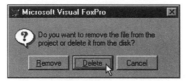

> **CAUTION**
>
> While this procedure is very convenient, you should take great care not to use it wholesale. If there is a chance that a project element is associated with another project, choose the Remove button in the Remove dialog box. This simply disassociates the project element from the project without deleting its file on the disk.

**N O T E**   A .PJX project file is a special type of free table. The Remove button marks records in the table for deletion, but does not perform a PACK. To PACK your project and dispose of the unwanted records, choose Project, Cleanup Project. ■

## Modifying Existing Project Elements

The Modify button in the Project Manager provides access to the native editor of every element in your projects. The following steps show how the modify button works.

1. Click the plus icon by the Other Files subheading.

2. Scroll down and highlight TTRADESM.BMP.

3. Choose Modify.

4. Exit the Paint application (the default application associated with BMP files for most systems).

5. Click the minus icon by the Other Files subheading.

If you had selected another OLE file or a native Visual FoxPro file, the Project Manager would have activated the appropriate editor as it does in Figure 15.7. This feature plays a key role in positioning the Project Manager at the heart of Visual FoxPro. As the amount of multimedia, hypertext help, and other features used in applications increases, you will consider the ability to integrate these into your development environment to be a major benefit.

**FIGURE 15.7**
Modify OLE files using the Project Manager.

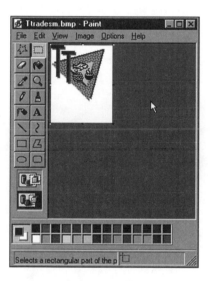

# Using the Project Manager as an Application Interface

You can already see how the new Project Manager aids the developer in organizing files by type and providing simple ways to create, modify, or even remove objects. If you aren't an application developer and got Visual FoxPro just to keep track of your own files, then the best is yet to come.

Visual FoxPro's new interface is much more intuitive than that of previous versions. In the next several sections you'll look at one button and how it uses context from the outline control to adjust its behavior.

## Running Programs and Forms from the Project Manager

When you highlight project elements listed under Programs, Forms, or Queries, the Project Manager displays a Run button. The Run button can be used to execute programs and queries and to activate forms. Use the following steps to run a program from the Project Manager.

1. Scroll up and click the plus icon by the Programs subheading.

2. Highlight the bolded program named MAIN.

**N O T E**  The bolded program indicates which program Visual FoxPro runs first when you bundle your application into an .APP or .EXE to distribute your applications to others. See the section "Setting a Main File" later in this chapter.  ■

3. Choose Run. This brings up the welcome screen from Tasmanian Traders as shown in Figure 15.8.

**FIGURE 15.8**
Run programs, forms, and queries straight from the Project Manager.

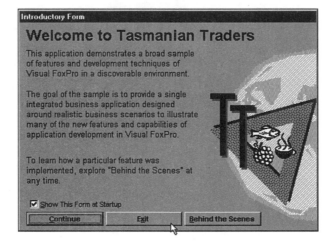

4. Choose Exit from the Tasmanian Traders welcome screen.

5. Click the minus icon by Programs.

## Previewing a Report

When you highlight project elements listed under Reports or Labels, the Project Manager displays a Preview button. The Preview button allows reports to be seen and reviewed on-screen prior to print or publication.

1. Scroll up and click the plus icon by Reports.
2. Highlight the LISTCAT report.
3. Choose Preview. An on-screen version of the report appears, much like the one in Figure 15.9.
4. Click the close preview icon.
5. Click the minus icon by Reports.

**FIGURE 15.9**
Proofread reports and labels using the Preview button.

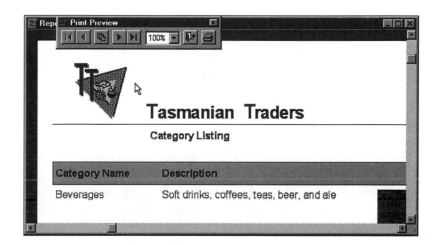

## Opening Databases and Browsing Tables

To take full advantage of Visual FoxPro's enhanced database engine, you need to create database containers. All of the database containers are listed under the Databases sub-heading. When you highlight a database container, the Project Manager displays an Open button. Because Database Containers merely contain definitions, rules, and relationships, opening a database container has no dramatic visual effects, but it does prepare Visual FoxPro to quickly access tables defined as part of the database. (If you have the standard toolbar open, you can see the database name in the database list box.) If a table is high-lighted, the Project Manager provides easy access to the data with a Browse button. Follow these steps to use the Browse button.

1. Click the plus icon beside Databases.
2. Click the plus icon beside TASTRADE.
3. Click the plus icon beside Tables.
4. Highlight EMPLOYEE, as shown in Figure 15.10.

**FIGURE 15.10**

View database elements from the Project Manager.

**N O T E** The exclude icon, which appears as a circle with a slash, denotes which files are left out of the .APP or .EXE when you build the project. Notice in Figure 15.10 how this icon shows up beside every table in the database. If these files were included in the project, they would get embedded in any .APPs or .EXEs that you might build. When embedded, they become read-only. Because most tables need to have data added and changed inside them, make sure they are marked as exclude. Fortunately, Visual FoxPro (unlike previous versions of FoxPro) defaults to this, but this flag can be changed. Make sure you really want a read-only table if you change this setting. See the section on including and excluding files later in this chapter to learn how to change this flag. ■

    5.  Choose <u>B</u>rowse. Your screen will look like Figure 15.11.

**FIGURE 15.11**

Quickly access table data from within your project.

| Employee_id | Last_name | First_name | Title |
|---|---|---|---|
| 1 | Buchanan | Steven | Sales Manager |
| 2 | Suyama | Michael | Sales Representative |
| 3 | King | Robert | Sales Representative |
| 4 | Callahan | Laura | Inside Sales Coordinator |
| 5 | Dodsworth | Anne | Sales Representative |
| 6 | Hellstern | Albert | Business Manager |
| 7 | Smith | Tim | Mail Clerk |
| 8 | Patterson | Caroline | Receptionist |
| 9 | Brid | Justin | Marketing Director |
| 10 | Martin | Xavier | Marketing Associate |
| 11 | Pereira | Laurent | Advertising Specialist |
| 12 | Davolio | Nancy | Applications Developer |
| 13 | Fuller | Andrew | Entry Clerk |

    6.  Close the Browse window.

    7.  Click the minus icon beside the Databases subheading in the outline control.

# Dragging and Dropping Project Elements

As mentioned at the beginning of this chapter, the Project Manager makes extensive use of drag-and-drop technology. The following series of steps work through a simple example of this. You'll want to experiment further to see the full range of Visual FoxPro's drag-and-drop capabilities. You can't hurt anything by experimenting because the Project Manager indicates where you can and cannot drop project elements.

1. Choose Window, Command Window from the Visual FoxPro system menu.
2. Choose Window, Arrange All.
3. Click the plus icon beside ABOUT under the Class Libraries subheading.
4. Click the left mouse button over the ABOUTBOX class and hold it down.
5. Move the mouse pointer over the Command window and release it. Visual FoxPro inserts the text aboutbox in the Command window, as shown in Figure 15.12.

**FIGURE 15.12**

Insert project elements into other project elements using drag-and-drop.

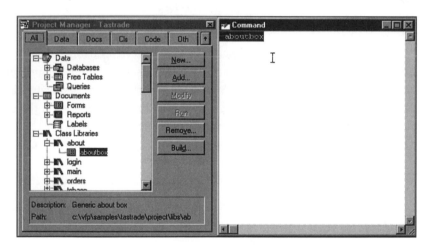

Many times during development you may decide to reclassify classes or rearrange your class libraries. The drag-and-drop feature proves helpful when you want to perform this task. Just drag the class from one library to the other. Remember to remove the class from the previous location to avoid duplication. When doing this, you will be prompted for reassurance that you do in fact want to remove the class, as shown in Figure 15.13.

**TIP**

Forms are a good place to start experimenting with drag-and-drop. Try dropping tables or visual classes on a form.

**FIGURE 15.13**

A screen pops up
when you remove a
class from its library to
ensure that you really
want to perform the
removal.

# Using Shortcuts with the Project Manager

As you can see, Visual FoxPro's Project Manager is full of helpful features. In fact, if you
are creating a database just for personal use, the Project Manager may be all the user
interface you require. In the previous section, you explored the functionality of the Project
Manager and how it helps you accomplish certain tasks more easily. This section focuses
on some shortcuts that provide convenient access to that functionality.

## Using the Tabs as Shortcuts to the Major Categories

As you've explored the Project Manager, you've probably noticed a one-to-one correspon-
dence between the major category headings in the outline control and the additional tabs
along the top of the Project Manager. They are nearly identical. Selecting the Data tab is
the same as clicking the plus icon beside the Data category in the outline control. Even
though they provide access to the same project elements, the tab and the outline category
may have different subheadings expanded, as you see in Figures 15.14 and 15.15.

**FIGURE 15.14**

Get the broad overview
using the outline
categories.

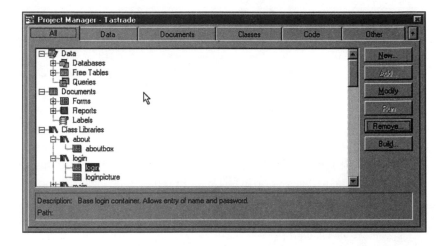

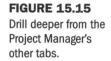

**FIGURE 15.15**

Drill deeper from the Project Manager's other tabs.

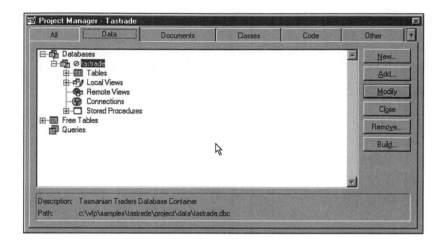

## Collapsing and Docking the Project Manager

For all its niceties, the Project Manager appears bulky. In the Visual FoxPro development environment, every inch of screen is a valuable commodity. Between Form Designers, Visual Classes, programs, and Property Sheets, Visual FoxPro needs as much "screen real estate" available as possible. In this regard, the Project Manager has deceived you; it does not have to take up a quarter of the screen. You've already seen how it can be resized, but then most of the tools in Visual FoxPro can be resized.

Choose the up-arrow button in the upper right-hand corner, and voilà, the Project Manager is minimized, collapsing like a magician's top hat. Although it appears that you've lost some functionality, you really haven't. First, choose the All tab and then click the right mouse button on any item in the list. Figure 15.16 demonstrates that all the functionality of the expanded Project Manager has been preserved in the right mouse button. You can also use the Project menu.

 Because Visual FoxPro was Microsoft's first Windows 95-compliant application, this right-mouse-button behavior is prevalent throughout the product. Try the right mouse button everywhere. You will find some very helpful shortcuts.

In this collapsed state, the Project Manager is a toolbar. If you drag it to the top of the screen, it docks there like any other toolbar. Additionally, you can drag a tab off of the collapsed Project Manager (regardless of whether or not it's docked). Drag the Document tab off the docked Project Manager, and your screen will look similar to Figure 15.17. Tabs dragged off the screen are referred to as *torn-off*.

**FIGURE 15.16**
The collapsed Project Manager takes up minimal screen space while readily supporting drag-and-drop to the designers.

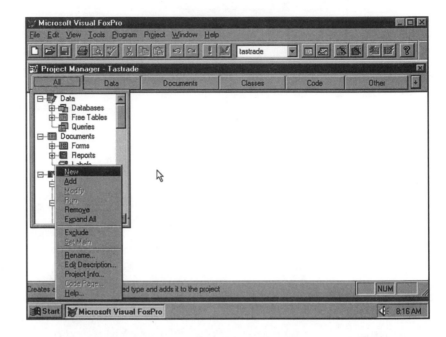

**FIGURE 15.17**
Drag tabs off the collapsed and/or docked Project Manager.

Pushpin

Windows 95 close button

Resize corner

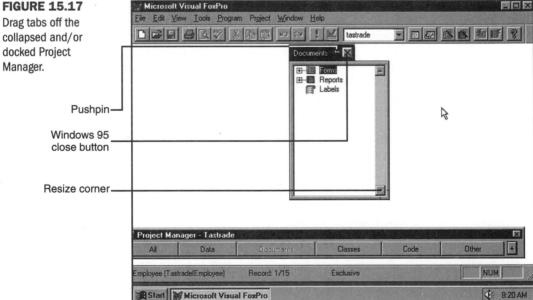

**TIP** Clicking the pushpin on a torn-off tab or property sheet forces it to stay on top. Clicking the pushpin on the Documents tab gives you quick and easy access to your forms, reports, and labels. Simply click the pushpin again to allow the tab to be covered up by other windows.

In its collapsed and docked form, the Project Manager acts like a very sophisticated menu system. Using the Project Manager in this fashion can be a great time-saver. It largely negates the need to program your own menu structure and helps you create a consistent interface to all of your databases.

If you choose to use Visual FoxPro as a menu system, you will want to take the following steps first:

1. Choose Tools, Options from the menu.

2. Select the Projects tab.

3. Select Run Selected File from the Project Double-Click Action radio button group, shown in Figure 15.18.

**FIGURE 15.18**
Change the double-click behavior in the Project Manager's outline control.

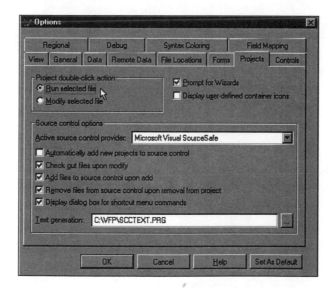

Now, whenever you double-click a project element, the Project Manager will run, open, browse, or preview it, as specified on the context-sensitive button.

# Using the Project Information Dialog Box

The Project Information dialog box can be brought up by choosing Project, Project Info (Ctrl+J) from the menu. The Project tab (see Figure 15.19) of the Project Information dialog box provides you with access to several varied but key settings such as debug info and encryption. The Files tab provides a more traditional overview of the files associated with your project as familiar to users of FoxPro 2.x. Finally, the Servers tab is used to define OLE servers.

**FIGURE 15.19**

Protect your programming investment with the Project tab of the Project Information dialog box.

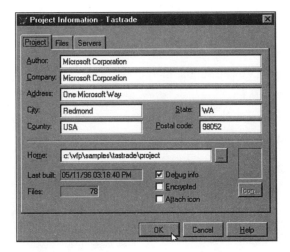

**Using the Author Information Fields**   The author information fields are very important. Filling in these fields in your projects can help establish your copyright. Generated code from menus gets branded with the supplied author information and the date. Providing this information protects your ownership of that code as a piece of intellectual property.

**Understanding the Home Directory, Last Built, and Files Field**   The Home directory is the root directory for your project. Typically, your project file, and all of the files specific to that project, should be in this directory or some subdirectory of this directory. This will not always be the case, particularly with class libraries, but it is a good practice to follow. As you saw in Figure 15.1, if you move a project file to a new directory, VFP automatically queries whether this new directory is project file's new home. If, for any reason, you cannot do this with the mouse and you need to do so with the keyboard, type the new home directory in the Home field or choose the ... button by tabbing over to it.

The Last Built field contains the last date and time that the project was built. The Files field counts the total number of files associated with the project.

**Using the Debug Info Flag**   The Debug Info check box tells Visual FoxPro whether or not to include source code line numbers in the compiled files. The source code line numbers allow the Trace window to track program operation in the compiled file and display it to you from the source code. This is essential to debugging your applications. Program and line number information can even be logged from the client's machine when an error occurs in the field. Unfortunately, leaving the debugging information in also provides more information for someone trying to decompile your code. Obviously, this is an issue that requires thought on a case-by-case basis. This option corresponds to the NODEBUG argument in the COMPILE command.

▶ **See** "Understanding Methods for Tracking Down Errors," **p. 646**

▶ **See** "Using Error Handlers," **p. 665**

**Using the Encrypted Flag**   The Encrypted check box tells Visual FoxPro whether or not to encrypt compiled files. While not infallible, this encryption adds a very real level of protection to your distributed applications. Decompiling an encrypted file to source code is a much more difficult proposition than decompiling a non-encrypted one. If you are worried about theft of your intellectual property, check the Encrypted flag.

 For maximum security when distributing an application, turn Debug Info off and Encrypted on.

**Setting the Default Icon for the Project**   Checking the Attach Icon to .EXE check box activates the Icon button. A File Open dialog box replete with an inset preview window helps you locate the desired graphic. Simply select an icon file and choose Preview to look at it. When you're satisfied with your selection, choose OK. The icon you select will be the icon displayed while the program is running.

**Getting the Most Out of the Files Tab**   Choosing the Files tab in the Project Information dialog box brings up a familiar sight to FoxPro 2.x users: a long list of files sorted by name. Although double-clicking these items does not modify or run them, this view is still much improved over previous versions. Choosing a column heading such as Type suddenly changes the sort order to type. This tab is most useful for checking and updating the include status on various project elements. The check box in the Included column is live. Clicking one of these check boxes toggles whether or not the file gets embedded into your .APP or .EXE file. By clicking Update Native Code Pages, you update the code page for every file to the native code. You cannot use this screen to change the code page for individual files, however. You can set a default code page in the Visual FoxPro configuration file.

Click the Included heading at the top of the table in the Files page. This sorts the files, listing those excluded first, then those included, and finally the main program. This is a great way to locate the main file in an old project. Simply scroll to the bottom of the list. There you will find a program, menu, or form with a filled-in check box like the one in Figure 15.20. The filled-in square indicates that this file is the main file for the project.

**FIGURE 15.20**

Use the Project Information dialog box's Files tab to locate a project's main file.

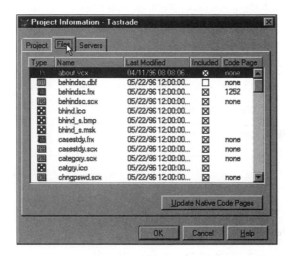

**Using Classes Located on Servers** The Server tab in the Project Information dialog box stores the location of the classes marked as OLEPublic, as shown in Figure 15.21.

**FIGURE 15.21**

Use the Project Information dialog box's Server tab to display information classes marked as OLEPublic.

When a class is marked as OLEPublic, an executable file (EXE) or a dynamic link library (DLL) containing the class can be created interactively in the Project Manager. The EXE or DLL is automatically registered with the operating system and becomes available to any OLE automation client. You can see a list of those available with the Server classes list box. When highlighting a listed item, you see the library name and the name of the class displayed. Also displayed is a description of the class name and a description of the library the selected class is based on. If you have created your own help files and have associated the class to a help topic, the help file and help context ID are also shown. Each class in the list has a corresponding .PJX file. This file is displayed in the Project name box. Instancing displays one of three choices: Single Use, Not Creatable, and Multi Use.

In *Single Use*, you can create an instance of the class within or outside Visual FoxPro using OLE automation. Each instance requested of the class by an OLE client outside the project causes a separate copy of the OLE serve to open.

*Not Creatable* indicates that you can create an instance only within Visual FoxPro.

*Multi Use* indicates that you can create an instance of the class within or outside of Visual FoxPro using OLE automation just like the Single Use; but if a copy of the OLE client is already running, it is provided as the OLE server for the requested instance as well.

▶ **See** "Creating Custom Classes," **p. 117**

# Building Visual FoxPro .APPs and .EXEs

Producing an application or executable file is probably the simplest thing you'll do in this chapter. Choose the Build button. Figure 15.22 appears; it shows the Build Options dialog box. Table 15.1 outlines the four build options displayed there.

**FIGURE 15.22**
Use the Build Options dialog box to create .APPs and .EXEs.

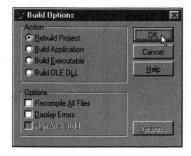

**Table 15.1   Build Options**

| Option | Description |
| --- | --- |
| Rebuild Project | This option goes through all the files in the project generating source code and/or checking for errors. |
| Build Application | This option builds the project as Rebuild Project does, and then bundles all the files marked for inclusion into an .APP file. Your clients must have their own copy of Visual FoxPro to use an .APP file. |
| Build Executable | This option builds and bundles the project as Build Application does, but in addition, an executable file header and the Visual FoxPro runtime loader are placed at the beginning of the file. You can distribute the Visual FoxPro runtime libraries with the .EXE. (Professional edition only!) |
| Build OLE DLL | This option creates the dynamic link library using the class information from the project file. |

Unless you check Recompile All Files, Visual FoxPro builds only files that have been modified since the last build. Checking Display Errors brings up a file at the end that lists all the syntax errors that Visual FoxPro encounters while trying to build this project. You also can bring this file up by choosing Project, Errors from the Visual FoxPro menu. Choosing OK initiates the build and brings up a Save As dialog box if necessary. If you like to view the project running immediately after you build an application or executable file (and who doesn't?), choose Run After Build; it automatically executes after the build is complete.

If you choose Build Executable or Build OLE DLL, the Version button is enabled. By clicking the Version button, you will display the EXE Version dialog box, which displays the Version Number and Information, as shown in Figure 15.23. This dialog box enables you to specify or automatically generate the version numbers that occur at each build. The Version Information displays the information set for various pieces of version information such as comments, company name, file description, legal copyright, legal trademarks, and product name.

**TROUBLESHOOTING**

**Sometimes, it seems that I build the project over and over, but my program always seems the same when I run it.** This is a great time to use Recompile All Files. Occasionally, your compiled file gets a date from the future or your source file gets a date from the past, and Visual FoxPro does not know to rebuild it even if you've made changes. Recompile <u>A</u>ll Files forces Visual FoxPro to look at all the files as if they'd never been compiled.

**Sometimes I try to build an .APP or .EXE, but it never creates the file.** You probably have an error in one of your files. Choose Pro<u>j</u>ect, Errors to locate the source of the trouble.

**FIGURE 15.23**

The Version dialog box enables you to specify information for the version.

## Setting a Main File

The file marked with the main icon (indicated by the bold file name) is the file that gets called when a client starts your .APP or .EXE. While it can be a form, menu, or program, a program is the recommended choice. The program need not do more than set up your databases, tables, and so on, and invoke your user interface, but it has several advantages. If you set a form as the main project element, then you have no way to name the form instance. If you use a menu, then the main setup code for your application is buried in some obscure snippet. A typical MAIN.PRG might look like:

```
...setup code...
DO main.mpr && setup main menu
DO FORM main.scx NAME mainform         && and/or setup main form
READ EVENTS && start event loop
...cleanup code...
```

This way you can refer to the MAIN.SCX form using the object name MAINFORM and all the setup and cleanup code is out in the open.

To change the main element in your program, do the following:

1. Click the plus in the outline control until you can see the form, menu, or program you want as your main file.

2. Highlight the project element by clicking it.

3. Choose Project, Set Main, or right-click the highlighted element and choose Set Main.

## Including and Excluding Files from Your .APPs and .EXEs

Including and excluding files can be the source of some confusion. You want every file in your project to end up on your clients' machines. Not all of them can be embedded in your .APPs and .EXEs, however. By default, Visual FoxPro excludes databases, tables, C library files called .FLLs, and .APPs from the embedding process. With the exception of certain tables, you never want to include any of those types of files. Databases and tables need to change and grow. Included files become static and read-only because .EXEs and .APPs are static once built. Clearly there is a fundamental problem with including databases and tables to these files.

**N O T E** A handful of exceptions to this rule apply to tables. Some lookup or code tables can benefit from being read-only on the client's machine to prevent damage or alteration. Additionally, FOXUSER.DBF and CONFIG.FPW can be included. In this read-only state, multiple users can access the settings contained in FOXUSER.DBF and CONFIG.FPW at the same time. ■

Even though .FLLs (or any other form of .DLL) and .APPs are static, there are technical reasons why they can't be included in the .APP or .EXE. Windows must be able to load .FLLs and .DLLs wherever it wants to in memory, hence the name Dynamic Link Library. If they were embedded in another file, Windows could not do this. If an .APP were inside another .APP, Visual FoxPro would be able to look for files inside of files *ad infinitum*.

Because these files won't be embedded in your .APP or .EXE, you have to make provisions for distributing these files, too. Fortunately, the Setup Wizard takes most of the hassle out of that.

## Building Projects from the Command Window

In addition to the Project Manager interface, the commands listed in Table 15.2 are available.

**Table 15.2 Project Command Window Equivalents**

| Command | Description |
| --- | --- |
| CREATE PROJECT MYPROJ | This command creates a project called MYPROJ.PJX and opens it in a Project Manager Window. |

| Command | Description |
| --- | --- |
| BUILD PROJECT MYPROJ FROM FILE1.PRG[, …] | This command creates a file called MYPROJ.PJX and associates FILE1.PRG, and so on, with it. |
| BUILD PROJECT MYPROJ | This is equivalent to selecting the Rebuild Project option from the Build Options dialog box. |
| BUILD APP MYPROJ FROM MYPROJ | This command creates a file called MYPROJ.APP based on MYPROJ.PJX. |
| BUILD EXE MYPROJ FROM MYPROJ | This command creates a file called MYPROJ.EXE based on MYPROJ.PJX. (Professional Version only) |

**CAUTION**

Do not confuse BUILD PROJECT with BUILD PROJECT FROM. BUILD PROJECT FROM overwrites your previous project file, and you lose all your original associations.

## Building Setup Disks to Distribute Your Application

Building setup disks is the final step in producing an application. The installation procedure, however, is the first thing your customers see. Certainly the old truism about first impressions applies here. You will not get a second chance to make a first impression. You've admired the slick yet simple Windows SETUP.EXE programs from commercial vendors, but have traditionally preferred to put your development efforts into a well-designed application rather than a slick setup.

Above and beyond the fact that a slick-looking setup program is impressive, Visual FoxPro is not a trivial system to install. Visual FoxPro's runtime modules, Object Linking and Embedding (OLE) 2.0, and maybe even the 32-bit version of the Open DataBase Connectivity drivers, in the case of a client/server application, must all be installed. In reality, the days are long past when you can simply unzip some files and start running your application.

Fortunately, Visual FoxPro Professional provides a very robust Setup Wizard that does virtually all the work for you.

# Using MAKEDIST Procedure in Preparation for the Setup Wizard

The only drawback to the Setup Wizard is its lack of integration with the Project Manager. The Setup Wizard requires you to create and maintain a separate directory tree that contains only the files you want to ship.

The MAKEDIST procedure in code listing 15PRG01.PRG bridges some of the gap between these two tools. In the form in which it is presented here, MAKEDIST does not fully challenge the Setup Wizard's abilities. The Setup Wizard re-creates entire directory trees below the directory you specify, and it faithfully re-creates any and all subdirectories of that directory. MAKEDIST functions as a scavenger picking up all the excluded project elements you might have forgotten to put in your distribution tree and places copies of them in a subdirectory called FILES. You can use this directory as your distribution tree even though it is not very elaborate.

 **TIP**  Think of the distribution directory tree as a blueprint that defines how you want the files to be laid out on the user's machine.

To use MAKEDIST, simply put 15PRG01.PRG, PIECES.DBF, and PIECES.CDX from the SE Using Visual FoxPro source disk in the Visual FoxPro path. Next, change to your project directory. Entering the following

```
DO MAKEDIST IN 15PRG01.PRG
```

in the Command window creates a subdirectory called FILES and one called DISKS for the numbered disk images, builds the project into an .EXE in FILES subdirectory, and finally, copies all the excluded project elements into FILES as well. One important note—MAKEDIST expects only one project per directory and ignores any others. If you would rather name the subdirectories something else, simply call MAKEDIST as follows:

```
DO MAKEDIST IN 15PRG01.PRG WITH "filedir", "diskdir"
```

Following is the listing for MAKEDIST:

**Listing 15.1   15PRG01.PRG**

```
***
***
**-    Note use of this program requires using the default file extensions
***
PROCEDURE MAKEDIST
PARAMETERS filedir, distdir
PRIVATE projname, makedistdir, badchar, destination, deleted, safety, temp

    IF EMPTY( m.filedir )
        m.filedir = "FILES"
```

```
    ELSE
        IF SUBSTR( m.filedir, LEN( m.filedir ) ) = "\"
            m.filedir = LEFT( m.filedir, LEN( m.filedir ) - 1 )
        ENDIF
    ENDIF

    IF EMPTY( m.distdir )
        m.distdir = "DISKS"
    ELSE
        IF SUBSTR( m.distdir, LEN( m.distdir ) ) = "\"
            m.distdir = LEFT( m.distdir, LEN( m.distdir ) - 1 )
        ENDIF
    ENDIF

    **- If no project, return to Command window
    IF ADIR( projs, "*.PJX" ) < 1
        RETURN
    ENDIF
    m.projname = UPTO( ".", projs[1] )
    RELEASE ALL LIKE projs*

    m.makedistdir = UPTOLAST( "\", SYS(16) )

    **- Create non-filename character filter
    m.badchar = ""
    FOR i = 0 TO 255
        IF   !(    CHR( m.i ) $ ":\._!$@#-" OR;
                ISDIGIT( CHR( m.i ) ) OR;
                ISALPHA( CHR( m.i ) );
            )
            m.badchar = m.badchar + CHR( m.i )
        ENDIF
    ENDFOR

    CLEAR
    ?
    ? "***"
    ? "**- MAKEDIST.PRG from SE Using Visual FoxPro "
    ? "**- Copyright 1995, Que Publishing"
    ? "***"
    ?

    **- Close all files, etc. to prepare for copy
    CLOSE ALL

    **- Create directory for distribution files
    m.temp = ON("ERROR")
    ON ERROR ? "Directory exists"
    MD (m.filedir)
    MD (m.distdir)
    ON ERROR &temp.

    m.safety = SET( "SAFETY" )
**-    SET SAFETY OFF      && Uncomment to always overwrite files without asking
```

*continues*

**Listing 15.1 Continued**

```
m.deleted = SET( "DELETED" )
SET DELETED OFF

**- Deposit EXE in the directory named in filedir
BUILD EXE (m.filedir + "\" + m.projname) FROM (m.projname)

**- Open project file as a free table
CREATE CURSOR project ( name M, type C(1) )
USE (m.projname + ".PJX") ALIAS projmst IN 0

**- Build project elements to copy cursor
SELECT projmst
SCAN FOR exclude
    INSERT INTO project VALUES ( projmst.name, projmst.type )
    IF DELETED( "projmst" )
        DELETE IN project
    ENDIF

    IF projmst.type = "d"
        SELECT 0
        USE (ALLTRIM( projmst.name )) ALIAS dbc
        SCAN FOR ObjectType = "Table"
            **- Extract table name from Property field
            m.temp = ""
            FOR i = 16 TO LEN( dbc.property )
                IF SUBSTR( dbc.property, m.i, 1 ) $ m.badchar
                    EXIT
                ENDIF
                m.temp = m.temp + SUBSTR( dbc.property, m.i, 1 )
            ENDFOR
            INSERT INTO project VALUES;
                ( m.temp , "D" )
            IF DELETED( "projmst" )
                DELETE IN project
            ENDIF
        ENDSCAN dbc
        USE
    ENDIF
    SELECT projmst
ENDSCAN projmst

**- Open pieces project element to file extension cross reference file
USE (m.makedistdir + "pieces") IN 0 ORDER type

**- relate each record (project element) in PJX to all of its files
USE IN projmst
SELECT project
SET RELATION TO type INTO pieces
SET SKIP TO pieces

**- copy excluded files to distribution directory
SCAN
    IF EMPTY( pieces.extension )
        m.temp = ALLTRIM( project.name )
```

```
        ELSE
                m.temp = UPTOLAST( ".", project.name, .T. ) + pieces.extension
        ENDIF
        m.destination = m.filedir + "\" + PASTLAST( "\", m.temp )

        DO CASE
                CASE !FILE( m.temp )
                        ? "No such file", m.temp, ". . ."
                CASE DELETED("project")
                        ? "Deleting", m.destination
                        DELETE FILE (m.destination)
**- Change the next CASE to an OTHERWISE to always overwrite files
                CASE !FILE( m.destination )
                        ? "Copying", m.temp, "to", m.destination
                        COPY FILE (m.temp) TO (m.destination)
                OTHERWISE
                        ? m.destination, "already exists!"
        ENDCASE
    ENDSCAN project

    SET DELETED &deleted.
    SET SAFETY &safety.

    CLOSE ALL

ENDPROC


***
**- Return string up to first occurrence of m.upto
***
PROCEDURE upto
PARAMETER upto, string
PRIVATE retval

    IF m.upto $ m.string
            m.retval = LEFT( m.string, AT( m.upto, m.string ) - 1 )
    ELSE
            m.retval = m.string
    ENDIF

RETURN m.retval


***
**- Return string up to and including last occurrence of m.uptolast
***
PROCEDURE uptolast
PARAMETER uptolast, string, pad
PRIVATE retval

    IF m.uptolast $ m.string
            m.retval = LEFT( m.string, RAT( m.uptolast, m.string ) )
    ELSE
            m.retval = m.string + IIF( pad, m.pastlast, "" )
```

*continues*

**Listing 15.1 Continued**

```
    ENDIF

RETURN m.retval


***
**- Return string up to and including last occurrence of m.pastlast
***
PROCEDURE pastlast
PARAMETER pastlast, string
PRIVATE retval

    IF m.pastlast $ m.string
        m.retval = SUBSTR( m.string, RAT( m.pastlast, m.string ) + 1 )
    ELSE
        m.retval = m.string
    ENDIF

RETURN m.retval
```

MAKEDIST sets a one-to-many relation from your .PJX project file to PIECES.DBF to make sure it picks up all the files associated with your project elements. PIECES.DBF contains pairs of project element type codes used by the Project Manager and file extensions. In this way, MAKEDIST can check for the existence of all the files needed for a table such as .DBF, .CDX, and .FPT. If you want to send the compiled code but not source code for programs, for instance, simply DELETE the record where extension = "PRG" and then PACK the table.

Depending on how you want to work, you may want to change MAKEDIST considerably. You might always want to overwrite files in the FILES directory, or you might want to create a more elaborate distribution tree, or model the directory tree in your project directory automatically.

After you have a distribution directory tree and a place to put the numbered disk images, most of the remaining work falls on the Setup Wizard.

**N O T E** If you find this procedure a useful tool, I would suggest renaming the program 15PRG01.PRG to "MAKEDIST.PRG" and take out the "PROCEDURE MAKEDIST" line in the program. ▧

**Specifying the File Location**    After choosing Tools, Wizards, Setup and allowing the wizard to create its distribution directory, you see Step 1, shown in Figure 15.24. The Setup Wizard is looking for your distribution directory tree. If you used MAKEDIST to create the tree and accepted its defaults, you would specify \PROJECT\FILES, where \PROJECT is your project directory.

**FIGURE 15.24**
Specify the root of the
distribution tree in
Step 1.

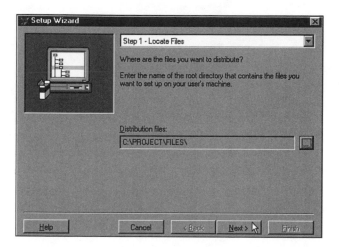

**Choosing the Optional Components**    Step 2, shown in Figure 15.25, asks which optional components you would like to include on the numbered distribution disk images. Unless your target user group already has Visual FoxPro, the FoxPro Runtime Library is required. Microsoft Graph 5.0 and ODBC with SQL Server Driver are necessary only if you plan to use those features. Checking the boxes underneath Required System Files includes the specific files needed to run under the listed operating systems.

**FIGURE 15.25**
Minimize your
installation size by
choosing only the
necessary options.

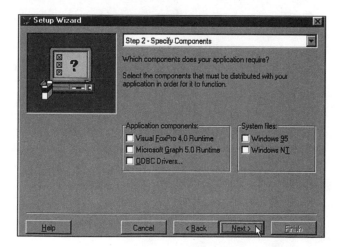

**Specifying the Disk Images Directory**    In Step 3, shown in Figure 15.26, you specify the disk images directory. If you used MAKEDIST to create the directory and accepted its defaults, then you would specify \PROJECT\DISKS, where \PROJECT is your project directory.

**FIGURE 15.26**

The Netsetup option is also an excellent choice for CD-ROM installations.

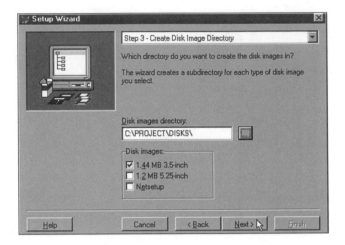

The Setup Wizard creates 1.44M disk images, 1.2M disk images, and a Netsetup. The Netsetup simply compresses the files into one directory. This is the most desirable choice whenever possible.

**Setting Up the Setup Options**  In Step 4, shown in Figure 15.27, the Setup Wizard enables you to enter three things: the Dialog Caption, the Setup Copyright, and the Post Setup Executable. The Dialog Caption is a nice place for the application title or the Setup is Initializing messages. The Setup Copyright notice is an important opportunity to assert your copyright in a place where the user can't ignore it. More practically useful, however, is the Post Setup Executable. This field is the place to include initial configuration programs, or just to extend the functionality of the default setup program.

**FIGURE 15.27**

Assert your intellectual ownership in Step 4.

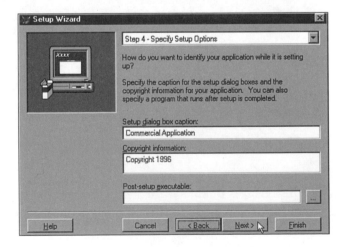

**Setting Up the Default Destination Directory** Users today expect to be able to put their software in any drive and directory they want. It is recommended that you write your applications in such a way that you can allow users to modify the directory and the Windows Program Manager group. Pictured in Figure 15.28, Step 5 of the Setup Wizard enables you to set directory and Program Manager group defaults.

**FIGURE 15.28**
Give your software a professional edge by allowing users to specify their own installation directories.

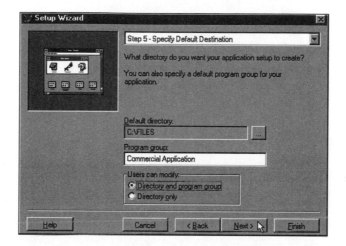

**Customizing File Installation** The File Summary grid in Step 6, shown in Figure 15.29, provides unprecedented control and ease-of-use. The combo boxes below Target Dir enable you, as the developer, to specify whether a file goes in the application's directory, the WINDOWS directory, or the WINDOWS\SYSTEM directory. You can use the OLE check box to specify whether a file is an Object Linking and Embedding file.

**FIGURE 15.29**
The PM item check box lets you add multiple icons from one set of setup disks.

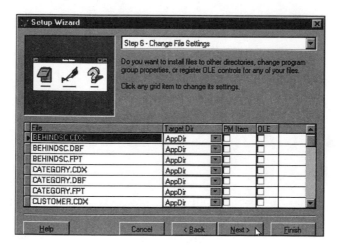

The dialog box in Figure 15.30 shows a great example of how to use this new feature. With one SETUP.EXE, you can specify several Program Manager items each with their own description text and icon.

**FIGURE 15.30**
Add icons for configuration programs, readme files, or external help systems.

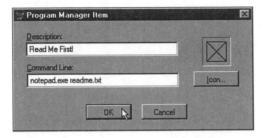

**Finishing Up** After Step 6, it's all in the wizard's hands. The wizard does the job in four passes:

1. It checks your distribution tree for new or updated files.
2. It updates its table of files.
3. It compresses all new or changed files.
4. It breaks these files into disk-size chunks.

Figure 15.31 shows the Setup Wizard in progress.

**FIGURE 15.31**
Generating the disk images is a lengthy process that you probably won't want to do until you are ready to ship your application.

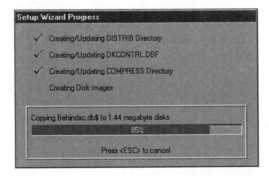

# Using Visual SourceSafe for Version Control in Team Development

One of the biggest headaches with a large project is managing the development by keeping track of the changes to your source code. Oftentimes team members have their own copies of the project's various source code in order to have the capability of referring to the code and making any changes necessary in order to customize the code for their needs. What often results in these situations is lost or overwritten code; and with too many versions of the same code floating around, the team members find it almost impossible to sort out, especially without knowing to whom the modifications belong. A solution to all this madness is to have a master copy of all project files and write access to one member at a time. Visual SourceSafe (VSS) can provide this functionality to a project with many other added benefits.

## Integrating VSS with Your Visual FoxPro 5.0 Project

The first step to integrate the functionality of version control is to install VSS on your system. Visual FoxPro 5.0 includes support for VSS. With proper VSS installation, VSS taps Visual FoxPro 5.0 on the shoulder and says, "Hey, I'm here to manage your project for you!" Visual FoxPro 5.0 welcomes the help and works very well with it. All you need to do is make sure you install VSS with the Server installation on the server where the master files will be stored, proceeding with installing VSS for each client. After successful installations, VFP 5.0 adds VSS to the Source Control options in the Tools Options dialog box on the Projects tab, as shown in Figure 15.32. From here, you can select Visual SourceSafe and set it as your default source control manager.

**FIGURE 15.32**
The Projects tab of the Tools Options dialog box gives you the option of integrating source control into your projects.

## Visual FoxPro 5.0 Configuration

The additional options shown in Figure 15.32 for Source Control are essential to your VFP/VSS configuration. In this section, VFP 5.0 defines whether or not files are to be automatically checked out upon modification, included in the master file upon addition of files to your local project or removal of local files upon removing them from the master project. You are also given the option to automatically add new projects to source control. If you don't choose to add this feature, you can always go back and add an existing project to VSS.

## Creating a Source Control Project

As long as you have set your Tools Project Options to automatically add new projects to source control, any project you create is automatically managed with the options that you have set. If you have a project already existing and wish to structure it into the source control environment, Visual FoxPro 5.0 gives you this option also. Open the project that you wish to add to source control. With VSS installed and configured to automatically add new projects to source control, you will get a VSS login window, as shown in Figure 15.33, even if the project is not currently controlled with VSS. Without users already specified, all you need to do is click OK. In the main menu, click Project and Add Project to Source Control.

**FIGURE 15.33**

You may have security in force for your version control files. If you don't, simply click OK to continue.

Figure 15.34 displays the VSS dialog box for adding a project to source control. Click Create to add your project to VSS. You are then given the option to type in a comment and after clicking OK, you get a list of files in your project. In this dialog box, shown in Figure 15.35, you have the option to deselect any files that you do not wish to have controlled—in other words, any file that you never want to be flagged as read-only, such as your data files. After VSS adds your files to the source control database, the files in your project that are controlled will display a lock beside them. As shown in Figure 15.36, the lock indicates that the files are read-only, or not checked out to your local project. We discuss these terms later on in this section.

> **CAUTION**
>
> Even though .DBC files may not be configured in VSS as a file type within Visual FoxPro's file group and you have your data in the project, Visual FoxPro 5.0 tries to add every file in the project to source control. Remember to deselect your data files for source control.

**FIGURE 15.34**
In the Add SourceSafe
Project dialog box you
are able to view
existing projects in the
specified directory
and add projects.

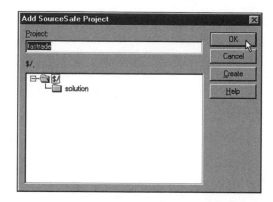

**FIGURE 15.35**
In the Add Files to
Source Control dialog
box, you can deselect
any files you don't
want controlled.

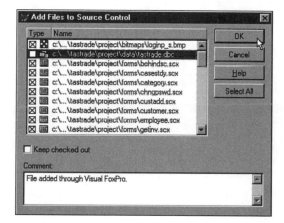

**FIGURE 15.36**
The Project Manager
shows files controlled
with VSS with a lock
beside the file.

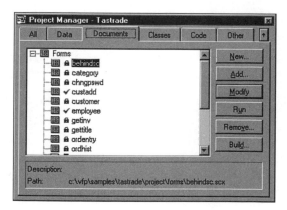

If you are configured for source control and you want to join a VSS project, you will notice a new menu item appearing in your file menu: Join Source Control Project. Selecting this option will open the SourceSafe Project dialog box as shown in Figure 15.37. Here is where you can view a list of all the source control projects in the specified directory. This procedure is for new team members who need a working copy, or local copy, of the master project file.

**FIGURE 15.37**
In the Open SourceSafe Project dialog box, you can view a list of projects with VSS and select a project to join.

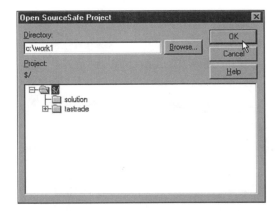

## Examining the Architecture of the Visual SourceSafe Project

The key concept in understanding how to work with VSS is the idea of a project. A project is a collection of files that you store in VSS. You add, delete, edit, and share files through projects. A project has much in common with an operating system directory, but there are significant differences.

- When you create a project that uses files in subdirectories on your operating system, VSS refers and treats these subdirectories as subprojects.

- The root directory (C:\) on your hard drive is the start of a hierarchy of directories. In comparison, ($/) refers to the start of a project tree hierarchy as the root project.

- VSS uses the forward slash (/) as opposed to the backward slash (\) to separate paths.

- When you make changes to a file, VSS saves the changes from the earlier versions to files referred to as reverse deltas.

- Users work with VSS commands to combine changes in different versions of files as compared to editing (cut and paste).

- VSS has built-in support for parallel streams of development.

When you store files in VSS, the files are in projects in the VSS database. Users cannot work on files stored in the VSS database. The file must be moved out of VSS to be worked on, referred to as checking out, and is placed in your working directory. The working directory is your personal home base for the project located on your local hard disk space or network drive that you use.

# Using Common Functions of Version Control with VSS

Any project in team development will benefit from the many functions that VSS provides. Following, we will discuss some of those functions and how VSS performs these tasks to give you a better understanding of version control concepts. Refer to your User's Guide, which VSS provides for a larger picture of the services VSS is capable of.

**Checking Files In and Out**   The check out command places a file into the working directory with read/write access. Once a file is checked out, it cannot be checked out by another user, unless VSS is configured to allow such, but this is not recommended. Depending on your configuration, clicking Modify in the Project Manager will automatically check a file out, or you can choose project from the main menu and select Source Control, then Check Out. The same items listed in the Control Source menu can be accessed by clicking the file in Project Manager. You will get a list of files to select for check out, if automatic check upon modify is not set. If you don't see your file listed, it is already checked out.

Checking in a file is just as easy. Selecting check in file from the Control Source items, or clicking the file in Project Manager, displays a list of files checked out by you and enables you to select the files you want checked in. You can use the comment box to log the changes that were made. VSS then replaces the master file and makes your local file read-only again.

**Undoing a Checkout**   This command cancels any changes made and audits the checkout.

**Tracking Versions**   Show History, Show Differences, and Source Control Properties all play a role in tracking the versions of your files. These options enable you to view the date/time stamps and the users who performed the changes. You can compare the master copy to the previous copies and basically do an audit on any file. VSS assigns version numbers to the files and this number is incremented every time the file is checked in.

**Sharing and Branching**   Sharing enables projects to access the same files; all actions that affect one of the shared files are automatically reflected in all the projects. Branching takes a shared file and breaks its link so it is not involved in any changes made from other projects. You can choose to branch after sharing a file, as shown in Figure 15.38. This is beneficial if a shared file is changed and becomes customized within a project. You can think of this as an un-sharing.

**FIGURE 15.38**
In the Share dialog box, you are given an option of branching after sharing, which takes a file from another project but makes a separate copy of it for the current project. This method is used for a customized file.

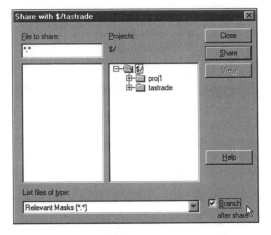

**Pinning** VSS provides the pin feature so that you can freeze older versions of files. This action is most useful when applied to shared files, although pinning is not limited to shared files. Pinning is different from branching in that you cannot make changes to it and it is not a copy. You are, in effect, sticking a pin into the file so that this particular version becomes the version that is shared in your project. You can execute this command on a file from the History of File options, as shown in Figure 15.39.

**FIGURE 15.39**
In the Show History dialog box, you are given an option of pinning a file, which freezes that version of the file.

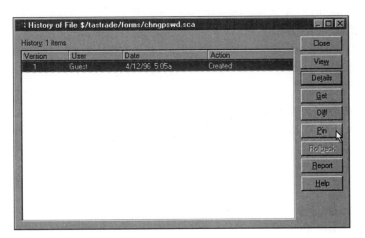

**Rolling Back Changes** Also in the Show History dialog box, Figure 15.39, you are given the option to rollback. This option is enabled if you select a file that has been modified and you can roll back the file to a specified version. This rollback makes all changes made later than the version rolled irretrievable. So be careful!

## Executing VSS Commands with VSS Server versus VSS Application

All the features and commands previously discussed in this chapter are made by VSS but VFP calls them. An alternative would be to switch to the VSS application and perform the commands there. The advantage of not using VSS as a server to VFP is that the processes perform more quickly. I suggest you study your User's Guide for VSS. You will find other options and configurations that you don't see in VFP menu items.

# From Here...

As you've seen in this chapter, the Project Manager is a very diverse tool. It can be an application when used as a catalog for your files. It can also help you create an application and distribute it with the help of the Setup Wizard. Whatever capacity you use it for, trust that this jack-of-all-trades has managed to be master, too.

Developing Visual FoxPro systems requires you to master a few trades as well. For more information on visual designers and creating applications, refer to these chapters:

- Chapter 5, "Using Wizards for Rapid Application Development," teaches you how to hit the ground running when developing applications. It also has a section on FoxDoc, the Documenting Wizard.

- Chapter 11, "Building Applications with Simple Form Structures," drills deeper into forms while maintaining an application-based approach.

- Chapter 20, "Creating On-Line Help," provides some background on using help in your applications and context-sensitive help.

- Bonus Chapter 02, "Other Visual FoxPro Tools," focuses on menus and toolbars. This chapter is located on the CD.

# Techniques from the Pros

# Error Detection and Removal

*by Michael Antonovich*

**A** program with errors cannot solve problems, save someone time, or make an organization more profitable. The bad news is that you will write few, if any, programs totally error-free right from the start. The good news is that you can learn how to detect and remove errors from code using a process called *debugging*.

The first case of debugging allegedly occurred many years ago when an insect caused some tubes to fail in one of the first computers. Thus, the term debugging came into use for getting the "bugs" out of a program. Whatever the origin, its purpose is to locate problems that cause programs to fail or produce incorrect results. Often, this process resembles a detective's investigation. You run the program and collect clues such as:

- Which procedures execute and in what order?
- What tables does the program open?
- Which index controls the table order?
- Why do certain variables contain the values they do?

**Identify and avoid common errors**

Learn to identify some of the common errors and how to avoid them.

**Use code modularization to reduce total errors and promote reusability**

Breaking code into smaller segments makes it easier to understand, test, and debug.

**Avoid multiple exits from loops and procedures**

When a program has multiple exits, code is often orphaned unintentionally, resulting in undefined or incorrectly defined variables.

**Handle file corruption**

Learn how to identify file corruption and what to do when it occurs.

**Create a multiple-level test plan**

Learn about a few different test plans, and see how a combination of test plans might best serve to debug your code.

**Track down errors with the Command, Trace, and Debug windows**

The new Debugger enables you to trace code, display variable values and object property values, display the call stack, and perform event tracking and coverage.

In fact, the more clues you collect, the more likely you will solve "The Case of the Program-Killing Error." ■

# Recognizing Common Coding Errors

There are hundreds of possible errors you can make when writing Visual FoxPro applications, at least if the number of error messages is any indication. (Visual FoxPro has more than 600 defined error messages.) Some errors are more common than others. Many are syntax-related and often result from simple typing mistakes. Others result from under-developed programming practices such as failure to check for EOF() before reading or writing a record. With so many possible errors, your common errors may not be the same as mine or your fellow programmers. In fact, every developer has a slightly different set of common errors that they seem to be constantly correcting.

Unfortunately, in most cases, there is really nothing your program can do after the error has occurred. Most error conditions cannot be fixed in a live application. The best that you can hope for is to document what happened and then roll back transactions, close tables, and exit the program. The real challenge of error handling is to prevent the errors from occurring in the first place by writing proactive code that anticipates possible errors. You can also become more aware of common errors and thereby avoid them.

This section looks at a fairly representative set of common errors that I have seen while working with other developers. Maybe you will recognize a few of them in your own coding—don't worry if you do. Recognition is the first step in developing better habits that will eliminate common errors from your coding habits.

## Syntax Errors

There are three major classes of errors in programming: logical, syntax, and exceptions. Of these, syntax errors are the easiest to find and correct. In fact, compiling your code is the fastest way to locate most of them. Some errors that are syntax-related do not show up during compilation, however. Common syntax errors include:

■ Forgetting an equal sign or other operator in an expression.

```
* Missing = sign after gnTotalDue

gnTotalDue pnNetDue * (1 + lnTaxRate)
```

■ Spelling a command or function name incorrectly.

```
* Missing second 'A' in DATABASE

OPEN DATBASE ptofsale
```

- Mispairing quotes around strings. This includes the common error of including the same type quote inside a string as used to delimit the string.

```
'This is Bill's statement'    && Fails

"This is Bill's statement"    && Succeeds
```

A variation on this error puts a single quote at one end of the string and a double quote on the other end.

**TIP** Visual FoxPro recognizes 'single quotes,' "double quotes," and [brackets] as string delimiters. If you need to use any of these characters inside the string, pick a different delimiter.

- Mispairing parentheses in complex expressions.

```
REPLACE pnboxno WITH PADL(VAL(pnboxno+1,'0',5)
```

- Using a reserve word for a memory variable or field name. Words Visual FoxPro uses for commands, functions, and keywords should not be used as variable names. This includes the use of four-character variable names that match the first four characters of a reserve word. When this happens, Visual FoxPro may try to interpret the variable or field name as the equivalent command. Usually, the command is out of context, resulting in an error. For example, the following statement generates the error `Invalid use of a Visual FoxPro function as an array`:

```
DIMENSION DATE[10]
```

- Not matching CASE...ENDCASE, DO...ENDDO, FOR...ENDFOR, IF...ENDIF, or SCAN...ENDSCAN commands, or using the wrong terminator (ending a DO structure with ENDIF). Visual FoxPro calls this problem a Nesting Error.

```
IF gnTotalDue > 100

= MESSAGEBOX("Get a supervisor's signature")

ENDDO                          && ENDDO should be ENDIF
```

A common syntax error not found during compilation is the passing of variables of the wrong type to a procedure. Because Visual FoxPro is not a strong typed language, memory variables can assume any variable type during execution. Therefore, VFP has no way to determine during compilation that the calling program will pass a numeric value when the procedure is expecting a character string. In any case, the program fails with a syntax error when this procedure call is run.

**NOTE** Although most of the chapter refers to compilation occurring as a separate step, you can have VFP compile your program code (PRG) every time you save it. This option can be set in the Edit Properties dialog box, discussed in Chapter 1, "Quick Review of Visual FoxPro's Interface." On the other hand, code stored as methods in forms, classes, and DBCs is compiled when these files are saved. ■

Part
IV

Ch
16

When you run a program, Visual FoxPro converts the source code to object code, if not previously compiled, and in the process detects references to other programs, procedures, and functions. It attempts to resolve these references within the current file or in other files included in the project. Suppose you attempt to call Procedure SOMETHIN. If Visual FoxPro cannot resolve it, it interrupts the compilation to display the following message:

```
Unable to find Proc./Function SOMETHIN
```

VFP also displays four buttons, labeled Locate, Ignore, Ignore All, and Cancel.

If you choose Locate, VFP displays an Open dialog box that enables you to find the missing file. Note, however, that this solves the problem only for the current compile. (Well, maybe. Suppose that you have the same-named file in more than one directory or on more than one server drive on a network system. Can you be sure that you or your users selected the correct file? I think not!) If you recompile the program later without correcting this reference, either within the code or by adding the file to the Project Manager, you get another error.

Sometimes, you can ignore one or more errors during compilation if you know the referenced procedure or function exists as a separate file or if it is an external reference. This often occurs when the compiler confuses an array reference with a function call. This problem can often be fixed by adding an EXTERNAL ARRAY <arrayname> in the program.

---

### Resolving External References

External can be used to resolve references to classes, forms, labels, libraries, menus, procedures, queries, reports, screens, and tables. The most common reason for requiring EXTERNAL to resolve the reference is because the program code uses macro expansion to define the object. The following code shows an example of memory variables required to determine which of three queries and reports to open. The EXTERNAL command is used to resolve these references to the compiler.

```
EXTERNAL QUERY LATE
EXTERNAL QUERY PASTDUE30
EXTERNAL QUERY PASTDUE60
EXTERNAL REPORT LATE
EXTERNAL REPORT PASTDUE30
EXTERNAL REPORT PASTDUE60
DO CASE
  CASE DATE() < INVDATE+30
    lcQry = "LATE"
    lcRpt = "LATE"
  CASE DATE() < INVDATE+60
    lcQry = "PASTDUE30"
    lcRpt = "PASTDUE30"
```

```
OTHERWISE
   lcRpt = "PASTDUE60"
   lcRpt = "PASTDUE60"
ENDCASE
DO (lcQry)
REPORT FORM (lcRpt) TO PRINTER
```

You can also choose to note, but ignore, unresolved references to permit VFP to complete the compile and log syntax errors into an error file. To log errors, choose Tools, Options, General page. Select the option Log Compilation Errors. (You can also use the command SET LOGERRORS ON.) Visual FoxPro then writes errors to a separate text file with the root name of the compiled file and an extension of .ERR. After compiling, you can open Project, Errors to see this error file (if you are compiling from the project). If you compile individual programs, you can view the error log by typing:

```
MODIFY FILE <filename>.ERR
```

If you do not log the errors, VFP merely shows the number of errors in the status bar at the end of the compile. Not a very informative solution, especially since this message disappears after a few seconds. Information reported with each syntax error in the log includes:

- The program line that caused the error
- A line number where FoxPro determines that the error exists
- An error message

When you recompile the corrected program, Visual FoxPro automatically removes this file as the program compiles without error.

**N O T E**  An important point about the line number is that it does not always point to the line containing the error. Yes, for missing parentheses or operators, the line number points to the exact line of the error. For a missing or mismatch of loop terminators (for example, ENDDO, ENDIF, ENDSCAN, or ENDFOR), the line number will probably be the end of the procedure. Visual FoxPro does not realize that an error exists until the procedure or program ends and the loop has not terminated properly.  ■

---

 **T I P**  Always SET LOGERRORS ON.

---

Closing the Methods window in a form object also performs a syntax check. For syntax errors discovered during compile, the alert box displays three options. You can Cancel the compile and return to the code to correct the problem. You can Ignore the error and check the balance of the code—until it finds another error or reaches the end of the code. Finally, you can Ignore All, which saves the code with all its errors. If you log errors, however, you can check the error log file to list the errors and resolve them one at a time.

If Visual FoxPro finds an error during execution that it does not find during compilation, it displays four options: Cancel, Suspend, Ignore, and Help. Cancel, of course, cancels the program. Suspend stops execution of the program and lets you enter the debugger to get more information about the error. Or you can simply use the Command window to print values of memory variables or table fields to determine the problem. The third button lets you ignore the problem; however, this is seldom a good choice. Finally, the Help button opens VFP Help to give you more information about the error message.

▶ **See** "Building Visual FoxPro .APPs and .EXEs," **p. 593**

Visual FoxPro cannot detect some syntax errors until the program executes. These errors may result from mixing the order of parameters, passing the wrong number of parameters, or other similar problems. They are usually fairly easy to detect and fix. The following code lines show some runtime syntax errors:

■ Mixing the order of parameters passed to a function. Visual FoxPro recognizes this error only if the switched parameters have a different type. It then responds with the Invalid function argument value, type, or count error. Mixing parameters of the same type generate logic errors at run time.

```
? TRANSFORM('$$$,$$$.99', gnTotalDue) && Parameters are switched
```

■ Entering an incorrect parameter to a command that has a limited number of possible values. For example, the ON KEY LABEL command expects specific key names. Anything else generatess an error, but only at compile time, as in the following statement:

```
ON KEY LABEL FJ9 ZOOM WINDOW PROPERTIES NORM FROM 0,0 ;
TO 10,10
```

■ Using the wrong number of parameters or no parameters in FoxPro functions. Passing too few parameters to a UDF is not automatically flagged as an error. The procedure may fail if it attempts to use the missing parameters, because VFP initializes them to .F.. This could result in a type error in subsequent statements. On the other hand, if you pass too many arguments to a procedure, you get the following error:

```
Must specify additional parameters
```

This may sound confusing, but look at it from the point of view of the procedure, which needs additional parameters to accommodate the number passed. The following code line attempts to use the TRANSFORM function to display a numeric variable, but does not pass the formatting string. This statement must fail because VFP will not know how to transform the value.

```
? TRANSFORM(gnTotalDue) && No PICTURE clause to format the value
```

■ A very common error is entering a comma instead of a period, or vice versa. The difference between these two characters is hard to see on many monitors. For example, the following statement fails because a period rather than a comma separates two parameters:

```
LPARAMETERS lnErrNum. lcErrMessage
```

This problem is made worse by the fact that these two characters occur next to each other on the keyboard. But, they are not the only character pairs likely to cause problems. Another commonly confused pair include the zero "0" and uppercase "O." Again, both characters occur close to each other on the keyboard and look almost identical on the screen. Another frequently confused pair is the number one "1" and the lowercase "l."

This list represents some common syntax errors, but not all of them. As you develop programs, you will recognize common syntax errors of your own. Some may even be in this list.

## Logic Errors

Logic errors are the second major category of errors. These errors are more difficult to detect and resolve. Compiling the program does not locate them. Sometimes, a serious logic error stops a program from executing, but not always; for example, referencing an array, or one of its elements, that does not exist results in a logic error. Perhaps the program defined the array in another procedure, but gave it a private scope rather than global. When VFP encounters any variable that does not exist, it stops the program's execution.

A similar type of logic error occurs when you overwrite existing variables when restoring variables from a memory variable file or a table. The RESTORE FROM command allows a program to use variables previously stored to a .MEM file. The following code line not only restores the .MEM file variables, it also erases all current memory variables. SCATTER MEMVAR performs a similar function when retrieving fields from a table and saving their values into memory variables. If a prior memory variable had the same name as a field in the table, its value will be replaced by a corresponding field in the current record.

```
RESTORE FROM Savevars.mem
```

or

```
USE CUSTOMER
SCATTER MEMVAR
```

If your program uses similar code and attempts to reference a previously defined variable, it could fail or at least generate incorrect results. The RESTORE FROM command actually causes more of a problem since it wipes out all prior memory variables before loading the ones from file. Fortunately, RESTORE FROM supports a clause to restore memory variable values without losing those already in memory. Simply include the ADDITIVE clause, as in:

```
RESTORE FROM Savevars.mem ADDITIVE
```

Of course, you may still overwrite an existing variable that also exists in the .MEM file.

Some logic errors create obviously wrong results. For example, you may see a string of asterisks in a field (****). It indicates a field overflow. In this case, either the field is too small or the value calculated is too large. Of course, errors do not have to be this dramatic. If a sales report calculates the total tax due as greater than the net cost of the items purchased, there is a problem. This error should be obvious to anyone who simply compares the sales totals before and after tax.

On the other hand, some errors are not obvious at all without an independent check of the calculations. Suppose that you have the following equation to calculate the number of acres in a square plot of land:

```
GnTotalAcres = (pnFront * pnSide) / 9 / 4480
```

This equation is valid and does not generate an error when executed. It multiplies the length of the front in feet by the length of the side and feet to get the area in square feet. It then divides by 9 feet per square yards. It divides the number of square yards by 4,480 rather than 4,840, however. Merely looking at the result may not reveal the fact that two digits were transposed. This type of error can go unnoticed for a long time.

Another difficult logic error to find occurs when using REPLACE. Suppose you try to change a field in a different table while the record pointer in the current table points to EOF. This error is subtle, as shown in the following code:

```
SELECT CUST
IF !SEEK(m.pcCustId)
  REPLACE ORDER.cCustId WITH 'NONE'
ENDIF
```

You may be surprised to find that this code fails. When FoxPro searches for the customer ID in table CUST and does not find it, it leaves the record pointer at the end of CUST. Even though the replace statement clearly uses an alias to replace cCustId in table ORDER, the default scope of NEXT 1 actually refers to the current work area, which is CUST, not ORDER. Because the record pointer in the current work area points to EOF, REPLACE fails. Obviously, the solution here is to precede REPLACE with a SELECT Order statement.

## Exception Errors

Exception errors, the third type of coding errors, occur due to circumstances outside of the program's direct control. For example, a program may fail because it cannot find a file it needs. Perhaps the file has been deleted or moved. Of course, if someone or some process deleted the file, there is no way for the program to continue. Even if someone has merely moved the file, you may not want to make the user responsible for finding it.

Said another way, you might not want users roaming around the file server looking for a "likely" table. First, they do not know where to look; second, they might open the wrong file causing even more problems. Yet an expert user, such as yourself, might be very qualified and able to perform this search. Even experts, however, make mistakes. In any case, your program should use the FILE() function to check if a file exists before attempting to use it. Then, based on the user level (assigned elsewhere), the code in Listing 16.1 shows one way to determine how to continue when the file does not exist. Of course, you may consider always calling a shutdown procedure when a file is not found by a program due to the ever-present possibility of accessing the wrong file.

### Listing 16.1   16PRG01.PRG

```
IF FILE('\VFP5BOOK\DATA\MYFILE.DBF)
* File found, open it
  USE \VFP5BOOK\DATA\MYFILE.DBF
ELSE
* File not found.
  WAIT WINDOW 'File: \VFP5BOOK\DATA\MYFILE.DBF NOT Found!' + ;
      CHR(13) + 'Press any key to continue'

* Can this user search for it?
  IF gnUserLevel > 1
    lcNewFile = GETFILE('DBF', 'Find MYFILE.DBF', 'SELECT')
    IF !EMPTY(lcNewFile)
      USE (lcNewFile)
    ELSE
      DO SHUTDOWN
    ENDIF
  ELSE
    DO SHUTDOWN
  ENDIF
ENDIF
```

The previous code can very easily be converted to a generalized form and made into a function that you can call from any program or procedure. Listing 19.2 shows one possible implementation.

**Listing 16.2   16PRG02.PRG**

```
IF FILE('\VFP5BOOK\DATA\MYFILE.DBF)
* File found, open it
  USE \VFP5BOOK\DATA\MYFILE.DBF
ELSE
* File not found.
  lcGetFile = FINDFILE('MYFILE.DBF')
ENDIF
*** REST OF PROGRAM CONTINUES

FUNCTION MYFILE
LPARAMETER lcFileNam

* Tell user what is happening.
  WAIT WINDOW 'File: &lcFileNam. NOT Found!' + ;
        CHR(13) + CHR(10) + 'Press any key to continue'

* Can this user search for it?
  IF gnUserLevel > 1
    lcNewFile = GETFILE('DBF', 'Find '+lcFileNam, 'SELECT')
    IF !EMPTY(lcNewFile)
      USE (lcNewFile)
    ELSE
      DO SHUTDOWN
    ENDIF
  ELSE
    DO SHUTDOWN
  ENDIF
RETURN lcNewFile
```

Another type of exception occurs when an index does not exist. If the table is part of a database, the program could retrieve the definitions for that table's indexes from the DBC file. It could then attempt to create the missing index. The potential problem here is that indexing requires an exclusive lock on the file. If the program cannot obtain that lock, the program should shut down gracefully.

Not all exception errors are as easy to deal with. In some cases, the best alternative may be to use an ON ERROR routine to document the system at the time of the error, rollback pending transactions, close all tables, and cancel the program.

**N O T E**  ON ERROR executes a single command when Visual FoxPro encounters any error condition. That command typically uses DO to execute an error-handling procedure. ON ERROR still provides a global mechanism for handling errors in Visual FoxPro. ■

The rest of this chapter shows additional methods of avoiding errors when possible, and how to track down errors that inevitably sneak in anyway.

# Modularizing Code to Minimize Errors

The number of errors in any program or procedure tends to increase as it grows in size. The reason is that it becomes increasingly difficult to remember all the details in the code. The demands on software grow daily as well. Very quickly, every programmer realizes that writing large single programs with hundreds or thousands of code lines causes more problems than several smaller programs that call one another. Obviously, the more errors, the greater the amount of time spent finding and removing them. On the other hand, dividing code into smaller functional units called procedures or functions reduces overall errors. It soon becomes obvious that each procedure or function should handle no more than one task. This process is known as *code modularization*.

Visual FoxPro facilitates code modularization. Any application can be thought of as a series of tasks. Tasks consist of data-entry screens, reports, or procedures that manipulate data. Menu choices provide access to each task. Each task often has two or more subtasks.

How do you go about breaking a task down into smaller units or subtasks? Think of a customer form as a single task. Within it, individual data fields represent subtasks. Individual pieces of information on that form may hold the customer's name, address, or telephone number. Visual FoxPro represents subtasks as control objects. Looking deeper into a control, you find individual methods that respond to various events. Object methods are used to:

- Set default values
- Determine a user's rights to a field
- Create pick lists
- Validate field entries
- Save or retrieve data
- Respond to mouse clicks or moves
- Display related forms

▶ **See** "Understanding the Event Hierarchy," **p. 527**

You have already seen how to generate forms. Each one represents a block of code functionally independent of the rest of the application. Within a form, methods further modularize the code needed to handle individual object events. You can create and store the code needed for a method in a variety of ways.

First, when you open a method in Visual FoxPro's form design mode, you can enter code directly. While this method works, it has several drawbacks. First, it limits the use of that code to one method in one `form`. Second, when you need to make a change, it takes a significant amount of time to load the form designer with the form. Then, you must open the method to make corrections. Finally, you must resave and recompile the application.

A better technique stores the code in a separate file. The event method then simply references it with a user-defined function (UDF) call. That's the easy part. The hard part is deciding where to store this separate code. Again, several possibilities exist.

The first one uses a separate PRG to store the needed procedures and functions used by that form. Its main program also calls the form. A prototype of this style code follows:

```
* Form setup code
  << Form Setup Code >>
* Call form
  DO myform.spr
* Cleanup code for form
  << Form Cleanup Code >>
RETURN

PROCEDURE PROC1
...
RETURN

PROCEDURE PROC2
...
RETURN
```

You can run this PRG directly, or you can have the application's main menu call this program rather than launching the form. In turn, the main program of this code launches the form. Visual FoxPro has no trouble finding the functions stored in the main program that calls the form.

This technique allows quicker editing of the code. It does not require the form designer just to change the code for a method. However, it does not allow sharing of code between objects with similar methods in different forms. This is a big negative when you begin to develop class libraries. The UDF call will be inherited when you subclass from the base object, but the source UDF may not be available.

Another technique stores all procedure code in a single but separate file. This file establishes a library of procedures and functions. Then, any screen with a similar method, even a subclassed screen, can call a common function. This technique makes changes to the code easier. If you need a new property or method, you add it in one place. Place the reference to the code in the appropriate method of the base class and place the code in the procedure library. If more than one form uses the same method code, it still appears in one place, not everywhere the object appears.

With VFP objects, you could build a subclass of the original class and include common method code in its definition. By encapsulating the method's code in the definition of the class itself, you don't have to worry about separate code libraries. By sharing the object through a class library, you still code it only once. This method works best when many forms use the same object with the same methods. An example might be VCR buttons used to control movement through a table's records.

**N O T E** Test objects, and their associated code, before you store them as custom classes in a class library. You can create a simple form and place the control in the form to test it. After you are satisfied with it, select the object and choose File, Save As Class. The resulting Save Class dialog box enables you to save the select controls with a class name in a class library. Debugging and modifying code after storing it in a class library requires more steps. ■

The point to this discussion is that object methods force you to divide code into individual tasks that are more easily comprehended and maintained. The theory is that if individual tasks work properly, then the sum of the tasks works properly.

Of course, you can achieve many of these same benefits in standard code by using procedures and functions that accomplish a single task. If a procedure performs more than one task, it can probably be split into two or more procedures.

Code modularization at the task level leads to another benefit, reusability. This has been mentioned before in terms of objects and object libraries, but it applies just as strongly to other common code tasks. If you write a procedure to handle movement through a table's records using a set of VCR buttons, you can use that same procedure with every table. The code remains unchanged. Developing this concept further, consider developing a library of common procedures to use in any application. You benefit from time saved by not having to write and test the same code repeatedly. Your applications also exhibit a consistent look and feel.

## Using Proper Parameter Passing

Another common error occurs during planned and unplanned parameter passing. First you may wonder what *unplanned parameter passing* means. Remember that Visual FoxPro makes any variable defined as a public or private variable automatically available to routines it calls. This can unintentionally redefine a variable when calling a lower-level routine that uses a variable with the same name. Visual FoxPro will not flag this as an error. After all, it assumes that you intended to do it.

As a general rule, never use the same variable names in programs that call one another or different procedures in the same program. If you must use a variable in a called procedure, pass the parameter by value and assign it a different name in the called procedure. Accidentally redefining variables in lower routines are extremely difficult errors to find.

**TIP** If you are not sure whether a variable has been used in a higher procedure, define the scope of the variable as LOCAL or PRIVATE in the called procedure.

**TIP** Pass parameters values into local variables by using the LPARAMETERS statement rather than PARAMETERS.

Another consideration is whether you pass parameters to procedures by value or by reference. When you pass a parameter by reference, the procedure uses the original variable. If the procedure changes the parameter value, the original variable's value changes also. Listing 16.3 shows this:

**Listing 16.3   16PRG03.PRG**

```
a = 5
DO newval WITH a
? a

PROCEDURE newval
PARAMETER b
b = 1
RETURN
```

On the other hand, if you pass the parameter by value, the procedure creates a new variable to store the parameter value. It does not pass changes back to the original. The equivalent code is shown in Listing 16.4.

**Listing 16.4   16PRG04.PRG**

```
a = 5
DO newval WITH (a)
? a

PROCEDURE newval
PARAMETER b
b = 1
RETURN
```

When calling a procedure, Visual FoxPro's default method passes parameters by reference unless you enclose it in parentheses. However, when calling a function, the default method passes parameters by value (observe, functions enclose parameters in parentheses). To pass a parameter to a function by reference, you can either:

- Type **SET UDFPARMS TO REFERENCE**
- Precede the parameter name with the @ character

**T I P**  If you need to pass an array to a procedure or function, pass it by reference. If you attempt to pass it by value, it passes only the first element.

▶ **See** "Passing Arrays to Procedures and Functions" in Bonus Chapter 04 located on the CD

 **T I P**  There is a limit of 24 passed parameters to procedures and functions.

Part
**IV**

Ch
**16**

# Eliminating Multiple Exits and Returns

Not too many years ago, the "new" programming paradigm promoted the elimination of all GOTO statements. FoxPro developers have never had a problem with GOTOs (other than GOTO TOP, GOTO BOTTOM) because the language does not support a GOTO branch statement. Instead they use IF, CASE, and DO structures for conditional code processing and loops. As a result, few FoxPro developers today miss GOTO statements and the resulting tangled code they created.

Unfortunately, many FoxPro developers still use multiple exits from structured loops and multiple returns from procedures and functions. In almost all cases, there is no need for this practice. All that is usually required is a minor revision to the loop's logic. Examine the following code example:

```
PROCEDURE GETPRODID
  IF EMPTY(m.lcProdId)
    RETURN
  ELSE
    < Code to test if lcProdId exists in PRODUCT.DBF >
    RETURN
  ENDIF
  USE
RETURN
```

This procedure has three exit points where only one is required. A restructured version of the same code follows:

```
PROCEDURE GETPRODID
  IF !EMPTY(m.lcProdId)
    < Code to test if lcProdId exists in PRODUCT.DBF >
  ENDIF
  USE
RETURN
```

Why be concerned about multiple exit and return points? First, it adds a level of unnecessary complexity to the code that makes tracing its path more difficult. But more importantly, it sometimes causes the program to skip critical code segments that it should execute. For example, in the earlier code, should the procedure close the current table (the USE command)? The first code example never closes the current file while the second one always does.

This illustrates another danger with multiple EXIT or RETURN commands. It is easy to *orphan* code, isolating it so that it never executes. The first example ends each branch of the IF statement with a RETURN. As a result, the USE statement never executes.

The EXIT command exits a DO...ENDDO, FOR...ENDFOR, or SCAN...ENDSCAN loop prior to completing the loop based on the loop condition. For example, the following program segment loops through rental product records to find the serial number of one still in stock. A simple SEEK finds a record that matches the product ID. Then, it must loop through all the records for that product until it finds the first one in stock.

```
USE RENTPROD ORDER PRODID
pcSerial = SPACE(4)
SEEK m.pcFindProdId
SCAN WHILE m.pcFindProdId = cProdId
  IF lInStock
    pcSerial = cSerial
    EXIT
  ENDIF
ENDSCAN
```

Observe that this code segment has two possible exits from the SCAN loop. If it finds at least one product in stock with a specific ID, it stores its serial number in variable pcSerial and exits. Otherwise, it continues to loop until the product ID changes.

A better way to write this code eliminates the extra exit. First, you need to recognize that you cannot simply eliminate the EXIT command. This would cause the loop to read through all records of the same product ID. The net effect would be to return the last available serial number rather than the first. The following code solves this problem by adding an extra conditional test to the SCAN:

```
USE RENTPROD ORDER PRODID
pcSerial = SPACE(4)
SEEK m.pcFindProdId
SCAN WHILE EMPTY(pcserial) AND m.pcFindProdId = cProdId
  IF lInStock
    pcSerial = cSerial
  ENDIF
ENDSCAN
```

Observe, in this case, that SCAN tests for an empty serial number memory variable first. If this field changes before the product ID does, an in-stock item has been found. This new condition also guarantees that the loop returns the first available serial number or a blank if there is no in-stock product.

**N O T E**  A case might be made that adding the extra condition test slows the loop and thus the extra EXIT actually improves the code performance. The programming world is loaded with tradeoffs.  ■

A similar case can be made for eliminating the use of EXIT in other loop structures. Thus, by careful use of IF blocks and additional conditional statements, you can eliminate most, if not all, multiple exits from programs. I hope that this will also eliminate another potential source of errors in your code.

# Developing Libraries of Testing Routines and Objects

Using libraries, program files containing common procedures and functions, is one of the most effective methods of reducing the number of errors in code. Of course, you must first thoroughly test routines before adding them to a library. Once tested, however, new applications can use them with virtual assurance that they do not contain errors.

**N O T E**  This concept of building common libraries of functions has grown up into the object world, in the form of class libraries.  ■

In fact, Visual FoxPro's builders and wizards provide the equivalent of a standard library to create forms, form controls, menus, queries, and reports. You do not have to write the basic code for these objects. Visual FoxPro provides error-free objects for you; all you have to do is tweak it to fit your particular application's needs.

You can also build your own libraries of functions and procedures to call from any program or object method. To create a library, store the functions and procedures in a single file and save it. Then in programs that use them, simply add a SET PROCEDURE statement before referencing them. The syntax for SET PROCEDURE is

```
SET PROCEDURE TO [FileName1 [,FileName2,...]] [ADDITIVE]
```

Visual FoxPro allows programs to reference more than one library. You can even reference additional libraries later in a program by including the ADDITIVE clause. Forgetting this clause closes any prior procedure libraries when opening the new one.

Procedure libraries provide an excellent way to store and use common routines. Create common routines to open files, create sorts, display messages, and perform other common functions.

▶ **See** "Creating Custom Classes," **p. 117**

In addition to procedure files, Visual FoxPro also lets you create object libraries of custom classes. To begin a custom class, use one of Visual FoxPro's basic classes. Then add additional properties or methods to it. For example, you could create a custom class consisting of a group of buttons to navigate through a file. You can then use this custom class in any form that needs file navigation buttons. To open and use a class library, use SET CLASSLIB. Its syntax is

```
SET CLASSLIB TO ClassLibraryName [ADDITIVE] [ALIAS AliasName]
```

As with SET PROCEDURE, you can have multiple class libraries open at the same time if you open each one with the ADDITIVE clause. Omitting this clause closes any previously opened class libraries.

# Handling Corruption in Files

Data files can easily become corrupted. Because data files often are larger than the amount of RAM memory in a machine, Visual FoxPro constantly moves some of the files between memory and disk. Normally, everything works fine. If, however, the user turns off the computer without properly exiting the program, the file may be incompletely written. This could happen when your program fails without a proper error handling routine that leaves tables open. This results in data corruption.

In Chapter 1, "Quick Review of Visual FoxPro's Interfaces," an example code called a procedure, REALQUIT, to prevent the user from accidentally exiting FoxPro by clicking the wrong Close Box. It proposed running a program when Visual FoxPro starts to initialize the ON SHUTDOWN event to execute REALQUIT. Alternatively, you can add the ON SHUTDOWN command to any program to prevent the user from exiting Visual FoxPro or Windows prematurely. The procedure in Listing 16.5  should be called by ON SHUTDOWN. It includes some additional commands to properly close down Visual FoxPro. If called from an error handler, you could even build a procedure consisting of the core code inside the IF...ENDIF block.

**Listing 16.5    16PRG05.PRG**

```
PROCEDURE SHUTDOWN
* Include any commands in this routine needed to return the system
* to a default environment. Applications running interactively
* require more attention than compiled standalone applications.
* Standalone applications might merely need to close down all
* files safely.
  IF MESSAGEBOX('Do you really want to exit Visual FoxPro?', 292) = 6
```

```
  * Reset common ON KEY definitions that the application uses.
    ON KEY LABEL BACKSPACE
    ON KEY LABEL ENTER
    ON KEY LABEL SPACEBAR
    ON KEY LABEL ESCAPE

  * Turn printer and file redirection off
    SET ALTERNATE OFF
    SET ALTERNATE TO
    SET PRINT OFF
    SET CONSOLE ON

  * Close transaction - TRAP ERRORS
 IF TXNLEVEL() > 0
       ROLLBACK
       END TRANSACTION
 CLOSE ALL

  * Release all variables (and objects)
    RELEASE ALL

  * Deactivate windows
    DEACTIVATE WINDOWS ALL
    DEACTIVATE WINDOW DEBUG
    DEACTIVATE WINDOW TRACE
    ACTIVATE WINDOW COMMAND

  * Deactivate any application menus
    SET SYSMENU TO DEFAULT

  * Clear macros
    RESTORE MACROS


 ENDIF
 RETURN
```

**Part**

**IV**

**Ch**

**16**

**N O T E** Unfortunately, there is no way to prevent a user from simply turning off the machine in the middle of a program. By adding a UPS (uninterruptible power supply) to your computers, you can protect against accidental losses of power. ■

Of course, the easiest way to fix a corrupted file is to restore a backup copy from tape or disk. If you perform daily backups, the most you lose is one day's worth of data. Even this minimal loss may be unacceptable. Several products exist to recover corrupted database files including utilities from Norton and Central Point. They are not as robust as dedicated tools such as dSalvage from Comtech Publishing Ltd. This product:

■ Fixes many errors in the file header

■ Recovers lost memo field data

- Recovers data removed with the ZAP command
- Recovers from cross-linked files
- Recovers lost cluster data
- Resets misaligned or offset data

In most cases, this program accomplishes its repairs without making another copy of the file. This can be important for very large data files or full disk drives where there is not enough room for a second copy of the damaged files.

Corruption in index files occurs more frequently than any other type of corruption. Often this results from improperly designed software. It also results from users who open and edit a database without opening all of the associated indexes. Thus, it is more common with the use of standard IDX indexes than with structural compound indexes (CDX). This is because FoxPro automatically opens structural indexes when it opens the table. Corruption can occur in any index, however.

Another common cause for a corrupted index occurs when someone copies a backup DBF to the current directory without copying its indexes. In this case, changes made to the original DBF exist in the index, but not in the copied DBF. Thus, the index may point to the wrong record, no record, or beyond the end of the table.

You can fix simple index file problems by reindexing the table; however, even REINDEX doesn't help if the index header is corrupted. Ideally, you should save index definitions in a separate table, a database, a data dictionary, or simply on a piece of paper. The DBC, while containing a record to reference each tag name in the structural compound index of the table, does not store the index expression; nor does it store information about any other index (stand-alone or nonstructural). Then, delete the corrupted index files, open the DBF, and re-create them.

**N O T E**   If your index file contains a primary key reference, it is not easy to simply delete an index file and re-create it. The problem is that the database container stores a reference to the primary key in two places, a tag record, and in the properties of the table record itself. Removing the tag record from the DBC is easy. Removing the primary key reference from the table properties is not. See additional information about working with the database container in Chapter 4, "Advanced Database Management Concepts." ■

Corrupted form, label, and report files present an additional challenge. Visual FoxPro stores information for these objects in both a DBF-type file and a memo file. Therefore, they are susceptible to the same types of damage and you can use the same tools and methods to fix them. Table 16.1 shows the corresponding file extensions for Visual FoxPro's key components.

**Table 16.1    File Extensions of Common Visual FoxPro Files**

| File | Data | Memo |
|------|------|------|
| DATABASE | DBC | DCT |
| MENU | MNX | MNT |
| OBJECTS | VCX | VCT |
| PROJECTS | PJX | PJT |
| LABEL | LBX | LBT |
| REPORT | FRX | FRT |
| SCREEN | SCX | SCT |
| TABLE | DBF | FPT |

Another tool for repairing damage to memo files is MemoPlus from Rory Data International. This product fixes corrupted tables that FoxPro reports as Not a Fox database. It also repairs corrupted memos that FoxPro reports as Memo file invalid or missing. It generates reports on memo contents and their addresses to assist in repairing as much of the file as possible. An interesting feature is its analysis of the memo contents to determine the optimal BLOCKSIZE.

With program files, it may be possible to edit and remove corruption. The safest solution, however, is to keep backup copies of all program and data files on floppy disks, a tape, or some other removable medium that can be stored off-site.

# Designing a Testing Plan

Testing your application should be considered a separate and planned task in its development. If you use a project planner, such as Microsoft Project, testing should be a separate task. There are many ways to design a test plan. Some developers test only after they completely write an application. The interactive nature of Visual FoxPro makes concurrent testing during development easier and more productive. The problem is that it is harder for management to track the time spent on concurrent testing. This section looks at various testing techniques and analyzes their pros and cons.

# Understanding Data-Driven versus Logic-Driven Testing

Testing an application consists of two elements: validity and coverage. Validity testing checks to see whether the application generates the expected results for a specific set of inputs. Coverage testing checks to see whether all code statements have been executed by the tests. Any code not executed could harbor a hidden bug. We will talk more about coverage testing later. First, let's examine validity testing.

There are two basic approaches to validity testing. The first approach is *data-driven*. It does not assume a prior knowledge of the way the program works. Rather, it focuses on selecting a variety of test data sets based on a random sampling of real-world or fabricated data. It then runs the program with the data to see whether it generates the expected results.

The second approach is *logic-driven* and requires extensive knowledge of the program's coding. It attempts to test every path the program can execute. It also tests how the program handles data limits by using data that pushes and exceeds known physical limitations.

Each method has advantages and disadvantages. The advantages to a data-driven approach include the fact that it does not consciously or subconsciously make assumptions about the program. Often a programmer "assumes" that a program never behaves a certain way and therefore fails to test it completely. Frequently, the parts of the program assumed to be correct are the very ones that fail. The primary disadvantage to a data-driven approach is that there is no guarantee that the test data sets cover all program paths and loops.

A logic-driven approach handles the weakness of data-driven testing. When properly designed, it tests every line of code in the entire system. The obvious disadvantage is that for a major application, fully testing every line of code requires multiple data tests. Further, it takes time to develop the necessary data sets to ensure testing of each line of code.

# Defining Testing Techniques

There are almost as many techniques for testing and debugging as there are programmers. Most techniques involve variations of just a few major techniques. The first several methods described here involve the design stage of a project. The more errors found and removed during the design phase, the less expensive the overall project becomes. It results in fewer false starts and less rework of code. This translates into reduced manhours and, thus, cost.

*Checking design documents* involves a review of forms, reports, table layouts, and relations developed during the design phase. This occurs prior to any coding.

An *informal group design review* involves a group of programmers, users, and designers meeting to discuss various aspects of the project. It does not require a formalized step-through of the design specifications.

*Formal design inspection* analyzes the critical parts of the system design and attempts to determine whether it accounts for all possible situations. It often uses decision-tree analysis diagrams to ensure coverage. Decision-tree analysis traces each major path and operation in an application and graphically displays them on paper. Due to the usual branching of options, the resulting diagram resembles the limbs of a tree and thus the name.

*Personal desk-checking* involves reviewing code listings and walking through the process on paper (or on-screen) without actually running the program. It often requires performing hand calculations using sample data in the actual code to check the results. Some developers refer to this technique as a *walkthrough*; however, the term walkthrough can also apply to other review types. This technique was more popular years ago when computer time was expensive and programmers were relatively cheap. Today, the reverse is true. Thus, this method may be used only to find non-trivial errors such as complex logic errors.

 **TIP** Test often and test early. The longer an error exists, the more expensive it becomes to find and remove.

Once coding begins, the focus shifts from paper and thought reviews to formal code reviews and actual physical testing. The following paragraphs describe a few of these techniques.

*Formal code inspection* involves careful scrutiny of critical code segments. It provides feedback about the code, standards, use of comments, variable naming, local and global variable usage, and so forth.

*Modeling* or *prototyping* uses available tools to quickly create an application shell. Its purpose is to show overall functionality of the system. With Visual FoxPro, this involves creating basic forms and reports linked together with a simple menu. While the forms are functional, they may not include final event trapping. Similarly, reports may not include selection and sorting options. A common term for this technique today is *RAD* (Rapid Application Development).

*Syntax checking* tests the basic correctness of the code. It checks the spelling of commands and text strings, the validity of expressions, and the basic structure of commands. FoxPro does most of this during compilation, although some syntax problems become evident only when you run the program.

**TIP** Visual FoxPro does not check spelling or syntax within strings, form captions, toolTips, status bar text, or messages. Yet these are the most visible parts of the program to users and could reflect on the entire system.

*Unit testing* exercises individual groups of statements. For example, when designing a new class definition, use unit testing to check the code associated with its methods. To perform unit testing, you must write a special program called a *driver*. The driver does not become part of the final code. Rather, you use it to set up the necessary program conditions, such as initializing variables, to test the code segment.

Even though you may test each procedure and function individually, their correct functioning does not guarantee that the program as a whole will work. However, it does narrow down the error possibilities. *System testing* specifically checks the interface connections between modules. Its purpose is to ensure that data and logic pass correctly to and from each module. This includes using proper parameter types and sizes. It can also look for unexpected changes to public or private variables redefined by a called procedure or function.

*Functional testing* checks that the major features of the program work as expected. When you select a report option from the menu, do you get the report you selected or another one, or perhaps even a form? If a form displays a message to press F2 for a list of possible values, it checks that the list really appears when you press F2. It does not necessarily include verification of the report results or that the list, which appears when you press F2, contains the correct data.

*Stress testing* checks boundary conditions of the program. It checks how the program responds to extreme data values. For example, if the program tracks weekly payroll, it might check what the program does if you enter 170 hours for the number of hours the employee worked this week. (In case you're wondering why to use 170, seven times 24 hours is only 168.) Stress testing on a network concerns itself with how the program performs when multiple users run it. Can the program handle simultaneous updates to data? Do record and file locks perform correctly while minimizing the time when other users cannot access the data?

The speed of a program falls under *performance testing*. Visual FoxPro provides the flexibility to code most features in several ways, but all ways do not perform equally. In fact, some methods substantially outperform others. Performance testing looks for areas to improve program speed by identifying which portions of the program require the most time. Then, you can try alternative programming methods to improve the speed.

Finally, *compatibility testing* looks at how the program works in different environments.

This may include different display monitor modes, different printers, and different directory structures. It may even involve the way the program displays regional or international fields such as time, dates, and money. Even the collating sequence of sorted data and the page code of tables become important issues when internationalizing an application.

# Determining When Testing Is Complete

One might successfully argue that testing is never complete until the application becomes obsolete. There are always new combinations of data. Furthermore, most programs change over time, adding a feature here or a field there. With each new feature, you introduce the possibility of errors. Program paths may change, new variables may overwrite similar variables in other routines, and other side effects may affect existing code.

Some developers use a *bug rate factor* to determine when to stop debugging. In other words, they measure the number of bugs found over time. While this gives a nice, neat, numeric way to determine when to cut off testing, several variations exist. For example, you could monitor the cost of looking for bugs compared to the cost of leaving them in. For example, the cost of leaving a spelling error in a text label is very low. However, the cost of an error that subtracts sales tax from total due rather than adding is higher. At a higher cost level is an error that returns the wrong product price when selecting products. Therefore, time is allocated for testing different parts of the program based on how serious an error would be in those parts.

No matter what method you use, it is nearly impossible to determine when all bugs have been found. Often, it is more of a subjective decision based on the cost of finding another bug compared to the cost of leaving it in. Conversely, declaring testing complete just to meet a schedule is dangerously shortsighted. Testing should continue until everyone involved feels confident in the application's performance.

The last section defined several techniques for testing software. The reason for so many different methods is that no one technique is perfect. In fact, a survey by Capers Jones, published in Programming Productivity, shows the effectiveness of the 10 most common techniques. Table 16.2 reproduces this table.

**Table 16.2   Effectiveness of Software-Testing Techniques**

| Technique | Minimum | Average | Maximum |
| --- | --- | --- | --- |
| Checking of design documents | 15% | 35% | 70% |
| Informal group design reviews | 30% | 40% | 60% |
| Formal design inspection | 35% | 55% | 75% |

*continues*

| Table 16.2   Continued | | | |
| --- | --- | --- | --- |
| **Technique** | **Minimum** | **Average** | **Maximum** |
| Formal code inspection | 30% | 60% | 70% |
| Modeling or prototyping | 35% | 65% | 80% |
| Personal desk-checking of code | 20% | 40% | 60% |
| Unit testing | 10% | 25% | 50% |
| Functional testing | 20% | 35% | 55% |
| Integration testing | 25% | 45% | 60% |
| Field testing | 35% | 50% | 65% |
| All of the above (used together) | 93% | 99% | 99% |

In this table, the three columns represent the minimum number of errors, as a percentage, found using each technique, the average number found, and the maximum number. These values assume one person is assigned to debug the code using one technique. The interesting point to the preceding table is that no one method guarantees error-free code. In fact, only a combination of methods finds close to all the errors.

Glenford J. Myers performed an interesting related study. He found that every programmer approaches debugging slightly differently. As a result, even the combination of as little as two programmers to the debugging process greatly improves the overall detection rate.

## Creating a Test Environment

There are two important issues concerned with creating a test environment: the hardware issues and the people issues. When testing an application, you should test it on the same hardware configuration that you plan to implement it on. If the application will run on a network, testing it on a stand-alone system can miss many of the potential problems related to record and file sharing.

**N O T E**   You can simulate a multiuser environment even on stand-alone machines by opening multiple instances of VFP. Of course, having additional memory helps improve the performance of this technique. ■

A similar problem occurs when the software must run on various display drivers. The same "perfect" form on one display may have fields and labels that fall off the screen when run with a different display adapter.

It is important to use real data when testing the system by the time it nears completion. For that reason, a recommended mode of development creates and implements those modules needed to collect data first. Then, users can begin using them to enter real data. This data can then serve as test data for subsequent development.

Of course, all development should occur physically separated from a live system and live data. Errors do occur during development that could destroy live data. For example, you could mistakenly enter the path of the live data rather than the test data and zap it. This also means that you should periodically back up even your test data and test programs.

Not everyone is good at testing. In fact, some people enjoy testing more than others. (These are often the same people who enjoy bureaucratic detail such as income tax forms.) Often the developers of an application make the worst testers. They know the program too well and tend to enter only correct data. They subconsciously don't want to make their own program fail, even if consciously they recognize the need for testing.

On the other hand, other staff members may not have the emotional attachment to a program and therefore prove ruthless in their testing. While "ruthless" testers may find more problems, they must exercise tact in discussing them with the developer. After all, a program is the product of someone's creativity and you do not want to suppress that.

Furthermore, Visual FoxPro provides many different ways to perform a task. Therefore, don't criticize a person's methods just because you might do it differently. If a better, more efficient way exists to perform a task, find a way to show the other developers how it is better. Help them to learn, don't force them to learn.

## Defining Test Cases that Exercise All Program Paths

Test data can consist of white box testing or black box testing. *White box testing* thoroughly checks all program paths. Because it requires knowing the logic of the program, it is also called logic-driven testing. *Black box testing* requires no knowledge of the program logic. It just gathers test data and runs it. There is no inherent assumption that the test data actually tests all the program paths simply because the paths are not known.

A side benefit of creating white box test data is the need to review the program carefully to identify these paths. This process often uncovers problems even before testing begins. There are two goals with white box testing:

- Identify and test all defined paths required for the application.
- Ensure that no possible path is missing or unaccounted for by the application.

## Defining Test Cases Using Copies of Real Data

Whenever programmers try to "generate" test data, they almost always, without fail, miss at least one special case. For that reason, a random sample of real data generally provides just as good a test of the real operating environment. Try to collect real data as early in the project as possible.

The best way to do this is to develop data entry forms or other programs that collect data with minimal functionality as early as possible. The Form and Report Designers make this relatively painless. Forms should include minimal data validation but may not include look-up tables, context-sensitive help, or other advanced features implemented through custom methods. Reports may not include all the calculated fields or groupings, but they must include enough information to verify the accuracy of the input data.

If the application involves several processes, the task of collecting real data becomes more complex. In a real system, the processing of data takes place continuously. Therefore, you really need to capture an instantaneous snapshot of the data. Any time delay that allows users to process data could cause the data to be unsynchronized. This causes *false* errors (errors due to bad data, not due to program logic) when testing the program. Significant time can be lost tracking down and resolving these "false" errors. If possible, collect a copy of live data from all tables when no one else is on the system, such as at 3:00 A.M.

## Documenting Test Cases

If you just randomly run test cases, you really know how thoroughly they test the procedure or application. Not only do you need to know how thoroughly the cases cover all possible program paths, you need to know what each case tests. Documenting test cases provides historical case results to compare future changes to the application against.

**N O T E**  While not specifically designed for Visual FoxPro, it is possible to create a series of scripts to test your application with Microsoft Test. ■

Testing is so important that the IEEE (Institute of Electrical and Electronic Engineers) has developed standards for documenting tests. They are summarized in the following list:

- Identify the test case, its purpose, and what features it tests.
- Identify features not involved in the test.
- Identify any requirements for the test (such as data files, indexes, relations, drivers, and so on).
- Identify any additional hardware or software requirements. For example, OLE tests require other programs, such as Excel, Word, or Mail.

- Identify any assumptions made in the test (such as minimum memory, hard disk requirements, and available floppy drives).
- Identify the steps needed to run the test.
- Identify the criteria for what constitutes passing or failing the test.
- Identify where the tester might want to suspend execution to examine the program path or variable values.
- Identify any conditions that could cause the program to stop prematurely and detail what the tester should do at that point.
- Maintain a history of tests performed for each case, who performed it, the results, and any corrective action made to the code.
- Make an estimate of the amount of time needed to set up and perform the test. After running the test, document the actual times.

## Using Additional Testing Guidelines

Following are some additional testing guidelines:

- Test early and test often. Basically, this means test code at the lowest level possible. If you use the Expression Builder, always click the Verify button to check the expression's syntax. If you are building custom classes, build a small driver program or form to test them before using them in an application. Test individual procedures and functions.
- Create a flow chart to diagram the major program paths.
- Identify calculations that require special consideration to test more thoroughly. For example, a routine that calculates the number of workdays between any two dates has more complexity than a calculation of total days between two dates. This routine can be made even more complex if it considers the effect of holidays.
- Be able to verify test results by some other independent means. This requires either the ability to perform the calculation by hand or to compare it to other results.
- Use generalized routines and class libraries as much as possible. After these are developed and tested, you need not test them again unless you change them. This saves considerable time that you can invest in other parts of the program.

Also, examine each input field and determine whether it needs:

- A default
- A picture clause
- Special formatting

- A lookup option
- Special validation or range checking

## Asking Questions During Testing

While it may never be possible to absolutely guarantee that you have found all errors, by asking several questions about each module you write, you can minimize the number of errors. The following list provides just a few of the possible questions you might ask. Over time, you'll undoubtedly expand on this list with your own questions.

- Examine the relations between fields. Do some fields require information from others, thus making the entry order important?
- Should the user be able to exit an incomplete form? And if so, what happens to the data?
- What does the program do if a required program does not exist? If a required index does not exist? If a form or report does not exist?
- Can the program use tables on any drive and directory or are the paths hard-coded?
- Must the user define the SET commands before running the program? And if so, how? For example, do you know that each form supports its own SET environment?

# Understanding Methods for Tracking Down Errors

Despite all the preceding preparation to avoid common errors and the development of test sets, errors still happen. Your first priority when an error occurs is to find it and fix it. You can later go back to your test cases to determine why they didn't discover it in the first place.

When an error occurs during program execution, Visual FoxPro displays an error box with a simple error message. Beneath the message, it has three buttons: Cancel, Suspend, and Ignore. Most of the time, you do not want to ignore an error. If you write programs for other users, you *never* want them to ignore an error. In fact, you probably don't want them to see this default error message. Rather, you want to trap all errors with your own error handler, which documents the system at the time of the error and gracefully exits the application.

As is true of any rule, however, there may be a few exceptions. If the program fails because it cannot find a colorset, you may want to ignore that error. Most other errors you cannot ignore. If VFP cannot locate a table, ignoring the problem does not allow the program to run anyway. It needs that table for a reason. So just document the problem and quit the program.

As a developer, you will find that SUSPEND is a valuable option during testing. It stops program execution without removing current variables from memory. Any tables currently open remain open with their record pointers in place. Most important, you can then open the Trace window of the Debugger. The Trace window displays the source code being executed, highlighting the current line. While suspended, time stops for the application, enabling you to examine details of the program and its variables. You can even use the Trace window to execute the program line-by-line.

Part
IV
Ch
16

Visual FoxPro includes several built-in functions to provide clues when errors occur. To use them, you must interrupt the default error handling of Visual FoxPro. Rather than display a sometimes cryptic message to the user, you want to pass control to an error-handling routine. Listing 16.6 shows the simple error routine that you should consider. It displays a little more information than the standard error window, using a multiline Wait window.

### Listing 16.6  16PRG06.PRG

```
ON ERROR DO ErrLog WITH ;
   ERROR(), MESSAGE(), MESSAGE(1), LINENO(1), SYS(16)
** Rest of the application **

PROCEDURE ErrLog
LPARAMETER lnErrorNo, lcMessage, lcErrorLine, ;
           lcErrLineNo, lcModule
  WAIT WINDOW ;
    'An error has occurred in: ' + lcModule + CHR(13) + ;
    'ERROR: ' + STR(lnErrorNo, 6) + ' ' + lcMessage + CHR(13) + ;
    'On Line: ' + STR(lcErrLineNo, 6) + ' ' + lcErrorLine
RETURN
```

The ERROR() function returns a number that represents the error. The appendix in the *Developer's Guide* lists all error numbers along with a brief description.

Perhaps more useful is the MESSAGE() function. When used without a parameter, MESSAGE returns an error message associated with the error. This message is usually the same one that appears in the Error dialog box, displayed by Visual FoxPro. As a bonus, MESSAGE(1) returns the program line that caused the error.

The function LINENO() returns the program line number that suspended the program. By default, this line number is relative to the first line of the main program. Because a typical application calls many procedures and functions, this value has less importance than the one returned by LINENO(1). This function returns the line number from the beginning of the current program or procedure. Use this value when editing a program by opening the Edit pull-down menu and selecting Goto Line. After entering the line number at the prompt, the editor places the insert cursor at the beginning of the error line. The default FoxPro text editor can display line numbers if you select Show Line/Column Position in the Edit page of Tools, Options.

PROGRAM(lnLevel) returns the name of the executing program if lnLevel is 0 and the main program if it equals 1. It reports deeper call levels as the value of lnLevel increases until it returns an empty string. Visual FoxPro supports nested program calls up to 128 levels deep. This function is similar to SYS(16) except that SYS(16) also includes the path. When the error occurs in a procedure or function, SYS(16) begins with its name. Then, it displays the path and the parent program name.

SYS(16,lnLevel) also supports a second parameter that tells it to print the program names at a specific level in the calling sequence. If lnLevel is equal to zero, the function returns the name of the currently executing program. A lnLevel value of 1 begins with the main program. Sequential values step through the procedure calling sequence until reaching the procedure or function containing the error. At that point, subsequent values of the parameter return an empty string. The code that follows traces the calling sequence up to the error:

```
lnLevel = 1
DO WHILE !EMPTY(SYS(16, lnLevel))
  ? SYS(16, lnLevel)
  lnLevel = lnLevel + 1
ENDDO
```

## Testing Errors in the Command Window

The easiest way to test the error line is to try it in the Command Window. First, suspend the program at the error. This keeps all memory variables and tables intact and open. You can print variable values to the screen, checking for undefined or unusual types. If you find an undefined variable, you at least know what to look for. You can examine the code preceding the current line for any clues as to why the variable has not been defined.

If all the variables look correct, enter and test the line that failed. If the line contains a complex expression, test portions of it to determine where it fails. If you find a simple error, first correct and test it while you are in the Command window.

 **TIP** Copying and pasting ensures that you don't add new syntax errors by retyping lines.

Suppose that the expression looks correct and all variables are defined, but the line still fails. You may have the wrong syntax for a function, be missing a parenthesis, or have some other syntax error. In this case, use FoxPro's online help to check the proper syntax for any command or function.

**TIP** To get fast help on a Visual FoxPro command or function, highlight it in the program edit or Command window, and press the F1 key.

▶ **See** "Getting Help from Visual FoxPro," **p. 80**

Part
**IV**
Ch
**16**

You cannot test all code in the Command window. If you need to test a block of code inside a loop structure, such as IF, DO, SCAN, or FOR, you need to create a small test program. You cannot create loop structures inside the Command window. Rather, cancel the original program, but leave the Trace window open. Next, open a new file and copy and paste the code that you want to test into it. Be sure to initialize any variables needed by the loop structure and open files and indexes as required. Then run the test file. You should see each line of code highlighted as Visual FoxPro executes it. After you determine what causes the code to fail, fix and test it while still using the test file. When it works, copy and paste the corrected code back into the original program. Don't forget to delete the old code lines.

Sometimes an error occurs in a section of code that you cannot test separately. BROWSE and SELECT statements often extend over many lines. When Visual FoxPro reports an error in these commands, it cannot tell you which line within the statement contains the error. For these long commands, it may be difficult to quickly spot the error. The SELECT statement that follows illustrates this situation with a complex SELECT that includes several tables as well as a union between two separate SELECTs.

```
SELECT A.cStoreId, A.cTicket, A.cItemId, A.nQuantity, ;
       A.nUnitPrice, A.nExtPrice, ;
       B.cEmplId, B.cCompanyId, B.cDeptNo, B.cBatch, ;
       B.dDate AS DATE, ;
       C.cCenterNo, D.cLastName, ;
       LEFT(E.cProdDesc,25) as ProdDesc, ;
       G.cCoName, H.cDeptName ;
  FROM TKTDETL A, TICKET B,  CENTERS C, CUSTOMER D, ;
       PRODUCT E, COMPANY G, DEPARTMT H ;
 WHERE A.cStoreId+A.cTicket = B.cStoreId+B.cTicket AND ;
       A.cStoreId+A.cTicket+A.cItemId = ;
       C.cStoreId+C.cTicket+C.cItemId AND ;
       &FiltStr1 ;
 UNION ALL ;
SELECT A.cStoreId, A.cTicket, A.cItemId, A.nQuantity, ;
       A.nUnitPrice, A.nExtPrice, ;
       B.cEmplId, B.cCompanyId, B.cDeptNo, B.cBatch, ;
       B.dDate AS DATE, ;
       SPACE(10) AS cCenterNo, D.cLastName, ;
       LEFT(E.cProdDesc,25) as ProdDesc, ;
```

```
         G.cCoName, H.cDeptName ;
  FROM TKTDETL A, TICKET B,  CUSTOMER D, ;
         PRODUCT E, COMPANY G, DEPARTMT H ;
  WHERE A.cStoreId+A.cTicket = B.cStoreId+B.cTicket AND ;
         A.cStoreId+A.cTicket NOT IN ;
            (SELECT F.cStoreId+F.cTicket from CENTERS F) AND ;
         &FiltStr2 ;
  INTO CURSOR MPA
```

Debugging a SELECT statement this complex is difficult without taking advantage of another technique called code reduction or decomposition. The purpose of code reduction is to reduce the amount of code used in a test. In this case, an obvious first attempt at reducing the test code is to split the individual SELECT statements. Then, test each one separately. After you determine which SELECT statement causes the error, you can remove additional code from it until it finally works. With a SELECT, further reduction can mean removing one table at a time along with its related fields and relations. Or, you could begin by removing sorts or groupings. With any method you choose, at some point the SELECT statement begins to work. It is then a simple matter to determine what is wrong with the code just removed.

After finding and correcting an error, you can proceed in several ways. You could take a pessimistic approach and incrementally rebuild the SELECT one table or feature at a time making sure it continues to work. You could also take an optimistic approach and test the changes in the original complete SELECT statement. Of course, there are levels in between. In this case, you may want to test the individual SELECT statement with the correction before copying it back into the union.

You can apply this same approach to any code, not just single commands like SELECT. Take any program or procedure that does not work and comment out functionality until it does. Whatever you mark as comments probably contains the error.

**N O T E** While you can comment out individual program lines by adding an asterisk in front of each one, this can become tedious for blocks of code. Select the lines of code you want to comment by clicking at the beginning of the first line and dragging through the lines. Then choose the Comment option from the Format menu. ■

A review of recent program changes provides another good clue to the error's cause. The most likely place to look when an error occurs in an existing program that ran fine previously is in any recent code changes. This is not a guarantee. After all, the error may reside in a code path that was not executed before. However, it is a good place to begin.

## Adding Wait Windows or Other Printed Output

Not all errors point to obvious lines of code. Sometimes a logic error originates in an entirely different section of the code from where the program finally fails or displays erratic behavior. In these cases, you need to spot check the program's activity at various points.

One way to check a program's path is to embed WAIT statements throughout the code using the following format:

```
WAIT WINDOW 'Beginning of PROCEDURE COPYDATA' NOWAIT
```

Part

**IV**

Ch

**16**

Every time execution passes a statement like this, a Wait window appears in the upper-right corner. The NOWAIT option allows the program to continue without pausing. (If you want the program to pause, skip the NOWAIT option or use the MESSAGEBOX( ) function with only the first argument to display a message.) Adding WAIT statements has an additional advantage for programs that perform extensive background processing. Even when used in a production environment, they assure the user that the program is still executing. Users who think a program has stopped may reboot the computer. This can lead to data corruption.

You can also halt the program at any point with the SUSPEND command or add commands to print or list information about the program such as those shown in Listing 16.7.

---

### Listing 16.7  16PRG07.PRG

```
lcMemFile  = 'MEM' + LEFT(CTOD(DATE()),2) + ;
             SUBSTR(CTOD(DATE()), 4, 2) + '.TXT'
lcStatFile = 'STAT' + LEFT(CTOD(DATE()),2) + ;
             SUBSTR(CTOD(DATE()), 4, 2) + '.TXT'
LIST MEMORY TO FILE &lcMemFile
LIST STATUS TO FILE &lcStatFile
```

---

Of course, you don't want these commands to execute every time a user runs the program. If you enter them as shown previously, there is a high risk that you may forget and leave them in the final user version. Because users do not need to see this output, you might want to bracket these commands with an IF...ENDIF like the following:

```
IF glDebugMode
     << Place any debug command here >>
ENDIF
```

You could then initialize the variable glDebugMode at the beginning of the program to turn these commands on or off. By using a variable and defining it in the main program, you need to change and compile only one routine to turn these statements on. A better technique stores the value for glDebugMode outside the program, perhaps in a configuration table or memory variable file. Then, you can activate the debug mode without having to recompile the system at all.

Even when these commands are inactive, they require memory, both for the additional program lines and the memory variable. An alternative uses the #DEFINE and #IF...#ENDIF directives to include or exclude the debug code at compile time.

```
#DEFINE glDebugMode .T.
#IF glDebugMode
   << Place any debug commands here >>
#ENDIF
```

The best solution, however, is not to hard-code any debug statement in the program. Visual FoxPro provides an excellent tool called the Debugger, which actually consists of a series of tools. One of these tools is the familiar Trace window used in previous versions. This window is joined by the Watch, Locals, Call Stack, and Output windows. The Watch window resembles the Debug window of previous versions, but it has a few differences.

## Using the Trace Window

Visual FoxPro Debugger provides the Trace window, a powerful tool, to debug code. Trace opens a window that displays the program's commands as they execute. It also enables you to step through the program one command at a time so you can see the exact path being followed. Figure 16.1 shows a typical Trace window.

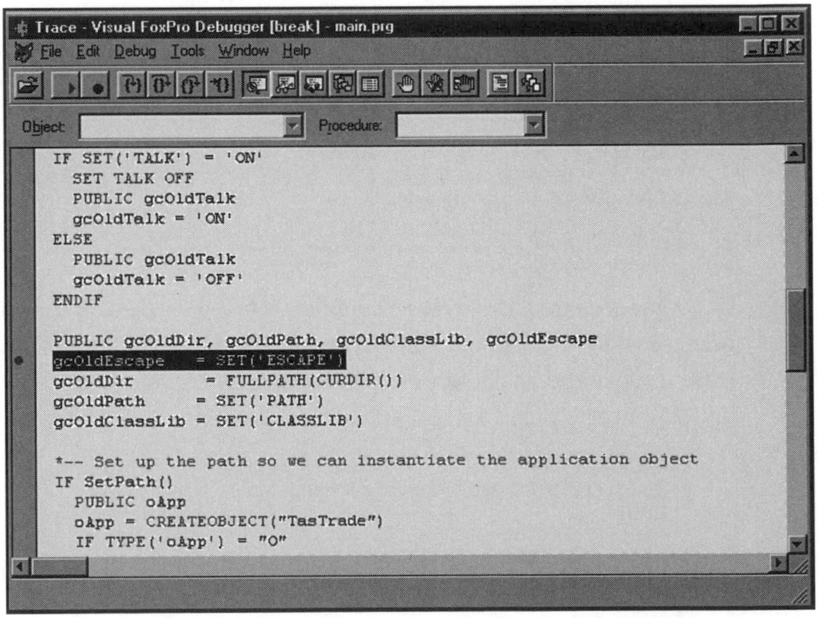

**FIGURE 16.1**
The Trace window shows code from TasTrade and a breakpoint set on the highlighted line.

> **CAUTION**
>
> Visual FoxPro executes programs referenced by a path in a different directory. However, it cannot reference source code in any but the current directory. If it cannot find the source code, it displays the message `Source Not Found`.
>
> Not only must it find the source code, but the date and time stamp must be later than that of the source. If not, VFP displays the message `Source Is Out of Date`.

There are several ways to enter Trace mode. One way is to place the command

```
SET STEP ON
```

in the code, recompile the program, and run it. When the program executes this command, it stops and displays a Trace window (refer to Figure 16.1). Early in the debug process, you may be tempted to put this command throughout the program. As with SUSPEND or hard-coded print statements, the danger is in forgetting to remove one or more of them.

Another way to open the Trace window is to select Debugger from the Tools menu before executing the program. This opens the Debugger, from which you can open the Trace window. If it is not already open, open the Trace window by selecting Windows Trace or by clicking the trace button in the toolbar. Notice that the Trace window activates other options in the Debugger's menu bar. Figure 16.2 defines the toolbar buttons.

To select an application or program, choose File, Open. This displays the Open dialog box. By default, it shows PRG, FXP, and MPR files in the current directory. It also shows APP and EXE files. If you select an APP file, a dialog box appears so you can select a program from within the application. If only FXP files can be found for the application, they are shown with dimmed text, because they cannot be used in the Trace window. You must have access to the source files.

---

### Activating and Deactivating Debugger Windows

If the Visual FoxPro Debugger window is open, you also can open the TRACE window with the command

```
ACTIVATE WINDOW TRACE
```

and close it with

```
DEACTIVATE WINDOW TRACE
```

Similarly, you can open the other Debugger windows with the following commands

```
ACTIVATE WINDOW WATCH
ACTIVATE WINDOW LOCALS
ACTIVATE WINDOW "CALL STACK"
ACTIVATE WINDOW "DEBUG OUTPUT"
```

*continues*

*continued*

and close them with

```
DEACTIVATE WINDOW WATCH
DEACTIVATE WINDOW LOCALS
DEACTIVATE WINDOW "CALL STACK"
DEACTIVATE WINDOW "DEBUG OUTPUT"
```

You can even deactivate the Debugger window itself, as follows:

```
DEACTIVATE WINDOW "Visual FoxPro Debugger"
```

Because deactivating a window does not remove it from memory, you can reactivate it with the following:

```
ACTIVATE WINDOW "Visual FoxPro Debugger"
```

**FIGURE 16.2**
All the windows in the Debugger share a toolbar with the buttons defined in this figure.

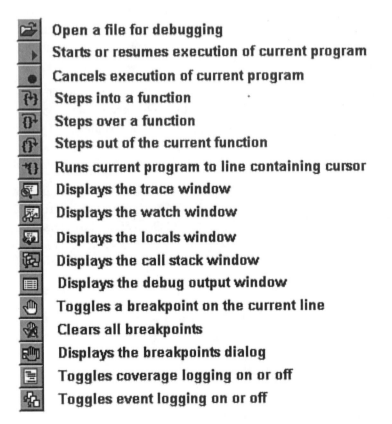

Open a file for debugging

Starts or resumes execution of current program

Cancels execution of current program

Steps into a function

Steps over a function

Steps out of the current function

Runs current program to line containing cursor

Displays the trace window

Displays the watch window

Displays the locals window

Displays the call stack window

Displays the debug output window

Toggles a breakpoint on the current line

Clears all breakpoints

Displays the breakpoints dialog

Toggles coverage logging on or off

Toggles event logging on or off

If you select a program (PRG) file, Visual FoxPro displays the source code in the Trace window. Notice that the Trace window also supports syntax coloring, just like the editor.

After selecting a program or application module, use the vertical scroll bar to display different lines of the module. If the line is wider than the width of the Trace window, you can scroll horizontally to see it all.

**N O T E** This capability to horizontally scroll the Trace window is great, but you should still try to limit the length of each line to the width of the editor window (assuming that the window is as wide as possible on your screen). Long lines are harder to read on-screen because of the need to keep switching from the vertical scroll bar to the horizontal one. Similarly, printed listings of the code with long lines are difficult to read. If you have a long command, split it across several lines by ending each line, except the last, with a semicolon. This punctuation tells Visual FoxPro that the command continues on the next line. ■

To mark a line with a breakpoint, double-click in the shaded margin bar next to the line, or place the cursor anywhere in it and press the space bar. You can also use the Toggle breakpoint button in the toolbar after selecting the line. If the line is an executable line, Visual FoxPro places a red circle to the immediate left of the line in the shaded margin bar. It serves as a visual reminder of the breakpoint. If you click a comment line, Visual FoxPro marks the next executable line after the comment. If you click one of a command's continuation lines, VFP marks the current command with the breakpoint. The circle is always placed on the last line of continuation lines.

Mark as many breakpoints as you need. Each time the program reaches a breakpoint, it treats it like a SUSPEND statement in the program and interrupts execution. It does not cancel the program. If you mark the wrong line, simply double-click it again or highlight it and press Enter to remove the mark.

While the program is suspended during a breakpoint, you can:

- Move forward or backward through the code using the scroll bar
- Switch to a different object or procedure using list boxes in the Trace window header
- Open the Data Session window to check the status of open files, their indexes, current record status, or even browse the data
- Enter commands in the Command window
- Select options from the main menu
- Change the current value of any memory or table variable
- Open other Debugger windows and check the current value of variables, the call stack, or set watch variables

The one thing you cannot do is change the executing program's source code.

### TROUBLESHOOTING

**During a suspend in the program execution, I examined several of the open tables to check the progress of the data updates. However, when I attempted to resume the program, it immediately failed.** Some changes made during a breakpoint can cause problems. If you move a record pointer or change the current work area, you must return everything to its original state. Otherwise, attempts to resume stepping through the program could fail.

If you want to trace an application, but do not want to set a breakpoint, just click the OK button when VFP displays the application module list. Visual FoxPro always begins execution of an application from the main module regardless of which module appears in the Trace window.

When you finish debugging your application, you need to remove all breakpoints. You can do this one breakpoint at a time in the Trace window. A more efficient method uses the Clear All breakpoints, which removes all breakpoints from the entire application. This saves you from the trouble of having to remember where you set breakpoints. After making a change to a module, Visual FoxPro recompiles it before running it. Recompilation removes breakpoints. Therefore, you may have to mark them again.

The Debug menu contains an option, Throttle, that controls the length of a pause between each executed line. The default of 0 means that there is no delay. This does not mean that programs executing with the Trace window active run at the same speed as a normal program. In fact, their speed is greatly reduced. The video drivers cannot keep up with the speed at which Visual FoxPro usually executes code. You may not be able to follow even this reduced pace. Therefore, you can increase the delay between each command from 0 to 5 seconds. While the trace is running, you can cut the speed in half by pressing any of the following keys:

> Ctrl
>
> Shift
>
> A mouse button

To cut it in half again, press any two keys at the same time.

**N O T E**   You can also set the throttle by changing the value of the system memory variable _THROTTLE, as in:

```
_Throttle = 1.0
```

The value again represents seconds and can range from 0 to 5, with 0 meaning no pause between executing lines. ■

If you click the Start button in the toolbar, select Debug Do!, or press F5; the program begins execution. Visual FoxPro highlights each code line in the Trace window as it executes. Of course, unless you can speed-read program code, you probably cannot keep up with it without increasing the Throttle value.

You can interrupt program execution while the Trace window is open by pressing the Esc key as long as SET ESCAPE is not OFF. You can set this feature by checking Cancel Programs on Escape in the General page of Tools, Options. This feature is useful to stop the Trace mode without running the entire program. Strongly consider adding the command SET ESCAPE OFF before distributing the application. This prevents users from aborting a program prematurely by pressing Esc.

While you are tracing a program, the toolbar provides four ways to step through your code:

Steps into a function

Steps over a function

Steps out of the current function

Runs current program to line containing the cursor

The most used toolbar button is the Step Into button. It tells Visual FoxPro to execute the next line of the code and then to pause again. Use it to step through a program one line at a time at your own pace. At any time, you can stop to check variables or tables. To continue, activate the Trace window and click this button again. If the next line happens to be a call to a procedure or a function, Trace continues stepping through the code in that procedure or function.

If you want to step through code only in the current procedure and not trace a procedure or function call, click the Step Over button. This tells VFP to execute the procedure or function, but not to trace the code. If you accidentally step into a procedure or function, use the Step Out button to execute the rest of the code in the current procedure or function and then return to trace mode when it returns to the calling program.

Another way to execute a block of code without tracing through it is to place the cursor in the line where you want to begin tracing again and then click the Run to Cursor button to execute the code without tracing until it reaches the line with the cursor. Note that if you do not select carefully, you could select a line that is not executed due to program loops or conditional statements. Thus, the program will not suspend again.

If you decide to stop tracing the code but want to finish executing it, click the Resume button (the same as the Start button). It tells Visual FoxPro to continue executing the program until it encounters either another breakpoint or reaches the end of the program. Click this option after stepping through a suspected problem area to complete the program normally. You also can terminate the program by clicking the Cancel button or by selecting Cancel from the Debug menu.

A new feature is the capability to set the next executable line while in trace mode. Normally, FoxPro executes each line one after the other sequentially. Only conditional statements, loops, and function/procedure calls change this sequential execution of code. Suppose, however, that you are testing a program that suspends due to an error in a line. You may not be able to change the line to correct it (with the Debug Fix option) without canceling the program. Suppose that you can enter the correct command line through the command window and then change the program line pointer to skip the problem line to continue execution without having to cancel the program. That is exactly how you can use the Set Next Statement option in the Debug menu. Just remember to go back and correct the program line later before running it again.

Another new feature is the Breakpoints dialog box. Click the third toolbar button from the right or select breakpoints from the Tools menu. This displays the dialog box shown in Figure 16.3.

**FIGURE 16.3**

The Breakpoints dialog box enables you to define four types of breakpoints: two based on a program line and two based on expression values.

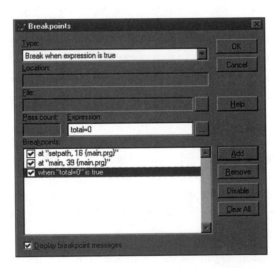

This dialog box defines options for each breakpoint. Notice the list box at the bottom of the dialog box. It lists all the breakpoints in the current module. Initially, no breakpoints are selected. Click one to see information about it.

The Location text box begins with the name of the program or function that contains the breakpoint and the line number from the beginning of that program or function. The File text box displays the name of the file where the program, procedure, or function is found. This includes the full path.

If you added the breakpoint by double-clicking to the left of the line or by using the Breakpoint toolbar button, the default breakpoint type is Break at Location. This means that the program merely pauses execution when it encounters this line. You have other options, however.

Even with the default breakpoint type, you can specify the Pass count at which trace begins. Suppose that you have an error inside of a loop. You know that the first 100 times through the loop, the calculation is valid; however, an error occurs shortly after that. You certainly don't want to step through the loop 100 times before reaching the error. An easier way is to set the Pass count to 100. This tells the Debugger to start trace mode only after it has reached the 100th pass through the loop.

You can change the breakpoint type by opening the Type drop-down list. The options include:

> Break at Location
>
> Break at Location if Expression Is True
>
> Break When Expression Is True
>
> Break When Expression Has Changed

The second type option is similar to the first but relies on an expression value rather than a pass count. For example, you might know that the error occurs when a specific variable is set to a specific value, but you don't know in which pass. Suppose that the variable TOTAL is zero when the expression attempts to use it as the dividend in an equation. Dividing by zero is not allowed. Therefore, you may want to set a breakpoint on the equation, but set the expression to TOTAL = 0. Note that you can also use the Expression builder button to the right of the field to help build the necessary expression.

Perhaps you would rather know when the variable TOTAL is set to zero. In this case, change the breakpoint type to *Break when expression is true*. Enter the expression TOTAL = 0 again and then click the Add button along the bottom right of the dialog box. This adds a new breakpoint to the list, but one that is not represented by a specific line in a specific code module. This option is equivalent to the way breakpoints were set to debug expressions in previous versions of FoxPro and Visual FoxPro.

Similarly, you can use the type *Break when expression has changed* to cause the program to enter trace mode when the value of the expression entered in the Expression text box changes. Again, this breakpoint type cannot be represented by a specific line in the code.

As you can see by the buttons in the bottom-right corner of the dialog box, you can also remove individual breakpoints by selecting them and clicking the Remove button. A new feature is the capability to disable a breakpoint without removing it. Click the Disable button while a breakpoint is selected to toggle the disable feature. Notice that this adds and removes the check in the box before the breakpoint description in the list box. This makes it easy to add breakpoints and selectively turn them on and off. Finally, the Clear All button lets you remove all breakpoints. Note that these buttons are the only way to remove breakpoints associated with expressions rather than lines.

> **CAUTION**
>
> Canceling a program while you are in trace mode can leave files and windows open, updates partially complete, and records and files locked. In addition, environment SET variables may have changed the environment and may not have been reset.

## Using the Locals Window

The Locals window remains empty until you run the program. Then, it displays all the variables as they are defined, along with their current value and type. This list is by procedure or function. So *local*, in this context, means all variables that are "seen" by the currently selected procedure or function. Figure 16.4 shows some of the local variables defined early in the execution of the Tastrade example.

**FIGURE 16.4**

The Locals window displays variables currently in use by the application, including objects.

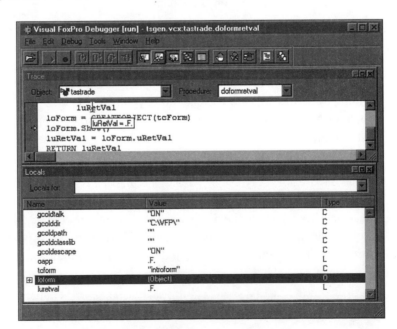

As you can see in Figure 16.4, the Locals window also shows object variables. Notice also in the Trace window, at the top of the figure, that the cursor is on the variable `luRetVal`. Beneath the cursor is a box with the current value of this variable. The Trace window lets you position the cursor over any variable in code that has already executed and display the value of that variable. Notice that this is the same variable and value that appears at the bottom of the Locals list. If your program is long and has dozens of defined variables, this ToolTip-type method of checking a variable value can be quite useful.

Back in the Locals window, the box with the + in it, before the variable name for an object, indicates that you can open this object to look inside. In fact, if you click this box, you can open the object to see the values for all its properties. If the object is a container object, you can see the objects it contains. These, too, can be opened. In fact, you can drill down through as many levels as you like to get to the base objects and their properties. Figure 16.5 shows three levels open in one of the objects from Tastrade. If you examine this code further, you will find that there are many more than three levels, and you can see them all.

**FIGURE 16.5**
The Locals window lets you view the variables currently defined by the running application, including objects and their properties.

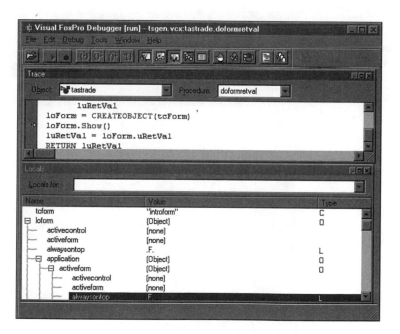

The drop-down list at the top of the Locals window enables you to look at the variables available in any of the procedures or functions that have executed. Just open the list and pick a different procedure or function to see what variables it can "see." Global variables are seen in all procedures, once defined. Private variables can be seen in the procedure where they are defined and any called procedures. Local variables can be seen only in the procedure where they are defined.

# Using the Watch Window

Sometimes, you don't want to see all the variables. Rather, you want to see only one or two to determine why they don't get the values you expect. In this case, it makes more sense to use the Watch window. Simply enter the variable names in the Watch text box. When you enter each variable, it appears in the list in the second half of the window. If the variable has already been defined by the current program, the second column displays its value, and its type appears in the third column. If the variable has not yet been defined or it is out of scope, the message (Expression could not be evaluated) appears in the Value column.

Figure 16.6 shows an example of this window using some of the fields from the Locals window. Note that while the Locals window can look at any routine and what variables are defined there, the Watch window sees only the variables in the current procedure or function.

**FIGURE 16.6**

The Watch window makes it easier to monitor the values of a few selected variables.

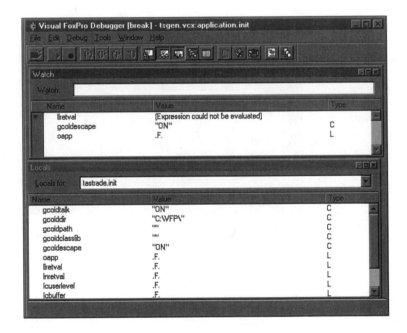

Note the circle in the left column next to the first watch variable. This shows another way to set a breakpoint on a variable. In this case, the program breaks whenever the value of llRetVal changes. To prove this, you can open the Breakpoints dialog box to see that the breakpoint, when llretval changes, appears in the list at the bottom of the dialog box.

## Using the Call Stack Window

When you are executing an application, it is very easy to get lost in the number of procedure and function call levels. In fact, sometimes the problem is that the program is calling procedures or functions in a sequence different from what you may have expected. One way to determine exactly how the program got to the current line is to open the Call Stack window, as shown in Figure 16.7.

Part
IV
Ch
16

**FIGURE 16.7**
The Call Stack window shows the sequence of procedure and function calls from the start of the program (bottom) to the current one (top).

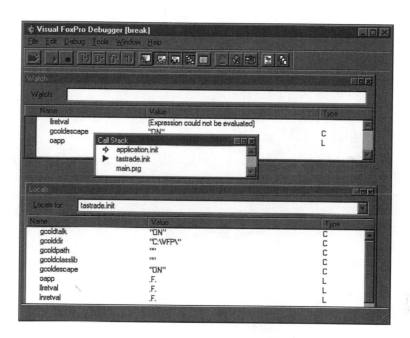

Just as the arrow in the Trace windows shows the current line being executed, the arrow in the Call Stack shows the currently executing procedure or function.

When you click any of the procedures of functions higher in the call stack, the Debugger automatically changes the procedure looked at by the Locals windows to show the variables *known* in that procedure. While you are looking at a procedure other than the current one, a black right-pointing arrow appears to the left of the procedure name. These changes do not affect which line is executed next.

## Using the Debug Output Window

This window displays character strings defined by the DEBUGOUT command. It also shows the names of system events that occur when event tracking is enabled.

The DEBUGOUT command has this syntax:

```
DEBUGOUT eExpression
```

This command can be placed in your program to print a string to the Debug Output window. Because output goes only to the Debug Output window, you can leave these commands in the code even when distributing the application to end users. Unless users have the full version of Visual FoxPro and have the Debug Output window of the Debugger open, they will never know that these commands are there. Yet, any time you need to debug the application, you can simply open the Debug Output window to watch the values that print.

Typical uses of DEBUGOUT include:

Print the current value of any variable

Print messages to indicate where the program is (at the beginning of procedures, object INITs, and so on)

## Using Event Tracking

Sometimes, it helps to know in what order events are fired for different objects. The real secret to object-oriented programming is knowing what code to place in the methods of each event so that they execute in the correct order. Sometimes, when your program just isn't working right, the easiest way to determine whether you have code in the correct method is to turn on event tracking.

While in the Debugger, Select Tools, Event Tracking to display the Event Tracking dialog box, as shown in Figure 16.8.

**FIGURE 16.8**

The Event Tracking dialog box lets you determine which events you want to echo statements from in the Debug Output window.

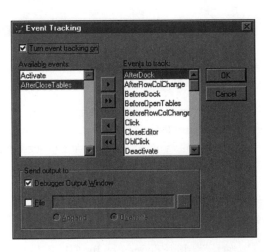

The top half of this dialog box lets you select which events you want to track. By default, all events are preselected, but event tracking is not enabled. Remember to click the check box at the top of the dialog box to enable Event Tracking. To move an event from one list to the other, select it and then click one of the buttons between the two lists. You can also double-click an event to move it from one list to the other.

The second half of the dialog box determines where VFP sends the output from event tracking. By default, the messages are sent to the Debug Output window of the Debugger. For large programs, this list can get rather long, and you may want to send it to a file and use the FoxPro Editor to search for specific event occurrences. Figure 16.9 shows an example of the Debug Output window with several event tracking messages.

**FIGURE 16.9**
Use the Debug Output window along with Event Tracking to determine the order in which events fire and thus the optimal location to add custom code.

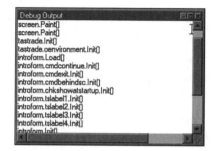

## Using Coverage

**At the time this chapter was written, it still was not certain whether the Coverage feature would exist in the final release of the product. Check our Web page with Que to see any last-minute changes that may affect this feature as the product is released.**

# Using Error Handlers

No amount of diligence in checking for common syntax, logic, or exception errors finds all errors. No amount of testing, even with the help of live data and the use of the Debugger window can guarantee an error-free program. Sometimes the application encounters a situation that you could not foresee and plan for. In many complex systems in use today, the number of combinations of possible data exceeds the national debt. Furthermore, no matter how foolproof you make a system, "fools" can be remarkably ingenious. It takes only one user to turn off the computer in the middle of a reindex to trash an entire file.

You have to accept the fact that at some point the program will fail. When it does, you do not want it to display a cryptic message to the user, who will probably just turn the machine off before calling you. At the very least, you want to direct the program to an error-handling routine using the ON ERROR trigger. The primary purpose of this error routine is to provide some information about the error. This command redirects execution to the procedure ERRLOG:

```
ON ERROR DO errlog WITH ERROR(), MESSAGE(), MESSAGE(1), SYS(16), ;
    LINENO()
```

Once in the procedure, you can determine the error type by checking the error number.

There are three primary classes of errors from the user's standpoint. First are trivial errors. These include errors as simple as a colorset not being found, or a printer or floppy drive that is not ready. In some cases, you can simply log the error and then skip the command causing the error and continue execution. This is the case when something trivial, such as a colorset, is missing.

In other cases, a simple message to the user followed by a RETRY or RETURN command handles it. Examples of when to use this approach might be when the program attempts to read a file from a floppy drive and there is either no floppy in the drive, the drive door is open (5.25-inch floppy disks), or the floppy is write-protected when the program attempts to write to it. A message to users telling them how to correct the program along with a RETRY button makes sense here.

For another example, suppose that while using SKIP to move through records, you overshoot the end of file. Visual FoxPro reports this error as End of file encountered. More specifically, it is error number 4. There is no need to cancel the program for this type of error. To correct the problem, the program can simply reset the record pointer on the last record in the table. The version of procedure ERRLOG shown in Listing 16.8 presents an outline of these techniques:

**Listing 16.8   16PRG08.PRG**

```
****************
PROCEDURE ERRLOG
LPARAMETERS lnErrorNo, lcMessage, lcErrorLine, ;
            lcmodule, lnErrorLineNo

* Check if beyond end of file, place on last record
  IF lnErrorNo = 4
    WAIT WINDOW 'AT LAST RECORD' TIMEOUT 2
    GOTO BOTTOM
  ELSE
    CANCEL
  ENDIF
RETURN
```

This example checks whether the error number equals 4. If so, it displays a window telling the user that it has moved the record pointer to the last record. It then exits the routine and returns to the line immediately after the one that caused the error. Presumably, this allows the program to continue executing. If any other error occurs, this routine cancels the program.

> **N O T E** When Visual FoxPro encounters RETURN in an error-handling routine, it attempts to
> continue execution from the line immediately after the one that caused the error.
> The RETRY command tells it to try to continue execution by reperforming the line that caused
> the error. You must determine which, if any, of these recovery methods apply to each error
> handled. ■

In addition to checking whether the record pointer is beyond the end of file, you can
check other conditions. Listing 16.10, at the end of this chapter, shows a few more. However, it is not meant to be an all-inclusive example. Rather, it merely shows the types of
ways you can handle selected errors.

A more serious error level is one that requires either more calculations or assistance from
the user, but is still recoverable. It might involve files or indexes. Sometimes, files get
deleted or moved, especially with systems on a network. In these cases, a program stops
with an error as soon as it attempts to open a file but cannot find it. Listing 16.9 uses the
GETFILE command to prompt the user to locate the file. Because GETFILE uses the
Open dialog box, users can search any drive or directory they have access to and
find it.

### Listing 16.9  16PRG09.PRG

```
****************
PROCEDURE ERRLOG
LPARAMETERS lnErrorNo, lcMessage, lcErrorLine, ;
            lcModule, lnErrorLineNo

* No table in use or table not found
  IF lnErrorNo = 1 OR lnErrorNo = 52
    LOCAL lcNewFile
    SELECT 0
    lcNewFile = GETFILE('DBF', 'Select a DBF:', 'SELECT')
    IF EMPTY(lcNewFile)
      CANCEL
    ELSE
      USE (lcNewFile) SHARED
      IF lnErrorNo = 1
        RETURN
      ELSE
        RETRY
      ENDIF
    ENDIF
  ELSE
    CANCEL
  ENDIF
RETURN
```

This example checks for two error values. Error number 1 indicates that the File does
not exist. This means that the named file does not exist in the current directory or in the

directory referenced by the program. The second error code, 52, says that No table is in use. This error occurs when the program attempts to perform any table related command while in an empty work area. In both cases, the program needs a file.

The previous code prompts the user to select a file using GETFILE. Of course, you may not want to do this for all users because they could easily load the wrong file; however, note that it is a possible solution. When the user selects a table, the program opens it. If the original error number is 1, the program probably is trying to open a file with the wrong name or directory. In this case, you want to continue execution on the line immediately after the error because the error handler just opened the file. Otherwise, the program continues to try to open the file in the wrong directory or with the wrong name. On the other hand, if the program assumes that the file is active and tries to perform a function on it, FoxPro generates error 52. In this case, you probably want to continue execution on the same line that failed. If the user selects CANCEL, GETFILE returns an empty string that cancels the program.

> **CAUTION**
>
> The authors do not recommend this technique as a general solution. It is too easy for the user to specify any file in any directory and potentially cause even greater damage. It is also possible that the file name could exist in more than one directory on the server and contain different data sets. In this case, they may continue executing, but with the wrong data and thus produce incorrect results. Generally, the best thing to do is to use the FILE command to check for the existence of the file in the expected directory. If it is not found, display a message to the user, log the error, and exit the program.

Unfortunately, most errors are not recoverable from a user's standpoint. These errors range from coding errors to corrupted files. The best that you can do as a programmer is to document as much as possible about the system when the error occurs. Program 16.10, at the end of this chapter, shows one way to do this. Then, have the routine display a message to users telling them what has happened and terminate the program.

Listing 16.10 shows a more complete version of an error-handling routine. Observe the code after the comment Unrecoverable Errors. This segment captures information about the system at the time of the error and saves it to a file. The file name is coded with the month, day, hour, and minute the error occurred. It handles even the possibility of multiple errors at the same time by changing the extension.

**Listing 16.10    16PRG10.PRG**

```
* Test driver for PROCEDURE ERRLOG
CLOSE ALL
ON ERROR DO errlog WITH ERROR(), MESSAGE(), ;
                        MESSAGE(1), SYS(16), LINENO(1)
```

```
* Test reindex
  SET DEFAULT TO \VFP5BOOK\DATA
  OPEN DATABASE ptofsale
  USE EMPL2
  SET ORDER TO TAG empl2

* Call a non-existent color set
  SET COLOR SET TO MIKEA

* Create a cursor and attempt to pack it
  SET DEFAULT TO \VFP5BOOK\DATA
  OPEN DATABASE ptofsale
  USE EMPL2
  SET ORDER TO TAG empl2
  SELECT * from empl2 INTO CURSOR mpa
  PACK

* Call for RESUME without a SUSPEND
  RESUME

* Use a file that does not exist
  USE MICKEY

RETURN

****************
PROCEDURE ERRLOG
LPARAMETERS lnErrorNo, lcMessage, lcErrorLine, ;
            lcModule, lnErrorLineNo
************************************************************
*                                                        *
* PROCEDURE ERRLOG                                       *
*                                                        *
* This routine demonstrates 3 ways to handle errors.  *
*                                                        *
* Parameters:                                            *
* lnErrorNo      - Error Number                          *
* lcMessage      - Error Message                         *
* lcErrorLine    - Line of code where error occurs       *
* lcModule       - Name of procedure where error occurs  *
* lnErrorLineNo  - Line number where error occurs        *
*                                                        *
* Copyright 1994 Michael P. Antonovich                   *
*                                                        *
************************************************************
LOCAL lcError, lnExitMethod
lnExitMethod = 0
WAIT WINDOW 'Error: ' + STR(lnErrorNo) TIMEOUT 1

* Avoid recursive loop if errlog contains an error
  lcError = ON('ERROR')
  ON ERROR

* Each case in this structure represents one error type
* It handles trivial errors first, followed by recoverable
```

*continues*

Part
IV
Ch
16

**Listing 16.10  Continued**

```
* errors. Finally, all other errors generate an ASCII text
* file with information about the system and error.
  DO CASE

*** Check for trivial errors
  * Check if beyond end of file, place on last record
    CASE lnErrorNo = 4
      GOTO BOTTOM

  * Check if before beginning of file, place on first record
    CASE lnErrorNo = 38
      GOTO TOP

  * Cannot pack a cursor
    CASE lnErrorNo = 1115

  * Check for Resume without Suspend
    CASE lnErrorNo = 1236

  * Colorset not found
    CASE lnErrorNo = 1642

*** Check for recoverable errors
  * No table in use or table not found
    CASE lnErrorNo = 1 OR lnErrorNo = 52
      LOCAL lcNewFile
      SELECT 0
      lcNewFile = GETFILE('DBF', 'Select a DBF:', 'SELECT')
      IF EMPTY(lcNewFile)
        lnExitMethod = 2
      ELSE
        USE (lcNewFile) SHARED
      ENDIF

  * Record is out of range
    CASE lnErrorNo = 5 OR lnErrorNo = 20
      LOCAL lcDBF, lcTagName, lcTagNo, lcTagExp, lcFilter, ;
            lcIndex, lcSafety, llExclusiveOn, lcUnique

    * Gather information about current DBF and index
      lcDBF     = DBF()                        && DBF name
      lcTagName = TAG()                        && Tag or IDX name
      lcTagNo   = SYS(21)                       && Index number
      lcUnique  = IIF(UNIQUE(), 'UNIQUE', '')  && Is index UNIQUE?
      IF VAL(lcTagNo) = 0
        WAIT WINDOW "No tag has been set. I don't know what to do"
        lnExitMethod = 2
      ELSE
        lcTagExp  = KEY()                     && Index expression
        lcFilter  = SYS(2021, VAL(lcTagNo))   && Index FOR condition
        lcIndex   = ORDER(1,1)                && Full Index name

        IF LEFT(lcIndex, 3) = 'IDX'
```

```
                * Open table without index
                  USE (lcDBF)

                * Turn safety off to allow reindex
                  lcSafety = SET('SAFETY')
                  SET SAFETY OFF
                  IF EMPTY(lcFilter)
                    INDEX ON &lcTagExp TO (lcIndex) &lcUnique ADDITIVE
                  ELSE
                    INDEX ON &lcTagExp FOR &lcFilter TO (lcIndex) ;
                             &lcUnique ADDITIVE
                  ENDIF
                  SET SAFETY (lcSafety)

                * Reopen table with new index
                  USE (lcDBF) INDEX (lcIndex)
                ELSE
                * Open table exclusively to remove and recreate tag
                  llExclusiveOn = ISEXCLUSIVE()
                  IF !llExclusiveOn
                    USE (lcDBF) EXCLUSIVE
                  ENDIF

                  DELETE TAG (lcTagName)
                  IF EMPTY(lcFilter)
                    INDEX ON &lcTagExp &lcUnique TAG (lcTagName)
                  ELSE
                    INDEX ON &lcTagExp FOR &lcFilter &lcUnique ;
                          TAG (lcTagName)
                  ENDIF

                  IF !llExclusiveOn
                    USE (lcDBF) SHARED
                    SET ORDER TO TAG (lcTagName)
                  ENDIF
                ENDIF
                lnExitMethod = 0
              ENDIF

      *** Unrecoverable Errors
        * Redirect output to a file
        OTHERWISE
          lnExitMethod = 2
          LOCAL lcChkDBC, lcCurDBC, lcErrorFile, lcSuffix, ;
                lnAnswer, lnCnt, lnWhichTrigger
        * Get a file name based on date and time
          lcErrorFile = SUBSTR(DTOC(DATE()), 1, 2) + ;
                        SUBSTR(DTOC(DATE()), 4, 2) + ;
                        SUBSTR(TIME(), 1, 2) + ;
                        SUBSTR(TIME(), 4, 2) + '.ERR'
        * Make sure the file name is unique by changing the extension
          lcSuffix = '0'
          DO WHILE FILE(lcErrorFile)
            lcErrorFile = STUFF(lcErrorFile, ;
                          LEN(lcErrorFile) - LEN(lcSuffix) + 1, ;
```

*continues*

**Listing 16.10    Continued**

```
                      LEN(lcSuffix), lcSuffix)
    lcSuffix    = ALLTRIM(STR(VAL(lcSuffix)+1, 3))
  ENDDO
  SET CONSOLE OFF
  SET ALTERNATE TO (lcErrorFile)
  SET ALTERNATE ON

* Identify error
  ? 'DATE:        ' + TTOC(DATETIME())
  ? 'VERSION:     ' + VERSION()
  ? 'FILE NAME:   ' + lcErrorFile
  ?

* Next identify the error
  ? 'Error:'
  = AERROR(laErrorArray)
  ? '    Number: ' + STR(laErrorArray(1), 5)
  ? '   Message: ' + laErrorArray(2)

  IF !ISNULL(laErrorArray(5))
    ? ' Parameter: ' + laErrorArray(3)
  ENDIF

  IF !ISNULL(laErrorArray(5))
    ? ' Work Area: ' + laErrorArray(4)
  ENDIF

  IF !ISNULL(laErrorArray(5))
    lnwhichtrigger = laErrorArray(5)
    DO CASE
      CASE lnwhichtrigger = 1
        ? ' Insert Trigger Failed'
      CASE lnwhichtrigger = 2
        ? ' Update Trigger Failed'
      CASE lnwhichtrigger = 3
        ? ' Delete Trigger Failed'
    ENDCASE
  ENDIF

  IF laErrorArray(1) = lnErrorNo
    ? '    Module: ' + lcModule
    ? '      Line: ' + lcErrorLine
    ? '    Line #: ' + STR(lnErrorLineNo)
  ENDIF
  RELEASE laErrorArray, whichtrigger
  ?

* Next identify the basic operating environment
  ? 'OP. SYSTEM:   ' + OS()
  ? 'PROCESSOR:    ' + SYS(17)
  ? 'GRAPHICS:     ' + LEFT(SYS(2006), AT('/', SYS(2006)) - 1)
  ? 'MONITOR:      ' + SUBSTR(SYS(2006), AT('/', SYS(2006)) + 1)
```

```
? 'RESOURCE FILE:   ' + SYS(2005)
? 'LAUNCH DIR:      ' + SYS(2004)
? 'CONFIG.FP:       ' + SYS(2019)
? 'MEMORY:          ' + ALLTRIM(STR(MEMORY())), 'KB OR ' + ;
                        SYS(12) + 'BYTES'
? 'CONVENTIONAL:    ' + SYS(12)
? 'TOTAL MEMORY:    '
? 'EMS LIMIT:       ' + SYS(24)
? 'CTRLABLE MEM:    ' + SYS(1016)
? 'CURRENT CONSOLE:' + SYS(100)
? 'CURRENT DEVICE:  ' + SYS(101)
? 'CURRENT PRINTER:' + SYS(102)
? 'CURRENT DIR:     ' + SYS(2003)
? 'LAST KEY:        ' + STR(LASTKEY(),5)
?

* Next identify the default disk drive and its properties
? '   DEFAULT DRIVE: ' + SYS(5)
? '      DRIVE SIZE: ' + TRANSFORM(VAL(SYS(2020)), '999,999,999')
? '      FREE SPACE: ' + TRANSFORM(DISKSPACE(), '999,999,999')
? '     DEFAULT DIR: ' + CURDIR()
? ' TEMP FILES DIR: ' + SYS(2023)
?

* Available Printers
? 'PRINTERS:'
IF APRINTERS(laPrt) > 0
  FOR lncnt = 1 TO ALEN(laPrt, 1)
    ? PADR(laprt[lncnt,1], 50) + ' ON ' + ;
      PADR(laprt[lncnt,2], 25)
  ENDFOR
ELSE
  ? 'No printers currently defined.'
ENDIF
?

* Define Workareas
? 'WORK AREAS:'
IF AUSED(laWrkAreas) > 0
  = ASORT(laWrkAreas,2)
  LIST MEMORY LIKE laWrkAreas
  RELEASE laWrkAreas
  ? 'Current Database: ' + ALIAS()
ELSE
  ? 'No tables currently open in any work areas.'
ENDIF
?

 * Begin bulk information dump
 * Display memory variables
 ? REPLICATE('-', 78)
 ? 'ACTIVE MEMORY VARIABLES'
 LIST MEMORY
 ?
```

*continues*

**Listing 16.10  Continued**

```
* Display status
? REPLICATE('-', 78)
? 'CURRENT STATUS AND SET VARIABLES'
LIST STATUS
?

* Display Information related to databases
IF ADATABASE(laDbList) > 0
  lcCurDBC = GETROOT(DBC())
  FOR lncnt = 1 TO ALEN(laDbList, 1)
    lcChkDBC = laDbList[lncnt, 1]
    SET DATABASE TO (lcChkDBC)
    LIST CONNECTIONS
    ?
    LIST DATABASE
    ?
    LIST PROCEDURES
    ?
    LIST TABLES
    ?
    LIST VIEWS
    ?
  ENDFOR
  SET DATABASE TO (lcCurDBC)
ENDIF

* Close error file and reactivate the screen
SET ALTERNATE TO
SET ALTERNATE OFF
SET CONSOLE ON

ON KEY LABEL BACKSPACE
ON KEY LABEL ENTER
ON KEY LABEL ESCAPE
ON KEY LABEL PGDN
ON KEY LABEL PGUP
ON KEY LABEL SPACEBAR

SET SYSMENU TO DEFAULT

WAIT WINDOW 'Check file: ' + SYS(2003) + '\' + lcErrorFile + ;
            CHR(13) + ' for error information'
lnAnswer = MESSAGEBOX('View Error Log Now?', 292)
IF lnAnswer = 6
  MODIFY FILE (lcErrorfile)
ENDIF
ENDCASE

* Type of exit
DO CASE
```

```
      CASE lnExitMethod = 0      && Retry the same line
        RETRY
      CASE lnExitMethod = 1      && Execute the next line of code
        RETURN
      CASE lnExitMethod = 2      && Cancel the program
        ON ERROR &lcError
        CANCEL          && SUSPEND during development
    ENDCASE
    ON ERROR &lcError
RETURN


*****************
PROCEDURE GETROOT
LPARAMETER lcFileName
**********************************************************
*                                                        *
* PROCEDURE GETROOT                                      *
*                                                        *
* This routine strips the extension and path from a     *
*      filename                                         *
*                                                        *
* Parameters:                                            *
* lcFileName    - Name of File                           *
*                                                        *
**********************************************************
LOCAL lndot, lnrslash
* Extract the root name for the file name passed as a parameter
  lndot    = RAT('.', lcFileName)
  lnrslash = RAT('\', lcFileName)
  IF lndot > 0
    lcFileName = LEFT(lcFileName, lndot-1)
  ENDIF
  IF lnrslash > 0
    lcFileName = SUBSTR(lcFileName, lnrslash+1)
  ENDIF
RETURN lcFileName
```

# Using Error Events in Objects

The previous example shows the typical way to handle errors using the ON ERROR statement. This method has been available in several earlier versions of FoxPro. In Visual FoxPro, however, you have a few more options. The most important one is that each object has its own error event. VFP first looks for an Error method in the current object when an error occurs. If you did not add code to this method, VFP then executes the global ON ERROR routine mentioned earlier. If you don't use a global ON ERROR routine, VFP uses its default error handler.

> **CAUTION**
>
> The default VFP error handler is about as useful to your users as sunscreen is to Eskimoes in the winter. It merely displays a message box containing the text of the error message and four buttons. The first says Cancel. Without other code, this could leave data transactions hanging uncommitted. If they are in the interpreted environment, they can Suspend the program (and do what?). The third button says Ignore. Very seldom do ignored errors just go away. The last says Help. How many users want to press Help just to get a more detailed error message, which does not generally tell them what to do next? The point is that you want to avoid letting the user ever see this default error handler.

The first thing you find is that the .ERROR method receives four parameters from VFP. These include:

An index number for the control if it is part of a control array to identify which control failed

The error number

The name of the method where the error occurred

The line number in the method where the error occurred

Currently, control arrays do not work quite as expected. Maybe in a future version of Visual FoxPro they will, but in the meantime, you can ignore this first parameter.

At this point, you could design a small routine to examine the error that occurred and display the information passed as parameter, possibly also writing it to an error log. Note, however, that you must keep this code as simple as possible because if another error occurs in your error-handling code, VFP throws you into its default error handler, even if you have an ON ERROR statement defined. We previously said that we never want to let the user see the default error handler with its limited button choices.

Another useful feature of Visual FoxPro is the AERROR( ) function. This returns an array with up to seven columns. The return value of the function identifies the number of rows in the array. Remember that some errors can actually generate a series of errors and thus the need for multiple rows. Table 16.3 defines the columns returned by AERROR( ) when the error occurs in Visual FoxPro code.

**Table 16.3    AERROR() Columns for Visual FoxPro Errors**

| Element | Description |
| --- | --- |
| 1 | A numeric value of the error number. Same as ERROR( ) |
| 2 | A string value of the error message. Same as MESSAGE( ) |

| Element | Description |
|---|---|
| 3 | Typically null unless the error has an additional error parameter such as those returned by SYS(2018) |
| 4 | Typically null, but sometimes contains the work area where the error occurred |
| 5 | Typically null, but if the error is the result of a failed trigger (error 1539), it returns one of the following values:<br>1 - Insert trigger failed; 2 - Update trigger failed; 3 - Delete trigger failed |
| 6 | Null |
| 7 | Null |

Part<br>IV<br>Ch<br>16

While it is true that most of this information can be obtained without resorting to the AERROR( ) function, the resulting array is easier to work with. Furthermore, this function returns important information not otherwise available if the error is the result of an OLE or ODBE error. Table 16.4 documents the returned column values for OLE errors (1426 and 1427).

**Table 16.4  *AERROR() Columns for OLE Errors***

| Element | Description |
|---|---|
| 1 | Numeric value containing 1426 or 1427. |
| 2 | Character value with text of Visual FoxPro error message. |
| 3 | Character value with text of OLE error message. |
| 4 | Character value with name of OLE application. |
| 5 | Null value typically. If a character value, holds the name of the application's help file. |
| 6 | Null value typically. If a character value, holds the help context ID for an appropriate help topic in the application's help file. |
| 7 | Numeric value with the OLE 2.0 exception number. |

Table 16.5 shows the column definitions for an ODBC error.

**Table 16.5  *AERROR() Columns for ODBC Errors***

| Element | Description |
|---|---|
| 1 | Numeric value containing 1526 |
| 2 | Character value with the Visual FoxPro error message |

*continues*

| Table 16.5   Continued | |
| --- | --- |
| **Element** | **Description** |
| 3 | Character value with the ODBC error message |
| 4 | Character value with the ODBC SQL state |
| 5 | Numeric value with the ODBC data source error number |
| 6 | Numeric value with the ODBC connection handle |
| 7 | Null |

Again, the point is not to fix the error, but to document it. Therefore, you will want to write formatted entries for each row in the array created by AERROR( ) to the error log.

When dealing with objects, you may not want to write an error code in every method, of every instance, of the object you create and use. Rather, it is better to create your own class library from the base classes provided with VFP. In these classes, define your error-handler code (as well as any other unique changes you need in all instances of the object). Then, build your forms and code from these base classes.

As you instantiate objects from your class library, each instance inherits the error method code from the parent class as long as—and only as long as—you do not add any additional code to the method. If you add any code to the .ERROR method of an instantiated class, the program no longer finds the error handler code in the parent class. Then, the user is thrown back into the default Visual FoxPro error handler.

While it is okay to handle code specific to an instance in that instance, remember to include a line at the end of the method to reference the parent code for those errors not specifically handled by the instance code. To do this, simply add the following line to the end of the instance error method code:

```
= EVAL(This.Class + '::ERROR(nError, cMethod, nLine)')
```

You can even add the following line to the classes in your class library to have them reference the error code from the containers in which you place them.

```
This.Parent.Error(nError, cMessage, nLineNo)
```

You may again need to use an EVAL statement similar to the first one in the container object's .ERROR method code if they handle specific instance errors.

Ultimately, if the error gets passed up through the class structure and into the containers and still cannot be handled, the program should resort to an ON ERROR error handler to document the error condition as much as possible before bailing out of the program.

(Author's note: Thanks to Malcolm C. Rubel for the preceding technique.)

The amount of time you spend debugging code before putting it into use depends on several factors:

- How quickly the users need it.
- How critical code failure is (such as software written to control aircraft or medical equipment).
- How management views the life cycle of projects. Do they expect it right the first time, or do they accept a break-in period?

There is no one correct answer for ensuring software quality. Similarly, there is no one correct way to write an error handler, especially when it comes to handling objects, OLE, and ODBC. But the more methods employed, the better the overall system performs, and when errors do occur, the easier it is to find them. Remember one thing that Malcolm C. Rubel says: "Most error conditions happen because you allow processing to continue into an error condition when you should have stopped processing before the error occurred." While I concur that in many cases this is true, I still believe in using error handler for those cases where I just did not anticipate everything.

# From Here...

Many of the notes and cautions throughout this book relate to things you need to watch closely to avoid errors in your code. The contents of this chapter samples additional concepts related to debugging and error handling. References in this area are relatively few. If you want to be a serious developer, you might want to check the few following listed references to learn more about debugging and software quality assurance:

- Chow, Tsun S. ed. *Tutorial: Software Quality Assurance: A Practical Approach*. Silver Spring, Md.: IEEE Computer Society Press, 1985.
- Glass, Robert L. *Building Quality Software*. Englewood Cliffs, N.J.: Prentice Hall, 1992.
- McConnell, Steve. *Code Complete*. Redmond, Washington: Microsoft Press, 1993.
- Myers, Glenford J. *Software Reliability*. New York: John Wiley, 1976.
- Schulmeyer, G. Gordon. *Zero Defect Software*. New York: McGraw-Hill, 1990.
- Schulmeyer, G. Gordon, ed. *Handbook of Software Quality Assurance*. New York: Van Nostrand Reinhold, 1987.

Finally, check out the next Visual FoxPro conference and look for any sessions it may have on error handling.

# Network Data Sharing

*by Arthur E. Young and Christopher R. Green*

**A**nyone who has worked with networked-based database applications for longer than a few months inevitably comes up against one of the principal issues of data processing: how to handle conflicts when two users simultaneously attempt to update data. In many computer operations, it's a case of the last one to save changes wins the updating game. This person's data is the last and final change made to the database, at the expense of any earlier updates, which ends up in the bit-bucket.

Microsoft's Visual FoxPro provides two methods for protecting your data in the multi-user environment. VFP5 offers developers the more traditional explicit record and table locking functions and commands and the new data buffer scheme that allows a more flexible approach to locking and updating data. With file and table locking, when the table, and consequent record(s) are accessed, a lock prevents anyone else from entering the area until the original user has finished his editing activities, and safely left the area. With buffering, the original records are saved, so that they can be restored if needed, and the developer can either lock the records once editing begins or after the data is saved.

**How to develop multi-user applications using Visual FoxPro**

The demands of the modern office require any developer to be able to create sophisticated multi-user applications.

**Common issues associated with developing multi-user applications**

When to lock, how long to lock, and when to release the lock are concerns in network-aware programs.

**How FoxPro implements buffering, and how to use it in your applications**

Buffering is becoming the preferred method of protecting your data.

In the FoxPro file-sharing environment, tables must be stored on a network drive in order to be sharable among users. In a single-user environment, where only one person at a time is working with data, there is little worry about file sharing and consequent data corruption. If you have the data, and Bob from Accounting wants something, you either provide him with the answer, or use the sneakernet shuffle. With the introduction of more people who desire access to your carefully guarded data, sharing becomes more important.

This chapter introduces you to the concepts surrounding the sharing of data in a networked environment, how to correctly build the interfaces that are required for such activity, and how to interact effectively within the shared-data world. This second concept is one that is becoming more and more common, and one that, in effect, renders the earlier, single-user, single computer arrangement obsolete. ■

# File Collisions, Contentions, and Deadly Embraces

Instead of one user having all the data resident on a local hard disk, information can be shared by a department or group of users. The usual solution is to remove the data from the local drive and to install it on a file server computer where access is guaranteed to everyone requiring it. An alternative is to make the local hard disk sharable. The first of these approaches is currently the most common one; however, the "peer-to-peer" types of networks are becoming more popular.

The next issue to resolve is how electronic conflicts are handled when two people try to access the same data. This activity is known as a *file contention*. Software designed to work in a shared environment must have some type of mechanism in place to avoid such impacts.

In a shared application, file contention occurs when two users try to simultaneously access the same record in the same file. Your application can guard against an event of this nature by negotiating file contention between different users.

A common occurrence in shared environments is known as a *deadlock* (also known as deadly embrace or, more colorfully, a fatal attraction). A deadlock occurs when one user has locked a record, or a table, and then tries to lock a second record or table that has been previously locked by a second user. At the same time, the second user is trying to lock the record that has already been locked by the first user. Consequently, each machine "hangs" waiting for the other user to finish her changes, which will never happen.

These paragraphs suggest an open architecture that permits anyone full access to whatever he wishes on the network. This management style may not always be acceptable, although it is in widespread use.

An incremental step upward to the next level of security suggests that a structured level of network security be employed, so that only certain users are allowed certain privileges. For example, you wouldn't want everyone fooling around in a table that printed checks to vendors for services rendered, but you might like to ensure that when the system administrator takes that well-earned vacation in Miami Beach that the system has been left intact with a responsible party. Network security is not covered in this chapter.

# Types of Locks

When developing multi-user applications, you need to contend with two types of locks—file and record. This section discusses the differences between these two locks and recommends approaches to implementing them in your applications. This section also discusses the difference between automatic and manual locks.

## Record versus File Locks

In applications that require access by multiple parties, care should be taken that access to data is granted only to those users who require it. A *record lock*, when correctly applied, prevents write access to a record by users other than the person requesting the lock. A *file lock*, on the other hand, locks the physical table to all outside parties, preventing anyone from writing data to the table while you are editing any one of a number of that table's records. Record and file locking do not prevent users from reading data from the locked records or files; it merely inhibits writing of data. Once file locking is enabled, access to the file and the records contained therein is denied until the original user releases the files from its locked position.

 **T I P** If you choose explicit locking, be sure to SET EXCLUSIVE OFF.

Generally, you primarily employ record locks on most of your applications, because record locks prevent access to individual records and not the entire table. Thus, while you are editing record number 80132 in the GERMFASK table, someone else can be working on record number 80920 within the same table—and both of you can save your changes without fear of stepping on the other's toes.

## Automatic versus Manual Locks

While record and file locking provide two related ways to secure your data, two methods of locking data, automatic and manual, are available for security from file manipulation.

Depending upon your needs, file locking can take place either automatically or through a manual method. VFP5 attempts to lock records automatically when specific data update commands are used (see Table 17.1). VFP5 also provides the ability to lock records manually, using a set of locking functions, which is discussed later. The following table illustrates many of the commands that automatically perform record and file locks.

Table 17.1 lists the commands that automatically lock database records and tables.

**Table 17.1   Commands That Automatically Lock Tables and Records**

| Command | Lock Coverage |
|---|---|
| ALTER TABLE | Automatically locks the entire table. |
| APPEND | Automatically locks the entire table. |
| APPEND BLANK | Automatically locks the table header. |
| APPEND FROM | Automatically locks the entire table. |
| APPEND FROM ARRAY | Automatically locks the table header. |
| APPEND MEMO | Automatically locks the current record. |
| BLANK | Automatically locks the current record. |
| BROWSE | Automatically locks the current record, and all of those records from aliased fields in the related tables. This takes effect once editing of a field commences. |
| CHANGE | Automatically locks the current record, and all of those records from aliased fields in the related tables. This takes effect once editing of a field commences. |
| DELETE | Automatically locks the current record. |
| DELETE NEXT 1 | Automatically locks the current record. |
| DELETE <n> | Automatically locks the file when <n> is more than one record. |
| DELETE SQL | Automatically locks the current record. |

| Command | Lock Coverage |
|---------|---------------|
| EDIT | Automatically locks the current record and all of those records from aliased fields in the related tables. This takes effect once editing of a field commences. |
| GATHER | Automatically locks the current record. |
| INSERT | Automatically locks the entire table. |
| INSERT SQL | Automatically locks the table header. |
| MODIFY MEMO | Automatically locks the current record when editing of that record begins. |
| READ | Automatically locks the current record and all records that come from aliased fields. |
| RECALL | Automatically locks the current record. |
| RECALL NEXT 1 | Automatically locks the identified record. |
| RECALL <n> | Automatically locks the entire table when <n> is more than one record. |
| REPLACE | Automatically locks the current record and all records that come from aliased fields. |
| REPLACE NEXT <n> | Automatically locks the current record and all records that come from aliased fields. |
| REPLACE <n> | Automatically locks the entire table and all records that come from aliased fields. |
| SHOW GETS | Automatically locks the current record and all records that come from aliased fields. |
| TABLEUPDATE() | Automatically locks the entire table. |
| UPDATE | Automatically locks the entire table. |
| UPDATE SQL | Automatically locks the entire table. |

If possible, it is better to use commands that lock individual records than commands that attempt to lock tables. This is due to two factors: the network overhead created by a file lock, and the possibility that the file cannot be locked by another user. In Visual FoxPro a file can be locked only if there are no record locks. In multi-user applications of any size, this could take a long time.

**N O T E** VFP5 documentation recommends that if you are updating multiple records in a table, locking the table is actually more efficient than locking the multiple records. Of course, this lock should be in effect during an update, and not for the duration of an editing session that includes lunch. ■

In the following example, a user wanting to lock the entire GERMFASK table uses the APPEND FROM command, which attempts to lock the table while appending data from another file:

```
SET EXCLUSIVE OFF
USE GERMFASK
APPEND FROM HOUGHTON FOR STATUS="CLOSED"
```

When the append task has concluded, the APPEND command releases any locks that it created.

**N O T E** A command that automatically creates locks releases those locks when the command is complete. ■

Manual locking functions test the lock status of a record or table. If the test determines that a record is unlocked, the record (or table) is locked, and the user may proceed to use the file.

To manually lock a table, you should use one of the LOCK( ), RLOCK( ), or FLOCK( ) functions. The RLOCK( ), and LOCK( ) are used to lock individual records or a group of records and are identical in their function and syntax (except for that R). The FLOCK( ) command is used to lock entire files. If you use these commands to lock a record or table, you should be sure to release the locks as soon as possible after your use has concluded. Unlocking allows other users to access the previously locked data.

 **T I P** To test your program's locking without bothering another person, run your code simultaneously in two windows.

In the following example, the FLOCK( ) command is used to lock the GERMFASK table, preventing any updates by other users. When the table is successfully locked, the REPLACE ALL command updates every record in the GERMFASK table. Finally, the UNLOCK command releases the file lock. If the file is unavailable for locking, in the case where another user has a record locked, an error message is displayed.

```
SET EXCLUSIVE OFF
SET REPROCESS TO 0
USE GERMFASK
IF FLOCK()
      REPLACE ALL LASTNAME WITH UPPER(LASTNAME)
```

```
                UNLOCK
        ELSE
                WAIT "Sorry, File is Being Used by Someone Else." WINDOW
    NOWAIT
        ENDIF
```

In Listing 17.1, the RLOCK( ) command is used to lock a group of records in the GERMFASK table:

**Listing 17.1   LOCKTEST.PRG—\* LOCKTEST.PRG**

```
    SET EXCLUSIVE OFF
    SET REPROCESS TO 0
    SET MULTILOCKS ON
    USE GERMFASK
    IF RLOCK( "5, 10, 15", "GERMFASK" )
            GOTO 5
            REPLACE LASTNAME WITH UPPER(LASTNAME)
            GOTO 10
            REPLACE LASTNAME WITH UPPER(LASTNAME)
            GOTO 15
            REPLACE LASTNAME WITH UPPER(LASTNAME)
            UNLOCK
    ELSE
            WAIT WINDOW ;
"Sorry, Record is Being Used by Someone Else."
NOWAIT
    ENDIF
```

If any of the records in the list is unavailable, none of the records is locked.

In Table 17.2, the commands to unlock records and files are explained. In many instances, the physical movement from one record or table to another record or table causes FoxPro to automatically unlock a temporarily locked item. If you have explicitly locked a table or record, however, you have to unlock it before the table is available for use by others.

**Table 17.2   Commands to Unlock Records and Tables**

| Command | Response |
| --- | --- |
| CLOSE | Releases all record and table file locks |
| CLOSE ALL | Releases all record and table file locks |
| END TRANSACTION | Releases all automatic locks |
| QUIT | Releases all record and table file locks |

*continues*

**Table 17.2   Continued**

| Command | Response |
| --- | --- |
| UNLOCK | Releases the record and file locks in the current work area |
| UNLOCK ALL | Releases all record and file locks in all work areas |
| USE | Releases all record and table file locks |
| SET MULTILOCKS OFF | Enables the automatic release of the current lock as a new lock to be created |
| FLOCK( ) | Releases all record locks in the affected file before locking the file |
| TABLEUPDATE( ) | Releases all locks before allowing the table to be updated |

**CAUTION**

If MULTILOCKS is off, and if you lock a record in a user-defined function (UDF), move the record pointer off, and then move back onto the current record; the lock on that record is automatically released.

# What to Do When the Record You Need Is Locked

There are times when you need to access a record within a table, only to find that it is being used by another user, or process. When this occurs, you see the error message Record is in use by another. This message is generated when the record or table has been locked by another user, or if the table was opened by a user under an exclusive command. If this happens, you'll need to wait to perform those edits.

When editing fields that are located in related tables, the related records are locked to prevent dual-editing. The lock attempt fails, however, if the current record or any of the related records are also locked by another user. Where the lock attempt is successful, FoxPro enables you to edit the record. The lock is released when you move on to another record, activate another window, or perform another activity.

If you elect to employ the Browse, Change, Edit, or Modify Memo commands for editing purposes, you find that the commands do not lock a record until the record is edited.

# Using Sessions

Visual FoxPro introduces to FoxPro developers, the concept of data sessions. *Data sessions* are data environments that are attached to a form. What this means is that you can attach, to a form, the tables that are to be used in its various operations. There are two types of data sessions: private and default. These data session types are discussed in the rest of the section.

Each data session is a separate data environment that attaches to a form. For instance, the data environment describes the work area: how cursors appear in the work area, the tables and their indices, and the relations among and between them. Data sessions allow multiple instances of a form to be created. An example of this is if a user wants to look at more than one customer record at a time. Rather than close the currently open form, the user simply requests another instance of the customer form.

A Data Session Property Value (*Form.DataSession*) attribute can be set to either 1 or 2. When changes are made to your form, the default property, 1, allows the changes that are made to the form to be reflected in all other open instances of that form. When the attribute is set to 2, or private data session, any changes that you make to one form are not automatically represented in the other instances of the same form. The number of open sessions that you can have are limited only by the available amount of system memory and disk space.

To begin a multiple data session from the form designer, set the DataSession property to 2. Alternatively, from the command window, type the following command: With the session set to 2, each instance of the form maintains a separate set of data, which includes a separate set of locks.

When the DataSession property is set to 2, Visual FoxPro creates a new data session for each instance of the form. Since an unlimited number of sessions can be opened, subject only to the size of your RAM and the available quantity of hard disk space, a session description can be modified through commands in the Load Event code, with the contents of the data session being observable from the View window. Each data session is numbered sequentially and identified with a data session identification number known as the DataSessionID.

In the following example, the DataSessionID property of a form called PoohForm is displayed:

```
DO FORM PoohForm
? PoohForm.DataSessionID
```

As an alternative, if the form is activated using the NAME clause, the data session identification number may be accessed with the following two lines of code:

```
DO FORM PoohForm Name one
? one.DataSessionID
```

You should avoid making changes to the data session identification number of a form, because data-bound controls lose their data sources when the data session identification number is altered. If you wish to ensure that a form's data environment is always available and always the same, the Data Environment dialog box found within the Form Designer can be used.

Where all instances of a form are supposed to access the same data and immediately reflect the changes to data common to all forms, an automatic data session assignment can be changed with an override property found in the Data Environment property sheet.

# Buffering Edits

VFP5 introduces form and programmatic data buffering. This improvement makes protecting data on a network far easier to implement than explicit locking. Buffering data enables you to better use local resources, limiting the contention for network and server resources. Buffering data stores any changes you might make to data in memory on the workstation. This data is not updated on the server until your application tells VFP5 to update.

This type of locking scheme is available with explicit locking and is implemented with the following steps:

1. While in the record that you are changing, do the SCATTER MEMVAR command to place all fields in memory variables.
2. Make your changes to the data in the memory variables, not the data in the table.
3. If you are satisfied with your changes, do the GATHER MEMVAR command to save your changes. If you want to perform an undo function, do the SCATTER MEMVAR command again to overwrite the data in the memory variables.

Buffering in VFP5 now does all this for you. There are two types of buffering schemes available: record and table buffering. *Record* buffering buffers edits on individual records. As soon as the updates to an individual record are completed, the data is flushed to a disk. This happens as soon as the record pointer is moved, or a TABLEUPDATE( ) function is issued. The second method is *table* buffering. This method stores to memory multiple changes to a table. This data is flushed when the table is closed or when TABLEUPDATE( ), with the lALLROWS parameter set to TRUE, is used, as follows:

```
lRetval = TABLEUPDATE( .T. )
```

Such buffers provide security within the data updating and data maintenance arenas when editing, deletion, and modification activities are made to both a single record and multiple records within multi-user environments. With VFP5 buffering, you no longer have to scatter your data to memory variables; you can directly edit the field, since the original data is safe until a TABLEUPDATE( ) is performed.

> **CAUTION**
>
> Once buffering is enabled for your session, it remains in effect until it is disabled or the table is closed.

With buffering, conflicts between data updating operations can be detected and resolved. During an editing operation, a current record is copied into a memory or a disk location that has already been identified and managed by VFP5. With this copy safely sequestered, other users can still access the original record. Once the record is moved back, FoxPro attempts to lock the record and verifies that no other changes have been made by other users. The resulting changes are written to the hard disk. This is commonly referred to as *optimistic locking*.

After the attempt to update data has been made, any other conflicts that are preventing the edits from being copied to the hard disk that are written back to the file must also be addressed and solved.

# Record Buffers

Record buffering should be employed when you are interested in accessing, modifying, or writing a single record at a time to a disk. The process allows the appropriate process validation and causes minimal impact on the data update operations of any other users in your multi-user environment.

# Table Buffers

Table buffering, on the other hand, is used when you want to buffer the updates to several records within a table. This method is ideally suited to records that exist within one table or to child records that exist in one-to-many relationships.

# Locking In Buffers

Record and table buffering can be employed in one of two different locking modes. These modes determine under what conditions one or more records are locked, and how and when those locked records can be released. The two modes are called pessimistic and optimistic.

The difference between these two types of locking mechanisms is seen when FoxPro performs its locks. *Pessimistic buffering* tells FoxPro to lock the record as soon as the edit begins. That is, as soon as you change a value in one of the buffered fields, the record is locked. This prevents changes to that record by other users until the update is completed. *Optimistic locking* locks the record when the data is updated to disk. This allows multiple users to edit the same record.

In Table 17.3, table buffering values for choices between one and five are offered. If buffering is proposed to access remote data, the buffering property should be set to 3 (optimistic row buffering) or to 5 (optimistic table buffering).

**Table 17.3    Table Buffering Values**

| Buffering and Locking Types | Suggested Buffering | Value |
| --- | --- | --- |
| No buffering | This is the default value | 1 |
| Pessimistic record locks | Locks the record, update when the pointer moves on, or upon the issuance of the TABLEUPDATE( ) command | 2 |
| Optimistic record locks | Waits until the pointer moves off of the current record before locking and updating the record | 3 |

| Buffering and Locking Types | Suggested Buffering | Value |
| --- | --- | --- |
| Pessimistic table locks | Locks the record, updates the information later when the TABLEUPDATE( ) command is issued | 4 |
| Optimistic table lock | Waits until the TABLEUPDATE( ) command is issued, whereupon, it locks, and updates the edited records | 5 |

The next five examples demonstrate methods of enabling buffering within your applications. The accompanying paragraphs provide an explanation of how the various record buffering commands are set with the CURSORSETPROP( ) function; a short explanation completes each section.

To enable pessimistic record locking, use the following command:

```
=CURSORSETPROP("Buffering", 2,"customer")
```

With this command, FoxPro first attempts to lock the record at the current pointer's location. If the attempt is successful, FoxPro places the record in the buffer and permits editing on that record. When the pointer is moved from the current location, or the TABLEUPDATE( ) command is issued, the software writes the buffered record back to the original table.

To enable optimistic record locking, use the following command:

```
=CURSORSETPROP("Buffering", 3, "customer")
```

With this command, FoxPro writes the current record out to a buffer. With this accomplished, editing on that record is then permitted. If the pointer is moved from its current location, or if a TABLEUPDATE( ) command is issued, FoxPro attempts to attach a lock onto the record. If this lock is successful, a comparison is made between the current value of the record located on the disk and the original buffer value. If those two values are identical, any edits are written to the original table. If the comparison generates differences, however, the edit is not made, and an error message is generated to alert the user to that fact.

To enable pessimistic locking of multiple records, use the following command:

```
=CURSORSETPROP("Buffering", 4, "customer")
```

This command makes an attempt at locking the record at the pointer's location. If the lock is successful, the software places the record into the buffer. Editing is then permitted on that record.

Part
IV
Ch
17

To enable optimistic locking of multiple records, use the following command:

```
=CURSORSETPROP("Buffering", 5, "customer")
```

This command writes the records out to the buffer, and then allows editing until such time as TABLEUPDATE( .T. ) is issued. When this command is made, the following sequential activities are performed:

1. Each edited record has an attempted lock placed on it.

2. If the lock is successful, FoxPro compares the current value of each disk-based record to the original buffer value.

3. If the comparison shows that the values are identical, FoxPro writes the original table values to the hard disk.

4. If the values are not identical, an error message is generated.

**N O T E**  For any of the buffering methods to work you need to execute the SET MULTILOCKS ON command. ■

If you are using a form (and you probably are), you set the buffering type using the BufferMode property (Figure 17.1). When setting buffering on a form, you specify only whether to use optimistic or pessimistic locking. Form-based buffering defaults to row buffering unless you are using a Grid control. In that case, the RecordSource table uses table buffering. This makes perfect sense, because you usually use the Grid control to display child or detail records. With table buffering, you can append records while you are in the Grid control and save all your work at one time, instead of a record at a time. If you are using a Data Environment, you can override the BufferMode property with the BufferModeOverride property of the selected table.

**N O T E**  When you are using table buffering, any records appended to the table before the TableUpdate( .T. ) command are given a negative record number. ■

## Performing Updates

Before any updates are made to your data, you must decide which buffering method and locking mechanisms you are going to use. Once the buffering and locking has been determined, record and table buffering can be enabled with code or from within the Data Environment of the form.

TABLEUPDATE( ) should be used to write edits to the original table. These edits can be canceled after a failed update operation in a table that is constrained by rules with the TABLEREVERT( ) command. The TABLEREVERT( ) command remains valid even if explicit table buffering isn't enabled.

**FIGURE 17.1**

This is an example of setting the BufferMode property of a form.

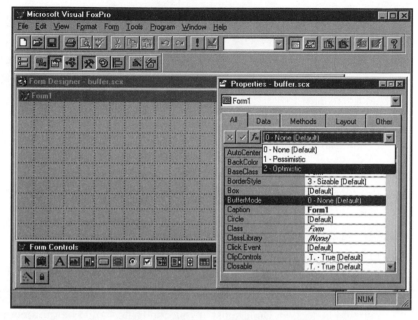

In Listing 17.2, records are updated with pessimistic record buffering enabled. In the form Init code, the table is opened and pessimistic record buffering is enabled. The pointer then goes through each field, checking each, in turn, to determine whether the field has been modified. Each record is then checked against the original to determine whether the original value has changed. If it has, the user is provided with the option of reverting the data back to the original data.

**Listing 17.2  PESSLOCK.PRG**

```
*PESSLOCK.PRG

    OPEN DATABASE BOOK
    Use Pages
    =CURSORSETPROP("Buffering", 2)
    1Modified = .F.
    For nFieldNum = 1 to FCOUNT()
         If GETFLDSTATE(nFieldNum)=2
              1Modified = .T.
              EXIT
         ENDIF
    ENDFOR
    If 1Modified
         nResult = MESSAGEBOX;
         ("Record has been Modified. Do You Want to Save it?",;
         4+32+256, "Data Change")
```

*continues*

**Listing 17.2  Continued**

```
        IF nResult = 7
              =TABLEREVERT (.F.)
        ELSE
            =TABLEUPDATE(.T.,.T.) && Force Changes to table.
        ENDIF
ENDIF
SKIP
IF EOF()
        =MESSAGEBOX("You're Already at the Bottom")
        SKIP -1
ENDIF
THISFORM.Refresh
```

# Detecting and Resolving Conflicts

It should go without saying that some degree of thought should go into any process that performs data updating operations. For example, you should carefully choose how and when to open tables and records, what buffering choices are best, and whether data should be locked. Uppermost in your thoughts should be the amount of time your data is considered to be at risk. You can help this by limiting the time a record or table is going to be opened.

*Conflicts* occur when, for example, the following scenario is independently occurring: One or more users simultaneously try to lock a record or table that is currently locked (and in use) by another user. Two users are not able to simultaneously lock and then access the same record or table. No one wins this particular skirmish.

A *deadlock* occurs when one user has locked a record, or a table, and then tries to lock a second record or table that has been previously locked by a second user. At the same time, that second user is trying to lock the record that has already been locked by the first user.

Your applications should be written in such a way as to handle situations similar to those just described. In the design of a multi-user application, or in those activities that add network support to a single-user system, FoxPro's record and table buffering systems simplify some of this work.

As you have already seen, if you attempt to lock a record or table that has previously been locked by another user, FoxPro returns an error message to alert you to that fact. If you employ locking within your code with the SET REPROCESS command, the ON ERROR routine, or the RETRY command, you are able to automatically deal with those situations that provide unsuccessful lock attempts.

In Listing 17.3, the SET REPROCESS, and the ON ERROR routines are used to manage user-based collisions. In the example, if an error occurs, a routine called ERR_FIX is run. Then the files are opened nonexclusively. Reprocessing of unsuccessful locks is performed automatically, and the table is opened. The code then performs a series of activities to append, replace, and add records. Finally, a routine (REP_CURR) replaces data in the current record before appending records from another file (ADD_RECS).

### Listing 17.3   ERR_FIX.PRG

```
*ERR_FIX.PRG

    ON ERROR DO errfix WITH ERROR(),MESSAGE()
    SET EXCLUSIVE OFF
    SET REPROCESS TO AUTOMATIC
    USE CLIENT
    IF !FILE('custcopy.dbf') COPY to CUSTCOPY
    ENDIF
    DO appblank
    DO repnext
    DO repall
    DO repcurr
    DO addrecs
    ON ERROR
     PROCEDURE repcurr
     PARAMETERS lnError, lcMessage
         WAIT WINDOW ;
"ERROR " + lcMessage + " at line" + STR(lnError)
RETURN

    PROCEDURE appblank
        Append Blank
    RETURN
    PROCEDURE repnext
        Replace Next 100 contact with Proper(contact)
    RETURN
    PROCEDURE repall
        Replace all contact with Proper(Contact)
        GO TOP
    RETURN
    PROCEDURE repcurr
        Replace contact with Proper(Contact)
    RETURN
    PROCEDURE addrecs
        Append from cus_copy
    RETURN
```

Part

IV

Ch

17

Without question, shared environments provide challenging opportunities for programmers and system administrators when data update operations are being performed. You may be required to determine which (if any) fields have been changed, what the original value of a field was, and to what value it has subsequently been changed. It should be a little easier for you to determine which fields have been changed, find the data that has been changed, and individually compare the current, original, and the new edited value before deciding how best to handle the error or conflict.

In the following example, the GETFLDSTATE( ) function is used to detect whether a change in a field has been made. This function should be performed after an update operation has been made:

```
1Modified = .F.
FOR nFieldNum = 1 to FCOUNT()
     if GETFLDSTATE(nFieldNum)=2
          1Modified = .T.
          EXIT
     ENDIF
ENDFOR
```

The GETFLDSTATE( ) function works only on buffered data. If you use GETFLDSTATE( ) in the code of a Skip button on a form, when the record pointer is moved, FoxPro checks the status of all the fields in the record. If you only want to check whether a change was made, and not the specific field that was changed, you can change the preceding example to the following:

```
1Modified = .F.
if '2' $ str( GETFLDSTATE( -1 ))
     1Modified = .T.
     EXIT
ENDIF
```

The -1 tells the GETFLDSTATE( ) function to return the change state of all the fields in the table. Table 17.4 shows the possible return values of GETFLDSTATE.

**Table 17.4  Table Buffering Values**

| GETFLDSTATE | Return Value |
| --- | --- |
| 1 | Data not changed in field of an existing record |
| 2 | Data changed in field of an existing record, or deletion flag was changed |
| 3 | Data not changed in field of an appended record |
| 4 | Data changed in field of an appended record, or deletion flag was changed |

You can then evaluate if the users can move to the next record, if changes have been made.

The GETNEXTMODIFIED( ) function returns the record number for the first modified record in a buffered table. This is a nice way to control the updating of records against the original data file. When combined with the CURVAL( ) and OLDVAL( ) functions, GETNEXTMODIFIED( ) enables you to develop "negotiation" routines for times when two users update the same data simultaneously. The CURVAL( ) and OLDVAL( ) fields can be used only with optimistic locking. To illustrate the usefulness of these two functions, consider a date field in an optimistic locked table. The value of the date field is everyone's favorite: 01/01/80. If a user changes value to 04/01/96 and saves it, and at the same time you change the value to 12/25/96 at your station, CURVAL( ) is equal to 12/25/96, OLDVAL( ) is equal to 01/01/80, and your edit control's value is 04/01/96. Your implementation choices are to allow your value to overwrite the change, revert your value, or let the system alert you that you have a conflict and enable you to make the decision.

Of course, the last of these is the best option, and it is easily implemented. Code similar to Listing 17.4 would be behind your SAVE button:

Part
IV

Ch

17

---

### Listing 17.4   CHKFLD.PRG

```
*CHKFLD.PRG

IF CURVAL( DateField ) <> OLDVAL( DateField )
    nOption = MESSAGEBOX( "Data has been changed by another user, do you wish
    ➥to overwrite?",;
                    4 + 48 + 0, "Update Conflict" )
    IF nOption = 7     &&NO
        =TABLEREVERT()
        RETURN
    ENDIF
ENDIF
=TABLEUPDATE( .T., .T. )
```

---

The second .T. in the TABLEUPDATE( ) function tells VFP5 to force the update despite the conflict. Otherwise, you still receive the conflict error message.

# Handling Errors

Using buffering to deal with life in a network environment brings with it a new set of errors.

▶ **See** "Using Error Handlers," **p. 665**

VFP5 gives you the AERROR function to help you decipher messages that you can receive from the buffering mechanism, the database container, and (if you are in a client/server situation) the ODBC drivers. You might have guessed that AERROR uses arrays in some manner. (Was it the A as the first letter?) AERROR takes an array name as its parameter. It fills this array with information concerning the error. Table 17.5 shows the return values for AERROR.

**Table 17.5    AERROR Return Values**

| Element | Type | Description |
|---|---|---|
| 1 | Numeric | Error number |
| 2 | Character | Error message |
| 3 | Character | Error parameter or .NULL. |
| 4 | Numeric or Character | The work area or .NULL. |
| 5 | Numeric or Character | Trigger failure (1 = insert, 2 = update, 3 = delete, or .NULL. ) |
| 6 | Numeric or Character | .NULL. (used for OLE & ODBC errors) |
| 7 | Numeric | .NULL. (used for OLE errors) |

What if you receive an error after entering several records of related information? The AERROR information is fine, but you may now have corrupted data, because you could not complete your save. This looks like a good place to introduce transaction processing.

# Using Transaction Processing

Even the most carefully laid plans can go awry at some point in an application. For that reason, Visual FoxPro's *transaction processing* helps you in the protection of your data during your updating and record recovery process.

Record and table buffering within the FoxPro environment greatly aid in the protection of your application by placing entire sections of data updates in a protected, but recoverable section of your hard disk. Transactions can also be nested and used to protect buffered updates.

Transactions act as a wrapper to temporarily store data update operations in memory or to the hard disk, instead of making the updates directly to the table. Although the actual updates are made at the end of the transaction, if for any reason those updates cannot be made, the entire transaction may be aborted, the updates canceled, and no update activities performed to your data, thereby protecting it from being accidentally overwritten.

Three commands are used to control a transaction: BEGIN TRANSACTION, END TRANSACTION, and ROLLBACK.

Table 17.6 defines these three commands.

**Table 17.6    Commands Used to Control Transactions**

| Command | Usage |
|---|---|
| BEGIN TRANSACTION | Initiates a transaction |
| END TRANSACTION | Locks records, commits all changes to the hard disk that have been made since the most recent Begin Transaction, and then unlocks the records |
| ROLLBACK | Reverses all changes that have been made since the most recent Begin Transaction command |

> **CAUTION**
>
> Operations that involve memory variables do not respect transactions. Any transactions that alter the contents of memory variables *cannot* be rolled back.

## Defining the Limits of a Transaction

Transaction processing should be used with record buffers, but not with table buffering activities. The exception is to include the TABLEUPDATE() function command within a transaction. With this command in place, a failed update can be rolled back. The reason for the failed update can be determined and corrected before the TABLEUPDATE() function is retried without fear of data loss.

## Rolling Back a Transaction

Simple transaction processing is not as volatile as you might first suppose. The system does not provide total insurance against system failures. When the system goes down, or some other anomaly strikes, such as the power failing on your system during the processing of your END TRANSACTION command, the data update is likely to fail, and data corruption can result.

In the following example, BEGIN TRANSACTION, END TRANSACTION, and ROLL-BACK commands are illustrated as a template.

```
BEGIN TRANSACTION
IF ...
      ROLLBACK
ELSE
      Field Validation
      IF ...ROLLBACK
      ELSE END TRANSACTION
      ENDIF
ENDIF
```

From the preceding example, observe the following rules with respect to transaction processing:

- You must bracket your transactions with the BEGIN TRANSACTION and END TRANSACTION commands. If you use one without the other, an error message is generated. A lock is imposed on your data at the time when a command directly, or indirectly, calls for it. Thus, any system or user direct or indirect unlock commands are cached until the completion of the transaction has been reached, as evidenced by either the END TRANSACTION or ROLLBACK commands.

- If you are using the FLOCK( ), and/or RLOCK( ) locking commands discussed at the beginning of this chapter, using the END TRANSACTION command does not release the lock; you must explicitly unlock any locks within a transaction before the data is released.

- If the ROLLBACK command is used without preceding it with the BEGIN TRANS-ACTION command, the ROLLBACK statement generates an error.

- Once you enter into a transaction process, the process remains in effect until either the corresponding END TRANSACTION or ROLLBACK command is reached. This process can be translated across all of your programs and functions until the application terminates, at which time a rollback begins.

- With respect to the queries that are involved in your transactions, the Visual FoxPro program always uses data that is cached in your transaction buffer before any disk-based data is used. A process of this nature ensures that the most current data is always used first.

- Whenever a transaction fails during execution, all operations fail, and the data remains untouched until the failure has been identified and corrected.

- Transactions only perform in a database container. You cannot use the INDEX command if using it overwrites an existing index file, or if any production index file has been opened.

# Nesting Transactions

In some instances, you want to employ transactions that are nested. Nested transactions are logical groups of table-update operations that are removed from concurrent processes. Where the need exists for nesting, the BEGIN and END TRANSACTION command pairs are not required to be located within the same function or procedure.

As with "regular" transactions, a different series of rules governs during transaction nesting:

- You can nest up to five BEGIN and END TRANSACTION pairs.
- The updates that are made with a nested transaction are not committed to your hard disk until the final END TRANSACTION command is reached.
- The END TRANSACTION is only functionable on the transaction that is initiated by the last-issued BEGIN TRANSACTION.
- ROLLBACK statements only operate on the transaction that is initiated by the last-issued BEGIN TRANSACTION command.
- The innermost update in a set of nested transactions on the same data takes precedence over any others within the same block.

In Listing 17.5, a nested transaction is performed. First, a cleanup process from previous transactions is performed. Then the environment for buffering is used by setting Multilocks to ON, and Exclusive to OFF. Optimistic table buffering is then enabled, with the program changing a certain set of records. If the update fails, the entire transaction is rolled back until the cause of the failure is determined and then corrected.

Part

**IV**

Ch

**17**

## Listing 17.5   NESTTRAN.PRG

```
*NESTTRAN.PRG

DO WHILE TXNLEVEL() > 0
     ROLLBACK
ENDDO
CLOSE ALL
SET MULTILOCKS ON
SET EXCLUSIVE OFF
OPEN DATA TEST
Use MRGTEST1
=CURSORSETPROP("Buffering", 5)
GO TOP
REPLACE FLD1 with "altered"
SKIP
REPLACE fld1 with "altered again..."
=MESSAGEBOX("modify the first field of " + ;
```

*continues*

**Listing 17.5 Continued**

```
"both records on another machine")
BEGIN TRANSACTION
1Success = TABLEUPDATE(.T.,.F.)
If 1Success = .F.
      ROLLBACK
      =AERROR(aErrors)
      DO CASE
      CASE aErrors[1,1]= 1539
      *-- Error handler code here
      CASE aErrors[1,1]= 1581
      *-- Error handler code here
      CASE aErrors[1,1]= 1582
      *-- Error handler code here
      CASE aErrors[1,1] = 1585
            nNextModified = getnextmodified(0)
            Do While nNextModified <> 0
                  GO nNextModified
                  = RLOCK()
                  For nField = 1 to FCOUNT()
                        cField = FIELD(nField)
                        if OLDVAL(cField) <> CURVAL(cField)
                        nResult = Messagebox;
                        ("This data has been modified by another user.;
Do you Want to Keep the Changes ?", 4+48,;
                        "Modified Record")
                        If nResult = 7
                              =TABLEREVERT(.F.)
                              UNLOCK record ;
                                    nNextModified
                              ENDIF
                              EXIT
                        ENDIF
                  ENDFOR
            ENDDO
BEGIN TRANSACTION
=TABLEUPDATE(.T.,.T.)
END TRANSACTION
UNLOCK
CASE aErrors[1,1]= 1700
      ...
      CASE aErrors[1,1]= 1583
      ...
      CASE aErrors[1,1]= 1884
      ...
      OTHERWISE
            =MESSAGEBOX("Unknown error ;
            message: " + STR(aErrors[1,1[))
      ENDCASE
ELSE
      END TRANSACTION
ENDIF
```

# Alternatives to Avoid Locking Issues

When developing multi-user applications, developers must understand that any locks placed on files, whether they be record or file locks, must be maintained in some way by the network operating system. It is not uncommon for a network to maintain thousands of locks at any given time. This lock maintenance comes at a cost. Maintaining locks on a network degrades its performance. There are some techniques for reducing the number of locks maintained by the network. This section briefly discusses some of these techniques.

## Using Object and Semaphore Locks

A common approach to handling multi-user applications is to implement some type of semaphore or object-locking technique. Such techniques use an additional field on a table to determine whether or not a record is in use. If the field is filled in, then the record becomes unavailable for update. The advantage of this approach is that it produces less network overhead. Reading data from FoxPro tables produces no network locks. Therefore, you can check to see if a record is locked by performing a read on that record, and then if it is empty, attempting the lock at that time. This method has some costs associated with it. They are the increased use of disk space and the chance that a record remains locked in the event of a disk failure.

Part

IV

Ch

17

## Storing Lookup Data in Arrays

Another approach is to store the contents of any lookup tables into memory. This provides no relief from network overhead but can reduce the number of files open at any given time. File handles, just like locks, must be maintained by the network operating system. Therefore, any time you can reduce the number of items for the system, the faster your applications will run.

## Using Temporary Files or Cursors

Multi-user applications tend to be slower than single-user applications, especially when multiple parties are banging away from several locations in order to meet some deadline requirement. If you are suffering from a slow server, you might consider some (or all) of the following suggestions to speed up the computer, and thus increase your application's throughput:

■ You can place temporary files on a local drive. For instance, if you are using indexes to perform ad hoc activities to which no one else requires access, those indexes could be relocated to your local drive. (The assumption is being made that you have a mappable, local, hard disk drive, and that you're not using a dumb terminal and monitor.)

■ Visual FoxPro for Windows creates all of its temporary files within the default directory (currently n:\VXP). If your local workstation computer has copious amounts of hard disk space, moving the temporary work files onto the local drive or into a RAM drive significantly increases the performance of the application by reducing the number of hits that are made to the network file server.

■ Creating cursors to do tasks that you might normally perform with temporary files helps keep down the number of unnecessary files with the .TMP extension that tend to clutter our systems. Cursors can be temporary, and when they are closed, they are automatically released by the system.

■ Alternative locations for your files can be specified by including any of the following statements in your CONFIG.FPW configuration file: EDITWORK, SORTWORK, PROGWORK, and TMPFILES. Additional information about aspects of the configuration file can be found in Appendix A, "Configuration Files."

## Using the EXCLUSIVE Command

The Exclusive command is one that enables you to open a table exclusively for your own use. The command prevents anyone else from opening the table while you have it under your control. When you've finished your editing session, closing the table as you go on to another task automatically releases the exclusivity of that table. The table is then available for use by another. Candidates for this activity include overnight updates, unique ad hoc requirements that apply to only one user, and so on.

The following commands cause a table to be opened exclusively. In the first example, the command is of two parts, each typed as a separate line into the Command window. The second example enables you to set a file to exclusive use with only one line:

```
SET EXCLUSIVE ON
Use POOH
```

or

```
USE POOH EXCLUSIVE
```

The following list contains a number of commands. Before employing these commands, you must first open the table under exclusive use. If you attempt to issue any of these commands without the exclusive legend, FoxPro warns you with an Exclusive Open of File Is Required message.

ALTER TABLE

INDEX

INSERT [BLANK]

MODIFY STRUCTURE

PACK

REINDEX

ZAP

> **CAUTION**
>
> The Zap command is one of the most dangerous commands that can be issued within FoxPro. Zapping a file erases all of your data from the table, but it leaves the table's structure intact. You cannot recover any data from a zapped file, except by restoring the information from previously-created backup files.

Part
**IV**

Ch
**17**

# From Here...

For more information on the subjects discussed in this chapter, you may want to review the following chapters of this book:

- Chapter 3, "Defining Databases, Tables, and Indexes," provides information about creating and using the database container that you have to protect in the network environment.

- Bonus Chapter 08, "Time for Client/Server," provides additional information on buffering, the CURSORSETPROP command, and related issues that show up in a client/server environment. This chapter is located on the CD.

# Data Dictionary Issues

*by Sandra Richardson-Lutzow and*
*Michael P. Antonovich*

A data dictionary is an important feature of successful application development. The contents of a data dictionary provide the information needed to perform tasks that would otherwise become complicated and time consuming. This chapter discusses what features a data dictionary can provide and how to structure it for functionality.

There are two ways you can go about creating your data dictionary: You can use and extend the database container provided with Visual FoxPro, or you can create your own. Your decision will depend on how far you wish to extend the data dictionary.

If you are a VFP 3.0 user, you are no stranger to the database container; however, you may not have taken the time to thoroughly explore all the possibilities that the database container can provide. This chapter will expose you to these possibilities.

If you are not familiar with the VFP's database container, this chapter begins with a quick overview of the concept, which basically allows you to store more information about your tables and fields than you ever could before. Furthermore, you have the option of expanding and enhancing the functionality of the Visual FoxPro database container as a data dictionary to make it work harder for you. ■

**Reference of data structures**

This chapter illustrates how to extend the data dictionary concept to track file locations.

**Validation of database and table structures**

Before an application starts, you can check that all required indexes and tables exist.

**Recovery of missing or corrupted files**

You can recreate missing indexes and even create entire table structures from the definitions in a data dictionary.

**Documentation on the data structures**

There are several ways to document your data structures. Some are passive such as reports and commands such as DISPLAY DATABASE. Others actively use an extended data dictionary.

**Data-driven operations**

You can use extended properties of the data dictionary to build additional functionality into your custom classes.

**Insurance of definition consistency**

Normalizing your field naming ensures that similar fields are always named and defined the same way in every table in which they appear.

# Using the Database Container as Your Data Dictionary

The database container is a table that stores the object definitions of a database and their properties. There is no requirement that the database container must reference all the tables used by an application. The proper way to decide what tables should belong in any database container is to look at the logical relations between tables. If tables are related to one another, they must be in the database container in order for Visual FoxPro to support referential integrity constraints. It is not possible to form referential constraints between tables that don't both belong to the same database.

By its very nature, the database container must be a free table. Furthermore, its base structure of eight fields cannot be modified; however, you can add new fields at the end of the structure. To open the database container as a table, in the command window type:

```
USE databasename.dbc
BROWSE
```

Figure 18.1 shows the basic structure of the database container.

> **CAUTION**
>
> It is very important that you not modify any of the data of this original structure, or the structure itself, manually; if you do, you will end up in a great deal of trouble. Principally, you may not be able to open any of your tables. This chapter discusses some of the problems that may occur and how to solve them.

**FIGURE 18.1**
Structure of VFP's database container.

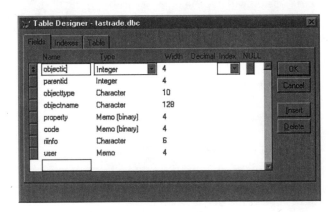

The following explains what exactly is stored for each object type by describing the fields of the database container.

**ObjectID.** The database container looks at each element of the database as an object. Visual FoxPro generates a unique integer to identify each object as it is added to the database container. While it may appear that some numbers are skipped, this is usually due to deleted records that are not shown. The next time the database is packed with the command PACK DATABASE, VFP renumbers all objects sequentially and makes other corrections to the ParentID field as needed. If you ever need to add records to the database container manually, be sure to use the next available sequential number. Do not duplicate numbers in the ObjectID field.

**ParentID.** This field stores the object ID of the parent object. A *parent object* is the object that the current object is contained in. A *database object* is parent to a table or view; a *table object* is parent to a field, an index, and a relation. (The child table of a relationship is parent of the relation object.) If a record has a ParentID that does not correspond to an existing ObjectID, Visual FoxPro treats this as an error. The record should either be removed or its proper parent should be identified to retrieve a valid ObjectID. When you free a table (remove it from the database container), VFP uses the ParentID field to locate all the related table records.

**ObjectType.** ObjectType is a character field that identifies the object types. The types of objects for which the database container stores data are listed below:

- Database
- Table
- Field
- Index
- Relation
- View

**ObjectName.** The name for an object is given by the user, such as table aliases, field names, index tag names, and view names. The database generates its own name for the database objects, such as Database, TransactionLog, StoredProcedureSource, and StoredProcedureObject and relations. The object name is a character field that can hold up to 128 characters.

**Property.** All property values for each object are stored in a single memo field. The specific properties stored depend on the object type. See Table 18.1 in Retrieving and Setting Property Values for a list of possible properties stored for each object along with the ID that identifies the property. Later in the chapter, utilities are provided that you can use to retrieve and set these properties through reading and writing the property values without using VFP functions or commands.

**Code.** Code is a memo field that stores the referential integrity code and other procedures. It is only used by the two database records StoredProceduresSource and StoredProceduresObject. The first of these stores all the source code for any stored procedure including referential integrity code generated by the referential integrity builder. However, it can also be used to store code called by table and field validation functions. The second record stores a compiled version of the stored procedure. This allows the code to be executed in a compiled application environment.

**TIP** When upgrading from Visual FoxPro 3.0, you need to recompile the code in the stored procedures before you can open the database container. Use the command COMPILE DATABASE.

**RiInfo.** The RiInfo field is a three character field that stores the type of referential integrity for Relation objects. Possible values are C=Cascade, R=Restricted, and I=Ignore. The first character represents the Update trigger, followed by the Delete trigger and finally the Insert trigger. Therefore, the string "CRI" indicates that Updates should be cascaded, deletes should be restricted, and inserts are ignored.

**User.** User is a memo that is currently unused by Visual FoxPro. You can use it to store your own custom properties. However, unless you use a formatted structure like in the Property field, you can only store a single value.

Figure 18.2 displays a browse window of the database container table for TASTRADE.DBC. You will notice how the data is structured and stored as explained previously.

## Customizing and Enhancing the Database Container

The database container stores the values for the basic properties of your table and index structures. What if you want to create and store your own custom properties?

First, look at field structures. Don't forget that the most important purpose of a data dictionary is to store the information on a field to allow for re-creation and reference operations. The field properties that the database container stores include:

- Default value
- Format
- Input mask
- Caption
- Comment
- Rules
- Triggers
- Display class

**FIGURE 18.2**
Browse window for
TASTRADE.DBC table.

| Objectid | Parentid | Objecttype | Objectname | Property | Code | Riinfo | User |
|---|---|---|---|---|---|---|---|
| 1 | 1 | Database | Database | Memo | memo | | memo |
| 2 | 1 | Database | TransactionLog | memo | memo | | memo |
| 3 | 1 | Database | StoredProceduresSource | memo | Memo | | memo |
| 4 | 1 | Database | StoredProceduresObject | memo | Memo | | memo |
| 5 | 1 | Table | setup | Memo | memo | | memo |
| 6 | 5 | Field | key_name | Memo | memo | | memo |
| 7 | 5 | Field | value | Memo | memo | | memo |
| 8 | 5 | Index | key_name | Memo | memo | | memo |
| 9 | 1 | Table | customer | Memo | memo | | memo |
| 10 | 9 | Index | company_na | Memo | memo | | memo |
| 11 | 9 | Index | customer_i | Memo | memo | | memo |
| 12 | 1 | Table | user_level | Memo | memo | | memo |
| 13 | 12 | Index | group_id | Memo | memo | | memo |
| 14 | 1 | Table | supplier | Memo | memo | | memo |
| 15 | 14 | Index | contact_na | Memo | memo | | memo |
| 16 | 14 | Index | company_na | Memo | memo | | memo |
| 17 | 14 | Index | supplier_i | Memo | memo | | memo |
| 18 | 1 | Table | shippers | Memo | memo | | memo |
| 19 | 18 | Index | company_na | Memo | memo | | memo |
| 20 | 18 | Index | shipper_id | Memo | memo | | memo |

Part
IV

Ch
18

You may want to create a program to verify and validate the existence and definition of all tables, fields, indexes, etc., for the application. In this case, you would compare the information in the data dictionary to the actual definitions. You would need to know how to retrieve the properties. Notice that the database container does not store the field type, size, or number of decimals. This information only exists in the DBF header. If the DBF is damaged, you may not have a way to determine this information. Therefore, these properties are prime candidates to add as custom field information in your data dictionary.

Now look at the properties that are available for a text box to affect the display or actions performed on the data—the properties of a form control. If you use the drag-and-drop method for adding a field to a form, the caption, class, comment, control source, format, input mask, maximum length, and width properties are automatically set to what the field definition provides. However, you may want to set the value of other properties for a field. We will discuss how to do this in a given situation.

Many times, privileged data is an issue in your development. You may want to set properties such as ReadOnly, Visible, or Enabled to a value other than the default for specific fields. Also, the value may depend on the user's security level. This information should be stored in your data dictionary, because it is a characteristic of the field. For each value that you want to store, simply add a field to the database container. Microsoft recommends that you name your custom fields with a prefix of U. VFP ignores fields with this prefix when working with the DBC. Remember not to change the original structure in any way and to add your additional fields at the end of the fields list.

Next, you can develop your application in such a way that it looks to your data dictionary for the security level of a field and sets the properties of the control accordingly. With VFP 5.0 and an effective data dictionary, this task is easy. You can create a class for each form control to dynamically seek your field name in the database container, retrieve the value of the security level of the field, and set the appropriate values.

Following is an example of a user-defined text-box control class that checks the security level per the data dictionary for the field and sets the values of the necessary properties. The code is placed in the Init event of the control, so don't forget your scope referencing if you put additional code in the Init procedure of an object of the class. This sample assumes that you have already opened the database container table in a work area.

**Listing 18.1   UDCCONTROLS.VCX—A Subclass of a Textbox to Set ReadOnly Property of the Textbox After Looking to the Data Dictionary for a Security Level of the Field**

```
**************************************************
*-- Class Library: udccontrols.vcx
**************************************************


**************************************************
*-- Class:  udctextbox (udccontrols.vcx)
*-- ParentClass: textbox
*-- BaseClass: textbox
*
DEFINE CLASS udctextbox AS textbox


      Height = 23
      Width = 100
      Name = "udctextbox"
```

```
        PROCEDURE Init
                lcCurrentAlias = ALIAS()
                SELECT testdata
                SET ORDER TO objectname
                lcFieldName =
LEFT(This.ControlSource,(RAT('.',This.ControlSource)-1))
                SEEK(lcFieldName)
                IF Security < 3
                        This.ReadOnly = .T.
                ENDIF
                SELECT (lcCurrentAlias)
        ENDPROC


ENDDEFINE
*
*-- EndDefine: udctextbox
*****************************************************
```

You can implement many other functions in a similar manner.

## Retrieving and Setting Property Values

The Property field in the DBC is formatted using a string of bytes which begins with a header to identify the property followed by its value.

The first four bytes define the length of the property including the header and the property value. It is stored as a 4-byte binary with the least significant byte first. For example, 20 0 0 0 indicates a 20-byte property field. Note that the 20 here represents the ASCII character value for the first byte. Use the following equation to calculate the property field length:

$$<B1> + <B2>*256 + <B3>*256*256 + <B4>*256*256*256$$

The next two bytes represent the length of the property ID code. Currently, there are less than 255 property IDs so these two bytes are usually: 1 0.

The next byte is the property ID itself. As mentioned previously, since there are less than 255 properties currently defined, only one byte is typically required here.

Finally, the rest of the bytes (as defined by the first four bytes) hold the value of the property with strings terminated with an extra byte of CHR(0).

With this information and the information found in Table 18.1, you can quickly decode the secrets of the property information field. Table 18.1 lists properties of the database container objects, ID, and the VPF functions that return and set the values of these properties.

**Table 18.1 Objects and Properties Stored in the Database Container**

| Object Type | ID | Property | Returns the Value | Sets the Value |
| --- | --- | --- | --- | --- |
| Database | 7 | Comment | DBGETPROP() | DBSETPROP() |
| | 24 | Version | DBGETPROP() | |
| Table | 1 | Path | * | * |
| | 2 | Reserved | | |
| | 7 | Comment | DBGETPROP() | DBSETPROP() |
| | 9 | RuleExpression | DBGETPROP() | ALTER TABLE [table name] CHECK [expression] or ALTER TABLE [table name] DROP CHECK |
| | 10 | RuleText | DBGETPROP() | ALTER TABLE [table name] ERROR [string] |
| | 14 | InsertTrigger | DBGETPROP() | CREATE INSERT TRIGGER or DELETE INSERT TRIGGER |
| | 15 | UpdateTrigger | DBGETPROP() | CREATE UPDATE TRIGGER or DELETE UPDATE TRIGGER |
| | 16 | DeleteTrigger | DBGETPROP() | CREATE DELETE TRIGGER or DELETE DELETE TRIGGER |
| | 20 | PrimaryKey | DBGETPROP() | ALTER TABLE [table name] PRIMARY KEY [key name] or ALTER TABLE [table name] DROP PRIMARY KEY |
| Field | 7 | Comment | DBGETPROP() | DBSETPROP() |
| | 9 | RuleExpression | DBGETPROP() | ALTER TABLE [table name] ALTER COLUMN [field name] CHECK [rule expression] or ALTER TABLE [table name] ALTER COLUMN [field name] DROP CHECK |
| | 10 | RuleText | DBGETPROP() | ALTER TABLE [table name] ALTER COLUMN [field name] ERROR [expression] |

*continues*

| Object Type | ID | Property | Returns the Value | Sets the Value |
|---|---|---|---|---|
| | 11 | DefaultValue | DBGETPROP() | ALTER TABLE [table name] ALTER COLUMN [field name] DEFAULT [expression] or ALTER TABLE [table name] ALTER COLUMN [field name] DROP DEFAULT |
| | 50 | DisplayClass | DBGETPROP() | * |
| | 51 | ClassLibrary | DBGETPROP() | * |
| | 54 | InputMask | DBGETPROP() | DBSETPROP() |
| | 55 | Format | DBGETPROP() | DBSETPROP() |
| | 56 | Caption | DBGETPROP() | DBSETPROP() |
| Index | 17 | Primary/ Candidate (Yes = 1, No = 0) | PRIMARY(TAGNO ([tagname of open CDX file]) or CANDIDATE(TAGNO ([tagname of open CDX file]) | * |
| Relation | 13 | ChildTag | * | * |
| | 18 | ParentTable | * | * |
| | 19 | ParentTag | * | * |
| Connection | 7 | Comment | DBGETPROP() | DBSETPROP() |
| | 29 | DataSource | DBGETPROP() | DBSETPROP() |
| | 64 | Asynchronous (Yes = 1, No = 0) | DBGETPROP() | DBSETPROP() |
| | 65 | BatchMode (Yes = 1, No = 0) | DBGETPROP() | DBSETPROP() |

**Table 18.1 Continued**

| Object Type | ID | Property | Returns the Value | Sets the Value |
| --- | --- | --- | --- | --- |
| | 66 | ConnectString | DBGETPROP() | DBSETPROP() |
| | 67 | ConnectTimeout (4-byte binary) | DBGETPROP() | DBSETPROP() |
| | 68 | DispLogin | DBGETPROP() | DBSETPROP() |
| | 69 | DispWarnings (Yes = 1, No = 0) | DBGETPROP() | DBSETPROP() |
| | 70 | IdleTimeout (4-byte binary) | DBGETPROP() | DBSETPROP() |
| | 71 | QueryTimeout (4-byte binary) | DBGETPROP() | DBSETPROP() |
| | 72 | Password | DBGETPROP() | DBSETPROP() |
| | 73 | Transactions (Yes = 1, No = 0) | DBGETPROP() | DBSETPROP() |
| | 74 | User Id | DBGETPROP() | DBSETPROP() |
| | 75 | WaitTime (4-byte binary) | DBGETPROP() | DBSETPROP() |
| | 78 | PacketSize (4-byte binary) | DBGETPROP() | DBSETPROP() |
| View | 2 | Local = 6, Remote = 7 | DBGETPROP() | DBSETPROP() |
| | 7 | Comment | DBGETPROP() | DBSETPROP() |
| | 9 | RuleExpression | DBGETPROP() | DBSETPROP() |
| | 10 | RuleText | DBGETPROP() | DBSETPROP() |

| Object Type | ID | Property | Returns the Value | Sets the Value |
|---|---|---|---|---|
| | 12 | Parameter List with the format <parameter name>,<parameter value>,<parameter name>,<parameter value>,...<parameter name>,<parameter value> | DBGETPROP() | DBSETPROP() |
| | 28 | BatchUpdateCount | DBGETPROP() | DBSETPROP() |
| | 32 | ConnectName | DBGETPROP() | * |
| | 36 | FetchMemo (Yes = 1, No = 0) | DBGETPROP() | DBSETPROP() |
| | 37 | FetchSize (4-byte binary, -1 for all) | DBGETPROP() | DBSETPROP() |
| | 39 | MaxRecords (4-byte binary, -1 for all) | DBGETPROP() | DBSETPROP() |
| | 40 | Share Connection (Yes = 1, No = 0) | DBGETPROP() | DBSETPROP() |
| | 41 | SourceType (Local = 1, Remote = 2) | DBGETPROP() | * |
| | 42 | SQL (Statement) | DBGETPROP() | * |
| | 43 | Tables (List of Tables used separated with commas) | DBGETPROP() | DBSETPROP() |

continues

Part
IV
Ch
18

**Table 18.1**   Continued

| Object Type | ID | Property | Returns the Value | Sets the Value |
|---|---|---|---|---|
| | 44 | SendUpdates | DBGETPROP( ) | DBSETPROP( ) |
| | 46 | UpdateType (SQL Update = 1, SQL Delete & Update = 2) | DBGETPROP( ) | DBSETPROP( ) |
| | 47 | UseMemoSize (4-byte binary) | DBGETPROP( ) | DBSETPROP( ) |
| | 48 | WhereType (Key Fields Only = 1, Key and Updatable Fields = 2, Key and Modified Fields = 3, Key and time stamp = 4 | DBGETPROP( ) | DBSETPROP( ) |
| Field in View | 35 | UpdateName | DBGETPROP( ) | DBSETPROP( ) |
| | 38 | KeyField (Yes = 1) | DBGETPROP( ) | DBSETPROP( ) |
| | 45 | DataType | DBGETPROP( ) | DBSETPROP( ) |

* No programmatic VFP function exists. See the section, "Using Database Container Utilities" for the process of retrieving and setting this property.

# Using Database Container Utilities

VFP 5.0 provides a program named GENDBC.PRG in the VFP\TOOLS directory. This program creates code to programmatically re-create the entire structure of the database. The program that GENDBC.PRG generates is named with your database name and the .PRG extension. To keep the program current, you need to run GENDBC.PRG after every structure change. Select any existing database and run this application. (You may want to use \VFP\SAMPLES\TASTRADE\DATA\TASTRADE.DBC.) After you run GENDBC.PRG, take a look at the resulting code. You will find that you can use pieces of the code as a guideline to create your own tools. For instance, you may decide to create a user interface to change the structure of your database. By "borrowing"code generated from GENDBC.PRG, you can easily create tools to perform modifications and creations of structures and properties.

**Using Utilities to Retrieve and Set Property Values**   You cannot set read-only properties with the DBSETPROP( ) function; VFP sets them as the user modifies the structure through the table, index, and relation design tools. Knowing the ID for the property in the Property field (Table 18.1) of the database container, you can write utilities to accomplish the task. The following class retrieves the selected properties of a table, changes their value with your input, and resets them to the value you specified. You can also find this class in the class library DATADICT.VCX included on the CD with this book.

**Part**
**IV**

**Ch**
**18**

---

**Listing 18.2   DATADICT.VCX—A Class to Retrieve and Set Various Properties of the DBC**

```
DEFINE CLASS udctblproperties AS custom

        *-- Name of the DBC
        rdbcname = ""
        *-- Name of the table
        rtablename = ""
        *-- Link or path to table
        rpathlink = ""
        *-- Primary index tag name for this table
        rprimaryindex = ""
        *-- Comments for this table
        rcomment = ""
        *-- Record Validation Expression
        rvalidexpression = ""
        *-- Record Validation Expression Error Text
        rvalidtext = ""
        *-- Update trigger
        rupdatetrigger = ""
        *-- Insert Trigger for this table
        rinserttrigger = ""
        *-- Delete trigger for this table
        rdeletetrigger = ""
```

*continues*

**Listing 18.2   Continued**

```
      Name = "udctblproperties"

      *-- Retrieve the property information for the selected table/DBC
      PROCEDURE mgetproperty
* Procedure: mGetProperty
* Description: This routine analyzes the PROPERTY field of the DBC for table
records and sets properties *     of this object to the individual values it
finds.
* Properties that need a value: rTableName
***** Notice.....: Copyright  1995 Michael P. Antonovich., All Rights Reserved.
*****
* Define local variables
 LOCAL lcCurDbc, lcDbcPath, lcProperty, ;
  lnCurPos, lnLength, lnNext, lnStart, lnType

* Open database container
 lcDBCPath = DBC()
 SELECT 0
 USE (lcDBCPATH) AGAIN

* Find record associated with this table
 LOCATE FOR UPPER(ObjectType) = "TABLE" AND UPPER(ObjectName) = This.rTableName
 IF FOUND()
* Assign defaults for stepping through field
 lnCurPos = 1
 lnNext = 1
 lnType = 0
 lnStart = 0
 lnLength = 0

* Initialize properties
 This.rPathLink  = ""
 This.rComment   = ""
 This.rValidExpression = ""
 This.rValidText = ""
 This.rInsertTrigger = ""
 This.rUpdateTrigger = ""
 This.rDeleteTrigger = ""
 This.rPrimaryIndex = ""

* Read the property field to identify all table properties
 lcProperty = Property
 DO WHILE lnCurPos < LEN(lcProperty)
  lnNext = ASC(SUBSTR(lcProperty, lnCurPos, 1)) + ;
    ASC(SUBSTR(lcProperty, lnCurPos + 1, 1)) * 256 + ;
    ASC(SUBSTR(lcProperty, lnCurPos + 2, 1)) * 65536
  lnType = ASC(SUBSTR(lcproperty, lnCurPos+6, 1))
  lnStart = lnCurPos + 7
  lnLength = lnNext - 8
 * Read individual properties
  DO CASE
  CASE lnType = 1
   This.rPathLink  = SUBSTR(lcProperty, lnStart, lnLength)
  CASE lnType = 7
```

```
    This.rComment    = SUBSTR(lcProperty, lnStart, lnLength)
    CASE lnType = 9
     This.rValidExpression = SUBSTR(lcProperty, lnStart, lnLength)
    CASE lnType = 10
     This.rValidText  = SUBSTR(lcProperty, lnStart, lnLength)
    CASE lnType = 14
     This.rInsertTrigger = SUBSTR(lcProperty, lnStart, lnLength)
    CASE lnType = 15
     This.rUpdateTrigger = SUBSTR(lcProperty, lnStart, lnLength)
    CASE lnType = 16
     This.rDeleteTrigger = SUBSTR(lcProperty, lnStart, lnLength)
    CASE lnType = 20
     This.rPrimaryIndex = SUBSTR(lcProperty, lnStart, lnLength)
    ENDCASE

  * Determine start of next property
  lnCurPos = lnCurPos + lnNext
  ENDDO && lnCurPos < LEN(lcProperty)
 ENDIF && FOUND()

 * Close database container as a table
 USE
 ENDIF
ENDPROC


PROCEDURE mSetProperty
*Description: This routine sets the value of the field PROPERTY for
*      the selected table in the DBC using values previously
*      stored in the object's other properties.
*Properties that need a value: rTablename
***** Notice.....: Copyright 1995 Michael P. Antonovich., All Rights Reserved.
*****

* Define local variables
 LOCAL lcDbcPath, lcProperty

* Open database container
 lcDBCPath = DBC()
 SELECT 0
 USE (lcDBCPATH) AGAIN

 * Find record associated with this table
 LOCATE FOR UPPER(ObjectType) = "TABLE" AND UPPER(ObjectName) = This.rTableName
 IF FOUND()
 * Build property string
  lcProperty = CHR(8) + CHR(0) + CHR(0) + CHR(0) + CHR(1) + CHR(0) + CHR(2) +
CHR(1)

 * Has a path property been supplied?
  IF !EMPTY(This.rPathLink)
  lcProperty = lcProperty + ;
     CHR(MOD(8 + LEN(This.rPathLink), 256)) + ;
     CHR(INT((8 + LEN(This.rPathLink) - INT((8 + LEN(This.rPathLink)) ;
      / 65536) * 65536) / 256)) + ;
```

*continues*

**Listing 22.2  Continued**

```
         CHR(INT((8 + LEN(This.rPathLink)) / 65536)) + ;
         CHR(0) + CHR(1) + CHR(0) + ;
         CHR(1) + This.rPathLink + CHR(0)
   ENDIF && !EMPTY(This.rPathLink)

 * Has a comment been supplied?
  IF !EMPTY(This.rComment)
  lcProperty = lcProperty + ;
         CHR(MOD(8 + LEN(This.rComment), 256)) + ;
         CHR(INT((8 + LEN(This.rComment) - INT((8 + LEN(This.rComment)) ;
         / 65536) * 65536) / 256)) + ;
         CHR(INT((8 + LEN(This.rComment)) / 65536)) + ;
         CHR(0) + CHR(1) + CHR(0) + ;
         CHR(7) + This.rComment + CHR(0)
   ENDIF && !EMPTY(This.rComment)

 * Has a validation expression been supplied?
  IF !EMPTY(This.rValidExpression)
  lcProperty = lcProperty + ;
         CHR(MOD(8 + LEN(This.rValidExpression), 256)) + ;
         CHR(INT((8 + LEN(This.rValidExpression) - INT((8 +
LEN(This.rValidExpression)) ;
         / 65536) * 65536) / 256)) + ;
         CHR(INT((8 + LEN(This.rValidExpression)) / 65536)) + ;
         CHR(0) + CHR(1) + CHR(0) + ;
         CHR(9) + This.rValidExpression + CHR(0)
   ENDIF && !EMPTY(This.rValidExpression)

 * Has a validation expression text string been supplied?
  IF !EMPTY(This.rValidText)
  lcProperty = lcProperty + ;
         CHR(MOD(8 + LEN(This.rValidText), 256)) + ;
         CHR(INT((8 + LEN(This.rValidText) - INT((8 + LEN(This.rValidText)) ;
         / 65536) * 65536) / 256)) + ;
         CHR(INT((8 + LEN(This.rValidText)) / 65536)) + ;
         CHR(0) + CHR(1) + CHR(0) + ;
         CHR(10) + This.rValidText + CHR(0)
   ENDIF && !EMPTY(This.rValidText)

 * Has an insert trigger been supplied?
  IF !EMPTY(This.rInsertTrigger)
  lcProperty = lcProperty + ;
         CHR(MOD(8 + LEN(This.rInsertTrigger), 256)) + ;
         CHR(INT((8 + LEN(This.rInsertTrigger) - INT((8 + LEN(This.rInsertTrigger));
         / 65536) * 65536) / 256)) + ;
         CHR(INT((8 + LEN(This.rInsertTrigger)) / 65536)) + ;
         CHR(0) + CHR(1) + CHR(0) + ;
         CHR(14) + This.rInsertTrigger + CHR(0)
   ENDIF && !EMPTY(This.rInsertTrigger)

 * Has an update trigger been supplied?
  IF !EMPTY(This.rUpdateTrigger)
  lcProperty = lcProperty + ;
         CHR(MOD(8 + LEN(This.rUpdateTrigger), 256)) + ;
```

```
       CHR(INT((8 + LEN(This.rUpdateTrigger) - INT((8 + LEN(This.rUpdateTrigger));
         / 65536) * 65536) / 256)) + ;
       CHR(INT((8 + LEN(This.rUpdateTrigger)) / 65536)) + ;
       CHR(0) + CHR(1) + CHR(0) + ;
       CHR(15) + This.rUpdateTrigger + CHR(0)
   ENDIF && !EMPTY(This.rUpdateTrigger)

 * Has a delete trigger been supplied?
  IF !EMPTY(This.rDeleteTrigger)
  lcProperty = lcProperty + ;
       CHR(MOD(8 + LEN(This.rDeleteTrigger), 256)) + ;
       CHR(INT((8 + LEN(This.rDeleteTrigger) - INT((8 + LEN(This.rDeleteTrigger));
         / 65536) * 65536) / 256)) + ;
       CHR(INT((8 + LEN(This.rDeleteTrigger)) / 65536)) + ;
       CHR(0) + CHR(1) + CHR(0) + ;
       CHR(16) + This.rDeleteTrigger + CHR(0)
   ENDIF && !EMPTY(This.rDeleteTrigger)

 * Has a primary index been supplied?
  IF !EMPTY(This.rPrimaryIndex)
  lcProperty = lcProperty + ;
       CHR(MOD(8 + LEN(This.rPrimaryIndex), 256)) + ;
       CHR(INT((8 + LEN(This.rPrimaryIndex) - INT((8 + LEN(This.rPrimaryIndex)) ;
         / 65536) * 65536) / 256)) + ;
       CHR(INT((8 + LEN(This.rPrimaryIndex)) / 65536)) + ;
       CHR(0) + CHR(1) + CHR(0) + ;
       CHR(20) + This.rPrimaryIndex + CHR(0)
   ENDIF && !EMPTY(This.rPrimaryIndex)

 * Update the DBC
  REPLACE property WITH lcProperty

 ENDIF && FOUND()
 * Close database container as a table
 USE
plFatal = .F.
ENDPROC
ENDDEFINE
*-- EndDefine: udctblproperties
```

The utilities for changing the values to the properties for the other objects of the database container are constructed in the same way, using the properties and their ID values as shown in Table 18.1. You can find the utilities for the table, field, and relation properties in the DATADICT.VCX class library on the enclosed CD-ROM.

One way to easily expand the functionality of the database container is to simply add additional fields to the end of the DBC structure. Just prefix these fields with U to identify them to VFP as user-defined fields. Do not insert these fields before any of the fields defined by Visual FoxPro. Also, do not change the order of the DBC fields defined by Visual FoxPro. If you add an additional column to the end of the database-container table structure defined as a memo field or use the memo field named "User," you can use a format structure similar to that used by VFP itself in the Property field to store multiple parameters in a single field. You can define values for your own properties, using the mSetProperty utility with the appropriate changes, to point to your new property field.

With this capability, you can infinitely enhance the functionality of the current DBC to handle any additional information that you want your application to support directly from the database container.

**Recovering from a Mismatch of Fields**   What would happen if someone copies an older database container file over the current database container file? If there have been no table or index structure changes between the two versions, nothing. However, what if the structure of the tables or indexes have changed? You can open the database, but when you try to open any tables that had their structures changed, VFP reports an error message. Even if something as simple as the index tags have changed, you still cannot open the table.

Suppose the fields have changed (added, deleted, renamed). If you attempt to open the table with the USE command, VFP first compares the fields in the table with those defined in the DBC. If there is not a match, VFP reports the following error:

```
Base Table fields have been changed and no longer match view fields.  View
fields properties cannot be set.
```

Similarly, if you enter the BROWSE command in the Command window and attempt to select the damaged table from the resulting Open dialog, VFP reports the error:

```
The fields in table '<tablename>' did not match the entries in the database.
```

Actually, this second error message is more informative, but neither lets you open the table to display its structure. The following program reads the header of the selected DBF and lists the fields, their type, size, and decimals as defined in the DBF.

### Listing 18.3   18PRG03.PRG—This Program Reads the DBF Header

```
CLOSE ALL
CLEAR ALL

DO WHILE .T.
  CLEAR
* Prompt for the DBF to read the header from
  cDbfName = GETFILE("DBF", "Examine DBF", "Examine", 0)
  IF EMPTY(cDbfName)
    EXIT
  ENDIF

* Open DBF with low level functions
  nHandle = FOPEN(cDbfName, 0)
```

```
    IF nHandle < 0
      MESSAGEBOX("File " + ALLTRIM(cDbfName) + ;
                 " could not be opened.")
      EXIT
    ENDIF

* Move byte pointer beyond the first 32 bytes
* to get to the first field record.
  nErr = FSEEK(nHandle, 32, 0)

* Begin a loop to read the field definitions
  iFld = 0
  DO WHILE .T.
    cStr = FREAD(nHandle, 32)
  * Check for field header section terminator
    IF ASC(LEFT(cStr,1)) = 13
      EXIT
    ENDIF

  * Read field data
    iFld = iFld + 1
    cFieldName = ALLTRIM(STRTRAN(LEFT(cStr, 10), Chr(0), Chr(32)))
    cFieldID = SUBSTR(cStr, 12, 1)
    DO CASE
      CASE cFieldId = "C"
        cFieldType = "Character"
      CASE cFieldId = "Y"
        cFieldType = "Currency"
      CASE cFieldId = "N"
        cFieldType = "Numeric"
      CASE cFieldId = "F"
        cFieldType = "Float"
      CASE cFieldId = "D"
        cFieldType = "Date"
      CASE cFieldId = "T"
        cFieldType = "DateTime"
      CASE cFieldId = "B"
        cFieldType = "Double"
      CASE cFieldId = "I"
        cFieldType = "Integer"
      CASE cFieldId = "L"
        cFieldType = "Logical"
      CASE cFieldId = "M"
        cFieldType = "Memo"
      CASE cFieldId = "G"
        cFieldType = "General"
    ENDCASE
    nFieldLength = ASC(SUBSTR(cStr, 17, 1))
    nFieldDecimal = ASC(SUBSTR(cStr, 18, 1))
    nFieldFlag = ASC(SUBSTR(cStr, 19, 1))
    cFieldFlag = ""
    IF INT(nFieldFlag/4) = 1 and cFieldId $ "CM"
      cFieldFlag = "Binary " + cFieldFlag
      nFieldFlag = nFieldFlag - 4
```

Part

IV

Ch

18

*continues*

**Listing 18.3    Continued**

```
    ENDIF
    IF INT(nFieldFlag/2) = 1
      cFieldFlag = "Nulls Allowed " + cFieldFlag
      nFieldFlag = nFieldFlag - 2
    ENDIF
    IF nFieldFlag = 1
      cFieldFlag = "System " + cFieldFlag
    ENDIF

  * Display field data
    ? "FIELD: " + STR(iFld,3) + "   " + PADR(cFieldname, 12, " ") + ;
      PADR(cFieldType, 12, " ") + STR(nFieldLength,3) + ;
      "." + PADR(ALLTRIM(STR(nFieldDecimal,2)), 2, " ") + ;
      cFieldFlag
  ENDDO

* Close the DBF with low level functions
  nErr = FCLOSE(nHandle)
  MessageBox("Done analyzing table &cDbfName..")

ENDDO
```

Compare the fields in the table's header with the ones that the database container has for that table. If the database has a field that the table's header doesn't have, delete that record from the database container. If the database doesn't have a field that the table's header lists, you need to add the field to the database container table, using the table's object ID for the parent ID of the new record. These corrections will enable you to open the table.

Next, you can remove the field, if necessary.

Keep in mind that if you need to keep the field and add it manually to the database container, you would have lost any properties that were set for that field. Assuming that you have generated an up-to-date program with GENDBC.PRG, reference the program code to see what properties were set for the field.

 Another alternative to trying to modify the database container manually would be to regenerate it from a recent output from GENDBC.PRG.

**Recovering a Corrupted or Missing Index File**    You may encounter a corrupted or missing index file from time to time. VFP has a command—VALIDATE DATABASE—that ensures that the locations of tables and indexes in the current database are current and that all index tags in the database exist. If you add RECOVER to the end of the command, VFP prompts you to locate any missing files.

If an index file needs to be re-created, you will have a problem setting a primary index. The database container stores the primary index in the Property field for the table object. If the table already has a primary index set, when you try to create another, it automatically makes it a Candidate index tag. To solve this problem, you need to remove the primary index reference from the database container. This task is made easy with the utilities discussed earlier in the chapter in the DATADICT.VCX class library.

Type the following in the Command window to simply remove the primary key reference of a table.

```
SET CLASSLIB TO DATADICT
oTblProp = CREATEOBJECT('udcTblProperties')
oTblProp.rDBCName = 'YOURDBC.DBC'
oTblProp.rTableName = 'YOURTBL.DBF"
oTblProp.mGetProperty
oTblProp.rPrimaryIndex = " "
oTblProp.mSetProperty
```

After removing the reference, you will be able to create another primary index.

**Moving a Table from One DBC to Another**    Imagine that you have a project that uses multiple databases. During development, you decide you want to move a table from one DBC to another without losing the property information. You cannot free the table from the database without losing the property information. The following utility enables you to perform this task.

On the CD

**Listing 18.4    DATADICT.VCX—This Class Moves a Table from One DBC to Another Without Losing Its Properties**

```
DEFINE CLASS udcdbfmove AS custom

*- Name of source DBC
rcOldDBCName = " "
*- Name of target DBC
rcNewDBCName = " "
*- Name of DBF file
rcDBFName = " "
*- Name of table
rcTableName = " "
*- Original Path to table that is moved.
rcOriginalPath = " "
*-Length in characters of the initial backlink in the DBF.
Rninitiallen = 0
*- Back Link Start Position in DBF to be moved
rnBAckLinkStartPosision = 0

*- Move a table from one DBC to another
PROCEDURE mDBFMove
```

*continues*

Part
IV
Ch
18

**Listing 18.4 Continued**

```
LOCAL lnPos, lcStr, lcDBC, lnInitialLen, lcPath, lnFHandle, lcNewStr, lcNewStr2;
  lcSuffix, lcPrefix, lnExt, lcRef, lnDup, llGood, lnSent, lcCurObjectId

*Locate the current backlink reference
lnFhandle = FOPEN(This.rcdbfname, 0)
This.rnBackLinkStartPosition = 0
lcStr = FREAD(lnFhandle, 32)
DO WHILE ASC (LEFT(lcStr,1)) # 13
 lcStr = FREAD(lnFhandle, 32)
 This.rnBackLinkStartPosition = This.rnBackLinkStartPosition + 32
ENDDO

* Reference start point found. Build string
lnPos = FSEEK(lnFhandle, This.rnBackLinkStartPosition + 1,0)
lcStr = FREAD(lnFhandle, 255)
lcDBC = LEFT(lcStr, AT(CHR(0), lcStr)-1)
lnInitialLen = LEN(lcDBC)

*Build the fully qualified file name for the DBC
lcPath = This.rcOriginalPath
DO WHILE LEFT(lcDBC, 3) "..\"
 lcDBC = SUBSTR(lcDBC, 4)
 lcPath = LEFT(lcPath, RAT('\', lcPath, 2)
ENDO
This.rcOldDBcName = UPPER(lcPath + lcDBC)

*Open New Database Container
SELECT 0
USE (This.rcNewDBCName) AGAIN ALIAS NEWDBC

*Open the old database container to retrieve records
 SELECT 0
 USE (This.rcOldDBCName) AGAIN ALIAS OLDDBC

*Find the reference to the moving table & get object ID
LOCATE FOR UPPER(objectname) = UPPER(This.rcOldDBCName)

*Could be using a long table name
IF EOF()
 SCAN FOR UPPER(ObjectType = "TABLE"
  lcNewStr = (LEFT(property, AT(".DBF", UPPER(property)) -1)
  lcNewStr2 = SUBSTR(lcNewStr, RAT(CHR(1), lcNewStr) + 1)
  IF RAT('\', lcNewStr2) > 0
  lcNewStr2 = SUBSTR(lcNewStr2, RAT('\', lcNewStr2) + 1
  ENDIF
  IF UPPER(lcNewStr2) = UPPER(This.rcTableName)
  EXIT
  ENDIF
 ENDSCAN
ENDIF
lcCurObjectID = ObjectId

*Move table record from old database to new one
SCATTER MEMO NAME MOVTBL
```

```
* RELREF() is another function provided in 22PRG02.PRG
lcRef = RELREF(This.rcNewDBCName, This.rcDBFName)
lnExt = (AT('.DBF', UPPER(MOVTBL.Property))
lcSuffix = SUBSTR(MOVTBL.Property, lnExt + 4)
lcPrefix = LEFT(MOVTBL.Property, RAT(CHR(1), LEFT(MOVTBL.Property, lnExt + 3)))
MOVTBL.Property = lcPrefix + lcRef + lcSuffix
SELECT NEWDBC
GOTO BOTTOM
lcNewParent = Objectid + 1
MOVTBL.ObjectID = lcNewParent
APPEND BLANK
GATHER MEMO NAME MOVTBL
SELECT OLDDBC
DELETE

* Now loop to retrieve all the related records
SCAN FOR ParentId = cCurObjectID
 SCATTER MEMO NAME MOVTBL
 SELECT NEWDBC
 lcObjectCnt = lcObjectCnt + 1
 MOVTBL.ParentID = lcNewParent
 MOVTBL.ObjectId = lcObjectCnt
 APPEND BLANK
 GATHER MEMO NAME MOVTBL
 SELECT OLDDBC
 DELETE
ENDSCAN
PACK

* Change the relative reference in the table
lnFhandle = FOPEN(This.rcDBFName,2)

*Move to reference start point & add new reference.
*Zero character fill if new reference is shorter.
LcRef = RELREF(This.rcDBFName, This.rcNEWDBCName)
lnPos = FSEEK(lnFhandle, This.rnBackLinkStartPosition + 1, 0)
lndup = MAX(This.rnInitialLen - LEN(lcRef),2)
lnSent = FWRITE(lnFhandle, lcRef + REPLICATE(CHR(0), lndup))
llGood = FCLOSE(lnFhandle)

*Close all databases and reset environment
SELECT OLDDBC
USE
SELECT NEWDBC
USE

ENDPROC
ENDDEFINE

*--EndDefine: udcdbfmove
```

Part

**IV**

Ch

**18**

This code has one major limitation. It does not attempt to transfer the stored procedure source or compiled code. There are several problems that would have to be resolved to do this.

When moving a table from one DBC to another, it easy to break any relational links in the original DBC, but impossible to second guess what links would be appropriate in the new DBC.

Store procedures are used for field and record validations. While it may be possible to look for and transfer the first level calls to functions, if these functions call other functions and procedures and they call others, and so on, the task quickly become very complex. In addition, what happens if the new DBC has another function or procedure with the same name as the old DBC?

Any attempt to clean-up the old DBC by removing unused functions or procedures would require scanning through all the remaining tables to discover what functions they require.

For the purposes of this example, these problems were not considered in the code. However, if you ran GENDBC.PRG on the database, you will find the stored procedures in a file named with the database name and the extension .krt. You can look at this file with MODIFY FILE to get an idea of what procedures were stored for the table, but obviously you will have to recreate the relationships and referential integrity to concur with the tables in the new database.

Looking at this code in the previous listings, you will notice a call to a function RELREF( ). This routine returns the relative reference between the path of the file passed as the first parameter and the path of the file passed as the second parameter. Following is the code for this routine, which is also included on the enclosed CD.

> **Listing 18.5   18PRG05.PRG—This Routine Returns the Relative Reference Between the Path of the File Passed as the First Parameter and the Path of the File Passed as the Second Parameter**

```
FUNCTION RELREF
LPARAMETERS cNewDbc, cMoveFile
LOCAL cTableName, cOrigPath

cTableName = SUBSTR(cMoveFile, RAT('\', cMoveFile)+1)
ctableName = LEFT(cTableName, AT('.', cTablename)-1)
cOrigPath = LEFT(cMoveFile, RAT('\', cMoveFile))

cPathNewDbc = LEFT(cNewDbc, RAT('\', cNewDbc))
cPathMoveFile = cOrigPath

IF cPathNewDbc == cPathMoveFile
  cNewRelative = cTableName + RIGHT(cMoveFile,4)
ELSE
* Check how much of path is common starting with the drive
  cDriveNewDbc = LEFT(cPathNewDbc,2)
  cDriveMoveFile = LEFT(cPathMoveFile,2)
```

```
   cPathNewDbc = SUBSTR(cPathNewDbc,3)
   cPathMoveFile = SUBSTR(cPathMoveFile,3)

   IF cDriveNewDbc # cDriveMoveFile
     cNewRelative = cDriveMoveFile + cPathMoveFile + cTableName +
RIGHT(cMoveFile,4)
   ELSE
     sublen1 = AT('\', cPathNewDbc,2)
     sublen2 = AT('\', cPathMoveFile,2)
     DO WHILE sublen1 > 0 AND sublen2 > 0
       chk1 = LEFT(cPathNewDbc, sublen1-1)
       chk2 = LEFT(cPathMoveFile, sublen2-1)
       IF chk1 == chk2
       * Throw away common directories
         cPathNewDbc = SUBSTR(cPathNewDbc, sublen1)
         cPathMoveFile = SUBSTR(cPathMoveFile, sublen2)
       * Check if more directories
         sublen1 = AT('\', cPathNewDbc,2)
         sublen2 = AT('\', cPathMoveFile,2)
       ELSE
         EXIT
       ENDIF
     ENDDO

     DO CASE
       CASE sublen1 = 0
         cNewRelative = cPathMoveFile + cTableName + RIGHT(cMoveFile,4)
       CASE sublen2 = 0
         cStr = ""
         FOR i = 2 TO LEN(cPathNewDbc)
           IF SUBSTR(cPathNewDbc, I, 1) = '\'
             cStr = cStr + '..\'
           ENDIF
         ENDFOR
         cNewRelative = cStr + cTableName + RIGHT(cMoveFile,4)
       OTHERWISE
         cStr = ""
         FOR i = 2 TO LEN(cPathNewDbc)
           IF SUBSTR(cPathNewDbc, I, 1) = '\'
             cStr = cStr + '..\'
           ENDIF
         ENDFOR
         cNewRelative = LEFT(cStr, LEN(cstr)-1) + cPathMoveFile + cTableName +
RIGHT(cMoveFile,4)
     ENDCASE
   ENDIF
ENDIF

RETURN cNewRelative
```

Part
IV

Ch

18

# Creating Documentation from the Database Container

Some of the most cumbersome tasks in application development are keeping track
of data and trying to keep your documentation up to date. Yes, I said documentation.

VFP provides functions and tools to create documentation. DISPLAY DATABASE displays information about the current database or fields, named connections, tables, or views in the current database. You can include the TO PRINTER or TO FILE clause to output the results to the printer or a file. Another alternative is to create a report directly from the database container table if you want a customized report.

▶ **See** "Custom Report Generation," **p. 555**

VFP also provides a documenting wizard, which formats and produces text files from your code in projects and program files. The wizard does not modify your code. Rather, it creates a text file to document the code. If you want the wizard to perform specific tasks, you are given the opportunity to customize the wizard.

▶ **See** "The Documenting Wizard," **p. 264**

# Designing Your Own Data Dictionary

This chapter wouldn't be complete without mentioning the possibilities and advantages of creating your own data dictionary database. In addition to performing the basic functions of a data dictionary, the data can be referenced for data-driven operations, such as the example earlier in this chapter that illustrated setting display control properties dynamically (Listing 18.1 in Display Class).

However, we do not recommend getting too carried away with data-driven operations for this creates a major impact on performance, or speed, of the application. As we all know, performance is the last sacrifice to make in your application and should be avoided whenever possible. The database container provides many of the data-driven operations seamlessly for you, especially during form design and data validation, so take advantage of them first.

However, there are many other reasons for a data dictionary. You may prefer to create your own data dictionary separate from the DBC. Maybe for reasons of not wanting to touch the database container for fear of creating problems, or you have so many additional properties to store that creating your own container in addition to VFP's makes just as much sense.

For a data dictionary database to be beneficial, it must be structured properly. Our experience with the implementation of a user-defined data dictionary proved that it can provide substantial functionality, with the proper structure. This section discusses the basic ideas behind the design but will leave the exact implementation open so that you can customize it to suit your specific needs.

First, you need to determine what data properties are important in your applications.

To begin with, you need a database container level. But that may not be the highest group level in your data dictionary. Remember that a database container is not necessarily specific to a single application. In fact, many applications in a company could share the same database container. Likewise, a single application can easily use more than one database container. Therefore, you may want to begin with a table defining the applications used by the company. In its simplest form, this table may consist of a single record for the current application. However, adding it at the beginning provides the flexibility for future growth. A typical structure for the application level might include the following fields:

```
APPLICATIONS
cApplicationName   C(40)    (Primary Key)
mApplicationDesc   M
```

Next you need a table to define the database containers used by all the applications that are part of the data dictionary. Note that this table is not a replacement to the VFP database container, but is supplemental to it. It also serves as a place to store database specific properties in addition to those supported by Visual FoxPro. Its structure might be shown as follows:

```
DATABASES
cDatabaseName      C(40)    (Primary Key)
cDatabasePath               C(80)
mDatabaseDesc               M
```

Because the relationship between these first two tables is a many-to-many, you need to create a table between them to normalize the structure. This table merely associates database containers with applications.

```
APPDBC
cApplicationName   C(40)
cDatabaseName               C(40)
```

In this case, both fields together define an appropriate primary key with the application name probably preceding the database container name. This table contains a record for every database container associated with an application. If, for example, database container A is associated with applications X, Y, and Z, there will be three records, one for each association.

Next you need a table to define the tables used by the system. Include in this table all table references, not just those bound to a database container. This way, you can always determine all of the tables, such as free tables, used by an application, not just those found in a DBC.

```
TABLES
cDbfName           C(20)              (Primary Key)
cTableAlias                 C(20)
cDbfPath           C(80)
cDatabaseName               C(20)
cTableDesc         M
```

Notice that this table includes a reference to the database container. Because a table can only be bound to one database container, it makes sense to include this information at the table definition level. If a table could be bound to more than one database container, we would need an intermediate table between TABLES and DATABASES.

Next, you need a table to define the fields used by any table, in any database, in any application. The purpose of creating a table to define field attributes is to ensure that fields with a common purpose always have the same name and are defined the same way. At the simplest level, you need to ensure that the field name is spelled the same, has the same type and the same size characteristics. You could also extend this concept to other field properties, but that would duplicate data already stored in the database containers. Also, you may want different defaults, validations, or captions when the field is used with different tables.

```
FIELDS
cFieldName       C(10)              (Primary Key)
cFieldDataType          C(1)
cFieldSize       N(3,0)
cFieldDecimal           N(2,0)
cFieldDesc       M
```

Notice that a field is only defined once, even if it is used by more than one table. This ensures that the field definition is normalized. However, it does not tell us which fields belong to which tables. For that, we need another table that contains a record for each field in each table.

```
TBLFLDS
cTableAlias      C(20)              Primary Key
cFieldName C(20)          Primary Key
```

Again, the combination of both fields define the primary key for this table. Note how it can associate a single field definition with multiple tables.

The corollary to the above is that if a field has a different name, it must either represent something different, have a different type, or a different size. For example, in a database that had several tables with the field cStyle, it may not be obvious whether this field represented the same thing in each table, especially if the field was defined with 6 characters in one table and 8 in another. However, by naming the fields cClothStyle, cYarnStyle, and cGarmentStyle, the differences become more evident.

Next, you want to store index information. The database container stores the name of primary indexes in the table record properties field. It also stores the names of all tags in the structural compound index. However, it does not store the tag definition. Nor does it store any information about non-structural indexes or standalone indexes. For these reasons, you may want to consider a table to document the index definition. The resulting fields in such a table might include the following:

```
INDEXES
cIndexName          C(10)     (Primary Key)
cTableName          C(20)
cTagName            c(10)
mIndExpression               M
mIndexPath          M
```

Finally, most developers will want to take advantage of the referential integrity feature provided by the database container. This information links two tables together through one or more common fields. This relation can also determine what types of changes can be made to one or both of the tables. For example, you can cascade changes from the parent record down to all the child records. This cascade of values specifically refers to the value of the linking field. You can also restrict changes. In other words, if a parent table record has child records, you can restrict any changes to the value of the connecting field.

Similarly, you can cascade deletes telling VFP to delete all the child records when a parent record is deleted. For example, if you delete an order record, you probably also want to delete all order detail lines. As with updates, you can also restrict a delete and ignore a delete.

Finally, you can restrict insert into the child table if there is no corresponding record in the parent table. Again you can ignore this restriction, but we do not recommend using ignore without careful consideration of the consequences.

The following list is an example of the table to store your persistent relationships.

```
RELATIONS
cParentName                  C(20)
cChildName          C(20)
cParentTag          C(10)
cChildTag           C(10)
cUpdateType                  C(1)
cInsertType                  C(1)
cDeleteType                  C(1)
```

You can expect that in the early stages of development, you will probably start with the basic information needed to define the tables and their indexes. Ideally, the best place to start is by defining the fields used by the application. Once you know what fields are required, you can begin organizing those fields into tables using the rules of normalization. Next you would define the indexes required to support common data searches, reports, and referential integrity. As development continues, you will likely add other fields to your data dictionary. You may require other attributes and other database structures beyond those provided by Visual FoxPro or those proposed here. In that case, simply add additional fields in the appropriate tables to support those properties with your code referencing the appropriate tables. For simplicity, and because your options are wide open at this point, we will stop here. Obviously though, you can go much further than this. See Figure 18.3 for an illustration of a custom-designed data dictionary database.

**FIGURE 18.3**
Database designed for a custom data dictionary.

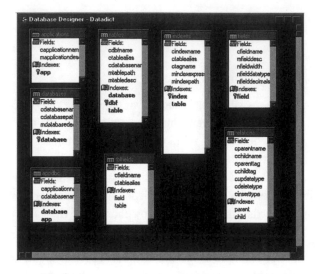

To help you get started, several utilities have been provided on the enclosed CD, which, in addition to the many functions that VFP 5.0 provides, will help you create a program to loop through your databases, tables, and fields, extracting the property values and storing them for initial population of your data dictionary.

# From Here...

This chapter has provided you with the information you need to create and maintain a data dictionary. Using VFP functions and user-defined utilities, the task of retrieving and setting properties and correcting data corruption of the database objects is made easy. Most of the utilities provided are in a class library named DATADICT.VCX. To use these utilities you should know how to work with classes and VPF's database container.

The following chapters will provide more information related to using classes and the database container:

- Chapter 2, "Introducing Object-Oriented Programming," will explain how to use and create custom classes.

- Chapter 3, "Defining Databases, Tables, and Indexes," will provide more information on how to create a database.

- Chapter 14, "Custom Report Generation," will explain how to design and create custom reports.

- Bonus Chapter 01, "Creating a Design Plan," will discuss the process of planning the design of your database. This chapter is located on the CD.

# Internet Support

*by Rick Strahl*

The Internet and the technologies that are driving it are hot these days! People are flocking to the Internet and the World Wide Web in particular by the millions, and new Web sites and other Internet-related businesses and institutions are keeping pace with the ever-increasing hook-up rates of new Web surfers. Building applications that are integrated with Internet technology and can connect databases to Web sites will likely become an important aspect in your software development, as companies like Microsoft integrate Web-based technology into every aspect of software from high-level applications down to the operating system.

While traditionally the Internet has been made of mostly static content, there is a tremendous rush under way to make dynamic data available. Database connectivity is key to this concept and Visual FoxPro is up to the task to provide the speed and flexibility to act as a database back end and integrate Internet functionality into existing applications. ■

**Why the Internet is important for database developers**

Find out why there is so much excitement about Internet-hosted applications and how the Internet is affecting the future of application development.

**How database development and Visual FoxPro fit into the Internet scheme**

Visual FoxPro's speedy database engine and its flexible object-oriented language make it a perfect tool for building Internet applications.

**How you can use Visual FoxPro to build Internet-enabled applications**

Internet-enabling your applications doesn't have to be difficult or require a rewrite of existing applications. Find out how to use add-on components and routines to Internet-enable your applications.

**How to use Visual FoxPro as a database back end to a Web server for providing dynamic content over the World Wide Web**

The World Wide Web is being hailed as the next big application platform. Find out about the tools that make it possible to use Visual FoxPro as a Web server back end to provide data access to Web applications.

# What's So Exciting About the Internet?

There is a lot of hype going around about the Internet and, to be sure, some of the new technologies are not all that they are cracked up to be. The use of the Internet for business application development is still in its infancy, and there are quite a few limitations when compared to the application development facilities that you might be used to using.

Nevertheless, the Internet is bringing about a major shift in the way applications are deployed by making it much easier to build solutions that are open and widely distributed, even open to the public over the World Wide Web. Over the last few years, you have probably developed or heard a lot about client/server development. The Internet is providing the full promise of what client/server was always meant to be: a platform that allows you to build widely distributed applications that can be centrally maintained using a common front end provided by a Web browser.

The driving force behind the popularity of the Internet and the World Wide Web in particular are:

- Universal client interface
- Wide distribution with centralized management
- Open standards

Let's take a look at these points in more detail in the following sections.

## The Universal Client: Web Browsers as a Common Interface

The World Wide Web and the Web browsers used to cruise it are changing the way we look at applications today. Web browsers have brought a universal interface to applications in a way that no other software interface before it has ever achieved.

Web browsers are easy to use and provide a very simple interface to the user. The use of simple controls for navigation (back and forward buttons, a list of the last places visited, a "favorites" list, etc.), make the browser interface just about self-explanatory. It also provides a consistent interface across applications developed with a browser in mind. A typical example of a dynamically generated Web page is shown in Figure 19.1.

The hyperlink-based nature of Web pages, where you can simply click on a highlighted area and immediately be transported to the location of the relevant information, makes it an extremely powerful tool for integrating information from various sources, both internally to a company as well as externally from out over the open Internet.

**FIGURE 19.1**

A Web page containing dynamically generated data. This order form shows items selected on a previous form allowing the user to fill out order info for an online purchase using a secure transaction.

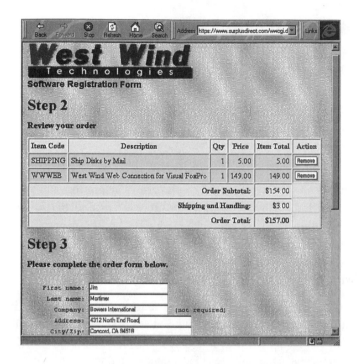

Ease of use is important, but even more compelling is the ubiquitous nature of Web browsers. Browsers exist for all the major computing platforms from Windows to Mac to UNIX. What this means is that an application interface developed for a Web browser will instantly run on all of the platforms that support a Web browser. Cross-platform development has been an often-overlooked part of software development in the past due to its complexities, but with the Web browser interface, this feature is included for free in the one-time Web application development process.

Finally, Web browsers free developers from distributing huge application runtimes that need to be installed on each client system. Take a typical stand-alone Visual FoxPro application, for example. To distribute an application across the company, you have to install the application runtimes on each of the machines. You distribute your EXE, the runtime, and various system files that get installed on the client system. With a Web browser, none of this happens. There is a one-time installation for the browser after which all Web-based applications are accessible. As long as the client system is equipped with a Web browser and access to the network that runs the application over either the public or company internal Web, the application can be run without any special installation procedures. Furthermore, the application can be run from *anywhere* whether the user is at the office, on the road, or on vacation as long as she has access to an Internet connection!

Part

IV

Ch

19

## Distributed Applications over the Web

The latter point is extremely important! The Web has made distributed computing a reality for the first time by making it relatively easy to install applications that can be accessed publicly over the Internet or privately over an internal network (which is called an *Intranet*). Prior to the Internet explosion, building a publicly accessible application was extremely difficult, inconvenient for end users, and very costly as proprietary communications and network protocols needed to be set up.

You've undoubtedly heard about client/server (C/S) over the last few years—the Internet is turning out to be the ultimate C/S platform! The promise of C/S has always been to create a distributed environment where there is a distinct line between the application interface and the database and business logic. The Web is providing this environment by clearly separating the client (the Web browser) and the server (the Web server and the back end applications tied to it) as well as providing an open platform (a network running the TCP/IP protocol) to connect the two.

Web applications make it possible to distribute applications widely, including the ability to allow public access at reasonable cost. But at the same time, the application is maintained centrally at the server with no pieces of the application actually residing on the client side. What this means is that updates to an application don't require updating any part of the client's system. All that's required is a code change on the back end application, and all clients are automatically updated.

## Open Standards

The Internet is based on open standards. While there are quite a few struggles to extend standards and push them into company-specific directions, by and large, all of the protocols and tools used are standards based and supported by a wide variety of products and vendors. This is extremely important as it allows different companies to build tools that can interact with one another.

In addition, the open nature of the Internet is forcing companies into trying to extend standards in non-proprietary ways. A good example is the struggle of extending HTML (Hypertext Markup Language) that is used for displaying output in Web browsers. The two leading browser vendors, Microsoft and Netscape, are the standard-bearers in this field; and both are trying to extend the standard beyond its current limitations. But unlike the past when extensions were often proprietary, both of these companies are making the specifications widely available for developers to start using them immediately, encouraging other browser vendors to pick up on the new extensions for use in their own products.

Many of the protocols used on the Internet are modular and relatively simple to implement. This means it's easy to integrate many of the connectivity features that the Internet provides with readily available protocols. Specs are publicly maintained and accessible over the Internet. Since most of the protocols used are simple to implement, a wide variety of tools is available to use with these protocols; or you can easily roll your own if you need specialized functionality.

All of this openness adds up to better interoperability of tools as well as immediate accessibility to the tools that are required to build advanced Internet applications.

## Limitations of Building Web-Based Applications

While the previous sections point out the glowing advantages of building Internet-based applications, it's important to keep in mind that this is a very young and still developing field. Most of the dedicated Web-only development tools that are available today are fairly limited. There are lots of solutions available to hook just about any kind of data to the Web, but the complexity or limits of the tools can often get in the way of building applications that provide the full breadth that a traditional stand-alone application can provide.

In this chapter, we will show you how you can use Visual FoxPro as a database back end that gets around some of the Web application development limitations. Still, there are limitations in interface design that will require a change from the way you might be accustomed to building applications with visual tools like Visual FoxPro.

For example, HTML and the distinct client/server interface that disallows direct access to the data from the Web browser requires building applications with the different mindset of server-based programming. HTML input forms are more reminiscent of the dBASE II days when you had to hand-code fields and had no immediate control over user input via field-level validation. All access to the data happens on the server end, so that each request for a data update requires calling the Web server and requesting it to update the current HTML page with new data. In essence, this process requires reloading of the currently displayed page with the updated information.

Web-based form input is transaction-based, where you first capture all the information entered in the Web browser, and then validate the input and return an error message relating to an entire input form on the Web server. While new HTML extensions provide more control over input forms and active HTML display, the fact that the Web browser has no direct access to data makes it difficult to build truly interactive input forms that can immediately validate input against the database rules. To update the input form or even send back an error message, the original form has to be submitted, sent to the server, and then be redrawn from scratch with the updated information retrieved from the server.

Another limitation to consider is that Web applications cannot easily print reports. All you can do is display a page as HTML and then print the result, but there's no full-fledged report writer to create banded and subtotaled reports. Instead of a report builder you have to hand-code.

While these limitations are real and something you have to consider when building Web-based applications, Microsoft and Netscape are addressing these issues with extensions to HTML that are starting to look more like the fully event-driven forms that we are used to with tools like Visual FoxPro. The not-too-distant future will bring tools to paint input forms with a form designer and allow attaching of validation code directly to fields. However, the lack of direct data access will likely continue to be a major difference between Web and desktop applications.

Limitations or not, the Web is hot and those who have taken the first step toward building Web-based applications rarely look back as the advantages of the distributed environment and the easy scalability that goes with it often outweigh the disadvantages just mentioned.

# Database Development on the Web

With the popularity of the World Wide Web, the need for database application development on the Web is exploding as more and more companies are realizing that to make maximum use of their Web sites, dynamic display of database information is essential to provide interesting and up-to-date content.

This section discusses the logistics of building database applications that run over the Web and how it affects the application development process and what's required to make it happen.

## Tools You Need to Develop Web Applications

To build applications to run over the World Wide Web, you need the following components:

- **The TCP/IP network protocol.** TCP/IP is available as an installable network protocol on Windows NT and Windows 95. Web servers require TCP/IP to receive requests. Although TCP/IP must be loaded on your machine, either bound to a network adapter or the dialup adapter (if you don't have a network adapter), you do not need a network to test a Web application. All components, Web server, Web browser, and your application can run on the same machine if required.

- **A Web server, preferably running on Windows NT Server.** A Web server is a piece of software that is responsible for serving Web content, as well as acting as an application server that handles routing requests to the appropriate helper applications. While Windows NT Server is the preferred platform for best performance and stability of Web services, you can also use Windows 95 or NT Workstation with many Web servers (the big exception is Microsoft's Internet Information Server).

- **A Web connector application.** A connector or script gets called by the Web server whenever it needs to generate dynamic output. A script is essentially an EXE or DLL application that runs in response to a Web request. A connector is a specialized script that passes on the requested information to a separate back end application like Visual FoxPro.

- **A fast (120MHz or better) Pentium-based machine with 32M or more of RAM.** Whereas you can get by with less, this configuration is a suggested minimum when running a Web server and a back end application. Web servers are resource-hungry services that suck up CPU cycles and memory. For optimal performance of high-volume online applications, multi-processor machines provide the best load distribution by allowing separate CPUs to handle the Web services and the database access.

- **A Web browser.** The Web browser is your interface to a Web-based application. Use either Microsoft's Internet Explorer (as all the examples here do) or Netscape, as both of these are the standard-bearers providing the most advanced features and 90+% of the browser market.

The preceding list provides a roadmap of tools you need to build Internet applications and test them on your local machine or over a local network. In addition, you must deal with the issue of connecting the application to the Internet. Several options are available:

- **Direct connection.** Your company or client might already have a direct connection to the Internet via a Frame Relay connection or full T1 or T3 access. This is the ideal setup when developing Internet applications, but also a very pricey one both in terms of the connection fees for Internet hookup as well as the network hardware requirements. A T1 runs from $2,500 to $5,000 monthly, depending on the type of connection.

- **Colocation.** Many Internet Service Providers (ISPs) allow you to stick a machine onto their network and provide you direct Internet access. You can then run your own Web server or use the machine only as a database server. In order for this to work, you must make sure you get full remote-control access to your machine. Typical fees for this service run between $300-$500 a month.

■ **Low-speed connection.** When getting started, it might be sufficient to hook your site into an ISP's network via a low-speed connection via Frame Relay, ISDN, or even modem hookup. You need to get a permanent connection from your site to one of the ISP's modems. You're usually responsible for the cost of your own hardware, the extra hardware required on the ISP's end (i.e., extra modem or router), plus the telco's monthly line charges. In addition, there's usually a surcharge on the ISP's monthly access charge over a standard dialup account. With ISDN, this can be set up as cheaply as $150 to $300 a month plus hardware expenses and one-time set-up fees.

## Running Applications over the Web

Database connectivity over the Internet is essentially a specialized form of client/server: You have a front end (the Web browser) that accesses a back end (the Web server), which, in turn, is connected to the application that provides the database access. The front end and the back end are connected via an Internet connection, which in most cases will be the World Wide Web and HTTP (Hypertext Transfer Protocol). Figure 19.2 shows the relationship between the Web browser and Web server.

**FIGURE 19.2**
The Web server is responsible for data access using server extensions, while the browser is responsible for display of output.

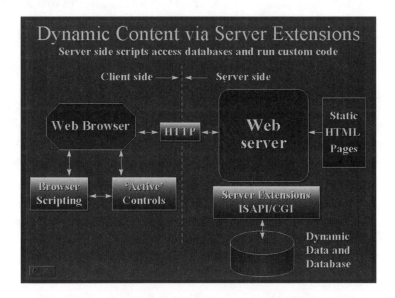

When you look at the diagram, keep in mind the clear distinction between the client and server sides—note the distinct line between the two! The Web browser has no direct access to the data, while the Web server on the other end has no direct access to the interface presented to the user. Think of the Web browser as the interface and the Web server as the database/application server. All interaction between the two is accomplished via a predefined protocol and transaction-based requests.

**Web Browsers Get Smart: Scripting and Active Controls**   On the browser side, you can see the Browser Scripting and Active Control options. Browser scripts are client-side browser extensions like Netscape's JavaScript and Microsoft's VBScript that provide programmable control over the browser's interface. These scripting languages provide additional control over the Form user interface used for input as well as provide programmable features for generating the HTML output—in essence, browser-side scripting provides logic smarts to the browser. Remember, though, there's no access to data from the browser.

Active controls refer to external controls that can be called by HTML pages and can be controlled by browser scripts. These controls can be automatically downloaded over the Web. In this context, active controls include Java applets and ActiveX custom controls (special-purpose, lightweight OLE controls that contain the logic to download and install themselves over the Internet) that can be executed or called by the scripting engines provided in the Web browser. Scripting languages provide the basic interface programmability, while the active controls can provide high-performance, optimized, and operating-system-specific features to a Web browser. Many multimedia-related tools and controls are implemented as active controls; and, in the future, we will likely see controls that match common GUI interface controls, such as popup calendars for date validations, shipping rate calculators, and so on.

But even these high-powered controls do not have direct access to the data that resides on the server.

**The Web Server: Providing the Link to Application and Database Connectivity**   On the other end of the Internet sits the Web server. When dealing with applications running over the Internet, the Web server acts as the intermediary that negotiates access to the application and database. The Web server on its own knows nothing about applications, but instead calls helper applications known as server scripts to perform this task for it.

The flow goes something like this: The Web browser requests access to data by sending a request to execute a script on the server side. A script is essentially a program that runs on the Web server machine in response to a hyperlink hit or the click on an HTML form button. Scripts can either be EXE files following the CGI (Common Gateway Interface) protocol, or a server-side API interface such as ISAPI (Internet Server API), which is available with Microsoft's Internet Information Server. The API level DLLs that are called in response to script links provide much better performance than the EXE-based CGI scripts because they are loaded in memory as in-process DLLs that don't need to be re-loaded on each hit.

Keep the server-side script concept in mind, as all dynamic Web access is accomplished by calling scripts. Don't confuse *server-side scripts* with scripting languages like JavaScript or VBScript either on the client or server side. Scripts in this context are external applications called by the Web server. These scripts can either be fully self-contained or can be used as connectors to call other applications such as Visual FoxPro to handle the database access, application logic, and the output display.

With each Web request, the browser makes available some information about itself: the browser type, its Internet address, along with any field values defined on an input form, and passes this information along to the Web server. When calling a server-side script, this information is passed to the script along with additional information the Web server makes available about itself. The script is then responsible for running its processing task and generating Web server-compliant output. The processing task could be anything from running a database query, adding records to a table, or simply sending back a plain HTML response page that shows the time of day.

Whenever a server-side script executes, it runs its own custom processing; but it is always required to return a response back to the Web server. In most cases, the response is an HTML document that displays the results of the request: the result of a query or a confirmation or error page stating the result status of the request that was just processed. While HTML output is the most common, other responses can also be sent such as a request to authenticate a user, a redirection to send a user to another location, or a trigger to display a standard Web server error message.

Typically, a server script provides the following three functions:

- Retrieves information from the Web browser, the Web server, and HTML form variables.
- Builds the actual request logic. Usually this means running a query, inserting records into a table, handling business rule validations, and so on.
- Generates the output. In most cases, this will be HTML output, but you can also generate requests for authentication, redirect the user to a different page, or generate an error page.

Keep these three points in mind because flexibility in handling each of these tasks is important when choosing a tool with which to build Web applications.

## How Visual FoxPro Fits In

Visual FoxPro makes for an excellent platform for building back end applications due to its extremely fast data retrieval speed against local data, its flexibility when accessing remote data, and its powerful object-oriented, database-oriented language, which is ideal for programming complex data access and business rule logic.

Please note that to standardize this text, the following examples all use the Microsoft Internet Information Server. Some of the tools to be described work with other Web servers; we will point out what servers are supported.

**N O T E** The rest of this chapter will focus on hooking Visual FoxPro databases to Microsoft's Internet Information Server (IIS), which is part of the operating system in Windows NT Server. Although some of the tools that will be mentioned work with other Web servers, we choose to standardize our discussion on IIS because it is built into Windows NT Server, which provides the ideal platform for hosting Web servers. Version 4.0 of Windows NT Server ships with this Web server; a version for Windows NT Server 3.51 can be downloaded for free from Microsoft's Web site (**http://www.microsoft.com/Infoserv/**). ■

Following are several mechanisms available for accessing Visual FoxPro data over the Web:

■ Access data via ODBC and a Web-server-based tool like the Internet Database Connector or ColdFusion.

■ Use a Visual FoxPro OLE server to respond to Web requests.

■ Use a Visual FoxPro application as a data server to process Web server requests.

ODBC-based tools are easy to set up and get started with and provide integrated solutions that are closely tied to the Web server. However, ODBC is comparatively slow when running against local data like Visual FoxPro and does not scale well if your server load gets heavy.

Using Visual FoxPro on its own for serving Web requests has distinct advantages over ODBC, as you get a significant database speed improvement and much better flexibility when building Web back ends using the full functionality of the FoxPro language.

To run Visual FoxPro as a stand-alone back end tool, Visual FoxPro must act as a data server, an application that is preloaded in memory waiting for requests. This is necessary to provide timely response to requests without having to incur the overhead of loading the entire Visual FoxPro runtime on each incoming hit. A data server can be implemented in a variety of ways, whether it's as a stand-alone application, an OLE server, or a DDE server. We will discuss several methods in the following sections.

## Why You Should or Shouldn't Use Visual FoxPro

There are a couple of things to keep in mind when using Visual FoxPro as a database back end.

The following are advantages of using Visual FoxPro:

Part IV
Ch
19

- Extremely fast data engine. ODBC does not even come close to matching Visual FoxPro's native speed.

- Flexible language to build complex business logic using a real database development tool rather than a general purpose scripting language.

- Object-oriented nature allows building an easily reusable framework for processing requests.

- Unlike ODBC with local data, Visual FoxPro applications can be scaled across the network.

The biggest advantage of using Visual FoxPro as the database back end is flexibility. Visual FoxPro is a high-end database tool, and you can take advantage of all the language and database functionality provided in it to create your Web application logic. You won't be limited by a cryptic general purpose scripting language, and there's no learning curve for new syntax (well, okay, you'll have to learn a little about HTML no matter how you slice it).

On the other hand, keep in mind the following disadvantages of using Visual FoxPro as a Web back end:

- Visual FoxPro is single-threaded; requests require multiple Visual FoxPro sessions to process simultaneously.

- Visual FoxPro is essentially detached from the Web server and requires a separate maintenance scheme.

At first glance, these limitations seem major. However, they are easy to overcome with proper implementation of the data server. Visual FoxPro's single-threaded nature can be handled by running multiple simultaneous sessions of the data server, which essentially simulates a multithreaded environment. While speed will decrease for simultaneous requests occurring in this fashion, the same is true for true multitasked tools. The CPU load is the real performance factor; and whether you're running one or ten simultaneous sessions or threads, the actual load that a single server can handle depends on the number and power of the CPUs available to handle that load.

The latter problem of maintenance is one to carefully consider. Running Visual FoxPro as a data server means that the application can respond to requests only while it's up and running—crash the server and you won't process requests. It's extremely important to build bulletproof code that can recover from any error and continue running.

Running Visual FoxPro as its own server also means that a separate startup procedure is required. It's easy enough to stick a shortcut to the data server into the system startup folder to have it load automatically when the system is rebooted; but unless you have the system log in automatically, some manual intervention for logging in is required. Unlike

Web servers, Visual FoxPro cannot easily be run as a system service. Running a Visual FoxPro OLE Server provides some automation of this process as the OLE server is treated as a system component that's accessible directly from the system.

Updating code or data also translates to shutting down the data server, and that means either physical access to the machine or accessing it via remote-control software such as pcAnywhere to make the changes online. With OLE servers, the Web server might need to be shut down to handle code updates.

For in-house Web installations, the latter points won't be much of a problem. However, these issues can be especially problematic if you plan to install your application on a third-party Internet Service Provider's network, as this will in essence mean that you get extensive security rights to access your data server. ISPs can be very touchy about what goes on their network and who is given access to network resources.

## The Internet Database Connector

*Requires Microsoft Internet Information Server Web Server*

The first and most straightforward method to access FoxPro data is one of the ODBC-based tools that is available with the Internet Information Server. IIS ships with the Internet Database Connector (IDC), which is a simple script-based tool that allows accessing Visual FoxPro tables or any other ODBC-accessible data source. Output is accomplished via a simple HTML-like scripting language that can be used to display the results from a SQL statement (SELECT, INSERT, UPDATE, DELETE, and so on).

**N O T E** The Internet Database Connector uses SQL syntax that follows the ODBC SQL guidelines, which vary slightly from the Visual FoxPro SQL implementations. For example, you cannot call FoxPro's built-in functions from the SQL command line, but instead have to use the ODBC/Transact SQL equivalent syntax. ■

To set up the Internet Database Connector for use with a FoxPro database or directory of data files, start by configuring an ODBC datasource using the Visual FoxPro ODBC driver:

1. Bring up the 32-bit ODBC manager from your taskbar menu.
2. Click the System DSN (button on the bottom of the list window of installed drivers). It's extremely important that you add the new ODBC datasource using the system data source rather than a standard ODBC source, or else IIS will fail to find your datasource and exit with an error! Figure 19.3 shows the resulting dialog.
3. Add a new datasource for the Visual FoxPro ODBC driver. For the demo, name the new data source QueVFP and point the driver at the directory with the sample data.

**FIGURE 19.3**

Create a new System DSN using the Visual FoxPro ODBC driver and point it at the directory that contains your DBC or directory containing free tables.

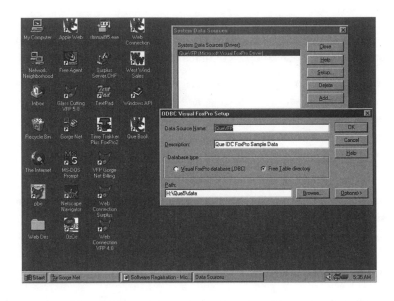

Once the ODBC driver is installed, you're ready to create the scripts that allow you to access this data. Take a look at Figure 19.4; see how the data travels from Web browser to Web server and your data and back to the browser.

**FIGURE 19.4**

An HTML form link accesses the .IDC script containing the query information. Results are displayed in the .HTX document.

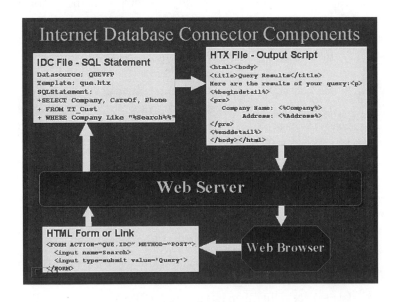

All in all, a request generated via the IDC requires three files: an HTML file that contains the link or form that launches the script, the .IDC file responsible for defining the query parameters, and the .HTX HTML file template that is used to display the output. The example provided here is extremely simple but should serve to illustrate the various pieces of the database connector.

The IDC and HTX files need to be placed into a directory that has been set up for execution rights in the IIS Service Manager application. By default, IIS assigns a **/scripts** directory for server scripts, but it's usually a good idea to create a separate directory for each of your applications. My example below uses a **/que** directory for this. To create this directory:

1. Bring up the IIS Service Manager.
2. Create a new Virtual Directory on the Directory tab (see Figure 19.5) of the Service Manager by clicking <u>A</u>dd.
3. Set the directory to the physical DOS path of the script directory that you are creating.
4. Set the Alias to the name that you would like to use as part of your URL. For example, **/que** translates to a full URL of **http://servername.com/que/**.
5. Make sure you set the Execute checkbox to allow the server to execute a script in this directory!
6. Read access is optional. If you place HTML files in this directory as well, check the Read checkbox.

**FIGURE 19.5**

Setting up a virtual directory involves mapping a physical directory to an alias that you can use over the Web. To run scripts from this directory, set the Execute Checkbox.

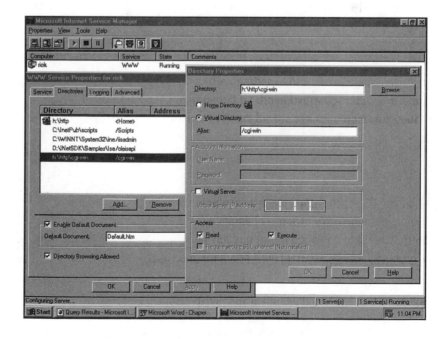

Once you've got the script directory set up on the server, you can get to work and call the HTML page. The HTML form that captures input from the user looks like this:

```
<HTML><BODY>
<FORM ACTION="/cgi-win/QUE.IDC" METHOD="POST">
  Enter Name to Lookup: <input name=Search size=20><br>
  <input type=submit value="Retrieve Names"></FORM>
</BODY></HTML>
```

The script is fired off by the ACTION tag of the input HTML Form. Here, we're retrieving input from the user and storing it to an HTML variable named *Search*.

---

### Running Server Scripts

You can also run an IDC script from an HREF link: `<A HREF="QUE.IDC?">Run Query</a>`

Note the trailing question mark when running in this fashion. The ? is required to tell the browser that the link is a script. Without the question mark, some browsers may attempt to download the script and display it.

The question mark serves as a delimiter to signify the end of the executable and the beginning of the *query string*, or the parameter list. You can pass additional parameters on the URL that can be evaluated inside of the script as if they were entered on a form:

`<A HREF="QUE.IDC?UID=00001&Name=Rick">`

These values can be retrieved in the .IDC file by using %UID% or %Name%.

---

When the user clicks the Retrieve Names button on this form, the QUE.IDC script is called. Behind the scenes, IIS calls an ISAPI DLL called httpodbc.dll that handles the routing, parameter translation, and evaluation of the IDC and HTX script files. The IDC script file contains all the parameters that are related to the query to run:

```
Datasource: QUEVFP
Template: que.htx
SQLStatement:
+SELECT Company, Careof, Phone
+ FROM TT_Cust
+ WHERE Company Like "%Search%%"
+ ORDER BY COMPANY
```

You can specify a host of other parameters that allow you to limit the number of records returned from the query, specify the name of the user for database access, and provide default parameter values.

You can also run multiple SELECT statements by including multiple SQL statement clauses in the .IDC file (multiple queries work only with IIS 2.0, which ships with NT 4.0), but keep in mind that these run one after the other immediately without allowing you to tie logic to them. If you're using SQL server, you can also execute Transact SQL syntax here and execute stored procedures.

The most important options are used in the preceding .IDC file: datasource name, the SQL Statement, and the name of the .HTX template file that is loaded when the query completes.

Output from this query is created with the .HTX template file, which is essentially an HTML document that contains embedded field values. The .HTX file looks like this.

**Listing 19.1    Que.htx: The HTX Template File that Generates the HTML Output**

```
<html><body>
<title>Query Results</title>
<h2>Internet Database Connector Result</h2>
<HR>
Here are the results of your query for company search string:
➥<b><%idc.search%></B>
<p>

<TABLE CELLPADDING=5 BORDER=2 WIDTH=95% ALIGN=CENTER>
<TR><TH>Company</TH><TH>Contact</TH><TH>Phone</TH>

<%begindetail%>
<TR><TD><%Company%></TD><TD><%CareOf%></TD><TD><%Phone%></TD></TR>
<%enddetail%>

</TABLE>
</body></html>
```

**FIGURE 19.6**

The output from the query example. The query retrieves the input form's **Search** variable and displays the selected records.

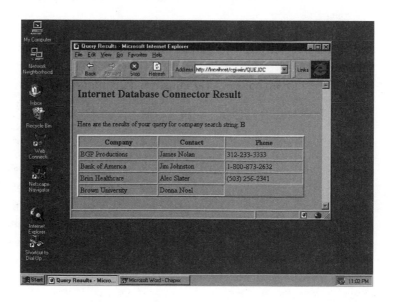

The `<%BeginDetail%>` and `<%EndDetail%>` tags provide a looping structure that runs through the result cursor. Any HTML in between these two tags is repeatedly generated for each of the records in the result set. Field names can be embedded inside of the page using the `<%FieldName%>` syntax that is used in the previous example. There are additional constructs available, such as a conditional `<%IF%>` (which can't be nested, though!). For example:

```
<%if idc.company eq "West Wind Technologies"%>
    <H2>Special Message for West Wind Technologies</H2>
<%else%>
   <H2>Standard Message for <%idc.company%> </H2>
<%endif%>
```

For more detailed information on the .IDC and .HTX format options, you can look in the **\IIS\IISADMIN\HTMLDOCS** directory and search the index on the Database Connector (the actual page that contains this info is in **\IIS\IISADMIN\HTMLDOCS\08_IIS.HTM**).

The Internet database connector provides an easy mechanism for simple access to your Visual FoxPro data. When using this mechanism for accessing your data over the Web, keep the following advantages and disadvantages in mind:

*Advantages:*

- Easy to set up and use.
- Relatively good speed using the Visual FoxPro ODBC driver. While not as fast as local Visual FoxPro data, it is still faster than any other desktop database ODBC driver.
- Ease of maintenance. The script files are fully self-contained and don't require any other application to run.

*Disadvantages:*

- Fairly limited in terms of functionality that can be implemented. The scripting language does not allow for complex logic, and you can't conditionally query the database from within a script.
- Single-transaction-based. Essentially, you can process only a single transaction at a time due to the inability to requery the data from within the script.
- ODBC access does not scale well. You can't offload processing to another machine (at least not with FoxPro data; you can with SQL servers), and multiple simultaneous hits against data can easily overload both the Web server and the ODBC engine.

■ No control over error handling. Database errors display cryptic ODBC message strings that are unsuitable for end users.

The advantage of the Internet Database Connector is that it is well integrated with the Web server and provides an easy way to get started connecting databases to the Web. On the downside, the scripting mechanism is limited in the functionality that is provided when accessing data and creating dynamic HTML output. Furthermore, ODBC is slow compared to running Visual FoxPro natively. ODBC makes good sense when running against remote server data, but provides limited scalability against local data such as FoxPro tables.

## Using Visual FoxPro as a Data Server

ODBC works well for small and simple Web applications; but for better performance and the ultimate in flexibility when creating applications based on FoxPro data, a Visual FoxPro data server is the ticket.

What exactly is a data server? The term implies that Visual FoxPro is used as a server that responds to requests rather than running as an interactive application. While it's possible to run a FoxPro EXE file directly in response to a Web server request, there are several problems with this approach: A Visual FoxPro EXE file takes several seconds to load under the best of circumstances; and loading the EXE directly in this manner causes the application to run invisibly on the desktop, which makes it next to impossible to debug your code should something go wrong. It's much more efficient for Visual FoxPro to be already loaded, waiting for incoming requests from the Web server, and instantly springing to life when a request is received. This always-on state is a requirement for Web applications where fast response time is crucial. Using a data server, it is possible to return data-based page responses in sub-second times.

To provide the data server functionality, it's necessary to use an intermediary piece of software, called a connector, that passes requests from the Web server to Visual FoxPro. These connector applications are usually small library-type routines that are written in C to provide a messaging interface that communicates between the Web server and a Visual FoxPro server that is waiting for incoming requests. Following are descriptions of two different implementations of FoxPro data servers using ISAPI-based connector applications.

Part
IV

Ch
19

# Using FoxISAPI and OLE Servers for Web Applications

*Requires an ISAPI-based Web server (MS IIS, Commerce Builder, Purveyor)*

Visual FoxPro's new capability to create OLE servers has brought about another slick option for implementing Visual FoxPro-based Web applications. What if you could use an OLE server to respond to a request placed from a Web page to handle the data processing and HTML page generation? With a tool called FoxISAPI that's provided with Visual FoxPro, you can do just that. You can find all the required files and an interesting example of an OLE server that makes use of FoxISAPI in \VFP\SAMPLES\SERVER\FOXISAPI.

Before trying out this mechanism, be sure to read this entire section, especially the areas on setting up and creating the OLE server. Configuration is critical in getting FoxISAPI to work correctly.

**How FoxISAPI Works**   FoxISAPI consists of a small connector script DLL that is called directly from an HTML page using a link similar to this:

```
<a HREF="/scripts/foxisapi.dll/
oleserver.myclass.mymethod?UID=1111&Company=Que+Publications">
```

The first thing that happens on a script call is that the FoxISAPI.dll is accessed. This DLL is implemented as an Internet Server API (ISAPI) extension, which is an API that extends Internet Information Server via an In-Process DLL interface. Since ISAPI extensions run in the same address space as the Web server, are multithreaded, and are coded in a low-level compiled language such as C, these extension scripts are extremely fast.

The task of the ISAPI DLL is to provide an OLE automation client that makes calls to your Visual FoxPro OLE server using the class Id (server, class, method) that is passed as part of the URL. The DLL parses out the class string, and makes an OLE Automation call to your OLE server accessing your class method directly. In response, your code should return a compliant result, which in most cases should be an HTML document. Figure 19.7 shows how a request travels from the Web server to your OLE server and back. Notice how FoxISAPI.dll is the mediator that receives both the outgoing script call and the incoming HTML output, sending the output to the Web server for display or processing.

**A Simple Example Server**   The FoxISAPI example provided by Microsoft in your \VFP\SAMPLES\SERVERS\FOXISAPI directory is a good way to check out some of the things you can do with a FoxPro-based data server. But a simpler example might be more adequate in showing how FoxISAPI works. Listing 19.2 demonstrates how FoxISAPI.dll calls a Visual FoxPro OLE server. The full example and a simplified class that handles many of the basic required tasks is included on the CD in FoxISAPI.prg.

**FIGURE 19.7**
FoxISAPI allows
calling OLE server
methods directly via
an HTML script link or
form submision.

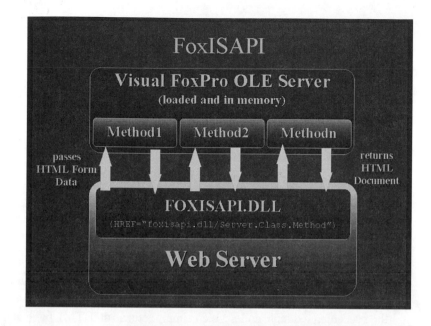

Part
IV
Ch
19

**Listing 19.2   FoxISAPI.PRG: This Snippet Demonstrates a Minimal Response OLE Server Using FoxISAPI**

```
#DEFINE CR CHR(13)+CHR(10)


****************************************************************
DEFINE CLASS QueVFP AS FOXISAPI OLEPUBLIC
****************************************************************


*****************************************************************************
* QueVFP :: HelloWorld
**********************************
*** Function: Minimal response method for handling FoxISAPI call.
*****************************************************************************
FUNCTION HelloWorld
LPARAMETER lcFormVars, lcIniFile, lnReleaseFlag
LOCAL lcOutput

*** HTTP header - REQUIRED on each request!
lcOutput="HTTP/1.0 200 OK"+CR+;
        "Content-type: text/html"+;
        CR+CR

lcOutput=lcOutput+;
"<HTML><BODY>"+CR+;
"<H1>Hello World from Visual FoxPro</H1>"+CR+;
"<HR>The current time is: "+TIME()+CR+;
"This page was generated by Visual FoxPro...<HR>"+CR+;
"</HTML></BODY>"
```

*continues*

---

**Listing 19.2  Continued**

```
RETURN lcOutput
ENDFUNC
* FoxISAPI

ENDDEFINE
* QueVFP
```

---

This example doesn't do much, but it demonstrates the basics of what's required of a method that responds to a call from the FoxISAPI DLL. The idea is this: FoxISAPI calls your OLE server method with three input parameters, so your method must always support these three parameters. The parameters provide all the information made available by the HTML input form as well as Web server and browser stats. You pull the appropriate information from these references in order to do your data processing. For example, you might retrieve a query parameter and, based on it, run a SQL Select statement. To complete the process, your code needs to then return an HTTP-compatible response to the Web server. In most cases, this response is an HTML document, as demonstrated by the preceding example code, which simply returns an HTML page along with the time, so you can assure yourself that the page is actually dynamically generated. Note that the output must include an HTTP header that is created by the first assignment to lcOutput.

Just like the HelloWorld example method, every response method must have three parameters. If your code has fewer than three parameters, the OLE call will fail, generating a FoxISAPI-generated error.

**Table 19.1  FoxISAPI Response Method Parameters**

| Parameter | Contents |
| --- | --- |
| cFormVars | This parameter contains all variable names and their contents in encoded form. |
| cIniFile | FoxISAPI creates an INI file containing Server/Browser variables which are stored in an INI file; the name and path of this file is passed in this parameter. |
| nReleaseFlag | Passed by reference, this variable determines whether FoxISAPI.dll releases the reference to the OLE server. You can set this value in your code and it's returned to the DLL. 0 is the default and means the server is not unloaded; 1 means it is unloaded. |

The first parameter is probably the most important as it contains the name and values of any fields that were filled out on an HTML form. All key/value pairs from an HTML form are returned—fields that are empty simply return an empty value. In typical CGI fashion and because browsers do not support certain characters on the URL line, the string is MIME-encoded using various characters to signify "extended" characters and spaces. Before you can use the string, you typically have to decode it. Here's an example of a string passed in lcFormVars:

```
UserId=000111&BookTitle=Using+Visual+FoxPro
```

Each of the key/value pairs is separated by an & and spaces are converted to + signs. In addition, lower ASCII characters are converted into a hex code preceded by an ampersand. For example, a carriage return would be included as %0D (hex 0D or decimal 13). The FoxISAPI class provided on the CD handles decoding the string for you as well as an easy way to pull an individual value from the string.

Listing 1.2 doesn't use the parameters passed to it, so let's look at another example that does. Listing 1.3 demonstrates how to retrieve the information provided by the Web server using a simple FoxISAPI class provided in FoxISAPI.prg. The code retrieves a couple of form variables passed on the URL of the request and then displays the entire INI file in a browser window for you to examine. Figure 19.8 shows most of the output from the request.

**FIGURE 19.8**

The HTML output from the TestMethod call demonstrates how to retrieve information from the Web server.

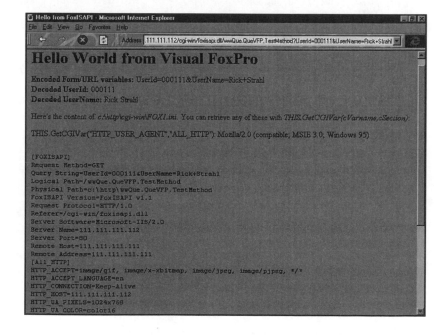

Part

IV

Ch

19

**Listing 19.3 FoxISAPI.prg: This Method Shows How to Retrieve Information Provided by the Web Server**

```
***************************************************************************
* QueVFP :: TestMethod
********************************
FUNCTION TestMethod
LPARAMETER lcFormVars, lcIniFile, lnReleaseFlag
LOCAL lcOutput

*** Decode the Form Vars and assign INI file to class property
THIS.StartRequest(lcFormVars,lcIniFile)

*** Must always add a content Type Header to output first
THIS.HTMLContentTypeHeader()

lcUserId=THIS.GetFormVar("UserId")
lcName=THIS.GetFormVar("UserName")

THIS.SendLn("<HTML><BODY>")
THIS.SendLn("<H1>Hello World from Visual FoxPro</H1><HR>")
THIS.SendLn("This page was generated by Visual FoxPro using FOXISAPI. ")
THIS.SendLn("The current time is: "+time()+"<p>")

THIS.SendLn("<b>Encoded Form/URL variables:</b> "+lcFormVars+"<BR>")
THIS.SendLn("<b>Decoded UserId:</b> "+ THIS.GetFormVar("UserId")+"<br>")
THIS.SendLn("<b>Decoded UserName:</b> " +lcName+"<P>")

*** Show the content of the FOXISAPI INI server/browser vars
IF !EMPTY(lcIniFile) AND FILE(lcIniFile)
   CREATE CURSOR TMemo (TFile M )
   APPEND BLANK
   APPEND MEMO TFile from (lcIniFile)
   THIS.SendLn("Here's the content of: <i>"+lcIniFile+"</i>."+;
               "You can retrieve any of these with <i>"+;
               THIS.GetCGIVar(cVarname,cSection)+"</i>:<p>")
   THIS.SendLn([For example to retrieve the Browser use ]+;
               [THIS.GetCGIVar("HTTP_USER_AGENT","ALL_HTTP"): ]+;
               THIS.GetCGIVar("HTTP_USER_AGENT","ALL_HTTP") )

   THIS.SendLn("<PRE>")
   THIS.SendLn(Tmemo.Tfile)
   THIS.SendLn("</PRE>")
   USE in TMemo
ENDIF

THIS.SendLn("<HR></HTML></BODY>")

RETURN THIS.cOutput
```

The code makes heavy use of the FoxISAPI class' internal methods to simplify retrieving information and generating the output. Table 19.2 shows the public interface to the FoxISAPI class from which the QueVFP class in the examples is derived.

**Table 19.2 FoxISAPI Class Methods**

| Method | Function |
| --- | --- |
| Send(cOutput, llNoOutput)<br>SendLn(cOutput, llNoOutput) | A low-level output routine that simplifies creating HTML output by using a method call. This is also useful for abstracting the output interface in case you want to modify the way output is generated later on. SendLn is identical to Send, but adds a carriage return to the output. |
| StandardPage(cHeader, cBody) | A simplified routine that creates a full HTML page by passing a header and body. The page created includes minimal formatting and a title directive. Both header and body may contain embedded HTML codes that are expanded when the page is displayed. |
| ContentTypeHeader(llNoOutput) | Generates the HTTP header required by FoxISAPI. Generates a default header for HTML documents. REQUIRED for each output page! |
| StartRequest() | Call this method to automatically decode the FormVariable string and set up the internal handling for retrieving form and server variables using the following two methods. REQUIRED for each request that retrieves Form or CGI variables using the internal methods. |
| GetFormVar(cVarName) | Returns the value for the form variable passed as the first parameter. Note, only single variables are returned—there's no support for multiselects. |
| GetCGIVar(cCGIVar,cSection) | Returns variables contained in the INI file that is passed by FoxISAPI. Pass the name of the variable and the section that it is contained in. The default section is FoxISAPI. |
| ReleaseServer() | A full request method that takes the standard 3 request parameters and sets the lnReleaseFlag to 1, thus forcing the FoxISAPI DLL to release the OLE server reference. |

Part
IV

Ch
19

In the Testmethod code, note the calls to THIS.StartRequest and THIS.ContentTypeHeader. StartRequest sets up the internal variable retrieval routines by assigning the input parameters to class properties so they can be easily referenced by the internal methods such as GetCGIVar and GetFormVar. Both of these routines make it easy to retrieve information related to the current request from the Web server's provided information. ContentTypeHeader creates the required header that must be sent back to the Web server in the result output. An HTTP header tells the server what type of content to expect and ContentTypeHeader obliges by providing the proper identification for an HTML document.

HTML output is accomplished by using the class Send method, which abstracts the output. Using this method is easier than concatenating strings manually and also provides the ability to build more complex output mechanisms that are required when your output gets longer than a few thousand characters. Behind the scenes, Send() does nothing more than add the text to a string property of the class. Note that at the exit point, a RETURN THIS.cOutput is used to return the final result text to the FoxISAPI DLL.

The next snippet outputs the original lcFormVars encoded string and then uses GetFormVar() to print the decoded values of the actual values that were passed on the URL. GetFormVar() takes the name of the key as a parameter and returns the decoded value. If the key does not exist or the key is blank, a null string ("") is returned.

CGI variables returned by the server provide information about the server, browser, and the environment. FoxISAPI.dll captures most of the relevant information into an INI file and the code wrapped in the IF statement outputs this file to the HTML page. Figure 19.8 shows the output of the entire page. All of the keys are accessible with the GetCGIVar() method which takes a keyname and section as parameters. For example, to retrieve the name of the Web Server in use, you can use the following code:

```
THIS.GetCGIVar("Server Software ","FOXISAPI")
```

Let's take another look at the customer list example we used with the IDC and see how to implement it with FoxISAPI. Here's the method code that accomplishes the task:

**Listing 19.4   This Sample Method Generates a Customer List Based on a Name Provided on an HTML Form**

```
************************************************************************
* QueVFP :: CustomerLookup
*********************************
FUNCTION CustomerLookup
LPARAMETER lcFormVars, lcIniFile, lnReleaseFlag
```

```
*** Decode the Form Vars and assign INI file to global var
THIS.StartRequest(lcFormVars,lcIniFile)

lcName=THIS.GetFormVar("Name")
lcCompany=THIS.GetFormVar("Company")
lcWhere=""
IF !EMPTY(lcName)
   lcWhere="UPPER(Careof)='"+UPPER(lcName)+"'"
ENDIF
IF !EMPTY(lcCompany)
   IF !EMPTY(lcWhere)
      lcWhere=lcWhere+" AND "
    ENDIF
    lcWhere=lcWhere+"UPPER(Client)='"+UPPER(lcCompany)+"'"
ENDIF
IF !EMPTY(lcWhere)
   lcWhere="WHERE "+lcWhere
ENDIF

SELECT Careof, Company, Address, Phone ;
   FROM (DATAPATH+"TT_CUST") ;
   &lcWhere ;
   INTO Cursor TQuery

IF _Tally <1
   THIS.StandardPage("No matching records found",;
                     "Please enter another name or use a shorter search string...")
   USE IN Tquery
   USE IN TT_Cust
   RETURN THIS.cOutput
ENDIF

THIS.HTMLContentTypeHeader()

THIS.SendLn([<HTML><BODY>])
THIS.SendLn([<H1>Customer Lookup</H1><HR>])

This.SendLn([Matching found: ]+STR(_Tally)+[<p>])

THIS.Send([<TABLE BGCOLOR=#EEEEEE CELLPADDING=4 BORDER=1 WIDTH=100%>]+CR+;
         [<TR BGCOLOR=#FFFFCC><TH>Name</TH><TH>Company</TH><TH>Address</TH>
         ➥</ TR>]+CR)

SCAN
   THIS.Send(;
         [<TR><TD>]+;
         TRIM(IIF(EMPTY(TQUery.Careof),"<BR>",Tquery.CareOf))+[</TD><TD>]+;
         TRIM(IIF(EMPTY(Tquery.Company),"<BR>",Tquery.Company))+[Company</TD><TD>]+;
         TRIM(IIF(EMPTY(Tquery.Phone),"<BR>",TQuery.Phone))+[</TD></TR>]+CR)
ENDSCAN
```

*continues*

**Listing 19.4  Continued**

```
THIS.SendLn([</TABLE><HR>])
THIS.SendLn([</BODY></HTML>])

USE IN Tquery
USE IN TT_Cust

RETURN THIS.cOutput
* CustomerLookup
```

**Setting Up for FoxISAPI**    It's extremely important to correctly set up the Web server, the FoxISAPI.dll script connector, and your Visual FoxPro OLE server to get them to properly run under Windows NT. Windows NT 4.0 especially requires special attention to OLE server access rights and user configuration rights in order to run OLE servers driven by the Web server.

Here are the configuration steps for using FoxISAPI with Internet Information Server under NT 4.0:

- Start by creating your public OLE server. See the following section for details on server creation. Make sure you compile the server as OLEPUBLIC and that you Create OLE Id for this server in the project's build options. If you run this server on an external machine, make sure you register the server on the Web server machine by using the *regserver* commandline switch on an EXE server or by running *regsvr32 yourdll.dll* against a DLL server. If you haven't created a server yet, you can copy and compile the wwQue example server from the CD. Before going any further with configuration, make sure your OLE server works correctly by instantiating it from the Visual FoxPro command window and testing the output!

- Copy FoxISAPI.DLL from the CD's CHAPTER19\CODE\FOXISAPI directory (or get the latest version at **http://www.microsoft.com/vfox**) to your \INETINFO\ SCRIPTS directory. Double-check and make sure that the **/scripts** directory is set up as a virtual directory in the IIS service manager and that the directory has "Execute" rights set on it.

- Make sure that your IUSR_XXXXX account is properly set up both in the IIS service manager as the default for the anonymous user and that this user exists in your user manager as a guest account. This account is for every Web user that accesses your Web server.

- If you are building an EXE-based OLE server, you have to run DCOMCNFG.EXE in your \WINNT40\SYSTEM32 directory. This utility sets the access rights for OLE servers in your system. Start by setting the selections on the Default Properties tab:

Enable DCOM and set Default Authentication to *Connect* and Default Imperson-ation to *Identify* (both of these are the default). On the Default Security tab, add the IUSR_XXXX account to the Access and Launch permission button lists. If you compile your server on the same machine as the Web server, you have to run DCOMCONFG *every time you recompile your program*. A faster alternative is to build the server on another machine and simply copy it to the server as this does not update the server's CLSIDs on the server. This DCOM configuration step is extremely important!!!

■ If you have created an EXE server and registered it, find it on the DCOMCNFG Applications tab. The name of the *class* should be found on this page. In the previous examples, the classname is QueVFP. Select it and click on Properties, then the Identity tab. Set the radio button to Interactive User, and then click Apply. This allows the server to access system libraries.

■ Start up the Web server if it isn't running already.

■ Start up your Web Browser and type: **http://localhost/scripts/foxisapi.dll/ wwque.quevfp.helloworld?**

**Deciding What OLE Server Instancing to Use**   Whenever you build an OLE Server, one of the important issues you need to deal with is server instancing. In Web applications, instancing is even more critical as timing and freeing up of the server for quick handling of requests are crucial to provide adequate Web performance.

Visual FoxPro is a single-threaded application and as such can handle only one request at a time. OLE servers, even Multiuse servers, are no different. If an OLE server is busy, it cannot handle another request until it finishes. Furthermore, although ISAPI DLLs are multithreaded, FoxISAPI blocks simultaneous OLE server access in its code to prevent Visual FoxPro from taking more than one request at a time.

Part
**IV**

Ch
**19**

Your instancing options are to use:

■ In-Process DLL Servers. This is the fastest implementation of an OLE server as it runs In Process of the Web server. Requests to the OLE server are queued. You can run only one DLL-based OLE server on a single machine! If you try to load a second DLL-based server, it will fail. DLL servers cannot be shut down unless the Web server is stopped. A crash in the OLE server DLL will likely bring down the Web server.

■ Multiuse EXE Server. This Out-of-Process OLE server creates a single, reusable instance of an OLE server. Slightly slower than a DLL-based server, as the server runs externally to the Web server. But since the instance stays loaded, there's no penalty for load time once it is loaded. Requests are queued, but you can run multiple *different* Multiuse servers (would require separate FoxISAPI.dll files since each OLE server call blocks additional OLE calls).

■ Singleuse EXE Server. This is the slowest server that forces a full load for each instance of a server. Speed is noticeably slower than the DLL or Multiuse servers, but multiple servers can load simultaneously. While this option provides simultaneous access, keep in mind that FoxISAPI actually serializes requests, so you can't even take advantage of the multiple server feature. Because of this and the slow load time, this option is not recommended. If you do use this method, keep a session of the VFP runtime loaded with an idle application. Once the runtime is in memory, startup speed can be reduced substantially.

The bottom line is that you should stick to DLL or Multiuse servers. DLLs provide the best speed but they are volatile as a crash in the OLE server can crash the entire Web server and will require a server shutdown. Multiuse servers probably offer the best compromise between performance and flexibility. Speed for these Multiuse servers is excellent and it is possible to shut them down without shutting down the Web server.

One major limitation for FoxISAPI to keep in mind is that you are limited in scalability. If you outgrow a single instance of your OLE server, FoxISAPI can't easily offload requests to another server. FoxISAPI can handle only one OLE Automation call at a time. It is possible to call *different* OLE servers simultaneously by making copies of FoxISAPI.dll and using a different name to call specific Multiuse OLE servers—essentially one ISAPI DLL per OLE server. But even using this workaround, you can't call the same server simultaneously.

As long as your needs can be served by a single machine and a single OLE server called serially, FoxISAPI provides a fast, efficient, and easily implemented interface to your FoxPro applications.

## Using Web Connection for Web Applications

*Requires ISAPI or Windows CGI-based Web server (MS IIS, Commerce Builder, Website, Purveyor for NT)*

FoxISAPI provides an easy, speedy interface for creating Web applications. But for maximum flexibility and scalability, a stand-alone Web application that runs as a data server can provide much better scalability, maintenance, and debugging functionality. FoxISAPI is limited to a single OLE server of the same type for handling like requests, which can be a serious limitation on busy sites. In contrast, when running a stand-alone Visual FoxPro application, it is possible to run multiple instances of Visual FoxPro to provide an imitation of multithreading for a Visual FoxPro-based Web application. Running only two sessions, I have tested up to 120,000 database requests per day on a single dual-processor Pentium Pro machine on a live site. With a tool like Web Connection, it's even possible to further scale the application to multiple machines across a network for even greater scalability by having remote nodes handle data processing over the network.

To provide working examples of how you can hook FoxPro code to process requests from a Web server, this section describes how to build Web applications using a third-party tool called Web Connection. A shareware version of the software is included on the Companion Disc (/WConnect) with which you can examine and check out the examples. To install, create a WCONNECT directory and unZIP the ZIP file with the /d switch to restore the directory tree.

Web Connection is a developer tool that provides a framework for connecting a Web server to Visual FoxPro. The framework provides many important features for developing industrial-strength Web applications—the ability to create external HTML pages with embedded FoxPro expressions to allow working with HTML designers, robust error handling and logging, automatic logging of Web hits, as well as an easy interface to retrieve information from and output HTML to the Web server.

Unlike FoxISAPI, which uses OLE as its messaging medium, Web Connection uses a file-based connector approach to communicate with the Web server. Figure 19.9 shows how data flows from the Web browser to the Web server to Visual FoxPro and your code.

Part
IV

Ch
19

**FIGURE 19.9**
With Web Connection, Visual FoxPro acts as an active server waiting for incoming requests from the Web server, responding by executing FoxPro code and generating an HTML page.

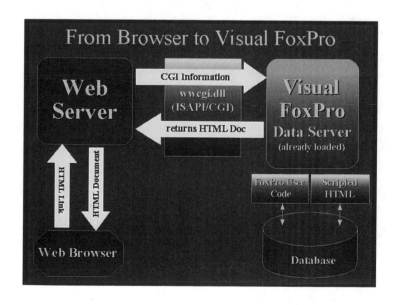

**From Web Server to Visual FoxPro** A typical request starts off on the Web browser where the user clicks either a hyperlink or the submit button of an HTML input form:

```
<A HREF="/cgi-win/wwcgi.dll?Test_Page">Simple CGI Test</A>
```

The wwcgi.dll script captures the information that the Web server and Web browser make available. Like FoxISAPI, Web Connection captures the content information, including the HTML form variables, into an INI file that can be easily accessed with the application framework provided.

Instead of using an OLE server as FoxISAPI does, Web Connection employs a Visual FoxPro application based on a set of framework classes that wait for an incoming message that is provided by the wwcgi.dll. The message comes in the form of a small file that contains the path to the Content INI file the DLL creates for each request. Web Connection picks up the file, retrieves the INI file path, and creates a CGI object that exposes all of the INI file's content.

**N O T E** If you'd rather use OLE messaging similar to FoxISAPI's instead of Web Connection's standard file messaging, you can also use Web Connection's OLE connector, which uses all of the Web Connection framework classes. You can access servers using the OLE object syntax and still use the CGI, HTML, and CGIProcess classes described here for generating your request code.

The OLE connector is included in the ZIP file and documented separately in the wwole subdirectory of the Web Connection installation. ■

The data server, which is responsible for picking up these requests, is implemented as form class running with a timer and retrieves the filename and creates an object that facilitates access to the INI file via a simplified class interface provided by the wwCGI class. Once the Web Connection server has received the message file from the Web server, it takes the newly created CGI object and calls a user-defined function, using the object as a parameter. This function is the hook that acts as an entry point for your own custom Visual FoxPro code.

Now it's your program's turn to take the information available via the CGI object and create HTML output. Your code can run any available FoxPro commands and functions, access class libraries, the data dictionary, views to remote data—the entire language is available to you at this point. Web Connection facilitates creation of the HTML output by providing a CGIProcess class that contains both the CGI object passed to the Process function as well as an HTML object that is preconfigured to output the HTML (in most cases the response is HTML, but you can actually return any HTTP-compliant result) result to the proper output file.

Once the HTML output has been generated, your custom code terminates and control returns to the wwCGIserver object, which, in turn, notifies the Web server that processing is complete. The Web server now takes the output file generated by your code and sends it over the Web for display by the Web browser.

**Setting Up Web Connection**   Setting up Web Connection requires running the included SETUP.EXE application shown in Figure 19.10, which sets up the example programs used for demonstrating the functionality of the product. The setup program's main task is to build the example programs in pages as a template from which you can build your own applications.

 **TIP**   Detailed Web Connection documentation is provided on the Companion Disk. There are detailed instructions for specific Web servers and many hints on Web server configuration.

**FIGURE 19.10**
The Web Connection setup program guides you through setting up the example programs to point at the temp, document, and script paths.

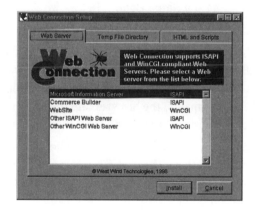

The basic installation steps are as follows:

1. Run SETUP.EXE from the Command window. Continue to review and set all options on the Temp Files and HTML and Scripts tabs of the setup program.

2. Select your Web server from the list of choices. If you choose IIS, Commerce Builder, or Website, the appropriate defaults are pulled from the registry and displayed for you.

3. Set the temporary file path. By default, this path will be your TEMP directory, but it can point anywhere. If you use a generic WinCGI server, make sure you figure out where the server is placing WinCGI temp files (usually your TEMP directory). If you're using NT and IIS, make sure that the INET_USER user account has write access in this directory!

4. Set the HTML document path. This is the path where the example HTML and image files are copied to. You will use this path to access the example pages.

5. Set the script file path. This is the most important aspect in getting Web Connection set up! This path determines where the wwcgi.dll or wwcgi.exe script files are copied to. This directory must be accessible via a Web browser and must have execution rights set. This means this directory must either be off the HTML root directory, or be set up as a virtual directory with a separate mapping in the Web server configuration. Whatever you do, make sure this directory has the Execute flag set on in the IIS control panel directory tab.

6. Click the Install button. Several files are copied and installed on your machine.

7. At the command box, type **DO CGITEST**.

8. Switch to your Web browser and access the demo pages. If you used the default setup options, this should be: **http://localhost/wconnect/wconnect.htm**. Hit the links and you should see activity in the data server form fired up with CGITest.

**A Look at the Components and the Setup Code**   Before we dig into the code, let's describe the components that make up Web Connection:

- **wwCGI.dll.** wwCGI is the script connector that is called by the Web server. wwcgi.dll is a small Internet Server API Extension library that handles the interface with Visual FoxPro. Its task is to let Visual FoxPro know when a request is incoming and pass along all the information the browser and the server are making available. Note that every Web request that accesses Visual FoxPro needs to call this script!

- **wwCGIServer class.** The wwCGIServer class handles requests that are generated by the external wwCGI program. The wwCGIServer class is responsible for receiving incoming CGI requests, decoding them, and passing a CGI object to a user-defined procedure of your choice.

- **wwCGI class.** This class encapsulates all the CGI information made available by the Web server. This includes the contents of form variables and status information about the Web server and the browser that called it. Your processing routine receives a wwCGI object as a parameter for you to use in generating an HTML document in response to the server's request.

- **wwHTML class.** The HTML class provides an optional high-level interface to creating HTML documents by providing a variety of methods that output HTML-formatted strings either directly to file or as string return values. The class supports single-method output of entire tables, display of pages from disk files or memo fields, and embedded FoxPro expressions or code in scripted HTML pages.

- **wwCGIProcess class.** The wwCGIProcess class is a wrapper class that encapsulates the wwCGI and wwHTML objects into an easy-to-use framework that makes creating your own requests as easy as creating a new method in a subclassed version of this class.

In its simplest form, startup of the Web Connection CGI server requires only a handful of lines of code:

**Listing 19.5   CGITest.PRG: Simplified Web Connection Server Startup Code**

```
*********************************************************************
FUNCTION CGITEST
******************
***    Function: Web Connection server startup program.
*********************************************************************
#INCLUDE WCONNECT.H

SET PROCEDURE TO CGIServ ADDITIVE
SET PROCEDURE TO CGI ADDITIVE
SET PROCEDURE TO HTML ADDITIVE
SET PROCEDURE TO CGIPROC ADDITIVE
SET PROCEDURE TO WWUTILS ADDITIVE

*** Starts up the server and gets it ready to poll
*** for CGI requests. Call Process UDF() on a request
oCGIServer=CREATE("wwCGIServer","Process")
IF TYPE("oCGIServer")#"O"
   =MessageBox("Unable to load the CGI Request Server",;
      MB_ICONEXCLAMATION,"Web Connection Error")
   RETURN
ENDIF

oCGIServer.SetCGIFilePath("c:\temp\")

*** This actually puts the server into polling mode - Modal Window
oCGIServer.show()

RETURN
```

The preceding code loads all the required code-based class libraries and simply creates a new wwCGIServer object. All of the actual CGI request retrieval logic is handled transparently by this server class. The only crucial item in this piece of code is the second parameter in the CREATE command. The second parameter, Process, specifies a function of your choice that is called with a wwCGI object parameter each time a request is generated by the Web server. Note the call to the SetCGIFilePath() method. The path specified here is inserted by the SETUP.APP installation program and should point at the location of the CGI temp files generated by each Web request. Once loaded, the form class displays a status window as shown in Figure 19.11.

Part
IV

Ch
19

**FIGURE 19.11**

The data server displays a status window while waiting for requests. Each hit is displayed in the message area.

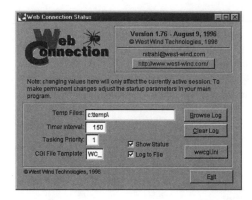

When a request from the Web server hits, the following code is called:

**Listing 19.5   CGITest.PRG: The Process Procedure Is Called By Any Incoming Request**

```
************************************************************************
FUNCTION Process
****************
***   Function: This is the program called by the CGI Server that
***             handles processing of a CGI request.
***
***             This example creates a process class, which
***             simplifies error handling and validation of
***             success. However, you can use procedural
***             code if you prefer.
***       Pass: loCGI -       Object containing CGI information
************************************************************************
LPARAMETERS loCGI

*** Now create a process object. It's not necessary
*** to use an object here, but it makes error handling
*** document and CGI handling much easier!
loCGIProcess=CREATE("MyCGIProcess",loCGI)

*** Call the Process Method that routes request types
*** to methods in the loCGIProcess class
loCGIProcess.Process

*** Debug: See what the input and output files look like
* RELEASE loCGIProcess   && Must release first or file isn't closed
* COPY FILE (lcIniFile) TO TEMP.INI
* COPY FILE (lcOutFile) TO TEMP.HTM
RETURN
```

This procedure is the entry point of the custom FoxPro code that can be executed in response to a Web server request. Note that this function expects a wwcgi parameter when it is called from the Web server.

While this routine creates another layer of abstraction by creating an instance of the CGIProcess class, this step is strictly optional (though highly recommended for ease of use). You could at this point use logic to retrieve the information passed by the Web server and start processing and generating HTML output right here. For maximum ease of use and maintainability, however, the CGIProcess class provides preconfigured settings that let you get to work immediately.

**The Process Class Putting Your Code to Work**   For maximum ease of use and maintainability the CGIProcess class created in the previous code snippet exposes a framework that provides development and debug mode error handling, an easy mechanism for routing requests to your code and preconfigured CGI and HTML objects. With this class, adding your own code becomes as easy as adding a method to a subclassed version of the class.

Let's see how this works. First, here's a typical URL that generates a request in the running Web Connection server:

```
<A HREF="wwcgi.dll?MethodToCall~Parameter1~Parameter2">Que Test Request</a>
```

Note the use of "parameters" on the URL to identify which method in the wwCGIProcess class to call.

When this request runs, the Web Connection server passes the request on to the Process function, which, in turn, creates a subclassed object of the wwCGIServer class as seen in the previous snippet. Once the object is created, its Process method is called.

Here's what a skeleton class definition looks like:

**Listing 19.7   CGITest.PRG: A Skeleton Class Definition for Setting Up Your Own Request Handlers**

```
****************************************************************
DEFINE CLASS webConnectDemo AS wwCGIProcess
****************************************************************
***   Function: This class handles the requests generated by
***             the wconnect.htm form and its results. The
***             class implementation makes error and output
***             doc handling much cleaner
***             Subclassed from a generic wwCGIProcess class
***             handler which provides error handling and
***             HTML and CGI object setup.
```

*continues*

**Listing 19.7 Continued**

```
**************************************************************
*** Properties defined by wwCGIProcess Parent Class
*** -----------------------------------------------
*** oCGI=.NULL.
*** oHTML=.NULL.
*** Methods defined by wwCGIProcess Parent Class
*** -----------------------------------------------
*** Init(oCGI)      && Initializes and checks HTML and CGI objects
*** Process         && Virtual Method that is always overridden used to route
                            ↪requests
*** Error           && Handles errors that occur in the Process code
*** ErrorMsg(cErrorHeader,cMessage)   && Quick Message Display
**************************************************************************
* webConnectDemo :: Process
***************************
***   Modified: 01/24/96
***   Function: This is the callback program file that handles
***             processing a CGI request
***       Pass: THIS.oCGI  Object containing CGI information
***     Return: .T. to erase Temp File .F. to keep it
**************************************************************************
FUNCTION Process
LOCAL lcParameter

*** Retrieve first 'parameter' off the URL
lcParameter=UPPER(THIS.oCGI.GetCGIParameter(1))

DO CASE
   *** Call the method if it exists
   CASE !EMPTY(lcParameter) AND PEMSTATUS(THIS,lcParameter,5)
     =EVALUATE("THIS."+lcParameter+"()")
   OTHERWISE
     *** Generate Error Response Page
     THIS.ErrorMsg("The server was unable to respond "+;
         "to the CGI request.<br>"+;
         "Parameter Passed: '"+PROPER(lcParameter)+"'...",;
         "This error page is automatically called when a "+;
         "Visual FoxPro code error occurs while processing "+;
         "CGI requests.<p>It uses the wwHTML::HTMLError() method to "+;
         "output two error strings and generic server information, "+;
         "as well as overwriting existing HTML output for this request.")
ENDCASE
RETURN .T.

Function CustomMethod1
 ... Your code here
EndFunc

Function CustomMethod2
  ... Your code here
EndFunc

ENDDEFINE
```

You'll always create a Process method which is used to route incoming CGI requests to the appropriate processing method within the wwCGIProcess subclass. This class can process requests generated by HTML tags with the following format:

```
/cgi-win/wwcgi.dll?Method~Optional+Parameter~Optional+Parm2
```

The method is an identifier that is used in the CASE statement to decide which method to call to process the request. The optional params are any additional parameters that you need to pass along when processing a request. Note that the ~ is used as a parameter separator that is recognized by the wwCGI::GetCGIParameter(ParmNo) method to separate parameters passed on the URL following the ?.

Because of the way the class is designed, it consists almost entirely of your own custom code. The Process method is provided here more for reference than anything else; the code is actually defined in the base class. However, you often will want to override the Process method to use a more complex parameter scheme that allows you to call different classes for request processing (see the CGIMAIN example in the Web Connection samples to see how to call multiple projects from one session).

The main task of the Process method is to route the request by figuring out which method to call. This logic is handled by retrieving the first parameter on the URL, then checking whether a method of that name exists with PEMSTATUS(). If the method exists, the EVALUATE() goes out and executes the method.

**N O T E**   PEMSTATUS() is an extremely powerful function for writing generic code that checks for the existence of class properties and methods. The function provides a mechanism to query all aspects of properties or methods. You can find out Public/Protected status, whether the value was changed from the default, whether the property is read only, and of what type a property is. ■

What all of this does is provide you with an easy mechanism to hook your own code: All you have to do is add a method to your subclassed version of the CGIProcess class, and the code is practically called directly from a URL link.

**Lights, Camera, Action**   So what does the actual code you write to respond to requests look like? Let's take a look at a couple of examples.

For starters, let's use the same simple example we used with the Internet Database Connector:

```
<HTML><BODY>
<FORM ACTION="/cgi-win/wwcgi.dll?CustomerList" METHOD="POST">
  Enter Name to Lookup: <input name=Search size=20><br>
  <input type=submit value="Retrieve Names">
</FORM></BODY></HTML>
```

To respond to this request, let's add a new method to the wwConnectDemo class started previously:

**Listing 19.8   CGITest.PRG: The Customer List Example Using Web Connection**

```
********************************************************************************
* wwConnectDemo :: CustomerList
********************************
***   Function: Returns an HTML table customer list.
********************************************************************************
FUNCTION CustomerList
LOCAL loCGI, loHTML

*** Easier reference
loCGI=THIS.oCGI
loHTML=THIS.oHTML

*** Retrieve the name the user entered - could be blank
lcCustname=loCGI.GetFormVar("Search")

*** Get all entries that have time entries (expense=.F.)
SELECT tt_cust.Company, tt_cust.careof, tt_cust.phone ;
   FROM TT_Cust ;
   WHERE tt_cust.company=lcCustname ;
   ORDER BY Company ;
   INTO CURSOR TQuery

IF _TALLY < 1
   *** Return an HTML response page
   *** You can subclass ErrorMsg to create a customized 'error page'
   THIS.ErrorMsg("No Matching Records Found",;
                 "Please pick another name or use fewer letters "+;
                 "to identify the name to look up")
   RETURN
ENDIF

*** Create HTML document header
*** - Document header, a Browser title, Background Image
loHTML.HTMLHeader("Customer List","Web Connection Customer List",;
                 "/wconnect/whitwav.jpg")

loHTML.SendLn("<b>Returned Records: "+STR(_TALLY)+"</b>")
loHTML.SendPar()
loHTML.SendLn("<CENTER>")

*** Show entire result set as an HTML table
loHTML.ShowCursor()

*** Center the table
loHTML.SendLn("</CENTER>")

loHTML.HTMLFooter(PAGEFOOT)
```

```
USE IN TQuery

ENDFUNC
* CustomerList
```

The logic of this snippet is straightforward. The code retrieves the value entered on the HTML form, runs a query, and then displays as an HTML table.

The important pieces in this code snippet are the uses of the CGI and HTML objects. As you can see, you don't need to create these objects because they are instantiated automatically when the CGIProcess object is created.

The `loCGI.GetFormVar()` method retrieves the single-input field from the HTML form. You can retrieve any field from an HTML form in this manner. Note that method always returns a string. If the form variable is not found, a null string ("") is returned, so it's safe in the preceding example to simply use the result in the query without further checks. The CGI class provides a ton of useful functionality. Here's a list of the most commonly used methods:

| wwCGI Method | Function |
| --- | --- |
| GetFormVar(cFormVar) | Retrieves a field entered on an HTML form |
| GetFormMultiple(aParams) | Retrieves multi-select field selections into an array |
| GetBrowser() | Returns the Browser Id string |
| IsHTML30() | Does the browser support HTML 3.0 extensions like tables |
| IsSecure() | Does the browser support secure transactions |
| GetPreviousURL() | Name of the page that generated this link |
| GetRemoteAddress() | Returns the IP address of the user |
| GetCGIVar(cKey,cSection) | Low-level CGI retrieval routine that allows retrieval of key values that don't have pre-defined methods. The section name defaults to the CGI section in the content INI file. |

Part

IV

Ch

19

The HTML class provides a simple output mechanism for generating HTML code. The class consists of both high-level and low-level methods that aid in creating your result output. At the low level are the Send() and SendLn() methods, which allow you to send string output to the HTML output file. It's entirely possible to generate your HTML output entirely using these two commands.

However, some of the higher-level functions can make life a lot easier. Here are a few of the functions available:

| wwHTML Method | Function |
|---|---|
| Send() | Lowest-level function. All output must go through this method to allow for different output methods. All of the methods in this class call this method for final output. |
| SendLn() | Identical to Send except it adds a carriage return/linefeed at the end. |
| HTMLHeader() | Creates a standard HTML header with a title line, browser window title, background image, as well as providing an easy mechanism to control HTTP headers passed back to the Web server. |
| HTMLFooter() | Adds <HTML><BODY> tags and allows for sending a standard HTML footer for pages. |
| ShowCursor() | Displays all fields of the currently open cursor/table as either an HTML table, or a <PRE> formatted list including headers and a title. |
| ShowMemoPage() | Displays HTML text from either disk file or a memo field contained in a system table (wwHTML.dbf). The file can contain embedded FoxPro character expressions. This function allows you to work with HTML designers for data-driven pages. |
| MergeText() | Merges text by translating embedded text expressions and returning the result. This function is more low level than ShowMemoPage and can be used for partial pages. |
| HRef() | Creates a hotlink. |
| List() | Creates various HTML list types. |
| HTMLError() | Creates an entire HTML page with a couple of text input parameters. Great for quick status displays or error messages. |
| SendMemoLn() | Formats large text fields. |

The preceding example uses ShowCursor() to display the result table with a single line of code. This powerful method takes the currently selected table and parses out the headers and fields, creating an HTML table as output. ShowCursor() has the ability to display custom headers passed into the method as an array and the ability to sum numeric fields.

Another extremely powerful method of the wwHTML class is ShowMemoPage(). This method makes it possible to build external HTML pages stored on disk or in a memo field that can contain embedded FoxPro expressions and even entire code snippets to be evaluated by the Web Connection engine.

Check out this more complex example that provides an interactive guest-book browser. This example centers around a single page that shows a guest-book entry form, which is implemented as a stand-alone HTML document that contains embedded FoxPro fields.

**Listing 19.9  ShowGuest.wc: The HTML Template Page for the Guest Book Application Contains Embedded FoxPro Expressions and Fields**

```
<HTML>
<HEAD><TITLE>West Wind Guest Book Browser</TITLE></HEAD>
<BODY Background="/wconnect/whitwav.jpg">
<p>
<IMG src="/wconnect/toolbar.gif" USEMAP="#entry" border=0, ismap HSPACE=20>
➥</A></TD></A>
<MAP NAME="entry">
  <!--- Image Map Coordinates here --->
</MAP>
<FORM ACTION="wwcgi.dll?ShowGuest~Save~##pcCustId##" METHOD="POST">
<INPUT TYPE="SUBMIT" VALUE="##IIF(pcCustId="NEW_ID","Add Info to","Update")##
➥Guestbook" WIDTH=40>
<p>

##IIF(!EMPTY(pcErrorMsg),[<hr><font color="#800000"><h3>]+pcErrorMsg+[</h3>
➥</font><hr>],"")##

<PRE>
     <b>Entered on:</b>
##IIF(EMPTY(guest.entered),DTOC(date()),DTOC(guest.entered))##

          <b>Name:</b> <INPUT TYPE="TEXT" NAME="txtName" VALUE="##guest. name##"
SIZE="39">    <b>Cust Id:</b> ##pcCustId##
       <b>Company:</b> <INPUT TYPE="TEXT" NAME="txtCompany" VALUE="##guest.company##"
SIZE="39">
          <b>Email:</b> <INPUT TYPE="TEXT" NAME="txtEmail" VALUE="##guest.email##"
SIZE="54">
<b>Checking in from:</b> <INPUT TYPE="TEXT" NAME="txtLocation"
VALUE="##guest.location##" SIZE="54">
</PRE>
<b>Leave a note for fellow visitors if you like:</b><br>
```

Part

**IV**

Ch

**19**

*continues*

**Listing 19.9 Continued**

```
<TEXTAREA  NAME="txtMessage" ROWS=5 COLS=75>##guest.message##</TextAREA>
<PRE>
        <b>Password:</b> <INPUT TYPE="TEXT" NAME="txtPassword"
        ➥VALUE="##pcPassword##" SIZE="8" MAXLENGTH="8"> (required to change
        ➥entry)
</PRE>
<CENTER> <b>##STR(RecCount())## visitors have signed the guestbook.</b><p>
➥</CENTER>
</FORM>
<CENTER>
[<A HREF="/cgi-win/wwcgi.dll?ShowGuest~Top~##pcCustId##">First</A>]
[<A HREF="/cgi-win/wwcgi.dll?ShowGuest~Previous~##pcCustId##">Previous</A>]
[<A HREF="/cgi-win/wwcgi.dll?ShowGuest~Next~##pcCustId##">Next</A>]
[<A HREF="/cgi-win/wwcgi.dll?ShowGuest~Bottom~##pcCustId##">Last</A>]
[<A HREF="/cgi-win/wwcgi.dll?ShowGuest~Add~##pcCustid##">Add Entry</A>]
[<A HREF="/cgi-win/wwcgi.dll?BrowseGuests">Browse Guests</A>]
</CENTER>
<hr>

<IMG SRC="/wconnect/wcpower.gif" ALIGN="LEFT" HSPACE=5 ALT="Powered by Web
➥Connection">
<FONT SIZE=-1><I>Query created by <A HREF="mailto:rstrahl@west-wind.com">Rick
Strahl</A><br>
<A HREF="/wconnect/wconnect.htm">Web Connection demo page</A>
</BODY>
</HTML>
```

You'll notice a bunch of ## ## embedded expressions inside of this HTML page. Between these delimiters you can find FoxPro character expressions that are evaluated by the ShowMemoPage() method. To use ShowMemoPage() in this manner, a Web Connection routine locates the record pointer(s) to the proper locations, then embeds the fields directly into the HTML form. When ShowMemoPage() is then called from code, it evaluates the character expressions and inserts the evaluated string in its place. Errors in expressions are automatically handled with an error string inserted instead.

The expressions can be database fields, variables, FoxPro expressions, even class method calls and User Defined Functions. By storing this page in an externally edited file, it's possible to edit this page visually using an HTML editor like FrontPage or WebEdit. As you might expect, this is easier and more maintainable than making changes inside of the actual FoxPro code. Furthermore, it allows you to design pages that can be edited by HTML designers who don't know anything about database programming.

Following is the entire code for the Guestbook application shown in Figure 19.12. The code is wrapped into two methods that are part of the wwConnectDemo process class started above. This example is lengthy and a bit more complex than the previous one, but it demonstrates a full range of features in a realistic example of a Web application (you can find the code for this and the previous examples in the Web Connection examples).

**FIGURE 19.12**

The Guest Book browser demonstrates how you can build interactive Web pages that act a lot like stand-alone applications.

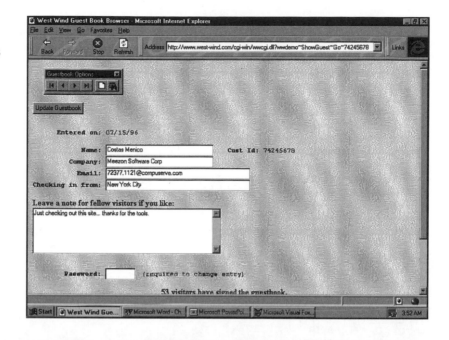

---

**Listing 19.10    CGITest.PRG: A Guest Book Application Implemented in Web Connection**

```
***************************************************************************
* wwConnectDemo :: ShowGuest
*********************************
***   Function: Guest Book Interactive Browser. Note that all this code
***             is not related to creating HTML at all, but rather
***             consists of setting up the logic for navigation and
***             adding editing entries.
***************************************************************************
FUNCTION ShowGuest
LOCAL lcCustId, lcMoveWhere, llError
PRIVATE pcErrorMsg, pcPassword

loHTML=THIS.oHTML
loCGI=THIS.oCGI

*** Retrieve the Operation option (Next, Previous etc.)
lcMoveWhere=UPPER(loCGI.GetCgiParameter(2))

*** Grab the commandline Customer Id
lcCustId=loCGI.GetCGIParameter(3)

pcPassword=""
pcErrorMsg=""
llError=.F.
```

*continues*

Part
**IV**

Ch

**19**

**Listing 19.10 Continued**

```
IF!USED("Guest")
  USE GUEST IN 0
ENDIF
SELE GUEST

IF EMPTY(lcCustId)
  lcMoveWhere="BOTTOM"
ELSE
  IF lcCustId#"NEW_ID"
    LOCATE FOR CustId=lcCustId
    IF !FOUND()
      pcErrorMsg="Invalid Record. Going to bottom of file..."
      lcMoveWhere="BOTTOM"
    ENDIF
  ENDIF
ENDIF

DO CASE
  CASE lcMoveWhere="GO"
    *** Do nothing - just display
  CASE lcMoveWhere="NEXT"
    IF !EOF()
      SKIP
      IF EOF()
        pcErrorMsg="Last Record in table..."
      ENDIF
    ELSE
      GO BOTTOM
    ENDIF

    IF EOF()
      GO BOTTOM
      pcErrorMsg="Last Record in table..."
    ENDIF
  CASE lcMoveWhere="PREVIOUS" AND !llError
    IF !BOF()
      SKIP -1
    ENDIF
    IF BOF()
      pcErrorMsg="Beginning of File..."
    ENDIF

  CASE lcMoveWhere="TOP"
    GO TOP
    DO WHILE EMPTY(guest.name) AND !EOF()
      SKIP
    ENDDO

  CASE lcMoveWhere="BOTTOM"
    GO BOTTOM
    DO WHILE EMPTY(guest.name) AND !BOF() AND !EOF()
      SKIP -1
    ENDDO
```

```
   CASE lcMoveWhere="ADD"
      *** Don't add record - move to 'ghost rec' to show blank record
      GO BOTTOM
      SKIP

      pcErrorMsg="Please fill out the form below and click the Save button..."

   CASE lcMoveWhere="SAVE"
      IF EMPTY(loCGI.GetFormVar("txtName")) AND
EMPTY(loCGI.GetFormVar("txtCompany"))
         THIS.ErrorMsg("Incomplete Input","You have to enter at least a name or
company.")
         USE IN GUEST
         RETURN
      ENDIF

      IF lcCustId="NEW_ID"
         APPEND BLANK
         REPLACE custid with sys(3), ;
                 entered with datetime(), ;
                 password with loCGI.GetFormVar("txtPassWord")
      ELSE
         *** Check password
         pcPassWord=PADR(loCGI.GetFormVar("txtPassWord"),8)
         IF UPPER(guest.password) # UPPER(pcPassword)
            pcErrorMsg="The password you typed does not allow you to change the
            ➥selected entry..."
            pcCustId=guest.custid
            pcPassword=""
            loHTML.ShowMemoPage(HTMLPAGEPATH+"Guest.wc",.T.,"FORCE RELOAD")
            RETURN
         ENDIF
      ENDIF

      REPLACE name with loCGI.GetFormVar("txtName"), ;
              company with loCGI.GetFormVar("txtCompany"),;
              location with loCGI.GetFormVar("txtLocation"),;
              Email with loCGI.GetFormVar("txtEmail"),;
              Message with loCGI.GetFormVar("txtMessage")


      pcErrorMsg="Record saved..."
ENDCASE

*** Prime pcCustId for all links
IF lcMoveWhere#"ADD"
   pcCustId=guest.custid
ELSE
   pcCustId="NEW_ID"
ENDIF
pcPassword=""

pcHomePath=HOMEPATH
```

*continues*

**Listing 19.10 Continued**

```
*** Display GUEST.WC - This HTML form contains the fields and
*** pcErrorMsg variable...
loHTML.ShowMemoPage(HTMLPAGEPATH+"Guest.wc",.T.,;
     IIF(ATC("MSIE",loCGI.GetBrowser())>0,"ForceReload","text/html"))

IF USED("Guest")
   USE IN Guest
ENDIF

ENDFUNC
* ShowGuest

*************************************************************************
* wwConnectDemo :: BrowseGuests
*******************************
***   Function: Shows a list of Guests in table form for the Guest
***             Sample application.
***             This example manually creates the Browse page.
*************************************************************************
FUNCTION BrowseGuests
LOCAL loHTML, loCGI, lcOrder

loHTML=THIS.oHTML
loCGI=THIS.oCGI

*** Retrieve the Order Radio Button Value - Name, Company, Location
lcOrderVal=TRIM(loCGI.GetFormVar("radOrder"))
IF EMPTY(lcOrderVal)
  lcOrderVal="Name"
ENDIF

*** Build an Order By expression
lcOrder="UPPER("+lcOrderVal+")"

*** Create Cursor of all Guests - Note the URL link is
*** embedded in the SQL-SELECT
SELECT [<A HREF="wwcgi.dll?ShowGuest~Go~]+custid+[">]+Name+;
       [</a>] as Guest, ;
   company, location,;
   &lcOrder ;
   FROM Guest ;
   ORDER BY 4 ;
   INTO CURSOR TQuery

*** Set up so we can us HTML tables
loHTML.SetAllowHTMLTables(loCGI.IsNetscape())

loHTML.HTMLHeader("Guest Book
Browser",,BACKIMG,IIF(ATC("MSIE",loCGI.GetBrowser())>0,"Force Reload","text/
➥html"))
loHTML.SendLn([ <FORM ACTION="wwcgi.dll?BrowseGuests" METHOD="POST">])
loHTML.SendLn([ Sort by: <input type="radio" value="Name" name="radOrder"
]+IIF(lcOrderVal="Name","checked=true","")+[>Name ])
```

```
loHTML.SendLn([ <input type="radio" value="Company" name="radOrder"
]+IIF(lcOrderVal="Company","checked=true","")+[> Company   ])
loHTML.SendLn([ <input type="radio" value="Location"
name="radOrder"]+IIF(lcOrderVal="Location","checked=true","")+[> Location<br>])
loHTML.SendLn([ <input type="submit" value="Change Order">])
loHTML.SendLn([ </FORM> <p>])

*** Explicitly set up headers so we only display first 3 cols
DIMENSION laHeaders[3]
laHeaders[1]="Name"
laHeaders[2]="Company"
laHeaders[3]="Location"

*** Display the table
loHTML.ShowCursor(@laHeaders)

loHTML.HTMLFooter(PAGEFOOT)

IF USED("Guest")
   USE IN Guest
ENDIF

ENDFUNC
* BrowseGuests
```

Looking at this code, you can tell that the majority of the logic that takes place has to do with the navigation aspect of the application rather than the actual Web/HTML dynamics; most of the display issues are wrapped up in the external HTML page stored on disk displayed in Listing 19.9.

One difference from a typical Visual FoxPro application is the fact that the application is implemented as a transaction-based process; every action is a request that is processed by a method call. There is no event-driven programming happening here, and all validation is happening at the FoxPro back end with error messages being sent back as a message on a regenerated HTML page. The actual error message is embedded on the HTML page with the following expression:

```
##IIF(!EMPTY(pcErrorMsg),[<hr><font
color="#800000"><h3>]+pcErrorMsg+[</h3></font><hr>],"")##
```

pcErrorMsg is a PRIVATE variable that is set in the code and then passed down to the Evaluation engine in ShowMemoPage(). Since the variable is PRIVATE, ShowMemoPage() can still access the pcErrorMsg variable, as it is still in scope. Thus, any variables that are declared PRIVATE or PUBLIC in the processing method can be accessed in a subsequent call to evaluate an HTML page processed with ShowMemoPage(). ShowMemoPage() (and MergeText(), which is the actual workhorse routine that ShowMemoPage() calls) also makes available the CGI and HTML objects as poCGI and poHTML, respectively. So, you could do something like this inside of the HTML page:

```
##poCGI.GetBrowser()##
##poHTML.ShowCursor(,,,.t.)##
```

The first expression displays the name of the browser used to access the current page. The latter expression displays a table of the currently selected cursor and embeds it inside the HTML page. Note that all of the HTML class methods can also be used to return a string rather than sending output directly to file, so that HTML class methods can be nested inside of each other. All HTML class methods have a logical llNoOutput parameter, which if set to .T. will return the output as string only.

## Working with Web Browsers

Browsers are the interface to the user; and while there's no direct interaction from the Web server back end application to the browser, the application does provide the interface in a non-interactive fashion by sending back an entire HTML page to display.

To give you an idea of just how important Web browsers are, Microsoft is integrating the Web browser interface directly into future versions of its Windows operating system. In Internet Explorer 4.0, there will be no distinction between the Web browser and the other interface components for file browsing and even for the display of desktop applications. With your desktop using a browser interface that is fully customizable, any application on your local box or out over the Internet is only a click away at all times. The browser is fast becoming the all-encompassing application that provides all the functionality required for navigating around the Web, your local network, and even your own computer and applications.

From the aspect of back end Web applications, browsers are very frustrating beasts in that they are both intensely visual and seemingly interactive, yet at the same time have a mentality that is reminiscent of the dumb terminal of the mainframe days. We already discussed the issue of no direct data connectivity between the browser and the server, which makes for a purely transaction-based interface to the data.

Nevertheless, browsers are getting smarter; and while the data connectivity is an issue that will not likely get resolved for some time given the infrastructure of the Web, a lot of logic is moving to the browser. New scripting languages like Java, VBScript, and JavaScript allow extending the browser interface beyond its limited display-only capabilities. With these scripting languages, it is possible to build some validation logic into the client-side HTML pages. For example, you can validate input as long as no data lookup is required (e.g., checking a phone number field for proper formatting, a credit card number to be valid, a state code being proper). In addition, these scripting languages are extending the Form control interface to be a lot more like a full GUI-based screen in that eventcode can be attached to input fields so that validation can be triggered automatically.

While Java is getting all the attention these days, the simpler scripting languages like VBScript and JavaScript make it easy to move some of the simpler validation-based and simple calculation-oriented functionality and implement it on the browser.

Because these scripting languages are implemented as HTML-embedded text that executes on the client side, you can use your Visual FoxPro back end application to actually generate script code that runs when the page is displayed on the Web browser. It's sort of like getting a double execution punch.

One thing to be aware of is that not all browsers support all of the features. Netscape and Microsoft are the market leaders with both of their browsers providing multitudes of extensions to their browsers. While the leading browsers from both companies are reasonably compatible and comprise 85% of the market, browsers from other companies do not support some of the more advanced features. If your site is public, hard choices have to be made whether to support only the most basic HTML features, or build state-of-the-art pages at the risk of turning away a small percentage of users with incompatible browsers.

Figure 19.13 shows an example of how taking advantage of browser-specific features can enhance the user interface. These two pages display the same information: one using Frames for IE 3.0 or Netscape 2.0 or later browser, and one using plain pages for all other browsers. The Frames version is much more visually appealing and provides a more functional interface for navigating the site. Note the option on the Frames page to go to No Frames—important for laptop and low-resolution users. This site is providing a dual interface to serve both the latest HTML extensions and the low-end browsers, but a fair amount of extra design effort is required to provide this functionality.

As a Web developer, you have to weigh carefully which features you want to implement. When building internal Intranet applications, it's likely that you have control over the browser to use, so you can choose the one that provides the most functionality for the job at hand. For public applications, though, there is a tradeoff between using the newest, coolest features and leaving some users who haven't upgraded to the latest and greatest in the dust.

**FIGURE 19.13**

Taking advantage of new HTML extensions can make your site easier to use.

One strategy is to develop two sets of pages to satisfy both the hottest new developments and the older browsers. For example, the following function (implemented with Web Connection) checks for browser support and returns a letter that identifies the browser type: "F" for Frames-based pages, "M" for Internet Explorer 2.0, and "" for all others:

```
**************************************************************************
* SurplusProcess :: PageType
**********************************
***   Function: Returns the PageType based on the Browser name
***       Pass: llNoFrames    -  Override flag to use or not use frames
***     Return: "F"rames for Netscape 1.2/IE 3 or higher, "M" for MSIE 2
***             "" for all other Browsers
**************************************************************************
FUNCTION PageType
LPARAMETERS llNoFrames
LOCAL lcBrowser, lcType

lcBrowser=UPPER(THIS.oCGI.GetBrowser())
lcType=""        && Default to non-frames page
IF  INLIST(lcBrowser,"MOZILLA/2.","MOZILLA/3.") AND !llNoFrames
   lcType="F"
ENDIF

*** Return "M" for MS Internet Explorer 2.0
*** only on the Homepage
IF llHomePage AND ATC("MSIE 2.",lcBrowser)>0
  lcType="M"
ENDIF
```

```
RETURN lcType
* PageType
```

When a page is loaded for display, it is then loaded with the appropriate prefix:

```
loHTML.ShowMemoPage(HTMLPAGEPATH+THIS.PageType(THIS.lNoFrames)+
➥"ShowCats.wc",.T.)
```

If all pages are dynamically loaded, it's now possible to load the appropriate page for the specified browser by checking for specific browsers that support frames. All static pages reference the appropriate frames pages with the F prefix while the nonframe pages point at the nonframe, nonprefixed page names.

## Web Development Issues in Working with Visual FoxPro

Web development feels a lot like two steps forward and one step back. When building FoxPro-based Web applications, here are several issues that you have to keep in mind:

- Speed is extremely important on the Web. Visual FoxPro's single-threaded nature makes it necessary to turn around requests as quickly as possible to free up the data server for the next request.

- Bulletproof code is not an option, it's a requirement! When running a data server, it's crucial that the code running on it does not crash. Crash the server and you bring the system to a stop. Good error-handling mechanisms are a must.

- HTML is graphic art! If you work on large-scale Web applications, be prepared to work with HTML designers. Don't code if you can build logic into external pages that can be loaded from within your VFP application—designers will expect this feature! It's also much easier to maintain a site this way, and you can leave page design to the graphic arts people!

- Web apps are transaction-based. It's not your typical GUI application, as database requests are sent from the browser to the Web server and your application in individual request chunks. Remember, the browser has no direct access to the data, and your application has no direct access to the user interface. Get used to hand coding where you might have used the screen builder or report writer before.

Part
IV

Ch
19

# Internet-Enabling Your Applications

Internet-enabling your applications doesn't have to be as complete as rebuilding them to run over the Web. Instead, you can use smaller and more easily integrated enhancements such as the ability to send e-mail over the Internet, uploading or downloading files via FTP, or accessing a Web site through a Web browser controlled with Visual FoxPro.

The following examples for SMTP e-mail and FTP functionality use third-party ActiveX controls from Mabry Software. Shareware versions of the Mabry controls are included on the CD in the \MABRY directory. To install these controls, run the individual EXE files in the directory.

The Web browser control example requires that you have Internet Explorer 3.0 installed on your system.

## Downloading a File via FTP

The File Transfer Protocol (FTP) is the primary protocol used to transfer files between client and server machines. While it's possible to download files directly over the World Wide Web simply by setting a link to point at a file, uploading files cannot easily be handled over the Web.

FTP is a widely used, relatively simple protocol. Using the Mabry FTP control, it's easy to build a class that allows sending and receiving of files via FTP. Figure 19.14 shows the class when running in visual mode, but the class also supports a programmatic interface that can run without displaying the form.

**FIGURE 19.14**
The wwFTP class lets you upload and download files from an FTP site. Uploads require a username and password, whereas downloads can often be anonymous.

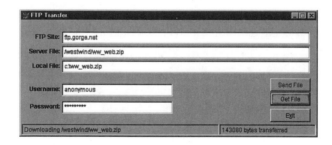

To create a form that contains the Mabry ActiveX FTP control, use the following steps:

1. Create a new form and grab two OLE container controls from the Form Controls toolbar. Insert the *Mabry Internet GetAddress Control* and the *FTP Control* from the "Insert Control" radio button selected list.

2. Assign ocxGetAddress and ocxFTP to the Name property of the controls in the property sheet.

3. Add the following properties to the class: cFTPSite, cRemoteFile, cLocalFile, cUsername, and cPassword. These fields correspond to the input fields that are used on the form shown in Figure 19.14. Create input fields for each of these variables

and point the datasource at the class properties you just created
(i.e., THISFORM.cFTPSite).

4. Add buttons for Sending and Receiving files. The Send button should call
   THISFORM.UploadFile(), whereas the Receive button should call
   THISFORM.GetFile().

5. Add the following GetFile and Uploadfile class methods:

**Listing 19.11  wwIPControls.vcx: The Getfile Method of the wwFTP Class Is
the Workhorse that Sends and Receives Files**

```
*-- Retrieves a file from an FTP site. All properties must be set prior to
    ➥calling this method.
PROCEDURE GETFILE
LPARAMETER llSendFile
LOCAL lcSite

#DEFINE RETRIEVE_FILE  7
#DEFINE SEND_FILE  6

#DEFINE BINARY = 2

IF llSendFile
   lnMode=SEND_FILE
ELSE
   lnMode=RETRIEVE_FILE
ENDIF

lcSite=TRIM(THISFORM.cFTPSite)

THIS.statusmessage("Retrieving IP Address for "+lcSite)
THIS.cIPAddress=THISFORM.ocxGetAddress.GetHostAddress(lcSite)

IF EMPTY(THIS.cIPAddress)
   THIS.statusmessage("Couldn't connect to "+lcSite)
   RETURN
ENDIF

THIS.statusmessage("Connected to "+THIS.cIPAddress)

*** Must Evaluate call to FTP Logon method since VFP balks at the Logon name
llResult=EVALUATE("THISFORM.ocxFTP.Logon( THIS.cIPAddress,TRIM(THIS.cUsername),;
                                    TRIM(THIS.cPassword) )")
IF !llResult
   THIS.statusmessage("Logon to "+lcSite+ " failed...")
   RETURN
ENDIF
THIS.statusmessage("Logged on to "+lcSite)

*** Assign files to upload/download
```

*continues*

---

**Listing 19.11 Continued**

```
THISFORM.ocxFTP.RemoteFileName = TRIM(THIS.cRemoteFile)
THISFORM.ocxFTP.LocalFileName = TRIM(THIS.cLocalFile)

IF llSendFile
   THIS.statusmessage("Uploading "+TRIM(THISFORM.cLocalFile) )
ELSE
   THIS.statusmessage("Downloading "+TRIM(THISFORM.cRemoteFile) )
ENDIF

THISFORM.ocxFTP.TransferMode = BINARY

*** Send or Receive File
THISFORM.ocxFTP.Action=lnMode
ENDPROC

*-- Uploads a file to the FTP site.
PROCEDURE uploadfile
THISFORM.GETFILE(.T.)  && .T. means send file
ENDPROC
```

---

The workhorse routine is the GetFile() method, which handles connecting to the FTP site, logging in, and then sending the file. The site connection is handled by the Mabry GetAddress Control which resolves the domain name on the form (**ftp.server.net**, for example) to an IP address in the format of **000.000.000.000** that is required by the FTP control. A simple call to the control's GetHostAddress() method with the domain name returns the IP Address. If the IP address cannot be resolved, a null string ("") is returned.

Once connected, the user must be logged into the FTP site. When downloading files from public sites, it's often acceptable to access the site anonymously by specifying "anonymous" as both the username and password. For other sites and for uploads in general, a specific username password may be required. The login operation is handled using the Login method of the ActiveX control, which takes an IP address and a username and password as a parameter. Due to a bug in Visual FoxPro, the Login method call is causing a compilation error, requiring the method to be called by embedding it inside of EVALUATE function call rather than calling the Login method directly:

```
llResult=EVALUATE(
"THISFORM.ocxFTP.Logon(THIS.cIPAddress,THIS.cUsername,THIS.cPassword)")
```

The actual file transfer operation is handled asynchronously—the LocalFile and RemoteFile properties are set with the filenames and the Action property is set to either RETRIEVE_FILE or SEND_FILE. As soon as a value is assigned to the Action flag, the transfer is started and control returns immediately to your program while the file transfer occurs in the background. You can use the following `IsBusy()` method of the FTP class to determine whether the current transfer is done:

```
*-- Returns whether a file transfer is in progress.
PROCEDURE IsBusy
#DEFINE FTP_IDLE 5
RETURN (THISFORM.ocxFTP.CurrentState <> FTP_IDLE )
```

You should also check this method prior to starting another transfer. To receive a completion message of the last file transfer, call the `GetErrorMessage()` method of the class.

Although this class is implemented as a form which can be activated with:

```
PUBLIC oFTP
SET CLASSLIB TO QueIP ADDITIVE
oFTP=CREATE("wwFTP")
oFTP.show
```

you can also control the class programmatically in code or from the command window:

```
oFTP=CREATE("wwFTP")

oFTP.cFTPSite="ftp.gorge.net"
oFTP.cRemoteFile="/westwind/ww_web.zip"
oFTP.cLocalFile="C:\ww_web.zip"

oFTP.cUsername="anonymous"
oFTP.cPassword="anonymous"

*!* oFTP.Show()     && If you want to show the form and property settings

oFTP.GetFile()
```

## Sending SMTP Mail

The Simple Mail Transfer Protocol provides a simple interface to sending mail over the Internet. The Mabry SMTP mail control allows you to take advantage of this protocol to send e-mail messages across the Internet with relative ease.

**NOTE** SMTP is an open protocol. When it originally was devised, it was designed to be accessible without any restrictions. This means a true SMTP mail server does not require a login and that anybody on the Internet can use the server to send mail.

Newer versions of SMTP servers implement IP address restrictions and login requirements based on a username/password scheme. The SMTP control on its own does not support this functionality; you have to use the POP3 control to log in to the mail server, then use that connection to send SMTP mail.

The example described here works only with SMTP mail servers that do not require a login. ∎

Part
IV

Ch
19

To create a form that contains the ActiveX SMTP control, use the following steps:

1. Create a new form and grab a couple of OLE container controls from the Form Controls toolbar. Add a Mabry Internet GetAddress Control and the SMTP control to the form.

2. Assign ocxSMTP to the control in the property sheet.

3. Add the following properties to the class: cSendToAddress, cFromAddress, cSubject, cMessage, cMailServerName. These fields correspond to the input fields that are used on the form shown in Figure 19.15. Create input fields for each of these variables and set their Controlsource at the form property (i.e., THISFORM.cSendToAddress). The form layout should look like Figure 19.15.

**FIGURE 19.15**

The wwSMTP class lets you send an e-mail message over the Internet. With its public class interface, you can populate the form programmatically.

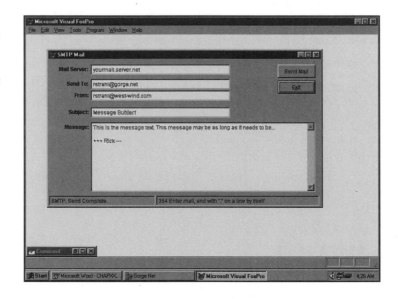

4. Add a Send button to the form. The Send button should call THISFORM.SendMail().

5. Create a new method named SendMail with the following code:

> **Listing 19.12   wwIPControls.vcx: The SMTP Class' Sendmail Method Is Responsible for Sending the Actual Message Once the Message Properties Have Been Filled**

```
*-- Used to send a message. Mail properties must be set prior to calling this method.
PROCEDURE Sendmail
LOCAL lcIPAddress
```

```
#DEFINE NORMAL_PRIORITY    3

IF EMPTY(THIS.cIPAddress)
    *** Resolve Mail Server IP Address - you can speed this up by not
    *** using this code and plugging the IP Address directly to the
    *** mail control
    lcSite=TRIM(THISFORM.cMailServerName)

    *** Clear out the IP Address first
    THIS.statusmessage("Retrieving IP Address for "+lcSite)

    lcIPAddress=THISFORM.ocxGetAddress.GetHostAddress(lcSite)

    IF EMPTY(lcIPAddress)
        THIS.statusmessage("Couldn't connect to "+lcSite)
    ENDIF
ELSE
    lcIPAddress=TRIM(THIS.cIPAddress)
ENDIF

THIS.statusmessage("Connected to "+lcIPAddress)

THISFORM.ocxSMTP.OriginatingAddress = TRIM(THIS.cFromAddress)
THISFORM.ocxSMTP.OriginatingName = TRIM(THIS.cFromName)
THISFORM.ocxSMTP.HostAddress = lcIPAddress
THISFORM.ocxSMTP.DomainName = "west-wind.com"
THISFORM.ocxSMTP.MailApplication = "West Wind Web Connection"
THISFORM.ocxSMTP.MailPriority = NORMAL_PRIORITY

THISFORM.ocxSMTP.DestinationUserList=TRIM(THISFORM.cSendToAddress)
THISFORM.ocxSMTP.CCUserList=TRIM(THISFORM.cCCAddress)
THISFORM.ocxSMTP.MailSubject=TRIM(THISFORM.cSubject)
THISFORM.ocxSMTP.MailBody=TRIM(THISFORM.cMessage)
THISFORM.ocxSMTP.MailAttachment=TRIM(THISFORM.cAttachment)

THISFORM.statusmessage("Sending Message to "+TRIM(THISFORM.cSendToAddress))
THISFORM.ocxSMTP.Action=1
RETURN
```

Part
IV

Ch

19

As with the FTP class example, this SMTP example also uses the Mabry GetAddress control to resolve the mail server's domain name (**mail.server.net**, for example) to an IP address which is required by the Mail control. Because it's quicker to not resolve the address, there's also an option to pass an IP Address in the classes cIPAddress property which causes the name lookup to be skipped.

Once the mail server is identified, the form properties are collected setting the Mail control's internal properties. Finally, the Mail control's Action property is set to 1, which causes the message to be sent and control is returned to your code immediately. As with the FTP class, an IsBusy() method tells whether a mail transfer is still in process:

```
*-- Determines whether the Mail Server is busy sending a message.
*-- While busy no other messages can be sent.
PROCEDURE isbusy
#DEFINE SMTP_IDLE 5
RETURN (THISFORM.ocxSMTP.CurrentState <> SMTP_IDLE )
```

In order to determine the final status of a sent message the Mail control's EndSendMail event is used to update the nErrorCode custom property set up on the form class:

```
*-- Fires when a message send is complete or failed
PROCEDURE ocxSMTP.EndSendMail
LPARAMETERS errornumber
THISFORM.nErrorCode=errornumber
THISFORM.statusmessage("Mail Transport done - Error Code:
"+STR(errornumber),;
                        THISFORM.geterrormessage(errornumber) )

ENDPROC
```

This code basically traps the error code and updates the form's status window with the error information. Once the error code is set, it stays set until the next message is sent.

Although the class is implemented as a form that can be run interactively with the following code,

```
SET CLASSLIB TO WwIPControls ADDITIVE

PUBLIC oSMTP
oSMTP=CREATE("wwSMTP")
oSMTP.show
```

you can also control the class under program control or from the command window:

```
PUBLIC oSMTP
oSMTP=CREATE("wwSMTP")

oSMTP.cMailServerName="mail.server.net"

oSMTP.cFromAddress="rstrahl@west-wind.com"
oSMTP.cFromName="Rick Strahl"
oSMTP.cSendToAddress="rstrahl@gorge.net"  && Use Commas to separate more
➥than one recipient
*oSMTP.cCCAddress="rstrahl@west-wind.com,rstrahl@gorge.net"

oSMTP.cSubject="Test Message from QUE's Using Visual FoxPro!"
oSMTP.cMessage="This is a test message generated by the SMTP example..."

* oSMTP.cAttachment="c:\autoexec.bat"
* oSMTP.Show()    && If you want to display the form

oSMTP.SendMail()
```

You can then use oSMTP.IsBusy() to determine if the control is still busy and oSMTP.GetErrorMessage() to determine the last result message of the mail message.

## Activating a Web Browser from Visual FoxPro

The following is a little routine that is handy for support features or cross-linking a FoxPro application to the Web. Windows 95 and Windows NT 4.0 support the ability to execute URLs directly via the OLE extension mappings supplied in the registry. If you have a browser installed in your system, and it's the default browser, when you click on an HTML document in your browser, you can use the following simple code to activate the browser and go to the specified URL:

**Listing 19.13   GoURL.prg: This Routine Fires Up the Registered Browser and Goes to the Specified URL**

```
*********************************************************
FUNCTION GoURL
******************
***    Function: Starts associated Web Browser
***              and goes to the specified URL.
***              If Browser is already open it
***              reloads the page.
***      Assume: Works only on Win95 and NT 4.0
***        Pass: tcUrl  - The URL of the site or
***                       HTML page to bring up
***                       in the Browser
***      Return: 2 - Bad Association (invalid URL)
*********************************************************
LPARAMETERS tcUrl

tcUrl=IIF(type("tcUrl")="C",tcUrl,;
          "http://west-wind.com/")

DECLARE INTEGER ShellExecute ;
    IN SHELL32.dll ;
    INTEGER nWinHandle,;
    STRING cOperation,;
    STRING cFileName,;
    STRING cParameters,;
    STRING cDirectory,;
    INTEGER nShowWindow

DECLARE INTEGER FindWindow ;
    IN WIN32API ;
    STRING cNull,STRING cWinName

RETURN ShellExecute(FindWindow(0,_SCREEN.caption),;
                    "Open",tcUrl,;
                    "","c:\temp\",0)
```

To activate a URL from code, you can then simply use:

```
GoURL("www.west-wind.com")
```

Part
**IV**

Ch
**19**

This function can be extremely useful for product support. You could stick a button containing a call to this function onto a form, thereby sending users directly to your Web site for support, upgrades, or other information.

If you need more sophisticated control of URL access, you can also place a browser directly onto a Visual FoxPro form. Figure 19.16 shows an instance of a browser class that's controllable via its class interface. The Microsoft Web Browser ActiveX control allows you to embed all of MS Internet Explorer's functionality directly into your Visual FoxPro forms. How's that for full-featured power?

Here are a few of the method calls available:

```
SET CLASSLIB TO WWIPCONTROLS ADDITIVE
oForm=CREATE("wwBrowser","www.west-wind.com")
oForm.Show()
oForm.GoUrl("www.transformation.com/foxpro")
oForm.GoUrl("www.microsoft.com")
oForm.BackBrowser()
oForm.RefreshBrowser()
oForm.StopBrowser()
```

**NOTE**  Unlike other ActiveX controls, the MS Web Browser is not fully self-contained and requires a full installation of MS Internet Explorer 3.0 to run. This means you cannot use this control on computers that do not have a copy of IE installed. ■

**FIGURE 19.16**

This is an example of the Web Browser control, which allows inclusion of all of Internet Explorer's advanced functionality into your own forms.

The Web browser control features a number of custom methods and events that allow you to control the browser's operation. The most obvious methods are for navigation of the browser. The following code snippets illustrate how to implement simple navigation with the control.

**Listing 19.14  wwIPControls: The Relevant Methods of the wwBrowser Class Allow Control over Browser Navigation**

```
*-- Init - allow pre-loading of URL
PROCEDURE Init
LPARAMETER lcUrl
THISFORM.GoUrl(lcUrl)
THISFORM.txtLocation.VALUE=lcUrl
ENDPROC


*-- Reloads the current URL
PROCEDURE refreshbrowser
THISFORM.ocxBrowser.refresh2()
ENDPROC


PROCEDURE stopbrowser
THISFORM.ocxBrowser.Stop()
ENDPROC


PROCEDURE backbrowser
THISFORM.ocxBrowser.GoBack()
ENDPROC


PROCEDURE forwardbrowser
THISFORM.ocxBrowser.GoForward()
ENDPROC


*-- Goes to the specified URL
PROCEDURE GoUrl
LPARAMETER lcUrl
lcUrl=IIF(TYPE("lcUrl")="C",lcUrl,"www.west-wind.com ")
THISFORM.ocxBrowser.Navigate(TRIM(lcUrl))
ENDPROC


PROCEDURE ocxBrowser.TitleChange
*** OLE Control Event ***
LPARAMETERS TEXT

THISFORM.CAPTION=TEXT
ENDPROC


*-- Form Resize handles browser and text control alignment
PROCEDURE RESIZE
loBrowser=THISFORM.ocxBrowser
```

*continues*

Part

**IV**

Ch

**19**

**Listing 19.14    Continued**

```
loBrowser.HEIGHT=THISFORM.HEIGHT - 50
loBrowser.WIDTH=THISFORM.WIDTH - 20

THISFORM.txtLocation.WIDTH= THISFORM.WIDTH - THISFORM.txtLocation.LEFT  - 10
ENDPROC

PROCEDURE txtLocation.INTERACTIVECHANGE
THISFORM.ocxBrowser.Navigate(TRIM(THIS.VALUE))
ENDPROC
```

There are a number of additional events and methods that can be called; unfortunately, at the time this chapter was written, there was no documentation on this interface yet, which made it difficult to explore many of them. By the time you read this, Internet Explorer should be available out of beta, along with additional information and documentation on the OLE program interface. Information about IE's object hierarchy and OLE Automation interface is available at **http://microsoft.com/intdev/sdk/docs/iexplore/**.

# From Here...

This chapter has shown you how you can use Visual FoxPro for Internet application development. You can extend your existing applications by embedding Internet functionality into old code as well as extend the reach of your FoxPro development by using Visual FoxPro as back end for Web application development.

For additional information on related topics, check out the following chapters:

- Chapter 12, "A Deeper Look at Object-Oriented Design," discusses how to use the Class Designer and object-oriented methods to create reusable components and tools.

- Bonus Chapter 06, "Sharing Data Through Automation and Using ActiveX Controls," describes how you can use OLE Automation and OLE linking to integrate functionality of other applications into your Visual FoxPro programs. This chapter is located on the CD.

- Bonus Chapter 07, "Extending Visual FoxPro with Third-Party Tools," describes in detail how to work with ActiveX controls. This chapter is located on the CD.

# Creating On-Line Help

*by Marl & Alice Atkins*

**A**ll your programming efforts will go to waste if your end users do not understand how to use the program you create—thus, the need for on-line Help. To create an effective on-line Help system, you must understand the type of Help system you are using, and you must understand the needs of the people who will use your program. Once you have that information you can use the features in your on-line Help system to help your end users operate your program with a minimum of effort.

This chapter was written to make understanding your users' needs and creating a Windows 95 Help system easy tasks. You will also learn about a few options that could make creating on-line Help even easier. ■

**Examine the kinds of on-line Help**

We will explore the different kinds of information you should include in your on-line Help system.

**Use Windows 95 Help Systems**

First, we will explore how a Windows 95 Help system is used.

**Design On-Line Help Systems**

We will cover professional on-line Help design techniques.

**Construct a Windows 95 Help System**

We will construct a working Windows 95 Help system.

**Evaluate current Help authoring tools**

Compares the features of the most popular Help authoring tools on the market today.

# FoxPro Supports Two Kinds of Help

It's a good idea to look at FoxPro's help files before you design your own. They are excellent help systems and are examples to follow when you design your own help. The default type of help is the windows or graphical style. You can activate it by pressing F1 or entering HELP in the command window. You'll see something like the image shown in Figure 20.1. The main help window contains the following elements: a menu, a button bar, and a main text area with graphics and text headings that list information contained in the help file.

**FIGURE 20.1**

Visual FoxPro's Help Topics using windows style Help.

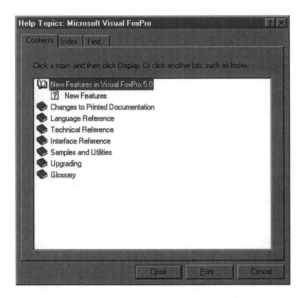

Windows style Help systems are similar across all windows applications. There are two components to a graphical Help system—the help file and the viewer. You create the Help file, and Microsoft provides the viewer in the form of WINHELP.EXE that ships with all flavors of the Windows family of operating systems. When you are viewing Windows style Help, you are actually running this viewer application. It's not directly linked to Visual FoxPro. This means you can take a Help system written for Visual FoxPro and use it in Excel or Word. Interaction with the Help file is done via the menu, buttons, and hot spots on images or text.

Now let's take a look at the DBF style Help as shown in Figure 20.2.

**FIGURE 20.2**

This figure shows a list box of topics in Visual FoxPro's DBF style help.

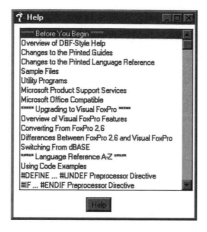

To activate DBF style Help you must tell Visual FoxPro to change help files. You can do this by issuing the following command:

```
SET HELP TO SYS(2004) + "\FOXHELP.DBF"
```

or in CONFIG.FPW

```
HELP = FOXHELP.DBF
```

**N O T E**  If you look for this file in your directory, don't be surprised not to find it. Visual FoxPro 5.0 no longer includes the DBF style help. However, if you installed over top of Visual FoxPro 3.0, which did include it, you may still have the file. In any case, the CD that comes with this book includes a much abbreviated version of the DBF style help file just so you can examine its structure. ■

When present, both styles of help files reside in the directory where you installed FoxPro. The SYS(2004) command returns the name of that directory, so we only supply the name of the file. Then press F1 to activate help as you did in the previous example. Visual FoxPro controls the viewing of this file and is required to enable DBF style help.

You can immediately see a big difference between the two types of help. DBF style Help is simpler and consists of a menu that lists all the help topics. You select a topic by clicking it. The window changes into a detail of the current topic along with additional navigation buttons. A comparison between the help styles for the topic ADATABASES( ) is shown in Figures 20.3 and 20.4.

Part

**IV**

Ch

**20**

**FIGURE 20.3**

DBF Help details.

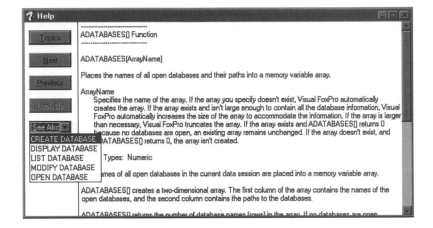

To return to the graphical style of help, enter the following:

```
SET HELP TO SYS(2004) + "\FOXHELP.HLP"
```

or in CONFIG.FPW

```
HELP = FOXHELP.HLP
```

Notice the "HLP" extension in the file name. All Windows-based Help systems use this default extension.

**FIGURE 20.4**

Windows Help details.

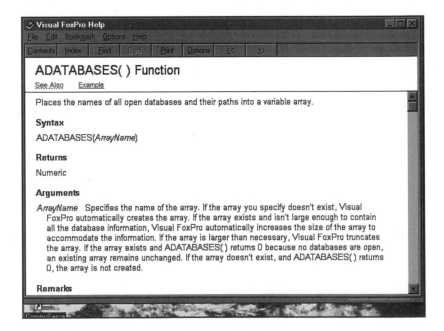

## Help Systems Compared

Before you design the help system, decide which help system suits you best. The main difference between the two systems is that DBF style Help can be augmented by your end user. You can include your own help file in an application and permit additional records to be added programmatically. This is accomplished by creating a form for entering user-specific help.

Graphical style help has become the standard and is more flexible. It provides more information but cannot be altered by the end user once it's compiled. To make changes, you must edit the source files and then recompile the application. This can be restrictive if your application requires constant help file updates.

Images and hypertext links are an integral part of Windows Help and are relatively simple to add or create. An image of a particularly difficult entry screen or graphic about a process goes a long way in assisting an end user faced with a problem. There also are macros and even capabilities to access external DLLs in the graphic version. The rest of this chapter concentrates on creating Windows style Help.

## Features of Windows Style Help

You can use many of the Windows graphical elements in your Help system. You can embed fonts, colors, and images into the help file. You can even launch applications or call subroutines from within the graphical help system. Your Help system can use key words to search for information or to link to images. The other distinguishing feature of graphical Help is the high degree of customization possible. You can create menus, hypertext links, hot spots on graphics, and even multiple windows in one help system. Windows Help is royalty free and, once compiled, it can be distributed without incurring any additional costs.

To build the help file, you need source information including text and images, the windows help compiler, and optionally, an authoring tool to help you with the development process.

This last component is not required, but I strongly recommend purchasing software to assist in building the help system, especially if you plan to create anything even mildly complicated. You create all Windows Help from a source file that uses a page markup method to describe individual pieces that make up the file. Keeping track of the separate components is awkward and time consuming. The page markup methods are simple enough, but it's difficult to manage all of them without a tool.

Graphical Help is transportable. This means you can create help in the Windows environment and take that file and run it under the Apple operating system without change. If your Help system must run on multiple platforms, it's important to keep the following limitations in mind. Some features are not available on the Macintosh, so review the technical documentation for the help compiler before beginning your project. For example, the following features are not currently supported in the Apple environment:

- Secondary windows
- Customizable menus
- Graphics in the Windows metafile format
- Support for DLLs

# Introducing Windows 95 Help Systems

Windows 95 Help systems are run by a Help engine that is built into the Windows 95 operating system. Windows uses the executable file, HCW.exe.

 You can open any Windows 95 Help system without being in the program it was written for. For example, turn on a computer that uses Windows 95 and open Windows Explorer. Click the folder for Visual FoxPro 5.0. You should be able to see an icon that looks like a book. You should now be in the FoxPro Help system. Click the close button in the upper righthand corner to exit.

You can open any Windows 95 Help system on your computer by opening Windows Explorer, locating the directory that the particular program is in and then clicking the book icon in that directory. As you can see, the Help system is run by Windows 95, not the individual application.

## The Windows 95 Help Interface

From Windows Explorer or from within the Visual FoxPro application, open Visual FoxPro Help.

The Visual FoxPro Help system appears. Its function is to help users understand how to use Visual FoxPro. We use it here only to describe the Windows 95 Help interface.

At the top of the window shown in Figure 20.5, you should be able to read "Help Topics: Visual FoxPro 5.0." You should see three tabs: "Contents," "Index," and "Find." Click "Contents."

## Contents

You should see three book icons. Double-click the book icon titled "Language Reference." Four more book icons appear along with two page icons. Your window should look like the window in Figure 20.5. Click the book icon titled "ActiveX Controls." Now nine more page icons appear.

**FIGURE 20.5**

Familiarize yourself with Visual FoxPro's Help Contents.

## Topic Windows

Click the page icon titled "Overview." Now you are in Visual FoxPro Help's main topic window for ActiveX controls.

Figure 20.6 shows a picture of Help's main topic window.

The title bar displays a Help book icon, the Help system's title "Visual FoxPro Help," and a minimize button, a maximize button, and a close button.

Below the title bar is Help's drop-down menu. Click "File" in the drop-down menu. A drop-down list appears providing options regarding files. Slowly move the mouse across each word in the menu to drop-down a list of options under each word. If a list does not appear, click the word.

Below the drop-down menu is a button bar.

Part

**IV**

Ch

**20**

**FIGURE 20.6**

Explore FoxPro Help's
Main Topic window.

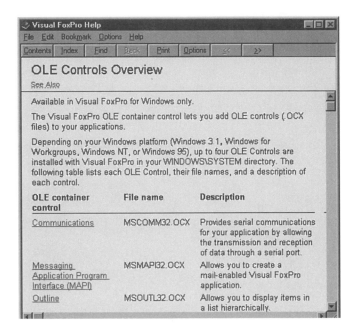

■ Click the Contents button to return to Help Contents.

■ Click the Index button to go to Help's Index.

■ Click the Find button to go to Help's full text search engine.

■ Click the Back button to back up to the last topic you viewed.

**N O T E** The Back button appears only after you have viewed more than one topic. ■

■ Click the Print button to print the topic you are viewing.

■ Click the Options button to access options regarding the manipulation of the topic text.

■ Click the << >> buttons to scroll sequentially forward or backward through numerous topics in a procedure.

Notice the scroll bar on the right side of the screen. If you scroll to the bottom of the topic, notice that the title and "See Also" remain at the top of the screen. This is the window's non- scrolling region.

Within topics, Windows 95 Help systems use highlighted (usually green) text, buttons, and locations in pictures to give users access to additional information. These locations are known as "Hotspots." The phrase "See Also" in the non-scrolling region shown in

Figure 20.6 is a hotspot. Hotspots create access to small pop-up windows containing small topics and jumps to other topics or locations within Help. Hotspots can also be used to run macros for opening dialog boxes or for performing tasks such as printing a test page.

## Index

In Windows Help, click the tab marked "Index." This is the Help Index (see Figure 20.7.) It contains words that the Help author decided to include to help users easily find the information they need. The words in the Index may or may not be used in the actual Help text. For example, a user may be interested in duplicating something. A good Help Index would include the word "duplicating" and offer "printing" and "copying" as possible topics to view.

**FIGURE 20.7**

Search for topics using Visual FoxPro's Help Index.

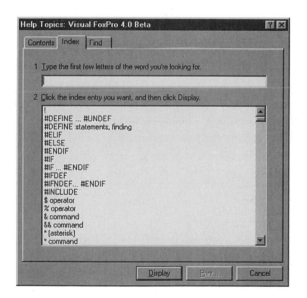

## Find

Figure 20.8 shows the first window of Help's Find Wizard. Click the "Find" tab on the Main Topic window to start a Help Wizard designed to search the entire Help text for words or phrases that the user is interested in reading about. The difference between "Find" and the "Index" is that the Index offers a list of words entered by the Help author. "Find" is a search engine that searchs the entire Help text for any and all instances of a word or phrase.

Now that you are familiar with the standard Help system you are about to create, we move on to explore a few different kinds of Help you may want to employ.

Part
IV

Ch
20

**FIGURE 20.8**
Search Help's entire text with Visual FoxPro's Find Wizard.

# Kinds of Help

The Help system you just explored is not the only kind of help available in Windows 95. On-line Help has become a very diverse and complex array of options. Programmers and authors have found amazing ways to convey specific information clearly and with a minimum of effort on the user's part. Most Help systems are written to help users operate computer applications. However, you can design any kind of book, catalog, or directory including full graphic animation and jumps directly to the Internet, using a Windows 95 Help system.

## Standard Help

Standard Help is the system you explored in Visual FoxPro Help. It is a document including a table of contents (Contents), information on the Help subject (Topics), and an index (Index). You can switch between an application and standard Help. Standard Help can even open a program and carry out a macro, but standard Help is also an application in and of itself. We view standard Help as being a kind of on-line user's manual.

## Using Context-Sensitive Help

You can learn about the interface of an application easily if its Help system employs one or more forms of context-sensitive Help. Following are two forms of context-sensitive Help available in Windows 95.

**What's This Help**    If an application employs "What's This" Help, the user can access information about a specific item on the application interface by performing one of the following actions:

1. right-clicking the item;
2. clicking the item and then hitting F1 or hitting Shift-F1 and then clicking the item;

3. clicking the button with the question mark in the right corner of the title bar and then clicking the item;

4. clicking a Help button on the toolbar and then clicking the item; or
5. clicking a Help button in the lower right corner of the interface and then clicking the item.

The user action necessary to call up context-sensitive Help is predetermined by the programmer. When the user performs the predetermined action, a little window appears explaining the item selected.

"What's This" Help can be used within a dialog box. Users have immediate access to information that is specific to the items within the dialog box. The user need not search the Help contents to obtain the information.

**Tooltip Help**   Some applications use Tooltip Help. In such applications, a user can position the mouse over buttons on any toolbar or form control and without clicking, get information about that button or form control.

# Designing On-Line Help Systems

When writing on-line Help, we try to keep the users' objectives in mind, to help authors write from a goal- or task-oriented perspective. Programmers often write from a features perspective. That is, programmers tend to describe application features and how they work. Users are generally interested in learning to perform specific tasks rather than learning all the features available. On-line Help authors strive to make specific goal-oriented information available to users with a minimum of effort.

## Types of Help Information

We can narrow down the types of information that Help authors need to be concerned with. Of course different circumstances require different kinds of information, but here are the basic information types that Help authors use.

**Overview**   Provides general information about the application or goals the user might wish to achieve. An overview would fill the user in on peripheral information that may aid the user's efforts or help the user avoid trouble.

**Goal**   Describes the user's intended result. If the author conveys this information well, the user can easily determine whether or not that information will be useful to achieve the intended result.

**Procedural**    Describes the step-by-step actions required to achieve the user's desired goal.

**Feedback**    Reinforces the user by describing the application's expected reaction. If the user carries out a step in the procedure correctly, feedback information will verify (by explaining the application's reaction) that the user acted correctly.

**Options**    Points out multiple options to the user.

**Side Effects**    Points out results that are not the desired result. Side effects may or may not be harmful to the user's efforts.

**System Operational Behavior**    Describes how the application operates with respect to a given topic.

# Topics

Help authors convey information by writing topics. We organize the information into individual topics because that enables users to "look up" specific bits of information (topics) from any number of locations. With the use of individual topics, a user can find all the information needed to achieve a goal without reading a lot of unnecessary information. Users can customize each Help session to their specific needs.

Needing to convey different types of information, Help authors write different kinds of topics. Each kind of topic reveals a certain kind of information. Here are the basic Help topics recognized by professional Help authors.

**Overview Topics**    Overview topics obviously convey overview information. We usually find overview topics in standard Help. They are generally lengthy and explain broad regions of background information.

**Procedural, Step-by-Step Instruction Topics**    Users access procedural topics to learn each step necessary to perform a specific task. Authors describe a procedure by writing numerous topics, each describing one action or series of actions, in the procedure. Procedural topics are almost always one of a group of topics. Help authors often utilize browse buttons to allow users to read the different topics of a procedure in sequential (or any author-designated) order. Different procedures may have certain actions in common. We use some of the same procedural topics to explain different procedures. Instead of continually repeating the same procedural topics, we use jumps and browse buttons to explain procedures.

**Application Interface Description Topics**   An easy way to explain everything in an application window is to take a picture of the window and to put it in the Help document. Using "hotspots," we can create pop-up windows to explain each part of the application window. In standard Help, if the user clicks a certain part of the picture, a pop-up window appears explaining what that item is, in the actual interface. This is sort of like "What's This" Help, except the user is only viewing an inactive picture of the interface, from inside standard Help.

**Command Topics**   Command topics describe the commands in a given dialog box. Although a user can access command topics from the standard Help contents, command topics are usually context-sensitive. The user can access the topic directly from within a dialog box. A list of all the commands and their functions for that dialog box are readily accessible. Command topics, unlike procedural topics, include all the commands for a dialog box in one topic.

**Context-Sensitive Interface Topics**   Users have access to information about the application interface without going into standard Help. Context-sensitive "What's This" Help is accessible by using an author-designated Help command. Context-sensitive topics generally describe items on the application's interface including its dialog boxes. Some context-sensitive topics include procedures needed to perform the tasks involving the specific items being queried. A user can open a dialog box within the application and learn all the functions pertaining to that dialog box by requesting context-sensitive Help.

**Keyboard Topics**   Keyboard topics describe the use of specific keys to carry out tasks and to point out multiple key commands. Keyboard topics usually point out short cuts.

**List Topics**   Hierarchies of headings in standard Help make finding specific information easy. List topics comprise part of a standard Help system or can be found in context-sensitive Help. A list topic amounts to no more than a list of jumps to different topics on a given subject.

**Definition Topics**   Every good Help system must have a glossary of some sort. Definition topics usually make up a glossary, and the word to be defined is highlighted as a hotspot in standard Help. When the user clicks the word, a pop-up window appears containing the word's definition. However, definitions are often found in context-sensitive Help.

**Troubleshooting Topics**   Troubleshooting topics help users diagnose and solve problems they are having with the application. Troubleshooting topics often include buttons for macros to open actual dialog boxes or to automatically perform certain tasks.

Part
**IV**

Ch
**20**

## Minimalist Writing

Many on-line Help authors adhere to a style of writing called minimalist writing. The idea is to convey enough information using the fewest words possible. One way to achieve that is to use pictures. People can usually get a lot more information from one picture than from many words. A consideration for Help authors is that some users are experienced with Windows 95 and perhaps with the application and therefore need very little information to complete their tasks. Other users, however, may not be experienced at all and would require instruction on every step and consideration necessary to achieve their goals. Minimalist writing could pose problems for these users.

## Layering Information

Help authors have found a solution to the minimalist writer's problem. Authors can segment information so that users can access it in layers. Users who only want basic information can access the basic topics, but users who want more information can access hotspots within the basic topics to get more detailed information.

# Construction of a Windows 95 Help System

Now that we have gone over what a Help system is, we can concentrate on actually creating one. To create an on-line Help system, you will need a way to create Help project files and assemble them with a Help compiler.

## The Help Authoring Tools that Ship with FoxPro

FoxPro ships with all the tools you need to create a Help system except a word processing program. You must have a Windows-based word processor that can save files to the Rich Text Format (*.rtf). MS Word works great for creating MS Windows 95 Help systems. WordPerfect and a few other word processing programs can also be used to create Help. FoxPro ships with the following Help authoring tools created by Microsoft.

**MS Help Workshop**    Help Workshop gives you the ability to perform four tasks necessary to authoring on-line Help:

- Create a project file
- Create a contents file
- Compile the help file
- Periodically view your help file as you work on it

**The Project File Creator/Editor**    Figure 20.9 displays the Help Workshop project creator/editor with an existing Help file loaded. Use this interface to create Help project or (*..hpj) files. The help project files store all the information the compiler needs to create the Help file. The interface offers many author options such as window customizing, adding buttons, and mapping context-sensitive Help for programmers.

**FIGURE 20.9**
Use this interface
to create Help
project files.

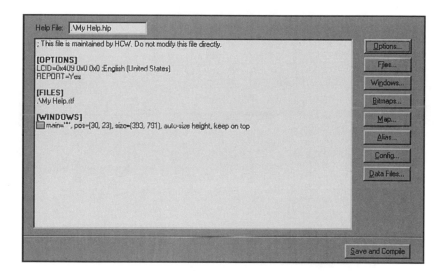

**The Contents File Creator/Editor**    Figure 21.10 displays the Help Workshop interface we will use to create a Help Contents (*.cnt) file. Use this tool to create Help hierarchies with book icons and to jump to topics with page icons. You can also designate what type of window a topic appears in when accessed from "Contents."

Part
**IV**

Ch
**20**

**FIGURE 20.10**
Use Help Workshop's
Contents interface to
create a Contents file.

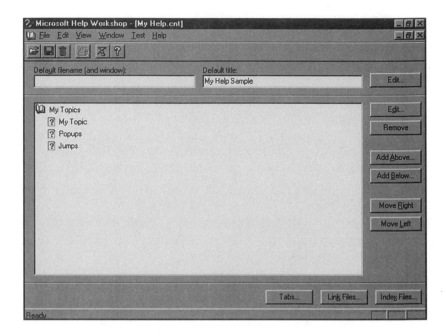

**_The Help Compiler_**    The compiler utilizes the project and contents interfaces to give you access to it. It compiles the information in the project and contents files to create a Help (*.hlp) file. A Help file is an executable file that users can access by clicking its icon.

**_The MS Hotspot Editor_**    In addition to Help Workshop, Visual FoxPro ships with the MS Hotspot Editor.

Figure 21.11 shows the Hotspot Editor with a sample graphic loaded. Two small squares mark two hotspots that have already been attached to the graphic using the Hotspot Editor. The Hotspot Editor creates graphic files with hotspots embedded, called SHED (*.shg) files.

**The Help Author's Guide**    This is a Windows 95 Help system just like the one we are about to create. Its purpose is to provide information about the creation of on-line Help systems using the Help Workshop and the Hotspot Editor.

**FIGURE 20.11**
Use the Hotspot Editor
Interface to create
hotspots on graphics.

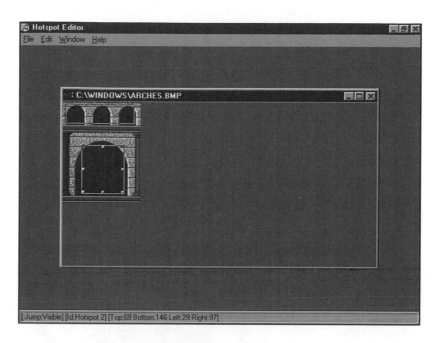

## Tutorial—Creating a Basic Help System

We will create a basic Help system with a jump and a pop-up window. First we will create a (*.rtf) file in MS Word. Next, we will use Help Workshop to create a project file. Finally, we will compile the Help file and then view it.

**Constructing Topics**   Open MS Word or your preferred word processing program to a new blank document. Click "View," and then click "Normal" to view the document in normal mode.

**N O T E**   Topic files can be created using any Windows-based word processor that can save to the Rich Text Format. This tutorial, however, demonstrates the construction of topics, using MS Word. ■

Now we will create three topics. The first will be an introductory topic, followed by a pop-up window and a jump. We will designate certain words within the text as hotspots for the pop-up and the jump.

1. Type the following line:

   `This, my first topic demonstrates a popup window and a jump.`

   This is your first topic. Hit Ctrl-Enter to add a page break after the topic.

2. Now type the following two lines:

   ```
   This is a popup window.
   This is a jump.
   ```

3. Hit Ctrl-Enter to add a page break after each topic. These lines represent the second and third topics. Now we must assign a topic ID for each topic.

4. Place the cursor at the beginning of the first topic on the drop-down menu bar. Click "Insert," and then click "Footnote."

5. When the dialog box opens (as Figure 20.12 shows) make sure "Footnote" is checked and then check "Custom Mark": In the field to the right of "Custom Mark," type a # symbol. This is the Help compiler's code to assign a topic ID to a topic.

**FIGURE 20.12**

Use the Footnote dialog box to assign topic IDs.

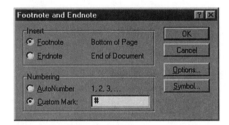

6. Click "OK."

   Now you should be in the MS Word footnote window (actually the end of the page).

7. Type the words `My Topic`, and then scroll back to the top of the page. Repeat this procedure to identify your second and third topics. Use the # in the "Custom Mark" field for each topic. Type `popup` in the footnote for the second topic ID and `jump` in the footnote for the third topic ID. When you finish, each topic should have a # at its beginning, marking a footnote. The end of each page should have a footnote, beginning with a # sign and a topic ID for the topic on that page. Your new topics should be "My Topic," "pop-up," and "jump."

   Now we must create a hotspot for the pop-up window and a hotspot for the jump.

8. In the first topic, double-click the word "pop-up" to select it.

9. From the drop-down menu click "Format," then click "Font."

10. When the dialog box opens find the "Underline" field and click the option drop-down button to its right. Refer to Figure 20.13.

**FIGURE 20.13**
Use MS Word's Font
dialog box to mark
text as a hotspot.

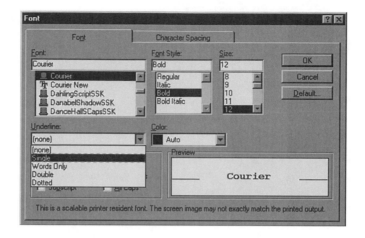

11. Select "Single" from the drop-down list, and then click "OK."

**TIP** Another option would be to click the button on the format toolbar. The objective is simply to underline the word "popup."

 By underlining a word in a topic you designate it as a hotspot for a popup window, not a jump or a macro. Now you must identify the topic that is to appear in the popup window.

12. Without adding a space, type the destination topic ID, **popup** after the word "pop-up."

13. Now use the mouse to select the topic ID "pop-up" (the second word "pop-up") in the first topic.

14. From the drop-down menu, click "Format," and then click "Font."

15. When the dialog box opens, check the "Hidden" field (in MS Word 7), and then click "OK." Figure 20.14 shows the font dialog box with the "Hidden" field.

    The second word "pop-up" that you just had highlighted, disappears.

    To see hidden text in MS Word:

16. Click "Tools" from the drop-down menu and then click "Options."

17. When the dialog box opens, select the tab labeled "View," and then check the "Hidden Text" field (see Figure 20.15) and click "OK."

    Now you should be able to see the second word "pop-up" again but with a dotted line underneath it. This word will not appear in the Help topic. Instead the word before "pop-up" will be colored green, signifying that it is a hotspot. If a user clicks the green word, a pop-up window containing the topic pop-up will appear.

    Now we must identify a hotspot for the jump to the topic, jump.

**FIGURE 20.14**

Use the Hidden field to hide the topic ID.

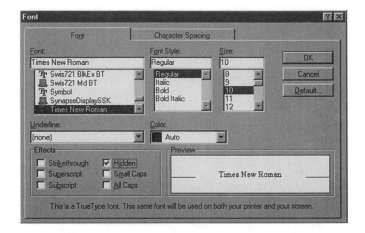

**FIGURE 20.15**

Check View Hidden Text to see the topic ID in your RTF file.

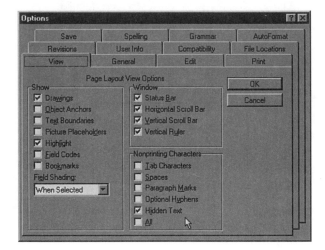

18. Within the first topic, double-click the word "jump" to highlight it.

19. From the drop-down menu click "Format," and then click "Font."

20. Click the  drop-down button for the "Underline" field.

21. This time select "Double" from the drop-down list and click "OK." The object is to double underline the word. By double underlining a word in a topic, you identify it as a hotspot for a jump and not for a pop-up window or a macro.

    Now we must identify the topic that the jump will go to.

22. Without adding a space, type the third topic ID `jump` after the double underlined word "jump" in the first topic.

23. Select the second word "jump" with the mouse to highlight it.

24. From the drop-down menu, click "F_ormat" and then click "F_ont." In the Effects field group, check the "H_idden" field. This allows Help Workshop to identify the topic without the topic ID appearing in the Help topic.

Your first topic should look like the following line:

> # This, my first topic demonstrates a popuppopup window and a jumpjump.

Each topic should be on a page of its own with its topic ID in a footnote at the bottom of the page.

Your first topic's footnote at the end of the page should look like this:

> # My Topic

**N O T E** Topic IDs are not case-sensitive. However, a topic ID cannot include spaces. Use underscores to replace them. ■

Now you must save your file in the Rich Text Format (*.rtf).

25. From the drop-down menu click "F_ile," and then click "Save A_s."

26. Figure 20.16 shows MS Word's Save As dialog box. When the dialog box opens, select a directory in which to store your sample Help files. Name your file "My Help."

**N O T E** You may need to create a directory for your sample Help in advance. ■

**FIGURE 20.16**
Save your RTF file using MS Word's Save As dialog box.

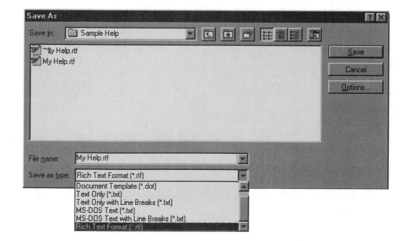

27. Click the drop-down button for the "Save as t_ype" field.

28. From the drop-down list select "Rich Text Format" (*.rtf), and then click "S_ave."

Now you have a Rich Text Format (\*.rtf) file that MS Help Workshop can use to create a Help system.

**Creating a Help File**    The next step in the process of creating a Help system is to create a project (\*.hpj) file. We will create a project file, and then compile and view the Help system.

1. From the Windows 95 desktop, click "Start" and then click Programs.
2. Click Microsoft Help Workshop, then click the icon labeled Help Workshop.
3. Once Help Workshop is open, click "File," then click "New."
4. When the dialog box opens select "Help Project," and then click "OK."
5. Select the folder you have chosen to store your sample Help files.
6. Name your new project file "My Help.hpj" and be sure to type the extension .hpj, then click "Save."

The Help Workshop project file interface appears in Figure 20.17, with your new project file My Help.hpj loaded. Now you must identify the "My Help.rtf" file with your topics in it, for Help Workshop to use.

**FIGURE 20.17**
Create Help project files using Workshop's project file interface.

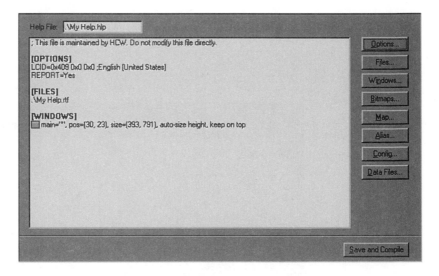

7. From the buttons on the righthand side of the interface, click "Files," and then click "Add."
8. A dialog box like the one shown in Figure 20.18 appears, allowing you to open a file.

The directory in the "Look In" field should already be the same directory in which you have your sample Help files. Also, the "Files Of type" field should already be set to "*.rtf". The file, "My Help.rtf," should be easy to select by clicking its icon or name in the window in the middle of the dialog box.

**FIGURE 20.18**

Import RTF files into your project file using this interface.

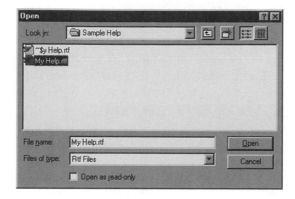

9. Click the icon or name for the file My Help.rtf.

10. Click "Open," then click "OK."

Now your project file has a Rich Text Format (*.rtf) file and, therefore, topics.

11. Click the compile button in the lower righthand corner.

**Viewing a Help File**　The Help Workshop window disappears for a second or two and then reappears. Now we will view the new Help system.

1. When Help Workshop reappears, click "File" from the drop-down menu, and then click "Run WinHelp," as shown in Figure 20.19.

**FIGURE 20.19**

When the window reappears, click File and then click Run WinHelp.

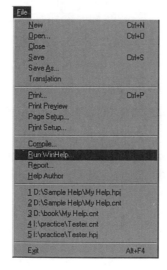

Part

**IV**

Ch

**20**

2. Now check the "A double-clicked file icon" field, and then click "View Help."

You should be looking at the first topic in your new Help system as shown in Figure 20.20. Two words should be colored green, pop-up and jump. Notice that when you place the mouse pointer over a green word it becomes a hand. This signifies that it is over a hotspot. Click the green word "pop-up." A little pop-up window appears containing your topic, pop-up. Now click the green word "jump." A new Help window appears that contains only the topic jump. Click the button labeled "Back" to return to your first topic.

**FIGURE 20.20**
View your new Windows 95 Help system.

# Tutorial—Adding Features to Your Help System

Now that we have a Help system, we can add features to make it easier to use and a bit more interesting. First, we will add a Contents. Then we will add a graphic and a graphic with hotspots. We will customize the Help window and, finally, create a non-scrolling region for a topic heading.

### Adding Contents

1. Open Help Workshop (if it is not open) and click "File," then click "New."

2. This time instead of selecting "Help Project," select "Help Contents."

3. Click "OK."

   Figure 20.21 displays the interface used to create a Contents for our Help system. Notice the button bar at the top and the one on the righthand side. Also, notice the drop-down menu above the toolbar (the top button bar).

4. In the "Default title" field type your new Help system's title, `My Help Sample`.

5. From the buttons on the right hand side, click "Add Above."

6. Check the "Heading" field.

**FIGURE 20.21**

Create a Contents file using this interface.

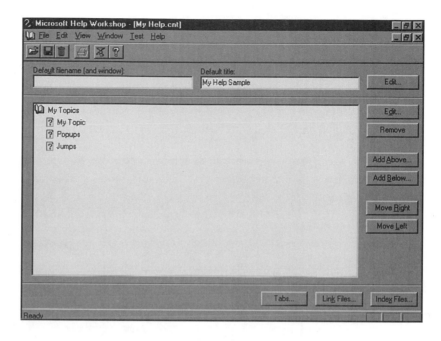

7. Now type your title **My Topics** in the "Title" field and click "OK" (see Figure 20.22.)

   Your first book icon appears in the Help Workshop window. It should be labeled "My Topics." Next we will add the topics to the Contents.

**FIGURE 20.22**

Create a Contents heading with MS Help Workshop's Creation dialog box.

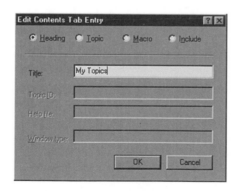

Part

**IV**

Ch

**20**

8. Click the button, "Add Below."

9. Once in the dialog box, check the "Topic ID" field.

10. In the "Title" field, type your topic title, **My Topic**. You can make up any title you like.

11. In the "Topic ID" field, type the topic name for your first topic, **My Topic**. Make sure you use the topic name exactly (case does not matter) as it is in the footnotes of the My Help.rtf file.

12. Click "OK."

   You should have your first page icon labeled "My Topic," in your new contents.

13. Now repeat this procedure to add your second and third topics. Remember to use the exact topic name (excepting case) in the "Topic ID" field.

   When you are finished, you should be able to see one open book icon and three page icons labeled with your topic titles as shown in Figure 20.23.

**FIGURE 20.23**

Your new Contents file should look like this.

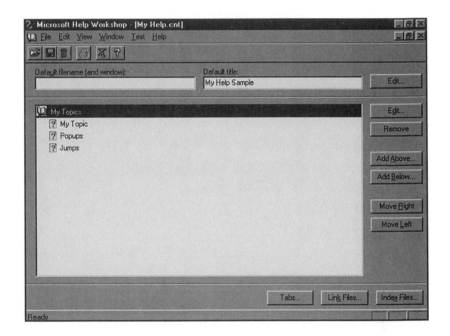

14. In the top button bar, click the Save button. This will save your new My Help.hpj file.

15. Select the directory that is storing your sample Help files and name your new contents file My Help.cnt.

16. Click "Save."

17. Now on the same button bar click the compile button.

   Figure 20.24 shows the interface that appears after you click the compile button in the Contents interface.

18. Check the field labeled "Automatically display Help file in WinHelp when done."

19. Now click the Compile button. Your new Help system should be compiled, and you should be viewing it.

20. If not, click "File" then click "Run WinHelp."

21. Click the "View Help" button.

**FIGURE 20.24**
Use the Contents
Compiler interface to
compile your Help file.

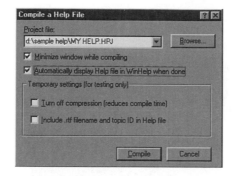

 You should be looking at the contents of your new Help system. Notice the title bar. You should see the words, "Help Topics: My Help Sample." If you double-click the book icon, page icons representing hotspots to your topics should appear. If you click any of the pages, they should take you to that topic.

**Adding Graphics**    Now we will add a graphic. You need a small graphic image file to accomplish this. You can find BMP files in your Windows directory.

Windows Help systems accept Windows bitmap (.bmp) files, Windows Metafiles (*.wmf), Windows Help SHED files with hotspots (*.shg), and Windows Help multiresolution files (*.mrb).

We suggest a small bitmap for this tutorial.

1. Open MS Word or your preferred word processing application.
2. Open the file My Help.rtf. and place the cursor at the end of the first topic.
3. Hit Enter on the keyboard to insert a return.
4. From the drop-down menu, click "Insert," then "Picture."
5. Now locate the graphic you have chosen for this tutorial, such as any one of the BMP files found in your Windows directory, and click "OK."

If you decide to compile and look at your graphic in My Sample Help, be sure to save all files that are involved, including the My Help.rtf file.

**Adding Graphics with Hotspots**    Now we will create a hotspot graphic.

1. From the Windows 95 Desktop, click "Start," then "Programs."
2. Click "Microsoft Help Workshop" and then click "Hotspot Editor."
3. When the application opens click "File," then click "Open."
4. When the dialog box opens, locate the directory that is storing your graphic file and open the file.

Part
**IV**

Ch
**20**

The Hotspot Editor appears with your graphic image loaded as shown in Figure 20.25.

**FIGURE 20.25**

Use the Hotspot Editor to create hotspots on graphics.

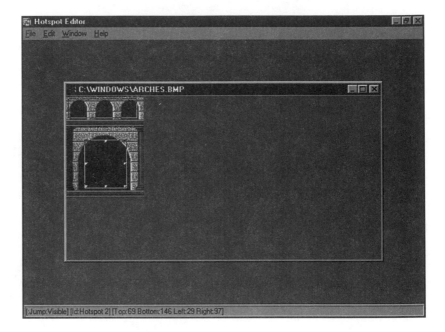

5. Drag the mouse from the top left corner of your image to the lower right corner of the image.

6. Click "Edit" and then click "Attributes."

7. When the "Attributes" dialog box opens as shown in Figure 20.26, type a new topic ID, **popup2**, in the "Context String" field.

**FIGURE 20.26**

Identify the hotspot using Hotspot Editor's Attributes dialog box.

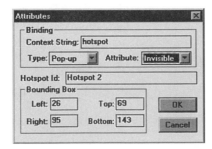

 8. Click the dropdown button for the "Type" field and select pop-up window from the drop-down list.

9. In the "Attribute" field click the  invisible button. Notice two smaller buttons immediately below it.

10. Click the higher of the two smaller buttons. The field changes to "INVISIBLE." This will keep the hotspot square from appearing on the image in the Help system.

11. Click "OK."

12. Now save your new graphic file as hotspot.shg. Make sure you save your file to the same directory that stores your sample Help files.

13. Return to the file My Help.rtf in your word processor.

14. Place your cursor at the end of the first topic.

15. Type the following line:

    `{bml hotspot.shg} This graphic is a hotspot.`

    - `{}` the braces signify that an object is to be placed in the location.

    - `bm` signifies that you intend to place a graphic image in the location.

    - `l` designates that you want the image at the left margin. A "c" designates that the image be placed in the center, and an "r" designates that the graphic be placed at the right margin.

    - `hotspot.shg`, of course is the filename for the image.

    We still need to create a pop-up window before this hotspot can call it to appear in Help.

16. Place the cursor at the end of the document, but before the footnote.

17. Now hit Ctrl-Enter to insert a page break.

18. Type the words `This topic is the graphic's popup window.`

19. Place the cursor at the beginning of the new topic and add a footnote. Use the # in the field marked "Custom Mark," and type `popup2` in the footnote for a topic ID. Make sure that the topic ID is exactly the same (excepting case) as what you typed in the "Context String" field, for the hotspot in the Hotspot Editor.

20. Save your file.

By all means, recompile and view your revised My Sample Help, if you are so inclined.

### Customizing Windows and Adding Buttons

1. Return to (or reopen) Help Workshop with your My Help.hpj file loaded.

2. Click the "Windows" button on the right hand side. Your window should look like Figure 20.27. This is the dialog box used to create, size, and color Help windows. You can also add buttons to the button bar and create access to macros.

Part
**IV**

Ch
**20**

**FIGURE 20.27**
Customize Help
windows using this
interface.

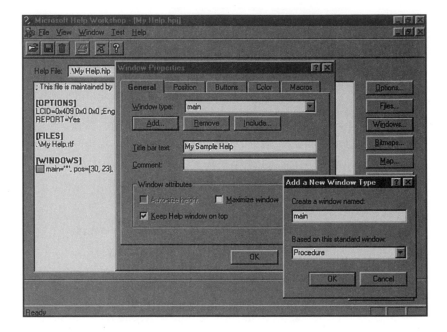

3. Click the tab marked "General," then click "Add."

4. In the "Create a window named" field, type the word main and click "OK."
   We are going to redefine the main Help window.

**NOTE** You can add secondary windows by giving each window a unique name. ■

5. Click the tab marked "Position" and then click the autosize button
   (see Figure 20.28).

6. Now you can place the mouse on the edges of the window and drag it to resize the
   window. You can also use the mouse to move the window.

7. When you like the size and location of your main window, click the OK button.

8. Now click the tab marked "Buttons." This interface is used to add or subtract
   buttons from the button bar.

9. Click the tab marked "Color."

   Notice two color change buttons. The top button changes the color of the non-
   scrolling region, and the lower button changes the color of the scrolling region.

   You can use the interface shown in Figure 20.29 to customize the color of scrolling
   and non-scrolling regions in any Help window.

**FIGURE 20.28**
Drag to size and position your custom Help windows.

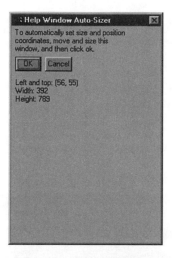

**FIGURE 20.29**
Customize your window colors using this interface.

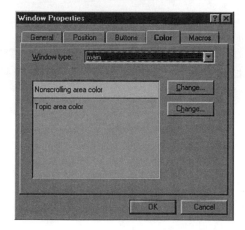

10. Click the top "Change" button, and click a color.

11. Click the lower "Change" button and pick a different color.

12. Click "OK."

13. Be sure to save your file.

The next time you view your first topic, it should include one of the new colors.

**Non-Scrolling Regions** Small Help windows have the ability to contain long topics with the help of scroll bars. However, authors can place titles and information such as overview information in regions above the scrolling window, that do not scroll up. The user can scroll to the bottom of a topic and still see the title and/or overview information.

Part
**IV**
Ch
**20**

1. In the file My Help.rtf, place the cursor at the beginning of the first topic.

2. Hit the Enter key, then place the cursor above the first line.

3. Type the following line:

   `NON-SCROLLING REGION`

4. Now select the entire line with your mouse.

5. From the drop-down menu click Format, then "Paragraph."

6. Select the tab marked "Text Flow," then check the "Keep With Next" field, as shown in Figure 20.30.

**FIGURE 20.30**
Use MS Word's Paragraph dialog box to mark non-scrolling regions.

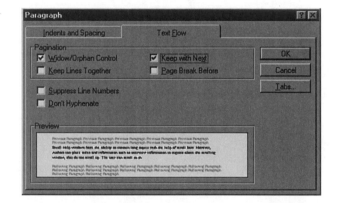

7. Click "OK."

8. Now place your cursor at the end of the text in the first topic and hit "Enter" to place the cursor below the text.

9. Hit "1 Enter," repeatedly until you use up a full page. The objective is to force the Help window to use a scroll bar.

10. Now save your file, compile Help, and view your first topic.

    You should be able to see the non-scrolling region in the color of your choice, as well as a scroll bar in the scrolling region. Scroll down and see that the non-scrolling region remains unmoved.

# More Features for Windows 95 Help Systems

Authors can add many features to a Windows 95 Help system. A few of the options available are:

1. Use of AVI and WAV files to add animation and sound to your Help system. Use WAV files to add verbal instruction to your Help system.

2. Creation of custom buttons to display pop-ups, jumps, or carry out macros. Using macros you can program Help to take the user directly to a specific application, in a specific dialog box, and the macro can even carry out procedures for users.

3. Creation of jumps directly to sites on the Internet.

4. Creation of up to 255 different, customizable styles of Help window for each Help system. You can designate any given topic to be displayed in a specific window style by inserting a footnote with a ">" in the "Custom Mark" field and naming the window style in the footnote. Help can display one of each window style simultaneously.

5. Creation of Browse Buttons to allow users to "browse" sequentially through procedures with multiple topics.

6. Creation of an Index, including any words the author believes the user might look up, whether or not they are in the Help text.

7. Creation of links between topics using K-Link (indexable) words and A-Link (hidden) words.

# Creating Windows 95 Context-Sensitive Help

Windows 95 applications using standard Windows dialog boxes, such as "Open," "Save," and "Print," and standard Windows buttons such as "OK" and "Cancel," already have context-sensitive Help built in. You do not need to create or map these topics.

Making a Help system interact with an application's interface requires a two-part procedure. First, you must create and properly identify the topics. This includes numerically mapping the topics in the Help project file so the application can identify each topic in its proper location. The second part of the procedure is to integrate the Help map into the application's interface, a programmer's job.

Part
IV

Ch
20

## Mapping Topics for Use in an Application's Interface

To make a Help topic context-sensitive you must first identify the topic with a prefix to identify it as being a context-sensitive topic. Note that the topic can also be in standard Help and/or in the Help Index. Second, you must identify each context-sensitive topic individually. To accomplish this, use numerical mapping in the Help project file.

**IDH_ Prefix**   You must add an IDH_ prefix to your topic ID in the (*.rtf) file to identify it as a context-sensitive topic. For example, you could add the following topic to your sample Help system.

# This is my context-sensitive topic.

# IDH_CONTEXT_SENSITIVE

The topic ID is IDH_CONTEXT_SENSITIVE. Notice that the topic ID includes underscores in place of spaces. A topic ID cannot contain spaces.

Help Workshop allows you to allocate prefixes other than IDH_ to identify context-sensitive Help. However, if you use prefixes other than IDH_ , you must specify them in the Map dialog box in Help Workshop.

### Numerically Mapping Context-Sensitive Topics

1. First open Help Workshop and load your Help project file.

2. From the buttons on the right click "Map…".

   Figure 20.31 shows the interface used to identify context-sensitive topics for the application.

**FIGURE 20.31**
Use Help Workshop's
Map interface to
identify topics within
application interfaces.

3. When the dialog box appears, type the topic ID in the "Topic ID" field.

   Type the number that is to identify the topic in the "Mapped numeric value" field.

   Click "OK" and click "OK" again.

From the dialog box shown in Figure 20.32 you can add, delete, or edit context-sensitive mapping in project files.

**FIG 20.32**
Use Help Workshop's
map edit interface
to edit context-
sensitive mapping.

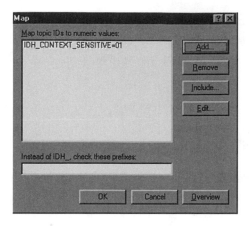

**Using a C Header**   From Help Workshop's project file interface, click "Map," then click "Include."

From the dialog box shown in Figure 20.33, you can use a C header file instead of or, in addition to, manually assigning numbers to topics in Help Workshop. If you use both, make sure that each topic is identified with a unique number.

Type the C header filename in the "File to include" field. If the file is not in the folder that the Help project is in, you must include the path to the file.

Click "OK."

**FIGURE 20.33**
Use the C Header
dialog box to integrate
programmers'
C Header files for
context-sensitive
mapping.

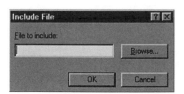

# Adding Help to Your Application

There are three basic types of help:

- A simple help menu option
- Context-Sensitive Help
- "What's This" Help

Part
**IV**

Ch
**20**

You can mix and match any of these help styles in your applications. In most cases, it is possible to implement all three from one basic help file. The rest of this chapter examines how to integrate help files created using the techniques in the first half of this chapter with your application.

## Loading a Help File

So far we've discussed the different types of help available and how to create them. At this point, you've created a help file so we'll now review what's required to integrate help into your application. The default setting for help is ON, but it doesn't hurt to make sure by entering the following:

```
SET HELP ON
```

You can turn help off by entering:

```
SET HELP OFF
```

Setting help on activates Visual FoxPro's help system, regardless of the file or type of help system you use. Next set help to your help file. Using SET HELP TO, enter the path, name, and extension of the help file you wish to use. The following activates a Windows style help system named MYHELP in the default directory.

```
SET HELP TO myhelp.hlp
```

## Activating Help

While it is possible to program any key combination using ON KEY LABEL to activate help (ON KEY LABEL F2 HELP), I suggest that you don't change it from F1. This is a windows standard, and programming other keys to activate help may confuse your users. You can always activate help by entering HELP from the command window or from your program.

## Building a Basic Help Menu

A help menu is the simplest help style you can create. It typically consists of an option in the menu bar called Help. It may simply open the Help Finder window shown in Figure 20.34 by issuing the HELP command in the menu option's code, or it may open a drop-down menu of related options that could include:

■ An option to open the Contents page of Help
■ An option to open the Index page of Help

- A reference to the company's Web page
- An option to list the types of technical support for the application and how to reach them
- An About box with copyright, version, and license information

**FIGURE 20.34**

The Help Finder Window can be programmatically opened with the command HELP.

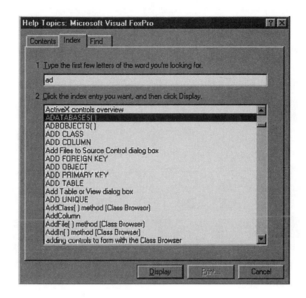

## Context-Sensitive Help

Context-sensitive help is a way of providing the users with help about their current activities. You've seen this behavior before. Open the form builder and press F1. Help about the form builder appears. You can do the same with the menu builder or report writer. This includes help for a procedure or help on a given screen. We want the help presented to focus on the action at hand, not just a scrollable list of items. There are several ways of implementing context-sensitive help. The easiest way to show this is by issuing the following at the command window:

```
HELP SEEK
```

Information about the SEEK command appears directly. In program code you can do this by issuing the following commands:

```
x="SEEK"
```

```
HELP &x
```

This method involves referencing help topics. If you tell Visual FoxPro what the topic is and it can find that topic reference, then help automatically activates that topic.

Part

**IV**

Ch

**20**

In Windows style Help, this means referencing the topic by using the keywords you defined with the "K" footnote.

With Windows help, using our sample help file, you would also enter:

```
SET TOPIC TO POPUP
HELP
```

Change the topic back to an empty expression once you're done, or else trigger help on the last requested topic by entering HELP from the command window.

> **N O T E**   There is also a mini-type of help available in Visual FoxPro. It's called tool tip text.
> These mini helpers are the yellow boxes that appear when you rest your cursor on a button or menu pad. You've probably seen them if you own Word or Visual Basic. You can add tool tips through the Properties dialog of the Form Designer. To learn more about form and control properties, look at the chapters about the Form Designer (Chapters 12 and 14). ■

## Adding Form-Level Context-Sensitive Help

Context-sensitive help gives users the ability to directly jump to a specific help topic based on what the user is currently doing. At its simplest level, context-sensitive help refers to the current form. However, you can also apply context-sensitive help to each and every control on the form.

To set context help at the form level, simply open the form using the Form Designer and change the property HelpContextID. By default, this property has a value of zero indicating that there is no available help topic. Simply change this value to an appropriate topic ID defined by the MAP file discussed earlier in this chapter. You can also set this property during runtime with a line like:

```
Thisform.HelpContextID = 15
```

Form level context-sensitive help opens a single help topic no matter which control currently has focus. This help topic should therefore provide information about the form itself and its purpose. However, it can also include jump points to:

- Explain specific controls.
- Provide step-by-step procedures.
- Explain other related actions the user should also perform.

Implementing form-level help can be as simple as including text that explains how to use the form or as complex as a multiple hotspot image of the form on which the user can click for detailed help on specific controls.

Adding context-sensitive help to individual controls is just like adding form-level help. Each base control has a HelpContextId property. Simply set each control on a form to its unique help topic using the Properties window of the Form Designer or set them interactively as follows:

```
cmdExit.HelpContextID = 78
txtFirstName.HelpContextID = 104
```

If you use object-level context-sensitive help for some objects on a form, you should use it for all. However, if you don't, Visual FoxPro moves back up to the form level to check it for a help topic if the object does not have one (HelpContextId = 0).

Keep in mind that when using field-level help, the help topic text should only pertain to the current field. If you need to reference information in other fields, use jumps to those topics. Similarly, if you have topics that define procedure steps, use jumps to them. Most important, "Don't repeat the same text in more than one topic." Write it once as a separate topic and create jumps to it.

Every object that can receive focus supports this property—even objects that you normally don't associate with receiving focus, like labels. Whether to use the HelpContextId or the WhatsThisHelpId is an issue taken up later in this chapter. For now, just know that you can define two different help topics IDs per object.

## Adding What's This Help

What's This Help is a new feature to Visual FoxPro 5.0.

To implement this feature, you must first turn on the WhatsThisButton in the form. Set this property to True to display a question mark button in the upper right side of the form's title bar. Figure 20.35 shows some of these settings.

You must also set the following properties:

- BorderStyle = (any value except 0 - None)
- WhatsThisHelp = True
- MinButton = False
- MaxButton = False

While other languages may support a WhatsThisButton feature, they may have other requirements for related properties. For example, Visual Basic automatically sets WhatsThisHelp to True.

When the user clicks this button, the mouse pointer changes to an arrow with a question mark. As shown in Figure 20.36, the user needs only to click this button and then click a control to display its corresponding help topic defined by the property WhatsThisHelpId.

**FIGURE 20.35**

The Properties window shows some of the settings for the WhatsThisButton feature.

**FIGURE 20.36**

To use the WhatsThisHelp feature, just click the question mark button in the title bar and the object you want help with.

> **N O T E**   You can programmatically enable the WhatsThis mouse pointer mode (arrow with question mark) by invoking the WhatsThisMode method of the form.
>
> ThisForm.WhatsThisMode ∎

You have to set the WhatsThisHelp property, also on the form. When set to True, the form uses the WhatsThisHelpId property to determine which help topic to display. Otherwise, it uses the HelpContextId property, even if you previously set the WhatsThisButton to True.

Finally, you need to set the WhatsThisHelpId. By default, the Form Designer sets this property to -1. If the user invokes help for such an object, it displays the message "No Help topic is associated with this item." A value of 0 tells VFP to look back up the object hierarchy for the first container that does have a help topic (this typically is a form, pageframe, or grid, but could be any container object). Any positive value searches the help file for a matching context ID. If the context ID is not found, it displays the message:

*The topic does not exist. Contact your application vendor for an updated Help file.*

**TROUBLESHOOTING**

**I've set the context IDs, but when I run the program and press F1, I still do not get any help displayed.** If you have defined HelpContextId values, you must set the WhatsThisHelp property for the form to False. If you want to use WhatsThisHelpID values, set WhatsThisHelp to True. Also be sure to set the help file to the correct file with SET HELP TO.

One final important point about WhatsThisHelp. It only displays the text in the topic title. This may be fine for a quick explanation, but to get detailed help, you must use the HelpContextId values. Note, however, that while the WhatsThisHelp property is set to True, pressing F1 also displays only the WhatsThisHelpId topic title text.

## Using Context IDs as Help

Each object within Visual FoxPro has a help context ID. The number entered within that property acts as a unique reference to a help topic.

In Windows help you must map each context string to a number and then pass that number to the help compiler. In the DEMO project file, we added a section like the following example:

```
[MAP]
QueryDesigner            100
```

Setting the HelpContextID to 100 and invoking help will now retrieve the correct help topic. There is yet another method in calling help from windows. You can access the Windows API with "FOXTOOLS.FLL" which ships with Visual FoxPro. The following code gives an example of invoking help using the Windows API.

```
#define_Help context           1
#define Help_quit               2
#define Help_index              3
#define Help_helponhelp         4
#define Help_setindex           5
#define Help_key               257
SET LIBRARY TO SYS(2004)+"FOXTOOLS.FLL"
winhelpi   = REGFN("WINHELP","LCIL","I")
lcHelpfile = "C:VFP\HC35\DEMO.HLP"
wCmd       = Help_context
dwdata     = 100
=callfn( winhelpi, mainhwnd(), lcHelpfile, wCmd, dwdata )
```

Part

**IV**

Ch

**20**

**N O T E**    Traditionally the F1 key has been used as the hot key to activate help. You can give
your users automatic help if they encounter a problem. Two areas that come to mind
are error conditions and problems within an application. I usually include an error handler as part
of any application. As soon as a problem is encountered, a screen pops up noting the problem
and prompts the user for input as to what the next action should be. Why not track how often your
users are having a problem and then automatically pop up the help for them? As an example, set
your auto help feature to appear after three errors in a row are returned from a validation routine.
The auto help is a program you've written. You would then activate the help engine with context-
sensitive information. Make sure you give the user the ability to turn off this feature. Some people
don't like to be told what to do when they make a mistake! ■

The menu system has changed little since FoxPro 2.6 and is one of the few things that has
not been converted into an object. As a result, there is no provision for assigning a help
context ID directly to the menu pads or bars. The best you can do is to a assign each
menu item a Message string in the Prompt Options box, which you can open through the
Menu Designer. Help is often overlooked when a new project is started. If you have multiple developers assigned to a project it's a good idea to keep track of context IDs. First,
consider assigning a range of numbers to each developer. Let's say there are three developers working on a project. Assign number ranges to each developer in increments of 100.
Developer A gets 1 to 100, developer B gets 101 to 200, and developer C gets 201 to 300.
When one of the developers exhausts the list of numbers, assign them another set of 100
numbers. Each developer should keep a separate table of the help context IDs, the topic
references, and the actual topics. The material would be combined at compile time.

# Help Authoring Tools

Now that you've actually created a small help file using the WinHelp 4 compiler, let's take
a look at a few options that can automate much of the mundane process of coding the help
file. To date, the most talked about help authoring tools include RoboHELP, Doc-To-Help,
and ForeHelp.

RoboHELP 95, by Blue Skies Software, is a full-featured help authoring system designed
to take advantage of the new Windows 95 Help conventions such as Contents, advanced
button capabilities, as well as high resolution graphics support and multimedia integration. RoboHELP 95 is designed to work in conjunction with Microsoft's Word 7. Robo-
HELP 95 adds its own tool bar and menu items to Word, so you can easily create jumps,
pop-ups, and hotspot graphics as you go. RoboHELP 95 also includes an export feature
that strips out all unnecessary help coding so that you can easily convert the help file to
printed manual.

Doc-To-Help 2.0, by Wextech Systems, Inc., is an almost fully-automated help authoring tool designed to create Windows 95 style help. Doc-To-Help's strongest feature is the ability to create one file for both the on-line help and printed document. Doc-to-Help 2.0 comes complete with templates to be used in conjunction with Word 7 to create attractive looking printed manuals. The focus of Doc-To-Help is to create the printed document in Word 7, then, with a click of a button, convert the DOC file to a help file. Doc-To-Help automatically converts cross-references and page numbers to hypertext jumps, changes margin notes to pop-up windows, adds the context IDs, footnotes, and any other necessary on-line help codes.

ForeHelp 2.0, by ForeFront, is a self-contained, full-featured help authoring tool that has its own word processor. ForeHelp's primary focus is on developing on-line help in a WYSIWYG environment. You do not see any of the help coding; instead, you see much of what the end user will see. Unlike both RoboHELP 95 and Doc-To-Help 2.0, there is no wasted time spent compiling the help file over and over again. ForeHelp's Test button lets you see what your file looks like without compiling. In fact, you do not have to actually compile the help file until you are completely finished with the project. ForeHelp also offers tools for creating a printed document.

# From Here...

This chapter described the different ways that Visual FoxPro allows you to add help to your applications. The simplest type of help uses status bar messages and toolbar help, but both of these methods are limited to a few words. For a more robust Help system, you need to create a DOS or Windows style Help system. Windows style Help systems are more flexible in that they provide the ability to add graphics and jump points, and they can even launch other applications. The resulting Help system can be run as a separate application whenever the user presses the F1 key, or it can be integrated as context-sensitive help.

To learn more about finishing your application, refer to:

- Chapter 11, "Building Applications with Simple Form Structures," to learn more about how to work with form properties.

- Chapter 15, "Organizing Components of an Application into a Project," to learn how to include your Help system in the project so that it becomes part of the distribution disks.

Part
IV

Ch
20

# Appendixes

# Configuration Files

*by Michael Antonovich*

**W**hen you start Visual FoxPro, it reads a configuration file, if one exists, to preset the environment to the way that you want to work. Most of the SET commands available in the language have equivalents in the configuration file. Also, additional commands affect the way that Visual FoxPro works with your hardware and applications.

This appendix takes a brief look at the types of things you can control through the configuration file. Before you begin, however, the first section takes a quick look at some command-line options that you can pass to VFP when you start it. ■

# Using Command-Line Options

The command-line options, also called *switches*, allow you to specify different options when Visual FoxPro starts. The -t option, for example, skips the initial splash screen and starts VFP directly in the desktop environment. There are also switches to specify a different configuration file, a different runtime DLL, and a different resource file. You can even have VFP ignore the configuration file and the registry settings. Table A.1 describes these options.

| Table A.1 | Command-Line Switches |
| --- | --- |
| **Switch** | **Function** |
| -A | Ignores the default configuration file and Registry settings. |
| -C | Allows you to specify a different configuration file. |
| -D | Allows you to use a different Visual FoxPro runtime DLL. |
| -L | Specifies a different resource file from the default. |
| -R | Refreshes the Windows Registry with file associations for Visual FoxPro; does not affect Option dialog settings stored in the Registry. |
| -T | Suppresses the sign-on (splash) screen; then Visual FoxPro starts. |

Suppose that you want to skip the splash screen and use a configuration file named C:\MYSTUFF\MYCONFIG.FPW. Then, use a startup command like the following:

```
\VFP\VFP.EXE -t -cC:\MYSTUFF\MYCONFIG.FPW
```

In Windows 95, choose the Run option from the Start menu. In the resulting dialog box, enter the preceding command to run VFP. Windows 95 stores the last several commands entered in the open field. To use an existing command, click the arrow to the right of the field to display a list, and select one.

If you have already installed a shortcut icon on your desktop for VFP (as described in Chapter 1, "Quick Review of Visual FoxPro's Interface"), right-click it and select the Properties option. Next, select the Shortcut page on the Visual FoxPro Properties dialog and place the preceding command in the Target text box.

# Configuring Your Startup Session with CONFIG.FPW

The preceding section mentions the use of a configuration file. Did you know that you can have many configuration files? You can have a development configuration file, application-specific configuration files, and even configuration files for each user. The following code shows a typical developer's configuration file (Listing A.1), along with a startup file (Listing A.2). (The details of your configuration file may vary, depending on the tools that you use and your directories.)

**Listing A.1   MYSTUFF.FPW:**

```
SAFETY = OFF
TALK = OFF
EXCLUSIVE = OFF
CENTURY = ON
DEVELOPMENT = ON
DEBUG = ON
PATH = D:\VFP;D:\FOXUTILS;P:\MYPROJ
RESOURCE = D:\VFP\MYRESORC.DBF
TITLE = NATASHA'S PLAY ROOM
TMPFILES = C:\TEMP
_STARTUP = "D:\VFP\MYSTUFF.PRG"
```

**Listing A.2   MYSTUFF.PRG:**

```
PROCEDURE MYSTUFF
LPARAMETER lcDevelopMode
PUBLIC _DevelopMode

* Clear Memory and Close data files
  CLEAR ALL          && Clear memory
  CLOSE ALL          && Close data files
  RELEASE WINDOWS    && Clear all orphaned windows
  ON KEY             && Clear ON KEY LABELs
  CLEAR              && Clear main window

* User defined system var for determining
* whether we're in development mode
  IF TYPE("lcDevelopMode")="C" .AND. UPPER(lcDevelopMode)="OFF"
    _DevelopMode=.F.
  ELSE
    _DevelopMode=.T.
  ENDIF
```

*continues*

**Listing A.2   Continued**

```
* Assign a few hotkeys for common access
  ON KEY LABEL F12 DO MACROS
  ON KEY LABEL F11 DO SYS(2004)+"browser.app"

* Now reset the system menu
  SET SYSMENU TO DEFAULT

* Load custom menu pads
  foxhome = SYS(2004)
  IF FILE(foxhome+"DEVELOPR.MPR")
    DO &foxhome.DEVELOPR.MPR
  ENDIF
  IF FILE(foxhome+"TIMETRAK.MPR")
    DO &foxhome.TIMETRAK.MPR
  ENDIF

* restore keyboard macros
  IF FILE(foxhome+"DEFAULT.FKY")
    RESTORE MACROS FROM &foxhome.DEFAULT
  ENDIF

* Editor Enhancement
  IF FILE(foxhome+"CEE5.APP")
    DO &foxhome.CEE5
  ENDIF

* Add shutdown check  -  (found in Chapter 1)
  IF FILE(foxhome+"REALQUIT.PRG")
    ON SHUTDOWN DO &foxhome.REALQUIT.PRG
  ENDIF
```

The location of the configuration file depends on how you want to use it. If you are satisfied with a single configuration file for all of your work, simply use the file CONFIG.FPW, located in the \VFP directory. You can either modify the existing file or create one with a different name. If you use one with a different name or path, however, you must pass that name to VFP by using the -C startup switch, described in the preceding section.

If you have different configuration files per application, you might want to store the configuration file in the main directory of the application. If you want FoxPro to automatically start the application whenever the user starts VFP, you can place the configuration file in a common directory, such as the VFP directory, and use the _STARTUP or COMMAND option to start the application.

Suppose that you have an application named INVOICE; you might want to add a configuration file in \VFP named INVOICE.FPW with the following line:

```
_STARTUP = \BUSINESS\AR\INVOICE.APP
```

You can use the same format to specify any of the other system variables (all defined with a leading underscore character).

Then start VFP with this command:

```
\VFP\VFP.EXE -cINVOICE.FPW
```

This is not all that you can put in the configuration file. In fact, you can define many options. The basic syntax for all commands is:

```
<Visual FoxPro Setting> = <Value>
```

To set talk off, for example, add the following line to the configuration file:

```
TALK = OFF
```

You can also place all SET commands in the configuration file by using a similar format, with the name of the SET command first, followed by an equal sign, and then the desired value. Table A.2 shows some of the more common SET commands found in configuration files:

**Table A.2   Common SET Values in Configuration Files**

| SET Command | Values | Definition |
| --- | --- | --- |
| TALK | ON \| OFF | Determines whether command results are echoed back to the screen. |
| DEBUG | ON \| OFF | Determines whether the Debugger option is available in the System menu. |
| DEVELOPMENT | ON \| OFF | Uses the creation time and date between the source and compiled file to determine whether the program needs to be recompiled before being run. |
| REPROCESS | 0-32000 \| AUTOMATIC | Determines how many times or how long VFP attempts to obtain a lock on a file or record. |
| EXCLUSIVE | ON \| OFF | Determines whether VFP attempts to open tables exclusive by default. In a single-user environment, setting EXCLUSIVE=ON improves performance. |
| PATH | <path;path...> | Defines the search path for locating files; is not affected by data sessions. |

Table A.3 defines some additional terms found in the configuration file.

| Table A.3    Configuration File Special Terms | |
|---|---|
| **Switch** | **Function** |
| EDITWORK | Defines where the text editor places temporary files. The best choice is a local drive. Speed of the drive in this case is not critical, but free space is. |
| INDEX | Allows you to define the default extension for index files other than IDX. |
| LABEL | Allows you to define the default extension for label files other than LBX. |
| MVCOUNT | Sets the maximum number of memory variables. The default is 1,024, but the setting can range from 128 to 65,000. |
| OUTSHOW | Toggles the use of Shift+Ctrl+Alt to hide open windows. |
| PROGWORK | Defines where VFP caches the program when running it. The best choice is a local drive. Speed of the drive in this case is critical. |
| REPORT | Allows you to define the default extension for report files other than FRX. |
| RESOURCE | Defines the location and name of the resource file. If RESOURCE is not specified, VFP uses FOXUSER.DBF in the directory \VFP. |
| SORTWORK | Defines where VFP places its temporary files when sorting or indexing a table. The available space should be at least twice the size of the largest file that you are going to sort. The best choice is a local drive. Speed of the drive in this case is critical. |
| TEDIT | Specifies an alternative text editor to be used with MODIFY COMMAND and MODIFY WINDOW. |
| TITLE | Specifies the title in the Title Bar of the VFP main window. |
| TMPFILES | This command defines where VFP places all temporary files (rather than setting EDITWORK, SORTWORK, and PROGWORK individually). The best choice is a local drive. Speed of the drive in this case is critical, as is total free space. |

**TIP** Options dialog-box settings are stored in the registry, but you can use the configuration file to override these defaults.

# Setting the Environment from Within Visual FoxPro

Not only can you set the VFP environment from the configuration file, but you can also set it with the Options dialog box. The changes made in this dialog box are shared by all users, unlike a set of configuration files, which can be configured per user. The values set in the dialog box are stored in the registry if you click the Set As Default button.

If you press the Shift key while you click the OK button to exit the Options dialog box, VFP echoes the equivalent SET commands to the Command window. You can copy these commands to a separate program file that you can execute any time. SET commands executed in the Command window, however, apply only to the current data session, whereas options set with Tools, Options apply to all data sessions.

SET commands define values in one of two ways:

- **ON or OFF.** Many SET commands require you to set an option on or off. Examples are SET TALK ON, SET EXACT OFF, and SET EXCLUSIVE OFF.

- **TO <value>.** Some SET commands apply a value to the setting in question. The type of value depends on the SET command that you're using. Examples are:

```
SET HELP TO C:\VFP\FOXPRO.HLP
SET POINT TO "."
SET ORDER TO names
SET REPROCESS TO 2 SECONDS
SET PROCEDURE TO MYFUNCS.PRG
```

You can clear any setting by using

```
SET <SetCommand> TO
```

without specifying a value. This code assigns a default value or clears the setting, depending on the individual SET command.

Table A.4 lists a few of the most common SET commands and briefly describes what they do.

**Table A.4 Commonly Used SET Commands**

| SET Command | Options | Function |
|---|---|---|
| BELL | ON/OFF<br>TO <nFrequency, nDuration><br>TO <cWavefile> | Turns the bell on or off.<br>Determines the sound that's created.<br>Plays the specified .WAV file when beeping. |
| BLOCKSIZE | TO <nMemoblocksize> | Size of the smallest block saved in Memo fields. |
| CENTURY | ON/OFF | Determines whether Date fields display the year. Four digits are used with ON; two are used with OFF. |
| CLASSLIB | TO <classlibrary> [ADDITIVE] | Loads a class library. |
| COLLATE | TO <cLanguage> | Allows sorting and indexing appropriate to the selected language. |
| CONFIRM | ON/OFF | When ON, typing the last character in a field does not move the cursor to the next field automatically. |
| CURRENCY | TO <cCurrencysymbol><br><br>TO LEFT/RIGHT | Changes the currency symbol from the default $.<br>Determines whether the symbol goes to the left or right of the number displayed. |
| CURSOR | ON/OFF | Controls the edit cursor display. |
| DATABASE | TO <cDatabase> | Selects a database. |
| DATASESSION | TO <nDataSession> | Allows a move to a different data session. |
| DEBUG | ON/OFF | Determines whether the Trace and Debug windows are available. |
| DEFAULT | TO <cPath> | Sets the current directory for Visual FoxPro. DEFAULT works like CD, except that it works with drives. |

App
A

| SET Command | Options | Function |
|---|---|---|
| DELETED | ON/OFF | Determines whether deleted records are included in displayed, scoped, and queried data. |
| DEVELOPMENT | ON/OFF | If ON, program files are checked for being up-to-date and are recompiled if necessary. |
| ESCAPE | ON/OFF | If ON, a running program can be interrupted by pressing the Esc key. |
| EXACT | ON/OFF | Determines whether comparisons involving the = operator are done exactly or using only the character length of the expression on the right. |
| EXCLUSIVE | ON/OFF | Determines whether files can be accessed by more than one user. |
| FILTER | TO <cFilterExpression> | Limits the records for a table by assigning a filter. |
| HELP | ON/OFF<br>TO <cHelpFile> | Turns help on or off.<br>Selects the help file used. |
| LIBRARY | TO <cAPILibrary><br>[ADDITIVE] | Loads an API library file. |
| MEMOWIDTH | TO <nColumnWidth> | Determines how a Memo field wraps when you are using the MEMLINES( ) and MLINE( ) functions. |
| MESSAGE | TO <cMessageText> | Puts message text in the status bar. |
| MULTILOCKS | ON/OFF | When ON, multiple records can be locked in a table. Otherwise, only a single record is locked. |
| NEAR | ON/OFF | When ON, a nonmatching search with SEEK( ) goes to the nearest matching record in the index order. When OFF, the search goes to the EOF( ). |

*continues*

**Table A.4   Continued**

| SET Command | Options | Function |
| --- | --- | --- |
| NULL | ON/OFF | Determines whether NULL values are allowed in a table. |
| ORDER | TO <cIndexOrder> | Sets the index order for a table. |
| PATH | TO <cPath> | Sets the search path for all files loaded from within Visual FoxPro. |
| PROCEDURE | TO <cProcedure> [ADDITIVE] | Sets a procedure file to use. |
| RELATION | TO <cRelation Expression> INTO <cRelated Table> [ADDITIVE] | Allows you to set a relation into another work area. |
| REPROCESS | TO <nTimeOut> \| AUTOMATIC | Determines how record-lock conflicts are handled. |
| RESOURCE | ON/OFF | Turns the use of a resource file on and off. |
|  | TO <cResourceFile> | Selects the resource file to use. |
| SAFETY | ON/OFF | When ON, Visual FoxPro warns before overwriting a file. |
| SKIP | TO <cTable> | Sets up a one-to-many relation by stepping through the parent file. |
| SKIP OF | MENU/PAD/POPUP/ BAR TO <lExpression> | Enables and disables menu options. |
| STEP | ON/OFF | Enables single-stepping through code, using the debugger. |
| SYSMENU | ON/OFF/AUTOMATIC | Shows and hides the system menu. |
|  | TO DEFAULT | Resets the system menu to its default. |
| TEXTMERGE | ON/OFF | Allows file output using text-merge commands. |
|  | TO <cOutfile> | Determines where the file output is sent. |
| TOPIC | TO "<cHelpTopic>" | Sets the current help topic to pop up when the Help key is pressed. |

# Retrieving a Setting

With all of the possible SET commands, you probably will need to have your programs determine what the current setting is before you change it. In most cases, a well-behaved program returns the original settings before exiting.

## Using the *SET()* Function

To retrieve the current setting of any SET command, use the SET() function. In a command, call SET() with a character string that specifies the SET option to query; the function returns the requested setting. The syntax is:

```
<setting> = SET(<SetCommand>, [<optional parameters>])
```

Some typical SET queries are:

```
lcCurExact = SET("EXACT")
lcCurHelpFile = SET("HELP", 1)
lcCurMemoWidth = SET("MEMOWIDTH")
```

Notice that ON and OFF settings are returned as character strings, but the same SET commands do not accept character strings. To solve this problem, use macro expansion, as shown in the following code:

```
lcOldNear = SET("NEAR")
SET NEAR ON
... code that searches table for records
SET NEAR &lcOldNear
```

The preceding example is a case in which macro expansion is the only option. SET NEAR (lcOldNear) fails. A few commands accept this alternative method, but you should test it in the Command window before adding it to your code. Macro substitution always works.

You may also have noticed that some SET commands, such as HELP, support more than one value. Usually, a default value is returned when no second parameter is returned. In the case of HELP, SET("HELP") returns either ON or OFF, specifying whether help is active. However, SET("HELP", 1) returns the name of the active help file. You can find additional commands that support multiple values by checking the online help system.

Some SET commands, such as MEMOWIDTH, return numeric values. In this case, you can use the returned value directly to reset the value without resorting to macro substitution. The following code shows an example:

```
lnCurMemoWidth = SET("MEMOWIDTH")
SET MEMOWIDTH TO 25
<<enter code that requires the new memo width>>
SET MEMOWIDTH TO lnCurMemoWidth
```

A good programming practice is to always restore the environment to the state in which you found it. One technique might be to call a library function from the INIT method of the first application form to capture the current environment settings and store them as properties in a nonvisual custom object. Then, the DESTROY method of the closing form could retrieve these properties and reset the environment.

You can use the same technique even within an individual procedure or function when the application requires a different setting. The bottom line is: Always clean up your environmental changes as soon as practical.

## Using the *ON()* Function

The ON() function works similarly to SET(), returning the settings of various ON commands, such as ON ERROR, ON KEY, ON KEY LABEL, ON SHUTDOWN, and ON ESCAPE. The following code snippet temporarily changes the ON ERROR statement for a few lines in a single procedure and then resets it:

```
LcCurError = ON("ERROR")
llError = .F.
ON ERROR Do MYERRPRG.PRG

* Try to open a file exclusively
  USE customer EXCLUSIVE

ON ERROR &lcCurError
```

Notice that to return the command associated with a specific key, you need to include a second argument in ON() to identify which key you want to examine, as in the following example:

```
lcSHIFTF1 = ON("KEY", "SHIFT+F1")
```

## Getting System Settings with *SYS()*

You can return even more information with more than 50 SYS() commands. These commands typically have no other command equivalent (a few do, however). The commands return a variety of functions related to the operating system, the network, the printer status, the setup, and the currently executing program. The syntax is:

```
<value> = SYS(<FunctionNumber>, [nOption])
```

The biggest drawback to this command is that you need to know the function's number, not its name. Although you may remember the numbers of a few functions that you use frequently, remembering them all is difficult. In addition, some functions (such as some SET commands) can return more than one value; therefore, they use a second parameter to identify which value to return. Table A.5 lists a few of the common SYS() functions.

### Table A.5  Common *SYS()* Functions

| Function | Return Value |
|---|---|
| SYS(0) | Network machine name. |
| SYS(1) | Julian date. |
| SYS(2) | Seconds since midnight when the session was started. Unlike SECONDS( ), this function does not reset to 0 at midnight. |
| SYS(3) | Unique file name, based on the time and date. |
| SYS(13) | Printer status. |
| SYS(16) | Currently executing program; provides more detail than PROGRAM( ). Through an additional parameter, you can determine the calling stack. |
| SYS(18) | Current control object. |
| SYS(2016) | Memory used by your programs and defined objects. |
| SYS(1037) | Printer Setup dialog box. |
| SYS(2003) | Current directory; use with SYS(5) for complete path information. |
| SYS(2010) | CONFIG.SYS file settings. |
| SYS(2011) | Query lock status without actually creating a lock. |
| SYS(2019) | Configuration file used at startup. |
| SYS(2020) | Size of default disk drive. |
| SYS(2023) | Temporary file drive and path, as set by TMPFILES. |

For additional information on the available SYS functions, check the on-line help system for topics related to SYS.

## Getting Operating-System Environment Information with *GETENV()*

Another valuable way to customize the Visual FoxPro environment is to retrieve the operating-system environment settings with the GETENV( ) function. Notice that you can define your own operating-system settings by using your own custom names in the AUTOEXEC.BAT file. In fact, some programs use this capability to soft-code search paths, user names, and other information, as shown in the following examples:

```
? GETENV("PATH")
? GETENV("MACHINENAME")
? GETENV("TEMP")
```

# The Resource File

*by Richard Curtis*

This appendix discusses the use and structure of resource and labels files. In previous versions of FoxPro, these files used the same structures, and in some cases, the information was stored in one file. Visual FoxPro 5.0 has changed the structure of the resource file and the location of the labels file. Figures B.1 and B.2 display field and Memo field information for the resource and label database files. ■

**FIGURE B.1**

The structure of
FOXUSER.DBF with the
two Memo fields
displayed.

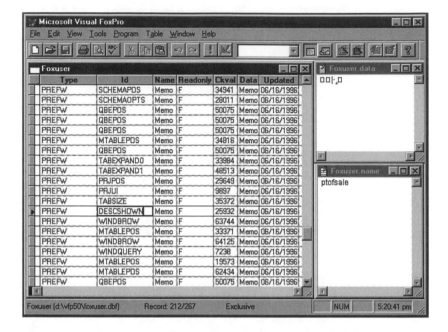

**FIGURE B.2**

The structure of
LABELS.DBF, with the
Memo field displayed.

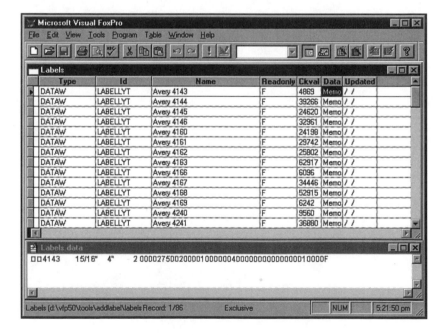

The resource file, FOXUSER.DBF, is the default file. The file stores information about Visual FoxPro or your applications, such as window and toolbar positions and browse configurations. Two ways to improve the performance of applications are:

- If the application does not require a resource file, include RESOURCE = OFF in the CONFIG.FPW file for that application.

- If the application requires a resource file but does not need to be updated, make the resource file read-only.

**TIP** Name the resource file with the same name as your application's .EXE to avoid confusion with other files that are in the system's path.

In network situations that require resource files, place the resource file on the local computer allowing storage of individual user information. A read-only resource file on a server or one included in the .EXE provides a standard resource file for all users.

Visual FoxPro 5.0 places ADDLABEL.APP and LABELS.DBF in the C:\VFP\TOOLS\ ADDLABEL directory by default. Earlier versions of FoxPro placed these files in C:\VFP, C:\FPW, C:\FPD, and so on. LABELS.DBF contains information for the Label Wizard to create Avery labels.

ADDLABEL.APP allows you to define custom label layouts for the Label Wizard to use. The first time you run ADDLABEL.APP, it creates USERLBLS.DBF to store label layouts. Figure B.3 shows the label layout designer.

**FIGURE B.3**

The New Label Definition form is contained in ADDLABEL.APP.

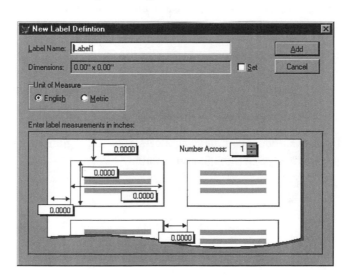

# Using the Resource File

Three Visual FoxPro commands for managing resource files are:

- SET RESOURCE
- SYS(2005) (current resource file)
- SET("RESOURCE")

The SET RESOURCE command sets the resource file ON, OFF, or TO [FileName]. The default condition, ON, saves changes in the Visual FoxPro environment to the resource file.

The SET RESOURCE OFF command turns off the saving of environment changes to the resource file. This command can result in faster program operation, because Visual FoxPro is not writing changes to the resource file.

SET RESOURCE TO without a file name opens FOXUSER.DBF. SET RESOURCE TO with a file name opens the specified file. Both commands invoke the default condition, SET RESOURCE ON.

The SYS(2005) command provides the name and path of the current resource file. The following command, used in a program or from the Command window, stores the name of the resource file and its full path in a memory variable:

```
cResourceFile = SYS(2005)
```

The following command displays the same information in a wait window:

```
WAIT WINDOW SYS(2005)
```

The SET("RESOURCE") command specifies the ON or OFF status of the resource file.

 **TIP**   Use the SET() command to save and restore the status of the resource file and other SET commands in your applications.

The SET("RESOURCE") command supports a second argument. The following command is the equivalent of the SYS(2005) command:

```
SET ("RESOURCE",1)
```

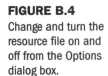

**FIGURE B.4**
Change and turn the
resource file on and
off from the Options
dialog box.

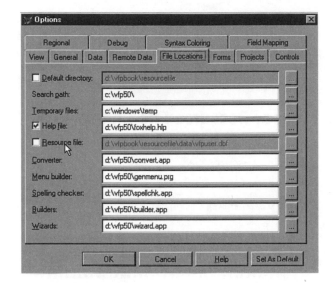

# Working with the Resource File

The resource file can be set and turned on and off from VFP's Options dialog box (see Figure B.4). However, most of the resource file changes are managed with code as shown in the following examples.

FOXUSER.DBF is the default resource file. You can create a resource file with a different file name in several ways. Two ways are demonstrated with the following commands:

```
USE SYS(2005) AGAIN
COPY STRUCTURE TO <filename>
SET RESOURCE TO <filename>
```

This opens the current resource file a second time, copies its structure to the specified file, and then sets the file as the current resource file.

These commands do the same thing:

```
USE SYS(2005) AGAIN ALIAS RSF
AFIELDS(<arrayname>,RSF)
CREATE TABLE <filename> FREE FROM ARRAY <arrayname>
SET RESOURCE TO <filename>
```

The second method has more lines of code, but when the array is created, it is available until it is released.

**NOTE** The Visual FoxPro resource file continues to grow unless it is read-only. Periodically check the record count of your file, and remove unnecessary records. Change the READONLY field to true (T) for those environment settings that you do not want changed. *Any structure change makes the resource file invalid.* ■

## A Programmed Tour of Resource File Changes

The program shown in Listing B.1 provides a sample of the types of environment information that are stored in a resource file.

### Listing B.1   VFPUSER.PRG

```
*/PROGRAM VFPUSER.PRG
*/RESOURCE FILE DEMONSTRATION
*/CAUTION - BEFORE RUNNING THIS PROGRAM SET THE RESOURCE FILE
*/TO VFPUSER.DBF
*/****************************************************************

LOCAL cMsgText
CLOSE DATABASE

*/TURN OFF THE RESOURCE FILE AND DELETE ALL RECORDS
SET RESOURCE OFF
USE SYS(2005) AGAIN
DELETE ALL
PACK
USE

*/TURN ON THE RESOURCE FILE
SET RESOURCE ON
cMsgText = "SYS(2005) Function: " + Chr(13) + ;
              SYS(2005)
=MESSAGEBOX(cMsgText, 0 + 64 + 0, "Resource File")

cMsgText = "SET('RESOURCE,1) Function: " + Chr(13) + ;
              SET('RESOURCE',1)

WAIT WINDOW cMsgText

cMsgText = "Please close the Form Designer" + chr(13) + ;
              "that appears after this message."
=MESSAGEBOX(cMsgText, 0 + 64 + 0, "Resource File")
MODIFY FORM VFPUSER

DO FORM VFPUSER
READ EVENTS
*/CHANGE THE DESKTOP COLOR TO GRAY
_screen.backcolor = RGB(192,192,192)
```

```
*/BROWSE THE DEFAULT RESOURCE FILE
=MESSAGEBOX("Browse FOXUSER.DBF", 0 + 64 + 0, "Resource File")
USE HOME()+ "FOXUSER.DBF"
BROWSE NOMODIFY
USE

*/CHANGE THE DESKTOP COLOR TO WHITE
_screen.backcolor = RGB(255,255,255)

USE SYS(2005) AGAIN
BROWSE
USE
RETURN
```

Before running VFPUSER.PRG, set the resource file to VFPUSER.DBF (included on the CD-ROM that comes with this book), or set the resource file to one other than FOXUSER.DBF.

**CAUTION**

All records in the current resource file are deleted when VFPUSER.PRG is run.

VFPUSER.PRG does the following:

- Displays techniques previously discussed in this appendix

- Browses the FOXUSER.DBF resource file

- Browses entries made in VFPUSER.DBF by VFPUSER.PRG

Compare the records in VFPUSER.DBF with the programmed events to determine which environment changes were recorded in the resource file (see Figure B.5).

**FIGURE B.5**

The resource file is updated by program VFPUSER.PRG.

| Type | Id | Name | Readonly | Ckval | Data | Updated |
|------|-----|------|----------|-------|------|---------|
| PREFW | PROPWIND | memo | F | 1535 | Memo | 06/30/1996 |
| PREFW | FORMINFO | Memo | F | 52747 | Memo | 06/30/1996 |
| PREFW | FTCLASSLIBS | Memo | F | 65535 | Memo | 06/30/1996 |
| PREFW | FORMTOOLS | memo | F | 60721 | Memo | 06/30/1996 |
| PREFW | TTOOLBAR | Memo | F | 4245 | Memo | 06/30/1996 |
| PREFW | TTOOLBAR | Memo | F | 27562 | Memo | 06/30/1996 |
| PREFW | WINDBROW | Memo | F | 21398 | Memo | 06/30/1996 |

# The Resource File and Performance

Applications run faster without a resource file. If the application does not require a resource file, don't use one. If a resource file is required, make it read-only, if possible.

If the resource file is not necessary throughout the entire application, turn it ON and OFF, as appropriate.

Provide an empty resource file or one with just the records that your application needs. Name the resource file that is included with your application so that you don't confuse it with other resource files on a system.

Include a LABEL.DBF, if labels are required. Visual FoxPro 5.0 does not store label information in the resource file. ●

# Optimizing
# Performance

*by Rick Strahl and Sandra Richardson-Lutzow*

**U**sers *always* want the most from their computers when it comes to speed, quick execution, and extremely short wait periods. By applying the ideas in this appendix, you can optimize the operating performance of Visual FoxPro and the applications that it is designed to run. The appendix deals with three main areas: using hardware, setting up Windows, and tuning your Visual FoxPro environment and applications. ∎

# Analyzing Hardware Requirements

Microsoft's Visual FoxPro is a professional application-development platform and, as such, requires some substantial hardware requirements for best performance. Remember that VFP provides all the functionality of previous versions of FoxPro, as well as an entirely new environment, including much-enhanced data handling and object-oriented features. As a result, Microsoft recommends the following minimum hardware for Visual FoxPro 5.0:

- An IBM-compatible computer with a 486 50MHz processor or better.
- A mouse. (You can perform most operations without a mouse, but the ease of use and flexibility justify the small cost of a mouse.)
- 8M RAM.
- 30M of hard disk space for a minimum installation and 80M for a full installation.
- For networks, a Windows-supported network and server. Visual FoxPro can also be run under Windows 95, Windows NT, and Microsoft LAN Manager.
- A VGA or higher-resolution monitor.

Notice that the preceding items are minimum requirements. You will get much better performance by adding more RAM. In fact, the greatest bang for the buck will be in adding memory to your system until you have at least 24M.

If you intend to use the Upsizing Wizard, you must install the Open Database Connectivity (ODBC) components. Also, the Upsizing Wizard works only with Microsoft SQL Server versions 4.x for Windows 95 and Windows NT and OS/2.

If you buy the CD-ROM version of VFP, you, of course, need a CD-ROM drive.

## Memory and Processor

The most important consideration in selecting hardware for use with Visual FoxPro is memory. Although at least a 486-class chip is required to run Visual FoxPro at reasonable speed, memory—or the lack thereof—has the most dramatic effect on performance. Although Microsoft claims a minimum requirement of 8M and a recommended minimum of 12M, these amounts are not really adequate for developing applications—and are barely adequate for running even small Visual FoxPro applications. A more reasonable minimum for both Windows 95 and Windows NT is 20M. If you plan to do serious work with Visual FoxPro, consider upgrading your memory all the way to 32M or more, so that you can comfortably run Visual FoxPro and several applications at the same time.

A 486-class chip (especially the 66MHz and higher versions) provides adequate performance. The newer Pentium chips provide better performance, of course, but make sure that you never shortchange memory in favor of the processor in any upgrades that you make. Visual FoxPro runs better with the extra memory, and you'll be able to multitask more applications reliably and without bringing your system to a standstill. If you are still running with a 386 processor in your system, you are likely to find Visual FoxPro's performance to be unacceptably slow; it's high time to upgrade to a more modern computer.

# Disk Drive

A full Visual FoxPro installation takes 80M of disk space. Although this install includes a great deal of supplemental material that is not required to run Visual FoxPro, you'll most likely install the additional support and sample files to have a ready reference for examples and documentation.

App
C

When you consider a new hard drive, don't even think about buying one smaller than 1G (1,000M). We're coming to the stage at which full installations of development tools are getting close to 100M, and mainstream consumer applications are weighing in at close to 50M—and a few of those are enough to fill a hard drive of lesser size in a hurry. In coming years, as users ask for ever-more-complex features, these requirements are only going to grow. Also, newer, larger drives in general have faster access times, which gives you an additional small performance boost.

It is well known that hard drives are more efficient when they are not chock-full. So, if you're starting to run out of disk space and need to make room just to make Visual FoxPro fit, you're likely to be ready for an upgrade to a larger drive. Free space on a disk partition should not fall below 10–15 percent to keep the disk at optimum performance and have room for a paging file.

Another factor to consider is that Windows 95 uses a virtual-memory swap file. This file grows and shrinks as the memory requirements of currently running applications change. The more applications you run simultaneously, the more disk space the swap file uses. Remember that the total memory available to the system is what counts. If you have only 8M of RAM, you will require more virtual memory than you would if you had a 32M-system. Some people even recommend adding memory until the hard disk use light goes out and stays out, unless you specifically access the hard disk to read or write data.

Hard disk maintenance also can have a big effect on performance. When you use Windows 95, make sure that you defragment the hard disk frequently (using DEFRAG.EXE or a third-party defragmenter). Defragmentation consolidates free disk space into larger contiguous areas, which the hard disk can access faster.

When you are building an application with Visual FoxPro, make sure that you break your project into its components and create separate directories for subportions of the application. A large number of files in a single directory can slow file-access performance dramatically, because Windows has to search through the long list of files to access a particular file. Although it takes about 250 files or more for this situation to become a problem, the performance degradation can become noticeable very quickly after you have a critical number of files.

## Video Cards

The type of video card that you use can have a dramatic effect on Windows' performance in general. Visual FoxPro is a highly visual product that works best at a high resolution (1,024×768 pixels or higher). High resolution enables VFP to fit the various toolbars, property sheets, and designers onto the screen, making the visual design of the user interface a reality. The high resolution and the nature of the graphic operations can greatly benefit from an accelerated local bus (PCI or VESA) video card that is optimized for Windows. The result is much faster screen draws and a more usable product.

If you are still using the video card that came with your system three years or more ago, it's time to check out accelerated cards and compare performance. You'll be amazed what a difference a new video card can make for your Windows experience.

# Configuring Windows

Visual FoxPro 5.0 is a Windows-only product at this time. (A Macintosh version may be available later.) Therefore, Visual FoxPro benefits from a properly tuned Windows environment, whether you are running Windows 95 or Windows NT. Notice that this release does not run under Windows 3.x or Windows for Workgroups; it is a 32-bit-only development environment.

When the appropriate hardware is in place, you can make a few adjustments to fine-tune your Windows environment. Because Visual FoxPro runs under Windows 95 and Windows NT, this appendix can't go into every detail; you should check a platform-specific book that helps you fine-tune your Windows version to its maximum performance. The appendix does touch on some of the big issues that can bring you immediate performance results.

Windows NT and Windows 95 include self-configuring virtual-memory and disk-caching options, which adjust themselves to the particular applications that are currently loaded while you are running Windows. It's recommended that you use these default auto-config options under these operating systems, because they provide the best performance under most circumstances.

## Windows 95

In Windows 95, virtual-memory settings are controlled via the Control Panel's System utility. The Performance property sheet displays a pair of options for setting the virtual swap-file settings. By default, Windows 95 manages the size of this swap file itself, adjusting the file's size according to available memory and applications in use. Windows 95 also automatically sets up a disk cache, which dynamically sizes itself depending on the amount of available memory. The only customization option for you to determine is the size of the swap file and where the file is located. In most cases, the default values provided by Windows 95 are very appropriate for a given setup. If you have a second hard drive in your system with a faster access time, however, you may want to force Windows 95 to place its swap file there.

Although this setup leaves little room for custom tuning, it is much improved over previous versions of Windows, in which trial and error was the best way to optimize performance. The good news is that the default settings that Windows 95 guesses at are really quite good; performance is excellent.

## Windows NT

In Windows NT, virtual-memory settings are also set via the Control Panel's System utility. The Virtual Memory command allows you to specify a paging-file size. The *paging file* is just another name for virtual memory used as a memory extension.

Windows NT provides guideline values for each drive, as well as for the available disk space on each drive. As a rule, the size of your swap file should be at least the amount of physical memory installed in your computer, plus 12M. As an absolute minimum, the swap file should be 22M, which is the amount that Windows NT requires internally for system-recovery purposes. A good starting point is a paging-file size of around 40M, which is likely what NT will provide as a default.

You can split paging files into separate files on different drives or partitions, in case you don't have enough space on a single drive to hold the entire file. Keep in mind that the combined value of the paging files applies to the guidelines mentioned earlier in this section.

Like Windows 95, Windows NT automatically sets up a disk cache, which is dynamically sized based on the amount of available memory while you are running applications.

App
C

# Configuring Visual FoxPro

In addition to tuning your hardware and Windows, you can fine-tune both the Visual FoxPro environment and the code that you write. Throughout this book, you find performance tips and notes that can help you in specific situations. This section provides a summary of more generic performance issues that have a global and immediate effect.

## Optimizing with Rushmore Technology

One of Visual FoxPro's strongest attributes over the years has been its use of the Rushmore technology, which provides extremely fast data-retrieval speeds on local tables. To take advantage of Rushmore and its speed enhancements, though, you have to know the rules.

**Creating Index Tags for Fields Often Used in Queries**    Rushmore uses index tags to optimize searches. Suppose that you have a table of names and addresses. If you expect to search or filter data by last name, you should have an index tag on last name. Similarly, to optimize a search on ZIP or postal code, you should have an index on that field. Basically, any field that you regularly search or filter data on should have an index to optimize the operation.

**Using Exact Expressions**    In short, Rushmore works by using index expressions to quickly retrieve data requested by compatible commands. The key is that the expressions that you use in SQL SELECT statements and in the FOR clauses of various data-access commands must *exactly* match those of index expressions that you created for a given table. For example, if you have a customer database and an index on UPPER(LAST), following is an example of a select statement written in two ways, one optimizable and the other not:

```
lcName = PADR("DOE",8)      && Name field length of 8

*** Optimizable
  SELECT * FROM customer ;
    WHERE UPPER(Last)=lcName

*** Not Optimizable
  SELECT * FROM customer ;
    WHERE Last = lcName
```

The second SQL statement is not Rushmore-optimizable, because the Last expression does not exactly match the index expression. If these two queries were run on a sizable customer table, the first SELECT would return the selected customer records almost instantly, whereas the second would take a while to sequentially run through the table (or possibly create a temporary index) to locate the selected records.

If you are not using exact tag expressions in a FOR clause, attach NOOPTIMIZE to the end of the expression. By attaching NOOPTIMIZE to the clause, VFP skips the first step of looking for an index.

To use Rushmore as much as possible, it is good practice to create an index tag on a field that you often use in query criteria. Be careful, though—if you end up with a large number of indexes, performance could be slow, because VFP must update each index every time that it adds, changes, or deletes a record. Thus, you should give less weight to indexes required by queries that are run once a month as opposed to those that are run once a day.

**Indexing on *DELETE()*** If your applications use SET DELETED ON, it's a good idea to create index tags for the deleted flag in all your tables. The reason is that if SET DELETED is set ON, the DELETED( ) flag of a record is implicitly included in all queries and FOR clause commands. If you don't have a tag on DELETED( ), all queries end up being only partially optimizable. To create an index tag on DELETED( ), use this code:

```
INDEX ON DELETED() TAG DELETED
```

**Reindexing** Make it a habit to reindex your tables periodically. Reindexing the data optimizes performance by defragmenting the indexes. Also, issuing the PACK command automatically reindexes after removing records marked for deletion.

You should also occasionally rebuild the index from its definition. If any data corruption enters the index, a simple reindexing may not solve the problem. In addition, using the REINDEX command may result in index-file bloat. In other words, VFP may remove the defragmentation by adding the index to the end of the index file a second time and marking it as the active index definition, leaving the original blocks of data intact. This larger file takes more time to read and cannot be cached as easily.

**Not *UsingEMPTY()* or *ISBLANK()*** It's often convenient to include EMPTY( ) and ISBLANK( ) in queries and filter expressions, but these functions are not optimizable under Rushmore. Instead, it's a good idea to create a blank value that matches the EMPTY( ) status for the field. If you have a last-name field, you might use the following:

```
*** Assign blank name to search for EMPTY()
  SELECT customer
  lcName = SPACE(FSIZE("Last", "customer"))

*** Optimizable
  SELECT * FROM customer ;
    WHERE Last = lcName
```

The non-optimizable statement would look like the following:

```
*** Not Optimizable
  SELECT * FROM customer ;
    WHERE EMPTY(Last)
```

App

C

**HAVING versus WHERE**    SQL-SELECT has two clauses that filter data: WHERE and HAVING.  SQL is not English, and looking at these two clauses as synonyms is a mistake. Many people think that WHERE is used for join conditions and that HAVING is used for filters; they're wrong. The conditions in a WHERE filters the original data, using index tags for optimization whenever possible, thereby producing an intermediate set of results. HAVING operates on the intermediate results, without using tags; therefore, it is not optimizable.

You should use HAVING any time that you group data with GROUP BY and want to filter the data on the result of the grouping.

## Executing Loops

When you create a loop that executes a fixed number of times, FOR is a better choice than DO WHILE. The counts and checks are built into a FOR; therefore, the process goes faster than the DO WHILE. When you have a basic loop construct, it should look like this:

```
FOR lnCnt = 1 TO lnMaxValue
     * execute commands
ENDFOR
```

The alternative, less efficient construct would look like this:

```
lnCnt = 1
DO WHILE lnCnt > lnMaxVal
     * execute commands
     lnCnt = lnCnt + 1
ENDDO
```

You shouldn't use DO WHILE where you can use SCAN, either. SCAN is designed to skip through records automatically, and it gets results much faster.

If DO WHILE is still the choice for constructing your loop, try not to execute commands in the loop condition. If a command doesn't depend on some characteristic of the loop or set any flags, it can probably go outside the loop. Following is an example of an efficient DO WHILE:

```
lnRowCnt = ALEN(aList,1)
lnRow = 1
DO WHILE aList[lnRow,1] = 'Searching for data' AND ;
   lnRow < lnRowCnt
      lnRow = lnRow + 1
ENDDO
```

The following is an example of an inefficient DO WHILE loop, accomplishing the same results:

```
llSuccess = .F.
lnRow = 1
DO WHILE NOT llSuccess AND lnRow < ALEN(aList,1)
```

```
            IF aList[lnRow,1) = 'Searching for data'
                 llSuccess = .T.
            ELSE
                 llSuccess = .F.
                 lnRow =  lnRow + 1
            ENDIF
      ENDDO
```

This proper construction eliminates repeated calls to ALEN( ) and the need for the
llSuccess variable.

# Using PROCEDURE or FUNCTION Clause

Take warning on using a PROCEDURE or FUNCTION clause at the beginning of a
stand-alone .PRG file. It takes three times as long to execute a PRG that begins with
PROCEDURE or FUNCTION as it does to execute one that doesn't have the header
statement—a tried-and-true discovery. So if you tend to place routines in stand-alone .PRG
files, comment out the header line and just start with the code. This practice will speed up
your applications considerably.

App
C

# Placing Temporary Files

If you are running Visual FoxPro from a network server, explicitly specifying where your
temporary files are going is important. Visual FoxPro creates temporary files for results
stored in cursors, for editing text, for caching program code, for temporary indexes, and
so on. These temporary files should be stored on the fastest hard drive on the local workstation whenever possible, thereby reducing network traffic. For fastest operation, the
hard drive should not be compressed. Temporary file locations are set with the
TMPFILES environment setting in the CONFIG.FPW file; for example:

```
TMPFILES = C:\VFPWORK\TMP
```

If this value (or the related SORTWORK, PROGWORK, and EDITWORK options) is not
specified, the temporary files go in the directory specified by the TEMP environment
variable defined in your AUTOEXEC.BAT file or your System Environment Variables
(Windows NT).

# Keeping Data Files Open

Opening and closing data files are among the slowest data-related operations in Visual
FoxPro. Unless a file is used only temporarily (for example, a one-time lookup table that is
loaded into an array for use in lists), data files should always be left open. Visual FoxPro
provides 32,767 work areas in each data session. Each form, form set, or report can have
its own data session. Even with all of these work areas, however, you can still have only

255 files open at one time, limited by memory or file handles. Although open files do take up file handles and a small amount of buffer memory, in most cases, the performance advantage is worth this overhead.

## Using SQL Commands versus Procedural Code

The various SQL commands available in Visual FoxPro are almost always faster than corresponding procedural code. When you are issuing VFP commands, if an order is set, Rushmore finds the records that match the criteria, but then it has to go back to the index to determine the order in which to display them. SQL-SELECT ignores any order set that may slow retrieval of records. Therefore, the SQL-SELECT command is almost always faster than using similar procedural code when you are gathering query results.

In addition, the required code is compacted into a single SQL statement. SQL-DELETE is faster than DELETE FOR, and SQL-INSERT INTO is much faster than APPEND BLANK followed by a string of REPLACE values.

## Compiling Applications to .APP or .EXE Files

Although you can run applications directly from their program, form, and visual class files, it's highly recommended that you compile them into .APP or .EXE files. These files bind all the program files into a single file from which the files are loaded. The files can be located much faster inside an .APP or .EXE file than on disk. The .APP also contains compiled code of program files. By comparison, when you are running .PRG files directly, those files need to be compiled into .FXP files when they are run.

## Minimizing Use of Interface Components

The slowest aspects of any GUI-based application are likely to be the interface components. Buttons, list boxes, pop-up menus, drop-down lists, grids—all these objects consume memory and require time to be written to the screen. The visual aspect is one of the most impressive features of Visual FoxPro, but it is also the biggest drain on performance. Make sure that you use the interface to its fullest, not wasting form real estate with neat toys that don't serve the purpose just perfectly. Be sure to apply the proper balance between form and function.

Between version 3.0 and 5.0, Microsoft greatly improved the performance of the GUI. The use of late binding, for example, allows forms with multiple-page page frames to come up faster. Despite these improvements, always remember that the more controls you have in a form, the longer it takes VFP to prepare and display that form.

## Avoiding Macro Substitution

The macro operator (&) is one of the most notorious xBase leftovers; it is both very powerful and very slow in execution. This operator lets you place a character string in the code at runtime, causing that line to be reevaluated at runtime and thus breaking the precompiled advantage that your code might have. You can do things such as create an entire command from a macro such as the following:

```
PARAMETER lcArchive, lcFiles
lcRunString = "RUN PKZIP.PIF " + lcArchive + " " + lcFiles
& lcRunString
RETURN
```

As you can see, the '&' operator is a very powerful feature that allows you to substitute just about any code at runtime. Nevertheless, limit the use of macro expressions to occasions when you have no alternative, especially if the macro ends up being used in a loop. xBase is notorious for the use of macro operators and for the slow and often sloppy code that accompanies them.

Unfortunately, in a few areas of Visual FoxPro, macro expressions are unavoidable—and even more desirable than other approaches. They include resetting SET and ON (SET TALK &lcOldTalk, for example) environment settings, full command substitutions (such as the RUN command in the earlier example), and parameterized SQL-SELECT statements that benefit from the one-time substitution versus a repeated conversion of the EVALUATE() function.

In general, see whether you can get around macro use by using the EVALUATE() function or by rewriting your code so that a macro is not required. Many xBase commands that used to require macro expressions now accept string expressions. USE (lcCustFile), for example, is the same as USE &lcCustFile.

## Referencing Object Properties

Object-property references are much slower than memory-variable references. If an object method references object properties frequently, it is more efficient to store the property's value to a memory variable as the following illustrates:

```
PROCEDURE btnDial.Click
LPARAMETER lcLocalArea

*** Assign phone number to local
  lcPhoneNum = THISFORM.txtPhone.value

  IF EMPTY(lcPhoneNum)
    RETURN .F.
  ENDIF
```

App
C

```
*** Strip off area code if it's local
  IF LEFT(lcPhoneNum, 4) = lcLocalArea
    lcPhoneNum = SUBSTR(lcPhoneNum,6)
  ENDIF
```

Along the same lines, you should be taking advantage of the new WITH structure when you work with a group of commands that involve an object's properties, such as the following:

```
*** Create new object and adjust properties
  THIS.parent.addobject("CloneObj", "Shape")
  WITH THIS.parent.CloneObj
    .top = THIS.top
    .left = THIS.left
    .width = THIS.borderwidth + 1
    .height = THIS.height
    .borderwidth = 0
    .fillcolor = IIF(llRaised, lnWhite, lnGrey)
    .fillstyle = 0
    .visible = .T.
  ENDWITH
```

In this example, the object reference of `THIS.parent.CloneObject` needs to be resolved only one time (at the top of the WITH structure statement), resulting in faster execution. ●

# Shortcut Keys, Function Keys, and Events

*by Michael Antonovich*

**K**eys are important in Visual FoxPro in two ways. First, they can be used throughout the program as shortcuts to simplify common procedures and keystrokes. In addition, you can use events, such as `KeyPress` or `Click`, to determine what happens when a user selects a particular key or control in a Visual FoxPro application. Developers who are familiar with the commands `INKEY( )`, `ON KEY`, and `READKEY( )` will discover new ways to perform the same functions in Visual FoxPro's object-oriented programming paradigm. ■

# Shortcut Keys

Many of the menus in Visual FoxPro include shortcuts that allow you to select a submenu item by pressing the Ctrl key and a letter key simultaneously. Table D.1 lists these shortcut keys.

**Table D.1   Shortcut Keys**

| Menu | Submenu | Shortcut Key |
|------|---------|--------------|
| File | New | Ctrl+N |
|      | Open | Ctrl+O |
|      | Save | Ctrl+S |
|      | Print | Ctrl+P |
| Edit | Undo | Ctrl+Z |
|      | Redo | Ctrl+R |
|      | Cut | Ctrl+X |
|      | Copy | Ctrl+C |
|      | Paste | Ctrl+V |
|      | Select All | Ctrl+A |
|      | Find | Ctrl+F |
|      | Find Again | Ctrl+G |
|      | Replace | Ctrl+L |
| Format | Bring to Front | Ctrl+G |
|        | Send to Back | Ctrl+J |
| Program | Do | Ctrl+D |
|         | Resume | Ctrl+M |
| Window | Cycle | Ctrl+F1 |
|        | Command Window | Ctrl+F2 |
| Table | Append New Record | Ctrl+Y |
|       | Toggle Deletion Mark | Ctrl+T |
|       | Change Partitions | Ctrl+H |
| Query | Run Query | Ctrl+Q |
| Menu | Insert Item | Ctrl+I |
|      | Delete Item | Ctrl+E |

You might notice that some of the shortcut keys are reused in different menus. At first glance, you might anticipate a problem—how can two different options be executed by the same shortcut key? The answer is that shortcut keys are enabled only if the menu itself is active and the submenu option is also enabled. Both the Edit and Format menus, for example, have the shortcut key Ctrl+G. While you are editing a report, both of these menus are active. The two submenu options are never enabled at the same time, however. Therefore, there is never a conflict. (Interestingly, when you are editing a form, both of these options are available, but the Bring to Front and Send to Back options do not have shortcut keys.)

# Function Keys

Visual FoxPro also allows users to define shortcuts with a series of function keys that issue commands in the Command window. Users who are familiar with previous versions of FoxPro will recognize these function keys, which are detailed in Table D.2.

**Table D.2    Function Keys**

| Key | Command |
| --- | --- |
| F1 | HELP |
| F2 | SET |
| F3 | LIST |
| F4 | DIRECTORY |
| F5 | DISPLAY STRUCTURE |
| F6 | DISPLAY STATUS |
| F7 | DISPLAY MEMORY |
| F8 | DISPLAY |
| F9 | APPEND |
| F10 | Moves cursor into menu |

App
D

# Events

Visual FoxPro offers several new features that in many cases replace the older key functions, such as INKEY( ), ON KEY, and READKEY( ). These features include the KeyPress, Click, and DblClick events, which are described in the following list:

■ *KeyPress event:* causes a command to execute when you release a key. The procedure syntax for this event is:

```
PROCEDURE <Object>.KeyPress
LPARAMETERS [nIndex,] nKeycode, nShiftAltCtrl
```

or

```
LPARAMETERS nKeyCode, nShiftAltCtrl
```

nIndex identifies the control, and nKeyCode contains a number that identifies the key pressed. This event is similar to the ON KEY function in previous versions of FoxPro.

A KeyPress event can apply to the following controls: CheckBox, ComboBox, CommandButton, EditBox, Form, ListBox, OptionButton, Spinner, and TextBox.

■ *DblClick event:* causes a command to execute when you double-click the left mouse button. The syntax is:

```
PROCEDURE <Object>.DblClick
[LPARAMETERS nIndex]
```

The DblClick event applies to the following controls: ComboBox, EditBox, Form, Grid, Header, Image, Label, Line, ListBox, OptionButton, OptionGroup, Page, PageFrame, Shape, Spinner, TextBox, and ToolBar.

■ *Click event:* occurs when you click the left mouse button. The syntax is:

```
PROCEDURE <Object>.Click
[LPARAMETERS nIndex]
```

A Click event works with the following commands: CheckBox, ComboBox, CommandButton, CommandGroup, EditBox, Form, Grid, Header, Image, Label, Line, ListBox, OptionButton, OptionGroup, Page, PageFrame, Shape, Spinner, TextBox, and ToolBar.

The preceding three events respond to things that the user does. However, you can also create a few events programmatically. The first command, KEYBOARD, has been around almost forever. This command places one or more characters in the keyboard buffer. These characters remain in the buffer until a VFP interrupt looks at the keyboard to see whether anything is there. Then VFP accepts these characters just as though they were typed from the keyboard. You can even simulate some of the special keys on the keyboard by using the KeyLabelName values listed in Table D.3.

**Table D.3   Special Keyboard Key Label Values**

| For This Key... | Specify This *KeyLabelName* Value |
| --- | --- |
| Left Cursor | LEFTARROW |
| Right Cursor | RIGHTARROW |
| Up Cursor | UPARROW |
| Down Cursor | DNARROW |
| Home | HOME |
| End | END |
| Page Up | PGUP |
| Page Down | PGDN |
| Delete | DEL |
| Backspace | BACKSPACE |
| Space bar | SPACEBAR |
| Insert | INS |
| Tab | TAB |
| Shift+Tab | BACKTAB |
| Enter | ENTER |
| F1 to F12 | F1, F2, F3... |
| Ctrl+F1 to Ctrl+F12 | CTRL+F1, CTRL+F2... |
| Shift+F1 to Shift+F12 | SHIFT+F1, SHIFT+F2... |
| Alt+F1 to Alt+F12 | ALT+F1, ALT+F2, ALT+F3... |
| Alt+0 to Alt+9 | ALT+0, ALT+1, ALT+2... |
| Alt+A to Alt+Z | ALT+A, ALT+B, ALT+C... |
| Ctrl+Left arrow | CTRL+LEFTARROW |
| Ctrl+Right arrow | CTRL+RIGHTARROW |
| Ctrl+Home | CTRL+HOME |
| Ctrl+End | CTRL+END |
| Ctrl+Page Up | CTRL+PGUP |
| Ctrl+Page Down | CTRL+PGDN |
| Ctrl+A to Ctrl+Z | CTRL+A, CTRL+B, CTRL+C... |

App
D

*continues*

| Table D.3    Continued | |
|---|---|
| **For This Key...** | **Specify This *KeyLabelName* Value** |
| Ctrl+0 | CTRL+0 |
| Right mouse button | RIGHTMOUSE |
| Left mouse button | LEFTMOUSE |
| Mouse button | MOUSE |
| Esc | ESC |

**N O T E**  Remember to enclose the KeyLabelName value in braces and quotes. Character strings can be simply in quotes. ■

Another command that creates events is MOUSE. MOUSE can simulate clicking, double-clicking, or moving the mouse, and even a drag operation. The MOUSE syntax is:

```
MOUSE [CLICK¦DBLCLICK][AT nRow1, nColumn1]
    ¦ DRAG TO nRow2, nColumn2, nRow3, nColumn3...]
    [PIXELS]
    [Window cWindowName]
    [LEFT ¦ MIDDLE ¦ RIGHT]
    [SHIFT] [CTRL] [ALT]
```

The CLICK and DBLCLICK clauses cause their respective events to occur. If you also include the AT command, you can specify the row and column over which the mouse pointer is positioned when the event occurs. This row-and-column position is relative to the VFP main window unless you include the WINDOW clause. Remember that a row corresponds to the height of the window font, and a column corresponds to the average column of the window font. You can also use PIXELS to position the mouse.

The DRAG clause can simulate dragging the mouse from one position to another. By default, the LEFT mouse button is pressed at the start of the move and released at the end.

You can specify which mouse button is clicked, as well as whether the mouse button is clicked along with the Shift, Ctrl, or Alt key.

Another event that you can create is an error. The ERROR command allows you to create an error programmatically. Why do this? The most common reason is to test error-handling routines during development. The syntax for ERROR is:

```
ERROR nErrorNumber ¦ nErrorNumber, cMessageText1 ¦ [cMessageText2]
```

Use this command to generate any error by its error number. You can also include a text string with your own error message. Finally, if you supply only a text message [cMessageText2], VFP reports error number 1098 with your message.

Remember to remove these command lines before distributing your applications to your users.

## Understanding ON KEY Codes

Although detailed tables for the INKEY( ) and READKEY( ) commands are no longer necessary in Visual FoxPro, KeyPress returns the same numeric codes that ON KEY uses, as listed in Table D.4.

**Table D.4    ON KEY Codes**

| Keystrokes | nKeyCode |
|---|---|
| Alt+Q, W, E, R, T, Y, U, I, O, P | 272–281 |
| Alt+A, S, D, F, G, H, J, K, L | 286–294 |
| Alt+Z, X, C, V, B, N, M | 300–306 |
| F1 to F10 function keys | 315–324 |
| Home | 327 |
| Up arrow | 328 |
| Page Up | 329 |
| Left arrow | 331 |
| Right arrow | 333 |
| End | 335 |
| Down arrow | 336 |
| Page Down | 337 |
| Ins | 338 |
| Delete | 339 |
| Shift+F1 to Shift+F10 | 340–349 |
| Ctrl+F1 to Ctrl+F10 | 350–359 |
| Alt+F1 to Alt+F10 | 360–369 |
| Ctrl+Prt Scrn | 370 |

App
D

*continues*

**Table D.4   Continued**

| Keystrokes | nKeyCode |
| --- | --- |
| Ctrl+Left arrow | 371 |
| Ctrl+Right arrow | 372 |
| Ctrl+End | 373 |
| Ctrl+Page Down | 374 |
| Ctrl+Home | 375 |
| Alt+1, 2, 3, 4, 5, 6, 7, 8, 9, 0, –, = | 376–387 |
| Ctrl+Page Up | 388 |

## Using Click and Other Events

To see a very simple example of a `Click` event in action, look at the Report form in the sample application, Tasmanian Traders, included with Visual FoxPro. To view the design of this form, choose File, Open, and select REPORTS.SCX in the C:\VFP\SAMPLES\TASTRADE\FORMS directory.

Right-click the Close command button, and choose Properties from the submenu to view the Properties window. Click the Methods tab to view the Click Event, which indicates that a User Procedure exists for this control. Double-click this event to view the User Procedure:

```
RELEASE thisform
```

As you will see, a simple RELEASE command executes when you click the Close button in this form.

The following example illustrates a more complex use of events. Run SOLUTION.APP, located in \VFP\SAMPLES\SOLUTION. Select Controls from the outline list. Then select Combo Box, followed by Add New Items to a Combo Box. Next, click the Run Sample button. The form that appears shows three ways to use combo boxes to select records from a table. In the first one, you need to enter the first few characters of the search string before pressing Enter to retrieve the records that match. In the second combo box, you must use the drop-down list to select an existing value. Finally, the last combo box uses an increment search technique, enabling the user to enter one character at a time to retrieve all records that match the characters entered. Figure D.1 shows this form.

**FIGURE D.1**

This figure shows several ways of working with combo boxes and their events.

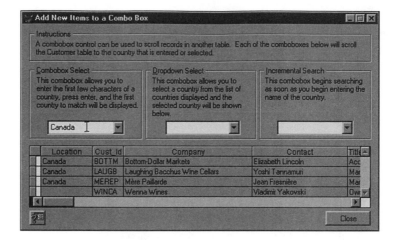

To see the properties and methods required for these combo boxes, return to the first screen, and click the See Code button. This button opens the Form Designer and allows you to look at the details of the form. If you look at the methods for the first combo box, you can see that code has been supplied for four events: GotFocus, Interactive Change, KeyPress, and LostFocus.

The first method, GotFocus, merely sets a form-level user-defined property called cboKeyEvent to .F., whereas the KeyPress event turns this property back to .T.. These two code lines appear:

```
THISFORM.cbokeyevent = .F.    && GotFocus
THISFORM.cbokeyevent = .T.    && KeyPress
```

This property value is used by the Interactive Change event in the following code:

```
IF !THISFORM.cboKeyEvent
   THIS.LostFocus
ENDIF
THISFORM.cboKeyEvent = .F.
```

Notice, if the property cboKeyEvent is false, any change to the combo-box text value causes this event to fire the Lost Focus event. This allows the user to enter as much text as he wants; nothing happens until he presses Enter or leaves the combo box (directly causing a Lost Focus event). Merely selecting a value from the list with the mouse does not cause a Lost Focus until the user moves out of the combo box or presses the Enter key.

As you may have guessed, the real work of retrieving records from the table is performed by the Lost Focus event using the code in Listing D.1.

App

D

**Listing D.1  APPD001.PRG**

```
#DEFINE C_NORECSFOUND_LOC "No records found."

LOCAL cDisplayValue,cCountryName

    cDisplayValue = ALLTRIM(THIS.DisplayValue)
    THIS.SelLength = 0
    IF EMPTY(m.cDisplayValue)
       RETURN
    ENDIF

    THISFORM.LockScreen = .T.

    IF THIS.Value = "(All)"
       SELECT country AS location,* FROM CUSTOMER;
             INTO CURSOR Custs
       thisform.grdcust.recordsource = "Custs"
    ELSE
       SELECT country AS location,* FROM CUSTOMER ;
        WHERE UPPER(ALLTRIM(Customer.Country)) = UPPER(m.cDisplayValue);
        INTO CURSOR Custs

       thisform.grdcust.recordsource = "Custs"

       IF _TALLY = 0
          MESSAGEBOX(C_NORECSFOUND_LOC )
       ELSE
          cCountryName = ALLTRIM(Custs.Country)
          IF ATC(m.cCountryName,THIS.RowSource)=0 AND !EMPTY(m.cCountryName)
             THIS.RowSource=THIS.RowSource+","+m.cCountryName
          ENDIF
          THIS.Value = m.cCountryName
       ENDIF
    ENDIF

THISFORM.ResetCombos(THIS)
THISFORM.LockScreen = .F.
```

Take a few moments to look at the code for these three combo boxes to see how they work. You can easily adapt this same technique into your code.

These are just three of the many examples provided in SOLUTION.APP that show how to use many of the base classes, their properties, and events. Studying these examples is certainly worth your time. Look at the other examples in SOLUTION.APP as well. ●

# Index

## Symbols

# C

# Licensing Agreement

By opening this package, you are agreeing to be bound by the following:

This software product is copyrighted, and all rights are reserved by the publisher and author. You are licensed to use this software on a single computer. You may copy and/or modify the software as needed to facilitate your use of it on a single computer. Making copies of the software for any other purpose is a violation of the United States copyright laws.

This software is sold *as is* without warranty of any kind, either expressed or implied, including but not limited to the implied warranties of merchantability and fitness for a particular purpose. Neither the publisher nor its dealers or distributors assumes any liability for any alleged or actual damages arising from the use of this program. (Some states do not allow for the exclusion of implied warranties, so the exclusion may not apply to you.)

# What's on the CD?

The CD included

ok, a collection of
demonstration a ware, and Web
page developme

The ten bonus c lesign plan to
extending the re on the CD:

- Bonus Ch
- Bonus Ch
- Bonus Ch
- Bonus Ch
- Bonus Ch
- Bonus Ch ctiveX Controls
- Bonus Ch s
- Bonus Ch
- Bonus Ch
- Bonus Ch 3.0

***Bonus Chapt*** ents located
in the root dir er to open
the document us chapters.
From there y

***Internet Exp*** vided Microsoft's
Internet Expl he \EXPLORER
directory on t

***BOOKCOD*** ok are provided
on the C directory of the
CD-ROM and

***BONUSCD*** D. To access the
chapter speci M.

***DEMOS:*** Que has included several third party tools, utilities, and resources to demonstrate the versatility and practicality of Visual FoxPro. These shareware items are located
in the DEMOS subdirectory of the CD-ROM.

***BOOK.HTM:*** An HTML page with links to cool FoxPro Web sites and various FoxPro-
related products and services is located in BOOK.HTM in the root directory of the
CD-ROM.